THE OXFORD H

PHILOSOPHY OF
EDUCATION

THE OXFORD HANDBOOK OF

PHILOSOPHY OF EDUCATION

Edited by

HARVEY SIEGEL

OXFORD

UNIVERSITY PRESS

OXFORD

UNIVERSITY PRESS

Oxford University Press, Inc., publishes works that further
Oxford University's objective of excellence
in research, scholarship, and education.

Oxford   New York
Auckland   Cape Town   Dar es Salaam   Hong Kong   Karachi
Kuala Lumpur   Madrid   Melbourne   Mexico City   Nairobi
New Delhi   Shanghai   Taipei   Toronto

With offices in
Argentina   Austria   Brazil   Chile   Czech Republic   France   Greece
Guatemala   Hungary   Italy   Japan   Poland   Portugal   Singapore
South Korea   Switzerland   Thailand   Turkey   Ukraine   Vietnam

Published by Oxford University Press, Inc.
198 Madison Avenue, New York, New York 10016

www.oup.com

First issued as an Oxford University Press paperback, 2012.

Oxford is a registered trademark of Oxford University Press

Library of Congress Cataloging-in-Publication Data

The Oxford handbook of philosophy of education / edited
by Harvey Siegel.
p. cm.
Includes bibliographical references.
ISBN 978-0-19-531288-1 (hardcover); 978-0-19-991572-9 (paperback)
1. Education—Philosophy. I. Siegel, Harvey, 1952–
LB14.7.O93 2009
370.1—dc22   2008046391

Printed in the United States of America
on acid-free paper

CONTENTS

....

CONTRIBUTORS

JONATHAN E. ADLER is Professor of Philosophy at Brooklyn College and the Graduate Center, CUNY. His main areas of research and publication are epistemology, philosophy of psychology and education, informal logic, and ethics. He is the author of *Belief's Own Ethics* (2002), co-editor (with Catherine Z. Elgin) of *Philosophical Inquiry: Classic and Contemporary Readings* (2007), and co-editor (with Lance Rips) of *Reasoning: Studies of Human Inference and Its Foundation* (2008).

DYLAN ARENA is a doctoral candidate in Learning Sciences and Technology Design at the Stanford University School of Education. In addition to philosophy, his interests include the teaching and learning of statistics and the use of games to foster learning.

ROBERT AUDI is Professor of Philosophy and David E. Gallo Chair in Ethics at the University of Notre Dame. He works in ethics and in related philosophical fields, especially epistemology. His books include *Action, Intention, and Reason* (1993), *The Structure of Justification* (1993), *Moral Knowledge and Ethical Character* (1997), *Religious Commitment and Secular Reason* (2000), *The Architecture of Reason* (2001), *The Good in the Right: A Theory of Intuition and Intrinsic Value* (2004), and *Moral Value and Human Diversity* (2007).

MARCIA W. BARON is Rudy Professor of Philosophy at Indiana University. She is the author of *Kantian Ethics Almost without Apology* (1995), and co-author, with Philip Pettit and Michael Slote, of *Three Methods of Ethics: A Debate* (1997), as well as articles on Kantian ethics, Hume's ethics, and philosophical issues in criminal law. Her recent articles include "Excuses, Excuses" in *Criminal Law and Philosophy*, "Justifications and Excuses" in *Ohio State Journal of Criminal Law*, and "Virtue Ethics, Kantian Ethics, and the 'One Thought Too Many' Objection" in M. Betzler, ed., *Kant's Virtue Ethics*.

LAWRENCE BLUM is Distinguished Professor of Liberal Arts and Education, and Professor of Philosophy, at the University of Massachusetts, Boston. He specializes in race theory, moral philosophy, moral education, and multiculturalism and is the author of *"I'm Not a Racist, But...": The Moral Quandary of Race* (2002), and *Moral Perception and Particularity* (1994).

THOMAS C. BRICKHOUSE is John Turner Professor of the Humanities and Professor of Philosophy at Lynchburg College. He is the co-author with N. D. Smith of five books and numerous articles on the philosophy of Socrates. They are currently working on a book-length study of Socrates' moral psychology.

HARRY BRIGHOUSE is Professor in the Philosophy department at University of Wisconsin, Madison. He specializes in political philosophy, philosophy of education, and education policy. Among his books are *School Choice and Social Justice* (2000), *On Education* (2006), and, with Adam Swift, a forthcoming book on the place of the family in liberal theory called *Family Values*. He is co-editor of the journal *Theory and Research in Education*.

NICHOLAS C. BURBULES is Grayce Wicall Gauthier Professor in the Department of Educational Policy Studies at the University of Illinois. His research focuses on philosophy of education, critical social and political theory, and technology and education. His most recent book is with Michael A. Peters and Paul Smeyers, *Showing and Doing: Wittgenstein as a Pedagogical Philosopher* (2008). He is the editor of *Educational Theory*.

EAMONN CALLAN is Pigott Family Professor in the School of Education at Stanford University. He is interested in questions about citizenship and justice. He is the author of *Creating Citizens* (1997).

DAVID CARR is Professor of Philosophy of Education at the University of Edinburgh. He is author and/or editor of several works of educational philosophy as well as of numerous philosophical and educational papers on ethics, epistemology, and aesthetics.

RANDALL CURREN is Professor and Chair of Philosophy and Professor of Education at the University of Rochester. His works in philosophy of education, ethics, legal and political philosophy, and the history of philosophy include *Aristotle on the Necessity of Public Education* (2000). He is the editor of *A Companion to the Philosophy of Education* (2003) and *Philosophy of Education: An Anthology* (2007), and co-editor of the journal *Theory and Research in Education*.

STEFAAN E. CUYPERS is Professor of Philosophy at the Catholic University of Leuven, Belgium. He works in philosophy of mind and action, epistemology, and philosophy of education. He is the author of *Self-Identity and Personal Autonomy* (2001) and, together with Ishtiyaque Haji, *Moral Responsibility, Authenticity, and Education* (2008).

CATHERINE Z. ELGIN is Professor of Philosophy of Education at Harvard Graduate School of Education, and an associate of the Edmund J. Safra Foundation Center for Ethics and the Professions at Harvard. Her scholarly work focuses on epistemology, philosophy of art, and philosophy of science. She is the author of *Considered Judgment* (1996), *Between the Absolute and the Arbitrary* (1997), and *With Reference to Reference* (1983), and co-author (with Nelson Goodman) of *Reconceptions in Philosophy and Other Arts and Sciences* (1988). She is editor of *The Philosophy of Nelson Goodman* (1997) and co-editor (with Jonathan Adler) of *Philosophical Inquiry* (2007).

RICHARD FELDMAN is Professor of Philosophy and Dean of the College at the University of Rochester. He specializes in epistemology. He is the author of over 70 articles and the author or co-author of three books: *Reason and Argument* (1999), *Epistemology*

(2003), and *Evidentialism* (with Earl Conee, 2004). He is a co-editor of a forthcoming book exploring philosophical issues about "reasonable disagreements."

RICHARD E. GRANDY is Professor of Philosophy and Cognitive Sciences at Rice University. His central interest is in the special human abilities to create and acquire knowledge of logic, mathematics, and science. These interests in philosophy of logic, mathematics, and science have led him to related questions in education, epistemology, metaphysics, and language as well.

AMY GUTMANN is the President of the University of Pennsylvania. Previously she was the provost of Princeton University and the founding director of Princeton's University Center for Human Values. A political philosopher, she has published numerous books and articles, among the most recent *Why Deliberative Democracy?* (with Dennis Thompson, 2004), *Identity in Democracy* (2003), and *Democratic Education* (revised edition 1999).

PHILIP KITCHER is John Dewey Professor of Philosophy at Columbia University; he is a past President of the American Philosophical Association (Pacific Division), a former editor-in-chief of the journal *Philosophy of Science*, and a Fellow of the American Academy of Arts and Sciences. In 2006 he was selected as the first recipient of the Prometheus Prize, awarded by the American Philosophical Association for lifetime achievement in expanding the frontiers of philosophy and science. He is the author of many articles in philosophy of science, epistemology, ethics, and social philosophy, and has published eight books, including *The Advancement of Science* (1993), *Science, Truth, and Democracy* (2001), *Living with Darwin: Evolution, Design, and the Future of Faith* (2007), and *Joyce's Kaleidoscope: An Invitation to Finnegans Wake* (2007).

MEIRA LEVINSON is Assistant Professor of Education at the Harvard Graduate School of Education, following eight years of teaching middle school in the Atlanta and Boston public schools. Her current research focuses on civic and multicultural education, especially in de facto segregated urban schools. She wrote *The Demands of Liberal Education* (1999) and was a contributing author to *Democracy at Risk: How Political Choices Undermine Citizen Participation, and What We Can Do About It* (2005).

GARETH B. MATTHEWS is Professor of Philosophy Emeritus at the University of Massachusetts/Amherst. He is the author of many articles and several books on ancient, medieval, and early modern philosophy, including *Socratic Perplexity and the Nature of Philosophy* (1999) and *Augustine* (2005). He is also the author of many articles and several books on philosophy and childhood, including *The Philosophy of Childhood* (1994).

ELIJAH MILLGRAM is E. E. Ericksen Professor of Philosophy at the University of Utah. Author of *Practical Induction* (1997) and *Ethics Done Right: Practical Reasoning as a Foundation for Moral Theory* (2005), his research focuses on the theory of rationality. His current historical interests include John Stuart Mill and Friedrich Nietzsche.

DAVID MOSHMAN is Professor of Educational Psychology at the University of Nebraska-Lincoln and book review editor for the *Journal of Applied Developmental Psychology*. His primary areas of expertise are adolescent development, intellectual freedom in education, and the psychology of genocide. He is the author of *Adolescent Psychological Development: Rationality, Morality, and Identity* (2nd edition, 2005), *The Daughters of the Plaza de Mayo* (political science fiction, 2006), and *Liberty and Learning: Academic Freedom for Teachers and Students* (2009).

NEL NODDINGS is Lee Jacks Professor of Education Emerita, Stanford University. Her latest books are *Critical Lessons: What Our Schools Should Teach* (2006) and *When School Reform Goes Wrong* (2007).

MARTHA NUSSBAUM is Ernst Freund Distinguished Service Professor of Law and Ethics at the University of Chicago, appointed in the Law School, Philosophy Department, and Divinity School. Her most recent book is *Liberty of Conscience: In Defense of America's Tradition of Religious Equality* (2008).

GRAHAM ODDIE is Professor of Philosophy at the University of Colorado at Boulder. He has written widely on issues in the philosophy of science, metaphysics, and the theory of value. His publications include *Likeness to Truth* (1986) and *Value, Reality and Desire* (2005).

D. C. PHILLIPS is Professor Emeritus of Education, and by courtesy of Philosophy, at Stanford University. He is a member of the National Academy of Education, and has been a Fellow at the Center for Advanced Study in the Behavioral Sciences. He is the author, most recently, of *Postpositivism and Educational Research* (with N. Burbules, 2000) and *The Expanded Social Scientist's Bestiary* (2000), and the editor of *Constructivism in Education* (the 99th Yearbook of the National Society for the Study of Education, 2000).

ROB REICH is Associate Professor of Political Science, Director of the Program in Ethics in Society, and co-Director of the Philanthropy and Civil Society Center at Stanford University. He is the author of *Bridging Liberalism and Multiculturalism in American Education* (2002), co-author of *Democracy at Risk* (2005), and co-editor of *Toward a Humanist Justice: The Political Philosophy of Susan Moller Okin* (2009).

EMILY ROBERTSON is Dual Associate Professor of Education and Philosophy in the School of Education and the College of Arts and Sciences at Syracuse University. Her primary research focus is on the development and defense of fostering rationality as an educational aim. She has also written on moral and civic education. Recent publications include "Teacher Education in a Democratic Society: Learning and Teaching the Practices of Democratic Participation" in the 3rd edition of *The Handbook of Research on Teacher Education* (2008).

AMÉLIE RORTY is Lecturer in the Department of Social Medicine at the Harvard Medical School and Visiting Professor of Philosophy at Boston University. She is the author of *Mind in Action* (1991) and editor of *Explaining Emotions* (1976), *Perspectives on Self-Deception* (1988), *Philosophers on Education* (1998), *The Many Faces of Philosophy* (2000), *The Many Faces of Evil* (2001), volumes on Aristotle's

Ethics, Poetics, and Rhetoric, and numerous papers in the history of moral psychology.

HARVEY SIEGEL is Professor and Chair of the Department of Philosophy at the University of Miami. He is the author of many papers in epistemology, philosophy of science, and philosophy of education, and of *Relativism Refuted: A Critique of Contemporary Epistemological Relativism* (1987), *Educating Reason: Rationality, Critical Thinking, and Education* (1988), and *Rationality Redeemed? Further Dialogues on an Educational Ideal* (1997).

MICHAEL SLOTE is Professor of Philosophy and UST Professor of Ethics at the University of Miami. He is the author, most recently, of *The Ethics of Care and Empathy* (2007); and his current research is on sentimentalist meta-ethics and on care-ethical moral education.

NICHOLAS D. SMITH is the James F. Miller Professor of Humanities at Lewis & Clark College in Portland, Oregon. He is the co-author with T. C. Brickhouse of five books and numerous articles on the philosophy of Socrates. They are currently working on a book-length study of Socrates' moral psychology.

THE OXFORD HANDBOOK OF

PHILOSOPHY OF EDUCATION

INTRODUCTION: PHILOSOPHY OF EDUCATION AND PHILOSOPHY

HARVEY SIEGEL

1. WHAT IS PHILOSOPHY OF EDUCATION?

PHILOSOPHY of education is that branch of philosophy that addresses philosophical questions concerning the nature, aims, and problems of education. As a branch of practical philosophy, its practitioners look both inward to the parent discipline of philosophy and outward to educational practice, as well as to developmental psychology, cognitive science more generally, sociology, and other relevant disciplines.

The most basic problem of philosophy of education is that concerning aims: what are the proper aims and guiding ideals of education? A related question concerns evaluation: what are the appropriate criteria for evaluating educational efforts, institutions, practices, and products? Other important problems involve the authority of the state and of teachers, and the rights of students and parents; the character of purported educational ideals such as critical thinking, and of purportedly undesirable phenomena such as indoctrination; the best way to understand and conduct moral education; a range of questions concerning teaching, learning, and curriculum; and many others. All these and more are addressed in the essays that follow.[1]

2. THE RELATION OF PHILOSOPHY OF EDUCATION TO PHILOSOPHY

For much of the history of Western philosophy, philosophical questions concerning education were high on the philosophical agenda. From Socrates, Plato, and

Aristotle to twentieth-century figures such as Bertrand Russell, John Dewey, R. S. Peters, and Israel Scheffler, general philosophers (i.e., contemporary philosophers working in departments of philosophy and publishing in mainstream philosophy journals, and their historical predecessors) addressed questions in philosophy of education along with their treatments of issues in epistemology, metaphysics, philosophy of mind and language, and moral and social/political philosophy. The same is true of most of the major figures of the Western philosophical tradition, including Augustine, Aquinas, Descartes, Locke, Hume, Rousseau, Kant, Hegel, Mill, and many others.[2]

On the face of it, this should not be surprising. For one thing, the pursuit of philosophical questions concerning education is partly dependent upon investigations of the more familiar core areas of philosophy. For example, questions concerning the curriculum routinely depend on epistemology and the philosophies of the various curriculum subjects (e.g., Should science classes emphasize mastery of current theory or the "doing" of science? What is it about art that entitles it, if it is so entitled, to a place in the curriculum? According to what criteria should specific curriculum content be selected? Should all students be taught the same content?). Questions concerning learning, thinking, reasoning, belief, and belief change typically depend on epistemology, ethics, and/or philosophy of mind (e.g., Under what conditions is it desirable and/or permissible to endeavor to change students' fundamental beliefs? To what end should students be taught—if they should be so taught—to reason? Can reasoning be fostered independently of the advocacy, inculcation, or indoctrination of particular beliefs?). Questions concerning the nature of and constraints governing teaching often depend on ethics, epistemology, and/or the philosophies of mind and language (e.g., Is it desirable and/or permissible to teach mainstream contemporary science to students whose cultures or communities reject it? Should all students be taught in the same manner? How are permissible teaching practices distinguished from impermissible ones?). Similarly, questions concerning schooling frequently depend on ethics, social/political philosophy, and social epistemology (e.g., Assuming that schools have a role to play in the development of ethical citizens, should they concentrate on the development of character or, rather, on the rightness or wrongness of particular actions? Is it permissible for schools to be in the business of the formation of students' character, given liberalism's reluctance to endorse particular conceptions of the good? Should schools be constituted as democratic communities? Do all students have a right to education? If so, to what extent if any is such an education obliged to respect the beliefs of all groups, and what does such respect involve?). This sort of dependence on the parent discipline is typical of philosophical questions concerning education.

Another, related reason that the philosophical tradition has taken educational matters as a locus of inquiry is that many fundamental questions concerning education—for example, those concerning the aims of education, the character and desirability of liberal education, indoctrination, moral and intellectual virtues, the imagination, authenticity, and other educational matters—are of independent philosophical interest but are intertwined with more standard core areas and issues (e.g., Is the fundamental epistemic aim of education the development of true belief, justified belief, understanding, some combination of these, or something else? In what sense if any can curriculum content be rightly regarded as "objective"? Given the cognitive state of the very young child, is it possible to avoid indoctrination entirely—and if not, how bad a thing is that? Should education aim at the transmission of existing knowledge or, rather, at fostering the abilities and dispositions conducive to inquiry and the achievement of autonomy?).

In addition, the pursuit of fundamental questions in more or less all the core areas of philosophy often leads naturally to and is sometimes enhanced by sustained attention to questions about education (e.g., epistemologists disagree about the identity of the highest or most fundamental epistemic value, with some plumping for truth/true belief and others for justified or rational belief; this dispute is clarified by its consideration in the context of education).[3]

For these reasons, and perhaps others, it is not surprising that the philosophical tradition has generally regarded education as a worthy and important target of philosophical reflection. It is therefore unfortunate that the pursuit of philosophy of education as an area of philosophical investigation has been largely abandoned by general philosophers in the last decades of the twentieth century, especially in the United States. The 1950s, 1960s, and 1970s saw quite a few general philosophers make important contributions to philosophy of education, including, among others, such notables as Kurt Baier, Max Black, Brand Blanshard, Richard Brandt, Abraham Edel, Joel Feinberg, William Frankena, Alan Gewirth, D. W. Hamlyn, R. M. Hare, Alasdaire MacIntyre, A. I. Melden, Frederick Olafson, Ralph Barton Perry, R. S. Peters, Edmund Pincoffs, Kingsley Price, Gilbert Ryle, Israel Scheffler, and Morton White.[4] But the subject has more recently suffered a loss of visibility and presence, to the extent that many, and perhaps most, working general philosophers and graduate students do not recognize it as a part of philosophy's portfolio.

The reasons for this loss are complex and are mainly contingent historical ones that I will not explore here. It remains, nevertheless, that this state of affairs is unfortunate for the health of philosophy of education as an area of philosophical endeavor, and for general philosophy as well. The "benign neglect" of philosophy of education by the general philosophical community—an area central to philosophy since Socrates and Plato—not only deprives the field of a huge swath of talented potential contributors; it also leaves working general philosophers and their students without an appreciation of an important branch of their discipline. One purpose of this volume is to rectify this situation.

3. THE CHAPTERS

The essays that follow are divided in a way that reflects my own, no doubt somewhat idiosyncratic understanding of the contours of the field; other groupings would be equally sensible. In the first section, concerning the *aims of education*, Emily

Robertson and Harry Brighouse treat the epistemic and moral/political aims of education, respectively, while Martha Nussbaum provides an account of and makes the case for the importance and contemporary relevance of liberal education.

The next concerns a variety of issues involving *thinking, reasoning, teaching, and learning*. Richard Feldman discusses epistemological aspects of thinking and reasoning as they are manifested in the educational context. Jonathan Adler offers an account, informed by recent work in cognitive science as well as epistemology, of the nature of fallibility and its educational significance. Eamonn Callan and Dylan Arena offer an account of indoctrination, while Stefaan Cuypers does the same for authenticity. David Moshman provides a psychological account of the development of rationality, while Gareth Matthews raises doubts concerning the contributions developmental psychology might make to the philosophical understanding of the various cognitive dimensions of education. Thomas Brickhouse and Nicholas Smith offer a nuanced account of Socratic teaching and Socratic method, while Amélie Rorty argues for the educational importance of imagination and sketches strategies for developing it in the classroom.

The third section focuses on *moral, value, and character education*. Michael Slote articulates and defends an empathy-based approach to moral education, while Marcia Baron defends a Kantian approach. Elijah Millgram focuses on moral skepticism and possible attendant limits of moral education. Graham Oddie offers a metaphysical account of value as part of a general approach to values education.

The next section treats issues arising at the intersection of *knowledge, curriculum, and educational research*. David Carr addresses general questions concerning the extent to which, and the ways in which, the curriculum is and ought to be driven by our views of knowledge. Philip Kitcher focuses on the work of Dewey, Mill, and Adam Smith, arguing that Dewey's philosophy of education has the resources to answer a challenge posed by Smith's economic analyses, and that philosophers ought to embrace Dewey's reconceptualization of philosophy as the "general theory of education." Catherine Elgin discusses the character of art and the centrality of art education to the curriculum. Robert Audi and Richard Grandy both address questions concerning science education—the first focusing on the ways in which religious toleration and liberal neutrality might constrain science education, and the second on contemporary cognitive scientific investigations of teaching and learning in the science classroom. Denis Phillips assesses extant philosophical critiques of educational research and discusses the scientific status, current state, and future promise of such research.

The fifth section addresses *social and political* issues concerning education. Amy Gutmann and Meira Levinson both address contentious questions concerning education in the contemporary circumstances of multiculturalism, while Lawrence Blum treats the problematic character and effects of prejudice and the prospects for overcoming them. Rob Reich investigates the moral and legal legitimacy of some varieties of educational authority, emphasizing the important but often overlooked interests of children.

The final section includes three papers that discuss particular approaches to philosophy of education: Randall Curren considers pragmatic approaches to the subject, Nel Noddings feminist approaches, and Nicholas Burbules postmodern approaches. All three provide useful overviews of and also critically address the promise of and problems facing the target approaches.

4. Bringing Philosophy of Education Back to Philosophy

All of these chapters exhibit both the deep and genuinely philosophical character of philosophical questions concerning education, and the benefits to be gained by sustained attention, by students and philosophers alike, to those questions. Most of them are written by distinguished general philosophers; they reflect both a sophisticated mastery of the core areas of philosophy (to which these authors have made independent important contributions) and a deep grasp of the significance of philosophical questions concerning education. All of them exemplify the benefits to be derived from a fruitful interaction between philosophy of education and the parent discipline.

The time is right for philosophy of education to regain its rightful place in the world of general philosophy. And it is for this reason that I am especially pleased to have been involved in the present project. Happily, there have been some positive developments on this score in recent years, as well as some honorable exceptions to the general neglect of philosophy of education in recent decades by the community of general philosophers.[5] My hope is that the volume will further contribute to the restoration of philosophy of education to its rightful place in the world of general philosophy, by playing some role in furthering the recent rekindling of interest among general philosophers in philosophy of education: in their taking seriously philosophical problems concerning education, and in putting the latter on their philosophical agendas.[6]

NOTES

1. For more detailed depictions of the field, see Curren 1998b, Phillips 2008, and Siegel 2007.

2. For contemporary assessments of the contributions to philosophy of education of these and other figures, made by an impressive roster of contemporary general philosophers, see Rorty 1998. A fine brief survey is provided in Curren 1998a. Phillips 2008 (section 1.2) issues a salutary reservation concerning the philosophical significance of the educational musings of the acknowledged great figures of the Western philosophical tradition.

3. See Siegel (2005).

4. For a brief and partial indication of the level of activity, see Archambault 1965, Doyle 1973, Frankena 1965, Hamlyn 1978, Langford and O'Connor 1973, *Monist* 1968, and Scheffler 1958/1966, 1960, 1965, 1973/1989.

5. I briefly mention some of them in Siegel 2005, p. 345, note 1.

6. Thanks to Jonathan Adler and Randall Curren for very helpful guidance and advice on the penultimate draft of this introduction.

REFERENCES

Archambault, Reginald D., ed. (1965). *Philosophical Analysis and Education*. London: Routledge & Kegan Paul.

Curren, Randall (1998a). "Education, History of Philosophy of." In *Routledge Encyclopedia of Philosophy*, ed. E. J. Craig (pp. 222–31). London: Routledge.

—— (1998b). "Education, Philosophy of." In *Routledge Encyclopedia of Philosophy*, ed. E. J. Craig (pp. 231–40). London: Routledge.

Doyle, James F., ed. (1973). *Educational Judgments: Papers in the Philosophy of Education*. London: Routledge & Kegan Paul.

Frankena, William K. (1965). *Three Historical Philosophies of Education: Aristotle, Kant, Dewey*. Glenview, IL: Scott, Foresman and Company.

Hamlyn, D. W. (1978). *Experience and the Growth of Understanding*. London: Routledge & Kegan Paul.

Langford, Glenn, and D. J. O'Connor, eds. (1973). *New Essays in the Philosophy of Education*. London: Routledge & Kegan Paul.

The Monist (1968). General Topic: Philosophy of Education. *Monist* 52:1.

Phillips, D. C. (2008). "Philosophy of Education." *Stanford Encyclopedia of Philosophy*, June 2008, http://plato.stanford.edu/entries/education-philosophy/.

Rorty, Amélie, ed. (1998). *Philosophers on Education: New Historical Perspectives*. London: Routledge.

Scheffler, Israel, ed. (1958/1966). *Philosophy and Education: Modern Readings*. Boston: Allyn and Bacon.

—— (1960). *The Language of Education*. Springfield, IL: Charles C. Thomas.

—— (1965). *Conditions of Knowledge: An Introduction to Epistemology and Education*. Chicago: Scott Foresman.

—— (1973/1989). *Reason and Teaching*. Indianapolis: Hackett.

Siegel, Harvey (2005). "Truth, Thinking, Testimony and Trust: Alvin Goldman on Epistemology and Education." *Philosophy and Phenomenological Research* 71(2): 345–66.

—— (2007). "The Philosophy of Education." *Encyclopaedia Britannica Online*, September 2007, http://search.eb.com/eb/article-9108550. Forthcoming in *Encyclopaedia Britannica*, print version.

PART I

AIMS OF
EDUCATION

CHAPTER 1

THE EPISTEMIC AIMS OF EDUCATION

EMILY ROBERTSON

[T]he educational ideal of rationality...[is aligned] with the complementary ideal of *autonomy*, since a rational person will also be an autonomous one, capable of judging for herself the justifiedness of candidate beliefs and the legitimacy of candidate values.

—H. Siegel, "Cultivating Reason"

Rationality sometimes consists in refusing to think for oneself.

—J. Hardwig, "Epistemic Dependence"

[T]he independent thinker is not someone who works everything out for herself, even in principle, but one who exercises a controlling intelligence over the input she receives from the normal sources of information whether their basis be individual or communal.

—C. A. J. Coady, "Testimony, Observation, and 'Autonomous Knowledge'"

EPISTEMOLOGY in the broadest sense is concerned with giving an account of knowledge. If educators ought to aim at having their students acquire knowledge, their *epistemic* aims are related to this goal. Knowledge is a familiar concept in public and professional debates about education.[1] People often consider what particular forms of knowledge ought to be included in the curriculum. Should schools offer a course on world religions, for example? Should they teach the theory of intelligent design in addition to, or in place of, the theory of evolution? But the epistemic aims of education do not concern curricular subjects, at least not directly. Rather, the issue concerns the way the work of the educator should be guided by an understanding of the nature of knowledge itself. What *is* knowledge? When does a student really know something as opposed to having simply guessed a correct answer, for example?

There are different types of knowledge, such as knowing that something is so, knowing how to do something, or knowing a person. Much philosophical inquiry has focused on what is required for knowing that something is so, commonly called *propositional knowledge.* There is considerable disagreement about the correct analysis of this type of knowledge.[2] Many hold, however, that having knowledge of a particular proposition requires justified true belief.[3] Thus if Professor Choi knows that social class differences in the United States affect educational attainment, she must believe the proposition, her belief must be true (i.e., it must be the case that class differences affect attainment), and she must be justified in believing the claim. On some accounts of justification, but not all, this means that she must have good reasons for her belief. What constitutes proper justification is one of the unresolved issues in the analysis of knowledge.[4]

It seems reasonable to assume that acquiring propositional knowledge is a major aim of education. If that assumption is correct, then the above analysis provides a starting point for our inquiry. If education aims at knowledge, and knowledge requires truth and justification, then they must lie among the epistemic aims of education.[5] But these aims, though central, cannot be the only epistemic aims, for several reasons. No one supposes that just *any* justified true belief should be included in an educational curriculum. Are there additional epistemic aims that guide the selection? Further, it's common to regard students not only as consumers of expert information but also as apprentices to the cognitive communities that produce knowledge (at least to the extent appropriate and possible given their goals and developmental levels). Is this assumption justified and, if so, what further epistemic aims does it entail? Even apprentices to cognitive communities can be regarded as subservient to the experts' construction of knowledge, however. Should educators aim more ambitiously at some degree of cognitive autonomy, making it possible, as Siegel (2003) puts it, for a student to be capable "of judging for herself the justifiedness of candidate beliefs" (p. 307)?

Answering these questions, as we will see, creates an abstract picture of the ideal knower whose characteristics embody a set of normative epistemic aims for education. I believe this picture is useful, indeed crucial, but it has also encountered significant challenges that should to be addressed in developing a defensible account. I'll discuss two main concerns:

1. Some have argued that the characterization of the ideal knower outlined above is too abstract (Alcoff and Potter 1993; Antony 2002; Code 1993; Daukas 2006; Haraway 1988; Harding 1991). It assumes that there are no epistemologically

relevant differences among knowers, that they can be regarded as the same for the purposes of producing a theory of knowledge. It does not take into account differences in the situation and features of potential knowers that are relevant, it is urged, to the knowledge (or theories of knowledge) they construct. Culture, gender, race, and group subordination or oppression, for example, are embodied features of those who construct knowledge that cannot be neglected if an adequate and helpful theory of knowledge is to result. At issue in this critique is not the abstractness of the characterization of knowledge per se, as if it were simply not concrete enough, but, rather, the way in which that abstraction denies or obscures the relationship between knowledge and power, a feature that an educationally useful (and morally and politically just) theory of knowledge cannot ignore. Thus, understanding the social and political conditions of the production and dissemination of knowledge is a crucial epistemic aim of education from this point of view.

2. The second issue concerns how epistemic educational aims should acknowledge each individual's dependence on the knowledge of others. On the one hand, it seems plausible that educators should teach students to think for themselves. On the other hand, we live in a world in which reliance on the testimony and expert judgment of others is pervasive. Is Hardwig (2006) right, then, that "Rationality sometimes consists in refusing to think for oneself" (p. 329)? Nor is the issue only a matter of whether and when it's appropriate to accept the claims of individual experts. As Elgin (1996) puts it, "Understanding and knowledge are collective accomplishments" (p. 116). The content of the curriculum that schools teach is the result of cognitive activity by communities of inquirers, the community of historians, for example. An individual learner's knowledge draws upon the resources of public bodies of knowledge created by these communities. There are, as Goldman (2002) argues, *social* pathways to knowledge. These pathways include not only communities of inquirers who create knowledge but also the disseminators of knowledge, the media and press, the educational system itself, for example. How should the social dimensions of knowledge be reflected in the epistemic aims of education?

The conclusion I'll argue for is that educators ought not to abandon the goal of thinking for oneself; yet thinking for oneself itself requires attention to the social conditions of knowledge. Thus I agree with Coady (1994) that the "independent thinker" is "one who exercises a controlling intelligence over the input she receives from the normal sources of information whether their basis be individual or communal" (p. 248). Understanding the social conditions of knowledge production, including the relationship between knowledge and power, is part of being an independent thinker in this sense. Yet even this conclusion has a largely individualist thrust in that it positions the individual knower at the center of the enterprise. In some respects, this focus is unavoidable, since educators do have a responsibility to help *individuals* think for themselves, or so I'll argue. On the other hand, given that knowledge creation and dissemination is a social enterprise, individuals should also understand their role as citizens, as well as knowledge producers, in supporting effective and just social pathways to knowledge. Here, consideration of the epistemic ends of education begins to merge with civic education.

1. KNOWLEDGE, TRUTH, AND JUSTIFICATION

Eventually we will need to broaden the epistemic aims of education beyond acquiring propositional knowledge, as I have already acknowledged. For example, the goal is not information per se, but, rather, knowledge that is significant and organized in patterns that contribute to perspective and understanding in orienting thought and action (Elgin 1996; Siegel 1988). Nevertheless, truth and justification—conditions of propositional knowledge—are arguably at the core of the educational enterprise. While teachers are not infallible, "we do not," Noddings (2007) observes, "defend the practice of teaching what we know to be false" (p. 123).[6] And Scheffler (1960) emphasizes the importance of teachers' justifying their claims to their students. Teaching, he says, requires teachers to submit themselves "to the understanding and independent judgment" of their students; to reveal their reasons for believing the claims they're teaching to their students and so submit them to the students' "evaluation and criticism" (p. 57). This is true, Scheffler (1965) holds, because teachers do not want merely "to bring about true belief, but to bring it about through the exercise of free rational judgment by the student" (p. 11).

1.1. Truth

It might seem evident that education should aim at truth. Those who think that knowledge is the proper goal are logically committed to the truth-aim given the standard analysis of propositional knowledge. Adler (2003) argues that, while justification has been the central educational interest, "one's reasons must genuinely establish one's belief as true" if the knowledge-aim of education is to be served (p. 287). Later we will consider whether education should aim at epistemic ends that involve skills and character, ends that are not evaluated in terms of truth or falsity, per se. If so, truth may not be a broad enough category to cover all the epistemic aims of education. Perhaps there are truth analogs in each of these cases. Skills should be effective in achieving their proper ends and character traits should be virtuous, for example. Or perhaps epistemic skills and virtues are valuable only instrumentally in terms of their effectiveness in generating true beliefs. But I am concerned here with the role of truth in the narrower educational domain of transmitting propositional knowledge.

The truth-aim is not without its critics. Here, I'll briefly consider four types of challenges to truth that have implications for education. I should admit at the outset that these are very large questions that cannot be fully explored here. I'll focus on the questions these positions raise for the epistemic aims of education.

1. It is sometimes argued that, since we have no access to truth independent of our reasons or justification for believing something true, truth itself can be dispensed with in favor of justification. For example, Rorty (1998) argues that there is no practical difference between truth and justification—that is, nothing that makes a difference to judgment or action. From this point of view, one might argue that the appropriate epistemic aim of education is justified or rational belief rather than justified *true* belief. This issue will be explored further in section 1.2.[7]

2. A second challenge to truth lies in observations from some feminists and postmodernists about the interconnections between knowledge and power (Code 1993; Foucault 1980, 1988). Much like Thrasymachus' claim in Plato's *Republic* that justice is what is in the interest of the stronger party, the worry here is that what counts as true will reflect the interests of those who have sufficient power to define the aims and rules of inquiry. This is a real worry, especially under conditions where some group's oppression places severe limits on its members' opportunities to participate in knowledge construction and limits the extent to which their experiences are part of the data to be understood and explained. Under these conditions, the dominant group tends to regard its perspectives and ways of thinking as the universal norm and all nonconforming views as deviant. But rejecting truth is surely not necessary for accepting the validity of this point. Exposing the workings of power leads not only to more inclusive theorizing but also to findings that are more nearly true (Siegel 1998). The position that the epistemic aims of education should include fostering critical perspectives that teach students to analyze theory and findings from this perspective will be explored further in section 3.

3. A third line of criticism rejects the idea that truth is objective or universal. Rather, truth is said to be relative to the organizing framework or perspective being employed. The world has no structure in itself, independent of the mind that represents it. According to the relativist, there is no scheme-independent way of deciding between competing frameworks, no possibility of determining truth in a way that transcends all schemes. In its strongest form, the thesis implies that a statement may be true relative to one framework and false relative to another. Some constructivist theorists of learning, for example, appear to hold the view that different persons can arrive at equally well-grounded but conflicting beliefs, each appropriately called knowledge.[8]

Whether relativism about truth is ultimately a coherent position or not cannot be decided here.[9] For our purpose of examining the epistemic aims of education, I note that, even if it is a coherent view, it is not a reason to dispense with a commitment to seek truth. Presumably, any useful and viable framework will contain methods of inquiry and standards of justification that allow for a distinction to be drawn between truth and error from within its perspective. Individual inquirers working within a framework cannot make any claim they like true; they are bound by the framework's standards. Neither is it possible to make any claim we like true by adopting a suitable perspective. Some claims lack plausibility from any reasonable perspective. Further, all individuals and groups seek to improve their fund of knowledge. They modify their beliefs in light of new experiences and information in an effort to arrive at beliefs that are more adequate. If we regarded *all* positions as equally valid, why would we be interested in learning or education at all? These facts give truth sufficient objectivity to make an admonition to seek truth a viable educational goal.

4. The final challenge to truth that I'll consider concerns the claim that truth does not necessarily trump all other values. In *Beyond Good and Evil*, Nietzsche (1966) wrote: "The falseness of a judgment is for us not necessarily an objection to a judgment.... The question is to what extent it is life-promoting, life-preserving, species-preserving, perhaps even species-cultivating" (pp. 11–12). Ellsworth (1997) takes a similar stance in her philosophy of education: "In what ways does the world rise or fall in value when a reader or groups of readers perform and let loose in the world this particular meaning or reading of a text or event? ... 'What counts' as a 'rise' or 'a fall' in the value of the world becomes a historical and social achievement—not a transcendental given waiting to be discovered.... Is this reading true or false, right or wrong, good or bad? is a question that drives toward closure, stasis, and the fixing of knowledge. But the question, What has this reading performed or let loose in the world? sends us out on an exploration" (127–28).

In both these claims, commitment to truth is simply deferred, not dispensed with. Presumably, investigating which judgments or readings are life-promoting or increase value in the world will require an inquiry whose end is discovering the truth of the causal connections in question. Nevertheless, Nietzsche and Ellsworth would be willing to give higher priority to noncognitive ends over truth in particular circumstances, just as many tell small lies rather than give offense to a friend or as a peace negotiator may care less about the truth of what happened and more about arranging a viable agreement (Robertson 2007). The desirability of such tradeoffs in particular circumstances does not challenge, however, the claim that truth is a primary *epistemic* goal.

1.2. Justification

On the standard account of propositional knowledge, a belief must be justified to count as knowledge. Under what conditions is a belief justified? Epistemologists have produced a daunting array of theories. Here, I consider one main disagreement concerning whether internalism or externalism is the correct view of justification.[10] According to internalists, justification must rest on factors accessible to the consciousness of the knower. Foundationalist internalists hold that justification ultimately depends on basic beliefs (foundational beliefs) that do not themselves depend on any other beliefs for their justification. Coherentist internalists hold that justification depends on mutual support among the agent's beliefs. For externalists, justification can depend on at least some factors outside the scope of the consciousness of the knower (and, indeed, any knowers) that are, nevertheless, in interaction with the agent's cognitive states. In one form, reliabilism, externalism holds that justified beliefs are those beliefs produced in the agent under appropriate conditions by a reliable and truth-conducive process (perception is an example). It's irrelevant from the externalist perspective whether the agent or anyone else knows that the causal processes involved are in fact truth-conducive. If they are, then the agent's beliefs arrived at under appropriate conditions through this process are justified (my belief that there is a computer in front of me right now, for example).

One way of understanding the internalist perspective is to suppose that internalists think justificatory criteria should provide guidance about what to believe; but if we lack access to the justificatory grounds for our beliefs, then those grounds cannot provide such guidance. As Elgin (1996) says, externalism is useless in our lives because, if we don't know when the right relationship obtains between our beliefs and the appropriate causal mechanisms, the criterion doesn't help us distinguish between true and false beliefs (p. 51).

Wherever the truth lies in epistemology, I believe that educators rightly adopt an internalist stance. From a first-person standpoint, there is no way to pursue truth except by searching for good reasons that are truth-conducive. Perhaps for this reason educational practice may seem to place greater weight on justification than on truth, a state of affairs noted by Adler (2003): "Because it is an external condition for knowledge, truth has been of less educational interest than the justification condition" (p. 286). There are, however, important educational reasons for the focus on justification. Educators should seek not merely to *transmit* knowledge but also to put students into a position where they can, to some extent, decide for themselves what to believe. It would be a poor education that transmitted a fixed body of facts without also developing the resources for arriving at new beliefs and evaluating old ones. Hence, the cogency of justifications that students offer for their beliefs is a prime concern of educators and leads to a central focus on conveying what sorts of reasons are good reasons for belief within a given domain. Thus, educators rightly want students to have access to the justificatory grounds for their beliefs.

Given an internalist perspective, is *justified* true belief too demanding an epistemic aim for educators? One might reasonably argue that knowing the evidential base for *every* belief is too strenuous even as an ideal. Students often come to believe what their teachers tell them or what their textbooks say, without necessarily knowing the reasons for these beliefs, for example. Are their beliefs in such cases unjustified? And what about the teachers' beliefs? Are their beliefs, the ones they are passing on to their students, fully justified on the internalist standard? What one says here will depend on whether beliefs based solely on the testimony of others can be justified and, if so, under what conditions. I defer discussion of this issue to section 3.

Since truth and justification are both conditions of knowledge, they cannot be educationally incompatible if knowledge is a proper educational goal. Nevertheless, the connection between justification and truth can come apart. Human claims to knowledge are fallible, since we have no way to truth except through our justificatory beliefs and strategies, and they can fail us. Sometimes these failures are unknown to anyone; they represent as yet unappreciated problems in the current state of knowledge. But there can also be, and frequently are, individual cases in which a person can appear to be justified in his or her belief, although the belief is not true and its falsity is known to others. Lehrer (1994) draws a distinction between "subjective" justification and "objective" justification to capture this situation. A person's belief is subjectively justified if the belief is supported by the other beliefs the person holds and he or she has arrived at the belief through appropriate reasoning and the belief would be sustained on reflection. If, however, known facts of which the person is unaware defeat the justification, the agent's belief is not objectively justified.

Educators often confront such cases. Sometimes teachers may more highly evaluate a student whose belief is false, but subjectively justified, than a student who has a true, but not subjectively justified, belief. Is it reasonable for educators to prefer subjectively justified false beliefs over unjustified true beliefs? Do educators rightly weight subjective justification more highly than truth, per se? If so, (subjective) justification would have a stronger claim to being the epistemic goal of education than knowledge, since knowledge requires truth.[11]

It is not unreasonable for teachers to prefer the former to the latter in their evaluations of students. A student who has learned to reason well is more likely to arrive at true beliefs in the future than one who has made a lucky guess or gullibly takes the word of another. On this view, justification is valued for its instrumental connection with truth. Or perhaps justification is valuable in its own right. Sosa (2003) proposes that, just as we value an archer's skill in hitting the bull's eye, we might also value not only "hitting the mark of truth" but also "*how* one accomplishes that. . . . On this conception, knowledge is not just hitting the mark but hitting the mark somehow through means proper and skillful enough" (p. 105). Or the educator might take a more deontological view of justification—that is, that it consists in fulfilling one's epistemic obligations. The subjectively justified student has better fulfilled those obligations. In education, these suggestions seem particularly apt: teachers are concerned not only about their students' holding true beliefs but also about the skills and virtues students display in doing so.

I believe that educators should aim at objective justification, however, and hence at what is believed to be true as judged from the perspective of the relevant disciplinary communities. The student whose belief is subjectively justified but false needs instruction just as much as the student whose belief is true but unjustified. Both truth and justification are educationally desirable. But that doesn't settle the proper pedagogy for changing the subjectively justified but false belief of a student. Merely telling the student what belief is best justified and why may not actually alter the student's belief structures and may undermine developing competence in rationality. Some constructivist pedagogies express reluctance to correct the views of those whose subjectively justified beliefs deviate from those of the relevant disciplinary community (Grandy 2007). But this strategy is in the interest of having the student construct his or her own knowledge rather than simply being told what is right by the teacher. Understood as a pedagogical response, constructivism need not deny that both truth and justification are proper epistemic aims of education.

2. Beyond Propositional Knowledge: Understanding, Skills, Virtues, and Judgment

I have argued that propositional knowledge, hence truth and justification, are central epistemic aims of education, but they do not appear to exhaust the domain. I'll not attempt to determine whether the additional aims, briefly mentioned in this section, are valuable in their own right or as means to achieving some unitary epistemic aim, truth, for example. For our purposes, it's enough that each has importance in an adequate educational program. Indeed, when educators speak of "knowledge" it is often assumed that these elements are included.[12]

2.1. Understanding

Even those in favor of students' memorizing lists of information agree that educators shouldn't aim at having students acquire *only* isolated bits of information. Students should understand the meaning and significance of the knowledge they acquire. Their knowledge should be organized in patterns and structures that contribute to perspective and understanding in orienting thought and action. Elgin (1996, 2007) argues that understanding, *not* propositional knowledge, is the goal of both inquiry and education. While I hold that knowledge and understanding are not incompatible goals (understanding generally requires a fair bit of knowledge), I'll not try to resolve this issue here. I agree, however, that understanding is a central epistemic aim of education. Knowledge of individual propositions is an abstraction from knowledge in a broader sense that encompasses understanding. Understanding requires a holistic grasp of an area that involves seeing the connections among the individual elements—how they fit together to generate an overall pattern or system. While some cases of understanding can be expressed in propositional form (e.g., understanding the meaning of a sentence), others arguably cannot (e.g., understanding a musical composition). Unlike propositional knowledge, understanding comes in degrees. A high school biology student's understanding of brain functioning is not equivalent to that of a neurologist's. But for the student's grasp to count as understanding it has to have *some* purchase on the phenomenon in question. A child who believes that the stork brings babies doesn't understand where babies come from. So understanding must meet an adequacy condition just as propositional knowledge requires truth (Riggs 2003; Roberts and Wood 2007, pp. 42–50). Still, there are degrees of adequacy of understanding, not simply the binary function of true or false associated with propositional knowledge.

2.2. Cognitive Skills and Know-how

Philosophers of education have argued that educators should be concerned not only to transmit expert knowledge with understanding but also to develop to some extent the cognitive skills required to produce and evaluate such knowledge. The development of such skills opens the possibility of the student's becoming a critical thinker (Bailin 1998; Siegel 1988, 2003). The cognitive skills aimed at may be general (e.g., appraising arguments for their validity) or specific to disciplinary fields (e.g., evaluating the merits of a musical performance) (Smith 2002).

Knowing how to produce and evaluate knowledge in a wide range of areas would be an impossible aim if it weren't the case that knowing how, like understanding, is in many cases achieved in varying degrees. A reasonable aim would be to enable students to develop cognitive skills to a degree appropriate to their stage of development and their specific educational goals. Knowledge of how to conduct a scientific experiment appropriate for high school biology students, for example, is not the same as the knowledge expected of doctoral students in the field.

The ability to engage in critical inquiry is not limited, however, to evaluating disciplinary claims. Critical thinking or critical rationality in education also aims at helping students to surface and criticize assumptions so deeply embedded in cognitive and cultural practices that they typically escape our scrutiny. This type of inquiry seeks to open up alternative perspectives as a way of evaluating current commitments and of creating new possibilities for thought and action. Inquiry that aims at uncovering assumptions that help to perpetuate forms of social injustice is one example (see section 4.2 for further discussion). What modes of thinking best foster such critical thought is contested (Thompson 2004). But at the very least, the aim of critical inquiry makes apparent a feature of cognitive skills that is also true of the practices described above: cognitive skills are not typically algorithmic, routinized performances. Their exercise often requires situation-specific knowledge and judgment.

Knowing how has not received the same attention from epistemologists as propositional knowledge. Some argue that knowing how *is* a species of propositional knowledge, at least in some senses (Sosa 2003; Stanley and Williamson 2001). Sosa (2003), for example, argues that knowing how may be a form of propositional knowledge, "of knowledge, with respect to a certain way of doing something, that one does it *that* way" (p. 101). Such knowledge is compatible with not knowing how to perform the action oneself. A soccer fan may know how a bicycle kick is performed, for example, without having the knowledge required to do a bicycle kick herself. Sosa calls the former a spectator sense of knowing how and the latter an agential sense. Both of these senses are further distinguished from the agent's ability to perform the act in question. Even someone with agential knowledge might cease to be able to perform the act given new physical disabilities, for example, without losing the relevant know-how.

Should educators aim at the spectator or agential sense of knowing how with respect to cognitive skills? Answering this question depends on the ultimate epistemic aim for teaching cognitive skills. Doctoral students, as the next generation of researchers, should be able to employ the relevant skills themselves, not simply know how it's done. But even at lower levels of the educational system, if the goal is generating some degree of epistemic autonomy, some capacity to think for oneself, then, to the degree possible, the agential sense is the proper aim.

2.3. Epistemic Virtues and Cognitive Emotions

Educators seek to embed cognitive knowledge and skills in an epistemic character. Not only should students be able to exercise the relevant cognitive abilities, they should also be disposed to exercise them in the right way in the appropriate circumstances. Recent work by virtue epistemologists on the cognitive virtues suggests a number of relevant virtues. Central commitments are a disposition to seek good reasons for one's beliefs and to base one's beliefs on them. Associated virtues include open-mindedness, willingness to entertain the views of others, responsiveness to the criticism of others, reasonableness, and self-reflectiveness (BonJour 2002; Burbules 1991, 1995; Hare 2003; Sherman and White 2003; Siegel 1988; Riggs 2003). Cognitive emotions—a love of truth or respect for good arguments, for example—are also part of a desirable epistemic character (Scheffler 1991; Sherman and White 2003).

The proper analysis of a virtue is disputed. For example, for some virtue theorists, virtue encompasses a competence condition while for others it is sufficient to have the proper motives (Riggs 2003). Suppose a person seeks reasons for her beliefs and bases her beliefs on her reasons, but frequently fails to achieve knowledge or understanding. Is such a person epistemically virtuous? Or does virtue require epistemic success? Teachers rightly give credit to students whose hearts are in the right place even if they fail to hit the mark, much as we may continue to admire the epistemic character of great thinkers from the past even if they were ultimately proved wrong. But whether competence is part of virtue or an additional element within the total set of epistemic aims of education, both competence (as the discussion above of cognitive skills indicates) and proper motivation have a place.

2.4. Judgment

Finally, educators rightly aim at the progressive development of intellectual judgment. What distinguishes experts from novices is not only their knowledge and skill but also the level of judgment they display (Dreyfus 2006). There are often no ultimate criteria, no algorithmic decision procedures, for settling intellectual disputes or solving intellectual problems. Still, there are better and worse reasons for taking one position rather than another. When a scientific experiment, for example, does not confirm the hypothesis being investigated, scientists must decide whether and, if so, where, to make accommodations in the theory that generated the hypothesis. Good intellectual judgment is not an independent epistemic aim, since success in developing judgment requires achieving the other aims described above. Sound judgment is impossible without the appropriate knowledge, understanding, skills, and virtues. And one cannot have fully achieved those aims without the development of judgment.

3. Epistemic Dependence

Goldman (1999) is not alone in claiming that "[t]raditional epistemology has long preserved the Cartesian image of inquiry as an activity of isolated thinkers, each pursuing truth in a spirit of individualism and pure self-reliance" (p. vii). That individualism can be seen in the above analysis, which is from the point of view of epistemic aims for the individual knower. The epistemic individualism of epistemology has influenced educational aims in the direction of an ideal of epistemic autonomy, expressed in Locke's claim that "The floating of other men's opinions in our brains makes us not one jot the more knowing, though they happen to be true" (*Essay*, I, iv, #23). Yet we live in a world in which reliance on the testimony and expert judgment of others is pervasive. This situation is not limited to laypersons in their relationships to experts. Scientists, for example, must rely on the reports of other scientists in doing their work since scientific inquiry itself requires collaboration (Hardwig 2006). Epistemic dependence results not only from dependence on the direct testimony of others (teachers, physicians, neighbors) but also from the social division of cognitive labor. We rely on social practices for creating and distributing knowledge, as social epistemologists have emphasized through a variety of perspectives and projects (Goldman 2002; Longino 1990; Nelson 1993; Schmitt 1994). We are all dependent on cognitive practices of others for producing knowledge—cognitive practices that individual scholars and experts help shape over time but that they also largely inherit. And we are dependent on social practices for the dissemination of knowledge. The media, the press, the textbook industry are collective and sometimes anonymous sources of our testimonial beliefs.

These "social pathways to knowledge," as Goldman (2002) calls them, present special challenges for the epistemic aims of education (p. ix). On the one hand, the educational system educates the experts in knowledge production, who, in the areas in which they work, are capable of judging directly the evidence for their knowledge claims. The preceding analysis of epistemic aims applies most robustly to them as they develop their areas of expertise. On the other hand, the system educates us all as consumers of knowledge that we are often unable to directly evaluate when it lies outside our fields of special expertise and our everyday experience. How should our epistemic educational aims acknowledge our dependence on the knowledge of others and on social pathways to knowledge?

As a window into these considerations, I will examine the epistemic status of beliefs acquired through the testimony of others—that is, through their telling us what is the case. A chief question will be the conditions under which a testimonial belief is justified and, hence, what stance educators should teach their students to take toward the testimony of others, including collective sources of knowledge production and dissemination. I explore in particular two sorts of educational projects that I believe are justified in light of epistemic dependence: (1) a critical stance toward our collective cognitive practices in order to consider ways in which they might embody biases that pervert the quest for knowledge and understanding; and (2) shared civic responsibility for supporting institutions that increase the likelihood of successful epistemic outcomes.

3.1. Testimonial Belief

It is evident that much of what any individual believes derives from the testimony of others, through what others have said or written.[13] Can these beliefs, if true, count as knowledge? The issue here concerns the conditions under which one's belief based on testimony will count as justified from the internalist perspective that, I've argued, is the proper stance for educators. Does one have to, as J. L. Mackie (1970) puts it, "know whatever it is off [one's] own bat," and what would that require (p. 254)? Does one have to appropriate the relevant evidence before the belief, if true, counts as knowledge? From this perspective, insofar as the educational system communicates testimonial beliefs, it at best aims at knowledge in the weak sense of true belief. Or does verifying the trustworthiness of the speaker count as justification? Or is testimony a basic ground of justification such that one is entitled to accept what another person says as true absent defeating conditions?[14]

No individual can investigate the grounds for any substantial proportion of the beliefs he or she has acquired through the testimony of others (including texts as well as face-to-face encounters) so as to base them on his or her own direct knowledge of the truth-making factors. It may be, as Adler (2002) argues, that beliefs initially gained through testimony are sustained through other forms of evidence, such as coherence of those beliefs with what we're told by other sources and through satisfactory experiences while acting on the beliefs in question (chap. 5).

Yet even Adler holds only that the gap between testimonial support and other forms has been exaggerated, not that we are never in the position of relying on testimony to sustain beliefs. And since we know that testimony is sometimes false, a policy of blind acceptance of all testimony, "gullibility" as Elizabeth Fricker (1994) calls it, is obviously a mistake. Under what conditions are beliefs based on testimony justified? Or, more weakly, even if they are not sufficiently justified to count as knowledge, how should one be able to defend a belief grounded in testimony so as to make its acceptance rational?

If one is thinking of education, what stance to take toward testimony is a particularly important question. Students are in a vulnerable epistemic position with respect to teachers, who are invested with societal, institutional, and (sometimes) parental authority that inclines students to accept their testimony. Further, teachers are not only telling students what to believe about the matters at hand. There are also explaining what the reasons are for a particular claim and, indeed, teaching students what counts as good reasons in a given domain. It is within their role to prepare students for a critical stance toward knowledge claims whether from individuals (including themselves) or from social sources such as newspapers and the media. What stance should teachers prepare their students to take toward testimony, their own included?

The philosophical literature on testimony suggests two basic options that educators might consider (Adler 2002; Goldman 1999; Matilal and Chakrabarti 1994; Selinger and Crease 2006b):

1. Regarding others as epistemologically trustworthy, and thus accepting their testimonial claims, is justified unless there are overriding reasons not to do so. On this view, hearers don't need reasons to be justified in accepting another's report but rather need reasons to distrust the speaker and reject the report. For example, if a stranger offers directions, we're normally justified in accepting them and acting on them. If, however, parts of the directions (e.g., US Interstate 40 runs through Santa Fe) contradict other things we know, we have reason to reject the speaker's claims.

2. One should always assess the speaker's trustworthiness. There are stronger and weaker versions of this requirement depending on the context.

   a. One should accept testimony only after one has personally verified the credentials of the speaker and satisfied oneself that he or she is likely to be trustworthy. Trustworthiness has two components: sincerity (intention to tell the truth) and competence within the domain of knowledge in question. Thus, we have good reasons to accept a testimonial claim on this account if we have good reasons for believing that the author of the claim is truthful and competent. This condition might apply to someone giving expert opinion, such as physicians, for example.

   b. In some contexts, particularly those dealing with everyday, commonsense claims (e.g., a speaker tells us the month of her birth), it is reasonable to accept what the speaker says if there are no evident reasons not to do so.

Thus far, this position seems equivalent to option 1. However, what distinguishes it from option 1 is a requirement that the hearer continue to monitor the speaker for evidence that the speaker is not to be trusted. Elizabeth Fricker (1994) puts this condition as a "counter-factual sensitivity" of the hearer: "it is true throughout of the hearer that if there were any signs of untrustworthiness, she would pick them up" (p. 154).

It is not entirely clear how distinct the active-monitoring condition expressed in 2b is from option 1. Presumably, defenders of option 1 would want the agent to abandon trust in the face of disconfirming evidence. Fricker holds that the difference lies in how *active* the hearer must be in searching out disconfirming evidence of the speaker's trustworthiness. To exhibit the proper "counter-factual sensitivity" the agent must engage in epistemic activity, must "be alert for" the presence of defeating conditions. Not so according to option 1, she argues, if it is truly to be a distinct option (p. 143).

3.2. Testimonial Belief and Educational Aims

On the above account of the two possible stances toward testimonial belief, it seems right that teachers should adopt the second position, encouraging students to be active and alert to disconfirming evidence, even under conditions where initial acceptance is warranted. Still there is considerable room for interpretation concerning the appropriate *degree* of epistemic activity. Knowing that teachers have been hired for their positions, and thus have presumably been judged competent by the hiring agencies, provides initial reasons for students to accept what the teacher says. Experience with particular teachers offers further opportunities for knowing something about their individual competence, as what they say is confirmed by other sources, for example. But should students simply be alert to inconsistencies that might reveal a lack of competence, or should they be more active in checking what the teacher says through other sources, for example? And do general reasons for holding their teachers trustworthy, such as their educational credentials, justify students in accepting particular utterances of theirs? In short, how active a stance should teachers encourage their students to take toward their own claims and the claims of others?

Likely there are no general answers to these questions, the appropriate degree of activity being subject to judgment and relative to context. For example, the experience of individuals or groups with experts in a given area can generate rationally grounded skepticism when it results from past violations of trust. If African Americans as a group have more negative experiences with police or the court system, for example, higher levels of skepticism and unwillingness to accept claims at face value would be warranted. Or, to suggest a second complicating feature, successful claims to expertise not only rest on competence within a given domain but also require recognition of that form of expertise by an audience (Selinger and Crease 2006a). Some people acknowledge practitioners of alternative medicine as experts and some do not, based on their beliefs about the validity of such practices, for example. Finally, a policy of automatic *mistrust* would require a high degree of epistemic activity that has costs, if only in terms of time and resources. Thus, overall prescriptions about stances toward expert claims need to be located within a complex social and experiential context.

Fricker's "counter-factual sensitivity" to conditions that might defeat acceptance of a testimonial report seems to count as an epistemic virtue in the terms of my previous analysis of epistemic aims. There are also skills of investigating the trustworthiness of testimonial reports that should be part of an educational agenda. These skills, unlike the cognitive skills in the previous section, are not ones that enable direct production or assessment of knowledge claims in terms of their evidential base but, rather, allow students to judge the acceptability of the *source* of the reported information or judgment. Common strategies in individual cases involve checking credentials, getting a "second opinion" in the sense of comparing the information to that available through other sources, or in the case of professional advice, seeking out references from other professionals or from former clients about the past effectiveness of the practitioner. Similar strategies may be devised for evaluating media, newspapers, and so on. These strategies are not always easy or even possible for laypersons to apply in all contexts, but they mitigate to some extent our need to blindly accept what others tell us.

One important mode of assessment involves examining our sources of knowledge for implicit biases. Knowing that a drug study has been funded by the drug's manufacturer, for example, may reasonably lead to some caution in accepting the results without further confirmation. Much recent work has focused on the ways in which factors such as the gender, race, class, or culture of the knowledge producers or disseminators may affect their theories or knowledge claims or the ways in which their theories or claims are received. Here are a few examples:

1. In a recent book, Miranda Fricker (2007) has introduced the notion of "epistemic injustice" in connection with assessments of testimony. A speaker suffers from one form of epistemic injustice if his or her claims are persistently accorded less credibility than is appropriate for reasons of prejudice connected with the speaker's social identity, where persons with that identity marker experience systematic structural social inequalities. If racial prejudice against African Americans, for example, leads white jury members to accord less credibility to testimony by African-Americans, then the African-American witnesses suffer from epistemic injustice. Not only is such a state of affairs unjust, it also leads to mistaken judgments. That is, in addition to being morally wrong and unjust, such prejudices have negative epistemic consequences.

2. Selinger and Crease (2006a) argue that expertise cannot be regarded simply as the embodied development of skilled behavior because its development is always socially and culturally embedded. Experts themselves will typically not be fully aware of the ways in which their social location shapes their judgments and performances. Anderson (2007) offers an example of a personnel manager

who created a tax-sheltered dependent-care account only to find that the staff members for whom it was largely designed (working mothers with children in day care) did not take advantage of it. What the manager had failed to appreciate was the inability of low-wage workers to afford to contribute to the dependent-care account while simultaneously paying for their children's day care. Their wages did not provide enough surplus funds to allow them to wait for later reimbursement. The manager's own economic position and lack of experience of the situation of the staff led to a less than optimal proposal.

3. Feminist scholars have argued that not only individual judgments and performances but also structures of knowledge, with their associated claims to truth, incorporate the biases and interests of their creators and do not serve well the interests of marginalized and oppressed groups who typically do not participate in knowledge production. Routinized measures for bias detection do not work well when the bias is shared by all the members of the group (Antony 2002; Harding 1991). Antony points out the misogyny that feminist philosophers have discovered in the Western philosophical tradition, for example. Features that are first argued to be central to what it is to be human (rationality, autonomy, acting on the basis of moral principles) are then said to be impossible for women, thus denying women fully human status.

Making students aware of issues of bias such as these is an increasingly embraced epistemic aim of education. While some feminists and postmodernists who have pointed out the need for such aims reject the concepts of truth and knowledge that have been described earlier, such rejection is not necessary for recognizing the validity of their observations (Siegel 1998). In general the relevant aim is to develop a critical perspective on one's own acculturated point of view and on the forms of knowing available in one's cultural and social context, examining them through a lens of privilege and power. Numerous anti-racist or multicultural educational programs have been devised with this end in mind at all levels of the educational system (Applebaum 2004; Hytten 2006; Michelli and Keiser 2005). Daukas (2006), for example, endorses Narayan's (1988) view that people in dominant groups would do well to develop an epistemic virtue of "methodological humility" when discussing issues of social oppression (p. 121). Such a stance requires recognizing that one "might be missing something" by virtue of one's privilege (Narayan 1988, p. 38).

3.3. Thinking for Oneself Revisited

The strategies I've canvassed above for being actively alert to defeating conditions for the acceptance of testimony are aimed at the individual knower. In some respects, the individualistic focus is unavoidable, since educators do have a responsibility to help individuals think for themselves, or so I've argued. But some theorists have proposed collective strategies of evaluation that may also have implications for the epistemic aims of education. I don't mean to suggest that knowers are communities rather than individuals, although that point of view has been argued (Nelson 1993). Rather, I have in mind ways in which achieving the epistemic aims of knowledge and understanding, given the facts of epistemic dependence, might be construed as a collaborative endeavor rather than a do-it-yourself project.

For Kant, the autonomous agent is a member of the "Kingdom of Ends" and joins in a public discussion that helps foster independent understanding. After all, *never* giving any weight to the opinions of others when they conflict with one's own is an epistemic vice just as much as total gullibility. The epistemic virtues previously mentioned include willingness to entertain the views of others and responsiveness to their criticisms. Are there social practices, actual or proposed, that could augment the individual strategies described above for assessing testimonial beliefs through generating a wider conversation?

Here are a few, largely tentative and programmatic, proposals. Goldman (2002) asks whether there could be "communicational intermediaries" that "might help make the novice-expert relationship more one of justified credence than blind trust?" (p. 160). In the *Public and Its Problems*, Dewey (1927) argued that the press could play a mediating role in making expert knowledge accessible to the public in the interest of solving public problems. Ihde (2006) argues for a practice of "science criticism" that would be similar to literary criticism. Such critics would have to be very well informed in the area of expertise, but not insiders, who might work in collaboration with scientists. Philosophers, perhaps, could play such a role. Said (2006) believes that increased specialization within universities has created a culture of noninterference across specializations and has limited critical conversation to insiders, rather than encouraging a broader intellectual conversation. He asks: "What is the acceptable humanistic antidote to what one discovers, say, among sociologists, philosophers, and so-called policy scientists who speak only to and for each other in a language oblivious to everything but a well-guarded, constantly shrinking fiefdom forbidden to the uninitiated?" (p. 377). Said forgoes any general answers to this question (e.g., interdisciplinary studies) in favor of encouraging heterogeneous interpretations within a broader intellectual community. Selinger and Crease (2006a) claim that, in some areas such as exposing cultural and other biases, outsiders can have better purchase on expert performance than the experts themselves and can improve it through their insights. They suggest that there could be forums in which experts are held accountable.

Since these practices are not, for the most part, yet actual, it would not make sense to prepare students for participation in them specifically. And many of the proposals I've described above require new categories of experts (counter-experts) as intermediaries between other expert groups and the public. Thus, if reliance on testimony is judged problematic, these strategies do not wholly solve the problem. But students should be aware of the ways in which we are both benefited by the division of intellectual labor and also challenged by it in our quest to think for ourselves.

The primary epistemic consequence of the acceptance of testimony as a source of justification lies in the shift from justification as reasons for the belief in question to reasons for believing others' claims. There is an important difference here, but the line can be drawn too sharply. In both situations, reliance on others is pervasive. Experts working in their areas of expertise and laypersons in everyday life rely on the knowledge of others even when they judge the matter at hand for themselves based on the available evidence for the claim in question. Conceptual frameworks, theories, cognitive strategies, and so on used in the evaluation are part of our social inheritance. The assessment of a particular claim often brings to bear background knowledge not directly assessed by the individual. As previously noted, in fields such as science, where research projects involve large teams of scientists, scientists accept the findings or data of others involved in the project without checking the results themselves. In both areas of expert knowledge and in everyday life, assessment of claims often involves dialogue with others, as one considers and responds to their objections and criticisms. So even justification understood as reasons for the belief in question is often a collaborative enterprise.

There is a difference, however, even if not an entirely sharp one, between knowing the reasons for a claim and accepting the testimony of others. Hardwig (2006) asserts that our dependence on testimony means that "'Thinking for oneself' is no longer at the heart of what it is to be rational" (p. 328); hence "Rationality sometimes consists in refusing to think for oneself" (p. 329). But this is too strong. On the view that rational acceptance of testimonial claims requires actively monitoring the situation for disconfirming evidence (a view it appears Hardwig accepts since he holds that justification requires our having good reasons for believing experts' claims), there is still an epistemic requirement to think for oneself about whether to accept testimonial claims as true.

Nevertheless, acknowledgment of the role of testimony demonstrates the need for assessments of the social context of knowledge production and dissemination if one is still to some extent to think for oneself. As Coady (1994) puts it, "[T]he independent thinker is not someone who works everything out for herself, even in principle, but one who exercises a controlling intelligence over the input she receives from the normal sources of information whether their basis be individual or communal" (p. 248). Such a conception of epistemic independence does not require the impossible task of extricating oneself from social influences but, rather, that one become capable of evaluating and criticizing particular received views, assessing the credentials of experts, and examining the potential biases of social pathways to knowledge if there is reason to do so. Such assessments and evaluations will often be a collaborative enterprise. Thus, I would add to Coady's account that there is a social and political dimension to becoming an independent thinker: individuals should be taught to understand the importance of supporting social institutions that make us all less gullible. Here, consideration of the epistemic ends of education becomes an aspect of civic education.[15]

NOTES

1. It is impossible to approach a topic of this size without making some assumptions that limit the scope of the inquiry. In this chapter I consider the normative epistemic aims of education in the context of the formal educational system. First, of course, education can be thought of in a more expansive way that includes the informal education that comes from participation in everyday life and enculturation into various communities of membership. Whether informal education invokes a different set of epistemic aims is not a question I address here. Second, the epistemic aims of education could be thought of as encompassing the fostering of practical rationality as well as the transmission of propositional knowledge and understanding. I confine myself to an account of the latter here.

2. For an overview of recent debates, see R. K. Shope 2002.

3. The account of propositional knowledge as justified true belief has come to be called the "standard analysis" of knowledge. See Scheffler 1965 for a still useful exploration of the standard analysis of knowledge in the context of education. Gettier 1963 has shown that justified true belief is not a sufficient condition for knowledge, thus challenging the standard analysis in this respect. See Zagzebski 1999 for discussion of the Gettier problem. My account of the epistemic aims of education does not assume that the standard analysis gives sufficient conditions for propositional knowledge but, rather, focuses on truth and justification as necessary conditions.

4. For an account of central positions in the debate, see BonJour and Sosa 2003.

5. I'll not give separate treatment to the belief condition for propositional knowledge, since philosophical attention has focused mainly on the truth and justification conditions. It seems to be largely agreed that one can't be said to know something one doesn't even believe. But see Shope 2002 for a review of some objections to the belief condition and Scheffler 1965 for discussion of the belief condition in the context of education.

6. It's true that sometimes teachers do not teach the exact truth because they need to simplify what they're teaching to fit the development level of students. But this pedagogical point is compatible with Noddings's observation; See Scheffler 1965, p. 12.

7. I'm sympathetic with Price's 2003 position that truth does make a difference of the sort Rorty denies: "truth is the grit that makes our individual opinions engage with one another" (p. 169). Aiming at truth is what turns difference into disagreement. Without the truth-aim, one could regard what another person says as an expression of that person, as what he or she thinks, but not as a reason to engage with the individual to resolve disagreement and determine what to believe or how to act.

8. For a helpful map of the various positions on constructivism, see D. C. Phillips 2007.

9. For further discussion, see Davidson 1984 (his chapter "On the Very Idea of a Conceptual Scheme"); Harre and Krausz 1996; Krausz 1989; Siegel 1987, 1998, 2004a. See also Blake et al. 1998, chap. 1, for an argument that poststructuralism should not be understood as endorsing relativism about knowledge.

10. This statement is a simplification of the issue, since externalists disagree among themselves about whether externalism is a theory of justification or a proposal for a different third condition of knowledge in addition to true belief. See BonJour 2002. See also BonJour and Sosa 2003 for a lively account of the internalism vs. externalism debate.

11. See Feldman 2002 for an argument that epistemic success consists in "having reasonable or justified cognitive attitudes" rather than "having knowledge" (p. 379). Schmitt 2005 argues that justified belief, not true belief, is the ultimate cognitive aim of

liberal arts education. But see Siegel (2005, 2004a) for an argument that both true belief and rational belief should be thought of as fundamental epistemic aims of education.

12. For example, see Carr 2003 on knowledge and education, pp. 132–33.

13. The philosophical literature on testimony seems largely to be framed in terms of face-to-face interactions between speakers and hearers, but I assume that the analysis is intended to cover writers and readers as well. Yet some strategies for establishing the trustworthiness of speakers can be difficult or impossible to apply to writers—knowing something of their character and circumstances, for example, or picking up on body language or other clues to lack of sincerity. I do not explore these issues further here.

14. I'm not addressing the question of whether there can be a global reduction of testimony to memory, perception, and inference as the basic sources of knowledge or whether testimony takes its place alongside them as itself a basic source of knowledge. The important question from an educational perspective is what stance to take toward any *particular* testimonial claim. Since we know that some claims are insincere or mistaken, a policy of total acceptance would not be justified even if testimony could be noncircularly established as a generally reliable pathway to knowledge under appropriate conditions. It's this question that I pursue in my discussion of testimony and education. (For discussion of the prospects for global reduction see Alston 1994, Coady 1994, and Fricker 1994 and 1995.)

15. Expertise is an area where epistemic and political aims intertwine. How are experts to be held accountable to the public in a democratic society if their expertise is publicly inaccessible? See Turner 2006 for further discussion.

REFERENCES

Adler, J. E. (2002). *Belief's Own Ethics*. Cambridge, MA: MIT Press.

—— (2003). "Knowledge, Truth, and Learning." In *A Companion to the Philosophy of Education*, ed. R. Curren (pp. 285–304). Oxford: Blackwell.

Alcoff, L., and E. Potter. (1993). "Introduction: When Feminisms Intersect Epistemology." In *Feminist Epistemologies*, ed. L. Alcoff and E. Potter (pp. 1–14). New York: Routledge.

Alston, W. P. (1994). "Belief-forming Practices and the Social." In *Socializing Epistemology*, ed. F. F. Schmitt (pp. 29–51). Lanham, MD: Rowman & Littlefield.

Anderson, E. (2007). "Fair Opportunity in Education: A Democratic Equality Perspective." *Ethics* 117: 595–622.

Antony, L. M. (2002). "Embodiment and Epistemology." In *The Oxford Handbook of Epistemology*, ed. P. K. Moser (pp. 463–78). Oxford: Oxford University Press.

Applebaum, B. (2004). "Social Justice Education, Moral Agency, and the Subject of Resistance." *Educational Theory* 54: 59–72.

Bailin, S. (1998). "Education, Knowledge and Critical Thinking." In *Education, Knowledge and Truth: Beyond the Postmodern Impasse*, ed. D. Carr (pp. 204–20). New York: Routledge.

Blake, N., P. Smeyers, R. Smith, and P. Standish. (1998). *Thinking Again: Education After Postmodernism*. Westport, CT: Bergin & Garvey.

BonJour, L. (2002). "Internalism and Externalism." In *The Oxford Handbook of Epistemology*, ed. P. K. Moser (pp. 234–63). Oxford: Oxford University Press.

BonJour, L., and E. Sosa. (2003). *Epistemic Justification: Internalism vs. Externalism, Foundations vs. Virtues*. Oxford: Blackwell.

Burbules, N. C. (1991). "The Virtues of Reasonableness." In *Philosophy of Education 1991*, ed. M. Buchmann and R. E. Floden (pp. 215–24). Normal, IL: Philosophy of Education Society.

—— (1995). "Reasonable Doubt: Toward a Postmodern Defense of Reason as an Educational Aim. In *Critical Conversations in Philosophy of Education*, ed. W. Kohli (pp. 82–102). New York: Routledge.

Carr, D. (2003). *Making Sense of Education*. New York: RoutledgeFalmer.

Coady, C. A. J. (1994). "Testimony, Observation, and 'Autonomous Knowledge.'" In *Knowing From Words: Western and Indian Philosophical Analysis of Understanding and Testimony*, ed. B. K. Matilal and A. Chakrabarti (pp. 225–50). Dordrecht: Kluwer.

Code, L. (1993). "Taking Subjectivity into Account." In *Feminist Epistemologies*, ed. L. Alcoff and E. Potter (pp. 15–48). New York: Routledge.

Daukas, N. (2006). "Epistemic Trust and Social Location." *Episteme* 3(1–2): 109–24.

Davidson, D. (1984). *Inquiries into Truth and Interpretation*. Oxford: Clarendon Press.

Dewey, J. (1927). *The Public and Its Problems*. New York: Henry Holt.

Dreyfus, H. (2006). "How Far Is Distance Learning From Education?" In *The Philosophy of Expertise*, ed. E. Selinger and R. P. Crease (pp. 196–212). New York: Columbia University Press.

Elgin, C. Z. (1996). *Considered Judgment*. Princeton, NJ: Princeton University Press.

—— (2007). "Education and the Advancement of Understanding." In *Philosophy of Education, An Anthology*, ed. R. Curren (pp. 417–22). Oxford: Blackwell.

Ellsworth, E. (1997). *Teaching Positions*. New York: Teachers College Press.

Feldman, R. (2002). "Epistemological Duties." In *The Oxford Handbook of Epistemology*, ed. P. K. Moser (pp. 362–84). Oxford: Oxford University Press.

Foucault, M. (1980). "Truth and Power." In *Power/Knowledge: Selected Interviews & Other Writings 1972–1977*, ed. C. Gordon (pp. 109–33). New York: Pantheon Books.

—— (1988). "On Power." In *Politics, Philosophy, Culture: Interviews and Other Writings 1977–1984*, ed. L. D. Kritzman (pp. 96–109). New York: Routledge.

Fricker, E. (1994). "Against Gullibility." In *Knowing From Words: Western and Indian Philosophical Analysis of Understanding and Testimony*, ed. B. K. Matilal and A. Chakrabarti (pp. 125–61). Dordrecht: Kluwer.

—— (1995). "Telling and Trusting: Reductionism and Anti-Reductionism in the Epistemology of Testimony." *Mind* 104: 393–411.

Fricker, M. (2007). *Epistemic Injustice: Power and the Ethics of Knowing*. Oxford: Oxford University Press.

Gettier, E. (1963). "Is Justified True Belief Knowledge?" *Analysis* 23: 121–23.

Goldman, A. I. (1999). *Knowledge in a Social World*. Oxford: Oxford University Press.

—— (2002). *Pathways to Knowledge*. Oxford: Oxford University Press.

Grandy, R. E. (2007). "Constructivisms and Objectivity: Disentangling Metaphysics from Pedagogy." In *Philosophy of Education, An Anthology*, ed. R. Curren (pp. 410–16). Oxford: Blackwell.

Haraway, D. (1988). "Situated Knowledges: The Science Question in Feminism and the Privilege of Partial Perspective." *Feminist Studies* 14(3): 575–99.

Harding, S. (1991). *Whose Science? Whose Knowledge?* Ithaca, NY: Cornell University Press.

Hardwig, J. (2006). "Epistemic Dependence." In *The Philosophy of Expertise*, ed. E. Selinger and R. P. Crease (pp. 328–41). New York: Columbia University Press.

Hare, W. (2003). "Is It Good to Be Open-Minded?" *International Journal of Applied Philosophy* 17(1): 73–87.

Harre, A., and M. Krausz. (1996). *Varieties of Relativism*. Oxford: Blackwell.

Hytten, K. (2006). "Education for Social Justice: Provocations and Challenges." *Educational Theory* 56: 221–36.

Ihde, D. (2006). "Why Not Science Critics?" In *The Philosophy of Expertise*, ed. E. Selinger and R. P. Crease (pp. 395–403). New York: Columbia University Press.

Krausz, M. (1989). *Relativism: Interpretation and Confrontation*. Notre Dame, IN: University of Notre Dame Press.

Lehrer, K. (1994). "Testimony, Justification and Coherence." In *Knowing From Words: Western and Indian Philosophical Analysis of Understanding and Testimony*, ed. B. K. Matilal and A. Chakrabarti (pp. 51–58). Dordrecht: Kluwer.

Longino, H. (1990). *Science as Social Knowledge*. Princeton, NJ: Princeton University Press.

Mackie, J. L. (1970). "The Possibility of Innate Knowledge." *Proceedings of the Aristotelian Society* 70: 245–57.

Matilal, B. K., and A. Chakrabarti, eds. (1994). *Knowing from Words: Western and Indian Philosophical Analysis of Understanding and Testimony*. Dordrecht: Kluwer.

Michelli, N. M., and D. L. Keiser, eds. (2005). *Teacher Education for Democracy and Social Justice*. New York: Routledge.

Narayan, U. (1988). "Working Together Across Difference: Some Considerations of Emotions and Political Practice." *Hypatia* 3(2): 31–48.

Nelson, L. H. (1993). "Epistemological Communities." In *Feminist Epistemologies*, ed. L. Alcoff and E. Potter (pp. 121–59). New York: Routledge.

Nietzsche, F. (1966). *Beyond Good and Evil*. Translated by W. Kaufmann. New York: Random House.

Noddings, N. (2007). *Philosophy of Education*, 2nd ed. Boulder, CO: Westview.

Phillips, D. C. (2007). "The Good, the Bad, and the Ugly: The Many Faces of Coinstructivism." In *Philosophy of Education, An Anthology*, ed. R. Curren (pp. 398–409). Oxford: Blackwell.

Price, H. (2003). "Truth as Convenient Friction." *Journal of Philosophy* 100(4): 167–90.

Riggs, W. D. (2003). "Understanding 'Virtue' and the Virtue of Understanding." In *Intellectual Virtue: Perspectives from Ethics and Epistemology*, ed. M. DePaul and L. Zagzebski (pp. 203–26). Oxford: Clarendon Press.

Roberts, R. C., and W. J. Wood. (2007). *Intellectual Virtues, An Essay in Regulative Epistemology*. Clarendon Press: Oxford.

Robertson, E. (2007). "The Value of Reason: Why Not a Sardine Can Opener?" In *Philosophy of Education, An Anthology*, ed. R. Curren (pp. 448–57). Oxford: Blackwell.

Rorty, R. (1998). *Truth and Progress: Philosophical Papers*, Vol. 3. New York: Cambridge University Press.

Said, E. W. (2006). "Opponents, Audiences, Constituencies, and Community." In *The Philosophy of Expertise*, ed. E. Selinger and R. P. Crease (pp. 370–94). New York: Columbia University Press.

Scheffler, I. (1960). *The Language of Education*. Springfield, IL: Charles C. Thomas.

—— (1965). *Conditions of Knowledge*. Chicago: Scott, Foresman.

—— (1991). *In Praise of the Cognitive Emotions and Other Essays in the Philosophy of Education*. New York: Routledge.

Schmitt, F. F., ed. (1994). *Socializing Epistemology*. Lanham, MD: Rowman & Littlefield.

—— (2005). "What Are the Aims of Education?" *Episteme* 1(3): 223–33.

Selinger, E., and R. P. Crease. (2006a). "Dreyfus on Expertise: The Limits of Phenomenological Analysis." In *The Philosophy of Expertise*, ed. E. Selinger and R. P. Crease (pp. 213–45). New York: Columbia University Press.

—— eds. (2006b). *The Philosophy of Expertise*. New York: Columbia University Press.

Sherman, N., and H. White. (2003). "Intellectual Virtue, Emotions, Luck and the Ancients." In *Intellectual Virtue: Perspectives from Ethics and Epistemology*, ed. M. DePaul and L. Zagzebski (pp. 34–53). Oxford: Clarendon Press.

Shope, R. K. (2002). "Conditions and Analyses of Knowing." In *The Oxford Handbook of Epistemology*, ed. P. K. Moser (pp. 25–70). Oxford: Oxford University Press.

Siegel, H. (1987). *Relativism Refuted: A Critique of Contemporary Epistemological Relativism.* Dordrecht: D. Reidel.

—— (1988). *Educating Reason.* New York: Routledge.

—— (1998). "Knowledge, Truth and Education." In *Education, Knowledge and Truth: Beyond the Postmodern Impasse*, ed. D. Carr (pp. 19–36). New York: Routledge.

—— (2003). "Cultivating Reason." In *A Companion to the Philosophy of Education*, ed. R. Curren (pp. 305–19). Oxford: Blackwell.

—— (2004a). "Relativism." In *Handbook of Epistemology*, ed. I. Niniluoto, M. Sintonen, and J. Wolenski (pp. 747–80). Dordrecht: Kluwer.

—— (2004b). "Epistemology and Education: An Incomplete Guide to the Social-Epistemological Issues." *Episteme* 1(2): 129–37.

—— (2005). "Truth, Thinking, Testimony and Trust." *Philosophy and Phenomenological Research* 71(2): 345–66.

Smith, G. (2002). "Are There Domain-Specific Thinking Skills?" *Journal of Philosophy of Education* 36(2): 207–27.

Sosa, E. (2003). "Knowledge and Justification." In *Epistemic Justification: Internalism vs. Externalism, Foundations vs. Virtues*, by L. BonJour and E. Sosa (pp. 99–118). Oxford: Blackwell.

Stanley, J., and T. Williamson (2001). "Knowing How." *Journal of Philosophy* 98(8): 411–44.

Thompson, C. (2004). "What are the Bounds of Critical Rationality in Education?" *Journal of Philosophy of Education* 38(3): 485–92.

Turner, S. (2006). "What Is the Problem with Experts?" In *The Philosophy of Expertise*, ed. E. Selinger and R. P. Crease (pp. 159–86). New York: Columbia University Press.

Zagzebski, L. (1999). "What Is Knowledge?" In *The Blackwell Guide to Epistemology*, ed. J. Greco and E. Sosa (pp. 92–116). Oxford: Blackwell.

CHAPTER 2

MORAL AND POLITICAL AIMS OF EDUCATION

HARRY BRIGHOUSE

WE subject children to education in the hope of influencing not only what opportunities they will have but also the people they will be. What kinds of people should we hope they will be? What opportunities should they have? And how should those opportunities be distributed among them?

It is convenient to think of the moral and political aspects of the educational system in three categories. I shall refer to the first as the "aims goals"; these goals describe the proper aims of education in the sense that they draw on ideals of what the educated person would be like and identify the values that underlie those ideals. When people disagree about whether children should be subject to character education, or religious education, deeper disagreements about aims goals often (but not always) underpin their arguments, which are fundamentally about what kinds of educational opportunities should be available. Second are what I refer to as "distributive goals"; these describe how educational opportunities should be distributed. Disagreements in the UK about whether children should be selected for an academic schooling at age 11 were often underlain by disagreements about distributional goals (broadly speaking, defenders of selection thought that educational opportunities should be distributed more generously to those with more talent, whereas opponents usually thought that they should be distributed equally); so are disagreements in the United States about busing and racial integration of schools. The final category is what I shall simply refer to as "constraints." Assume that there is complete agreement on the ideal aims and distribution of educational opportunities; still, there could be disagreement about the extent to which it is permissible for the government to override the preferences of parents to achieve those goals or the degree of coercion schools can use to get children to comply with discipline. These disagreements are often underpinned by commitment to the existence of certain moral constraints on what may be done to pursue ideals.

1. AIMS GOALS

Theorists, obviously, disagree about aims goals. In this section I argue for five aims goals: personal autonomy; the ability to contribute to social and economic life broadly understood; personal flourishing; democratic competence; and the capacity for cooperation.

Autonomy

Children have a right to the opportunity to make and act on well-informed and well-thought-out judgments about how to live their own lives. The animating idea behind the goal is that, for human beings to enjoy a good life, they have to find a way of life that is suited to their particular personalities. Think about religious choice. Some people may flourish brilliantly within the constraints laid down by Roman Catholicism, but others may find that those constraints make it impossible to live well. We make our choices about whether to be Roman Catholics based on a judgment of fit between the chosen life and ourselves; the better the fit, the better we flourish. But it is important that we have knowledge about other religious views and nonreligious views because, for some (those who cannot flourish within Catholicism), flourishing will depend on being able to adopt alternatives. Not only do we need knowledge of the alternatives, we also need the self-knowledge, habits of mind, and strength of character to make the appropriate alternative choices.

I've framed the choice as a religious choice because religion is the aspect of life around which debates about autonomy most usually revolve. But there are many other less obvious, but perhaps equally important, ways in which we ought to be able to rely on our own judgments in our lives. Think about the choice of occupation. Some children find themselves under very heavy parental pressure to pursue a particular occupational path. The nonautonomous person might reject the path out of spite or, alternatively, succumb to the parental pressure without enthusiasm. The autonomous person, by contrast, has sufficient knowledge of the relevant variables and sufficient fortitude to make the parental pressure a very small influence on his choice; whether, ultimately, he chooses for or against will depend on his own, independent, judgment of the fit between the occupation and his interests.

Think, finally, about sexual identity. Suppose (plausibly) that heterosexuality and homosexuality are morally equivalent; that it is, in other words, exactly as possible to live well as a homosexual as it is to live as a heterosexual. Someone whose constitution is, for whatever reason, incompatible with flourishing as a heterosexual needs to grow up with an awareness that there are other legitimate and morally innocent ways of living and needs to be raised with enough ability and inclination to seek self-knowledge that she has a real chance of finding out who she is and the ways of being in which she, given who she is, can flourish. She needs, in other words, to be able to be autonomous.

The autonomous person is reflective, and responds to reasons, whether those reasons concern his own well-being or that of others; he is *not* merely calculating and rationally self-interested. He can see the force of other people's needs and interests and can respond appropriately to them, for example. But he does not do so slavishly, any more than he responds to his own interests slavishly. The autonomous person evaluates the demands of others, and responds to those that are legitimate, but rejects those that are tyrannous; he does exactly the same with respect to his own demands (the selfish person is not autonomous, but is both a tyrant and a slave).[1]

Contributory Effectiveness

Capitalist economic institutions place a heavy influence on economic self-reliance, at least for those who are not fortunate enough to be supported by wealthy parents. And, in capitalist economies, it is especially important for schools to equip students to be able to be economically self-reliant; in the absence of social institutions designed to guarantee that everyone can have a decent life, it is a precondition of an individual's ability to flourish that she be able to work for an income or be attached to a family unit in which others do. But even in a capitalist society, income is not the only valuable reward that work brings. People also flourish at work, if they are lucky enough to have work that they find interesting and an environment in which they have some control over what they do and when. Fortunately, people vary in what they find interesting; Sid finds the sight of blood sickening, and has very little interest in people, so he would find being a family doctor something akin to torture, but he is thrilled by the challenge of flying an airliner; Ken has a fear of flying, but enjoys company and problem solving with people. A good deal of research suggests that people flourish primarily through engagement with family and friends, but work can provide a diversity of challenges and rewards that can sometimes compete with, and sometimes enhance, the fulfillment of personal relationships. So the general principle that everyone should have a wide set of opportunities to flourish supports educating them so that they have the opportunity to find rewarding work and can judge the relative importance of work and other activities in their lives.[2]

That said, no one is *truly* self-reliant, and so there is therefore something artificial about anyone's *sense* of self-reliance. Even capitalist economies are essentially cooperative; nobody makes a contribution that would be worth the income he derives from it if others were not also contributing in other valuable ways. The efforts of others make our own efforts valuable. The incomes we derive from those efforts are only distantly related to the relative importance of our contributions. Nobody has a right to a sense of self-reliance; what they have a right to is that parents and teachers enable them to develop their talents so that they can make effective and genuine contributions to the cooperative economy.

So there is a powerful interest in being able to be an effective contributor, and in being able to derive an income and some sense of self-reliance from making that contribution. It is worth noting, though, that we seem to have a self-serving tendency to think of ourselves as deserving our salary, whatever that salary is, and our sense of self-reliance rests on this thought. But, in fact, our salaries, and even the kinds of job available to us, are a consequence of a multiplicity of choices and decisions over which we had no control and which could have been different. Tiger Woods enjoys a much higher income than he would have enjoyed, even in an advanced economy, if television had never been invented, or if it had been invented but had been regulated everywhere to prohibit advertising. Top soccer players now enjoy much higher incomes relative to the population than they did forty years ago. This is partly because the rest of the population has much larger disposable incomes (which it chooses to spend on watching soccer), partly because of techno-logical changes (television, and the use of satellite technology), but also because of major changes in labor-market regulation over which they had no control (for example, the erosion of the ability of national sports leagues to limit employment of foreign players). It has very little, if anything at all, to do with the increased natural talents of players; but the players on the whole think of themselves as deserving their incomes. Successful white male lawyers in the American South in the 1950s had a strong sense of responsibility for their own success; but most of them would have been somewhat less wealthy and less successful if there had been no Jim Crow laws and their black peers had been allowed to compete effectively with them and if social norms had not excluded women from becoming lawyers. While it is clearly important for a sense of self-worth, the sense of self-reliance is, to a considerable extent, socially constructed.[3]

Equally important for their sense of self-worth, for many people in many societies, has been the sense that they are making a meaningful contribution to the life of the community. One problem in an economic system dominated by the formal economy and the cash nexus is that many meaningful contributions are not validated by society as a whole because they are not part of the cash economy, and so it is harder for those people who perform them to come to see them as contributions. Minding a neighbor's child, raising one's own child, caring for an elderly invalid, tending a communal garden, coaching a kids' soccer team—these are among the numerous contributions to the flourishing of the community as a whole that garner little public recognition in a capitalist economy, but are no less important for that fact. An education system is obliged to equip children to contribute to society in these and other ways, not only because the activities are valuable for others but also because those who engage in them derive a sense of self-worth from making such contributions.[4]

Flourishing

At the foundation of the arguments for preparing children to be autonomous and preparing them for the labor market is the idea that these are extremely valuable for them to be able to live flourishing lives. The school should see itself as having an obligation to facilitate the long-term flourishing of the children.

We have a good deal of evidence about what makes people happy and what does not make them happy. We also know that children have certain tendencies that make it very difficult for their families, even if they are well-willed and good judges of their children's interests, fully to prepare them for a flourishing life. Finally, we know that in our society there are certain quite specific barriers to living a happy and flourishing life that many of our children will have to negotiate, and that we cannot anticipate accurately which barriers children will encounter or which children will be particularly hindered by them.

Here's the relevant evidence about what makes people happy. We know, in particular, that people are made happy neither by materialism nor by the wealth that materialism brings. We know that poverty makes people unhappy and restricts considerably their ability to flourish, even when poverty is conceived in relative rather than in absolute terms. The low status and stress that accompany relative poverty, and the lack of control over one's conditions of life, diminish people's ability to flourish. But once people have achieved a reasonable level of financial security, additional income and wealth do not make them happier, especially if they are premised on the need to spend more hours at work and away from family and friends. The income from remunerated labor helps people to have more control over their lives, and more security, up to a point, but it does not help much beyond a certain point. We also know that people are happier when they are connected in social networks. Close connections to, and successful relations with, family and friends correlate closely with reports of subjective well-being. Being able to spend time with, and relate intimately to, other people is a tremendously important precondition of flourishing for most of us.

Another important source of flourishing is the exercise of skills that are difficult to master.[5] Those people who are lucky enough to have interesting jobs that suit their personalities and talents will flourish from the exercise of those talents.[6] But it is also common for people to enjoy activities in which they do not, by any absolute criteria, excel but that make the appropriate demands on them— frequently outside of their jobs. Someone may find writing doggerel a challenge and obtain great satisfaction in producing ditties that just make his children or his friends laugh; or someone might enjoy playing cricket as well as he can on a weekend team, not just for the companionship but also for the sense of stretching his limited capacities. For many people it is in their leisure time that they will find the meaning in their life.

But we also know that children, as they grow into adults, will face significant challenges, built into the structure of our society, in engaging with the world in a way that facilitates their flourishing. First, we know that family life is increasingly complicated by at least two factors. The first is that close to 50 percent of marriages end in divorce, and a very high proportion of those divorces occur while children are still in the home.[7] This means that most children who themselves marry will be in a relationship in which one partner has parents who are not married to one another. Furthermore, most people remarry, or re-enter a relevantly marriage-like relationship. So, as adults managing their own lives, they will have to engage with at least three, rather than the previously normal two, parental households. First, the time, energy, and emotional demands on a remarried parent are greater than those on an undivorced parent; the child of a remarried parent is not only negotiating with more households but has more competition for the attention and interest of her parent. Second, the dramatically increased geographic mobility in our society weakens the connections among adults within families. Parents, adult children, and adult siblings are less ready courses of mutual support and care when they live at great geographic distances from one another, so that even intact families are frequently less connected to one another in adulthood than was an expectation even thirty years ago.[8]

Democratic Competence

Citizens need to be able both to use democratic institutions to press their interests and to recognize the legitimate interests of others through them. The knowledge and skills needed for democratic competence are various and may depend on context. A basic understanding of the history of a society's political institutions is usually valuable, as is a basic ability (and inclination) to scrutinize claims and arguments other people make in the light of evidence and reason. Many policy issues are hard for citizens to evaluate because they lack a good understanding of both the way the institutions work and the possible side effects on other institutions of any reform. This is made much harder in a political culture like ours, which provides incentives for obfuscation and in which the very wealthy have enormous power over the character of public debate. But even in a society in which political debate is well structured and carried out with good will, citizens need to be equipped with knowledge and skills that competitive political forces may not themselves be eager to supply.[9] Schools are a natural location for such education; it is too much to expect institutions in civil society to provide the needed education to citizens without schools' providing a sound grounding.

Cooperative Capacity

One of the first priorities for any kindergarten teacher is to establish order in the classroom. This involves teaching the children how to make space for one another, how to share and engage in give and take. In Anglophone education systems, cooperation is usually taught in the first instance for the sake of creating order, but it is also valuable in itself; most children will have better lives if they are able to cooperate with others as equals, and most will have better lives if others are able to and inclined to cooperate with them as equals. As I've said, even capitalist economies are essentially cooperative, and so are successful intimate (and even distant) personal relationships. Cooperation is not something we learn simply from being in the world, especially because conflict and competition are also pervasive—think of the capitalist economy that depends on cooperation for its success, but within which competition is also a driving force. So, from a very early age, the cooperative capacities of children need to be elicited, fostered, and practiced, so that as the children grow they can deploy those capacities both to their own advantage and for the decent treatment of others.

2. DISTRIBUTIVE GOALS

Assuming there is agreement about the aims goals, how should educational opportunities be distributed?

One popular view, and the one that is worth using as the baseline for comparison in this section, is educational equality: the view that in some sense of good, everyone should have an equally good education. Even politicians and theorists who would reject egalitarianism *tout court* often invoke some sort of educational egalitarianism in justification of policy initiatives. Recent legislation in the United States aims at reducing the "achievement gap," whereby that is understood as the gap between proportions of children from higher and lower socioeconomic classes, or of racial or of ethnic groups, reaching some threshold of competence in various basic academic tasks. Some British policymakers have insisted on a goal of completely delinking academic performance from social class background. In both cases, the concern is that socioeconomic disadvantage leads to inequality in educational achievement. In most developed countries, further efforts are taken to ensure that children with disabilities in general areas, and in learning-related areas in particular, have opportunities to learn in excess of those they would have if they were accorded only the same level of resources as other children.

Unlike demands to equalize overall conditions, educational egalitarianism is closely associated with meritocracy: the idea that inequality of outcomes is justified as long as the competition for those outcomes is fair and rewards some combination of talent and effort. The principle of educational equality does the work of ensuring that, despite unequal social starting points, children have equal opportunities to develop the talents that the competitions are structured to reward. So, whereas there is nothing wrong, according to the educational egalitarian, in having a wide wage gap, there is something wrong if some children have much better chances of getting the jobs to which high wages are attached because they got superior chances to develop their talents.

Meritocratic Educational Equality

But what, exactly, is the principle of educational equality?[10] From the preceding discussion it is easy to see that there must be several versions. The dominant version is meritocratic educational equality, which states, consistent with the motivation set out in the previous paragraph: *An individual's prospects for educational achievement should be a function only of that individual's effort and talent, not of his or her social class background.* This principle, or something like it, lies behind a good deal of contemporary rhetoric. But, as stated, it faces several challenges, of which three bear closer investigation.

The first is that it is unstable. In singling out social background as an unacceptable source of influence on outcomes, the principle arbitrarily favors the talented, who merit no more credit for their natural advantages than the well-born do for their social advantages. Why should the naturally talented get special access to unequally distributed rewards?

A second challenge objects that the means that would be needed to realize the principle are unacceptable because they would undermine other values. For example, some people think that prohibiting, or imposing punitive taxes on, elite private schooling would violate parental liberty. Perfectly realizing the principle would probably require even more intrusive measures; interfering with the ordinary childrearing practices of middle-class parents who prepare their children to take good advantage of the opportunities presented in school (like teaching them to read at home, reading them bedtime stories, and teaching them middle-class manners).

In fact, observing a conflict between two values in particular circumstances does not establish that either principle is wrong. Even radical educational egalitarians tend to agree that when the principle comes into conflict with ordinary childrearing practices that lie at the heart of family life, it should give way to the value of the family. But this does not render it inert. Those radicals will usually maintain that although parental liberty is important, it is not so important that it requires us to permit parents to purchase elite private schooling for their children. And, even if a successful argument could be given for why that was so important, the principle of educational equality might still require governments to take other measures, like improving state schools so that they were effectively competing with elite private schools; or limiting inequality of wealth; or reducing child poverty, concentrations of which are a major barrier to providing good educational opportunities for less advantaged children.

The third objection appeals to efficiency. It is, or at least can be, socially inefficient to do what would be required to produce meritocratic educational equality, because it would result in a leveling down of educational provision and, consequently, reduced investment in the total stock of human capital and, ultimately, of social wealth. At least in some circumstances this seems likely, and egalitarians are unlikely to dispute it. But social wealth is only one value; fairness in the competitions to access it and how it is distributed also matter. Educational egalitarianism describes a principle of fairness concerning access to the stock of social wealth, and egalitarians accept that justice will sometimes conflict with growth. Depending on how much weight is placed on the principle, different judgments will be made concerning the likely trade-offs.

A corollary of the motivation for the meritocratic principle is the idea that, as inequalities of outcome narrow, educational equality becomes less important because education has a less important role in allocating people to advantages in the labor force. But education is not only valuable because it helps its recipients in social competitions; it is also intrinsically valuable, contributing as it does to personal growth and flourishing. So most egalitarians have a residual concern about the unfairness of some people getting more of the benefits intrinsic to education than others through no effort or merit of their own. This concern has force even if noneducational outcomes are equalized.

Radical Education Equality

The objection that rewarding natural talent but not social class is arbitrary suggests a much more radical principle of educational equality—one that attempts to compensate for inequality of talent, as well as for inequality of social-class background: *An individual's prospects for educational achievement should be a function only of that individual's effort, not of his or her social class background or natural talent.*

This principle reflects the correct observation that natural talent is just as arbitrary from the moral point of view as is social class. But it has two obvious problems. One is that, taken alone, it seems to justify concentrating massive resources on children with cognitive disabilities; the other is that it seems to justify leveling down educational achievement to the highest level that the lowest achiever reaches. Both consequences are unappealing.[11]

Benefiting the Least Advantaged

The efficiency objection to educational equality is sometimes posed specifically in terms of benefit to the least advantaged. In this version, the objection suggests an alternative principle to either version of educational equality that places a principled limit on the resources devoted to students with disabilities, and a reason not to level down achievement, viz: *Education should be distributed in the way that maximizes the prospects for overall well being of those whose prospects are poorest.*

This principle has not been well explored in the literature.[12] Adopting it effectively abandons the idea, tacit in the other previous principles, that there is a special principle of justice for education. Instead, it directly subordinates educational policy to an overarching principle of justice that demands maximizing the prospects of the least advantaged. It is nevertheless a genuine and viable alternative to the versions of educational equality above. It has the nice feature, compared with the radical version of educational equality, that it does not demand the leveling down of educational outcomes. But it also has the nice feature, compared with the meritocratic version, that it does not arbitrarily favor the talented; the talented get better educated, if they do, because that will benefit other less fortunate people. It is also worth noting that other values can be pressed against this principle; and it might be plausible that trade-offs need to be made between it and values such as educational excellence or parental liberty.

Adequacy

A second alternative to educational equality is the principle of educational adequacy. There are several versions, all of which have the following form, but which specify *X* differently: *Everyone should receive an education adequate for them to X.*

At the most austere end of adequacy theorists is James Tooley, who demands education adequate to functioning in the economy; at the most demanding end are theorists like Debra Satz, Elizabeth Anderson, and Amy Gutmann, who tie adequacy to the developed capacity to participate as an equal in political (Gutmann) and social (both Satz and Anderson) life.[13] Adoption of a principle of educational adequacy seems in most cases to be motivated by a more fundamental connection to the idea that adequacy, rather than equality or maximizing the position of the least advantaged, is what justice demands regarding the distribution of resources all told.[14] Tooley explicitly grounds his support for educational adequacy in the sufficientarian critique of a principle of equality of resources, rather than directly criticizing the case for educational equality. Anderson and Satz are both more direct in their criticism of various versions of the principle of educational equality, but Anderson at least has also endorsed a general principle of sufficiency as the core commitment of a theory of social justice, which is in turn grounded in a very extensive critique of equality as a general principle of justice. Educational egalitarians, furthermore, generally accept that achieving an adequate education for all is very urgent—much more so than achieving equality. However, no principle of adequacy seems adequate, as the following scenario suggests.

Imagine that everyone is adequately well educated (understanding "adequacy" however you might plausibly understand that). Now, imagine that new resources enter the educational system and that whomever they are spent on, it will remain the case that everyone is adequately well educated. If adequacy were the sole distributive principle, then there would no reason of justice at all to spend those resources on the least advantaged students. But this seems implausible; there is such a reason, which is that they, through no fault of their own, will have a worse education than others, and by spending the money on them we can alleviate that condition. That reason may not outweigh reasons to spend the money elsewhere— for example, if spending the money on more advantaged students would predictably secure better overall prospects for the less advantaged, which might well constitute another reason of justice. But the principle of educational adequacy, offered as the sole principle of educational justice, cannot recognize any reason of justice to spend it one way or another.[15]

Maximizing Excellence

A final alternative to educational equality focuses on the value of educational achievement itself. John Wilson makes the following proposal: *Educational resources should be distributed to those who can make the most use of them.*[16]

The principle gets its appeal from some sort of principle of efficiency with regard to the production of educational excellence; to maximize excellence we would have to invest optimally, so it would be most urgent to invest in those whose capacity for achievement is high and can be developed inexpensively. This principle would benefit some of the most able children enormously, but only some of the most able. For example, if an enormously able child is sufficiently socially difficult, the cost of developing her talent might be so great that it would be more efficient to invest in a more docile, but less able, child; and children who speak an unusual foreign language might be expensive to invest in, even though highly able. But the central problems with this criterion are that it fails to recognize that if academic achievement is valuable, then we *all* have a powerful interest in being able to achieve, academically, and that we cannot detach educational achievement from the distribution of other rewards.

Hybrid Views

One might take the view that each of the starkly stated principles above captures a rational kernel, which has a place and needs to be weighed against the rational kernel in the other views. There is a reason to reduce the effect of social class, and of natural talent, on outcomes, but there are also reasons to seek higher levels of excellence, among them the desirability of producing higher levels of human capital that can be harnessed to the overall benefit of the least advantaged; and there is a reason to seek an adequate education for all. Or one might take the view that there is a rational kernel to some, but not all, the principles. The task, then, of constructing a theory of distributive justice for education is that of identifying these reasons and showing how much weight they should have relative to one another.

3. CONSTRAINTS AND TRADE-OFFS

Assume that we can get agreement concerning what the aims of education should be and how educational opportunities should be distributed. Are there constraints on what may done in pursuit of those goals? Of course, there may be pragmatic constraints—it may be impossible to get political support for all of the goals. My question is not about that; it is about whether there are moral constraints—constraints of principle, which one would be morally bound not to exceed even if one could get political support for doing so.

The philosophical literature has elaborated, in great detail, one such constraint, which concerns the interests or rights of parents. Much less attention has been paid to a second constraint, concerning the interests of the children being educated even though, increasingly, public attention is, indeed, being paid to the latter. In this section I shall briefly elaborate both, giving them equal billing.

Parent-Centered Constraints

Children are raised, normally, in families, by parents who invest a great deal of time, energy, and emotion in the well-being of their children. Suppose that there was a readily available way of effectively promoting the aims and distributive goals above, but it required removing all children from their parents for twelve hours a day, six days a week, fifty weeks of the year, from the age of 24 months. Would it be morally acceptable to do so? Most readers will be inclined to demur; parents have a strong interest in being able to have ample time to spend with their children, in being the people primarily in charge of their well-being, and the time left over by the described policy would be insufficient for them to realize that interest, even if it did no harm to the children. Allowing parents to establish and maintain intimate relationships with their children is a constraint on the pursuit of the goals I've elaborated above.[17]

This much is easy to accept. But the debates about parent-centered constraints become harder to decide when more is claimed. Some theorists, in line with the dominant strain of human rights declarations, argue that parents have an absolute right to direct the education of their children in line with their own values. If that were so, the constraint would be very strong, indeed; it would prevent the government, for example, from facilitating children's autonomy against the wishes of their parents, or facilitating their flourishing by providing them with basic sex education against parental wishes, or for facilitating educational opportunity by prohibiting or taxing elite private education. Nathan Glazer suggests the motivation for the very strong understanding of the constraint as follows:

> To be sure, the case for both [racial] integration and equality of expenditure is powerful. But the chief obstacle to achieving these goals does not seem to be the indifference of whites and the non-poor to the education of non-whites and the poor. . . . Rather, other values, which are not simply shields for racism, stand in the way: the value of the neighborhood school; the value of local control of education and, above all, the value of freedom from state imposition when it affects matters so personal as the future of one's children.[18]

Glazer hints at a very strong reading of the constraint; one that actually has a good deal of resonance with, for example, the provision of the Universal Declaration of

Human Rights that parents have a "prior right to choose the kind of education that shall be granted to their children." If we understand this right as absolute, it acts as a very strong constraint on attempts to achieve the goals in the previous sections. Assume for a moment that some measure of racial integration is needed to achieve democratic competence, and that a child's peers constitute part of her education. On the strong reading, parents have a right to demand that their children be educated only with peers of the same race or in ideologies that are fundamentally undemocratic.

Such a strong understanding of the constraints set by parents' rights is not necessary. Suppose, instead, that parents merely have a moral right to have a close relationship with their children; this would give them little latitude over what went on in school as long as the school day and school year were short enough for them to have plenty of time with their children outside school, and as long as the ethos of the school does not undermine their relationship. But it takes philosophical work on the precise content of the moral rights that parents have concerning their children to establish how severe the constraint is; this, I take to be one of the central tasks of the philosophy of education and the philosophy of the family.[19]

Child-Centered Constraints

A good deal of work on the aims of education is forward-looking; all the aims goals I described above are about how the child is supposed to turn out as an adult. But children are not just adults-in-formation; childhood is itself a significant part of a person's life, and the quality of a childhood is intrinsically important, independent of its consequences for the quality of an adulthood. Recent work in the sociology of childhood has emphasized this, and it is implicit, too, in practitioners' concerns about matters like bullying and testing.

It is worth remembering, too, that schooling is compulsory. Children have no choice but to spend a significant number of their waking hours in the classrooms where their parents and teachers have placed them, and among other children whom they have not chosen, and many of whom they would not choose, as their companions. This places a special burden of justification on us when it comes to the quality of the time the children spend there, even though there are good enough reasons to require them to be in school.

Philosophers, while none of them denies the independent importance of childhood as a stage of our lives, have not done much work figuring out how it constrains the delivery of education, or even what constitutes a good childhood other than the goods in childhood that prepare us well for adulthood. It is easy to imagine, though, that some of the means that would most improve a child's prospects for academic achievement might diminish the quality of his school days. It is plausible, for example, that in some circumstances frequent and rigorous testing would be involved in the most effective method for improving low-end achievement, but it would make some low-end achievers excessively anxious at the time. Even if we were confident that a rigorous testing regime was crucial for the best strategy for improving a child's performance, we might feel justified in sacrificing some of that achievement for the sake of not making his school days miserable.

Trade-offs

Just as we are sometimes required to trade off important educational goals against the parent-centered and child-centered constraints, there are sometimes trade-offs among those goals themselves. Consider the meritocratic version of educational equality. That principle requires that social origin have no influence over educational outcomes and, therefore, in a highly unequal society, that talented children from lower socioeconomic classes have excellent educational prospects. But whereas children from higher socioeconomic classes may expect that their parents will celebrate and understand their educational success, and that it will lead them to have lives recognizably like those of their parents, educational success for many working-class children would exact the high price of alienating them culturally from their parents, siblings, and communities. If commonalities with one's family members are needed for relationships to remain close, and close familial relationships play an important role in underpinning a flourishing life, the social mobility generated by meritocratic educational equality may conflict with the flourishing of the socially mobile child. A full theory of the moral and political aspects of education would give guidance in managing these trade-offs when they arise.

4. Concluding Comment: Institutions

I have paid little direct attention to public political debates about the structure and reform of educational institutions; in a volume devoted to philosophy of education, it seems appropriate to discuss the distinctively philosophical questions. But throughout it will be clear that disagreements at this philosophical level will influence disagreements about reform and even pedagogy. The interest in autonomy, for example, suggests that it is important for all children to be exposed to a range of moral and political perspectives, and to be educated to become critical thinkers; many theorists who reject the aim of autonomy believe that pursuing it involves excessive interference in the ability of parents to control their children's environment. If you reject the demanding conception of democratic citizenship I have proposed, you are much less likely than if you support it to favor civic education. What will not be so clear is that reforms can sometimes find support across fundamental normative disagreements. For example, there are strong anti-egalitarian, and strong egalitarian, supporters of school-choice reforms.

Anti-egalitarians frequently support school choice because they see it as giving power to parents to decide how their children will be educated.[20] Some egalitarians support it because it distributes parental power more equitably than neighborhood schooling, which effectively gives power to wealthy, but not to poorer, parents.[21] Similarly, public support for religious schools is sometimes supported on the ground that parents have the right to educate their children in their religious faith, and sometimes on the ground that such a policy will support integration of religious and nonreligious children in ways that promote autonomy in particular circumstances.[22] Simply knowing what values are at stake does not suffice to evaluate current arrangements or proposed reforms; but an understanding of what values are at stake, and how to weigh them against each other, is essential for evaluation.

NOTES

1. Joseph Raz, *The Morality of Freedom* (Oxford: Oxford University Press, 1987), provides a nice account of the value of autonomy. Amy Gutmann, *Democratic Education* (Princeton, NJ: Princeton University Press, 1989), and Eamonn Callan, *Creating Citizens* (Oxford: Oxford University Press, 1997, especially chapter 6), provide accounts of how its value is important in education and childrearing. For more skeptical approaches, see Shelley Burtt, "Religious Parents; Secular Schools," *Review of Politics* 56 (1994): 51–70, and William Galston, "Two Concepts of Liberalism," *Ethics* 105 (1995): 516–34.

2. For a powerful recent statement of this interest, see Paul Gomberg, *How to Make Opportunity Equal* (Oxford: Blackwell, 2007).

3. An article in the *New York Times* includes the following quotes from two of the wealthiest people in the history of humanity. "I think there are people, including myself at certain times in my career, who because of their uniqueness warrant whatever the market will bear" (Leo J. Hindery, Jr.); "In the current world there will be people who will move from one tax area to another. I am proud to be an American. But if tax became too high, as a matter of principle I would not be working this hard" (Kenneth Griffin). While most of the wealth these people have accumulated is the result of their good luck in being born with certain traits in an environment that accords great rewards to people with those traits, and a good deal of luck, they are not at all atypical in believing that the root cause of their wealth accumulation lies in themselves (their "uniqueness" and "hard work"). See Louis Uchitelle, "The Richest of the Rich, Proud of a New Gilded Age," *New York Times*, July 15, 2007.

4. See Amy Gutmann, *Democratic Education*, chapter 2, and Elizabeth Anderson, "Fair Opportunity in Education: A Democratic Equality Perspective," *Ethics* 117, no. 4 (2007): 595–622.

5. For recent surveys of the literature on what makes people happy, see Richard Layard, *Happiness* (London: Penguin, 2002), and Tim Kasser, *The High Price of Materialism* (Boston, MA: MIT Press, 1998).

6. See Paul Gomberg, *How to Make Opportunity Equal* (Oxford: Blackwell, 2007), for a powerful statement of this, and an argument concerning its implications for the organization of work.

7. According to the U.S. Census Bureau's snapshot figures for 2006, 67 percent of all children under the age of 18 lived with both their original parents. If that figure sounds

surprisingly high, remember that the proportion of 1-year-olds living with their original parents is likely to be much higher than the proportion of 15-year-olds. Most children will not be living with both their original parents by age 18.

8. My thoughts about flourishing in education have been influenced by conversations with Christine Sypnowich about her in-progress book manuscript, *Equality Renewed*. For more thoughts specifically about education, see John White, *The Curriculum and the Child* (London: Routledge, 2003). See also Martha Nussbaum, *Cultivating Humanity* (Cambridge, MA: Harvard University Press, 1997), for an account of the humanistic purposes of higher education.

9. See Amy Gutmann, *Democratic Education*; Eamonn Callan, *Creating Citizens*, and Stephen Macedo, *Diversity and Distrust* (Cambridge, MA: Harvard University Press, 2000), for a sample of different arguments for the conclusion that promoting democratic competence is an important aim of education.

10. See Christopher Jencks, "Whom Must We Treat Equally for Educational Opportunity to be Equal?" *Ethics* 98 (1988): 518–33, for an exploration of the difficulties of specifying the content of the principle of educational equality; and Adam Swift, *How Not to be a Hypocrite* (London: RoutledgeFalmer, 2004), for an example of the meritocratic version of the principle. See also Harry Brighouse and Adam Swift, "Putting Educational Equality in its Place," *Educational Policy and Finance* 3, no. 4 (2008): 444–66, for a hedged defense of the meritocratic version of the principle.

11. See further exploration of these problems in my *School Choice and Social Justice* (Oxford: Oxford University Press, 2000), chapter 7.

12. See John Rawls, *A Theory of Justice* (Cambridge, MA: Harvard University Press, 1971); Matthew Clayton, "Rawls and Natural Aristocracy," *Croatian Journal of Philosophy* 1 (2001): 239–59; Harry Brighouse and Adam Swift, "Equality, Priority and Positional Goods," *Ethics* 116 (2006): 471–97, for arguments in favor of prioritizing the interests of the less advantaged in social policy generally.

13. For variants of this view, see Amy Gutmann, *Democratic Education*, pp. 128–39; Randall R Curren, "Justice and the Threshold of Educational Equality," *Philosophy of Education* 50 (1995): 239–48; John White, "The Dishwasher's Child: Education and the End of Egalitarianism," *Journal of Philosophy of Education* 28 (1994): 173–82; James Tooley, *Disestablishing the School* (London: Institute of Economic Affairs, 1996); Elizabeth Anderson, "Fair Opportunity in Education: A Democratic Equality Perspective," *Ethics* 117, no. 4 (2007): 595–622; Debra Satz, "Equality, Adequacy, and Education for Citizenship," *Ethics* 117, no. 4 (2007): 623–48.

14. See Harry Frankfurt, "Equality as a Moral Ideal," *Ethics* 98, no. 1 (1987): 21–43, and Joseph Raz, *The Morality of Freedom*, chapter 5, for statements of this view.

15. For a detailed criticism of adequacy, see Harry Brighouse and Adam Swift, "Educational Equality versus Educational Adequacy: A Critique of Anderson and Satz," *Journal of Applied Philosophy* 26, no. 2 (2009): 117–28.

16. John Wilson, "Does Equality (of Opportunity) Make Sense in Education?" *Journal of Philosophy of Education* 25 (1991): 27–31, at 29. See also David Cooper, *Illusions of Equality* (London: RKP, 1980), for a trenchant statement of the principle that educational excellence is more important than concerns about the distribution of educational resources or achievement.

17. See Harry Brighouse and Adam Swift, "Parents' Rights and the Value of the Family," *Ethics* 117 (2006): 80–108.

18. Nathan Glazer, "Separate and Unequal," *New York Times Book Review*, September 25, 2005, pp. 12–13, at 13.

19. See Francis Schrag, "Justice and the Family," *Inquiry* vol 19, no. 2 (1976): 193–208; William Galston, *Liberal Pluralism*; Callan, *Creating Citizens*; Matthew Clayton, *Justice and Legitimacy in Upbringing* (Oxford: Oxford University Press, 2006), and Brighouse and Swift, "Parents Rights" for various accounts of the content and limits on parents' rights.

20. See, for example, Milton Friedman, *Capitalism and Freedom* (Chicago: University of Chicago Press, 1962), chapter 6; see also James Tooley, *Reclaiming Education* (London: Continuum, 2000).

21. For example, Herbert Gintis, "The Political Economy of School Choice," *Teachers College Record* 96 (1995): 462–511; Harry Brighouse, *Choosing Equality* (London: Social Market Foundation, 2002).

22. See Eamonn Callan, "Discrimination and Religious Schooling," in Will Kymlicka and Wayne Norman, eds., *Citizenship in Diverse Societies* (Oxford: Oxford University Press, 2000), pp. 45–67, and Harry Brighouse, "Faith Schools in the UK: An Unenthusiastic Defence of a Slightly Reformed Status Quo," in Roy Gardner et al., eds., *Faith Schools: Consensus or Conflict?* (London: RoutledgeFalmer, 2005), pp. 83–90, for secularist arguments for permitting, and even supporting, religious schools.

CHAPTER 3

....

TAGORE, DEWEY, AND THE IMMINENT DEMISE OF LIBERAL EDUCATION

....

MARTHA NUSSBAUM

We may become powerful by knowledge, but we attain fullness by sympathy.... But we find that this education of sympathy is not only systematically ignored in schools, but it is severely repressed.

—Rabindranath Tagore, "My School"

Achievement comes to denote the sort of thing that a well-planned machine can do better than a human being can, and the main effect of education, the achieving of a life of rich significance, drops by the wayside.

—John Dewey, "Democracy and Education"

1. The Education Crisis

....

I begin with four examples, which illustrate, in different ways, a profound crisis in education that faces us today, although we have not yet faced it. All illustrate the loss of insights contained in the statements by Tagore and Dewey, two of our greatest educational reformers and thinkers about the role of education in a pluralistic society.

1. It is a hot March in Delhi, in 2003. I am attending a high-level and very impressive conference on pluralism and the Indian democracy at Jawaharlal Nehru University. Much of the conference is concerned with issues of education. All the papers on education focus on the content of required national textbooks, which are to be memorized and regurgitated on examinations. The Hindu Right, still in power, has been pushing for a content that supports their view of India's history, introducing new national textbooks for that purpose. The conference presenters, all opponents of the aims of the BJP (Bharatiya Janata Party, the political wing of the Hindu Right), inveigh against this aim and propose textbooks with a different, more Nehruvian content. But nobody mentions the children: the stultifying atmosphere of rote learning in classrooms, the absence of critical thinking and all cultivation of imagination. Tagore once wrote a fable called "The Parrot's Training" in which lots of smart people talk about how to educate a parrot, preparing a fine gilded cage and lots of fancy textbooks. Nobody notices that along the way the bird itself has died. The education debate at JNU, typical of much of the larger debate in India, reminds me uncomfortably of that story.[1]

2. It is a surprisingly warm November in Chicago, in 2005, and I go across the Midway to the Lab School, the school where John Dewey conducted his path-breaking experiments in democratic education reform. The teachers are having a retreat, and I've been asked to address them on the topic of education for democratic citizenship, something that I undertake with some trepidation because I am sure they all know so much more about this topic than I do. As I defend the legacy of Dewey, focusing particularly on the sympathetic imagination, and introduce them to the very similar writings of Tagore, I discover that I'm not where I thought I was, the safe home of Dewey's ideas. I'm on a battleground, where teachers who still take pride in stimulating children to question, criticize, and imagine are an embattled minority, increasingly suppressed by other teachers, and especially by wealthy parents, intent on testable results of a technical nature that will help produce financial success. When I present what I thought of as a very banal version of Dewey's vision, there is deep emotion, as if I've mentioned something precious that is being snatched away.

3. One week later, again in the fall of 2005, I keep a phone appointment to talk with the head of the committee that is searching for a new Dean for the School of Education in one of our nation's most prestigious universities. Hereafter I'll just refer to the university as X. They want my advice, or think that they want it. Since, as a result of the first two

incidents and many others of a similar nature, I'm already alarmed about the future of the humanities and the arts in primary and secondary education, I lay out for this woman my views about education for democratic citizenship, stressing the crucial importance of critical thinking, knowledge about the many cultures and groups that make up one's nation and one's world, and the ability to imagine the situation of another person, abilities that I see as crucial for the very survival of democratic self-government in the modern world. To me it seemed that I was saying the same thing I talk about all the time, pretty familiar stuff. But to this woman it was utterly new. How surprising, says she, no one else I've talked to has mentioned any of these things at all. We have been talking only about how X University can contribute to scientific and technical progress around the world, and that's the thing that our President is really interested in. But what you say is very interesting, and I really want to think about it. Taken aback by her surprise at what I thought was mainstream humanism, I start imagining the future of education in my country and in the world: initiatives focusing narrowly on scientific and technical training, producing many generations of useful engineers who haven't a clue about how to criticize the propaganda of their politicians, and who have even less of a clue about how to imagine the pain that a person feels who has been excluded and subordinated.

4. Finally: last year, I was invited by another great university, also in my own country, let's call it Y, to speak at a symposium celebrating a major anniversary. I was asked to speak as part of a symposium on "The Future of Liberal Education." A few months before the date of the event itself (February 2006), I am told by the Vice-Provost that the nature of the occasion has been changed: there will no longer be a symposium on the future of liberal education, and I am therefore urged to give a single lecture on whatever topic I like. When I arrive on campus, I press for an account of the reasons behind the change. From a helpful and nicely talkative junior administrator, I learn that the President of Y has decided that a symposium on liberal education would not "make a splash," so he has decided to replace it with a symposium on the latest achievements in science and technology. My lecture, a tiny wavelet that is no longer part of a large "splash," argues for the great importance of the arts and humanities for a decent public culture, both critical and sympathetic, able to transcend suspicion and fear of the different. But of course at this point, with no public symposium, I'm preaching to the converted, an audience of humanities faculty and students.

We are living in a world that is dominated by the profit motive. The profit motive suggests to most concerned politicians that science and technology are of crucial importance for the future health of their nations. I have no objection to good scientific and technical education, and I have no wish to suggest that nations should stop trying to improve in this regard. My concern is that other abilities, equally crucial, are at risk of getting lost in the competitive flurry, abilities crucial to the health of any democracy internally and to the creation of a decent world culture. These abilities are associated with the humanities and the arts: the ability to think critically; the ability to transcend local loyalties and to approach world problems as a "citizen of the world"; and, finally, the ability to imagine sympathetically the predicament of another person. Since Tagore and John Dewey were among the most important thinkers about these abilities, I will develop my argument by drawing on their writings and their educational practice. One should bear in mind, however, that these ideas about the student's self-critical and imaginative activity are far older; they have their roots in the ancient Greek and Roman tradition, in Socrates' educational practice and Seneca's famous Letter concerning liberal education.[2]

Rabindranath Tagore and John Dewey do not seem to have met, and I am unable to find evidence that either one ever read the work of the other. They worked at approximately the same time, and it seems likely, at any rate, that Dewey was aware of Dartington Hall, the Tagore-inspired school founded in England in the 1930s by Tagore's friend Leonard Elmhirst, who spent a long time in Santiniketan. Despite this lack of direct connection, their thought was similarly inspired: by the deadness of traditional education, its failure to stimulate criticism of tradition, and its failure to cultivate sympathy. In their insistence on the crucial importance of a pedagogy that enlivens and activates, they are kindred spirits, whose shared legacy is today deeply threatened.

2. THREE ABILITIES

Let me begin by outlining three abilities that are, in my view, crucial for citizenship in a pluralistic democratic society that is part of an interlocking world. Because I have written a book on this topic,[3] I shall simply summarize, in each case connecting my thoughts to the ideas of Tagore and Dewey—and then I shall turn to the current crisis. In my book I focused on liberal education in colleges and universities, but it was always my view that these values need to be cultivated appropriately by primary and secondary education, which are Tagore's and Dewey's central focus. Colleges won't get very far unless students have begun much earlier.

Three values, I argue, are particularly crucial to citizenship in such a nation and for such a world. The first is the capacity for Socratic self-criticism and critical thought about one's own traditions. Although some parents may object to this sort of teaching, as they always have since the time of Socrates, who lost his life on the charge of "corrupting the young," we may give them Socrates' own answer: democracy needs citizens who can think for themselves, rather than deferring to authority, who can reason together about their choices rather than simply trading claims and counter-claims. Socrates, appropriately, compared himself to a gadfly on the back of a noble but sluggish horse: he was waking democracy up, so it would conduct its business more responsibly.[4]

Although Tagore was not explicitly thinking, at first, of the prerequisites of democracy, he was animated throughout his life by a hatred of dead convention and a love of independent thought. Most education, he said, is "a mere method of discipline which refuses to take into account the individual ... a manufactory specially designed for grinding out uniform results."[5] At Santiniketan, by contrast, independence of mind and questioning of convention was strongly encouraged. Tagore was particularly passionate about the education of women for a more Socratic life. He cultivated independence of mind and expression on the part of female students, who elsewhere were more or less always brought up to be passive receptacles of tradition. This commitment grew only stronger as time went on. In a 1936 lecture, he urged women to "open their hearts, cultivate their intellect, pursue knowledge with determination. They have to remember that unexamined blind conservatism is opposed to creativity."[6]

Dewey explicitly connected the importance of critical thinking to the health of democracy. Democracy, he stressed, "is more than a form of government; it is primarily a mode of associated living, of conjoint communicated experience."[7] A society that is going to overcome traditional barriers of race, class, and wealth must "see to it that its members are educated to personal initiative and adaptability."[8] Criticism of custom, which Dewey saw as lying at the heart of democracy since its inception in ancient Athens, is a linchpin of this formation of citizens.[9] In ancient Athens, "custom and traditionary beliefs held men in bondage."[10] People were led to think Socratically, with a focus on rational argument, by the evident inadequacy of tradition for democratic life.[11] Education then and now must support "the struggle of reason for its legitimate supremacy."[12]

The second key ability of the democratic citizen, I would argue, is the ability to see oneself as a member of a heterogeneous nation, and world, understanding something of the history and character of the diverse groups that inhabit it. For Dewey, this was not a major focus, but it followed from his insistence that education must produce flexible citizens who can adapt their thought to the nature of the current reality. Tagore's school was perhaps more focused on this cosmopolitan idea, given Tagore's development of a universalistic "religion of man." The school cultivated this ability in the way in which, as Amita Sen tells us, students learned about all the major religions and even celebrated their holidays. Always the effort was to root the student's education in the local, giving each a firm grasp of Bengali language and traditions, and then to expand their horizons to the whole world (as the name of Visva-Bharati University indicates that goal).

Today, given the nature of global interdependence, and given the fact that many of our interactions as global citizens are mediated by the impoverished norms of market exchange, we need this second ability more than ever. In *Cultivating*

Humanity, I argue that all young citizens should learn the rudiments of world history and should get a rich and nonstereotypical understanding of the major world religions, and then should learn how to inquire in more depth into at least one unfamiliar tradition, in this way acquiring tools that can later be used elsewhere. At the same time, they ought to learn about the major traditions, majority and minority, within their own nation, focusing on an understanding of how differences of religion, race, and gender have been associated with differential life-opportunities. All of this, I believe, would have been entirely congenial to Dewey, and is even more in the spirit of Tagore.

The third ability of the citizen, closely related to the first two, can be called the narrative imagination.[13] This means the ability to think what it might be like to be in the shoes of a person different from oneself, to be an intelligent reader of that person's story, and to understand the emotions and wishes and desires that someone so placed might have. The cultivation of sympathy, which I take to be the central public task of ancient Athenian tragedy and thus of ancient Greek democracy, has also been a key part of the best modern ideas of progressive education. Both Dewey and Tagore gave it major emphasis. Dewey argued that the arts were modes of intelligent perception and experience that should play a crucial role in education, forming the civic imagination. He protested against the usual sort of education, in which "Achievement comes to denote the sort of thing that a well-planned machine can do better than a human being can." Similarly, in India, Tagore wrote, concerning the role of the arts in his school at Santiniketan, "We may become powerful by knowledge, but we attain fullness by sympathy.... But we find that this education of sympathy is not only systematically ignored in schools, but it is severely repressed." Both felt that the cultivation of imaginative sympathy was a key prop to good citizenship; that children had this ability to be tapped, if it was not killed off; but that it had to be made more sophisticated and precise through education.

The education of sympathy is being repressed once again today, as arts and humanities programs are increasingly being cut back in schools in many nations, in favor of a focus on technical and scientific education, which is seen as the key to a nation's financial success.

Instruction in literature and the arts can cultivate sympathy in many ways, through engagement with many different works of literature, music, fine art, and dance. But thought needs to be given to what the student's particular blind spots are likely to be, and texts should be chosen in consequence. For all societies at all times have their particular blind spots, groups within their culture and also groups abroad that are especially likely to be dealt with ignorantly and obtusely. Works of art can be chosen to promote criticism of this obtuseness, and a more adequate vision of the unseen. Ralph Ellison, in a later essay about his great novel *Invisible Man*, wrote that a novel such as his could be "a raft of hope, perception and entertainment" on which American culture could "negotiate the snags and whirlpools"[14] that stand between us and our democratic ideal. His novel, of course, takes the "inner eyes" of the white reader as its theme and its target. The hero is invisible to white society, but he tells us that this invisibility is an imaginative and educational failing on their part, not a biological accident on his. Through the imagination we are able to have a kind of insight into the experience of another group or person that it is very difficult to attain in daily life—particularly when our world has constructed sharp separations between groups and suspicions that make any encounter difficult. For Tagore, a particular cultural blind spot was the agency and intelligence of women, and his instruction, in consequence, insisted on giving women expressive leading roles.

So we need to cultivate our students' "inner eyes," and this means carefully crafted instruction in the arts and humanities, which will bring students into contact with issues of gender, race, ethnicity, and cross-cultural experience and understanding. This artistic instruction can and should be linked to the "citizen of the world" instruction, since works of art are frequently an invaluable way of beginning to understand the achievements and sufferings of a culture or group different from one's own.

The arts are also crucial sources of both freedom and community. When people put on a play together, they have to learn to go beyond tradition and authority if they are going to express themselves well. And the sort of community created by the arts is nonhierarchical, a valuable model of the responsiveness and interactivity that a good democracy will also foster in its political processes.

Finally, the arts are great sources of joy for children, and indeed for adults as well. Participating in plays, songs, and dances fills children with joy, and this joy carries over into the rest of their education. Memoirs of the school show how all the "regular" education in Santiniketan, the education that enabled these students to perform very well in standard examinations, was infused with passion and delight because of the way in which education was combined with dance and song. Children do not like to sit still all day; but they also do not know automatically how to express emotion with their bodies in song and dance. Tagore's extremely expressive, but also extremely disciplined dance regime, for example, was an essential source of creativity, thought, and freedom for all pupils, but particularly, perhaps, for women, whose bodies had been taught to be shame-ridden and inexpressive.

There is a further point to be made about what the arts do for the spectator. As Tagore knew, and as radical artists have often emphasized, the arts, by generating pleasure in connection with acts of subversion and cultural criticism, produce an endurable and even attractive dialogue with the prejudices of the past, rather than one fraught with fear and defensiveness. That is what Ellison meant by calling *Invisible Man* "a raft of hope, perception and entertainment": entertainment is crucial to the ability of the arts to offer perception and hope. It's not just the experience of the performer, then, that is so important for democracy; it's the way in which performance offers a venue for exploring difficult issues without crippling anxiety. Tagore's notorious performance in which women of good family danced highly emotional and sensuous roles on the Kolkata stage were the milestones for women that they were because they were artistically great and extremely enjoyable.

In the end, the audience could not sustain habits of shock and anger, against the gentle assault of beautiful music and movement.

3. DEMOCRATIC EDUCATION ON THE ROPES

How are the abilities of citizenship doing in the world today? Very poorly, I fear. Education of the type I recommend is doing quite well in the place where I first studied it, namely the liberal arts portion of U.S. college and university curricula. Indeed, it is this part of the curriculum, in institutions such as my own, that particularly attracts philanthropic support, as rich people remember with pleasure the time when they read books that they loved and pursued issues open-endedly.

Outside the United States, many nations whose university curricula do not include a liberal arts component are now striving to build one, since they acknowledge its importance in crafting a public response to the problems of pluralism, fear, and suspicion their societies face. I've been involved in such discussions in the Netherlands, in Sweden, in India, in Germany, in Italy, in India and Bangladesh. Whether reform in this direction will occur, however, is hard to say, for liberal education has high financial and pedagogical costs. Teaching of the sort I recommend needs small classes, or at least sections, where students get copious feedback on frequent writing assignments. European professors are not used to this idea, and would at present be horrible at it if they did try to do it, since they are not trained as teachers in the way that U.S. graduate students are, and they have come to expect that holding a chair means not having to grade undergraduate writing assignments. To some extent this is true in Asia as well. And even when faculty are keen on the liberal arts model, bureaucrats are unwilling to believe that it is necessary to support the number of faculty positions required to make it really work. Thus, at the University of Oslo a compulsory ethics course has been introduced for all first-year students, but it is taught as a lecture course with 500 people and a multiple-choice examination at the end. This is worse than useless, since it gives students the illusion that they have actually had some philosophical education, when they have had only a gesture toward such an education. In Sweden, at the new urban university Sodertorn's Hogskola, a large proportion of whose students are immigrants, the faculty and the Vice-Chancellor (philosopher Ingela Josefson) badly want a liberal arts curriculum based on the idea of preparation for democratic citizenship. They have sent young faculty to U.S. liberal arts colleges to study and practice this type of small-classroom teaching, and they have constructed an exciting course on democracy. As yet, however, they do not have enough manpower to hold the class in small sections with lots of group discussion and copious writing assignments, some-thing that is crucial if the class is to succeed. Only in small idiosyncratic institutions, such as the Institute for Humanist Studies in Utrecht, is the liberal arts idea a reality in Europe.

Another problem that European and Asian universities have is that new disciplines of particular importance for good democratic citizenship have no secure place in the structure of undergraduate education. Women's studies, the study of race and ethnicity, Judaic studies, Islamic studies—all these are likely to be marginalized, catering only to the student who already knows a lot about the area and who wants to focus on it. In the liberal arts system, by contrast, such new disciplines can provide courses that all undergraduates are required to take, and can also enrich the required liberal arts offerings in other disciplines, such as literature and history. Where there are no such requirements, the new disciplines remain marginal.

So the universities of the world have great merits, but also great problems. By contrast, the abilities of citizenship are doing very poorly, in every nation, in the most crucial years of children's lives, the years known as K through 12. Here the demands of the global market have made everyone focus on scientific and technical proficiency as *the* key abilities, and the humanities and the arts are increasingly perceived as useless frills, which we can prune away to make sure our nation (whether it be India or the United States) remains competitive. To the extent that they are the focus of national discussion, they are recast as technical abilities themselves, to be tested by quantitative multiple-choice examinations, and the imaginative and critical abilities that lie at their core are typically left aside. At one time, Dewey's emphasis on learning by doing and on the arts would have been second nature in any American elementary school. Now it is under threat even at the Dewey Laboratory School. National testing has already made things worse in the United States, as national testing usually does: for at least my first and third ability are not testable by quantitative multiple-choice exams, and the second is very poorly tested in such ways. (Moreover, nobody bothers to try to test it even in that way.)

Thus the humanities are turned into rapid exercises in rote learning, packaged, often, in state-approved textbooks, and the whole political debate comes to be focused on the content of these textbooks, rather than on the all-important issue of pedagogy. At this point I cannot resist introducing Tagore's short story, called "The Parrot's Training," which provides a very good picture of education in our time, as in his.

A certain Raja had a bird whom he loved. He wanted to educate it, because he thought ignorance was a bad thing. His pundits convinced him that the bird must go to school. The first thing that had to be done was to give the bird a suitable edifice for his schooling, so they built a magnificent golden cage. The next thing was to get good textbooks. The pundits said, "Textbooks can never be too many for our purpose." Scribes worked day and night to produce the requisite manuscripts. Then, teachers were employed. Somehow or other they got quite a lot of money for themselves and built themselves good houses. When the Raja visited the school, the teachers showed him the methods used to instruct the parrot. The method was so stupendous that the bird looked ridiculously unimportant in comparison. The Raja was satisfied that there was no flaw in the arrangements. As for any complaint from the bird itself, that simply could not be expected. Its throat was so completely choked with the leaves from the books that it could neither whistle nor whisper.

The lessons continued. One day, the bird died. Nobody had the least idea how long ago this had happened. The Raja's nephews, who had been in charge of the education ministry, reported to the Raja:

> "Sire, the bird's education has been completed."
> "Does it hop?" the Raja enquired.
> "Never!" said the nephews.
> "Does it fly?"
> "No."
> "Bring me the bird," said the Raja.

> The bird was brought to him, guarded by the kotwal and the sepoys and the sowars. The Raja poked its body with his finger. Only its inner stuffing of book-leaves rustled.
>
> Outside the window, the murmur of the spring breeze amongst the newly budded asoka leaves made the April morning wistful.[15]

This wonderful story hardly needs commentary. Its crucial point is that educationists tend to enjoy talking about themselves and their own activity, and to focus too little on the small, tender children whose eagerness and curiosity should be the core of the educational endeavor. Tagore thought that children were usually more alive than adults, because they were less weighted down by habit. The task of education was to avoid killing off that curiosity, and then to build outward from it, in a spirit of respect for the child's freedom and individuality rather than one of hierarchical imposition of information.

I do not agree with absolutely everything in Tagore's educational ideal. For example, I am less anti-memorization than Tagore was. Memorization of fact can play a valuable and even a necessary role in giving pupils command over their own relationship to history and political argument. That's one reason good textbooks are important, something that Tagore would have disputed. But about the large point I am utterly in agreement: education must begin with the mind of the child, and it must have the goal of increasing that mind's freedom in its social environment, rather than killing it off. (I note that good nongovernmental organizations that conduct literacy programs for women and girls in India, a large part of what I have studied, do everything Tagore would have wanted and everything that my three-part structure recommends. They do not fall victim to rote learning, because they know that their students won't stay around unless education is enlivening, and they use the arts and literature very productively to stimulate criticism of imprisoning traditions.)

Today, however, these insights of Tagore and Dewey are ignored in favor of an education for economic success. Whether a nation is aspiring to a greater share of the market, like India, or struggling to protect jobs, like the United States, the imagination and the critical faculties look like useless paraphernalia, and people even have increasing contempt for them.

Thus in West Bengal, Tagore's path-breaking Santiniketan school, which produced Amita Sen, Amartya Sen, Satyajit Ray, and many more gloriously independent and imaginative world citizens, is now viewed with disdain as a school for problem children. Long ago, Jawaharlal Nehru sent his daughter Indira there, though she spoke no Bengali. (And it was the only happy time at school she had, though she attended many famous schools.) Today nobody from outside West Bengal wants to go there, and the school itself has become routinized. Meanwhile, a parent's glory is the admission of a child to the Indian Institutes of Technology and Management. Meanwhile, in the United States, at the Dewey Lab School, the arts requirement is being watered down under pressure of the drive for success on the part of parents and administrators. Worse yet, the sheer burden of homework in all disciplines makes it impossible for children to enjoy the use of their critical and imaginative faculties.

The United States has some resilience still, thanks to its traditions of local autonomy. Thus Indian-American friends of mine wistfully compare the education their children receive here—where young children learn about the civil rights struggle, for example, by putting on a play in which one of them is the person who has to sit in the back of the bus—with the education they themselves never had in India, where rote learning rules the roost. But the United States is moving toward India, not vice versa.

Indeed, most outrageously and thoughtlessly, the United States is currently egging on other nations to emulate our worst, not best, traits. The two major universities I have mentioned are both very strongly concerned with educational initiatives abroad. Needless to say, given my examples, these initiatives do not focus on the creation of sympathy and the cultivation of critical thinking.

What will we have, if these trends continue? Nations of technically trained people who don't know how to criticize authority, useful profit-makers with obtuse imaginations. What could be more frightening than that? Indeed, if you look to Gujarat, which has for a particularly long time gone down this road, with no critical thinking in the public schools and a concerted focus on technical ability,[16] one can see clearly how a band of docile engineers can be welded into a murderous force to enact the most horrendously racist and anti-democratic policies. And yet, how can we possibly avoid going down this road?

I believe that outrage is called for, on the part of every person who cares about the future of democracy in the world, and I think intellectuals should be leading the expression of outrage. Perhaps if we say these things loud enough and eloquently enough, we may actually make a difference.[17]

Democracies have great rational and imaginative powers. They also are prone to some serious flaws in reasoning, to parochialism, haste, sloppiness, selfishness. Education based mainly on profitability in the global market magnifies these deficiencies, producing a greedy obtuseness that threatens the very life of democracy itself. We need to listen, once again, to the ideas of Dewey and Tagore, favoring an education that cultivates the critical capacities, that fosters a complex understanding of the world and its peoples, and that educates and refines the capacity for sympathy—in short, an education that cultivates human beings and their humanity, rather than producing generations of useful machines. If we do not insist on the crucial importance of the humanities and the arts, they will drop away because they don't make money. They only do what is much more precious than that: make a world that is worth living in, and democracies that are able to overcome fear and suspicion and to generate vital spaces for sympathetic and reasoned debate.

NOTES

1. See my discussion of the Indian situation in "Education for Democratic Citizenship," *The Little Magazine* (New Delhi), fall 2005, also published by the annual yearbook of Jamia Milia Islamia, New Delhi.

2. See discussion in my *Cultivating Humanity: A Classical Defense of Reform in Liberal Education* (Cambridge, MA: Harvard University Press, 1997), chapters 1 and 2; the letter in question is Moral Epistle 88.

3. Nussbaum, *Cultivating Humanity.*

4. Here and elsewhere, my proposals are very similar to those richly and rigorously developed by Israel Scheffler: see for example *Reason and Teaching* (New York: Routledge 1973); see also the collection in Scheffler's honor, *Reason and Education: Essays in Honor of Israel Scheffler,* ed. Harvey Siegel (New York: Springer, 1997).

5. "My School," in *Personality* (extract in *A Tagore Reader,* ed. Amiya Chakravarty [Boston: Beacon Press, 1961], pp. 218–24). Compare "To Teachers," in *A Tagore Reader,* pp. 213–17.

6. "Nari" ("Women"), extract translated in Sumit Sarkar, "*Ghare Baire* in its Times," in *Rabindranath Tagore's The Home and the World: A Critical Companion,* ed. P. K. Datta (New Delhi: Permanent Black, 2003), pp. 143–73, at 168.

7. John Dewey, *Democracy and Education* (Chicago: University of Chicago Press, 1903), p. 83.

8. Ibid, p. 84.

9. Ibid. See pp. 251–52, 264–65.

10. Ibid, p. 252.

11. Ibid, pp. 264–65.

12. Ibid, p. 252.

13. This, too, is a favorite theme of Scheffler's: see his wonderful essay, "In Praise of the Cognitive Emotions," in *In Praise of the Cognitive Emotions and Other Essays in the Philosophy of Education* (New York: Routledge, 1991), pp. 3–17.

14. Ralph Ellison, *Invisible Man* (New York: Modern Library, 1994), p. xxxi.

15. From V. Bhatia, ed., *Rabindranath Tagore: Pioneer in Education* (New Delhi: Sahitya Chayan, 1994).

16. For details, see my *The Clash Within: Violence, Hope, and India's Future* (Cambridge, MA: Harvard University Press, 2007), chapters 1 and 9.

17. A good beginning is made by *College Learning for the New Global Century*, issued by the National Leadership Council for Liberal Education and America's Promise (LEAP), a group organized by the Association of American Colleges and Universities (Washington, DC: LEAP, 2007), a valuable riposte to the dismal Spellings Commission Report, *A Test of Leadership: Charting the Future of U. S. Higher Education*, 2007, available online at http://www.asiaing.com/a-test-of-leadership-charting-the-future-of-u.s.-higher-education.html.

PART II

THINKING, REASONING, TEACHING, AND LEARNING

CHAPTER 4

THINKING, REASONING, AND EDUCATION

RICHARD FELDMAN

It is a truism, and therefore true, that one goal of education is to teach students the thinking and reasoning skills they need to be effective and responsible citizens.[1] These skills are necessary, but obviously not sufficient, for them to deal reasonably and intelligently with the information they need to make sensible decisions, both about their own lives and about the public issues that come before them when they vote, serve in community groups, or otherwise engage in public action.

One way to attempt to teach some of these reasoning skills is through courses on critical thinking or argument analysis. For many years, I have a taught a fairly conventional course of this sort. The purpose of my course is to teach students to identify, interpret, and evaluate arguments as they are presented in nontechnical sources such as newspapers, magazines, and books. I have always paid little attention to the generally worthless material that fills the typical letters to the editor of a local newspaper and focused primarily on the somewhat more sophisticated material in the more serious newspapers, magazines, and books that I hoped my students would regularly read. I take these to be principal sources of information for educated citizens and thus believe that helping students to be capable consumers of this material is a worthy goal. I aim to improve their ability to digest and assess this information. I've tried to do this by presenting a method for taking the arguments found in the relevant written material and reconstructing them as precise arguments that can be assessed for their logical structure and for the merits of their premises. I'm sure many instructors who seek to teach their students critical thinking or reasoning have goals somewhat similar to mine, even if the details of the methods they present differ. Indeed, people teaching in many disciplines are apt to include this as part of what they hope to accomplish. I continue to think that this is a worthy goal.

It would be a mistake to think that argument analysis is all there is to effective thinking. However, it would be a major mistake to think that it is not a key component of the desired skills. It would also be a mistake to think that there is a unique, correct way to teach the skills of argument analysis. No doubt, different techniques will work with different degrees of effectiveness for students at different levels of sophistication. Nevertheless, I think that there are some general points about arguments that students must grasp if they are to develop the key skills. In this chapter I describe a few of these key points. I emphasize them here both because I think that they are fundamental—without them, there's little hope of success—and because I think that they sometimes get lost in the philosophical debates about the nature and goals of argument.

1. Persuasion, Agreement, and Understanding

In my experience, students are often woefully confused about the goal of engaging in critical reflection about an issue. What should we tell them about this? A good way to approach this question is by imagining a discussion with students who have been asked to analyze the arguments in an essay. For the sake of discussion, I will consider an example in which the essay in question is about capital punishment. I will assume that the essay takes a particular stand on some issue concerning capital punishment. And I will consider the point of the exercise by focusing on a student who comes to the discussion with a point of view about this issue opposed to the one defended in the essay. Suppose this student asks why she is doing this; what is the point of this analytical exercise? What should the response be?

I can imagine at least three general types of response. Each has its merits. Indeed, I think that each connects in an important way to a goal that people might have when they engage in argument. The three responses are:

Response 1: The purpose of analyzing this argument about capital punishment is to learn a general skill concerning arguments. It is valuable to be able to engage rationally with people you encounter and to respond effectively to arguments with which you disagree. You need to be able to analyze arguments such as this one so that you can show those who accept the argument where it goes wrong. This will also help you construct your own arguments so that you can more effectively convince others of your point of view.[2]

Response 2: The purpose of analyzing this argument about capital punishment is to learn a general skill concerning arguments. Arguments are a key tool used for reaching agreement and achieving consensus among rational people. By analyzing this argument, you will learn how this process works when it is done in a rational and respectful way. For a democratic society to thrive, it is essential that citizens are able to do this.[3]

Response 3: The purpose of analyzing this argument about capital punishment is to learn a general skill concerning arguments. Arguments are statements of reasons to believe conclusions. By examining this argument, you will learn something about how arguments are formulated and assessed. You will then be able to determine whether the author of the argument has in fact made a rationally compelling case for its conclusion. The understanding thereby achieved can be applied to arguments about other topics, so that you can assess the merits of these other arguments, thereby increasing your understanding of these other issues.[4]

These three responses represent three perspectives concerning arguments. The first comes from the perspective of one who sees arguments as tools of persuasion: an argument is something one uses to persuade others of one's point of view. One wants to understand arguments so that one can use this tool effectively and can resist arguments having conclusions one disagrees with. The second response comes from the perspective of one who sees arguments as dialectical tools used in discussions aimed at resolving disagreements. One wants to understand arguments so that one can better achieve such resolutions. The third response comes from the perspective of one who sees arguments as logical tools used to spell out in clear and precise ways the supporting case for a point of view. One wants to analyze arguments so that one can better assess a line of thought (allegedly) supporting a view, and perhaps adjust one's thinking in response. This third approach takes an approach more in keeping with the individualist strand in contemporary epistemology. One's emphasis, on this approach, is to use argument analysis in an effort to help answer for oneself the question, "What should I believe now?" In contrast to views that emphasize persuasion or agreement, this one emphasizes one's own rational attitudes. I will sometimes characterize this approach by saying that it seeks understanding, meaning by this only that it sees argument analysis as a tool one uses in one's effort to better understand an issue.[5]

There is something to be said in behalf of each of the three responses. We do use arguments to persuade others. We use much else as well. Rhetorical devices of all sorts, including emotional appeals, logical slight of hand, humor, and more can be effective. It is useful to know about this, both to persuade when that is one's goal and to resist when others use such tools on oneself. We also use arguments to resolve differences. In any number of social situations, whether with one's family, one's colleagues, or one's community organization, there are disagreements that must be resolved. Rational discussion of argument is no doubt an extremely valuable tool to have in such situations. We also use arguments as tools of inquiry. We do this when we want to understand something and use a case made for one position or another in an effort to achieve that understanding. Thus, arguments are used to persuade, to resolve disagreements, and to achieve understanding.

Although arguments do have the three uses just characterized, I want to make a case for the centrality of their role in seeking understanding and then to draw out some consequences of the centrality of this role. There is no doubt that persuasion is sometimes our primary goal. Advertisers, defense attorneys, and advocates of all kinds have as their assignment persuading others of a particular conclusion. What that conclusion is depends on the particular role the person has. In such cases, the conclusion to be argued for is already determined and the arguments can be brought in to support it. But surely this is not our central goal in teaching students to reason. We want to teach them how to deal with information they receive, not how to manipulate that information in the service of some antecedently determined conclusion.

There is also no doubt that achieving agreement is a socially valuable thing. It surely is a good thing if students can learn to resolve their differences via rational argument. However, one can reach agreements in which the conclusion that is agreed upon is supported by the available facts and one can also reach agreements in which this is not the case. There are all sorts of ways to reach agreement that have nothing to do with rationality. For example, we could adopt the policy that everyone should accept the view asserted by the person who shouts the loudest or talks the longest. What is desired, surely, is rational agreement, where this means something like agreement on the conclusion that in fact is best supported by the evidence. Thus, the sort of rational agreement highlighted in Response 2 depends on the rational evaluation and understanding highlighted in Response 3. If people properly understand arguments, and share their information, then they will agree. (I here set aside differences arising from matters of taste or differing basic preferences.) If this is right, then those who see arguments as vehicles for resolving disagreements should see arguments as fundamentally tools for gaining understanding, and then can note then when parties to a disagreement are able to deal effectively with arguments in this way, they will reach agreement.

If this is right, then the crucial role for arguments is as a tool for understanding. We must carefully separate understanding (rational belief about an issue) from persuasive power or effectiveness in reaching agreement. My own survey of materials for courses on argument and critical thinking reveals some conflation of these points. Popular discussion of argument, particularly political argument, is so focused on persuasion that the goal of understanding is almost absent. And, for reasons that will come up in Section 2, I think that many students tend to shy away from seeing arguments as tools of understanding. If we are to teach students to be effective reasoners—that is, if we are to teach them to deal effectively with arguments—it is imperative that we tell them something about what a good argument actually is.

I think that a starting point in discussing this topic with students must be a clear and direct discussion of the difference between persuasion and understanding. We can acknowledge that if one's goal is purely to persuade, then whatever will in fact be persuasive is a good means to one's goal. When one wants to encourage someone to buy a product, catchy phrases, attractive salespeople, uplifting music, humor of various kinds, and any number of other techniques can be effective. However, it is obvious on reflection that persuasive techniques of the sort just mentioned have little to do with rationality and understanding. Suppose one's goal is to determine whether a particular product is in fact worth buying, whether a particular candidate merits one's vote, or whether a view on a controversial issue is correct. Students can rather easily see that what tends to persuade on the topic can be of little consequence in trying to answer such questions. What matters is what in fact provides good support for a conclusion. Having the skills necessary to assess material to determine whether it provides good support for a conclusion enables people to gain the requisite understanding.

It is difficult to overemphasize the importance of the distinction between persuasion and understanding. If you think of reasoning and argumentation as tools to be used in an effort to persuade others of your antecedent point of view, then they are not well designed for the critical examination of your own prior views. Perhaps one can test one's arguments by seeing whether they convince others. And perhaps some people are sometimes able to ask whether they really are persuaded by arguments that they previously have found convincing. But to take the stance toward issues that I take to be the key to effective reasoning, one has to see its goal to be the production of rational belief and not the persuasion of others.

What, then, makes for a good argument? The short answer is that a good argument provides a good reason to believe its conclusion. In the remainder of this section, I will expand upon this answer.[6]

To begin, note that the account to be presented makes the notion of a good argument "relative," in the sense that what can be a good argument for one person need not be a good argument for another person. This is not a matter of taste or preference—an argument is not a good argument for you simply because you endorse it or approve of it. Rather, it is a consequence of the fact that the account of good arguments is epistemic—that is, it relies on the concept of good reasons. Because people can differ in their background information, an argument that provides one person good reason to believe something may fail to provide another person good reason to believe that same thing.

According to my epistemic account of good arguments, a good argument must satisfy three conditions. First, arguments provide rational support for their conclusions only if the premises are justified (reasonable) ones. Arguments can have true premises that a person has no reason to accept. Such arguments do not provide the person with good reason to believe their conclusions. Moreover, arguments with false but well-justified premises can provide good reasons to believe their conclusions. So, an argument is a good one for you only if you are justified in believing (the conjunction of) its premises.

Second, good arguments must have premises that connect to their conclusion in a suitable way. Assuming that we have a notion of validity or necessary connection that applies to arguments expressed in ordinary language, we can say that valid arguments meet this condition. But we should allow for good arguments that are not valid. I use the word *cogent* to describe the structure of such arguments. Let's say that when an argument is either valid or cogent, the premises are "properly connected" to the conclusion and the argument is "well formed." Now, imagine an argument that is in fact valid, but the connection between the premises and the conclusion is enormously hard to see. You don't have any reason to think that the premises do support the conclusion. In that case, the argument does not provide you with any reason to believe its conclusion. It's not a good argument for you. This leads me to say that what's required is that you justifiably believe that the argument is well formed—that is, that you justifiably believe that the premises are properly connected to the conclusion.[7]

Finally, there must be a "no-defeater" condition. Cogent arguments can have premises that are well justified, but the argument can nevertheless fail to provide one with a good reason to believe its conclusion because you have defeating evidence. A simple inductive argument might have premises that you know to be true and a conclusion that is highly probable on their basis. For example, an argument for the conclusion that it is not raining now might have just the right form—generalizing from premises about the weather conditions yesterday and past patterns. But you might have defeating evidence from direct perception that defeats this otherwise strong argument.

Thus, my proposal is that an argument is a good argument for a person provided the person is justified in believing the conjunction of its premises, and the person is justified in believing that the premises are properly connected to the conclusion, and the argument is not defeated for the person. When a person encounters a good argument for a conclusion, then it is reasonable for the person to believe that conclusion. Thus, good arguments guide rational belief.

Each of the three conditions just described includes an element whose satisfaction is dependent upon the background information available to the individual. People can differ with respect to which premises are justified for them, which patterns they know to be well formed, and which cogent arguments are defeated. Such differences can make an argument a good one for one person but not for another. Again, this is not a matter of taste or preference, but one of reasons and evidence. On this account, when assessing an argument, a person raises three questions: Are these premises justified? Do the premises connect in a proper way with the conclusion? and (in the case of cogent arguments) Is the argument defeated? A rational person will modify beliefs in light of a good argument, when the conclusion conflicts with a previously held belief. In this way, one can learn from arguments.

Understanding arguments in this way invites students to approach arguments by asking, "What should I think now, having encountered this argument?" That strikes me as exactly the right the question to ask. It treats arguments as potential sources of information and understanding. It encourages students to modify beliefs in the light of arguments that provide good reason to believe a conclusion not previously accepted. It properly focuses on issues of rational support rather than persuasion. Highlighting it is, I think, a fundamental component of an effective approach to teaching reasoning.

2. Truth and Objectivity

The following point is probably more controversial than the first, but it seems to me that it is equally fundamental. If students do not think that there is some truth that they are trying to reason toward, then it is very difficult for them to make any sense of the project of analyzing arguments. If one does not think that there are truths (or facts) in a domain, then one cannot make clear sense of arguments purporting to establish truths in that domain. Yet, students, and sometimes their instructors, seem to think that certain controversial realms are mere "matters of opinion" about which there is no "absolute truth" or no "objective truth." I think that it is crucial that students achieve some kind of clarity about these matters if they are to learn to reason effectively.

In developing this point, it will be useful to discuss separately factual issues, including controversial issues about which there is no expert consensus, and broadly moral or policy issues, which of course also often fail to attract consensus. It will be useful to contrast issues of these two kinds with simple matters of taste. I will assume a naive view about simple matters of taste.

Let us begin with matters of taste. Suppose that I like vanilla ice cream but not chocolate and you have just the opposite preferences. This difference could be expressed as a difference about which flavor of ice cream "tastes better." In a sense, we do disagree. And if we have to share a dessert, we may have to find a way to resolve this disagreement. It is further true that we might each be able to say something about why we prefer what we do. However, in some crucial sense, we have no rational disagreement. There are no competing views to defend. There are no arguments for our preferences that can be assessed or criticized. There is no need to defend our views. We simply have different preferences. Our "disagreement" is not the sort of thing that critical thinking courses are about.

To say that there is no point of rational disagreement, and no view that can be rationally defended, when we simply have different preferences is not to say that there are no related factual issues about which we might formulate arguments. In fact, there are many. We could construct arguments about which flavor of ice cream is preferred by the most people, which flavor has the greatest health benefits, and so on. But when I say that vanilla tastes better, I do not mean to report any of these facts. I am simply reporting my preference. We could, of course, disagree about whether that really is my preference. There is a fact about what I prefer. But to present arguments about that proposition would, in most situations, be an unusual and pointless exercise.

The simple and naive view about taste, then, is that there is no truth—no fact—about which flavor is "better." There are simply different preferences. Hence, this not a topic about which we typically construct arguments, and it is not the sort of thing that is the subject matter of critical thinking courses. I want to emphasize that the discussion to follow does not depend on the idea that this simple view about taste is correct. It is mentioned simply for contrast. That is, the idea is that other issues are not like this.

It is possible to express this point about taste by saying that there are no "absolute" or "objective" truths about which flavor is (simply) better. In putting the point this way, we do risk some confusion. As noted, there are "absolute" or "objective" facts about which flavor tastes better *to me* and which tastes better *to you*.[8] What's true is that there is no unrelativized truth about which flavor tastes better *simpliciter*. In this respect, sentences about what tastes better are perfectly analogous to sentences about matters having nothing to do with preferences. For example, a sentence such as "The pants fit" (meaning that they are not too small to get into) is the same. One might say that there is no "absolute" or "objective" truth about the fitness of pants. Again, the key point is that there is no truth that is not relative. That is, the truths in the vicinity might be that the pants fit one person but not another. There is no unrelativized fitness. But the relativized fitness claims are perfectly "objective." The same is true about taste.

The central idea, then, is that matters of taste—claims made by saying things such as "Vanilla ice cream tastes better than chocolate"—are typically not the sort of thing that serves as the conclusion of arguments and are typically not the sort of thing that are addressed in critical thinking classes. Students have to see that the claims that are the focus of these courses are unlike these simple matters of taste.

On topics that we would regularly describe as "factual" or "empirical," it is fairly easy to get students to understand that there are truths, even if they are hard to know. It is also relatively easy to get them to see the place of arguments and reasoning about such topics. For example, consider the thesis that the death penalty deters crime. This clearly needs to be spelled out more fully to have something that we can argue about, but such amplifications of the point can be made. We can identify the kinds of crimes in question, the kinds of societies in which the punishment is alleged to have a deterrent effect, and any other factors left vague in the initial formulation. With that in place, it is clear that there is a correct answer, that various items might support or undermine the statement, and that this is a topic that we can reason about. In this, it contrasts with the statement about ice cream. In other words, these are topics in the realm of reasoning and argumentation.

When it comes to questions in the domain of values or policies, such as whether we ought to use capital punishment, the issues become murkier. To think effectively about this, it is imperative that one carefully distinguish questions about what we ought to do, or what the best policy is, from a host of related clearly factual questions. These related questions include questions about the effect of capital punishment, its status in countries around the world, the public sentiment about it, the frequency with which attempts to implement it fail, the amount of pain and suffering those who are executed feel, the amount of psychological value the practice has for the family and friends of the victims of the criminals who are executed, the frequency with which innocent people have been (or will be) executed, and so on.

All of the questions just identified are fairly readily seen to be objective factual questions. They are questions about which evidence can be assembled and conclusions drawn. The point I want to emphasize here is that if students are to learn to reason effectively, they must see that there is an additional question to be addressed once these are answered (though the answer to the additional question may depend on the answers to these other questions). The additional question concerns what we ought to do in light of these other facts, or in light of those of them that are relevant. I will call questions such as this "moral questions." I intend to use the phrase "moral questions" very broadly, to include all questions about what ought to be done, what is right, what is best, or what is morally acceptable. For present purposes, differences among these questions will not matter.

Much of what comes up for discussion in politics, many of the key social questions that societies must face, are in this sense moral questions. I think that it is clear that one of the key goals in courses about thinking and reasoning is to help students to deal more effectively with moral questions, where these questions are taken in the broad sense just described. If one is to rationally address moral questions, then one must see them as genuine questions to which there are potentially correct and incorrect answers. If there is no truth to the matter, if there is no objective fact, then there is nothing to argue about. There cannot be a good argument, in anything like the sense specified above, in this domain unless the conclusion of the argument is something in the objective realm. Students must understand this if they are to make sense of arguments in this domain.

It is important to be clear about what this does not imply. It does not imply that moral truths are in no way dependent on human choices and constructs. For example, it may be that the expectations people have developed on the basis of social arrangements they have made play some role, major or minor, in determining how people ought to behave. It may be that these factors differ from society to society, so that the only truths along these lines will be relativized. In this way, moral truths will be comparable to sociological truths. That is, just as there are truths about the common practices in various societies and perhaps few if any universal truths along these lines, the moral facts may be similarly relative. If this is the case, then moral issues are more like issues of taste than I have suggested. However, there would remain a key difference: while there is rarely any point in formulating and assessing arguments about whether a particular person prefers one thing or another, there may well be genuine value in arguing about whether our social arrangements determine that we ought to behave in one way or in another. That is, even if the moral facts are socially relative in this way, they may remain open for legitimate rational debate.

In teaching this material, I find that many students are resistant to the idea that morality is "objective" in anything like the sense characterized here. My impression is that there are a few simple confusions that lead to this resistance. For one thing, they conflate the idea that there are objective truths about moral issues with the idea that there are simple universal truths about moral issues. Thus, for example, they assume that an objectivist about morality must assume that if an action of a particular type is wrong in one circumstance, then it is wrong in all circumstances. Of course, this is clearly mistaken, since one can think that many facts about the context of an action contribute to the determination of its status.

Another potential confusion comes from running together epistemic and metaphysical issues. To claim that there are objective truths about moral matters is to make a metaphysical claim, not an epistemic claim. The objectivity claim has no implications concerning our ability to know what the moral truths are. It is consistent with a profound moral skepticism. And it is worth noting that the most interesting forms of moral skepticism imply a kind of objectivism: they imply that there are moral truths but we cannot know what they are. One who holds that there are no moral truths will of course have to concede that there is no moral knowledge, but only because there are no truths to be known.

Another confusion, not unrelated to the first two, that can get in the way in this area comes from focusing only on the most controversial moral issues. If you think about only controversial issues, such as abortion or capital punishment, you can find yourself wondering whether there is a truth of the matter. If you are also thinking that the truth must be universal—abortion is always wrong, or always permissible, or that capital punishment is always wrong—then you might even more easily reject the objectivity claim. However, focusing on some simpler, less controversial issue may help to reduce this inclination.

A final source of resistance, I believe, is the desire to be tolerant and open-minded. Some students want somehow to allow that everyone is "right" in moral disputes because everyone is entitled to his or her opinion. This kind of tolerant attitude may be admirable, and it is fine if it leads to respectful treatment of others. But it should not be taken to imply that everyone's belief is not untrue, that there is no fact of the matter, or that morality is in any sense not objective.

I think that clearing away some of these confusions can help diminish the resistance to the idea that morality is objective. In saying that students need to see that morality is objective in order to engage successfully in reasoning about morality, I do not intend to be taking a stand on contentious philosophical debates. I mean only that they must see it as something that it is possible to argue about, something to which reasons are relevant. For it to be something to argue about, moral statements must be the sort of thing that can be the conclusion of an argument. For them to be conclusions, they have to be the sort of things to which evidence and reasons are relevant. And thus they must be the sorts of things that can be true or false. What kinds of things make moral statements true or false is another matter entirely.

There are sophisticated antirealist positions about morality that are designed to leave room for genuine argument about moral issues. I do not intend to contest those views here. What I do think is crucial is that students see that moral issues are not in relevant ways like issues about unrelativized statements of taste ("Vanilla tastes better"). If they were, then they would not be things to which arguments are relevant. And if a student does not see moral statements as objective in this limited sense, then the effort to teach that student to reason effectively about them is apt to be futile. The arguments will be seen by such a student as a muddled attempt to prove something that is not susceptible to proof.

It is also worth noting that a potentially effective way to get students past the naive relativism or naive antirealism that so many of them purport to endorse is to get them to reflect on their own practices. If there are any issues about which they struggle, wondering what to think about them, then their struggling about them will likely consist in considering the factors that they think bear on the issue. But once they can see that this is what they are doing when they assess an issue, they have already acknowledged something that takes them beyond the naive relativism or naive antirealism that they profess. This is because those views cannot in the end make sense of the idea that these factors really do bear on the issue that they are struggling with.

Another way to put the point I am making here is that moral reasoning and argumentation make sense only if somehow or other there are facts that make some difference to morality. This is what students must be made to understand. Thus, I think that some sort of discussion of these meta-ethical issues is a crucial component of educating students to reason well.

I fear that asserting anything like the view that morality is "objective" is fraught with difficulty. Laudable efforts to be open-minded and inclusive, to avoid "imposing" one's views on students, contribute to the difficulty. Still, it is crucial that students recognize that there is objectivity in this domain, or else they will simply be unable to see what the point of reasoning about moral issues can be (other than persuasion or resolving disagreement). I conclude this section by highlighting some points that can help alleviate these difficulties.

One reason, though not the only reason, that controversial issues are controversial is that the evidence we have about them is limited or inconclusive. That is, they are topics about which there is, or ought to be, considerable uncertainty. Add to this two points briefly mentioned earlier. One point is the ease with which we can conflate related issues such as the moral status of capital punishment with other facts about its effectiveness, constitutionality, and the like. The other point is the ease with which we can confuse simple universal generalizations with other more restrictive generalizations. Claims about the morality or immorality of particular practices are often generalizations with unspecified quantifiers. Is the claim that capital punishment is wrong a universal claim about the practice, or one limited to particular social settings? Being clear about this can help alleviate concerns about saying that there is an objective truth about moral issues such as this.

In any case, students must see moral issues as real issues about which we can argue if they are to analyze arguments about such issues effectively. This requires that they see the issues for what they are. They must see them as genuine issues, perhaps difficult to resolve, to which there are correct answers. The correct answers may be complex and they may be unreachable given the available evidence. This does not undermine the need to see them accurately.

3. Fallacies

In this final section I want to address briefly something that I think students really do not need to learn in order to become effective reasoners.[9] Indeed, it is something that I think is potentially detrimental. Teaching students to identify the so-called informal fallacies—allegedly common errors in reasoning—is one popular way to teach students reasoning. Having a classification of reasoning errors can seem to be a useful and effective way to facilitate argument analysis. In my view, this is a subject best avoided.

Anyone reading the literature on fallacies will see that there is considerable disagreement about exactly what counts as a fallacy. Some people think that only arguments can be fallacies: a fallacy is an invalid argument. Others think that fallacies are violations of the rules of conversation. Still others count as fallacies related things such as misleading persuasive techniques. Some think any bad argument counts as a fallacy, while others think that only bad arguments that appear to be good or tend to persuade people count as fallacies. Some think that a fallacy must have a structural defect, while others think that different sorts of defects, such as a mistaken premise, is enough to categorize the argument as a fallacy. For the present discussion, such details can be ignored. Furthermore, anyone reading the literature on fallacies will notice that there is considerable disagreement about exactly how to define the various fallacies, with some making ever finer distinctions and presenting a greater array of categories.[10] Whether there is a useful classification scheme that is internally coherent is an open question. I will not pursue this point here. It will not matter for the discussion that follows.

Assume, then, for the sake of discussion that it is possible to produce a catalogue, or taxonomy, of errors made in arguments. Is this something that we should teach our students about? I think that the answer is no. In this final section, I briefly explain why. I acknowledge at the outset that my defense of this answer is far from decisive. A well-defended answer would require information about the effects of teaching using the various methods. We cannot properly sit in our armchairs and figure out what will happen if we use these methods. To think otherwise is to commit "the speculative fallacy."

There are, however, plausible grounds to worry about the practical effects of teaching the fallacies.[11] One worry is that learning about the fallacies induces mindless, negative classification. Students play "name that fallacy" instead of thinking hard about arguments. A second worry is that the existing classifications are confusing, so it is hard to believe that students can know what to do with them. Third, the classification scheme adds unnecessary complication to the project of evaluating arguments.

This last point strikes me as particularly forceful, and I will develop it here in more detail. Here's an imperfect analogy: suppose that you want to be able to grow lilies in your garden. Lilies are relatively easy to grow, but they are subject to a few diseases and pests. There are growing conditions to avoid and remedies to apply when problems strike. As far as I know, for the average home gardener, the same remedy will be applied in the same way to many of the problems that arise. Teaching the average home gardener to distinguish all the different diseases and their variations is likely to be counterproductive. They'll end up trying to differentiate minute details that make little difference to what they want to do. I think that something similar is true of the fallacies.

The thing that I find most striking about teaching the identification of informal fallacies is that it is completely unnecessary. Students armed with the account of good arguments presented at the beginning of this essay will have exactly what they need to assess an argument. Students using the epistemic account of good arguments will ask themselves three questions: First, do the premises support the conclusion? Second, am I justified in believing the conjunction of the premises? Three, does my background evidence defeat this argument? If the argument succeeds on all three points, then the argument is a good one for them and they ought to believe the conclusion on the basis of the argument. If not, then they should not believe the conclusion on the basis of the argument. The classification of arguments as fallacies is just a fifth wheel in this process. Things that are properly classified as fallacies will come out to be bad arguments (or not arguments) on the epistemic account. Things that are not fallacies will be judged to be good arguments (barring defects not classified as fallacies). But students simply do not need to consider which sort of allegedly bad argument it is. And they do not need to spend their time learning the names of the various fallacies, nor do they need to spend their time trying to classify the arguments they encounter into the categories deemed fallacious. They can just assess the arguments.

The simplicity of this description of the method for evaluation of argument no doubt masks the complexities that can arise in carrying it out. It can be hard to tell what supports what, and it can be difficult to determine whether one is justified in believing a set of premises. Factoring in background evidence often muddies the issues. Still, if you answer these questions, you'll have done the job. It just does not matter whether the basis for a negative evaluation also provides the basis for categorizing the argument as an instance of one fallacy or another. Identifying the fallacy strikes me as a confusing and unnecessary extra step.

Furthermore, for students to grasp what the fallacies are—to have the idea of a bad argument that tends to persuade people—they will need to have some grasp of the concept of a good argument. So they need the general idea anyway. It is hard to see what of value is gained by having a multitude of names for the various errors. We can do without the fallacies.

4. CONCLUSION

In this chapter I have assumed without argument that a central goal of education is to teach students the essential reasoning and thinking skills needed to be effective citizens. I described what I contend to be two key features that ought to be included in courses teaching these skills. The first feature concerns the nature and purpose of arguments. I contrasted three general approaches, one focusing on arguments as tools of persuasion, one emphasizing their role in the achievement of agreement or consensus, and one emphasizing their use in reaching rational beliefs about issues. I argued briefly in favor of the third, or epistemic, approach, and spelled out some of the details of my preferred version of this approach. The second key feature concerns the objectivity of morality. I argued that moral claims are among the things about which students need to learn to reason. But to make sense of moral argument, students must learn to see moral claims as things that can be right or wrong, things to which evidence and reasons apply. And this requires disabusing them of the naïve views to the contrary that they often hold. Finally, I suggested that students do not need, and possibly would be better off without, discussion of the so-called informal fallacies.

NOTES

1. This view is widely held. See, for example, Siegel 1988. For discussion, see Marples 1999.

2. This is intended to represent the views of those who take a rhetorical approach to argument. A notable example is Tindale 1999.

3. This is intended to represent the views of those who take a dialectical approach to argument. Notable examples are van Eemeren and Grootendorst 2004.

4. This is intended to represent the views of those who take an epistemic approach to arguments. For an extensive discussion of this approach, see the essays in Lumer 2005, 2006.

5. Lumer's introductory essay in Lumer 2005 provides an excellent overview of theories of arguments, with emphasis on the epistemological approach.

6. The ideas developed here summarize the views I defended in Feldman 1994. For a detailed defense of a different version of the epistemic account, see Biro and Siegel 1992, 2006a, 2006b, and Siegel and Biro 1997, 2008. For additional discussion, see Lumer 2006.

7. Some philosophers who largely share my perspective on arguments are apt to disagree on this point. Harvey Siegel suggests (in correspondence) that defenders of an

epistemic approach to arguments develop a conception of good arguments that is not relativized in the way I proposed. On his account, a good argument must have a proper structure, but there is no condition requiring that a person grasp this fact. What matters is just that it in fact have a proper structure (and that its premises be justified for the person). But this seems to me to have an unwelcome consequence. Suppose that (i) I know some premises to be true, (ii) these premises entail some controversial proposition, and (iii) I have no idea that this entailment holds. It seems to me that I would not be justified in believing this conclusion on the basis of an argument having these premises. That is, an argument with these premises and this conclusion does not provide me with reasons justifying belief in the conclusion. Yet on Siegel's suggested view, this would be a good argument. Siegel must therefore abandon the connection between good arguments and rational belief—that is, he must admit that reasonable people need not believe things even though they have good arguments for them. The concept of "good argument" that I'm working with takes a good argument to be one that does rationally demand acceptance of its conclusion. However, I acknowledge that there are multiple concepts of "good argument" that can play a useful role in thinking about arguments.

8. I should acknowledge a complication involving the claim that there are these relativized facts, or facts about what flavor I prefer. There are actually many facts in the vicinity, and it is not always clear which one is expressed by the sentence, "I prefer vanilla ice cream to chocolate." I may prefer vanilla over chocolate in some circumstances but not others, or I may prefer some kinds of vanilla ice cream to any kinds of chocolate ice cream, but prefer some chocolates to inferior vanilla. Reflection on these facts brings out that the sentence "I prefer vanilla ice cream to chocolate" is in certain ways incomplete or obscure.

9. For discussion of the various issues raised in this section, see Hamblin 1970 and Hansen and Pinto 1995.

10. For a recent textbook taking this approach, see Walton 2008. My own text, Feldman 1999, avoids discussion of the informal fallacies.

11. See Hitchcock 1995.

REFERENCES

Biro, John, and Harvey Siegel. (1992). "Normativity, Argumentation, and an Epistemic Theory of Fallacies." In *Argumentation Illuminated,* ed. F. H. van Eemeren, R. Grootendorst, J. A. Blair, and C. A. Willard (pp. 85–103). Amsterdam: SICSAT.

—— (2006a). "Pragma-Dialectic Versus Epistemic Theories of Arguing and Argument: Rivals or Partners?" In *Considering Pragma-Dialectics: A Festschrift for Frans H. Van Eemeren on the Occasion of His 60th Birthday,* ed. Peter Houtlosser and Agnes van Rees (pp. 1–10). London: Routledge.

—— (2006b). "In Defense of the Objective Epistemic Approach to Argumentation." *Informal Logic* 26: 91–101.

Feldman, Richard. (1994). "Good Arguments." In *Socializing Epistemology,* ed. Frederick Schmitt (pp. 159–88). Lanham, MD: Rowman and Littlefield.

—— (1999). *Reason and Argument,* 2nd ed. Upper Saddle River, NJ: Prentice-Hall.

Hamblin, C. H. (1970). *Fallacies.* London: Methuen.

Hansen, Hans V., and Robert C. Pinto, eds. (1995). *Fallacies: Classical and Contemporary Readings.* University Park, PA: Pennsylvania State University Press.

Hitchcock, David. (1995). "Do the Fallacies Have a Place in the Teaching of Reasoning Skills or Critical Thinking?" In *Fallacies: Classical and Contemporary Readings*, ed. Hans V. Hansen and Robert C. Pinto (pp. 319–27). University Park, PA: Pennsylvania State University Press.

Lumer, Christoph, ed. (2005). *Informal Logic* 25. Special Issue on the Epistemological Approach to Argumentation, Part 1.

—— (2006). *Informal Logic* 26. Special Issue on the Epistemological Approach to Argumentation, Part 2.

Marples, Roger, ed. (1999). *The Aims of Education*. London: Routledge.

Siegel, Harvey. (1988). *Educating Reason: Rationality, Critical Thinking, and Education*. London: Routledge.

Siegel, Harvey, and John Biro. (1997). "Epistemic Normativity, Argumentation, and Fallacies." *Argumentation* 11: 277–92.

—— (2008). "Rationality, Reasonableness, and Critical Rationalism: Problems with the Pragma-dialectical View." *Argumentation* 22: 191–203.

Tindale, Christopher W. (1999). *Acts of Arguing: A Rhetorical Model of Argument*. Albany, NY: SUNY Press.

van Eemeren, F. H., and R. Grootendorst. (2004). *A Systematic Theory of Argumentation: The Pragma-dialectical Approach*. Cambridge: Cambridge University Press.

Walton, Douglas. (2008). *Informal Logic: A Pragmatic Approach*. Cambridge: Cambridge University Press.

CHAPTER 5

WHY FALLIBILITY HAS NOT MATTERED AND HOW IT COULD

JONATHAN E. ADLER

1. FALLIBILITY AS THE EASILY IGNORED INDUCTIVE POSSIBILITY OF ERROR

FALLIBILISM is the dominant epistemology in education. Leite (in press) explains the doctrine of fallibilism clearly:

> an anti-dogmatic intellectual stance or attitude: an openness to the possibility that one has made an error and an accompanying willingness to give a fair hearing to arguments that one's belief is incorrect.... So understood, fallibilism's central insight is that it is possible to remain open to new evidence and arguments while also reasonably treating an issue as settled for the purposes of current inquiry and action.

Despite widespread adherence, fallibilism plays little role in education or even in contemporary philosophy of education. A recent major—638-page—collection in the philosophy of education (Curren 2003) contains no reference in the index to fallibilism or to fallibility, though I expect that the authors all endorse fallibilism. Why does fallibility or fallibilism lack bite in education? Should it be otherwise and, if so, how?

An obvious start to answering the first question is: complete victory. The battle against epistemologies that aspire to certainty or incorrigibility is won. No serious educational proposal will guarantee success. Knowing that future changes will alter current policies does not differentiate among prospective policies. Without contenders for controversy, there is no visibility.

But this is only a part of the explanation: even if fallibilism has no battles to fight, it could provide substantial guidance to policies. Democratic ideals, the authority of the teacher in the classroom, students' use of textbooks, the centrality of mathematics in the curriculum are hardly contestable, but still inform policy.

The major culprit is fallibility, which is the doctrine on which fallibilism rests. The problem is that fallibility, as it is commonly understood, is too weak to justify the significant recommendations or attitudes of fallibilism, as described above.

The standard understanding of fallibility identifies it with the *ineliminable possibility of error* for judgments or beliefs, however well formed. The model is inductive inference, which can be warranted, yet the denial of its conclusion is compatible with the truth of the evidence. (Elgin 1996, p. 11).[1] Can this understanding yield recommendations for procedures to lessen prospects of error? Can so minimal a fallibility serve as the pillar of fallibilism—providing a reason to remain open-minded? If not, we have a strong candidate to explain fallibility's (or fallibilism's) lack of bite.

Elgin draws the sought-for connection between fallibility and correction:

> Forced to concede fallibility, imperfect procedural epistemology [the view she advocates] demands corrigibility. Rather than treating acceptability as irrevocable, it incorporates devices for reviewing accepted commitments and correcting or rejecting them should errors emerge.   (Elgin 1996, p. 132; see also p. 121)

But how can fallibility motivate Elgin's recommendation? For the minimal inductive possibility of error cannot be eliminated or even diminished by corrective devices. A factory is motivated to implement a new quality-control system only because the new system promises to lower its rate of manufacturing defective products. It would hardly be motivated if the outcome is guaranteed not to lower the rate.

Given the current understanding of fallibility, the response to the discovery of one's error may just as well be the indifferent response to which we are all familiar: "I believed *p*, but I was wrong. So what? I'm fallible." The response can go even one step below indifference: "I believed *p*, but it turned out false and I replaced it with the correct belief. I learned from my mistake, so I am now more assured."

Although the logical compatibility of the evidence and the denial of the inductively reached conclusion is incontestable, the move from it to the possibility of error is not. The possibility is supposed both to represent the logical evidence-conclusion gap and to rule out the conclusiveness or necessity of the evidence-to-conclusion relation.

Yet, we do often describe inductive inference in conclusive terms (of the necessity of the conclusion given the premises): "John *must* still be in his office. I saw him go in a minute ago and no one has come out since." Conclusiveness characterizes knowledge—I know John is in his office only if, given the evidence, it could not be otherwise. It is contradictory to think "I know that John is in his office, but it is possible that he is not" or even "John is in his office, but it is possible that he is not."

These coherence-of-thought tests provide for a contrast with desire: of any particular belief, I cannot think that it might be false. To do so is already to lose that belief. By contrast, one can know that a particular desire, like the desire for a hot fudge sundae, is bad to satisfy. Yet, there it remains.

The failed test implies that when a possibility of error remains one cannot know. Fallibility, as the ineliminable possibility of error, is called upon to serve as a pivotal premise for radical skepticism. The linchpin of the dreaming argument is that, compatible with the appearances before me now of, for example, a computer screen, I cannot know that it is a computer screen, since I cannot exclude the (way-out) possibility that I am now the subject of a very realistic dream. If someone affirmed, as above, that John must be in his office and you insist that it is still possible that he is not, on a judgment that is so obvious, you could cast into doubt most any knowledge claim.

A prominent candidate to explicate knowledge is, in fact, the elimination of possibilities of error (Lewis 1996). If you stay at a friend's house and you are searching for coffee, once you find none in either the refrigerator or the cabinet, you are sure, by elimination, that the coffee is in the freezer, if there is any open container. These are the only three places in the home where open coffee containers are normally kept. If correct, you know that the coffee is in the freezer, when you have eliminated all the places (possibilities) but one.

These claims about possibility do not rest on an exotic or demanding notion of knowledge. There is no claim that knowledge implies certainty. Urging fallibility as a reason to replace knowledge as the central epistemological concept or goal with justified belief or warranted assertibility does not help. Only when you have eliminated all other possibilities are you warranted in asserting "The coffee is in the freezer."

A related understanding of fallibility, taken by Peirce, Dewey, and Popper, is that future inquiry may (or will) upset current conclusions.[2] Godfrey-Smith writes: "Popper placed great emphasis on the idea that we can never be *completely sure* that a theory is true. After all, Newton's physics was viewed as the best-supported theory ever, but early in the twentieth century it was shown to be false in several respects" (2003, p. 59; see also Dewey 1986, chap. 2).

In a book that attempts to develop a Popperian philosophy of education, the authors write in their introduction:

> fallibilism is a philosophical perspective which rests on the assumption that people can never be certain that their ideas or beliefs are absolutely true. For a fallibilist, all that is known today will very likely be superseded by very different and potentially better ideas. Just as Newtonian physics was revolutionized by Einstein's theories about the universe, *it is quite possible* to envision a new physics that will render the ideas developed by Einstein relatively obsolete.
>   (Swartz, Perkinson, and Edgerton 1980, p. xi, my emphasis)[3]

But since we did uncover flaws in Newton's theory, which discoveries required examining a wider variety of evidence than believed necessary at Newton's time, are we not entitled to far greater assurance that Einstein's theory is basically correct, rather than less? I do not doubt the heuristic value of the fate of Newton's theory for teaching a powerful example of fallibility in scientific theorizing. Rather, I doubt whether this case should serve as a paradigm for secure, but nevertheless fallible, beliefs. Would not much better candidates be Descartes' "two and three added together are five" and "a square has no more than four sides"; or, if a clearly empirical or contingent example is sought, how about "The earth was at some time habitable" or "There are rocks" or "There is no Santa Claus"?

These latter examples have, unlike Newton's theory, withstood the test of time, and it is not believable that they will be discovered false in the future. We are *certain* (in ordinary usage) of them—counterexamples to the ringing claim that people "can never be certain that their ideas or beliefs are absolutely true." If fallibility is the universally applicable doctrine that is alleged, why can't we readily produce examples like these, where yet the belief turned out false? These beliefs are not only painfully obvious, but they are also implied by many other beliefs. The surrendering of Newton's theory hardly made a ripple in our corpus of beliefs. However, if any of my mundane examples were surrendered, the disruption would be profound.

The fallibility I am challenging can only maintain its antiskepticism by introducing specialized usages for "certain" and "possibility." This is evident also in the use of "quite possible" in the previous quote, which exhibits an urge for a strong fallibilism, but a fear to affirm it. The authors really want to say something like that a new physics is "very easy to envision," but they dodge that more challenging claim because, presumably, the latter calls for evidence or detailed argument that is not forthcoming. I expect that they are prisoners of both their own treatment of fallibility as the minimal, inductive "possibility" and the dilemma I present in the next section.

2. ROBUST FALLIBILITY

Is there another way to understand fallibility than the minimal constancy view, which would support a significant educational role for the possibility of error?[4] I will answer both parts in the affirmative, though an adequate defense of the former would enter deep epistemological waters that I cannot do here.

We want an interpretation of a thought like "I know that the coffee is in the freezer, though I *might* be wrong" or an assertion like "The coffee is in the freezer, though I might be wrong" that is consistent. The second ("might") conjunct is not a possibility incompatible with knowledge. Even if the evidence does conclusively establish the conclusion, I can conceive ways, from the position I am in to judge, that I am wrong. One may coherently think: "The coffee is in the freezer, but it seems to me, from the (epistemic) position in which I make that judgment, that others are in a position to put forward, as a warranted claim, a similar judgment, and I cannot discriminate their position from my own."

If this alternative understanding works, does it help us to formulate a *robust fallibility* that can motivate open-mindedness and self-corrective efforts in order to lessen the prospects for error?[5] Those who promote taking fallibility seriously will want to advocate for robust fallibility, yet, in adhering to the standard view, they find themselves boxed in by a dilemma:

> If fallibility is minimal, it holds of each of our beliefs without empirical evidence. However, if fallibility is more than minimal, either it would not apply to each of our beliefs and it would vary in applicability to individuals or if it did apply universally, it would require evidence against the warrant for those beliefs, which would, implausibly, amount to an empirically grounded radical skepticism. So, a nonskeptical robust fallibility would be too variable for any general implications or educational recommendations (to encourage open-mindedness and related intellectual virtues).

The view of fallibility put forth above and to be developed rejects or qualifies both horns of this dilemma.

To pursue the epistemic import of a robust fallibility, recall Descartes' very general, yet natural, line of thought in *Meditation I* to shake his confidence in even "obvious" or necessary truths like that $2+3 = 5$: "since I judge that others sometimes make mistakes in matters that they believe they know most perfectly, may I not, in like fashion, be deceived every time I add two and three or count the sides of a square, or perform an even simpler operation, if that can be imagined?" (Descartes 2002, p. 461).[6]

Descartes' line of thought comes close to how we invoke fallibility to disturb those we think of as overly confident or dogmatic. John is driving well over the speed limit. When you tell him to slow down, he responds that he is a very good driver. You observe that many of those who precipitated bad accidents thought of themselves as good drivers for reasons seemingly as good as his own. Psychological studies confirm a kind of "Lake Wobegon" effect in ratings for oneself: in a wide range of self-judgments, (nondepressed) subjects rate their abilities as better than others in peer groups—for example, friendlier, less biased, better drivers, less conformist.[7]

Now these overratings may be so high as to generate a liability to error that is evidence against one's believing that one is, e.g., a good driver. But only if they are so high is the overrating incompatible with knowing that one is a good driver. (Do the high divorce rates imply that no one can know that his or her own marital prospects are good?) But if not, they still rationally lower one's confidence. Your pointed observation does not directly challenge John's belief that he is a good driver. Instead, you are proposing to him that he can easily envisage others, whom he takes to be similarly situated, who did precipitate accidents. Consequently, John should lessen his confidence and rethink his speeding.

However, the Cartesian line, also implicit in the Newton-Einstein comparison, requires a qualification. Descartes' worry arises in comparing his own confidence with that of others of equal assurance, whom he takes to have been mistaken. However, first, individuals' strength of attitude is sensitive to changes in their circumstances that do not constitute reasons supportive or undermining of beliefs. A student becomes less confident of his geometry proof for a final exam than merely for homework, though his reasons—the steps in the proof—remain the same. Second, the conclusion sought of one's liability to error requires the further assumption that one's current position does not compensate for those errors. In earlier times, people were sure of a child's temperature by touch with the back of one's hand or of the lines in a poem by memory. Now we have thermometers and books or computers, respectively.

A robust fallibility takes account of what we learn from experience. So it is one's *epistemic position*—for brevity, one's claim and the evidence for it—that is crucial for ascribing likeness of circumstances, not merely one's confidence or assurance. One's epistemic position may be better than that of others, though they appear to one as similar. One's judgment is still fallible, when it is correct and warranted, even though one is unable to discriminate one's own position from others, similarly situated, who fail to be warranted or correct.

3. Weaknesses in Reasoning and the Study of Error

Robust fallibility is about our proneness to error, not just its (constant, minimal) possibility. If there is such a proneness, there should be evidence for it. If so, that evidence is worth study by educators to evaluate curricula and by students to appreciate their own errors, including the sources of those errors (poor understanding, confusion, hasty judgment, forgetfulness, false assumptions, distraction ...). Studying that evidence should contribute to the students' self-understanding and to weakening that proneness.8 The proposal, consonant with appreciation of our robust fallibility, is then for the study of errors, relying on research on reasoning as evidence for our proneness to error.

Explanation is a central concept of epistemology, education, and human understanding. In an investigation of how we explain prima facie discrepant occurrences, subjects are asked to answer a set of questions for which open-ended, discursive, answers are sought on a variety of topics. One question concerns baseball batting averages: "After the first two weeks of the baseball season the leader has a batting average that is over .450. Yet, no batter ever finishes a season with a better than .450 average. What do you think is the most likely explanation for the fact that batting averages are higher early in the season?" (Jepson, Krantz, and Nisbett 1983, p. 500).

A typical answer is: "As the season commences a player will, I think, become less motivated to impress people with a powerful bat—he is taking a sort of ho-hum attitude about it" (compare to Kahneman and Tversky 1982). The favored response is grounded in chance—more specifically, the law of large numbers and regression. Earlier in the season, with far fewer times at bat, deviation from a well-established average is more likely. With the much greater number of times at bat by the end of the season, the chance influences on deviations from average performance are more likely to balance out to smaller deviations from that average. Batting averages that reflect greater times at bat are less subject to the influence of chance and so provide better evidence "as to how well a batter hits" (Jepson, Krantz, and Nisbett 1983, p. 500). In general, the experimenters found that "Most of these answers [of subjects] presumed, either tacitly or explicitly, that the sample was adequate and showed no recognition of the uncertain or probabilistic nature of events of the kind presented in the problems" (p. 496).

A related example is to explain the alleged sophomore slump, whereby outstanding rookie baseball players do substantially worse their second year. Subjects give similar answers—for example, success spoiled them—in response to which Nisbett and Ross (1980) comment: "by chance alone, some mediocre athletes will perform exceptionally well in their first year but perform less well in subsequent years" (p. 164). The explanations that subjects offer—for example, that the batter became too cocky—fit common patterns: performers who become conceited owing to their success in a skilled, demanding activity relax their efforts and then do worse.

The weaknesses in reasoning revealed by these studies should fuel, I assume, efforts to promote an education that seeks to develop an informed and critical citizenry. Although I will provide further and varied illustration of such weaknesses, I cannot undertake to establish this assumption here, since it requires showing that many faulty judgments in public policy rely for their support on distortions of evidence, argument, and reasoning, which exploit the weaknesses that the above studies and their neighbors expose.

Distortions in argument can anticipate success at persuasion because our curiosity and what we accept as explanations to satisfy that curiosity can be turned on us, as the baseball examples suggest. Another captivating example is in Michael Schermer's column in *Scientific American* ("Mr. Skeptic Goes to Esalen"): "Once it become known that Mr. Skeptic was there [at Esalen Institute], for example, I heard one after another 'How do you explain *this?*' story, mostly involving angels, aliens, and the usual paranormal fare" (p. 38). The request for an explanation is really a challenge: if Schermer cannot supply a better explanation, he is rationally bound to endorse the one offered. In accepting the legitimacy of the "why" question, we bias ourselves against explaining-away some of the alleged surprising phenomena with a chance account: "Look, there is no 'why' to it. It's just chance."

Another set of studies is from elementary physics (mechanics), and I quote from Howard Gardner's (1991) presentation:

> Researcher Andrea DiSessa devised a game called Target, which is played in a computerized environment with a simulated object called a dynaturtle. The dynaturtle can be moved around a computer screen by means of commands like FORWARD, RIGHT, LEFT, or KICK, the latter command giving the

dynaturtle an impulse in the direction that the simulated object is currently
facing. . . .

The goal of the game is to give instructions to the dynaturtle such that it will
hit a target and do so with minimum speed at impact. . . .

So described, the game sounds simple enough . . . Yet nearly everyone at both
levels of expertise fails dismally. The reason, briefly, is that success at the game
requires an understanding and application of Newton's laws of motion. To
succeed, the player must be able to take into account the direction in which and
the speed with which the dynaturtle has already been moving. Whatever their
formal training, however, players of this game reveal themselves to be dyed-in-the-
wool Aristotelians. They assume that, so long as they aim the dynaturtle directly at
the target, they will succeed, and they are mystified when the KICK does not result
in the desired collision.   (pp. 152–53)

Gardner concludes that "This is not a case of simple ignorance of the principle
under investigation; many of the students know—and can state—the laws on
which they would be drawing. Nor is it a case of factual errors; the students are
not being asked whether the sun is a star, or a dolphin is a fish" (p. 155).

These two illustrations can be marshaled against another instance of the above
false dilemma that made robust fallibility itself appear impossible. The dilemma
in this configuration concludes that robust fallibility cannot be of educational import:

Propensities to err are either very weak, in which case, though they may apply
generally, they provide neither direction for policy nor sufficient prospective
benefits to warrant investment; or else they are substantial, in which case they will
be too variable across individuals and domains to serve as a basis for general
(uniform) policies.

Against this false dilemma, I offer the empirically based illustrations above, which
stand for many others, of widespread difficulties that most any student would
confront. The fallacies derive from entrenched and heavily used ways of thinking.
They are evidence of a substantial proneness to error, and yet, contrary to the
dilemma, they hold generally without implying a radical skepticism.

The faults that the research uncovers have been construed as impediments to
learning, across the liberal arts curriculum. In presenting these problems in *The
Unschooled Mind* (also his *The Disciplined Mind*), Gardner means to show:

just how great is the disjunction between scholastic ["correct-answer"] and
nonscholastic [expert] forms of understanding has become apparent only in
recent years.   (1991, p. 150)

In the case of science and science-related areas, I will speak of *misconceptions* that
students bring to their studies. In the case of mathematics, I will speak of *rigidly
applied algorithms*. Finally, in the case of nonscientific studies, particularly those in
the humanities and arts, I will speak of stereotypes and simplifications.   (p. 151)

The weaknesses in reasoning exposed by this research are likely to be impediments to learning across the curriculum because of the generality of reasoning:

reasoning embraces all the ways in which we attempt to reach rational conclusions by inference, whether about what to believe or about what to do. The research provides evidence that our proneness to error is not just a conceptual possibility but also an empirically sustained proneness that is not restricted in application to particular domains of thought or inquiry.

The two previous illustrations are, however, initially problematic as evidence for a robust fallibility. For fallibility teaches its sharpest lesson when it applies to judgments or beliefs that are warranted, which does not hold in these cases (participants are wrong about how to explain the baseball discrepancies or how to kick the dynaturtle). The lesson of fallibility is close by, though: One can reasonably think one's judgment warranted—and it not be. But fallacious patterns of reasoning can even be involved in judgments that are warranted. Those who failed with di Sessa's dynaturtle test can nevertheless succeed at a wide range of judgments of motion. Students who commit well-known fallacies with conditionals, like affirming the consequent, can be warranted in judging valid that "if today is Tuesday, I have class. So since today is Tuesday, I do have class" and invalid that "if I do not practice, I will not make the varsity. So if I do practice, I will make it."

The proneness to error of fallacious patterns of reasoning need not reveal itself in a substantial actual rate of error. To the contrary, these patterns may not only guide successful action, but they will be reinforced, within our narrow confines of experience, by the success of those actions. The weaknesses are uncovered only by going beyond those confines or by contriving tests where failures are more vivid and precise, as with the dynaturtle experiments.

It is not only the world that may be misleadingly cooperative as far as exposing limits on patterns of reasoning but also pervasive human activities. In the baseball cases, the exclusion of the chance account is reinforced by ordinary conversation. To ask why there is the discrepancy between early and late batting averages, or freshman and sophomore batting performance, is to *presuppose* that the discrepancy calls for explanation and so it is not a chance phenomenon. Since hearers normally accommodate to a speaker's presupposition, we are conversationally disposed to place a chance account off the table, as assumed above. (There are, of course, other reinforcers to this nonchance, deterministic explanation for the discrepancy in batting performance.)

The problem of limited experience and pragmatic presuppositions' furthering flawed patterns of reasoning is exacerbated by the *self-protective*, though porous, nature of reasoning. In the above illustrations, contrary observations and experiences are available, but these experiences are not even so registered (as contrary). Our beliefs oppose a description of those experiences as falsifications of themselves.

The standard pattern of learning from experience is that—for example—you are trying to get to the 50th Street stop from Chambers Street. You take the first uptown train to arrive on the line with a 50th Street stop—the #2. But the #2 does not stop at 50th Street, proceeding from Times Square (42nd Street) directly to the 72nd Street stop. Realizing the error, you check the map to discover that 50th Street is a local stop and the #2 is an express train. You lose your original belief that any train on the line with your destination station and heading in its direction will stop at the station. You replace that belief with a qualified one to take account of the difference between express and local stations. This pattern can be represented as:

belief → action → recognized failure → revision (modification, qualification)

of belief, where the arrow stands for some immediate (e.g., intentional, causal, epistemic) connection. (This is roughly the pattern taken as central in Ohlsson 1996.)

The cases that we are concerned with are those in which the first three steps, especially the middle two, are not evident in normal experience. There are no simple actions or predictions that could yield clear falsifying observations. In short, you must endorse your own reasoning. The reasoning by which you draw a conclusion thereby also provides you with sufficient reason neither to question that reasoning nor to conceptualize various outcomes as falsifying. The explanation of the discrepancy in batting averages as due to the batters' becoming too cocky and cutting down on practice will deter me from putting that explanation to the test or to take real notice of whether it holds up over time and across players. To the contrary, that explanation satisfies me. So it undermines motivation to pursue further analysis, while rendering salient those cases that appear confirmatory.

Contrast this self-protection with reasoning from desire to action. Given my desire to eat a hot fudge sundae, I reason practically to what I might do to obtain and eat one. The reasoning does not nullify the reasons I have to criticize the desire. Or, to recall an earlier example, if I conclude that the coffee is in the freezer by elimination, but I do not find it there, the guiding belief that there is no further location to search is noticeably jeopardized.

The problem of self-protectiveness is akin to worries over conflicts of interest: The circumstances that generate the potential conflict of interest thereby generate a barrier to impartially judging whether one is really in a conflict of interest. If you are concerned that your own bias might interfere with determining what position in the batting order your son should bat on his baseball team, which you coach, that bias will affect your judging whether you can judge the order fairly (Adler 2002b).

Although the problem of flawed reasoning as self-protective is far-reaching, it is nevertheless subject to exaggeration. Clearly, in the dynaturtle case the students do discover that their judgment (prediction) is erroneous, although the discovery requires reassurance that the experiment is on the up-and-up, as well as the sharp focus induced by the computer model.

Limits on the conceptual problem of self-protection are best addressed by returning to a similar and familiar problem. The problem drew on Kuhn's *The Structure of Scientific Revolutions* and the Quine-Duhem thesis (that hypothesis testing is always mediated by further beliefs), and it enjoyed exponential growth to reach the conclusion of the impossibility of decisive falsification. I want to forestall such a grand reading of the modest problem I pose.

Persuasive presentations are subject to testing or to critical examination, not only subsequent to acceptance but also prior to it. They are subject to *plausibility* assessments that, in extreme cases, justify rejection of a starkly incredible conclusion without examination of premises. Why is it that even if a speaker wants to deceive you into making an unnecessary trip to a local Wichita, Kansas, dance club, he will not tell you that the Rolling Stones are playing there this Friday, so that you should rush over to get tickets? You will not believe him. Since the speaker knows this, he will not waste his breath trying to convince you otherwise. It is starkly implausible that the Rolling Stones would perform at a small club in Wichita without well-publicized inducement.

Students, even young ones, already have vast stores of knowledge that regularly awake them in conversation to highly implausible claims, regardless of the arguments or evidence alleged for them. You cannot wildly fool many of the people much of the time. That background knowledge is one resource limiting the problem of self-protective reasoning. Studying error should bring to the forefront, and build upon, this powerful resource that students carry with them and regularly apply effortlessly. Learning increases that resource: the more one knows in a domain, the more claims are subject to plausibility assessments, so students are less susceptible to bad reasoning or to false persuasion.

Unfortunately, this optimism works only to expose the strikingly implausible. Optimism sinks rapidly for claims and conclusions that require reflection to draw out the implausibility. The example I turn to is another of Gardner's illustrations of widespread and deep-seated misconceptions. Gardner writes:

> If one is told that there are six times as many students as professors and that there are ten professors, nearly everyone can compute the number of students. . . . But when students are asked to write out a formula that captures the relevant proportion, using S for students, and P for professors, the majority of college students fail. . . . The majority of college students write the formula $6S = P$. (1991, p. 160)

Gardner comments: "Yet this formula would yield the astonishing conclusion that if there are 60 students, there would be 360 professors!" (p. 160).

Gardner's counterexample is a knock-down objection to the solution. Students, who answer wrongly, already have the competence to recognize that their solution is baldly mistaken. But, of course, Gardner can only offer the example to illustrate misconceptions because the students do endorse their answer. They fail to activate, or worse, they deactivate, their own powerful critical resources.

The students who give the incredible answer find no discomfort in their reasoning. They do not recognize a reason to check their answer, let alone to check it in a novel way, which is another surfacing of the problem of self-protective reasoning. Bad reasoning does not come so marked, and whether reasoning is good or bad, it provides grounds for a judgment, which are thereby grounds not to doubt that judgment. In cases like the algebra one, as well as the earlier ones, the great lesson of fallibility is to be found in discovering that one's own error is obstructed by the reasoning that yields that error.

4. MORE DETAILS ON THE STUDY OF ERROR

Nothing in the proposal to study errors is a challenge to subject-matter coverage, but only of how some of that material is covered. The study would be a contribution to improving meta-cognition, which research on expert-novice comparisons shows is more fruitful as it is richly embedded in domain-specific knowledge.[9]

An addition that the study of errors does require for the higher grades is the study of reasoning, focusing on probability and statistics; explicitness of steps (assumptions) in proofs and arguments; and the appreciation of correlative concepts of chance, causality, randomness, proof, consistency, implication, and explanation. A more demanding suggestion is that more of science be taught historically with original texts, as part of a larger place for the history of ideas.[10] Real errors, modifications, and dead-ends become apparent, yet placed in a web of beliefs where those errors emerge sensibly.[11]

The study of errors has a number of dimensions, which I will list and illustrate from our examples so far, with further ones to be introduced. The lessons to be drawn next will be in sharper focus if the errors illustrated are contrasted with simple errors of, say, spelling, calculation, memory, or formulation, even if each is evidence of fallibility.

4.1. Surprise and Puzzlement

The discovery that you are wrong in the two main illustrations is very surprising. Subjects confidently believed p to be true, but it turned out to be false. The surprise is second-order: I come to believe that what I believed, or thought I knew, was wrong. (Adler 2008) Surprise, and appreciation of fallibility, cannot arise in an area of recognized ignorance, but only where one thinks one knows. The surprise brings salience and focus to the outcome or observation, as contrary to one's expectation and to one's poor understanding.

The surprise is the surprise of puzzlement, and not just of a contrary-to-expectation occurrence. Discovering the right answer in the motion case is a long way from the students' knowing why their answer is wrong. The puzzlement arises because these errors are incongruous with the students' understanding. Even when the right answer is known, understanding does not accommodate it until there is correction in a range of beliefs. Puzzlement is an intrinsic motive to learn and a stronger motive than just for a contrary-to-expectation occurrence, which will arise when any confident judgment fails, such as when misremembering a historical date.

4.2. Self-Protective Barriers to Discovery or Falsification

As already emphasized, in the main two illustrations there were numerous, ordinary experiences that presented contrary evidence, which the students or subjects missed. In watching lots of baseball games, for example, subjects had the opportunity to discover by observation alone that their account is mistaken.

In any of these examples, once an error is detected in a belief, the belief is surrendered, as in the subway case. But that detection requires seeing the event under a description of it as a counterinstance, which ordinarily cannot be counted on—an aspect of the self-protection problem. The falsifying description in the motion case is compelled by the computer simulation, which eliminates all variables but the ones essential to the Newtonian processes.

Still, even the contrivances of the computer environment do not wholly eliminate the latitude to explain-away the observation. In di Sessa's (1982) study, described earlier by Gardner, the reaction of the students, when they observe their dynaturtle miss its target, is that there is cheating going on—the software is deceiving them. It takes reassurance and further testing to convince them otherwise. In the cases that we have presented, normal experience does not even yield the formation of the specific beliefs. Instead, it yields only clusters of assumptions, vaguely related beliefs, and patterns of thought. In the baseball examples, the beliefs that immediately yield the judgments are partly induced by the experimenter's question. Previous to that question, subjects are simply not sufficiently focused on the comparison of batting averages to even notice the discrepancy.

4.3. Dependence

The students' discovery of their error with little latitude for evasion required external guidance, as by teachers (or computer simulations). It cannot, except by accident or happenstance, derive from normal experience—a crucial premise to argue for the study of errors in the liberal arts curriculum.

The teacher's role is not just to guide students to a better understanding of the relevant subject and to help them to develop knowledge of it, but also to bring students to recognize their own misconceptions. An important lesson of the study is of the extensive dependence on others, which is also a lesson in humility, a facet of fallibilism. The correlative lesson is the importance of discerning good authorities or experts, and respecting a division of (epistemic) labor among one's peers in social inquiries.

4.4. Comfort with One's Understanding and Discomfort with Abstraction

Each of these cases, and this is typical of the reasoning studies, involve a conflict between our ordinary understanding and a more abstract, less contextualized understanding. The real "why" of a chance (regression) account in either baseball case is in discord with natural ways of thinking about such phenomena—discrepancies from a trend are to be explained by a change of circumstance. But the chance account denies that there is any real discrepancy. ("Natural" does not imply "inevitable." We each have explained-away discrepant phenomena and coincidences by saying "It's just chance.")

Teaching to correct these erroneous patterns is through abstraction.[12] In the baseball cases, the abstraction requires viewing the performance, not as an outstanding start in hitting followed by a comparatively mediocre one, but as noted earlier as any outstanding (positive or negative) performance followed by one that is closer to the norm. Taken that way, the alteration is no real discrepancy, but simply an expected—unsurprising—outcome of regression.

The anticipated discomfort of abstraction teaches a minimal realism, complementary to fallibilism. The world is complex. It operates independent of me, yet I must form and test judgments about it with limited information. The two main illustrations show that despite our regular interaction and responsiveness to the world, we can badly misunderstand.

Appreciation of this minimal realism also prepares students to admit ignorance, which is especially valuable when confronted, as Schermer was at the Esalen Institute, with those who offer a ready account for seemingly puzzling phenomena. In addition to the humble "I do not know," intellectual courage is called for to maintain this discomforting puzzlement and to resist accepting the account offered, merely because it is the only one available.

4.5. Alternatives and Suppositional Reasoning

In the reasoning studies, the correct and discomforting alternative patterns of reasoning or analysis are not merely less preferred to the ones that students and subjects rely upon. These alternatives are not generated. The simple thought-experiment for constructing a blatant counterexample is not even attempted in Gardner's algebra example. In the baseball cases, randomness or chance does not even appear to subjects as a candidate account of the discrepancy in averages. (Studies on individual differences in reasoning show that when arguments that back subjects' conclusions are explicitly compared to arguments for the preferred answer (e.g., to factor into the motion problem the resolution of vectors), subjects shift, mainly favoring the latter; Stanovich 1999.)

The generation of alternatives—by way, prominently, of suppositional (or counterfactual) reasoning—is a crucial part of robust fallibility teaching. Deanna Kuhn (1991, chaps. 5, 8, 10), in her studies of how ordinary people argue, finds great shortcomings in our ability to generate serious alternative accounts for social phenomena, despite their clear distance from the subjects' own competence—for example, what are the causes of unemployment?

The next example, an extended one from history, illustrates the importance of appreciating the full set of options in correcting for recurrent sources of human fallibility: a narrowing of the set of options either by not noticing genuine alternatives, as has preoccupied discussion so far, or by treating them as off-the-table. The example is particularly distressing for the grave importance of the events and the false restrictions that many experts and leaders imposed, despite extensive time and resources for informed deliberation.

In his book *Humanity: A Moral History of the Twentieth Century*, Glover (1999) develops a contrast between the leadership of 1914, involved in World War I, and that involved in the Cuban Missile Crisis of 1962. To enormously simplify a comparison that runs over five chapters, the crucial contrast is in the responses to what Glover refers to as "traps," which position leaders so that there appears no exit to a highly risky course of action. Even when they desperately did not want a major war, the leaders of the nations involved in World War I and their advisers took themselves to be so bound by treaties, political pressures, and sensitivities of national pride, as well as caught in miscommunication, misunderstanding, and haste, that they entered the war almost as an act of resignation. Glover writes: "The political and psychological traps combined with this inadequate mode of thinking to cause the statesmen collectively to bring about the disaster. It was a disaster unwanted, certainly by most of them, and probably by all of them" (p. 199).

The inadequate mode of thinking that Glover's "this" points to is social Darwinism, which viewed conflicts among nations as inevitable, as another leader's apology for the war affirms: "It is in accord with this great principle ['mankind's struggle for existence'] that the catastrophe of the world war came about inevitably and irresistibly as the result of the motive forces in the lives of states and peoples, like a thunderstorm which must by its nature discharge itself" (Glover 1999, p. 195).

Glover's contrast with the peaceful resolution of the Cuban Missile Crisis of 1962 is that when devastating costs are a serious expectation from a course of action, leaders must rethink the starting presupposition that there are no other alternatives. In the Cuban Missile Crisis, leaders recognized a substantial probability that if the current trajectory continued, the U.S.–Russia confrontation would escalate to nuclear war. Both Kennedy and Khruschchev took this as a gamble that should be refused. They both, though, appear trapped, especially by public opinion and national pride. However, "The other side of the crisis is the way the two governments managed to slip out of the trap. They did not pull tight the knot of war. In this they succeeded, but they nearly failed" (Glover 1999, p. 212).

Neither Kennedy nor Kruschchev acted in haste, despite intense political and military pressure to act. They took time to reflect (on the origins of World War I, specifically), one benefit of which was that the anger "was replaced by fear" (p. 214). There was a change in "tone of voice" and something approximating explicit acknowledgment of their respective traps, so that "they can then turn escape from the trap into a shared project" (p. 215). As in 1914, the thinking in 1962 was "limited by dangerously crude assumptions," including influential hawks who thought that the idea of escalation to nuclear war was "preposterous" (p. 218).

By contrast, "The doves placed much emphasis on uncertainty and human fallibility" (p. 218). They found unacceptable even a small risk of nuclear war, and they favored their emotional reaction and "great imaginative awareness" (of the potential devastating outcomes) over the calculations of rational choice theory. Ultimately, both leaders generated and chose alternatives that, because of negative consequences, were previously outside the set of feasible options that had defined their respective traps:

> Kruschchev had to make what was widely seen as a humiliating climbdown. And Kennedy, in order to defend his reputation for toughness, had to deceive the public about the existence of the deal. . . .
>
> Through climbdown and deception they avoided war. After the crisis, Krushchev wrote to Kennedy that "we had to step over our pride, both you and [me], in order to reach this agreement." This stepping over pride was what the statesmen of 1914 had not been able to do to their sense of national honour. The humiliating climbdown, the necessary deception, and stepping over one's pride: they should each have their honoured place in a modern account of the political virtues.   (Glover 1999, pp. 222–23)

In the closing section, Glover draws an important lesson from taking fallibility seriously: "At a deeper level people are trapped by the limitations of their view of the world" (p. 230).[13] And further trapped by those limitations obscuring recognition of them as limitations.

5. Motivation, Economy, Intellectual Virtues, and Self-Correction

The positive part of the study of errors is to determine how the errors might have been avoided. One obvious way was just discussed: to generate alternatives. There are two closely related barriers we have come across that hide possibilities for a systematic lessening of fallibility; that is, the reasoning that yields one's judgment both blocks the recognition of potential errors and generates a self-protective cloak against classifying failures as such.

As already indicated, science is subject to an analog of the self-protective cloak, yet science lessens various sources of error and, more pertinently, it regularly corrects its error. In an educational forum, Timothy Feris (2002) observes that science is a "self-correcting system of inquiry, in which errors—of which there are, of course, plenty—are sooner or later detected by experiment or by more careful analysis" (p. 20).

The main reason that recognition and self-protection are not serious barriers to self-correction for science is that science's formulation and testing of hypotheses is ongoing, requiring no special motivation. In that ongoing testing, the role of previously accepted hypotheses in developing new, testable predictions routinely places those (former) hypotheses at risk without any reason to doubt them. Scientists are varied in ideas and commitments, and they act free of others' control. They are motivated to perform original and creative work, including the generation of new hypotheses and the criticism of previous claims, not only by internal drive and curiosity but also by an extensive reward system (Kitcher 1993).

Given that scientific hypotheses and theories yield observable predictions only as heavily mediated by further assumptions, why can we, as individuals, not also expect that our errors will be "sooner or later detected?" Why do we need to rely much more on design and intervention? What are the limits or obstacles (without contrivance) to our approximating science as a self-corrective system—besides the obvious differences, such as our pursuing a wide range of inquiries as individuals, compared to a huge, trained professional community devoted to specialized inquiries?

One broad and positive implication for education is that students need to be taught to generate (imagine) alternatives and other potential grounds of self-criticism, and to impose mechanisms of critical control that are most effective to the extent that they are *independent* of the beliefs or judgments to which their findings are potentially contrary. Teachers already impose independent mechanisms toward self-correction. For example, mathematics teachers have students check their answers; English teachers ask or require students to hand in revisions of their papers. Computer programming is practically impossible without numerous, easy, corrective simulations—successive approximation.

The additional need in teaching is for explicit mention of the connection to fallibility and a suitable common vocabulary for facilitating a focus on error. Few mathematics and English teachers encourage, I expect, reflection on the basis for their recommendations: even when students are sure their work is impeccable, they should check and revise. The meta-lesson of fallibility is not so conceptualized and presented. Fallibility appreciation is a meta-cognitive lesson in monitoring your own understanding and progress; planning your steps in learning; and generating, and heightening access to, self-knowledge of weaknesses, biases, and past errors—and when (and from whom) to seek more information and assistance.

Drawing these conceptual connections is crucial to developing a surrogate for science's reward system. How can education encourage the imposition of self-corrective mechanisms that function fairly independently of the reasoning and correlative judgments that they should correct? The encouragement must address—conceptually, intellectually, and by practice—three motivational needs: intrinsic, extrinsic (prospective benefit), and ease or economy of use and acquisition.

Intellectual virtues of honesty, open-mindedness, humility, and disposition to challenge oneself offer potential solutions to these motivational needs. Their acquisition is intrinsically valuable as a way to lessen fallibility. Acquired as habits, these virtues serve an ongoing monitoring and corrective process, like the plausibility filter of our own knowledge. They promise to improve one's success in action, even if not immediately, in accord with truth as what believing itself claims. In the case of humility, we already observed these three ingredients: humility dictates that one defer to those better positioned to know. Deference eases the burden on oneself. Since the ones to whom one defers are more reliable than oneself, one is thereby more likely to reach a correct judgment.

In routine cases, when these intellectual virtues are applied automatically, rather than calling upon deliberation they are expected to provide guidance beyond the school setting. Well-acquired habits are reliable and economical. Cognitive science teaches that learning is facilitated by ease of usage and the lessening of burdens on thought.

Given our limited time and resources, a crucial role for good judgment ("practical wisdom") in guiding the application of these intellectual virtues is a high degree of selectivity. Greater efforts are invested as the potential cost of error or the importance of being correct is greater.[14] We are more open-minded in those domains and to those questions that we believe are less well established—those domains in which we are likely to be more robustly fallible. It is worse than pointless to be open-minded about whether the sun will rise tomorrow, even granted that it is (inductively) possible. Intellectual virtues, especially open-mindedness, can easily be overwhelmed, if you are indiscriminately open-minded, since time and attention are very limited resources (Adler 2004).

However, these intellectual virtues are not as promising applied to problems of benefit, reward, or self-interest. These virtues involve rendering oneself vulnerable to criticism or counterevidence and to tolerating new, discomforting assumptions, as arise by generating alternatives. They involve positioning oneself to invest time, resources, and effort into activities and reflection whose most justifying outcome will be to unsettle beliefs that, by implication, deny that the investment will pay off.

Intellectual honesty involves admitting the influences of others' work, and so downplaying one's originality. It imposes burdens of explicitness about assumptions and precision in formulating claims that foreclose "plausible deniability." In writing an opinionated essay, pleasure is with style, which dictates varying terms and other devices of enjoyable reading. But clarity of argument is enhanced by stating only what cogency requires and so leads to homogenizing terms. When confidence in a particular belief is diminished, a self-critical person attends to his belief from a detached perspective on himself, which is neither natural nor in accord with inclination.

The conceptual connections among belief, fallibility, correction, and the intellectual virtues are links to reward and benefit. Fallibility, as proneness to error, is in conflict with belief's aim of truth. Even more motivating practically than this internal or conceptual demand of belief for truth is the external value of truth: your actions are expected to largely succeed only if the beliefs guiding them are true. If I think the name of the person approaching me at a party is "Bill" and my wife reminds me that it is "Tony," I gladly surrender my belief, acquire hers, and look forward to greeting him without embarrassment with, "Hi, Tony."

By acquiring intellectual virtues like open-mindedness, which keeps us "open to new evidence and arguments," we can expect to diminish our fallibility. Given the obstacles to self-correction, it is hard to know what other means could promise to work as well. By drawing the conceptual connections of belief, truth, and fallibility with these virtues, their acquisition is shown to be ultimately consonant with inclination or pleasure. Fallibility thus provides an internal motive for students to acquire those virtues, as well as stimulating their manifest external motive of wanting their actions to succeed.

The self-understanding as to why students should conform to the virtues because of their conceptual ties to fallibility and the claims of belief may not be as effective, practically, as are rewards or threats (tests, grades). Nevertheless, understanding the conceptual ties contributes to the stability and resilience of the virtues across diverse settings, particularly when the dictates of these virtues conflict with self-interest. It is harder to negotiate away the demands of intellectual honesty when one grasps the arguments for it—arguments that reveal the depth of one's commitment.

The initial examples implicate the students' own self-understandings. They are, then, gripping evidence of a significant fallibility in reasoning, rather than a lapse in memory or patience. The description is essentially first-person: "I did not really know, though I thought I did," representing an intrinsic reason to learn and to correct one's error. The study of error engages students' interests easily because it addresses their own preconceptions and misconceptions, challenging them at the borders of their understanding.[15]

Students will enjoy, or be stimulated by, the surprises and the challenges to their self-understanding. This interest, of course, threatens to be a detour away from disciplinary studies and toward self-absorption. But the risk is not severe, for reasons already mentioned. The misconceptions and faulty reasoning are common, and common as impediments to learning. The tendencies that research on reasoning and the study of error uncover, however, are human tendencies, not isolated or idiosyncratic ones.

NOTES

1. Fallibility is also attributable to methods or procedures.

2. Some identify fallibilists as those who accept the assumption, crucial to the "preface paradox," that we should each believe that "Some of my beliefs are false." For arguments against this assumption, see my 2002a, chap. 7.

3. Popper's (e.g., 1959) philosophy of science is a bad model for a substantive role for fallibility, since he denied that there could be (inductive) learning from experience. However, in his concern with seeking out and examining errors, as well as problem solving, his is a useful view, which inspires Swartz, Perkinson, and Edgerton 1980.

4. The proposal to come is related to the second-order view that is advocated by Evnine 2001 and Adler 2002a, chap. 11, and 2004.

5. Throughout I am concerned only with Type I error when one accepts a false hypothesis. One commits a Type II error when one rejects a true hypothesis (or, we can add,

does not accept a true hypothesis, presented to him). The omission is not merely for brevity: 1. As with self-interest, our natural disposition is toward acceptance (gullibility, hasty generalization . . .), so the main worries are over false acceptance or error. 2. James's two objectives—seek truth; avoid error—are not equal. The latter is an absolute demand— once error is even suspected, the belief is erased. However, on the "seek truth" aim, a person may agree that the evidence points toward a conclusion, but hesitate to accept it because he is very cautious. 3. Since a type II error, where one remains ignorant or forgets one's rejection, will involve not believing that one knows, Type I errors are bound to be more costly, in general.

6. The analysis to follow depends on a distinction between belief and confidence, elaborated in Adler 2002a, chap. 10.

7. For references and insightful reflections, see Elga 2005. Below, I deny, however, Elga's thesis that the ratings are always *evidence* of self-overrating.

8. *Objection*: If we study errors, we study what is wrong. But right ideas are always more valuable, all other things equal. So, given limited time, the course of study should deal only with what is correct—that is, what we believe now.

Reply: But labeling errors as such does amout to teaching truths. Moreover, the objection assumes that students will learn better only if they study just what we regard as true or known, given limited time. But why accept this, particularly when taking account of students' quality of thought outside and subsequent to school? We do not, after all, think that the structure of knowledge in a discipline is the same as the structure of how it should be taught.

9. Although transfer is limited in that way, meta-cognitive practices and strategies do show some transfer. For discussion and citations, see Bransford, Brown, and Cocking 2000.

10. Here, as elsewhere, I am not treating specialized training—for example, the training of future scientists. On science education, see Siegel 1988, chap. 6.

11. Another addition is that of much more use of argumentation in disciplinary studies; see Kuhn 2005, part III.

12. On tendencies to contextualization, rather than abstraction, as explaining some fallacious reasoning, see Stanovich 1999.

13. Cross-cultural contrasts are an excellent way to teach these limits and the fallibility of taking one's perspective to be universal.

14. Rescher (2007) distinguishes between the gravity or seriousness of error and its extent, or "how wide off the mark a mistake happens to be" (p. 4).

15. The relevance of such engagement to learning is cited in Bransford, Brown, and Cocking (2000, pp. 14–15). For further examples, see their chap. 7.

REFERENCES

Adler, J. E. (2002a). *Belief's Own Ethics*. Cambridge, MA: MIT Press.
—— (2002b). "Conundrums of Doxastic Self-Control." *The Monist* 85: 456–67.
—— (2004) "Reconciling Open-Mindedness and Belief." *Theory and Research in Education* 2:127–42.
—— (2008). "Surprise." *Educational Theory* 58: 149–73
Bransford, J. D., A. L. Brown, and Cocking, R. R. (2000). *How People Learn: Brain, Mind, Experience, and School*, expanded ed. Committee on Developments in the Science of Learning. Washington, DC: National Academy Press.

Curren, R. (2003). *A Companion to the Philosophy of Education*. Oxford: Blackwell.

Descartes, R. (2002). *Meditations on First Philosophy*. In *Classics of Western Philosophy*, 6th ed., ed. S. M. Cahn (pp. 452–86). Indianapolis: Hackett.

Dewey, J. (1986). *Logic: The Theory of Inquiry*. Vol. 12: 1938. *The Later Works, 1925–1953*. Carbondale, IL: Southern Illinois University Press.

di Sessa, A. (1982). "Unlearning Aristotelian Physics: A Study of Knowledge-Based Learning." *Cognitive Science* 6: 37–75.

Elga, A. (2005). "On Overrating Oneself. . . . and Knowing it." *Philosophical Studies* 123: 115–24.

Elgin, C. (1996). *Considered Judgment*. Princeton, NJ: Princeton University Press.

Evnine, S. (2001). "Learning from One's Mistakes: Epistemic Modesty and the Nature of Belief." *Pacific Philosophical Quarterly* 82: 157–77.

Feris, T. (2002). "The Whole Shebang." *American Educator* 26 (Fall): 20–23, 43–45.

Gardner, H. (1991). *The Unschooled Mind*. New York: Basic Books.

—— (1999). *The Disciplined Mind*. New York: Simon and Schuster.

Glover, J. (1999). *Humanity: A Moral History of the Twentieth Century*. New Haven, CT: Yale University Press.

Godfrey-Smith, P. (2003). *Theory and Reality: An Introduction to the Philosophy of Science*. Chicago: University of Chicago Press.

Jepson, C., D. H. Krantz, and R. E. Nisbett. (1983). "Inductive Reasoning: Competence or Skill?" *Behavioral and Brain Sciences* 6: 494–501.

Kahneman, D., and A. Tversky. (1982). "On the Psychology of Prediction." In *Judgment under Uncertainty: Heuristics and Biases*, eds. D. Kahneman, D. Slovic, and A. Tversky (pp. 48–68). Cambridge: Cambridge University Press.

Kitcher, P. (1993). *The Advancement of Science*. Oxford: Oxford University Press.

Kuhn, D. (1991). *The Skills of Argument*. New York: Cambridge University Press.

—— (2005). *Education for Thinking*. Cambridge, MA: Harvard University Press.

Leite, A. (in press). "Fallibilism." In *Blackwell's Companion to Epistemology*, 2nd ed., eds. E. Sosa and M. Steup. Oxford: Blackwell.

Lewis, D. (1996). "Elusive Knowledge." *Australasian Journal of Philosophy* 74: 549–67.

Nisbett, R., and L. Ross. (1980). *Human Inference: Strategies and Shortcomings of Social Judgment*. Englewood Cliff, NJ: Prentice-Hall.

Ohlsson, S. (1996). "Learning from Performance Errors." *Psychological Review* 103: 241–62.

Popper, K. (1959). *The Logic of Scientific Discovery*. New York: Harper.

Rescher, N. (2007). *Error: On Our Predicament when Things Go Wrong*. Pittsburgh: University of Pittsburgh Press.

Schermer, Michael. (2005). "Mr. Skeptic Goes to Esalen." *Scientific American*, December, p. 38.

Siegel, H. (1988). *Educating Reasoning: Rationality, Critical Thinking and Education*. London: Routledge.

Stanovich, K. E. (1999). *Who Is Rational? Studies of Individual Differences in Reasoning*. Mahwah, NJ: Lawrence Erlbaum.

Swartz, Ronald N., Henry J. Perkinson, and Stephanie G. Edgerton, eds. (1980). *Knowledge and Fallibilism: Essays on Improving Education*. New York: New York University Press.

CHAPTER 6

....

INDOCTRINATION

....

EAMONN CALLAN AND
DYLAN ARENA

1. INDOCTRINATION AS WRONGDOING

....

A pejorative meaning is now firmly attached to the word *indoctrination*.[1] A much older use of the word as a synonym for *instruction* was gradually overtaken by another that now clearly connotes moral wrongdoing.[2] That linguistic shift provokes a question: What is the distinctive wrong allegedly done when accusations of indoctrination are made?

Suppose we have observed you teaching a class of children, and we tell you that what we witnessed was indoctrination. You would not be flattered. Without further elaboration, the content of our accusation would be vague, but its rough outlines might still be clear enough for immediate purposes. Our common recognition of those outlines is revealed by the fact that competent language users could very easily agree in identifying many unjustified accusations of indoctrination. Thus, if we went on to point out that your performance in the classroom had been hopelessly disorganized and listless, that you had mangled all your half-hearted attempts at explanation, and you had left your students at the end as disaffected and ignorant as they had been at the beginning of the class, you would reasonably infer that, although we did intend to accuse you of morally irresponsible teaching, we did not understand *indoctrination* in its pejorative sense as it is ordinarily understood. No one could deny that to teach so carelessly that students learn nothing is wrong. Yet indoctrinated students learn something, perhaps a great deal, and their indoctrinator may be immensely skillful and determined in bringing that learning about. Still, some serious moral failing afflicts the teaching that results in their learning, or so we are apt to assume.

When charges of indoctrination are made, the imputation of moral wrongdoing has to do with a systematic distortion of some kind in the teacher's presentation
of subject matter—a distortion that elicits, or could reasonably be expected to
elicit, a corresponding distortion in the way students understand the subject
matter. Furthermore, the distortion is not, at least in paradigm cases, to be
explained by the intellectual laziness or indifference that often explains merely
ineffective teaching, but by an ill-considered or overzealous concern to inculcate
particular beliefs or values.[3] The connection to beliefs seems ubiquitous. Charges
of indoctrination do not ordinarily apply to the teaching of skills or know-how:
driver education is no doubt a practice in which wrong can be done, but teaching
people how to steer a car or brake safely is not a context in which indoctrination
can intelligibly occur.

These rough criteria constitute our established pejorative concept of indoctrination. In a word, indoctrination entails some kind of distortion in teaching that
produces belief, a distortion liable to induce some corresponding failure in students' understanding of the relevant subject matter, and the practice is prompted,
at least characteristically, by a misplaced or excessive concern on the part of the
teacher to inculcate particular beliefs. Therefore, if you were accused of indoctrination you could demand, given the criteria we have specified, that the accusation
be substantiated with some evidence about the intimidating or overly partisan
manner in which you addressed objections to your views from students, a lack of
impartiality or objectivity in the way you contrasted rival theories, intolerance
toward dissent in the classroom, or the like.

The cautious phrase "or the like" in our last sentence is intended to register the
fact that, so far as ordinary language goes, *indoctrination* as the name for a species
of morally objectionable teaching has no more than rough conceptual boundaries.
Therefore, the attempt to find a philosophically useful interpretation of the concept will inevitably gravitate toward more precision than established usage reveals.[4]
But precision just for its own sake is not what we should want; the point is rather to
elucidate the morally important considerations that properly interest us when
teaching seems to be contaminated with intellectual distortion of the kind sketched
above. For example, does the relevant distortion apply only when objectionable
teaching methods of some kind are used? When propositions whose epistemic
status is especially contestable ("doctrines") are taught as true? When teaching is
characterized by some intention that warrants the condemnation that *indoctrination* imputes?

How we should interpret our ordinary concept in light of these questions—
how we develop an adequate conception of the concept,[5] in other words—is far
from obvious. For the notion of intellectual distortion in the presentation of
subject matter is elusive as it stands. A sound philosophical conception should
certainly keep faith with the criteria that constitute the ordinary concept; otherwise
it cannot capture whatever moral concerns have driven the concept's emergence as
something to be contrasted with acceptable pedagogy, assuming for the moment
that these concerns have merit. But if it is to provide guidance in hard cases, it must

yield principled answers to questions that cannot be answered merely by attending to ordinary language.

The basis of the moral condemnation that accusations of indoctrination have come to convey is also unclear in the absence of philosophical argument. If one indoctrinates, is the alleged wrongdoing so grave that it could not be justified, regardless of circumstances, or is it only prima facie wrong—the sort of thing that generally warrants condemnation but can be justified, all things considered, in some circumstances? In fact, we should be open to the possibility that the descriptive content in what *indoctrination* designates and the negative emotive force that has become attached to the word will come apart, so to speak, under philosophical scrutiny. We might discover that no clearly identifiable pedagogy in the roughly demarcated conceptual territory the word now picks out warrants even presumptive condemnation. This is not to deny that we should be seeking criteria that can reasonably be said to warrant moral condemnation when we assess candidate conceptions of indoctrination. But whether we can find any that really fill the bill is an open question. Maybe too much depends on the variable contexts in which indoctrination allegedly occurs for any condemnation to be appropriate in abstraction from particular cases. After all, the moral evaluations our vocabulary embodies at any point in time are not necessarily justified.

Consider in this regard some remarks on indoctrination in George S. Counts's famous pamphlet, "Dare the School Build a New Social Order?" Counts was writing at a time when *indoctrination* as a term of reproach was beginning to acquire the salience that it has now. But he was at least a little doubtful about the assumptions that the emerging concept seemed to harbor:

> And when the word indoctrination is coupled with education there is scarcely one among us possessing the hardihood to refuse to be horrified. This feeling is so widespread that even Mr. Lunacharsky, Commissar of Education in the Russian Republic until 1929, assured me on one occasion that the Soviet educational leaders do not believe in the indoctrination of children in the ideas and principles of communism. When I asked him whether their children become good communists while attending the schools, he replied that the great majority do. On seeking of him an explanation of this remarkable phenomenon he said that Soviet teachers merely tell their children the truth about human history. As a consequence, so he asserted, practically all the more intelligent boys and girls adopt the philosophy of communism. I recall also that the Methodist sect in which I was reared always confined its teachings to the truth! (Counts 1932, pp. 10–11)

Counts's considered view on the moral status of indoctrination is not clear. But on one reasonable interpretation at least, he wanted to dispel what he saw as over-blown liberal anxieties about the means by which teaching tries to reach worthy educational ends. If the ends are indeed worthy, then scruples about indoctrination in the means to achieve the ends are perhaps misplaced. At least that is a possibility to which we should return when a more exact interpretation of the concept is available.

2. METHOD, CONTENT, AND INTENTION

Some attempts to specify a philosophical conception of indoctrination have claimed as constitutive criteria the methods used to impart beliefs, the propositional content of the beliefs being imparted, or the intention of the party doing the imparting. None of these three ways of characterizing indoctrination adequately interprets the concept.

The attempt to define *indoctrination* by reference to methods appeals to our intuitive qualms about teaching methods that fail adequately to engage learners' capacity to reason. But succeeding in this attempt requires more than a list of methods that indoctrinators use. Instead, as John Kleinig says, we must ask "[w]hat is it about particular methods which makes them indoctrinatory?"(Kleinig 1982, p. 58). P. J. Sheehan describes them as "those . . . which induce beliefs in a way which bypasses the reasoning process of the person to which they are applied, or coerce his will and are systematically applied over a prolonged period" (quoted in Kleinig 1982, p. 58). But the most flagrant indoctrinators will frequently appeal to chains of reasoning when teaching their beliefs. Religious or political indoctrination, for example, will commonly involve instruction in standard arguments that purport to disclose the erroneous reasoning on which heresies are based. And some (though certainly not all) instances of indoctrination occur in venues entered into voluntarily by those who become victims of indoctrination.

An additional objection to any definition that hinges on the use of nonrational methods is the fact that these are often used in unambiguously innocent contexts to teach multiplication tables, elements of spelling and grammar, or the like. Responding to this objection, David Cooper has argued that nonrational methods are indoctrinatory "if these methods are employed *despite the availability of other, rational methods*" (Cooper 1973, p. 54, emphasis in original). However, Cooper's amendment misses the fact that nonrational methods are often used without any justified reproach, merely for convenience: it would be possible, though tedious, to teach the multiplication tables solely by appeal to multiplicative reasoning instead of memorization. Since uncontroversial instances of indoctrination can occur without nonrational methods, and nonrational methods can uncontroversially be used without indoctrinating, their use cannot be central to a satisfactory conception of *indoctrination*.

A notable variation on Sheehan's definition is offered by Cooper (1973): "[I]ndoctrination will be identified . . . by the tendency of the activities involved to produce certain effects, e.g., to result in non-evidentially held beliefs" (p. 53). Although Cooper's definition refers to outcomes, he is primarily concerned with methods rather than outcomes, for two reasons: first, Cooper wants to be able to describe a teacher as indoctrinating even if, after instruction, no one is indoctrinated; and second, Cooper wants to protect from charges of indoctrination teachers whose conscientious use of exemplary teaching methods happens to instill in a student what we would want to call indoctrinated beliefs.

The first of Cooper's aims rests on the idea that we can observe a scene in which no particular learning outcome has yet been achieved and still say, "Person A is indoctrinating Person B." What Cooper fails to explain is why it should be important for us to be able to say that rather than, "Person A is attempting to indoctrinate Person B and may soon succeed in doing so." If the latter conjecture were to turn out to be wrong—if Person B were to leave Person A's presence unconvinced of the truth of what Person A had been saying—then we could surely amend our observation: "Person A tried to indoctrinate Person B but failed to do so." Cooper's focus on the tendency of certain methods to produce a certain outcome misses this successful-outcome requirement of indoctrination.

Cooper's second aim is to show that the charge of indoctrination is unjustified if a teacher's lesson, although a model of morally responsible pedagogy, instills in a student the same learning that indoctrination would produce. In other words, such teachers' innocent methods should suffice to save them from accusations of indoctrination, despite an outcome identical to that of indoctrination. Cooper believes that indoctrination is inherently blameworthy, and that it would be unfair to blame the teacher in the absence of malicious intent or negligence.

However, if we accept the premise that a teacher's lesson (and not some other confluence of factors that fortuitously coincide with the lesson) has produced some belief in the student that we would want to call indoctrinated, then what we have is better viewed as a case in which indoctrination sheds its usual normative overtones. By analogy, instances of killing other human beings may prompt us to look for malicious intent or negligence on the part of the killer, but we often fail to discover these. Similarly, in a situation such as the one imagined by Cooper, the correct response to the teacher would seem to be, "Alas! It appears that, through no fault of your own, you have indoctrinated this student." In the section below on indoctrination and moral responsibility, we deal with just such a nonstandard case.

Several alternative attempts to form a philosophically cogent interpretation of indoctrination have focused on its supposedly distinctive propositional content. Perhaps the most influential version of the content criterion has been that a sufficient, or at least a necessary, criterion of indoctrination is the teaching of doctrines (e.g., Flew 1972). But this cannot be right. First, however broadly or narrowly *doctrine* might be defined, we can surely impart doctrines without resorting to indoctrination. The Marxist teacher in Stalinist Russia and the teacher of Marxism in a contemporary American university teach certain doctrines, and yet it would be rash to assume that the latter is fated to indoctrinate just because the former was almost certain to do so. Indeed, even if the latter were a self-described Marxist, it would be unjust to infer that she must be an indoctrinator without evidence other than her own doctrinal commitments. So the teaching of doctrines cannot be a sufficient condition of indoctrination. And neither can it be a necessary condition, for indoctrination might occur without imparting anything ordinarily recognized as a doctrine. For example, we might imagine a teacher indoctrinating his pupils to believe that the *Apollo* moon landing was actually filmed on a sound stage or that the U.S. government has secret knowledge of extraterrestrial intelligence.

Another variation on the content criterion is that the teaching of false beliefs as true is the heart of the matter. We return to this idea later on when we use it to throw our own conception of indoctrination into sharper relief. It suffices for now to note that it could not be the whole story, for the simple reason that the indoctrination of true beliefs is obviously possible. Suppose we happen upon a student who insisted that 2 is the only even prime number, but the character of her belief and what we know of how it came about incline us to impute indoctrination. The student is intensely dogmatic about her mathematical beliefs, seems wholly indifferent to their rational basis, and persistently appeals to the intellectual authority of her teacher whenever challenged to justify what she believes. Now, suppose another student is like the first in all respects except that the second one believes that 2 is not the only even prime number. The only difference between the first and the second student is that the first has a true belief whereas the other has a false one. But it is counterintuitive to on that ground alone say that the second is a victim of indoctrination whereas the first is not.

Many attempts to define indoctrination have claimed that the intention of the indoctrinator is essential. According to J. P. White, indoctrinating someone is trying to get him to believe that a Proposition P is true in such a way that nothing will shake that belief (White 1967).This formulation runs aground because it does not yield a sufficient condition of teaching we have reason to deplore. Consider the teacher who tries to get her students to believe that 2 is the only even prime number using analysis of the definitions of the concepts *even* and *prime number* along with careful reasoning about divisibility. Suppose the consequence of her efforts is that nothing will shake their belief. White's formulation would entail that this teacher is indoctrinating, which is clearly wrong.

A slightly different formulation by I. A. Snook does hit on something crucial. Someone indoctrinates P (a proposition or set of propositions) if she teaches with the intention that the learner believes P regardless of the evidence (Snook 1972, p. 47). The crucial consequence of indoctrination noted by Snook is that the student will disregard evidence that may bear on the truth or falsity of P. Insufficient regard for evidence is essential to an adequate conception of indoctrination, or so we shall argue. However, Snook's formulation and all other variations of the intention position implausibly deny that a teacher might indoctrinate without intending to do so. As we shall see, indoctrination without any deplorable intention is a familiar phenomenon.

3. THE OUTCOME OF INDOCTRINATION

The philosophical literature on indoctrination discussed thus far concentrates on features internal to the activity of teaching rather than its effects on students' learning. Even when those effects have figured in analysis, they have often received scant scrutiny. White argues that indoctrination entails the intention to instill unshakable belief, but says almost nothing about what such belief entails. Snook claims that the intention to teach belief that is held regardless of the evidence is the heart of the matter, while leaving the object of that intention unanalyzed. Cooper equates indoctrination with methods that instill belief nonevidentially whenever evidential methods are available, suggesting at least that evidential belief (once the belief can be evidential) is the normal outcome of educationally responsible teaching. But he leaves the distinction between evidential and nonevidential belief unexamined. Still, White, Snook, and Cooper gesture toward something important in their references to the outcome of indoctrination that is worth exploring further, even though what they suggest cannot be quite true as it stands.

If indoctrination must result in unshakable belief, then its effects could never be undone. But we cannot rationally infer that someone who, as an adult, abandons beliefs that were inculcated during childhood must therefore have acquired those beliefs without indoctrination. The bare fact that one changes one's mind cannot suffice to show that no indoctrination occurred in the first place. Children who were instilled with Nazi ideology in the Hitler Youth Movement were in most cases able to abandon that ideology after the war ended, though it hardly follows that they were never indoctrinated. Still, White is on the track of something important insofar as excessive resistance to revision does seem to be symptomatic of the indoctrinated mind, as we intuitively understand that condition.

Snook's conception leans in a similar direction. To hold a belief regardless of the evidence does not mean that one gives no regard to evidence. Those whom we suspect of being indoctrinated may devote themselves to winning converts and exposing the errors of all who disagree with them, and that cannot be done without heeding relevant evidence. But when belief is held regardless of the evidence, its maintenance has been divorced from consideration of the evidence, however extensive that consideration may be for other purposes, such as proselytizing. This condition of nonevidential maintenance, like unshakable belief, is also redolent of the intellectual rigidity we intuitively associate with being indoctrinated.

Snook's conception takes us a little further than White's because it suggests that the effect of indoctrination has to do not with the sheer strength of conviction, as unshakable belief would imply, but with some illicit breach between conviction, on the one hand, and the assessment of evidence, on the other. Because strong conviction is so often desirable in our lives, a conception of indoctrination that entailed its wholesale derogation could not be right. But the idea that some wrong or harm is done when conviction and the evaluation of evidence are sundered from each other is a familiar ethical idea. Cooper's reference in his analysis of indoctrination to the inculcation of nonevidential belief when evidence is available takes us very close to that idea.

That our convictions are properly based on the evidence that can be adduced in their support is evidentialism, a principle famously expounded by W. K. Clifford in the nineteenth century and defended by many contemporary philosophers as well (Clifford 1977/1999; Wood 2002; Conee and Feldman 2004). But the claim that we do wrong when conviction is cut adrift from the assessment of evidence is not unique to philosophers. The very fact that to describe someone as close-minded is also to ascribe what is taken to be an intellectual vice attests to a concern with the ethics of belief embedded in our ordinary language that is at least akin to evidentialism.[6] To believe Proposition P close-mindedly is to be unable or unwilling to give due regard to reasons that are available for some belief or beliefs contrary to P because of excessive emotional attachment to the truth of P. People who are characteristically close-minded are thus liable to cling to beliefs that cannot be justified by the best evidence and argument to which they have access. Still, close-minded belief need not be so utterly disengaged from the assessment of evidence that it can be characterized as holding regardless of the evidence; the point is that regard for evidence in close-minded belief is deficient, not that it must be nonexistent.

The idea of close-minded belief is a more promising candidate for the relevant outcome of indoctrination than either unshakable belief (White's candidate) or belief held regardless of the evidence (Snook's candidate). Unlike White's candidate, it allows for the possibility that indoctrination may occur even when its victims are disabused of their indoctrinated beliefs at a later date. A closed mind need not be irrevocably shut. Snook's candidate limits the scope of indoctrination to the most extreme cases, where the disregard of evidence is total. Yet if a total disregard of evidence on the part of the learner might warrant moral reproach to the teacher who induced that attitude, the teacher surely cannot escape reproach just because the induced disregard of evidence is a bit less than total. So if we are trying to make sense of indoctrination as a practice that warrants moral disapproval, then the concept of close-mindedness, which admits varying degrees, seems better suited to capture the full range of relevant outcomes than Snook's candidate.

We said that close-minded people are unable or unwilling to give due regard to reasons that are available for revising their current beliefs. But although this is necessary, it cannot be sufficient for close-mindedness because sheer intellectual laziness or credulity might make people unwilling to show such regard, and it would be odd to describe anyone as close-minded just because she cared too little to use her mind.[7] (That is not to say that intellectual sloth and credulity are not vices; it is only to say that they are different vices from close-mindedness, and that nothing is to be gained by confusing them.) What also seems necessary is a special emotional investment in the truth of some belief that an open mind regarding that belief would threaten: the belief has become integral to the individual's understanding of who she is and why her life matters so that seriously considering evidence contrary to the belief is threatening to her very identity.

Protection from the threat might be achieved by attaching to the belief a moralistic second-order belief. The content of the second-order belief would be: it is always wrong/shameful to entertain doubt about this belief.[8] But moralistic second-order beliefs are not strictly necessary because close-mindedness may also be the effect of two closely related intellectual vices that create resistance to doubt.

One is intellectual cowardice, the other intellectual arrogance. The pursuit of knowledge and understanding will sometimes require intellectual courage, and those who fearfully close their minds when evidence to abandon some cherished conviction is available are guilty of intellectual cowardice. Similarly, the pursuit of knowledge and understanding will sometimes require intellectual humility. That happens when fresh evidence against some belief we have proudly defended shows that others have been right where we were wrong. Those whose vanity closes the mind to such evidence are intellectually arrogant.

We said that close-mindedness can be evident to varying degrees. This is what we might call its psychological depth, a standard that registers the intensity with which the individual is prone to resist countervailing evidence to beliefs already held. But another important dimension is breadth, which reflects how widely close-mindedness affects particular components within the overall system of the individual's beliefs. There is no necessary connection between the depth and breadth of close-mindedness. A deep close-mindedness of narrow scope, localized around a few cherished convictions, might coincide with a laudable open-mindedness beyond the sphere of those convictions. By the same token, a broader close-mindedness that ramifies widely across the entire structure of someone's belief system might be relatively mild. If a subset of beliefs is almost freestanding, with few implications for other items within the system, then a localized close-mindedness might be easy to keep localized. This could be true, say, of your beliefs about the glorious history of your favorite baseball team and the exalted skills of its players. But a close-mindedness of narrow scope is not feasible with comprehensive religious, moral, or political doctrines that are specifically intended to have an architectonic role within the believer's life. These will inevitably have far-reaching implications across belief systems, and precisely because the falsification of what they imply will cast doubt on the underlying doctrine, close-minded adherence to the doctrine will naturally motivate close-minded resistance to whatever would falsify its implications.

This point may help to explain more fully why it is a mistake to stipulate that indoctrination requires the inculcation of doctrines. Comprehensive doctrines are commonly at the core of our individual identities, and so they are readily allied with the intellectual cowardice or arrogance that evidential threats to identity are liable to provoke and commonly fortified with moralistic second-order beliefs to keep the threats at bay. Yet because the implications of these doctrines extend so widely, a pedagogy that ensures fidelity to any one of them may have to secure close-minded adherence to implications remote from the normative core of the doctrine. Some (by no means all) Christians believe that the implications of their faith cannot be reconciled with evolutionary biology, and that belief motivates efforts to defend creationism, "intelligent design," or the like, as better alternatives to evolutionary biology. Whether such people are right about the implications of Christianity or not, there is plainly a risk that attempts to instill the faith as they conceive it will modulate, for example, into efforts to teach children that the bacterial flagellum (an appendage that lets bacteria swim) is too complex to have developed through natural selection. But if instilling close-minded religious conviction is indoctrination, then surely eliciting closed-minded belief about how the bacterial flagellum came to be is also indoctrination, given that both might be integral to the same (anti–)educational process.

4. INDOCTRINATION AND MORAL RESPONSIBILITY

To be close-minded is not necessarily to have been indoctrinated. Human beings would appear to be entirely capable of learning to be intellectually arrogant and cowardly, or to develop misplaced scruples about doubting particular beliefs, without being taught to be or do these things by anyone else. But close-mindedness can also be the product of teaching, and where it is, responsibility for its occurrence will shift at least somewhat from learner to teacher.

That fact also shows what is appealing and yet misleading in the idea that indoctrination entails the intention to indoctrinate. If indoctrination presupposes a teacher who is responsible (to some degree) for the close-mindedness of the learner, then the intention to produce that outcome is plainly sufficient for responsibility. But we are commonly and rightly held to account for some outcomes that may be flatly at odds with our intentions. If I drive my car at excessive speed and kill a pedestrian, the fact that I intended to kill no one does not make me blameless. The accusation of negligence has purchase here. As a driver, I have a legal and moral duty to drive at a safe speed, and injury to a pedestrian caused by my failure to discharge that duty is injury for which I will be held accountable, regardless of my intentions. The idea of moral negligence must apply to teaching if teachers have educational responsibilities to their students. For whenever unintended harm is caused by a culpable failure to discharge those responsibilities, the charge of negligence will be justified. The claim that unintended indoctrination is a species of moral negligence derives from the reasonable assumption that among the educational responsibilities of teachers is the avoidance of social influences that conduce to close-mindedness. Teachers should be reasonably vigilant about avoiding such influences, which easily seep into their practice whenever a belief is taught that has broad and fervent social consensus in its support, and merely forswearing the intention to indoctrinate is not enough for adequate vigilance.

The wider social context of belief is an important consideration in addressing moral responsibility. An ingenious example developed by Rodger Beehler will help to show what is at stake here. Beehler asks us to imagine the predicament of a young man with a high-school education who is hired as a teacher in Canada's Northwest Territories during the 1930s (Beehler 1985). Among his responsibilities is the task of teaching students in the first three grades about "the native peoples of Canada and their relation to the immigrant white population." The teacher has never met any of Canada's native people, and none live close to the town where he teaches. But he is intellectually scrupulous, and he reads all he can find about the topic. All he reads represents Canada's indigenous peoples in a derogatory fashion. The uniformity of the picture that emerges from the only materials to which he has access means that when he tries to stress the evidential basis of his pedagogy, a wildly inaccurate stereotype of Canada's native peoples is reinforced.

Is this indoctrination? The case is ambiguous, and we think our conception is helpful in explaining this ambiguity. As a complacently colonial society whose legitimation depended on justifying the dispossession of its indigenous peoples, Canada in the 1930s had a vested interest in portraying that population negatively. School textbooks, and mainstream scholarship and political discourse, all spoke with one voice in supporting that invidious portrayal. Beehler's depiction of the young teacher makes it wrong to think of him as close-minded, rather than just very badly mistaken, and his efforts to make students form their beliefs on the basis of available evidence could hardly be more strenuous. All that makes it somewhat plausible to say that he is not guilty of indoctrination. For if open-mindedness requires due regard for relevant evidence and argument, those who practice the virtue, and try to teach it to others, are still constrained by bias, selectivity, and outright lies in the evidence available to them in a given sociohistorical context. And one might rationally hope that if the students came to emulate their teacher's open-mindedness in such circumstances, they would be cognitively primed to reject the stereotypes they are taught when counterevidence one day becomes available to them.

Yet a very different line of interpretation of the case is also reasonable. This begins with the hypothesis that the evidence available to white Canadians during the 1930s about the country's indigenous population was so badly corrupted because of white Canadians' collective self-image as a righteous people who had wrested control of a vast wilderness from undeserving savages. The defense of the self-image would naturally lend itself to close-minded resistance to whatever would falsify its presuppositions. Thus in what parents or pastors said to children outside school, what children heard on the radio, read in newspapers when they were old enough, and the like, the image of an impeccably virtuous white citizenry would be powerfully affirmed, and a concomitant close-minded resistance instilled to whatever would threaten their self-image. Therefore, we need to interpret the conduct of Beehler's teacher in the classroom against the background of a broader racist process of societal indoctrination to which his pedagogy is inevitably related. A reasonable surmise is that because the evidence to which the teacher has access is so utterly corrupted, his efforts effectively support the societal process of indoctrination by sealing a veneer of evidential rectitude on the very same beliefs that students are taught to believe close-mindedly outside the school. And that makes is at least somewhat plausible to say he does engage in indoctrination, despite not being morally responsible for what he does.

The ambiguity of Beehler's and similar cases does not matter much so long as we stay alert to why we are inclined to respond to them in contradictory ways. One way to maintain the necessary alertness is to distinguish between standard and nonstandard cases of indoctrination. In the standard case, the teacher bears some moral responsibility for the inculcation of close-minded belief, typically by being negligent in the duty to do all that might reasonably be done to avoid social influences on her teaching that conduce to close-mindedness. Still, in some unfortunate (and nonstandard) cases, teachers might do all that could be reasonably done and yet the outcome of their best efforts causally reinforces some wider process of indoctrination that pervades the society as a whole.

5. THE CONCEPT AND CONCEPTION OF INDOCTRINATION

We suggested earlier that our ordinary concept of indoctrination connotes some intellectual distortion in the presentation of subject matter that elicits a corresponding distortion in the minds of students. We also said that at least in paradigm cases, the distortion is not to be explained by intellectual laziness or indifference, but by an ill-considered or overzealous concern to inculcate particular beliefs. The question we face now is whether the conception of indoctrination we have outlined is consistent with the criteria that constitute the ordinary concept and whether our conception opens the way, as we argued it should, to a clearer grasp of the moral considerations at stake in accusations of indoctrination than we would otherwise have.

Academic subject matter can be distorted in many different ways in teaching. False beliefs might be presented as true. The risk of that happening is obviously great when teachers fail to keep abreast of intellectual progress in the subjects they teach, but it cannot be avoided just by staying attuned to recent research. For if the history of science reveals anything, it surely tells us that scientific progress will expose much that we now take as true to be false, and that being so, teaching what is false as if it were true would seem to be an almost inevitable misfortune in the educational process rather than a culpable distortion for which anyone could be held to account. How do we best cope with the inevitability of that misfortune?

Perhaps the most obvious strategy is to remind students regularly of the corrigibility of even our best theories. These are the best approximations to the truth that we can currently construct, and will in many cases be superseded through the progress of inquiry. No doubt that caveat is wholesome good sense, but the incantation of the caveat at regular intervals seems unlikely to do much good if what occurs between the incantations is not teaching conducive to open-mindedness. Only open-mindedness enables us to make the best use of fresh argument and evidence to improve our understanding of the world. If what we take to be our corpus of established knowledge is almost certainly riddled with errors that we cannot yet identify, the only reliable means of identifying these as promptly as we can is by keeping an open mind to whatever might expose them as errors. That being so, close-mindedness would seem to be a particularly formidable obstacle to the timely correction of error. The inculcation of close-mindedness counts as a particularly grievous form of intellectual distortion in the presentation of subject matter, and its condemnation in an intellectual culture sensitive to our susceptibility to error is just what we should expect.

A conceivable instance of inculcating close-minded belief is a teacher consciously formulating the intention to do precisely that and then acting on that intention. But a more common phenomenon is surely the teacher who indoctrinates but lacks the level of self-awareness that such examples entail. Perpetrators of indoctrination will often be past victims of indoctrination, and the more successful their victimization, the more apt they may be to regard themselves as paragons of open-mindedness, whose intensity of conviction is merely a consequence of how thoroughly they appreciate the compelling evidence for what they believe. Given that self-ignorance, they will be primed to indoctrinate others without any intention, conscious or not, to encourage close-mindedness. Thus on the conception we have championed, it is easy to understand why in paradigm cases the relevant distortion in the presentation of subject matter is not to be explained by intellectual laziness or indifference but by an ill-considered or over-zealous concern to inculcate particular beliefs. On our conception, what makes the teacher's motivation ill-considered or overzealous is precisely the close-mindedness that students are explicitly or implicitly taught to emulate.

6. THE MORAL STATUS OF INDOCTRINATION

If the inculcation of close-minded belief is indoctrination, then one can obviously be indoctrinated to believe what is false. But as we noted earlier, one can also be indoctrinated to believe what is true. No doubt indoctrination in support of truth is preferable to indoctrination in defense of falsehood. But does that preference mean that indoctrination is a morally neutral means to an end, to be commended when it serves laudable ends and condemned only when its ends deserve condemnation? This is the question that our earlier quotation from George Counts provokes.

Two considerations suggest that open-mindedness has an important human value that cannot be reduced to its role as a means to protecting and achieving true belief or other worthy ends, and that being so, indoctrination is bad to the extent that it thwarts the realization of that value even when it secures other values. The first consideration has to do with the epistemic value of understanding; the second with the moral value of autonomy.

Suppose for the moment that the best form of government ever invented is American constitutionalism, and that Jane has been indoctrinated to accept this true belief. One risk Jane must incur is that many other beliefs might be true for reasons that would seem to cast some doubt on her belief that American constitutionalism is the best form of government, and the close-minded character of her belief is liable to disincline her to evaluate those reasons impartially, and hence block the acquisition of whatever other true beliefs the reasons support. If American constitutionalism is the best form of government, its success might still presuppose conditions that are sometimes absent in extant human societies—a tradition of largely peaceful accommodation between rival religious groups, or the like. Taking to heart Voltaire's adage that the best is the enemy of the good, we might find ourselves with some reasons to believe that human beings should often settle for political regimes that differ substantially from American constitutionalism. These reasons will apply when the presuppositions of the American model have yet to be satisfied. The cogency of these reasons is entirely consistent with the belief that American constitutionalism is indeed the best form of government. But if Jane believes the latter close-mindedly, she will also feel psychologically threatened by any arguments that seem to dilute or qualify the grounds for her belief. She is thus less well situated than people who hold the same belief open-mindedly to profit from such arguments.

It would be a mistake to infer from this that the harm close-mindedness causes Jane is an overall deprivation of knowledge. For her close-mindedness might well be combined with a passionate curiosity about American constitutionalism, and that might prompt her to become as knowledgeable about the object of her passion as anyone could be. Where close-mindedness will inhibit the acquisition of knowledge is in those particular matters she perceives (not necessarily consciously) to pose a threat to her faith in the superiority of American constitutionalism. Why should that loss concern us if she accumulates a great store of other knowledge about the same object? The short answer is that however much knowledge Jane might pick up, her close-mindedness is sure to limit her to a decidedly lopsided understanding of the object of her passion.

According to Jonathan Kvanvig "understanding requires . . . an internal grasping or appreciation of how the various elements in a body of information are related to each other in terms of explanatory, logical, probabilistic and other kinds of relations" (2003, pp. 192–93). On Kvanvig's account, understanding is the product of a mind primed to sift through the multifarious relations that link items in a body of information. That task requires not only imagination, logical skills, and kindred intellectual abilities but also an emotional readiness to follow thought in directions that might cast unexpected doubt on some central organizing idea within that connect items of information to each other. The problem for Jane is that much of the information about American constitutionalism that comes her way will disclose, for example, its possible imperfections or dependence on conditions that might not be widely replicated in other countries. To adequately integrate these into her understanding of the topic would not require her to give up any true belief. But it would require her tenaciously to pursue the implications of facts and probabilities that critics of American democracy stress in their arguments, imaginatively to entertain possible beneficial departures from American constitutional norms, and so on. What these intellectual activities have in common is both the prospect of achieving a deep understanding of American forms of government and the risk of entertaining at least episodic doubts, which might even become settled doubts in time, about her true belief that American democracy is best. Unfortunately, the prospect cannot be achieved without incurring the risk, and Jane's close-mindedness blocks her from taking the risk.

The harm done by indoctrination to our capacity for understanding will vary with the depth and breadth of the close-mindedness it fosters. But except in the uncommon case when the inculcated belief is about some relatively trivial matter and is a more or less freestanding module within one's system of beliefs, indoctrination must count as a substantial impairment of understanding, regardless of other values with which it might coincide.

The alleged impairment of the capacity for understanding that indoctrination will bring about presupposes that without indoctrination, the victim could have achieved a better understanding of matters related to the indoctrinated belief through educationally responsible teaching. That presupposition might well be false in some particular cases, and in such cases, indoctrinated true belief could well be a better outcome than any feasible alternative, such as open-minded but catastrophically false belief. This point reveals an interesting connection between the belief that human cognitive capabilities are very unequally distributed and a willingness to resort to indoctrination on paternalistic grounds. The connection is abundantly evident in Plato's notorious argument in *The Republic* in defense of an education for the masses of citizens that instills steadfast adherence to true beliefs with no understanding of the grounds of those beliefs. The argument affronts our egalitarian sensibilities. Nevertheless, if Plato were right that the recipients of political indoctrination were capable of no greater understanding than their indoctrination gives them, we could not say that it denies them the value of greater understanding.

The argument about the ethics of indoctrination threatens to become mired at this point in empirical disputes about the distribution of human cognitive capabilities. But an alternative line of argument promises a way around that impasse. The alternative stresses indoctrination's status as a violation of the autonomy to which all persons within some wide range of normal cognitive functioning are rightfully entitled, irrespective of substantial differences in intellectual endowment among those within the range. This argument assigns a distinctively moral rather than an epistemic loss to the victim of indoctrination. The autonomy argument against indoctrination has been cogently pursued elsewhere (Kleinig 1982, p. 65; Siegel 1988, p. 88), and we wish to add only a small addendum here.

The powerful intuition at the root of the autonomy argument is the idea that people should be free to determine their own lives within wide boundaries set by the rights of others, and that intellectual self-determination (which entails open-mindedness) is intrinsic to that freedom. When someone exploits the asymmetry of power between teacher and learner by instilling close-minded belief, the intellectual self-rule that befits rational beings has been violated. But a good question that might arise here has to do with the quality of thinking that people exhibit when they think for themselves. If some people think badly when they think for themselves, why is intellectual autonomy preferable to having other people (the benevolent indoctrinators perhaps) think for us by instilling true close-minded beliefs? The question seems to take us back to those disputes about the distribution of cognitive capabilities from which the autonomy argument promised an escape.

Two points can be said about this. First, if we abandon indoctrination for an education that systematically cultivates the open mind, it would be foolish to suppose that teaching students to think for themselves should be our only goal. We should also try to teach them to think rigorously, clearly, imaginatively, and the like. Honoring learners' intellectual self-determination signifies no indifference to intellectual quality. But by itself, that claim will cut no ice with Platonic pessimists who believe that most ordinary mortals have at best modest potential to think well when they think for themselves. This takes us to our second point.

For the sake of argument, suppose we agree with Platonic pessimists that many, perhaps most children who receive the best feasible education might still often think and choose badly when they are encouraged to be autonomous and, therefore, open-minded. Does it follow that once we take this bleak view of ordinary mortals' educable capacity for rational self-determination we must now take a favorable view of indoctrination when it is undertaken with the paternalistic intent of securing adherence to the truth? The inference that we should is very odd because it combines moral and intellectual pessimism about those who are likely to be on the receiving end of indoctrination with an astonishing optimism about those who would be its practitioners. If the outcome of the best feasible education still leaves us with an acute susceptibility to error, how can anyone be trusted with the power to indoctrinate anyone else? Even if paternalistic indoctrinators are sincere—they genuinely believe that what they teach is true and profoundly important—their assurance is no guarantee against error. And is it not likely that in many cases what they choose to indoctrinate will be whatever serves their own predatory interests, regardless of what they believe to be true? The moral argument against indoctrination requires no sunny optimism about open-mindedness as the easy route to truth and justice; it is better served by a tough-minded realism about the vulnerability to abuse that besets all unequal human relations, including that between teachers and students.

NOTES

1. The approach to indoctrination canvased here was profoundly influenced by Hare's seminal work on open-mindedness (1979, 1985). Our endorsement of an "outcome criterion" also builds on several important contributions to the philosophical literature on indoctrination that pioneered this approach (Green 1964/5; Siegel 1988; Kleinig 1982). Many thanks to Harvey Siegel and Bill Hare for helpful comments on an earlier draft.

2. It may well be true that attempts to distinguish a concept we would now label *indoctrination* long antedates this linguistic change. For an intriguing argument along these lines, see Sommerville 1983. It is also not clear just when the pejorative usage begins, though John Stuart Mill in a letter from 1852 is suggestive: "What the poor as well as the rich require is not to be indoctrinated, is not to be taught other people's opinions, but to be induced and enabled to think for themselves." (Mill 1852/1972, p. 80). Thanks to Bill Hare for this reference.

3. Some readers will want to distinguish between values and beliefs on the grounds that beliefs imply some commitment to the truth of a proposition whereas values have no content that could be strictly true or false. We shall use "belief" as shorthand where some readers might prefer to see "beliefs and values."

4. That point was acknowledged even during the heyday of ordinary language philosophy (Flew 1972, p. 87).

5. The distinction between concepts and conceptions was introduced in Rawls 1971. The best elucidation of the distinction is in Dworkin 1986, pp. 70–72.

6. To acknowledge the epistemic vice of close-mindedness, as it is specified here, does not make us take sides in the debate between evidentialists and their most notable contemporary critic, Alvin Plantinga. Any evidentialist must concede that some beliefs are "properly basic" in the sense that they are not rightly inferred from evidence: for example, your belief that you are reading this text right now. Plantinga argues that the scope of properly basic belief is much greater than Enlightenment-inspired evidentialists have traditionally supposed, and even includes the creedal core of Christianity (Plantinga 2002). But Plantinga acknowledges that very many other beliefs are properly evidential. To fail to maintain those beliefs evidentially is necessarily, on his terms, to fail to give due regard to relevant evidence, and hence to be close-minded in the sense defined here. Moreover, he concedes that the propriety of basic belief, in Christian theism, for example, will depend on our ability to refute whatever rational objections to which it is susceptible, and that brings him closer to the evidentialist camp than he might seem at first glance. Still, we do not believe that Plantinga's attempt to put Christian belief beyond evidentialist challenge is successful, and therefore, we regard his argument as no more than a very ingenious defense of a close-minded Christian piety. But whether we are right about that is far too big an issue adequately to address here, though it is certainly relevant to the topic of religious indoctrination in Christian and other faiths.

7. This is where we might take issue with Siegel's analysis. Siegel says that students "are indoctrinated if they are led to hold beliefs in such a way that they are prevented from critically inquiring into their legitimacy. . . . Indoctrination may be regarded as the collection of those modes of belief inculcation which foster a non-evidential, or non-critical, style of belief" (1988, p. 80). Credulity and intellectual sloth may prevent critical inquiry and nourish nonevidential styles of belief, but they are not the same as close-mindedness and, therefore, the teaching that produces them is not the same as indoctrination. Credulity and intellectual sloth are commonly the upshot of bad teaching that plies students with content to be memorized or brings no spark of intellectual excitement to subject matter. No doubt these species of bad teaching should be deplored, but as we argued in the opening section, not all kinds of bad teaching are indoctrination. There seems no reason to suppose that indoctrination is necessarily morally worse than teaching that instills other kinds of invidiously nonevidential belief. But maybe indoctrination is especially worrying to the extent that close-mindedness entails an active resistance to counterevidence and argument that credulity or intellectual sloth does not

entail. Other things being equal, close-mindedness would seem a more formidable obstacle to the correction of error than these other intellectual vices.

8. The point is well made by Kleinig: "Where ... particular beliefs become closely identified with a person's feelings of security, or take on strong moral associations such that questioning them would induce guilt-feelings, we could expect them to be indoctrinated" (1982, p. 63).

REFERENCES

Beehler, Rodger. (1985). "The Schools and Indoctrination." *Journal of Philosophy of Education* 19: 261–72.

Clifford, W. H. (1977/1999). *The Ethics of Belief and Other Essays.* New York: Prometheus.

Conee, E., and R. Feldman. (2004). *Evidentialism: Essays in Epistemology.* Oxford: Oxford University Press.

Cooper, E. (1973). "Intentions and Indoctrination." *Educational Philosophy and Theory* 5: 43–55.

Counts, G. S. (1932). *Dare the School Build a new Social Order?* New York: John Day.

Dworkin, R. (1986). *Law's Empire.* Cambridge, MA: Harvard University Press.

Flew, A. (1972). "Indoctrination and Doctrines." In *Concepts of Indoctrination*, ed. I. A. Snook (pp. 152–61). London: Routledge & Kegan Paul.

Green, T. F. (1964/5). "A Typology of Teaching Concepts." *Studies in Philosophy of Education.* 3: 284–19.

Hare, W. (1979). *Open-mindedness and Education.* Montreal: McGill-Queen's University Press.

——— (1985). *In Defence of Open-mindedness.* Montreal: McGill-Queen's University Press.

Kleinig, J. (1982). *Philosophical Issues in Education.* London: Croom Helm.

Kvanvig, J. L. (2003). *The Value of Knowledge and the Pursuit of Understanding.* Cambridge, U.K.: Cambridge University Press.

Mill, J. S. (1852/1972). "Letter to the Rev. Henry William Carr." In *Collected Works of John Stuart Mill Volume XIV: The Later Letters, 1849–1873*, ed. F. E. Mineka and D. N. Lindley (pp. 80–81). Toronto: University of Toronto Press.

Plantinga, A. (2002). *Warranted Christian Belief.* Oxford: Oxford University Press.

Rawls, J. (1971). *A Theory of Justice.* Cambridge, MA: Harvard University Press.

Siegel, H. (1988). *Educating Reason: Rationality, Critical Thinking, and Education.* London: Routledge.

Snook, I. A. (1972). *Indoctrination and Education.* London: Routledge & Kegan Paul.

Sommerville, C. J. (1983). "The Distinction Between Indoctrination and Education, 1549–1718." *Journal of the History of Ideas* 44: 387–406.

White, J. P. (1967). "Indoctrination." In *The Concept of Education*, ed. R. S. Peters (pp. 177–91). London: Routledge & Kegan Paul.

Wood, A. W. (2002). *Unsettling Obligations: Essays on Reason, Reality, and the Ethics of Belief.* Stanford, CA: Center for the Study of Language and Information.

CHAPTER 7

EDUCATING FOR AUTHENTICITY: THE PARADOX OF MORAL EDUCATION REVISITED

STEFAAN E. CUYPERS

1. INTRODUCTION: METAPHYSICS OF FREE WILL AND PHILOSOPHY OF EDUCATION

THEMES in the philosophy of education often involve a perplexing blend of conceptual and empirical issues. In as much as philosophy of education does not coincide with developmental psychology or other branches of the social sciences, it is, to a large extent, considered "applied philosophy". Philosophers of education either apply concepts borrowed from metaphysics, epistemology, and ethics to the particular case of educating (and teaching) children, or they draw educational consequences from positions held in these core domains of "pure" philosophy. For instance, curriculum theorists draw on conceptual resources from the theory of knowledge and the metaphysics of value; some educational theorists explore the nature of moral education, borrowing heavily from the discussion on virtue-ethics and deontological and utilitarian morality; and yet others sort out the implications of the debate between political liberalism and communitarianism for educating for democratic citizenship.[1] However, the connections between "pure" philosophy and philosophy of education are not only extrinsic, as in the application case, but also—and more importantly—intrinsic. In this chapter, I focus on one such intrinsic connection: the inherent relationship between the metaphysics of free will (or autonomy) and *educating for authenticity*. To show how chief problems in the metaphysics of free will essentially connect with key issues in the philosophy of education, I sketch the debate on free will.[2]

Determinism is "the thesis that there is at any instant exactly one physically possible future" (van Inwagen 1983, p. 3). If this thesis is true, the facts of the past, together with the laws of nature, entail all truths. Indeterminism is the denial of determinism. Compatibilism is the view that free will, free action, and moral responsibility are compatible with determinism; incompatibilism is the denial of compatibilism. Libertarians are incompatibilists who believe that at least some of us, at times, perform free actions for which we are responsible. Included in the arsenal for incompatibilism is the alluring manipulation argument. (Other arguments include the consequence and the direct argument.[3]) The manipulation argument helps us to appreciate intimate associations between the metaphysics of free will and the philosophy of education. So, let me summarize a few salient things about this argument.

A causal history involving apt *manipulation* by means of, for example, secret hypnosis or clandestine brainwashing—a manipulated causal history—is generally taken to undermine free action and, hence, responsibility. Yet a deterministic causal history, incompatibilists contend, is pertinently like a manipulated one: an action that is causally determined, just like an action whose etiology involves manipulation, issues from sources—the past and the natural laws—over which the agent lacks any control. Pertinent incompatibilists submit that compatibilists cannot distinguish, in a relevant and principled way, an action that results from freedom-undermining manipulation from an action that has a more ordinary deterministic causal history. Compatibilists respond differently to this manipulation argument.[4] On the assumption that at least certain elements of a person's psychology—especially desires, preferences, values, and other pro-attitudes—play an essential role in the constitution of autonomy, *internalism* is the thesis that facts about how the person acquired these psychological elements in the past are completely irrelevant for his or her autonomy now. With certain qualifications, internalists claim that it doesn't, for example, matter whether the causal source of these elements is the result of manipulation or "natural" factors. *Externalism* is the thesis that facts about one's past or history in the external world that bear on the acquisition of one's psychological elements are pertinent to whether one's actions are free and, hence, pertinent to whether one can be morally responsible for them. Again, with various caveats, externalists affirm that it does matter whether the causal source of the psychological elements is infected with manipulation and thus is autonomy-subverting, or is "natural" and so autonomy-preserving.

This is not the place to adjudicate the in-house debate among compatibilists who divide into internalists and externalists.[5] For the purpose of this chapter, I limit attention to the externalist compatibilist theory. To be viable, externalism must draw a principled distinction between an appropriate causal history and an inappropriate one. Given that everything has a causal history on the assumption of determinism, causal origin and genesis can only make a difference if causal histories can be sorted out into two separate sets: the set of the "right," or autonomy-preserving histories, and that of the "wrong," or autonomy-subverting ones. Now, it is precisely in undertaking the formidable task of formulating such a principled distinction in the causal domain that the externalist compatibilist metaphysics of free will intrinsically connects with central issues in the philosophy of education. Compatibilist free will theorists cannot deal with *the problem of an externalist criterion* without making *the educational problems of authentic upbringing and indoctrination* their own. The complementary issues of manipulation and autonomy in the metaphysics of free will cover, to a large extent, the same domain as that of indoctrination and authenticity in the philosophy of education. David Zimmerman identifies the chief problem for externalism in the debate as "*the puzzle of naturalized self-creation in real time*: How do some children manage to develop the capacity to *make up their own minds* about what values to embrace, by virtue of having gone through a process in which they play an increasingly active role in *making their own minds*, a process that begins with their *having virtually no minds at all* ?" (Zimmerman 2003, p. 638; emphasis in the original) And he specifies the problem of an externalist criterion as follows:

> In short, responsibility-grounding autonomous agency develops with the appropriately *continuous and active participation of the emerging person herself.* The positive historicist thus wishes to clarify the difference between patterns of psychological development that a good liberal would praise as "education" or "cultivation," on the one hand, and condemn as "indoctrination" or "psychological manipulation," on the other....
>   The difficulty, however, is to ... [make] room in the developmental picture for a difference between the kinds of early preference-acquisition that eventually lead to autonomous agency and those that block the child from transcending its early and inevitable heteronomy. This is what I have referred to as the difference between liberal education and authoritarian indoctrination.   (pp. 647, 655)

I agree with Zimmerman that the educational issues of "authoritarian indoctrination" and "liberal education" are of crucial concern to the externalist compatibilist metaphysics of autonomy.

In what follows, I address "the puzzle of naturalized self-creation in real time." I proceed in this fashion: I first revisit Richard S. Peters's attempt to deal with this puzzle and identify an important remaining problem with his resolution of "the paradox of moral education." I then examine Robert Noggle's contemporary attempt to resolve "the paradox of self-creation" and indicate why I find it wanting. Subsequently, I offer my own forward-looking account of educating for authenticity that, I submit, overcomes both Peters's and Noggle's difficulties. Finally, I extract an externalist criterion from this account.

2. R. S. PETERS'S PARADOX AND THE PROBLEM OF EDUCATIONAL AUTHENTICITY

A recurrent theme in major debates in the philosophy of education is the appeal to the child's (or pupil's) authenticity. The idea is that the child is, in some sense variously specified by different theorists, the *ultimate source* of her experiences, desires, beliefs, values, principles and actions. The child has, in that specified sense, a life that is "truly the child's own"; she is the real originator of her own walk of life.[6] Reflection on this theme of educational authenticity leads to Peters's paradox of moral education.

According to Peters, authenticity is a component of the analysis of "freedom." He writes:

> The lynch-pin of the analysis is the notion of man as a chooser, a rational being placed in what I have called the situation of practical reason. . . . In education, however, we are usually concerned with more than just preserving the capacity for choice; we are also concerned with the ideal of personal autonomy, which is a development of some of the potentialities inherent in the notion of man as a chooser.   (1973, pp. 16–17)

As for the notion of personal autonomy, he explains:

> There is . . . a gradation of conditions implicit in the idea of autonomy. The first basic condition is that of authenticity, of adopting a code or way of life that is one's own as distinct from one dictated by others. The second condition of rational reflection on rules is one espoused by most believers in autonomy.   (1973, p. 16)

Peters further details the first basic authenticity-condition of autonomy:

> Etymologically, "autonomy" suggests that a person accepts or makes rules for himself. . . . It denies that the individual's code of conduct is simply one that he has picked up from others or adopted in any second-hand way. The rules which he lives by are not just those that are laid down by custom or authority . . . this is represented as what the individual really wants as distinct from what conformity dictates.   (1973, p. 15)

I interpret Peters's second condition of autonomy—associated with assessment and criticism—also as an authenticity-condition, be it a less basic one: "The individual is conceived of as being aware of rules as alterable conventions which structure his social life. He subjects them to reflection and criticism in the light of principles and gradually emerges with his own code of conduct" (1973, pp. 15–16).

"To be a chooser is not enough for autonomy," Stanley Benn remarks, "for a competent chooser may still be a slave to convention, choosing by standards he has accepted quite uncritically from his milieu" (1976, p. 123). For that reason, the "free man" not only is a free chooser but also possesses an authentic code of conduct in the light of which he chooses. Taking my cue from Peters, I propose that a choice (or decision) is autonomous if and only if its agent both has control in making it and is authentic with respect to it. The control and authenticity component of autonomy each merits independent scrutiny.

A mental action, such as a decision (an action of intention formation) is autonomous only if its agent has control in performing it. Various accounts of this control have been proposed in the metaphysics of free will. Some theorists, for example, have argued that a person has the right sort of control only if he had genuine alternatives; he "could have done otherwise" (Ginet 1996; van Inwagen 1983). Others have suggested that a person has the required control only if he is appropriately sensitive to reasons; he would, under specified conditions, have arrived at some other decision were apt reasons present (Fischer and Ravizza 1998; Haji 1998). Still others have maintained that a person has the pertinent control just in case he identifies with the action's motivating desires (Frankfurt 1971, 1988). And yet others have defended the view that the germane control consists in the action's being produced nondeviantly by causal antecedents such as desires, beliefs, values, and so forth that satisfy certain constraints (Mele 1995). This is not the place to assess these or other substantive accounts of control. That there is *some* control condition on autonomous choices is not controversial.

The authenticity-component says that a choice is autonomous only if it causally issues from antecedent springs of action, such as beliefs and desires, which are "authentic" or "truly the agent's own," as opposed to being inauthentic or alien. Varieties of manipulation that subvert agency and undermine autonomy bring out the pertinent contrast between pro-attitudes—for example, desires and values—that are authentic and those that are alien. Globally manipulated agents, for example, are agents who, unaware of being finagled with, fall victim to manipulation that results in significant alteration of their psychological constitution. Consider one of Alfred Mele's examples of global manipulation in which indolent Beth is, in relevant respects, turned into the psychological twin of industrious Ann (Mele 1995, p. 145). Ann and Beth are both philosophy professors, but Ann is far more dedicated to the discipline. Wanting more production out of Beth and not scrupulous about how he gets it, the dean of the university procures the help of New Wave neurologists who "implant" in easy-going Beth Ann's hierarchy of values. The global induction results in Beth's being, in *relevant respects*, the psychological twin of Ann. So, for instance, the induction leaves unscathed values, beliefs, desires, and so forth that pre-manipulated Beth possessed and that can co-exist more or less harmoniously with the implanted pro-attitudes. Such psychological tempering is, thus, consistent with preserving personal identity: premanipulated Beth is identical to her postmanipulated self. Intuitively, the subject of such manipulation is not autonomous with respect to (at least) the first few choices that issue from the alien, engineered-in springs of action. Despite satisfying the correct control condition (whatever this may be), globally manipulated Beth's posttransformation choices lack autonomy, since they issue from elements that are not truly Beth's own. Alternatively, B. F. Skinner's fictional character Frazier, who is the founder of *Walden Two*, gives a suggestive description of autonomy-subversive manipulation when he says that in his community persons can do whatever they want or choose, but they have been conditioned since childhood to want and choose only what they can have or do (Skinner 1948). Whatever sort of control the denizens of this utopian world exercise over choice, they are not autonomous with respect to their choices because they are the causal output of beliefs, desires, values, and the like that are alien to them.

I am now in a position to take up and further substantiate my earlier claim that the complementary issues of manipulation and autonomy in the metaphysics of free will parallel those of indoctrination and authenticity in the philosophy of education. We are well aware that judicious Pavlovian or Skinnerian conditioning and authoritarian indoctrination or extreme paternalism are effective means of getting others, including children, to do our bidding. Desires, dispositions, and other pro-attitudes instilled at the opportune, vulnerable time may leave the child without autonomy in various spheres of her life. Such "implanted" pro-attitudes may be practically unsheddable. As Mele explains, a pro-attitude is practically unsheddable for a person at a certain time if, given her psychological constitution at that time, ridding herself of that attitude is not a "psychologically genuine option" under any but extraordinary circumstances (1995, p. 172) The child, for example, may not be able to refrain from a certain religious practice—her relevant actions would express choices stemming from unsheddable, antecedent causal elements that are not truly the child's own—because of the way in which the religious "training" took place. There is a sense in which the germane springs of action that constrain the child's pertinent choices are inauthentic; the suitably indoctrinated child's choices are not autonomous because they issue from pro-attitudes that are alien.

Intuitively an authentic education, as opposed to an inauthentic one such as a fundamentalist religious or Nazi education, seems perfectly possible, even in the earliest stages of the child's development. Reflection on the very possibility of such an education, however, generates the problem of authentic upbringing. As education is a process of molding or influencing, it necessarily involves *interferences*[7]; it requires instilling in the child, among other things, salient choice-guiding and action-producing elements such as values and other pro-attitudes, deliberative and other principles. But if such elements are implanted—their acquisition totally bypassing the child's rational capacities of reflective assessment and criticism because these capacities are absent or latent at this early stage—then is the child not also a victim of a kind of autonomy-subversive manipulation much as the inhabitants of *Walden Two* are? Would these instilled elements not be just as inauthentic as those engineered into the populace of *Walden Two*? As the requisite, pertinent interferences during any process of education seem no different in kind from those of behaviorist conditioning and extreme paternalism that appear to subvert autonomy, these necessary educational interferences also seem incompatible with authenticity. Hence, some may argue, authoritarian indoctrination is unavoidable, and despite our initial intuition to the contrary, an authentic education is impossible and just a pipe dream.

Peters formulates this problem of educational authenticity as the paradox and problem of moral education:

> given that it is desirable to develop people who conduct themselves rationally, intelligently and with a fair degree of spontaneity, the brute facts of child development reveal that at the most formative years of a child's development he is incapable of this form of life and impervious to the proper manner of passing it on ... Nevertheless, in spite of the fact that a rational code of behaviour ... is beyond the grasp of young children, they can and must enter the palace of Reason through the courtyard of Habit and Tradition. ... The problem of moral education is that of how the necessary habits of behaviour ... can be acquired in a way which does not stultify the development of a rational code ... at a later stage. (Peters 1963, pp. 271–72)[8]

In this revealing passage, the phrase "people who conduct themselves rationally, intelligently and with a fair degree of spontaneity" may be interpreted as "agents in possession of an authentic code of conduct," while the terms "Habit and Tradition" signal the danger of authoritarian indoctrination in the necessary educational interferences. The problem of moral education is that of the apparent incompatibility between Reason (authenticity) as the end, on the one hand, and Habit and Tradition (indoctrination and paternalism) as the necessary means, on the other: "Is it the case that we have to use [such] irrelevant 'extrinsic' techniques [Habit and Tradition] to get children going so that eventually they can take over for themselves, without needing any longer such extrinsic incentives or goads? Or does the use of such extrinsic techniques militate against intelligent, spontaneous, and intrinsically directed behaviour [Reason] later on?" (p. 274). Can a rational or authentic code of conduct be acquired in a nonrational or inauthentic way? And, if so, how then can moral autonomy be arrived at heteronomously?

Peters's resolution of the paradox of moral education essentially consists in distinguishing between two types of habit. Although the inculcation of moral habits is a necessary condition for acquiring a rational code of conduct, "the formation of *some* types of habit may not necessarily militate against adaptability and spontaneous enjoyment" (1963, p. 274; emphasis in the original), which are usually associated with reason and authenticity. The type of habit we have in mind when we use phrases like "out of habit," "through force of habit," or "that is a matter of sheer habit" is modeled after bodily reflexes, auto-regulative processes, and other rigid stimulus-response mechanisms. On this conception of habits as "pretty stereotyped and narrowly conceived things, which are usually fired off by familiar stimuli" (p. 278), habits evidently exclude intelligent adaptability—they resist rational moulding—and spontaneity. Yet on an alternative conception, habits are tendencies to act that have a fair degree of plasticity or open-endedness, and whose ensuing actions are variable with the situation and adaptable to the purpose at hand. Habits, in this sense, are *rationally* permeated tendencies to act; in principle, they have reasons behind them, and although they usually operate automatically, we are at liberty to stop them. By an appeal to this second type of habit as a tendency to act over which we have, to a considerable extent, rational control, Peters closes the gap between the necessary formation of moral habits and the acquisition of a rational or authentic code of conduct: "For there is no *necessary* contradiction between the use of intelligence and the formation of habits" (p. 277; emphasis in the original).

Peters's analysis of moral habit in terms of intelligent adaptability and openness to reason to resolve the paradox of moral education faces, however, an important remaining problem. Peters articulates the contrast between intelligent habits with respect to moral rules—those that are conducive to acquiring a rational or authentic code of conduct—and unintelligent ones as follows. An open-ended, moral habit is a tendency to act *on* a moral rule, whereas a "conformist moral" habit is a capacity to act *in accordance with* a moral rule.[9] This conformist capacity—"e.g., to inhibit actions of which authority figures disapprove, or to inhibit a narrowly conceived range of movements" (Peters 1963, p. 277)—does not presuppose that the person—that is, the child—who so acts possesses the *moral concepts* under which his actions fall. Yet possessing such concepts is indispensable for intelligently understanding the moral rule on which one acts. So, in contrast, the open-ended tendency does presuppose the possession of the relevant moral concepts to understand the specific moral rule on which one acts. Moral concepts are the constituents of *moral beliefs and desires*, such as the belief that theft is wrong and the desire always to respect others' property, the belief that keeping promises is right and the desire always to tell the truth. Hence, the child's acquisition of moral habits in the requisite, authenticity-conducive way presupposes the instillment in the child of pertinent moral concepts, beliefs, and desires. However, as to the *status* of the initial instillment of these prerequisite elements of adequate moral habits, Peters remains silent. He does not say whether these prerequisite elements *themselves* can be authentically acquired and, if so, how they can be acquired without stultifying the development of a rational or authentic code of conduct at a later stage. Consequently, regarding the acquisition of the pertinent moral concepts, beliefs, and desires required for the formation of adequate moral habits conducive to adaptability and spontaneity, we are confronted with the problem of educational authenticity all over again.

3. ROBERT NOGGLE ON AUTHENTIC EDUCATION

To address Peters's major remaining shortcoming, I turn to Noggle's recent attempt to resolve the paradox of self-creation.[10] To examine his position, it will be helpful to distinguish between two stages in a child's development: the stage prior to which the child has become a so-called normative agent—the *pre*–normative stage (before *t*)—and the *post*–normative stage (after *t*).[11] Children are not born as normative agents; they start off as nonnormative beings and gradually develop into partially normative individuals until they finally become fully normative ones (at *t*). A (fully) normative agent is an individual capable of (1) intentional action, (2) rational deliberation or practical reasoning, and in the possession of (3) an evaluative scheme in the light of which he guides his deliberation and action. In Peters's and Benn's terminology, a normative agent is a "rational chooser," while an evaluative scheme is a "code of conduct." During the prenormative stage the child gradually acquires an *initial* evaluative scheme. In the postnormative stage of childhood, adolescence, and adulthood an individual acquires a scheme that results from modifications to his initial scheme—he acquires an *evolved* evaluative scheme. Such an evolved, or minimally completed, initial scheme is made up of the following constituents: (i) normative standards the agent believes (though not necessarily consciously so) ought to be invoked in assessing reasons for action, or in evaluating beliefs about how the agent should go about making choices; (ii) the agent's long-term ends or goals he deems worthwhile or valuable—his "pro-attitudes"; (iii) deliberative principles the agent utilizes to arrive at choices about what to do or intentions how to act; (iv) and lastly, motivation both to act on the normative standards specified in (i) and to pursue one's goals of the sort described in (ii) at least partly on the basis of engaging the deliberative principles outlined in (iii). So, evaluative schemes contain both doxastic propositional attitudes (beliefs) and motivational elements (desires and other pro-attitudes).

Our scrutiny of Peters's paradox reveals that the problem of educational authenticity is most pressing as regards the child's acquisition of an initial evaluative scheme at the prenormative stage. Most theorists, including Peters, Noggle, and myself, agree that changes in an already existing authentic evaluative scheme—an authentic evolved one—at the postnormative stage may be perfectly compatible with preserving authenticity on the condition that those changes take place under *the agent's own deliberative rational control*.[12] Such self-control involves the exercising of deliberative capacities, including (a) the capacity critically to reflect on beliefs and pro-attitudes, (b) the capacity rationally and morally to assess these attitudes, and (c) the capacity to change their strength, or to revise and even to eradicate them, or to foster new attitudes in the light of (a) and (b).[13] Exercising these deliberative capacities is authenticity-preserving in virtue of the agent's "engaging" elements constitutive of his authentic evolved scheme. By contrast, if an agent's authentic evaluative scheme is not engaged in, for instance, acquiring a pro-attitude—if its acquisition bypasses all of the agent's capacities of deliberative control—then this pro-attitude is inauthentic. Whereas a solution along these lines of the problem of authentically modifying evolved schemes is relatively uncontroversial, theorists are in a quandary about the "hard" problem of educational authenticity—that of authentically inculcating initial schemes. Given the importance of rational reflection for authenticity at the postnormative stage, how can educators authentically instill in young children, for example, *the belief that critical self-evaluation is important* at the prenormative stage, where the young are short of pertinent deliberative capacities?

Noggle's notion of a "core self"—consisting of "core attitudes"[14]—and that of an "evaluative scheme" are co-extensive, while his distinction between an "*initial* [core] self" and an "*existing* [core] self" coincides with that between an initial and evolved evaluative scheme (2005, pp. 99–100, 104). An existing self is an "authenticating self" because, assuming it is itself authentic, it is the source of constituting the authenticity of other psychological elements, just like the engagement of an authentic evolved scheme is authenticity-conveying. Noggle elucidates:

> we might say that both historical [externalist] and structural [internalist] theories [of autonomy] are, so to speak, "self-referential" in that they define the authenticity of an element by its connection to the self. On this view, the self is, by definition, the determiner of authenticity or inauthenticity, because the authenticity of a psychological element depends on its relationship to the self. In the context of a self-referential theory, this *authenticating self*... is the source of authenticity. (2005, pp. 94–95)

Noggle proposes that the "authenticating self first arises gradually" (2005, p. 99).

Turning, now, to the issue of pressing interest to us—authentic springs at the prenormative agent stage of development—how does such an initial self arise? Noggle writes:

> Infants and very young children do not yet have the two key psychological ingredients [core attitudes] for the kind of self that we are supposing is the determiner of authenticity.... The earliest core desires, as well as the initial elements of the child's cognitive conceptual scheme, arise via processes that would be considered authenticity undermining if they were used to implant beliefs and desires into an adult. Such processes apparently include operant, aversive, and classical conditioning; role model imitation; blind obedience to and subsequent internalization of behavioral norms; uncritical acceptance of propositions on the authority of parents and teachers; and so on. Out of a seemingly unpromising beginning—a sort of chaotic psychological "soup"—the child's [initial] self gradually emerges as her cognitive and motivational systems develop the kind of structure and stability and the rational and reflective capacities necessary for the existence of a coherent and stable self that can be the source of authenticity. (2005, p. 101, note omitted)[15]

At first blush, the indoctrinative "standard child-rearing techniques" Noggle (2005, p. 103) refers to are incompatible with the authentic acquisition of the earliest core attitudes. How, one might ask, can the (minimally completed) initial self then be the source of authenticity if the necessary educational interferences on the basis of which it arises "would be considered authenticity undermining if they were used to implant beliefs and desires into an adult"? Noggle answers:

> If we accept a self-referential condition of authenticity, an element is authentic to a person just in case it bears the right relation to her true [core] self. Before the self initially arises, there is no other self for the initial self to bear any authenticity-grounding relation to.... When that initial self forms, it is the only self that there is. Sadly, that initial self is the only game in town, so to speak. Now if we ask whether some *element* of that initial self is authentic, then the answer

simply has to be "yes." After all, the element belongs, *ex hypothesi*, to the only self that exists. If the self is fully formed and the elements are related to it in the right way (with the right way depending on what theory of authenticity we finally adopt), then that is all there is to their being authentic.   (p. 103)

According to Noggle, the logic of the concept of authenticity instructs us "that it is really a two-place relation: Some element is authentic *to* a particular person [self]." (p. 103). In the case of an existing self, the relation of authentication can hold unproblematically. By contrast, in the case of a gradually arising initial self, the relation cannot hold since one of the two relata is absent. But although there simply is no authenticating self present at the beginning of the prenormative stage, there will be a minimally completed, authentic initial self in existence on the verge of the postnormative stage. To resolve this paradox of self-creation, Noggle proposes that the original elements—the earliest core attitudes—which gradually build up the initial self are *ipso facto* authentic ones. All the "first" attitudes are, so to speak, "good" ones. While there is much with which I agree in Noggle's account, I believe that the implication of his account that any doxastic or pro-attitudinal element in the child's gradually developing initial evaluative scheme at the prenormative agent stage qualifies as authentic is seriously flawed. I briefly indicate why that is so.

On Noggle's account, authenticity is a necessary but not a sufficient condition for autonomy: "Depending on how we fill out the theory of autonomy, it is possible that a person's behavior could be caused by authentic elements of her psychology without her being autonomous. For example, coercion may be thought to rob an agent of autonomy, even though the coerced agent's behavior may be caused by authentic desires (e.g., to avoid harm)" (2005, p. 88). Noggle would presumably endorse my analysis of "freedom," introduced in section 2, according to which a choice (or decision) is autonomous if and only if its agent both has control in making it and is authentic with respect to it. Assuming this analysis of autonomy in terms of an authenticity and a control component, imagine the following. A religious, fundamentalist leader successfully manages to implant at the prenormative agent stage in the young who are forced to attend his sermons core desires that are irresistible or practically unsheddable, so that the novices at a later stage cannot refrain from daily performing ritual actions caused by such unsheddable elements. On Noggle's account, these first core pro-attitudes are *authentic* despite their being irresistible. Qualifying them as authentic is, however, implausible since these unsheddable pro-attitudes would presumably undermine later autonomous choice and action stemming from such attitudes by undermining the control autonomy requires. It seems much more plausible that they are *inauthentic* precisely because they are autonomy-subverting: they subvert the control that autonomy requires. Hence, not all first attitudes seem *ipso facto* good ones.

Moreover, the "inauthenticity" of such irresistible pro-attitudes (and other actional elements) has implications for the authenticity of various other pro-attitudes (and actional elements) that the adolescent into whom the "religiously indoctrinated" child develops will come to possess. Suppose inauthentic desires (including hierarchical ones) and beliefs, instilled at the prenormative agent stage, are later implicated in the "fully formed" self's deliberations regarding changes to her core attitudes. Then, it seems, these deliberations inherit the taint of inauthenticity owing to some or all of the primary "inputs"—the first instilled elements—to deliberation being inauthentic themselves. It should come as no surprise, then, that the "output" of these deliberations—"altered" beliefs or desires—may themselves not be authentic. This could be so even though the deliberations of the "existing self" at the postnormative stage involve no empirical errors or logical confusions.

First core attitudes—*ipso facto* authentic ones—are instilled by means of standard child-rearing techniques that "would be considered authenticity undermining if they were used to implant beliefs and desires into an adult." To avoid paradox, Noggle adds: "it makes a great deal of difference whether such processes are being used to build an *initial* self, or whether they are being used to implant psychological elements into an *existing* self" (2005, p. 104; emphasis in the original). In both cases, a self is created. The "big difference" depends on the logic of authenticity central to Noggle's self-referential theory. In the case of an existing self, an inauthentic self is created by manipulatively tampering with an already existing one. In the case of an initial self, the question whether the resulting self is an authentic descendent of an earlier one is meaningless since there is no earlier self around in the prenormative agent stage. But why exactly, one might insist, would the impact of manipulative techniques on self-creation be crucially different in early childhood? Why would indoctrinative processes of child-rearing be less, or even fail to be, completely authenticity undermining in the prenormative agent stage? Noggle's answer to whether a first core attitude that is "beaten into" a child, or instilled via "shock therapy," at the pre-normative agent stage is authentic is a resounding yes. This implication of his self-referential theory of authenticity is, however, hard to swallow. The fact that there is no self around at this early stage seems irrelevant to whether or not first core attitudes implanted via such "harsh methods" are authentic. If, as a result of the way in which the early religious "training" took place, the novice finds at a later stage that he cannot refrain from punctiliously going through the ordained rituals in virtue of irresistible first core attitudes that are still with him, then these pro-attitudes were *inauthentically* implanted for the reason previously adumbrated: They are inauthentic because their indoctrinative mode of instillment subverts autonomy by subverting the control condition. Again, not all first attitudes are *ipso facto* good ones or authentic.

4. A FORWARD-LOOKING ACCOUNT OF EDUCATING FOR AUTHENTICITY

The model I propose as a solution to the hard problem of educational authenticity may be dubbed "forward-looking."[16] On the view that I (and my co-author) defend, there is nothing like "plain authenticity" or "authenticity per se or *sans phrase.*" Rather, we defend a relational view of authenticity according to which springs of action, such as beliefs and desires, are authentic or inauthentic only relative to whether later behavior that issues from them is behavior for which the normative agent into whom the child will develop can shoulder moral responsibility. Our view on authentic education is in this sense forward-looking: although pertinent psychological elements instilled in the child during the prenormative stage are not authentic per se, they can be authentic with an eye toward future moral responsibility. So, on our relational conceptualization of authenticity, elements constitutive of an initial evaluative scheme are not authentic in their own right, but only authentic relative to future responsibility.

On Peters's and Noggle's view, authenticity is a component of autonomy (freedom), whereas on ours it is a component of moral responsibility. This is not, however, an important difference because their analysis is included in ours. The sort of autonomy Peters and Noggle are interested in is *responsibility-grounding autonomy* and, accordingly, autonomy—which comprises control and authenticity—is a necessary condition for moral responsibility. Since my goal here is to give an account of the notion of authenticity—in relation to that of moral responsibility—in an educational context, it is important, first, to elucidate the concept of moral responsibility and, second, to indicate the role of moral responsibility in the process of education. I start with this latter preliminary.

It is undeniable that a primary aim of educating children is to make sure that they become moral agents—a specific kind of normative agents. However different in other respects, other diverse views concerning the aims of education rest on a presupposition that has received insufficient attention: children must be raised so that they develop into free agents who are capable of shouldering moral responsibility for their behavior. Even communitarians, many of whom regard liberalistic education as inimical to a valued way of life, do not—indeed, cannot—deny that a pivotal goal of education is to turn children into morally responsible agents. A distinguishing mark of moral persons, as opposed to mere members of the species *Homo sapiens*, is that persons are responsible agents. So, whatever other secondary goals, such as autonomy, critical thinking, well-being, or democratic citizenship, one wants to promote (Marples 1999; Winch 2006), fully-fledged personhood seems indisputable as a primary goal of education.

Elaborating, part of what it is to be a moral agent is to be a competent participant in the array of practices constitutive of moral responsibility. Among other things, to become a moral agent, the child must see himself as an appropriate candidate of the morally reactive attitudes such as resentment and gratitude and must be such a candidate (P. Strawson 1962/1982). It is received wisdom that, whereas certain forms of training or upbringing are conducive to attaining this goal, various forms of authoritarian indoctrination or paternalism are detrimental to its realization. We suggest that "harsh" paternalism threatens attainment of this goal, when it does, primarily by virtue of the fact that it threatens achievement of the desideratum that the child will be an apposite candidate of things like moral praise and blame. Paternalism of the relevant sort thwarts the fundamental goal of education because the severely afflicted child may not be a moral person, as opposed to a mere human being; paternalism foils the complex, intentional process—what is fundamental to *authentic* education—of transforming a child from being simply a member of *Homo sapiens* into a moral agent. We may, indeed, regard such paternalism, or more generally, unacceptable educational interferences, as mere training as opposed to authentic education. By contraposition, then, authentic education, as opposed to indoctrinative training, consists of necessary educational interferences that are conducive to the attainment of the primary educational aim of transforming children into morally responsible agents.

If a key goal of education is to ensure that children blossom into morally responsible agents, educational theorists also need to attend to the concept of moral responsibility. Apart from general agency requirements—only normative agents are appropriate candidates—moral responsibility specifically has epistemic, freedom or control, and authenticity requirements. A normative agent S cannot be morally responsible for a particular action A unless (i) S knows that S is doing wrong (or right) in performing A; (ii) S exercises responsibility-relevant control in doing A; and (iii) A stems from psychological antecedents that are constituents of S's authentic evaluative scheme. For present purposes, I confine attention primarily to the third condition.[17] Earlier I noted my alliance with the standard view that modifications to an authentic evolved evaluative scheme at the postnormative stage are authenticity preserving as long as they are initiated "under the agent's own steam." The "big issue" that requires tackling head-on is this: How, precisely, does authenticity originate in the *initial* evaluative schemes of children who gradually develop into normative agents? Addressing the prenormative agent stage—early childhood before a full-fledged evaluative scheme has been attained—is there a reasonable sense in which a child's cognitive and pro-attitudinal elements, constitutive of the initial scheme it will acquire, are authentic?

Regarding the child's initial evaluative scheme, I argue for the view that its constituent elements can be relationally authentic in the manner previously indicated: they can be authentic relative to respecting or ensuring future moral responsibility. So the hard problem of educational authenticity is solved in two steps. First, we invoke the view that authenticity per se or *sans phrase* of an initial scheme's constituents is a myth: educators can only succeed in authentically implanting pertinent cognitive and pro-attitudinal elements if these elements play an appropriate role in the child's development into a morally responsible agent (and continue to play that role after the child has become a minimally competent normative agent). Second, we show that things such as authoritarian indoctrination or harsh paternalism (when responsibility-thwarting), unlike authentic ways of instilling salient psychological elements, make use of ways that undermine such *responsibility-relative authenticity*. To appreciate this strategy, reflect on mental illness, coercion, or deception—factors all parties readily grant frequently affect moral responsibility. Such factors subvert moral responsibility, when they do, if they undermine one or more of the requirements of responsibility, such as epistemic or control requirements. If a person acts on the basis of a belief that is false, the belief having been acquired as a result of deception, then (assuming that the person is nonculpably ignorant) the person is "off the hook." Similarly, if a person acts on a surreptitiously implanted desire that is irresistible, so that action issuing from the desire is action that is not under her control, then once again the person has a genuine excuse. Against the backdrop of these considerations, I propose that a cognitive or pro-attitudinal element or its mode of acquisition is *inauthentic* if that psychological element, or the way in which it is acquired, will *subvert* moral responsibility for behavior, which owes its proximal causal genesis to the element, of the normative agent into whom the child will develop. Subversion of moral responsibility would occur as a result of either the epistemic or control requirement—*independently*, of course, of the authenticity requirement itself—of moral responsibility being thwarted. I now supply details of this sketch.

Joel Feinberg remarks that the extent of a child's role in his own shaping is a process of continuous growth begun at birth. He continues:

> Always the self that contributes to the making of the newer self is the product both of outside influences *and* an earlier self that was not quite as fully formed. That earlier self, in turn, was the product both of outside influences and a still earlier self that was still less fully formed and fixed, and so on, all the way back to infancy. At every subsequent stage the immature child plays a greater role in the creation of his own life, until at the arbitrarily fixed point of full maturity, he is at last fully in charge of himself, . . . That is the most sense that we can make of the ideal of the "self-made person," but it is an intelligible idea . . . with no paradox in it. Perhaps we are all self-made in the way just described, except those who have been severely manipulated, indoctrinated, or coerced throughout childhood. *But the self we have created in this way for ourselves will not be an authentic self unless the habit of critical self-revision was implanted in us early by parents, educators, or peers, and strengthened by our own constant exercise of it.* (1986, pp. 34–35; emphasis in last sentence added)[18]

In this insightful passage, Feinberg suggests that authenticity requires both a certain sort of maturation—one free of things like indoctrination or coercion—*and* deliberate interferences in the processes that shape the child. For instance, he proposes that the habit of critical self-revision must be *implanted* in us early if we are to acquire authenticity. On Feinberg's view, then, some deliberate interferences in shaping the child are perfectly compatible with and are, indeed, required for authenticity.[19] With this view of Feinberg's, and the proposal that instillment of doxastic and pro-attitudinal elements that subvert responsibility for subsequent, relevant behavior suffices for the inauthenticity of these pro-attitudes in mind, ponder these examples.

To be *morally* responsible for an action, an agent must be minimally morally competent. An agent must have elementary moral concepts, such as those of right, wrong, and obligation, and she must be able to appraise morally—even if imperfectly—reasons, choices, actions, consequences of action, and so on in light of the normative standards that are partly constitutive of her evaluative scheme. A minimally morally competent agent has a grasp of the notions of guilt, resentment, praise-, and blameworthiness or of the concepts of related reactive attitudes or feelings and has at least a rudimentary appreciation of when such attitudes or feelings are appropriate.

Now, suppose a child, call him Émile, is trained so that he lacks knowledge of the relevant moral concepts and norms, with the result that he is not even minimally morally competent. Then lack of instillment of the appropriate moral concepts and norms is responsibility-subversive because without the conceptual wherewithal, Émile won't satisfy responsibility's epistemic requirement. Or consider instillment in Émile of a pro-attitude or disposition—on a par with an irresistible desire—the influence of which on his behavior he cannot thwart. Instilling such a pro-attitude would presumably undermine responsibility for later conduct arising from that pro-attitude by undermining the control moral responsibility requires. Or suppose instilled in Émile is a powerful disposition always to act impulsively. Here, again, we would not want to hold Émile morally responsible for much of his later impulsive behavior. Or, finally, consider an interference that prevents Émile from engaging in critical self-reflection. This may subvert Émile from being morally responsible for some of his later behavior, on occasions of choice, by significantly narrowing the range of Émile's options, alternatives he may have considered had he acquired "normal" habits of critical self-reflection. In sum, some interferences—"untoward ones"—are incompatible with Émile's being morally responsible for his subsequent behavior that issues from these interferences. Such interferences subvert later moral responsibility while others do not. We propose that the subversive ones are *responsibility-wise inauthentic*.[20] Setting aside the authenticity requirement of responsibility, if these interferences subvert later moral responsibility, they will do so by subverting *other* requirements of responsibility, such as epistemic or freedom requirements.

So far, our discussion has been limited to responsibility-relative authenticity of the "objects" of instillment, such as dispositions, or pro-attitudes in general. What about the methods or techniques of instilling such things? Are some of these responsibility-wise authentic and others not? Assume that to ensure prevention of subverting moral responsibility for later behavior, it is necessary to instill in the child the disposition to be moral. Different modes of instillment of this disposition could affect responsibility-relative authenticity of this very disposition itself. For example, suppose that given the mode of instilling the moral disposition in Émile—perhaps the disposition was "beaten into" Émile or instilled via "shock therapy"—Émile subsequently finds that he cannot refrain from doing what he perceives to be morally right and to do what is, for instance, in his best self-interest. On occasions of choice, he is stricken with inward terror even at the faintest thought of not doing what he deems moral. Intuitively, Émile would not be morally responsible for much of his later behavior because the mode of instillment of the moral disposition subverts responsibility-grounding control. Modes of instilling pro-attitudes and the like are responsibility-wise not "truly one's own"—that is, are responsibility-wise inauthentic—if the modes subvert responsibility for later behavior. Again, if these modes of acquiring pro-attitudes undermine later moral responsibility, they will do so by subverting one or more of responsibility's requirements (other than the authenticity requirement).

Apart from pro-attitudes, a normative agent's evaluative scheme comprises *cognitive* constituents. Again, with the young child whose evaluative scheme is in embryo, it may well be the case that certain beliefs will have to be willfully instilled to ensure responsibility-relative authenticity. As Feinberg suggests, one will, perhaps, have to instill in the child *the belief that critical self-evaluation is important* because without this belief, moral responsibility for later behavior may well be threatened in the manner indicated above. In addition, the child's having of such a belief, it would seem, would be morally permissible and perhaps even morally required. Instilling beliefs of this sort, in consequence, via modes or methods that themselves do not subvert later responsibility, would not threaten responsibility-relative authenticity. Various sorts of belief, though, *would* undermine or seriously imperil moral responsibility for later conduct. The following sorts, for example, seem to be responsibility-wise inauthentic: beliefs formed as a result of deception (and self-deception), beliefs implanted on the basis of coercive persuasion or subliminal influencing, and beliefs inculcated in such a way that the agent is subsequently never encouraged to seek supporting evidence for them and his reason assessment capacity is permanently suppressed. The agent, presumably, would not be morally responsible for actions performed in the light of such beliefs.[21]

We may now formulate a general criterion for the authenticity of initial evaluative schemes. I have suggested that, possibly, having some doxastic and pro-attitudinal elements is required to ensure moral responsibility for later behavior; having them ensures that necessary conditions—other than the authenticity condition itself—of moral responsibility can (later) be satisfied by the agent or by her behavior that stems from them. Such required attitudes are *authenticity demanding*. I have also suggested that having some doxastic and pro-attitudinal elements is incompatible with moral responsibility for later behavior that issues from them; having these elements precludes satisfaction of necessary conditions, such as epistemic or control conditions, that moral responsibility requires. Such incompatible attitudes are *authenticity destructive*. Lastly, I have suggested that some modes of instilling doxastic and pro-attitudinal elements are irreconcilable with moral responsibility for later behavior; such modes of instillment subvert later responsibility by thwarting satisfaction of necessary conditions of responsibility apart from the authenticity condition itself. These irreconcilable modes of attitude-acquisition are *authenticity subversive*. I propose, then, the following criterion as one that governs responsibility-relative authenticity of *initial* schemes of developing agents at the pre-normative stage.

> *Criterion of Authenticity*: A child's initial evaluative scheme is responsibility-wise authentic if its doxastic and pro-attitudinal elements (i) include all those, if any,

that are required to ensure that the agent (into whom the child will develop) will be morally responsible for his or her future behavior; (ii) do not include any that will subvert the agent's being responsible for future behavior that issues from these elements; and (iii) have been acquired by means that, again, will not subvert the agent's being responsible for his or her future behavior.

The crux of this criterion is that the child's initial evaluative scheme is not the child's own if its doxastic and pro-attitudinal elements subvert, to a substantial degree, moral responsibility for later behavior that issues from these elements.

All the ingredients for a solution to the hard problem of educational authenticity are now in place. Solving this big issue involves distinguishing at the pre-normative agent stage necessary educational interferences that are authentic (authentic education) from inauthentic ones (authoritarian indoctrination). I draw this crucial distinction in terms of the Criterion of Authenticity. To ensure that the child matures into a normative agent, certain doxastic and pro-attitudinal elements must be instilled in the child. But neither these instilled elements nor their mode of instillment need subvert the child's being morally responsible, at the age when it can be so responsible, for behavior that causally issues from these instilled elements. Instilling pertinent beliefs or desires is authentic if their acquisition does not subvert, in a characteristic way, moral responsibility for later behavior that (at least partly) issues from these elements.

The characteristic way is this: The acquisition of these elements subverts moral responsibility by compromising necessary requirements of responsibility, such as epistemic or control ones, with the exception of the authenticity requirement itself. These elements are, then, in the terminology introduced, *relative-to-future-responsibility authentic* and gradually build up a child's authentic *initial* evaluative scheme. But some instilled elements or their modes of instillment undercut moral responsibility for later behavior by undermining fulfillment of necessary conditions of responsibility other than the authenticity condition itself. Offensive manipulation, harsh paternalism, hideously depraving conditions, or experiences traumatic to the child may have this effect. If they do (and empirical evidence is required to confirm whether they do), then in these sorts of cases, the instilled elements are (relationally) inauthentic—not "truly the child's own."

5. AN EXTERNALIST CRITERION IN THE FREE WILL DEBATE

From our excursion in the philosophy of education we can, in conclusion, collect fruitful results for the metaphysics of free will. At the outset I remarked that the major task for externalism is to draw a principled distinction in the causal domain between the "right" or autonomy-preserving histories and the "wrong" or autonomy-subverting ones—in Zimmerman's (2003) words, "to make room in the developmental picture for a difference between the kinds of early preference-acquisition that eventually lead to autonomous agency and those that block the child from transcending its early and inevitable heteronomy" (p. 638). This problem of distinguishing autonomy from heteronomy—and thus manipulation—at deterministic worlds can usefully be construed as a problem of contrasting "normality" with "deviance." In troubling cases of manipulation, psychological elements such as beliefs and desires, among other things, are acquired via causal routes that are deviant relative to causal routes deemed normal. Exploiting the Criterion of Authenticity, I propose, then, that the externalist compatibilist theory of free will adopts the following criterion.

> *Externalist Criterion*: A causal route to the acquisition of salient doxastic and pro-attitudinal elements is normal, if either (i) the elements are authenticity demanding; or (ii) they are not authenticity destructive; and (iii) these elements have been acquired by means that are not authenticity subversive. If some salient psychological element is not acquired via a normal route, the route to its acquisition is deviant.

Roughly, a causal route to acquiring things such as beliefs or desires is normal if their acquisition does not subvert responsibility for later behavior that (at least partly) issues from these elements by compromising necessary requirements of responsibility, such as epistemic or control ones, with the exception of the authenticity requirement itself. Once a "normal" (authentic initial) evaluative scheme is in place, the condition for a causal route's being normal will be governed primarily by the principle that deviant routes are routes that result in salient springs of action being acquired—in bypassing the agent's own deliberative rational control—independently of the agent's engaging her already existing, normal evaluative scheme.[22]

NOTES

1. As illustrations of such "applications," see, for example, pertinent chapters in Blake et al. 2003 and in Curren 2003.

2. For more, excellent information on this debate, see Kane 2002, 2005.

3. For these arguments, see van Inwagen 1983.

4. Internalism (or structuralism) is defended by, among others, Frankfurt 1988; Double 1991, part I; McKenna 2004, 2008. Externalism (or historicism) is defended by, among others, Christman 1991; Mele 1995, chaps. 9–10; and specifically applied to moral responsibility by Fischer and Ravizza 1998, chaps. 7–8.

5. For my critique of internalism, see Cuypers 2004; for that of externalism, see Cuypers 2006. For our defense of a position that navigates between internalism and externalism, see Haji and Cuypers 2007.

6. For various ways in which different educational theorists construe the notion of authenticity, see Cuypers and Haji 2007, pp. 78–81.

7. Let "interference" be a general term for things like suppression of innate propensities and dispositions; or implantation of certain beliefs, desires, habits, values, and principles; or deliberate lack of instillment of various doxastic and pro-attitudinal elements.

8. I limit discussion of Peters's paradox to the child's acquisition of "a rationally held and intelligently applied moral code" (p. 268) and omit Peters's parallel considerations pertaining to the child's initiation into "the 'language' of a variety of [good or worthwhile] activities" (p. 272).

9. See Peters 1963, p. 277. Compare this contrast with Kant's between "acting from duty (*aus Pflicht*)" and "acting in accordance with duty." For an excellent discussion of Kant's classic distinction, see Stratton-Lake 2006.

10. Noggle's 2005 attempt is representative of accounts that construe educational authenticity as "plain authenticity" or "authenticity per se or sans phrase" (psychological elements, such as beliefs and desires, are authentic in their own right). Other examples are Zimmerman (2003, pp. 658–61), Rousseauist, child-centred theorists and some proponents of children's rights (see note 6). As against these (mistaken) theories, I defend a relational account of educational authenticity in section 4.

11. The borderline between these two stages (time *t*) is, to a certain extent, arbitrary; some might place it at 12 years or even earlier, others at 16 or only later at the conventional 18 years. For a useful discussion of this demarcation problem in the context of children's rights, see Archard 1993, chap. 5, and 2003, chap. 1.

12. For Peters's second autonomy-condition of rational reflection—"deliberative control"—which I interpreted as an authenticity-condition, see section 2. According to Noggle (2005, pp. 100–101), once a person has acquired "a core self," she has the ability to adjust and revise the doxastic and motivational elements of it: "Often, such changes are, to a large degree, 'internally motivated' in such a way that they seem to be intelligible reflections of the contents of the core attitudes. . . . When psychological changes happen this way, it seems correct to say that the new configuration of the self is an authentic continuation of the previous configuration. On the other hand, a psychological change—especially a change to the core attitudes—that does not occur in this way produces a new configuration that is not an authentic continuation of the previous one."

13. For a detailed account of the deliberative capacities of normal, healthy human agents, see Mele 1995, pp. 166–72; 183–84.

14. Noggle (2005, pp. 99–100) speculates that a person's desires and beliefs are structured around a core, consisting of "those beliefs that constitute her most basic cognitive organizing principles and fundamental assumptions and convictions, together with the desires that constitute her deepest, most significant goals, concerns, commitments, and values."

15. Noggle expands on this; see Noggle 2002.

16. I developed this model together with Ishtiyaque Haji, especially in Haji and Cuypers 2004, 2007.

17. As knowledge entails truth, some theorists (for example, Smith 1983) endorse the "objective" view that an agent is morally responsible for an action only if performing that action is objectively wrong (or right). Others (for example, Haji 1998, chap. 9) maintain the "subjective" view: a belief condition—the agent's believing that performing the action is wrong (or right)—is sufficient to fulfill the epistemic requirement. As the control requirement for moral responsibility coincides with the control component of autonomy,

see section 2 for the various accounts of the pertinent type of control that have been proposed.

18. See also Feinberg 1980/1992, p. 96.

19. Galen Strawson (1986, p. 293) suggests that the implantation or fostering of the attitude or disposition of seeing oneself in control of one's actions, as a suitable subject of moral responsibility, may well—at least in the very initial stages of development—be required to ensure moral responsibility for subsequent behavior. Fostering this sort of attitude is presumably morally required. For a similar view, see Fischer and Ravizza 1998, p. 208.

20. Specifically, imagine an agent like a young child who does not yet have an initial scheme. Such an agent's, S's, having pro-attitude P is responsibility-wise inauthentic if S's having P, as a result of instillment, subverts S's being morally responsible for S's behavior that stems from P; the having of P precludes S from being morally responsible for behavior stemming from P. "Stems from" requires analysis that shall not be undertaken here save for the following. A causal theory of action (which I endorse) assumes that actions causally arise from desires, or desire/belief pairs, or a cluster of psychological elements. On this theory, when an action issues from a certain desire (as opposed to another), this desire (as opposed to the other, typically together with other actional elements) is causally implicated in the production of the action. I presuppose whatever account of "issues from" that causal theories of action presuppose. For such theories, see Davidson 1963/1980 and Mele 1992.

21. Harvey Siegel 1988 also offers a forward-looking solution to the problem of indoctrinative belief-inculcation in the context of educating for critical thinking. For a congenial discussion of the authentic instillment of the "reason assesment" and "critical spirit" components of critical thinking, see Cuypers and Haji 2006.

22. We discuss and defend further this externalist criterion in Haji and Cuypers 2008. I want to express my gratitude to Ishtiyaque Haji for his extremely valuable comments and advice.

REFERENCES

Archard, David William. (1993). *Children: Rights and Childhood*. London: Routledge.
—— (2003). *Children, Family and the State*. Aldershot: Ashgate.
Benn, Stanley I. (1976). "Freedom, Autonomy and the Concept of a Person." *Proceedings of the Aristotelian Society* 76: 109–30.
Blake, Nigel, Paul Smeyers, Richard Smith, and Paul Standish, eds. (2003). *The Blackwell Guide to the Philosophy of Education*. Oxford: Blackwell.
Christman, John. (1991). "Autonomy and Personal History." *Canadian Journal of Philosophy* 21: 1–24.
Curren, Randall, ed. (2003). *A Companion to the Philosophy of Education*. Oxford: Blackwell.
Cuypers, Stefaan E. (2004). "The Trouble with Harry: Compatibilist Free Will Internalism and Manipulation." *Journal of Philosophical Research* 29: 235–54.
—— (2006). "The Trouble with Externalist Compatibilist Autonomy." *Philosophical Studies* 129: 171–96.
Cuypers, Stefaan E., and Ishtiyaque Haji. (2006). "Education for Critical Thinking: Can It Be Non-Indoctrinative?" *Educational Philosophy and Theory* 38: 723–43.

—— (2007). "Authentic Education and Moral Responsibility." *Journal of Applied Philosophy* 24: 78–94.

Davidson, Donald. (1963/1980). "Actions, Reasons, and Causes." In *Essays on Actions and Events*, D. Davidson (pp. 3–19). Oxford: Clarendon Press.

Double, Richard. (1991). *The Non-Reality of Free Will.* Oxford: Oxford University Press.

Feinberg, Joel. (1980/1992). "The Child's Right to an Open Future." In *Freedom and Fulfillment*, J. Feinberg (pp. 76–97). Princeton. NJ: Princeton University Press.

—— (1986). *Harm to Self.* New York: Oxford University Press.

Fischer, John, and Mark Ravizza. (1998). *Responsibility and Control. A Theory of Moral Responsibility.* Cambridge: Cambridge University Press.

Frankfurt, Harry G. (1971). "Freedom of the Will and the Concept of a Person." *Journal of Philosophy* 68: 5–20.

—— (1988). *The Importance of What We Care About.* Cambridge: Cambridge University Press.

Ginet, Carl. (1996). "In Defense of the Principle of Alternative Possibilities: Why I Don't Find Frankfurt's Argument Convincing." *Philosophical Perspectives* 10: 403–41.

Haji, Ishtiyaque. (1998). *Moral Appraisability. Puzzles, Proposals, and Perplexities.* Oxford: Oxford University Press.

Haji, Ishtiyaque, and Stefaan E. Cuypers. (2004). "Responsibility and the Problem of Manipulation Reconsidered." *International Journal of Philosophical Studies* 12: 439–64.

—— (2007). "Magical Agents, Global Induction, and the Internalism/Externalism Debate." *Australasian Journal of Philosophy* 85: 343–71.

—— 2008. *Moral Responsibility, Authenticity, and Education.* New York: Routledge.

Kane, Robert, ed. (2002). *The Oxford Handbook of Free Will.* New York: Oxford University Press.

—— (2005). *A Contemporary Introduction to Free Will.* New York: Oxford University Press.

Marples, Roger, ed. (1999). *The Aims of Education.* London: Routledge.

McKenna, Michael. (2004). "Responsibility and Globally Manipulated Agents." *Philosophical Topics* 32: 169–92.

—— (2008). "A Hard-line Reply to Pereboom's Four-Case Manipulation Argument." *Philosophy and Phenomenological Research* 77: 142–59.

Mele, Alfred R. (1992). *Springs of Action. Understanding Intentional Behavior.* New York: Oxford University Press.

—— (1995). *Autonomous Agents. From Self-Control to Autonomy.* New York: Oxford University Press.

Noggle, Robert. (2002). "Special Agents: Children's Autonomy and Parental Authority." In *The Moral and Political Status of Children*, ed. D. Archard and C. MacLeod (pp. 97–117). Oxford: Oxford University Press.

—— (2005). "Autonomy and the Paradox of Self-Creation." In *Personal Autonomy. New Essays on Personal Autonomy and Its Role in Contemporary Moral Philosophy*, ed. J. S. Taylor (pp. 87–108). Cambridge: Cambridge University Press.

Peters, Richard S. (1963/1974). "Reason and Habit: the Paradox of Moral Education." In *Psychology and Ethical Development. A Collection of Articles on Psychological Theories, Ethical Development and Human Understanding*, R. S. Peters (pp. 265–80). London: George Allen & Unwin.

—— (1973). "Freedom and the Development of the Free Man." In *Philosophy of Education. Major Themes in the Analytic Tradition. Volume II: Education and Human Being*, eds. P. H. Hirst and P. White (pp. 11–31). London: Routledge.

Siegel, Harvey. (1988). *Educating Reason. Rationality, Critical Thinking, and Education*. New York: Routledge.

Skinner, B. F. (1948). *Walden Two*. New York: Macmillan.

Smith, Holly. (1983). "Culpable Ignorance." *The Philosophical Review* 92: 543–71.

Stratton-Lake, Philip. (2006). "Moral Motivation in Kant." In *A Companion to Kant*, ed. G. Bird (pp. 322–34). Oxford: Blackwell.

Strawson, Galen. (1986). *Freedom and Belief*. Oxford: Clarendon Press.

Strawson, Peter F. (1962/1982). "Freedom and Resentment." *Proceedings of the British Academy* 48: 1–25. Reprinted in *Free Will*, ed. G. Watson (pp. 59–80). Oxford: Oxford University Press.

van Inwagen, Peter. (1983). *An Essay on Free Will*. Oxford: Clarendon Press.

Winch, Christopher. (2006). *Education, Autonomy and Critical Thinking*. London: Routledge.

Zimmerman, David. (2003). "That Was Then, This Is Now: Personal History vs. Psychological Structure in Compatibilist Theories of Autonomous Agency." *Noûs* 37: 638–71.

CHAPTER 8

THE DEVELOPMENT
OF RATIONALITY

DAVID MOSHMAN

EDUCATION, almost everyone agrees, should promote rationality. Many have made stronger claims. It has been argued that the promotion of rationality is the only legitimate aim of education, or the central aim that explains and justifies all others, or at least the most important of all possible aims of education. There is much to be said for these stronger claims but there is no need to say it here. Even if education has multiple important aims, there is no doubt that rationality is among these. Whatever disputes there may be about the centrality of rationality in education, there appears to be a longstanding consensus that education should promote rationality (Siegel 1988, 1997).

But how is rationality to be promoted? If we assume students come to us as nonrational or irrational beings, and naturally tend to remain that way, then our task is to transform them into rational agents. If we assume they are fundamentally illogical, we must teach them logic. And woe to us all if we fail. There will be little rationality in the world, in this view, unless we succeed in promoting it.

Research on cognitive development, however, provides a very different picture. Even by age 4 or 5, if not long before, children have reasons for their beliefs and actions, and routinely make appropriate and useful inferences, including strictly logical deductions. That is, young children are rational agents in the sense that they have reasons, and often logical reasons, for what they think and do. Rationality continues to develop, moreover, for many years. The promotion of rationality, then, must recognize that students, as early as kindergarten age, are already rational agents who make logical inferences and that they are already developing. The promotion of rationality in education cannot consist of the transformation of nonrational or irrational beings into rational agents or the instilling of logical norms. It must consist, at its core, of the promotion of development.

What, then, do we know about development beyond early childhood? It seems intuitively obvious that 5-year-old children are less rational than adults, but it is surprisingly difficult to specify just how this is so. What are young children lacking? What remains to develop?

Research on cognitive development, especially since the late 1970s, suggests that what develops, in a word, is *metacognition*, broadly construed to include conceptual knowledge about knowledge and inference as well as knowledge about, and control of, one's own cognitive structures and processes. Specifically, over the course of the elementary school years children make dramatic progress in their conceptual knowledge about the nature of inference, reasoning, and logic, and they take greater control of their own inferential processes. In adolescence and beyond, many individuals construct abstract knowledge about the fundamental nature and justification of knowledge. Preschool children may be more rational than we used to think, but there is nevertheless dramatic progress in metacognition over the course of childhood, and often beyond. The trend toward increasing knowledge and control of our inferential processes, and thus of the resulting structures of knowledge, can be considered the development of rationality.

1. Rational Agency

To be rational is to be a rational agent (Sokol and Chandler 2003; Sokol, Chandler, and Jones 2004). Even preschool children are rational agents in the sense of having reasons for their beliefs and actions. Imagine a hungry 4-year-old looking for candy. She remembers seeing some placed in the bottom drawer of the kitchen cabinet so she looks there. Why is she looking for candy? In order to eat it. Why does she look in the drawer? Because she believes that's where the candy will be. Why does she believe it will be there? Because she saw it placed there. She is a rational agent in the sense that she has reasons for her beliefs and actions.

Such reasons are enriched by appropriate inferences. Suppose the drawer has two compartments. If the candy is not in the first, our 4-year-old will readily infer that it is in the second and will look for it there. We can say she has made a disjunctive inference. Young children's inferences are sometimes mistaken, of course, but so are those of adults. When a conclusion can be deduced directly from available information, people of all ages readily make correct deductions (Braine and O'Brien 1998).

By the time they reach kindergarten, then, children are already rational in important ways (see also Robinson, Haigh, and Nurmsoo, 2008; Wellman, Cross, and Watson 2001). Even in the early years of elementary school, the promotion of rationality does not start with a blank slate. The challenge is determining what remains to develop, and what we can do to promote such development.

2. AWARENESS AND EVALUATION OF INFERENCE

Inference is an elementary cognitive function central to perceiving, interpreting, and remembering. Immediate, automatic inferences are routine from infancy (Moll, Koring, Carpenter, and Tomasello 2006) through adulthood (Moors and De Houwer 2006). What develops beyond infancy, it appears, is metacognition with respect to inference, including awareness, evaluation, and control of inference.

There is no age, it should be emphasized, when automatic inference gives way to metacognition. We continue to make automatic inferences throughout our lives and could not function otherwise. Beginning about age 6, however, we increasingly understand that we and others make inferences and increasingly recognize when an inference has been made. Our inferential processes, to be sure, remain largely unknown to us. Even when adults are unaware of their inferences, however, they know that they make inferences. It is often efficient and adaptive to combine conclusions with premises in an undifferentiated structure of knowledge, but adults understand in principle the distinction between a conclusion and the premises from which it is inferred. Preschool children, in contrast, are not just unaware of particular inferences but seem unaware of inference itself. The problem for pre-schoolers is not simply that they lose track of what they have inferred from what. The problem is that they fail to make a distinction between premises and conclusions. The developmental difference is not that preschool children are unable to make inferences or even that they are less likely than adults to do so. The difference is that they are unaware of inferential processes, both their own and those of others, and thus cannot distinguish the output of such processes from the input.

By age 6, however, children recognize inference as a potential source of knowledge for both themselves and others. An early demonstration of this was provided in 1987 by Sodian and Wimmer. Imagine a container of red balls. A ball is removed from the container and placed in an opaque bag without your seeing which ball was transferred. What color is the ball? You readily infer it to be red. Moreover, because you are aware that this conclusion can be inferred, you recognize that another person who also did not see the transfer will make the same inference you did and will know the color of the ball in the bag without having seen it.

Sodian and Wimmer presented variations on this task, including a variety of control tasks to rule out alternative explanations, to children aged 4 through 6 years. They found that children of 4 or 5 years routinely made correct inferences about the color of the ball in the bag but showed no recognition that another person could infer that color. Even when the other person correctly indicated the color of the ball, they attributed this to a lucky guess. Six-year-olds, in contrast, recognized that the other person would make the same inference they did and thus would know the ball's color. Even the 4-year-olds in Sodian and Wimmer's study, however, understood that a person who had seen the transferred ball would know its color even if they themselves did not. They understood that perception could be a source of knowledge but were oblivious to inference as a source of knowledge, although they were routinely making proper inferences.

Awareness of inference, then, apparently emerges about age 6 (see also Rai and Mitchell 2006). This is not, however, a matter of turning on, once and for all, the lamp of metacognition. Awareness of various sorts of inferences in diverse contexts continues to develop for many years (Beal 1990; Miller, Hardin, and Montgomery 2003; Pillow 2002; Pillow, Hill, Boyce, and Stein 2000), consistent with the view that such awareness, far from switching on like a light, is actively constructed (Piaget 1977/2001, 1980/2006).

Of fundamental significance for the development of rationality, increasing awareness of inference allows one to consider the possibility that some inferences are better than others in the epistemic sense that the conclusions they generate are more justifiable. In a series of two experiments, Pillow (2002) presented sets of inference-related tasks to 112 children, ranging in age from 5 through 10 years, and to 16 college undergraduates. The tasks included deductive inference, inductive inference, guessing on the basis of partial information, and pure guessing. All participants were highly certain of their conclusions in the case of deductive inferences and less certain in the case of nondeductive inferences and guesses. Even the youngest children (ages 5–6) had significantly more confidence in deductions than in guesses and justified their deductive conclusions by referring to relevant premises. By ages 8–10, children had significantly more confidence in deduction than in induction and significantly more confidence in induction than in pure guessing. Adults showed a clear hierarchy with certainty significantly higher for deductive than for inductive inferences, for inductive inferences than for informed guesses, and for informed guesses than for pure guesses.

Related research is consistent with the conclusion that children have at least some intuition of the greater certainty associated with deduction as early as age 5 or 6, but that understanding of various metalogical distinctions—deduction versus induction, inference versus guessing, informed versus pure guessing—continues to develop across childhood and beyond (Galotti, Komatsu, and Voeltz 1997; Pillow and Anderson 2006; Pillow et al., 2000).

3. Control of Inference: Thinking and Reasoning

In addition to *awareness* and *evaluation* of inference, development is marked by increasing *executive control* of our inferences. To an increasing extent, we deliberately apply and coordinate our inferences to serve our purposes. With this in mind, *thinking* may be defined as *the deliberate application and coordination of one's inferences to serve one's purposes* (Moshman 2004b, 2005). This definition recognizes that thinking is intrinsically inferential without assuming that all inferences are acts of thinking. It thus reserves the term *thinking* for deliberate processes of the sort that are typically labeled problem solving, decision making, judgment, planning, or argumentation. Such processes, and their development during childhood and beyond, have been extensively studied (Holyoak and Morrison 2005; Jacobs and Klaczynski 2005; Kuhn 2005; Kuhn and Franklin 2006).

Our increasingly ability to control our inferences, moreover, parallels our increasing ability to evaluate them. Over the course of development we increasingly apply and coordinate our inferences with the intent of conforming to what we take to be appropriate inferential norms (Smith and Vonèche 2006). When we attempt to reach justifiable conclusions by normatively constraining our own inferences, we may be said to be reasoning. *Reasoning,* in other words, is *epistemologically self-constrained thinking* (Moshman, 2004b, 2005).

Thus, our increasing control of our inferences constitutes the development of thinking, and our exercise of such control with increasing attention to normative considerations constitutes the development of reasoning. Thinking and reasoning, however, do not replace automatic inference. Not all of our inferential processes come under our control. Quite the contrary: rapid, automatic inferences are crucial to everything from immediate intuitions to recognizing faces to understanding what we read. However often we think, and however well we reason, we continue to make automatic inferences throughout our lives (Klaczynski 2004, 2005; Sloman 1996; Stanovich 1999; Stanovich and West 2000).

With respect to the development of rationality, however, it is the emergence and development of thinking and reasoning that are of central concern. To the extent that we deliberately apply and coordinate our inferences to serve our purposes, we are rational agents; to the extent that we constrain our inferences on epistemic grounds, our rationality is enhanced. Rationality is thus fundamentally metacognitive in that it entails awareness, evaluation, and control of inferential processes. Given the ubiquity and sophistication of inference through the life span, the development of rationality cannot consist of the emergence of inference or a transition from bad inferences to good ones. Rather, the development of rationality is largely the development of metacognition. To the extent that our inferences are automatic and outside our awareness, we are not rational agents even if we make what logicians deem to be good inferences. To the extent that we comprehend, evaluate, and control our inferential processes, on the other hand, we are indeed rational agents, even if we make mistakes (for related philosophical arguments see Hanna 2006; Lehrer 1990).

Flavell, Green, and Flavell (1995) conducted a series of fourteen studies that examined young children's ability to distinguish thinking from looking, seeing, doing, touching, talking, and knowing; their attributions regarding whether others are thinking and what they are thinking about; and their introspections with regard to their own thinking. The researchers concluded that preschool children (ages 3–5) understand thinking as an internal mental activity people engage in that refers to real or imaginary objects or events, but are strikingly poor at determining when they or someone else is thinking and what they or the other is or is not thinking about. Children this age, they suggest, see thinking as a matter of isolated and largely inexplicable thoughts. This is consistent with evidence discussed earlier that children under age 6 have little or no awareness of inference.

Amsterlaw (2006) studied the ability of school-age children to distinguish reasoning from nonreasoning and better reasoning from worse. In one study, 20 children in each of grades 1, 3, and 5 (roughly ages 6, 8, and 10 years, respectively), plus 20 adults, were presented individually with a series of scenarios intended to exemplify *reasoning* (such as figuring out why plants are wilting by manipulating variables and observing their effects), *shortcut problem solving* (such as flipping a coin or recalling an answer), or *automatic action* (such as removing one's hand from a hot stove or jumping out of the way of an oncoming truck). Children of all ages, as well as adults, distinguished reasoning from shortcut problem solving, evaluating the reasoning protagonists as showing more thinking and effort and taking more time. The first-graders, however, although recognizing that reasoning would also require more time than automatic action, did not distinguish reasoning from automatic action with respect to amount of thinking or mental effort. Only beginning in third grade were such distinctions seen.

In a second study, 40 children in each of grades 1, 3, and 5, and 40 adults, were asked to evaluate the quality of thinking displayed in each of a series of scenarios designed to contrast (a) thoughtful decision making vs. arbitrary selection, (b) consideration of alternatives vs. jumping to a conclusion, (c) gathering evidence vs. acting on a hunch, and (d) considering pros and cons vs. considering only pros. In the absence of outcomes, first-graders showed inconsistent preferences for good reasoning; by third grade such preferences were consistent and substantial. For half the participants at each age, however, the presentation of the scenario and reasoning was followed by an outcome statement that, in the crucial conditions, indicated a good outcome after poor reasoning (e.g., a bike chosen randomly turns out to be great) or a poor outcome after good reasoning (e.g., despite consideration of alternatives a conclusion turns out to be false). Outcome information influenced judgments about the quality of reasoning at all ages, but its influence declined sharply with age. First-graders tended to evaluate poor reasoning with good outcomes higher than good reasoning with poor outcomes; by fifth grade the pattern was reversed. Adults strongly preferred good reasoning despite bad outcomes to bad reasoning with good outcomes, though not so strongly as they preferred good to bad reasoning in the absence of any outcomes at all (Amsterlaw 2006).

Thus, elementary school children have considerable and increasing knowledge of inference, thinking, and reasoning. As we will now see, they also have considerable and increasing knowledge about logic.

4. METALOGICAL UNDERSTANDING

Logic can be identified in the sensorimotor behavior patterns of young infants and shows systematic development over the first two years of life as infants increasingly coordinate their sensorimotor action-schemes (Langer 1980, 1986). As we have seen, moreover, deductive inference is also elementary. Development in the domain of logic beyond the preschool years consists in large part of progress in metalogical understanding. We have already considered two important aspects of metalogical understanding: (1) awareness of inference as a process that generates conclusions from premises; and (2) understanding that some inferences are better than others. In addition, as we will now see, metalogical understanding includes knowledge about the logical properties of propositions, inferences, and arguments.

We are properly more certain of our deductive inferences than our inductive inferences. Deductive inferences are not just better than nondeductive inferences in the sense of allowing a somewhat higher level of certainty, however. In the case of a deductive inference, the conclusion follows necessarily from the premises. Motivated initially by the centrality of necessity in Piaget's (1981–83/1987, 1977/2001, 1980/2006) theory (see Smith 1993), there has been substantial research on the development of conceptions of necessity.

A classic measure of children's understanding of logical necessity is the Piagetian class inclusion task (Inhelder and Piaget 1964). Show a child five roses and three daisies and ask if there are more roses or more flowers. Children under age 7 or 8 typically respond that there are more roses. Although they know that roses are flowers, they compare the roses to the daisies, a class at the same level in the hierarchy of flowers. Beginning about age 7 or 8, however, children, like adults, answer that there are more flowers. Asked to justify this response, moreover, they rarely count out five roses and eight flowers to demonstrate empirically that there are indeed more flowers. Rather, they explain that there *must* be more flowers, as a matter of logical necessity, because all of the roses, plus the daisies, are flowers. Children as young as 5 can infer that if a "zog" is a rose it is a flower, an implicit transitive inference relying on their knowledge that all roses are flowers. Only beginning about age 7 or 8, however, do they usually comprehend the logical necessities intrinsic to hierarchical classification (Deneault and Ricard 2006; Perret 2004; Perret, Paour, and Blaye 2003; but see Siegler and Svetina 2006 on learning in 5-year-olds).

In a more general approach to the issue of necessity, Miller, Custer, and Nassau (2000) interviewed 100 children of ages 7, 9, and 11 about logical necessities (e.g., a light must be on or not on), mathematical necessities (e.g., 3 is bigger than 2), definitional necessities (e.g., triangles have three sides), physical laws (e.g., letting a pencil go will result in it falling), social conventions (e.g., students wear shoes in school), and an arbitrary fact (whether there was chalk in a particular box). Questions focused on spatial universality ("Is this true everywhere?"), changeability ("Could this ever change?"), and the imaginability of any alternative (including, for a sample of items, a request to draw an alternative such as "a triangle that does not have three sides"). Even the 7-year-olds showed some appreciation of necessary truths as holding everywhere and never changing. With increasing age, children made increasingly sophisticated differentiations among the various sorts of knowledge and increasingly recognized that violations of necessary truths were literally unimaginable.

Other research has generated results consistent with this picture. Children show some understanding of logical necessity, consistency, possibility, and impossibility beginning about age 6 (Beck, Robinson, Carroll, and Apperly 2006; Ruffman 1999; Somerville, Hadkinson, and Greenberg 1979; Tunmer, Nesdale, and Pratt 1983). Research also shows continuing development in the comprehension of necessity, possibility, sufficiency, indeterminacy, and associated concepts over the remaining years of childhood (Byrnes and Beilin 1991; Morris and Sloutsky 2001; Piaget 1981–83/ 1987; Pieraut-Le Bonniec 1980; Ricco 1997; Ricco, McCollum, and Wang 1997), and age-related constraints on the ability to learn such concepts (Klahr and Chen 2003).

Not surprisingly, the development of metalogical understanding continues into adolescence. Consider these arguments:

1. Elephants are plants or animals.
   Elephants are not plants.
   Therefore, elephants are animals.
2. Elephants are animals or plants.
   Elephants are not animals.
   Therefore, elephants are plants.

Even a young child would readily endorse the first argument as logical. Children as old as age 9 or 10, however, reject arguments such as number 2 as illogical (Moshman and Franks 1986) and most fail to profit even from systematic efforts to elicit understanding (Morris 2000). Most adolescents and adults, on the other hand, especially given sufficient opportunity to consider their responses, recognize in cases of this sort that the two arguments have the same logical form and are both valid. The second argument has a false second premise and a false conclusion, which is why children reject it, but it is nonetheless a valid argument in that the conclusion follows necessarily from the two premises. If the premises were true, adolescents and adults understand, the conclusion would necessarily be true as well. Even without formal coursework in logic, adolescents and adults have an understanding of logical form and validity that is largely absent in children.

5. Epistemic Cognition

Not only do people have knowledge about logic, they have knowledge about knowledge. As we will now see, children as young as age 4 have knowledge about beliefs, older children increasingly understand the interpretive and constructive nature of the mind, and adolescents and adults often develop more general under-standings about the nature and justifiability of knowledge. The development of epistemic cognition consists in large part of progress in knowledge about the nature and relation of objectivity and subjectivity.

A good place to begin the developmental story of epistemic cognition is with what has come to be known as the false-belief task. In a typical version, with typical results, you ask a 3-year-old what is inside a candy box and she says "candy." Then she opens the box and finds pencils, not candy. What, you ask her, would another child who had not yet opened the box expect? Pencils, she replies. And what had she expected? Pencils. Really? Yes, she insists. By age 4 or 5, in contrast, children respond like adults. They recognize that the new child will see a candy box and expect candy. They remember saying that there would be candy in the box and they understand that the new child will be tricked, as they were. Children of age 3 may succeed on easy versions of the task, and even 4-year-olds may have trouble with more difficult versions, but the evidence is clear that knowledge about the possi-bility of false beliefs develops dramatically between the ages of 3 and 5 (Wellman, Cross, and Watson 2001).

Understanding that people—including yourself—can hold false beliefs is widely seen by developmentalists as foundational to epistemic cognition and has been deemed evidence of at least an implicit "theory of mind." There is plenty of room for further development, however. In the classic false-belief task, a belief is false owing to lack of access to information. The other child has a false belief because she or he has been denied the evidence necessary to know the truth. Even 4-year-olds understand this. Children this age, however, do not understand that two individuals can interpret the same evidence differently.

Carpendale and Chandler (1996) presented children of ages 5, 6, 7, and 8 with tasks in which two puppets disagreed with each other about the interpretation of (a) ambiguous figures (such as the classic "duck-rabbit"); (b) lexical ambiguity (e.g., "wait for a ring"); or (c) ambiguous referential communication (e.g., specify-ing the *red* object in the face of two red objects). Every child also received, and passed, a standard false-belief task, but the 5- and 6-year-olds seemed mostly unable to comprehend the legitimacy of different interpretations in the main tasks of the study. The 7- and 8-year-olds, in contrast, often recognized and explained that the two interpretations were both reasonable given the ambiguous nature of the stimulus and that the response of a new child could not be predicted.

It appears, then, that children typically begin to develop an interpretive theory of mind about age 7 (see also Lalonde and Chandler 2002). Epistemic development continues well beyond this age, however. Over the course of the elementary school years children increasingly appreciate the active nature of human information processing with respect to diverse phenomena of attention, perception, compre-hension, memory, inference, thinking, and reasoning. The distinction between knowing and not knowing, originally dichotomous, comes to be seen as a contin-uum that acknowledges degrees of certainty. More generally, elementary school children become increasingly cognizant of their own subjectivity and that of others.

That is, they develop constructivist theories of mind (Fabricius and Schwanen-flugel 1994; Pillow 2002; Rowley and Robinson 2007; Schwanenflugel, Fabricius, and Noyes 1996).

As we have seen, however, elementary school children also have substantial and increasing metalogical understanding about objectively demonstrable necessities. In addition, they increasingly recognize a domain of taste that they see (as do most adults) as entirely subjective (Carpendale and Chandler 1996; Kuhn, Cheney, and Weinstock 2000; Rowley and Robinson, 2007). By late childhood, if not before, children are making differentiated epistemic judgments. Interpretation, they recognize, has both subjective and objective aspects. More than one interpretation is possible, but not every interpretation is equally reasonable. On one side of the domain of interpretation lies an objective domain of verifiable facts and logical necessities, perhaps including moral necessities, where disagreements can be definitively resolved. On the other side of interpretation lies the subjective domain of taste, perhaps including idiosyncratic values, where resolution is not to be expected (Moshman, 2008; Wainryb, Shaw, Langley, Cottam, and Lewis 2004).

Even as late as age 10 or 11, however, children's epistemic cognition is oriented toward understanding the epistemic properties of particular beliefs and inferences. One can consider whether a particular proposition is true, or better justified than another, without thinking explicitly and abstractly about knowledge and justification. In adolescence and beyond, to varying degrees, we see the development of conceptual knowledge about the nature and justification of knowledge in general (Chandler 1987; Chandler, Hallett, and Sokol 2002). Only beginning in adolescence, then, do we see epistemologies in a deeper and more general sense. Although theoretical accounts differ in detail and terminology, the advanced development of epistemic cognition is generally seen by developmentalists to begin with an objectivist epistemology. If development continues, it consists of a transition to a subjectivist epistemology and then, in some cases, to a rationalist epistemology, with substantial individual differences in the rate and extent of progress (Chandler 1987; Chandler et al. 2002; King and Kitchener 1994, 2002; Kuhn 2005; Kuhn et al. 2000; Kuhn and Franklin 2006; Mansfield and Clinchy 2002; Moshman 2005, 2008).

At the level of abstract epistemology, the objectivist, who may be an adolescent or adult of any age, believes objective knowledge consists of ultimate truths that can be discovered through evidence, logically proven or learned from the proper authorities. The objectivist has understood since middle childhood that diverse minds may construct divergent interpretations in particular cases, but children do not generalize their insights about the subjectivity of specific beliefs into abstract forms of epistemic relativism or skepticism, and neither do many adolescents and adults. Thus, a constructivist theory of mind, developed in middle childhood, is compatible with the objectivist epistemologies that may be constructed in adolescence and last a lifetime.

Many adolescents, however, reflecting more deeply on their subjectivity, construct a subjectivist epistemology within which truth is not only constructed from but also determined by one's point of view. Truth is thus relative; everything is, ultimately, a matter of opinion, which is to say a matter of taste. Such an epistemology reflects genuine insight into the inescapable nature of subjectivity.

Some adolescents and adults, however, construct rationalist epistemologies that recognize the possibility of coordinating diverse perspectives and advancing knowledge through evidence and argument. Without expecting to achieve an absolute or final truth, the rationalist believes ideas and viewpoints can be meaningfully evaluated, criticized, and justified, and subjective biases transcended, through rational processes of reflection, coordination, and social interaction. Thus, the rationalist agrees with the subjectivist that there is no simple truth but nevertheless believes that some ideas can be rationally judged better than others and that inquiry and argument therefore serve epistemic purposes.

It appears, then, that we can distinguish two levels in the development of epistemic cognition: a basic level associated with childhood and an advanced level associated with adolescence and adulthood. At the basic level, children come to distinguish at least three epistemic domains: an objective domain of truth, a subjective domain of taste, and a rational domain of reasonable interpretation. At the advanced level, adolescents and adults theorize about which of these domains is the domain of knowledge. The objectivist takes verifiable facts and logical proofs as paradigm cases of knowledge. The subjectivist sees knowledge, if we even call it that, as opinion, and opinion as a matter of taste. Finally, the rationalist, coordinating objectivity and subjectivity, construes knowledge, in a world of interpretation, as justified belief.

6. Autonomy, Morality, and Identity

The development of rationality, it appears, is in large part the development of our knowledge and control of our inferential processes and of the resulting knowledge. Awareness, evaluation, and control of our inferences and knowledge enhance our autonomy. But to be autonomous is not to act without constraint. Rather, to be autonomous is to constrain oneself on the basis of what one takes to be justifiable norms. The development of rationality, then, is the development of normative self-constraint, which constitutes autonomy.

The development of autonomy, moreover, is accompanied by increasing recognition of, and respect for, the autonomy of others. Theorizing in a Kantian mode, Piaget (1932/1965) famously construed morality as a logic of social interaction and highlighted the fundamental role of peer interaction in the construction of moral reciprocity. Kohlberg (1981) described increasingly abstract levels of perspective taking, culminating in the formulation of universalizable principles. Subsequent research and theory have provided richer conceptualizations of the moral domain consistent with the guiding assumption of a rational basis for morality and its development (Gibbs 2010; Moshman 2005).

In adolescence and adulthood people often construct *identities*—explicit theories of who they are as persons, including their most fundamental beliefs, goals, and commitments. To have an identity is to see oneself as a singular and continuous rational agent despite behavioral differences across contexts and changes over time. Identities provide self-constructed and enduring reasons for action and thus enhance autonomy and, potentially, rationality (Moshman 2005).

But identity is also a threat to rationality. To the extent that our beliefs are strong, and especially to the extent that they are central to our conceptions of ourselves, we are motivated to maintain them and to reject alternative beliefs. As a result of such self-serving biases, we uncritically accept and accumulate evidence and arguments consistent with our beliefs, especially those beliefs central to our identities, while subjecting alternative beliefs, evidence, and arguments to more critical scrutiny (Klaczynski 2004, 2005). Entire societies, in fact, maintain their moral self-conceptions by processing relevant information in systematically self-serving ways (Moshman 2004a, 2007).

We are, nevertheless, rational agents, and to varying extents we are committed to seeing ourselves as such, which is why we try to explain and justify our beliefs and actions to ourselves and each other. To the extent that this is centrally important to our self-conceptions, we may be said to have rationalist identities. No identity guarantees good reasoning, but a rationalist identity may motivate deliberate efforts to identify and overcome biases in seeking and processing information (Moshman 2005). Although research on rationalist identities is sparse, it seems plausible that such identities are the basis for the dispositions and attitudes that philosophers of education have associated with a "critical spirit" (Siegel 1988, 1997) and with "critical thinking in the strong sense" (Paul 1990).

7. Construction and Promotion of Rationality

Implicit in a metacognitive conception of rationality is a constructivist conception of its development. This is not to deny the logic intrinsic to our early modes of functioning, nor is it to deny the possibility and value of learning various thinking skills. But the development of rationality is not just the emergence of a logic programmed in our genes, nor is it simply the acquisition of skills taught by parents and teachers. Rather, if rationality is fundamentally a matter of knowledge and control of our knowledge and inferences, it presumably develops through processes of reflection and coordination. Rationality may be promoted, then, by encouraging and facilitating such processes.

Metacognitive reflection and coordination often occur in the context of social interaction. This includes parent/child and teacher /student interactions. In addition, there is a developmental tradition dating back to early Piaget (1932/1965) suggesting that peer interaction is especially likely to enable the self-regulated reflections and coordinations central to the development of rationality (Carpendale and Müller 2004; Kuhn 2005; Kuhn and Franklin 2006; Moshman 2005; Moshman and Geil 1998; Piaget 1965/1995). In arranging for developmentally beneficial social interactions, educators should recognize the unique value of peer interactions among students.

If rationality develops, then the promotion of rationality is the promotion of that developmental process. As a basis for addressing the promotion of rationality, then, the aim of this chapter has been to provide an account of its development.

ACKNOWLEDGMENT

I thank Dan Abbott, Deanna Kuhn, Annick Mansfield, Liz Robinson, Martin Rowley, Harvey Siegel, and Les Smith for feedback on an earlier draft.

REFERENCES

Amsterlaw, J. (2006). Children's beliefs about everyday reasoning. *Child Development, 77,* 443–64.

Beal, C. R. (1990). Development of knowledge about the role of inference in text comprehension. *Child Development, 61,* 1011–23.

Beck, S. R., Robinson, E. J., Carroll, D. J., and Apperly, I. A. (2006). Children's thinking about counterfactuals and future hypotheticals as possibilities. *Child Development, 77,* 413–26.

Braine, M. D. S., and O'Brien, D. P. (Eds.) (1998). *Mental logic.* Mahwah, NJ: Erlbaum.

Byrnes, J. P., and Beilin, H. (1991). The cognitive basis of uncertainty. *Human Development, 34,* 189–203.

Carpendale, J. I., and Chandler, M. J. (1996). On the distinction between false belief understanding and subscribing to an interpretive theory of mind. *Child Development, 67,* 1686–1706.

Carpendale, J. I. M., and Müller, U. (Eds.) (2004), *Social interaction and the development of knowledge.* Mahwah, NJ: Erlbaum.

Chandler, M. (1987). The Othello effect: Essay on the emergence and eclipse of skeptical doubt. *Human Development, 30,* 137–59.

Chandler, M. J., Hallett, D., and Sokol, B. W. (2002). Competing claims about competing knowledge claims. In B. K. Hofer and P. R. Pintrich (Eds.), *Personal epistemology: The psychology of beliefs about knowledge and knowing* (pp. 145–68). Mahwah, NJ: Erlbaum.

Deneault, J., and Ricard, M. (2006). The assessment of children's understanding of inclusion relations: Transitivity, asymmetry, and quantification. *Journal of Cognition and Development, 7*, 551–70.

Fabricius, W. V., and Schwanenflugel, P. J. (1994). The older child's theory of mind. In A. Demetriou and A. Efklides (Eds.), *Intelligence, mind, and reasoning: Structure and development* (pp. 111–32). Amsterdam: North-Holland.

Flavell, J. H., Green, F. L., and Flavell, E. R. (1995). Young children's knowledge about thinking. *Monographs of the Society for Research in Child Development, 60*(1), Serial. No. 243.

Galotti, K. M., Komatsu, L. K., and Voeltz, S. (1997). Children's differential performance on deductive and inductive syllogisms. *Developmental Psychology, 33*, 70–78.

Gibbs, J. C. (2010). *Moral development and reality: Beyond the theories of Kohlberg and Hoffman*, 2nd ed. Boston: Allyn and Bacon.

Hanna, R. (2006). *Rationality and logic*. Cambridge, MA: MIT Press.

Holyoak, K. J., and Morrison, R. G. (Eds.) (2005). *The Cambridge handbook of thinking and reasoning*. Cambridge, UK: Cambridge University Press.

Inhelder, B., and Piaget, J. (1964). *The early growth of logic in the child: Classification and seriation*. London: Routledge.

Jacobs, J. E., and Klaczynski, P. A. (Eds.) (2005). *The development of judgment and decision making in children and adolescents*. Mahwah, NJ: Erlbaum.

King, P. M., and Kitchener, K. S. (1994). *Developing reflective judgment*. San Francisco: Jossey-Bass.

—— and Kitchener, K. S. (2002). The reflective judgment model: Twenty years of research on epistemic cognition. In B. K. Hofer and P. K. Pintrich (Eds.), *Personal epistemology* (pp. 37–61). Mahwah, NJ: Erlbaum.

Klaczynski, P. A. (2004). A dual-process model of adolescent development: Implications for decision making, reasoning, and identity. In R. V. Kail (Ed.), *Advances in child development and behavior, Vol. 32* (pp. 73–123). Amsterdam: Elsevier.

—— (2005). Metacognition and cognitive variability: A dual-process model of decision making and its development. In J. E. Jacobs and P. A. Klaczynski (Eds.), *The development of judgment and decision making in children and adolescents* (pp. 39–76). Mahwah, NJ: Erlbaum.

Klahr, D., and Chen, Z. (2003). Overcoming the positive-capture strategy in young children: Learning about indeterminacy. *Child Development, 74*, 1275–96.

Kohlberg, L. (1981). *The philosophy of moral development*. San Francisco: Harper and Row.

Kuhn, D. (2005). *Education for thinking*. Cambridge, MA: Harvard University Press.

—— Cheney, R., and Weinstock, M. (2000). The development of epistemological understanding. *Cognitive development, 15*, 309–28.

—— and Franklin, S. (2006). The second decade: What develops (and how)? In D. Kuhn and R. Siegler (Eds.), *Handbook of child psychology, Vol. 2: Cognition, perception, and language* (6th ed.) (pp. 953–93), W. Damon and R. Lerner, series eds. Hoboken, NJ: Wiley.

Lalonde, C. E., and Chandler, M. J. (2002). Children's understanding of interpretation. *New Ideas in Psychology, 20*, 163–98.

Langer, J. (1980). *The origins of logic: From six to twelve months*. San Francisco: Academic Press.

—— (1986). *The origins of logic: One to two years*. Orlando, FL: Academic Press.

Lehrer, K. (1990). *Metamind*. Oxford: Oxford University Press.

Mansfield, A. F., and Clinchy, B. M. (2002). Toward the integration of objectivity and subjectivity: Epistemological development from 10 to 16. *New Ideas in Psychology, 20*, 225–62.

Miller, S. A., Custer, W. L., and Nassau, G. (2000). Children's understanding of the necessity of logically necessary truths. *Cognitive Development, 15*, 383–403.

——Hardin, C. A., and Montgomery, D. E. (2003). Young children's understanding of the conditions for knowledge acquisition. *Journal of Cognition and Development, 4*, 325–56.

Moll, H., Koring, C., Carpenter, M., and Tomasello, M. (2006). Infants determine others' focus of attention by pragmatics and exclusion. *Journal of Cognition and Development, 7*, 411–30.

Moors, A., and De Houwer, J. (2006). Automaticity: A theoretical and conceptual analysis. *Psychological Bulletin, 132*, 297–326.

Morris, A. K. (2000). Development of logical reasoning: Children's ability to verbally explain the nature of the distinction between logical and nonlogical forms of argument. *Developmental Psychology, 36*, 741–58.

Morris, B. J., and Sloutsky, V. (2001). Children's solutions of logical versus empirical problems: What's missing and what develops? *Cognitive Development, 16*, 907–28.

Moshman, D. (2004a). False moral identity: Self-serving denial in the maintenance of moral self-conceptions. In D. K. Lapsley and D. Narvaez (Eds.), *Moral development, self, and identity* (pp. 83–109). Mahwah, NJ: Erlbaum.

——(2004b). From inference to reasoning: The construction of rationality. *Thinking and Reasoning, 10*, 221–39.

——(2005). *Adolescent psychological development: Rationality, morality, and identity* (2nd edition). Mahwah, NJ: Erlbaum.

——(2007). Us and them: Identity and genocide. *Identity, 7*, 115–35.

——(2008). Epistemic development and the perils of Pluto. In M. F. Shaughnessy, M. V. J. Veenman, and C. Kleyn-Kennedy (Eds.), *Metacognition* (pp. 161–74). New York: Nova Science.

—— and Franks, B. A. (1986). Development of the concept of inferential validity. *Child Development, 57*, 153–65.

—— and Geil, M. (1998). Collaborative reasoning: Evidence for collective rationality. *Thinking and Reasoning, 4*, 231–48.

Paul, R. (1990). *Critical thinking*. Rohnert, Park, CA: Center for Critical Thinking and Moral Critique, Sonoma State University.

Perret, P. (2004). Logical necessity in class inclusion development and the ability to process transformations. *Journal of Cognitive Education and Psychology, 4*, 220–31.

——Paour, J.-L., and Blaye, A. (2003). Respective contributions of inhibition and knowledge levels in class inclusion development: A negative priming study. *Developmental Science, 6*, 283–88.

Piaget, J. (1932/1965). *The moral judgment of the child*. New York: Free Press.

——(1981–83/1987). *Possibility and necessity*. Minneapolis: University of Minnesota Press.

——(1965/1995). *Sociological studies*. London: Routledge.

——(1977/2001). *Studies in reflecting abstraction*. Hove, UK: Psychology Press.

——(1980/2006). Reason. *New Ideas in Psychology, 24*, 1–29.

Pieraut-Le Bonniec, G. (1980). *The development of modal reasoning: Genesis of necessity and possibility notions*. New York: Academic Press.

Pillow, B. H. (2002). Children's and adults' evaluation of the certainty of deductive inferences, inductive inferences, and guesses. *Child Development, 73*, 779–92.

——and Anderson, K. L. (2006). Children's awareness of their own certainty and understanding of deduction and guessing. *British Journal of Developmental Psychology, 24*, 823–49.

Pillow, B. H., Hill, V., Boyce, A., and Stein, C. (2000). Understanding inference as a source of knowledge: Children's ability to evaluate the certainty of deduction, perception, and guessing. *Developmental Psychology, 36,* 169–79.

Rai, R., and Mitchell, P. (2006). Children's ability to impute inferentially based knowledge. *Child Development, 77,* 1081–93.

Ricco, R. B. (1997). The development of proof construction in middle childhood. *Journal of Experimental Child Psychology, 66,* 279–310.

——McCollum, D., and Wang, J. (1997). Children's judgments of certainty and uncertainty on a problem where the possible solutions differ in likelihood. *Journal of Genetic Psychology, 158,* 401–10.

Robinson, E. J., Haigh, S. N., and Nurmsoo, E. (2008). Children's working understanding of knowledge sources: Confidence in knowledge gained from testimony. *Cognitive Development, 23,* 105–18.

Rowley, M., and Robinson, E. J. (2007). Understanding the truth about subjectivity. *Social Development, 16,* 741–57.

Ruffman, T. (1999). Children's understanding of logical inconsistency. *Child Development, 70,* 872–86.

Schwanenflugel, P. J., Fabricius, W. V., and Noyes, C. R. (1996). Developing organization of mental verbs: Evidence for the development of a constructivist theory of mind in middle childhood. *Cognitive Development, 11,* 265–94.

Siegel, H. (1988). *Educating reason: Rationality, critical thinking, and education.* London: Routledge.

——(1997). *Rationality redeemed? Further dialogues on an educational ideal.* London: Routledge.

Siegler, R. S., and Svetina, M. (2006). What leads children to adopt new strategies? A microgenetic/cross-sectional study of class inclusion. *Child Development, 77,* 997–1015.

Sloman, S. A. (1996). The empirical case for two systems of reasoning. *Psychological Bulletin, 119,* 3–22.

Smith, L. (1993). *Necessary knowledge: Piagetian perspectives on constructivism.* Hillsdale, NJ: Erlbaum.

—— and Vonèche, J. (Eds.) (2006). *Norms in human development.* Cambridge, UK: Cambridge University Press.

Sodian, B. and Wimmer, H. (1987). Children's understanding of inference as a source of knowledge. *Child Development, 58,* 424–33.

Sokol, B. W., and Chandler, M. J. (2003). Taking agency seriously in the theories-of-mind enterprise: Exploring children's understanding of interpretation and intention. In L. Smith, C. Rogers, and P. Tomlinson (Eds.), *Development and motivation: Joint perspectives* (pp. 125–36). *British Journal of Educational Psychology Monograph Series II, No. 2.*

——Chandler, M. J., and Jones, C. (2004). From mechanical to autonomous agency: The relationship between children's moral judgments and their developing theories of mind. *New Directions for Child and Adolescent Development, No. 103,* 19–36.

Somerville, S. C., Hadkinson, B. A., and Greenberg, C. (1979). Two levels of inferential behavior in young children. *Child Development, 50,* 119–31.

Stanovich, K. E. (1999). *Who is rational? Studies of individual differences in reasoning.* Mahwah, NJ: Erlbaum.

—— and West, R. F. (2000). Individual differences in reasoning: Implications for the rationality debate? *Behavioral and Brain Sciences, 23,* 645–65.

Tunmer, W. E., Nesdale, A. R., and Pratt, C. (1983). The development of young children's awareness of logical inconsistencies. *Journal of Experimental Child Psychology, 36,* 97–108.

Wainryb, C., Shaw, L. A., Langley, M., Cottam, K., and Lewis, R. (2004). Children's thinking about diversity of belief in the early school years: Judgments of relativism, tolerance, and disagreeing persons. *Child Development, 75,* 687–703.

Wellman, H. M., Cross, D., and Watson, J. (2001). Meta-analysis of theory-of-mind development: The truth about false belief. *Child Development, 72,* 655–84.

....

CHAPTER 9

PHILOSOPHY AND DEVELOPMENTAL PSYCHOLOGY: OUTGROWING THE DEFICIT CONCEPTION OF CHILDHOOD

....

GARETH B. MATTHEWS

JEAN PIAGET (1897–1980), the greatest and most influential developmental psychologist of the twentieth century, divided childhood into four stages: (1) the *sensorimotor* stage (from birth to about 2 years), (2) the *preoperational* stage (from about 2 to 7), (3) the stage of *concrete operations* (from 7 to 11), and (4) the stage of *formal operations* (from 11 on).[1] According to Piaget, the infant in the sensorimotor stage experiences the world through its own movements. The great cognitive achievement of this period is the infant's understanding that physical objects tend to persist ("object permanence"). Motor skills are then the chief achievement of the pre-operational stage. During the stage of concrete operations, the child develops the capacity to think logically, but only about concrete objects and events, or, as Piaget puts it, "tangible objects that can be manipulated and subjected to real action."[2] It is only in the last stage, the stage of formal operations, that the child develops a capacity for abstract reasoning.

How does philosophical thinking fit into this Piagetian picture of cognitive development? It doesn't really fit at all. Since philosophy requires abstract reasoning, it seems that, according to Piaget's developmental scheme, philosophy could not appear before the advent of formal operations—that is, at about 11 or 12 years of age. Yet there is credible evidence of philosophical thinking as early as the "preoperational" stage and throughout the stage of merely "concrete operations." Consider these examples:

1. Steve, 3 years old, was watching his father eating a banana. "You don't like bananas, do you Steve?" said the father. "No," Steve agreed and thought a moment. "If you wuz me, you wouldn't like bananas," he said. Steve reflected another moment and then asked, "Then who would be the daddy?"[3]

2. Some question of fact arose between James and his father, and James said, "*I know* it is!" His father replied, "But perhaps you might be wrong!" Denis, 4 years, 7 months, than joined in, saying, "But if he knows, he can't be wrong! *Thinking's* sometimes wrong, but *knowing's* always right!"[4]

In the first example, Steve raises a problem with what philosophers call "counterfactual identicals." If Gandhi were Hitler, would Gandhi be a warmonger or would Hitler be an advocate of passive resistance? Although philosophers have recently made great strides in understanding counterfactual reasoning, they have not, in my judgment, come up with an adequate account of counterfactual identicals. Thus, Steve's question, 'Then who would be the daddy?' is not just a philosophically interesting question; it actually poses a serious challenge to even the most sophisticated accounts of counterfactual conditionals available today.

In the second example, Denis makes a philosophically interesting comment about what it is to know something. Although there is no consensus among philosophers even today about the proper analysis of knowledge, some philosophers, beginning perhaps with Plato in his *Republic*,[5] have insisted that genuine knowledge is infallible. In any case, Denis's comment suggests this view, and the view has a distinguished pedigree. There is reason to think that Denis's remark was a teasing one. But it wouldn't be successful as a teasing remark unless it were at least plausible to think that in knowing something one cannot be wrong.[6]

These two examples of philosophical thinking in children whose age puts them at Piaget's "preoperational" stage are especially striking. But other, less dramatic examples of philosophical thinking in very young children could also be given. Can such examples be shoehorned into a developmental scheme, such as Piaget's?

Piaget sometimes suggested that he thought ontogeny recapitulates phylogeny—that is, that the development of the individual recapitulates the development of the race, or species.[7] Following this idea, the development of philosophical thinking in children would recapitulate the history of philosophy. But Piaget warned his readers against supposing that children have any well-worked-out or systematic views. "It goes without saying," he wrote, that the child does not actually work out any philosophy, properly speaking, since he never seeks to codify his reflections in anything like a system. Even as Taylor was wrong in speaking of the "savage philosophy" as that which concerns the mystic representations of primitive society, so also one cannot speak, other than by metaphor, of the philosophy of the child.

And yet, however unconnected and incoherent the spontaneous remarks of children concerning the phenomena of nature, of the mind and the origin of things may be, we are able to discern in them some constant tendencies, reappearing with each new effort of reflection. These are the tendencies that we shall call "children's philosophies."[8]

It turns out that the tendencies Piaget refers to here include such things as "childhood animism," which Piaget regarded as a primitive way of thinking to be overcome as one becomes a mature thinker. However, the examples above, and the further examples I supply in *Philosophy and the Young Child* and *The Philosophy of Childhood*, are not primitive.

Still, the idea that young children might have ideas that resemble early philosophical thought, say, pre-Socratic philosophy, is intriguing. I report in my book *The Philosophy of Childhood* some of the thoughts of Kristen, age 5, that resemble the thinking of the pre-Socratic philosopher, Parmenides:[9]

> Sitting on her bed talking to her father, [Kristen] commented, "I'm sure glad we have letters."
>
> Kristen's father was somewhat surprised at that particular expression of gratitude. "Why?" he asked.
>
> "Cause if there was no letters, there would be no sounds," explained Kristin. "If there was no sounds, there would be no words.... If there was no words, we couldn't think ... and if we couldn't think, there would be no world."

Kristin's reasoning is certainly not primitive; indeed, it is profoundly philosophical. Insofar as it resembles a saying of Parmenides,[10] it is also pre-Socratic, which conforms to the recapitulationist idea. But it hardly fits into a Piagetian developmental scheme. It certainly does not count as what Piaget called "pre-operational thinking," the kind of thinking Piaget expects from a 5-year-old. It doesn't even fit Piaget's characterization of the stage of concrete operations. If it is to be fitted into Piaget's stage scheme at all, it belongs to the stage of formal operations.

There is a general problem about trying to find children recapitulating the history of philosophy. As I try to show in my book *Philosophy and the Young Child*, one can certainly link the questions, comments, and lines of reasoning one finds in young children with passages in the writings of the great philosophers. But one cannot count on their turning up as a standard or "normal" phenomenon in every, or even in most, children. Moreover, even when one finds something in what a child says that seems to echo the thought of Descartes, or Plato, or Parmenides, or Hume, one certainly cannot expect that the child will first go through, first, a pre-Socratic phase, then enter a Platonic phase, then move on to Aristotle, and so on, up to Ludwig Wittgenstein, Martin Heidegger, and, finally, Jacques Derrida.

Piaget's most explicit suggestion about children and philosophy is that systematic thinking, anyway, appears first in adolescence, in the stage of formal operations. Thus, he writes:

> By comparison with a child, an adolescent is an individual who constructs systems and "theories." The [pre-adolescent] child does not build systems. Those which he possesses are unconscious or preconscious in the sense that they are unformulable or unformulated so that only an external observer can understand them. In other words, he thinks concretely, he deals with each problem in isolation and does not integrate his solutions by means of any general theories from which he could abstract a common principle. By contrast, what is striking in the adolescent is his interest in theoretical problems not related to everyday realities. . . . What is particularly surprising is his facility for elaborating abstract theories.[11]

In fact, developmental psychology, as Piaget envisioned it and as it is pursued today, is bound to have difficulty accounting for philosophical thinking in young children. The genius of Piaget was to identify cognitive developments that could be analyzed into distinct age-related stages, such that each stage would have its own logical structure, and the series would culminate in a fully developed structure we can find in a mature human being—that is, in the standard or normal adult. In *The Child's Conception of the World*, Piaget discusses the stages in which children come to develop a mature conception of thinking, of dreaming, of consciousness, and of life (that is, of what it is to be alive). In each case, Piaget identifies three or four stages in this development and, in each case, the series culminates, he supposes, in a mature—that is, an adult—conception.

Similarly, in his work on the conservation of substance, weight, and volume,[12] Piaget identifies four stages in a sequence that culminates in what he regards as an adult conception of how substance, weight, and volume are conserved, as when a ball of clay is flattened but there remains the same amount of substance; or when the liquid is poured into a container with a very different shape but the volume of liquid remains the same; or when grains of popcorn are popped but the weight of the popped grain remains the same as that of the unpopped corn.[13] Thus, the stage sequences are thought to map a development from immaturity in thinking to maturity.

Perversely, however, what Piaget has to say about the stages of concept acquisition in young children often avoids what is philosophically problematic, and so what is philosophically interesting, about those very concepts. In fact, the children Piaget interviews sometimes show sensitivity to what is philosophically problematic about the concept being investigated when Piaget himself shows no such sensitivity. Consider the concept of dreaming.

Piaget devotes a fascinating chapter, Chapter 3 of *The Child's Conception of the World*, to dreams. He tells us in that chapter that children first think that a dream "comes from the outside and remains external" (pp. 91*ff*). At the second stage, he says, they think a dream "arises in us but is external to us" (pp. 106*ff*). Only at the third and final stage, according to him, do they realize that a dream is "internal and of internal origin" (pp. 117*ff*). So, Piaget's probing question to his child subjects about dreaming is always, "Is the dream inside you or outside?" Children who say "outside" are placed at stage one. Children who say "both inside and outside" are placed at stage two. And children who say simply "inside" are located at the final stage, stage three.

As we soon realize, what Piaget means by saying that dreams are "inside us" is not that they can be found by opening us up. What he means is that dreams are subjective in the sense that the dreamer alone experiences the dream. But, of course, we can always talk about what was in a dream we had. And, in fact, one may oneself appear in the dream one has had. The two uses of in:—where "is in us" means "is merely subjective" and where "in the dream" means "is part of the content of the dream"—are both perfectly legitimate.

One child in Piaget's study, Fav, age 8, reports having had a dream in which the devil confronts him and wants to boil him. Fav has produced a drawing of his dream. In Fav's drawing, Fav appears twice, once in bed and once in the room, confronted by the devil, who wants to boil him. And that seems entirely sensible. After all, he was in his bed, asleep, during the time in which he had the dream. Moreover, in his dream, he was in his room, outside the bed, confronted by the devil.

Piaget concludes that Fav is only at stage two in developing an adequate concept of dreaming because Fav insists both that the dream was in him (while he was lying in bed, asleep) and also that he was in the dream he had. "When I was in bed," he says, "I was really there, and then when I was in my dream I was with the devil, and I was really there as well" (p. 111).

In this conversation with Fav, Piaget squandered a wonderful opportunity to reflect with Fav on how he could be in two places at once—in the bed all the time he was dreaming and in the dream, outside the bed confronted by the devil. Disappointingly, Piaget ignored the puzzle that Fav's dream presents and simply assigned Fav to stage two in his understanding of "where" a dream is.

What would happen, we might well want to know, if one deliberately encouraged children to pursue philosophical questions, perhaps questions that they themselves had formulated or perhaps ones that we suggested to them. In *The Philosophy of Childhood*, I offer this rather striking example of a philosophical discussion among children Piaget would have assigned to the stage of merely concrete operations:

> "Do you think there could be any such thing as the beginning of time?" I asked the dozen third and fourth graders in my philosophy discussion group in Newton, Massachusetts. (We had been trying to write a story about time travel.)
>
> "No," several of the kids replied.
>
> Then Nick spoke up. "The universe is everything and everywhere," he announced, and then paused. "But then if there was a big bang or something, what was the big bang *in*?"
>
> Nick's question had long puzzled me, too. In my own case, hearing lectures on the "big bang" theory of the origin of the universe given by learned

astrophysicists and cosmogonists had never quelled the conceptual worry that Nick articulated so simply and directly.

At the time of this discussion Nick had just turned nine years old. The others in the group were anywhere from nine to ten and a half.

Not only did Nick have a genuine puzzle about how the universe could have begun, he also had a metaphysical principle that required beginnings for everything, the universe included. Everything there is, he said, has a beginning. As he realized, that principle reintroduces the problem about the universe. "How did the universe start?" he kept asking.

"The universe," said Sam, "is what everything appeared on. It's not really anything. It's what other things started on."

"So there always has to be a universe?" I asked.

"Yeah," agreed Sam, "there always has to be a universe."

"So if there was always a universe," I went on, "there was no first time, either."

"There was a first time for certain things," explained Sam, "but not for the universe. There was a first time for the earth, there was a first time for the stars, there was a first time for the sun. But there was no first time for the universe."

"Can you convince Nick that the universe has to always be there?" I asked Sam.

Sam replied with a rhetorical question. "What would the universe have appeared on?" he asked simply.

"That's what I don't understand," admitted Nick.[14]

Among several interesting things about this discussion is the fact the Nick, only 9 years old, has this grand metaphysical principle: Everything there is, including the universe itself, has a beginning. Nick also supposes that the universe is everything and everywhere. Furthermore, he seems to assume that everything that comes into being comes into being somewhere—that is, *in* something, or as Sam puts it, *on* something. But, if there has to be something for the universe itself to come to be *in*, or *on*, then, as Nick realizes, the universe cannot be everything and everywhere. This is hardly a discussion one would expect from children who can think only in terms of concrete operations on objects that can be "manipulated and subjected to real action."

It is common for children who are told that God made the world to ask, "And who made God?" Similarly, it is common for grown-ups who are told about the Big Bang theory of the origin of the universe to ask, "And what caused the Big Bang?" To both questions the reply may be "Don't ask!"

There is, however, so far as I know, no identifiable time in the course of a child's cognitive development when we can expect that child to ask, unprompted by theology or science, how the universe came into being—or whether it could have come into being at all. Still, as the discussion above illustrates, young children are quite capable of having very interesting things to say about the origin of the universe.

Consider another spontaneous discussion among a group of children, some even younger than those involved in the exchange above. This one is recorded by Susan Isaacs, a progressive English educator early in the twentieth century:

At lunch the children talked about "the beginning of the world." Dan [six years, one month] insists, whatever may be suggested as "the beginning," there must always have been "something before that." He said, "You see, you might say that first of all there was a stone, and everything came from that—but" (with great emphasis), "*where did the stone come from?*" There were two or three variants on this theme. Then Jane [eleven years], from her superior store of knowledge, said, "Well, I have read that the earth was a piece of the sun, and that the moon was a piece of the earth." Dan, with an air of eagerly pouncing on a fallacy, "Ah! But where did *the sun* come from?" Tommy [five years, four months], who had listened to all this very quietly, now said with a quiet smile, "I know where the sun came from!" The others said eagerly, "*Do* you, Tommy? Where? Tell us." He smiled still more broadly, and said, "Shan't tell you!" to the vast delight of the others, who thoroughly appreciated the joke.[15]

So here is a genuinely philosophical topic (how the universe itself could have come to be) that young children can discuss with imagination and fervor. Yet there is no standard age when all or even most children take to this topic. And there is no obvious sequence of stages in which they will come to a mature competence in handling it.

Suppose that philosophical thinking in children cannot be shoehorned into any Piagetian-style developmental schema. Does that matter?

We might think that it doesn't matter at all. Developmental psychology studies competencies that children are not born with, but which develop in predictably age-related stages and which normal adults can be expected to have mastered. If philosophical thinking is not such a capacity, why should we care?

One important reason we should care is this. Developmental psychology has become so prominent in our culture that many of us tend to look to developmental psychologists, rather than to parents or teachers, to tell us what our children are like—or, even more important, what they *should be* like, if they are developing normally. In particular, we look to developmental psychologists to tell us what we can expect the thinking of a 4-year-old, or a 10-year-old, or an adolescent to be like. If developmental psychologists are not going to have anything of much interest to say about philosophical thinking in children, we adults, as their parents and teachers, are likely to leave philosophy out of our expectations for the children around us.

Moreover, since our faculties of education include, as indeed they should, the study of developmental psychology in their research and teaching, the influence of that discipline on teacher training encourages our teachers to think that they need make no room for philosophical thinking in the classroom. Even more perniciously, teachers of pre-adolescents may be encouraged by their study of developmental psychology to think that the stage of their children's cognitive development makes these children unfit for discussions like the two reported above. Discussion of the Big Bang, and whether we must suppose that the Big Bang had a cause, could well be thought to be "age-inappropriate" for their second- or third-grade class, which would be a shame.

Consider the example of an elementary-school teacher in a school near where I live in Massachusetts. Let's call her "Monica." One year Monica decided to have the kids in her combined first- and second-grade, bilingual class read *The Real Thief* by William Steig. She wanted to use some materials one of my associates and I had written to go with the story to stimulate philosophical discussion of issues the story raises. The vocabulary in this story is rated as appropriate for about a fourth-grade level. Monica divided her class into pairs, with a strong reader and a weaker reader in each pair. The stronger reader was to help the weaker reader with unfamiliar words.

All the characters in this story are animals. The mouse, Derek, has found, to his surprise, that he has tunneled into the King's treasury. Overwhelmed by the beauty of the gems around him, and confident that the King does not need to have all these jewels simply sitting in his treasury, Derek takes a couple home to his hovel. Later he returns to pick up another, and another, until finally he takes the King's prize jewel, the Kalakak diamond.

The King finally realizes that someone is stealing his precious stones, but he does not know whom to suspect. The only one, besides himself, who has a key to the King's treasury is the trusted guardian of his treasury, Gawain, a goose. Unable to think of anyone else who might have stolen the gems, the king decides it must have been Gawain and so puts him on trial for the theft.

Derek is actually a good friend of Gawain's. He certainly doesn't want Gawain to be convicted of stealing jewels that he, Derek, actually stole. He resolves to confess to the crime, if Gawain should be convicted. Gawain is, indeed, convicted on purely circumstantial evidence. But before he can be taken off to jail, he flies away and goes into hiding. (There is much more to the story, including elements worthy of philosophical discussion, which I omit here.)

My materials raise issues on this first part of the story, including issues about circumstantial evidence. Children are to be asked, among other things, about whether a parent or teacher has ever thought, on the basis of purely circumstantial evidence, that they had done something naughty when, in fact, they were quite innocent of the crime. And there are several follow-up questions.

The children in that first- and second-grade class became fascinated with the idea of evidence. The mother of one of the kids in the class was a lawyer. Monica asked her to visit the class to talk about legal evidence. The lawyer's presentation further increased the interest of the kids in questions of evidence. Indeed, evidence became a topic of discussion for the rest of the school year. They could be discussing a topic in history or social studies or science or mathematics, when suddenly one of the children would ask, "What evidence do we have for that?"

Monica was undaunted. Even when she had nothing in her lesson plan about evidence—in fact, even when she had never herself thought of asking for evidence for, for example, the seven times table—she was prepared to discuss evidence with the kids in her class. In this way her curriculum turned out to have a special focus on the theory of knowledge—what philosophers call "epistemology."

What a gift to the children in that class to have in Monica a teacher who was willing to reconceive her curriculum to take in, at their initiative, questions about the epistemology of history, science, and even mathematics! Her willingness to do that showed remarkable respect for the minds of those children and forged an unusual partnership in inquiry between herself and her pupils.

No doubt Piaget would have frowned on Monica's openness to inquiry-based philosophical learning. He would have thought that epistemology should wait, if not for the college or university classroom, at least until adolescence, when as he supposed a young person first enters the stage of formal operations and acquires the capacity for abstract thought about, for example, kinds of evidence and about the role that evidence plays in knowledge acquisition.

I turn now from questions about evidence to another philosophical topic that can engage the interest of schoolchildren. The inquiry I shall report on concerns the nature of happiness—in fact, the idea of total or perfect happiness. The stimulus to discussion this time is a story I made up based on a passage in Plato.

Certainly many philosophers have tried to explain what happiness is. But none of them has come up with an answer that satisfies everyone. Yet there is a way in which each of us knows perfectly well what happiness is. As Aristotle puts the point, happiness (*eudaimonia*) is that of which the following two things are true: (1) virtually everyone wants it (*Nicomachean Ethics* 1.4); and (2) no one wants it for the sake of something else, but all want it for its own sake (*Nicomachean Ethics* 1.7). A dramatic way of putting the second point is to say that it is absurd to ask *why* we want to be happy.

To dwell for a moment on the second point, suppose you tell me that you want to buy a new dress or suit. I may sensibly ask you why you want to buy a new dress or suit. You might tell me that the old one is now out of fashion. I might then ask you why you want to wear something fashionable. You might say that you want to look good at work, or at a party, and to do that you need to be wearing something fashionable. But if, somewhere along the line, you answer that you just want a new dress or suit to make you happy, it would be absurd or nonsensical for me to ask, "And why do you want to be happy?"

So these two characteristics of happiness—that virtually everyone wants it and that is absurd or nonsensical to ask *why* one wants it—provide what we can call a "formal" characterization of what happiness is. But they do not really give us any help in determining the *content* of the concept of happiness. This is what philosophers have disagreed about, and what should now engage our attention.

We might pause for a moment to note that our situation with respect to happiness is quite like that with respect to many other philosophically interesting concepts. Take the concept of a cause, or the concept of time. In a way we all know what a cause is and we all know what time is. If you tell me that the cause of the water's boiling is that it has been heated to 100° Celsius, I will understand you. And if you ask me what time it is now, I will understand what sort of answer will satisfy you. But there is also a way in which we are probably unclear about what time is and what a cause is. The way in which we do not understand what time is or what causality is is that we do not have an adequate analysis of the concept of time, or of the concept of causality, that will satisfy a tough-minded critic. Even if we ourselves think we have a pretty good analysis, there may be problems in explaining it or defending it against objections. Thus, for example, if I follow Aristotle and say that time is the measure of motion with respect to before and after, I may still not know what to say about whether everything in the universe could be completely still for a period of time, so that there would be no motion to measure time. Surely it is conceivable that the whole universe has been motionless for a time. But what could time have been then, if time were indeed the measure of motion with respect to before and after?

Happiness is like time and causality and most of the other philosophically interesting concepts. When we try to go beyond what I am calling the "formal" features of happiness, we may well find ourselves unable to say in any satisfactory way what happiness is. And yet it is important that we reflect on happiness and try to come up with at least a moderately satisfactory understanding of how it should be conceived. It is important to do this for several reasons. For one thing, since the pursuit of happiness is the overall aim that motivates our lives, it is good for us to be as clear as we can be about what, for us, happiness consists in. Moreover, since the pursuit of happiness is also the overall aim of other people around us, reflection on what *they* seem to understand as happiness will help us understand them better.

Plato, in his dialogue, *Gorgias*, has Socrates compare the various desires and appetites we have to jars—in fact, to *empty* jars, or at least *somewhat* empty jars, in the case of appetites and desires that have not been satisfied, and to *full* jars in the case of those that have been satisfied. The self-controlled person, Socrates suggests to his conversation partner, Callicles, has full jars, whereas the undisciplined person has leaky jars, which constantly need filling. Socrates thinks that the person with full jars, being a contented person, is the happier one, whereas Callicles disagrees. "The one who has filled himself up has no pleasure anymore," Callicles says (494a). By contrast, according to him, the person who has lots of appetites that constantly need to be satisfied will be the happy person.

Socrates decides to put the "leaky jar" thesis of Callicles to the test. "Tell me," he says, "whether a man who has an itch and scratches it and can scratch it to his heart's content, can be happy." (*Gorgias* 494c). Socrates's idea seems to be that scratching an itch is like trying to fill a leaky jar. Scratching the itch will not make the itch go away. Instead, the itch will go on itching. Thus, even if one gains pleasure from the scratching, scratching does nothing to relieve the itching, and so does not amount to true happiness.

Callicles finds Socrates's example disgusting, which it certainly is. But Socrates persists. Under pressure from Socrates to answer the question, Callicles finally agrees that a person who takes great pleasure in scratching himself, and scratches himself to his heart's content, will be perfectly happy.

Callicles could have protested that, according to what he had said before, to be perfectly happy one would have to have many different empty jars, or at least many partly empty jars—that is, many different unsatisfied desires. But he doesn't say that. Instead, he lets Socrates make him think about the case in which someone is so preoccupied with the pleasure of scratching that, at the moment anyway, he doesn't want anything else besides that pleasure. Callicles reluctantly concedes that such a person would be happy.

This passage in Plato inspired me to write the following story, which I call "Perfect Happiness."[16]

> "What happened in school today, Tony?" asked Tony's mother as she served him his helping of spaghetti and meatballs. The Allen family was seated around the dinner table for their evening meal.
>
> "Actually, there was something kind of cool," replied Tony. "This new kid in the class, I think his name is Roy, he cracked everybody up by something he said."
>
> "What did he say?" asked Tony's sister, Heather.
>
> "Well, you see," explained Tony, "our teacher, Ms. Hernandez, was talking about this story in which some kid said that she wanted to be totally happy. Ms. Hernandez asked us if we could think of a time when we were perfectly happy."
>
> "That's an interesting question," put in Tony's father.
>
> "Yeah, well, what this kid, Roy, said was that if he had an insect bite on his seat, you know, on his rear end, and it itched like crazy and he could scratch it as hard as he wanted to, he would be perfectly happy."
>
> "That's pretty gross," said Heather, making an ugly face.
>
> "Yeah, it was pretty gross all right," Tony agreed, "but it cracked everybody up. Kids laughed so loud you couldn't hear Ms. Hernandez trying to get us to shut up."
>
> "That was a disgusting thing to say," said Tony's mother disapprovingly.
>
> "Yeah," agreed Heather, "it was a yucky thing to say, but, you know, it's right! If scratching a very itchy insect bite gives you so much pleasure that, at that moment, you don't want anything else, then you're perfectly happy."
>
> "I wouldn't call that perfect happiness," protested Tony.
>
> "Why not?" insisted Heather. "Perfect happiness is just enjoying something, it doesn't matter what it is—scratching an insect bite, stuffing yourself with chocolate cake, whatever—enjoying it so much that you don't at that time want anything else. Do you have some other explanation of what perfect happiness is?"
>
> Tony decided to change the subject. He wished he hadn't told his family about what Roy had said in school. He didn't think Heather was right about what perfect happiness is, but he didn't know how to prove she was wrong. She was always winning arguments. He hated that.
>
> Still, Tony was puzzled about what happiness is, and especially about what perfect happiness is. Is it just enjoying something so much that the thought of everything else is blanked out? Somehow that didn't seem right to him. But what could he say about total happiness that he could defend against Heather?

A few years ago I discussed this story with a class of 5th-graders in Osaka, Japan. The Japanese children focused rather quickly on the limitation inherent in satisfying only a single desire—namely, the desire to scratch an insect bite. As Yoshimoto put his objection, "No matter how happy a person is, that person should have more desires than just this one." Callicles, in Plato's dialogue, would have been sympathetic to Yoshimoto's point. As we have already noted, Callicles portrays the fully happy person as having many desires and having the never-ending pleasure of continuing to satisfy them all.

Another child in Japan, Karini, raised the issue of the duration of one's pleasure. She refused to accept the idea that one could be perfectly happy at a single moment. "Happiness," she said, "must last a long time to be perfect."

One Japanese child, whose name I didn't get, added a humorous note. "If scratching an insect bite is complete happiness," she said, "what happens when you have many insect bites? How will you even know which insect bite to scratch?" Although this comment was humorous, it raises an important point. Some pleasures can certainly be combined with others. Thus, I can sit in front of a warm fire on a cold night and, at the same time, take pleasure in eating a piece of cake and also, perhaps, take pleasure in hearing some beautiful music. But it may be difficult or even impossible to combine distinct pleasures through a single sense modality—say, sight, or hearing, or taste, or touch.

Still, despite the problem of combining pleasures, those Japanese children insisted that perfect happiness must involve a number of different pleasures, perhaps arranged in some mutually enhancing configuration. Another child whose name I did not get put the point this way: "Scratching an insect bite and enjoying it so much that, at the moment, you don't want anything else, is only one petal of the flower of happiness."

I have also discussed this story with a 5th-grade class in an elementary school near my home in Massachusetts.[17] Very early on in that discussion, Juliane made clear how limited Tony's conception of happiness really is. According to him, as she put it, "Total happiness is just enjoying what you are doing right now and not thinking of all the other things that you want." This is a trenchant remark. It invites us to reflect on an important assumption that gives Tony's conception of happiness whatever plausibility it has. If we want to give that assumption a name, we can call it "solipsism of the present moment."

Unqualified solipsism is the view that only I and my impressions and thoughts exist. The world, other people—everything else besides me—is only a thought or impression I have, or perhaps a collection of my thoughts and impressions. Solipsism, so understood, is not, of course, a position any important philosopher defends. There would be no point in defending solipsism. If solipsism were true, there would be no one else to convince of its truth. What could be the point of my trying to convince you that you are only a figment of my imagination? In fact, the only challenge that unqualified solipsism poses is the challenge of proving that it is wrong.

Solipsism of the present moment is more interesting. It is the claim that there is nothing of value or importance except what one can appreciate at the moment. On this assumption, it is quite plausible to conclude that, if I am now enjoying something in such a way that, at the moment, I don't want anything else, I am totally happy. Juliane's comment should remind us that there may be many things we want that we are not even thinking about just now. But if those other things we want are put out of our minds by some simple pleasure we are now enjoying, we should not conclude, according to her, that this simple contentment amounts to perfect happiness.

Andrew underlined Juliane's point with an example. "You could be playing with something at your desk," he said as he himself played at his desk with his pencil, "and not paying attention to anything else." He then added in disbelief, "And that would be perfect happiness?" The implication of his tone of voice was that such a supposition was quite implausible. The broader implication was that solipsism of the present moment must be rejected.

Matt tried another tack. He, too, wanted to focus on much more than a pleasure of the present moment. But what he required for total happiness was some major accomplishment in one's life. His idea was that the satisfaction of having accomplished some major goal in life would give one happiness for a lifetime. His own choice for a major accomplishment was to become a football star—in fact, to become, as he put it, "the very best wide receiver ever."

Nathan seemed to agree with Matt. "Even after you retire," he said, "you could have the satisfaction of knowing that you were the very best." But Marissa was not convinced that one major achievement in life would guarantee total happiness. "You can get bored doing what you do best," she insisted.

Kristle was also skeptical about Matt's proposal. But the grounds for her skepticism were different from Marissa's. "You can't be happy forever," she said; "sad things will happen." Here, again, these children touched on a theme philosophers have pursued since ancient times. Plato thought that an ideally good person would be invulnerable to misfortune. Goodness, and with it happiness he thought, are conditions of one's *psyche*, or inner self. According to Plato, if one has achieved an ideally good state of one's psyche, not even torture will be a threat to one's happiness.

Of course, the achievement Plato was talking about was different from the achievement Matt had in mind. Matt thought that excellence at football—what we might call "football virtue"—would be an achievement that would guarantee happiness for a lifetime. Plato thought that the needed achievement was virtue or excellence of soul, or inner self. Yet, structurally, Matt's and Plato's suggestions were similar.

Aristotle, in contrast to Plato, thought that even the most virtuous of us is vulnerable to the vicissitudes of fortune. Mary, another pupil in that class, echoed Aristotle's caution. "Something bad can always happen," she warned, "something not in your control."

The verdict of most of the kids in that class was not just that Tony had the wrong conception of what perfect happiness is. Rather, in their view it is a mistake to aim for perfect happiness. They considered that an unattainable goal. "You can be overall happy," they agreed, "but not perfectly happy."

So those are two different discussions of perfect happiness—one in Japan and one in the United States. Does it matter whether children have the stimulus and opportunity to have discussions like this about happiness? I think it does. Education is about, among other things, helping young people to become competent, informed, thoughtful, and responsible human beings. To achieve that goal it is necessary to reflect on what it would be for one to be a flourishing human being. It is obvious that, for many people, the attraction of drug- or alcohol-induced euphoria is irresistible. But a little philosophical reflection should help us all see that such euphoria cannot be perfect happiness. Perhaps it is not even one petal of the flower of happiness. To live a happy life we need to think about what it would actually be like to live such a life.

Let's move now from reflection on happiness to philosophical reflection more generally. Why is it important to make room for such reflection with our children?

If the relationship we adults have to our children is focused solely on those competencies that we can be assumed to have and our children can be assumed to lack, then it will be no surprise if our attitude toward our children is completely paternalistic. We will picture our children according to what I call the "deficit conception of childhood." If, however, we make space for discussions with them on issues that they can help us think about freshly—discussions with them in which we, too, have something to learn, if only because we are forced to examine assumptions we have not articulated for ourselves—we will thereby foster a climate of respect otherwise missing from adult interactions with children. By respecting their questions and comments we will be helping them to respect themselves.

I do not wish to denigrate the value of what we can learn from developmental psychology. I wish only to plead that we not allow the quite understandable focus of developmental psychology to structure completely our conception of our children or our relationship with them. To learn to hear what our children have to say and to engage with them in genuinely philosophical discussions—whether at their initiative or at ours—is to get beyond what might otherwise be merely a deficit conception of childhood. It is also one of the very best ways available to us to give them, ourselves, and our relationship with them, an open future.

NOTES

1. See, for example, Ginsburg and Opper 1969.
2. Piaget 1978, p. 62.
3. Matthews 1983, pp. 18–28.
4. Isaacs 1930, p. 355. See also Matthews 1980, especially chapters 1–3.
5. Book V, at 477e.
6. Actually what is most plausible is this: it is impossible for one both to know something and also to be wrong about that very matter. I would say that that is not only plausible but also correct.
7. See the discussion of Piaget in Gould 1977, pp. 144–47.
8. Piaget 1933, p. 534.
9. Matthews 1994, p. 15.

10. A famous line from the great poem of Parmenides, "For the same thing is there both to be thought of and to be," seems to have the implication that only what can be thought of exists.

11. Piaget 1978, p. 61.

12. Piaget 1974.

13. See Piaget 1974 and my discussion of this work in Matthews 1994, chapter 4.

14. Matthews 1994, pp. 10–11.

15. Matthews 1980, p. 22.

16. Matthews 2008, pp. 33–36.

17. Matthews 2008, pp. 38–39.

REFERENCES

Ginsburg, Herbert, and Sylvia Opper. (1969). *Piaget's Theory of Intellectual Development.* Englewood Cliffs, NJ: Prentice-Hall.

Gould, Stephen. (1977). *Ontogeny and Phylogeny.* Cambridge, MA: Harvard University Press.

Isaacs, Susan. (1930). *Intellectual Growth in Young Children.* London: Routledge & Kegan Paul.

Matthews, Gareth B. (1980). *Philosophy and the Young Child.* Cambridge, MA: Harvard University Press.

—— (1983). "Philosophical Reasoning in Young Children." *Phenomenology and Pedagogy* 1: 18–28.

—— (1994). *The Philosophy of Childhood.* Cambridge, MA: Harvard University Press.

—— (2008) "Getting Beyond the Deficit Conception of Childhood." In *Philosophy in Schools*, ed. Michael Hand and Carrie Winstanley (pp. 27–40). London: Continuum.

Piaget, Jean. (1929). *The Child's Conception of the World.* London: Routledge & Kegan Paul.

—— (1933). "Children's Philosophies." In *A Handbook of Child Psychology*, ed. Carl Murchison, 2nd ed. rev. (pp. 534–47). Worcester, MA: Clark University Press.

—— (1974). *The Child's Conception of Quantities.* London: Routledge & Kegan Paul.

—— (1978). "The Mental Development of the Child." In *Six Psychological Studies*, ed. D. Elkind (pp. 3–73). New York: Vintage Press.

CHAPTER 10

SOCRATIC TEACHING AND SOCRATIC METHOD

THOMAS C. BRICKHOUSE AND NICHOLAS D. SMITH

1. INTRODUCTION

IN recent years a great deal of learned attention has been paid to what has become known as the "Socratic Method," or the "Socratic Method of Teaching," from scholars specializing in the study of ancient Greek philosophy, as well as from specialists in educational theory. Despite scholarly interest, the actual ancient texts that serve as our best sources on what Socrates himself actually said and did present several puzzles for those interested in the subject.[1] Here is a sample:

> For my whole life shows that I am this sort of person whether I did anything in public or in private, namely one who never gave in to anyone at all contrary to what's just, nor to any of those whom my accusers say are my students. I've never been anyone's teacher. But if anyone, young or old, wants to hear me talking or carrying out my own work, I never refused him, nor do I carry on a conversation when I get paid but not when I don't get paid. Instead, I make myself question rich and poor and by answering if anyone wants to hear what I have to say. And if any of those who listen becomes good or not, I couldn't rightly be held to be the cause, since I've never promised any of them any knowledge, nor have I ever taught anyone anything. If anyone says that he's ever learned anything from me or heard in private something that everyone else hasn't heard, you can be sure he's not telling the truth. (Plato, *Apology* 33a-b[2])

Why would one of the world's best-known teachers not only disclaim actually being a teacher but also contend that no one had ever learned anything from him? And if he did not teach and no one learned from him, what are we to make of the notion of a "Socratic Method of Teaching"?

2. SOCRATIC IRONY

The ground Socrates gives for disclaiming being a teacher is, as he often says in many of Plato's dialogues, that he lacks the knowledge he would need to have in order to be a teacher. In at least some instances of Socrates' profession of ignorance, however, we have some reason to think that the profession itself plays a strategic role that has led some scholars to doubt Socrates' sincerity. Consider, for example, what Socrates tells Critias, in Plato's *Charmides*:

> "But Critias," I replied, "you are talking to me as though I professed to know the answers to my own questions and as though I could agree with you if I really wished. This is not the case—rather, because of my own ignorance, I am continually investigating in your company whatever is put forward." (*Charmides* 165b-c; Sprague trans. [in Cooper 1997])

Socrates' reluctance to answer others' questions—when he is so very good at insisting that others answer his own—on the ground that he is ignorant himself has struck some as a transparent pose. Plato himself has one of his characters refuse to accept Socrates' tactics. In Book I of the *Republic*, Thrasymachus refuses to allow Socrates to continue in his normal way.

> If you truly want to know what the just is, don't only ask and gratify your love of honor by refuting whatever someone answers—you know that it is easier to ask than to answer—but answer yourself and say what you assert the just to be! (*Republic* I.336c; Bloom trans.)

In response, Socrates makes his familiar claim of incompetence, but Thrasymachus will have none of it:

> He listened, burst out laughing very scornfully, and said, "Heracles! Here is that habitual irony (*eironeia*) of Socrates. I knew it, and I predicted to these fellows that you wouldn't be willing to answer, that you would be ironic and do anything, rather than answer if someone asked you something." (*Republic* I.337a; Bloom trans.)

It is plain that Thrasymachus does not believe Socrates when the latter claims not to be able to answer questions. Rather, Thrasymachus supposes that Socrates only claims ignorance in order to maintain the upper hand in his discussions with others, for "it is easier to ask than to answer." Socrates' claim of ignorance, then, is actually "that habitual irony of Socrates"—in other words, it is feigned rather than real. And Thrasymachus is not the only one who suspects that Socrates is not telling the truth when he disclaims knowledge. Even now, the *Compact Oxford English Dictionary* gives the following definition for *irony*:

> noun (pl. **ironies**) 1 the expression of meaning through the use of language which normally signifies the opposite, typically for humorous effect. 2 a state of affairs that appears perversely contrary to what one expects. —ORIGIN Greek *eironeia* "simulated ignorance."

Several ancient and modern readers, as well, have shared Thrasymachus' suspicions about Socrates. So Quintilian claims that Socrates "was called 'ironical' because he played the part of the ignoramus who revered others as sages" (*Institutio oratoria* 9.2.46, trans. McAvoy), and in modernity, L. R. Shero (1927, p. 109), Norman Gulley (1968, p. 69), and Gregory Vlastos (1971, pp. 7–8), though the last of these later reversed his view, all regarded Socrates' profession of ignorance (as Gulley put it) as "an expedient to encourage his interlocutor to seek out the truth, to make him think that he is joining with Socrates in a voyage of discovery" (p. 69).

But if, as Thrasymachus and these others have suspected, Socrates' profession of ignorance is not entirely sincere, then we might also be suspicious of his disclaimers to be a teacher as well, for the two disclaimers are linked. Moreover, some modern scholars—especially those eager to put Socrates back on trial and to find him guilty a second time—are not only eager to find that Socrates was a teacher but they are also prepared to give some of Athens' most notorious men to Socrates as pupils.[3]

Now, there can be no doubt that sometimes Socrates lavishly praises the wisdom of interlocutors he actually regards as fools, or worse (see, e.g. *Euthyphro* 5a, *Ion* 430b-c, *Protagoras* 328d-329b, and *Euthydemus* 295e), and these episodes plainly fit the claim that Socrates is at least sometimes ironical with his interlocutors. But it is one thing to regard Socrates' praise of others as ironical and another to suppose that his self-deprecation about his own knowledge is ironical. So let us look more closely at precisely what the famous Socratic disclaimer of knowledge actually disclaims, so we can be in a better position to see whether he really did regard himself as having knowledge to share with others by instructing them.

3. SOCRATIC KNOWLEDGE

Those disinclined to count Socrates' professions of ignorance as ironical have sometimes gone so far as to say that Socrates claimed not to know anything at all.[4] In fact, however, Socrates occasionally allows that he knows something or other. For example, at *Apology* 29b, Socrates claims to know that it is always wrong to disobey one's superior. Nonetheless, because he lacks any special grounding for this bit of knowledge, he never identifies himself as a teacher of anything. So, in Plato's *Euthydemus* we find Socrates challenged by Euthydemus:

> Very well, he said, just answer. Do you know anything?
> Yes, I said, many things, but only little things.
> (*Euthydemus* 293b; Sprague trans. [in Cooper 1997])

Elsewhere, he allows that there are some things that "anyone could know" (*Ion* 532d-e), and lots of things that others know that he does *not* know, but which nonetheless do not make their possessors less ignorant than Socrates is (*Apology* 22d).

But if Socrates' famous "profession of ignorance" is not a confession that he does not know anything, then what exactly does he disclaim? Socratic ignorance is nowhere better explained than in the famous passage in Plato's *Apology*, in which he explains how the oracle at Delphi declared that no one was wiser than Socrates. In this passage (20e-23c), too long to quote here, Socrates explains how he was dumbfounded to hear that the oracle had said such a thing about him, "for I'm aware that, in fact, I'm not wise at all" (21b). Socrates is also convinced, however, that the god of Delphi cannot lie, but is notorious for riddling, and so he seeks to refute the superficial meaning of the oracle, to attempt to discern what the possible meaning of the riddling answer might be. So he goes first to a famous politician— one renowned for his wisdom—and is surprised to discover, on questioning him closely, that the politician indeed was *not* wiser than Socrates (*Ap.* 21c-d).

Socrates goes on to examine more politicians, and then some poets—again, men celebrated for their great wisdom—only to find that each one of them fails in precisely the same way to be wiser than Socrates. Whereas Socrates is aware of the extent and degree of his own ignorance, these others suppose they know what they do not know. At last, Socrates searches among more modest men, the craftsmen. Among these, he actually does find genuine knowledge—the knowledge of their crafts—but also among these, too, he finds the pretense of wisdom: the craftsmen also believe they are wise about "the most important things" when they are not (*Ap.* 22d-e).

On the basis of these investigations, Socrates draws the conclusion that he really is the wisest of men.

> But what's likely, men, is that the god is really wise and that in this oracle he means that human wisdom is of little or no value. And he appears to mean that such a person is Socrates and to have used my name, taking me as an example, as if to say, "This one of you, O human beings, is wisest, who—as Socrates does— knows that he's in truth worthless with respect to wisdom." (*Apology* 23a-b)

We can see, then, why Socrates claims not to be a teacher, and why he says no one ever learned anything from him: What knowledge he actually has is entirely ordinary and commonplace, and although others have knowledge that really is worth teaching (the knowledge of crafts, for example), Socrates does not have such knowledge. In the subjects he is most interested in—"the most important things"—neither he nor any other human beings have knowledge, and so neither does he teach anyone when he talks about these subjects nor does anyone learn anything from him.

4. DOCTRINAIRE TEACHING

Socrates' claim not to have been anyone's teacher may seem somewhat forced to us, for anyone who reads Plato's dialogues will come away convinced that Socrates has done quite a bit of teaching in his conversations with people. No doubt this very strong impression is part of why some have been inclined to regard Socrates' disclaimers as ironical and not to be taken literally. But we should understand Socrates' claim not to be a teacher within the context in which he made the claim—at his trial. Socrates had been charged with impiety, a charge that requires further specification to detail the exact way or ways in which the defendant is alleged to have offended religion or the gods. In Socrates' case, the three specifications are these: (1) Socrates fails to recognize the gods that are recognized by the state, (2) Socrates introduces new (bogus) divine things, and (3) Socrates corrupts the youth. It is the third specification that pertains to the question of teaching: Socrates, according to his prosecutor (Meletus), teaches the youth not to believe in the gods (*Apology* 26c), and to believe that the sun and moon are not gods, but that the sun is a stone and the moon is earth (*Apology* 27d). These accusations are obviously intended to fit with the general prejudices against Socrates, which he explains as "what's commonly said against all philosophers—'what's in the heavens and below the earth,' 'doesn't believe in gods,' and 'makes the weaker argument the stronger'" (*Apology* 23d). The kind of teaching that Socrates is accused of doing, by which he allegedly corrupts the young, is what might be called "doctrinaire" teaching—the kind of teaching by which one compels or persuades one's students to accept certain *doctrines* as truths the students did not know or believe prior to being taught them. So when Socrates denies that he is a teacher and denies that anyone has learned anything from him, he is denying that he is a teacher of doctrines and denies that anyone has learned any doctrines from him.

5. SOCRATIC QUESTIONING: THE *ELENCHOS*

Socrates' claim not to be a doctrinaire teacher accords well with what we actually see Socrates doing in his many conversations with others, for these conversations are at least usually refutations *ad hominem*: Socrates produces arguments *against* some thesis or a series of theses proposed by his interlocutor, and does so mostly by eliciting other claims made by the interlocutor, which Socrates then shows are inconsistent with the thesis or theses the interlocutor initially proposed. Although Socrates did not assign a special name for the ways he questioned others, scholars have come to call this distinctively Socratic style of philosophizing "the Socratic *elenchos*" ("refutation"; some scholars Latinize the word: *elenchus*), and have treated this term synonymously with the term "Socratic method." The question is: Did Socrates believe that those he questioned could actually learn anything of value from this sort of refutative questioning, and, if so, might that learning rightly be seen as the (nondoctrinaire) product of what can only be called "Socratic teaching"?

This question may be the most contentious of all of the questions scholars have tried to answer about Socrates. On the one hand, if all that Socrates does with interlocutors is bring to light inconsistencies in their beliefs—as good as it might be for them to recognize this about themselves—nothing in Socratic conversations will help the interlocutors figure out which of the inconsistent beliefs must be revised or eliminated. On the other hand, Socrates sometimes speaks to his interlocutors as if his refutations have *proven* something positive. This pair of features of Socratic questioning was dubbed by Gregory Vlastos as "*the* problem of the Socratic elenchus" (Vlastos 1994, pp. 3–4).

Scholars have offered various solutions to this problem, but none have managed to create much of a consensus. One major obstacle to scholarly agreement has been Vlastos's view that Socrates supposed himself to be *proving* something in his elenctic arguments. Vlastos's best direct textual evidence for this claim was *Gorgias* 479e. There, Socrates says, in what is admittedly remarkable language for him, "Hasn't it been proved that what was said is true?" (Vlastos trans.). However, Socrates immediately goes on to note that "what was said" is entirely conditioned upon other things his interlocutor (Polus) had agreed to, and Socrates plainly indicates that he is not committed to those other things (480e). A thorough review of the texts finds no more compelling evidence than this passage in the *Gorgias*, moreover, that Socrates conceives of himself as *proving* anything positive in his refutations.[5] Without more positive evidence that Socrates took himself to be *proving* anything, accordingly, it seems reasonable to conclude that Vlastos's "problem of the elenchus" is a nonproblem.[6]

Another obstacle to resolving scholarly disputes over the Socratic *elenchos* has been the failure of all attempts to explain precisely what "the Socratic method" actually is and what it requires. Perhaps the scholar most dedicated to this task—other than Vlastos himself—has been Hugh H. Benson, whose "doxastic constraint" provides both a necessary and sufficient condition of elenctic argument:

> (DC) Being believed by the interlocutor is a necessary and sufficient condition for being a premise of a Socratic elenchos.   (Benson 2000, p. 38)

Plainly, the advantage of this condition is that is captures well the *ad hominem* nature of Socratic philosophizing. But even if this condition actually did apply, it would provide only the thinnest possible analysis of "Socratic method," for one can readily imagine any number of kinds of arguments flowing from the mere requirement that Socrates' interlocutors believe the premises of the arguments they develop in their discussion. Moreover, if this condition were both necessary and sufficient, we should expect that the very *most* anyone could get from a Socratic discussion is a bit of self-knowledge—namely, the recognition that some of one's beliefs are inconsistent with others. This result does not trouble Benson, of course, because he is convinced that the *elenchos* was never intended, and never taken, by Socrates to teach anyone anything in a constructive way. But it also leaves very little room for those of us interested in "Socratic teaching" to see much in the way of teaching in Socratic conversations, doctrinal or otherwise.

But even this thinnest of analyses of how the *elenchos* works does not succeed, for one finds several cases of elenctic arguments in which the putatively required condition fails to apply. Although it is evident that Socrates actually often does encourage his interlocutors to express *only* their own beliefs (e.g., at *Crito* 49c-d, *Euthydemus* 286d, *Gorgias* 500b, *Protagoras* 331c and 359c-d, and *Republic* I. 337c and 346a), he will sometimes allow especially recalcitrant interlocutors to evade this condition in order to allow a fruitful conversation to continue (e.g., at *Gorgias* 497b, 499b, 501c, 504a-c, 505c, 506c, 510a, 513c, 516d, 519d-e, and 522e; *Protagoras* 333b-c, *Republic* I.350e, 351c, d, and 352b). At other times, he quite obviously leads his interlocutors in ways they find very difficult to follow, and to such a degree that it would be unreasonable to take their willingness to agree to the premises subsequently introduced as indications of genuine beliefs they actually hold (e.g., at *Euthyphro* 12a*ff*).

Perhaps it is not surprising that others have argued that we should understand the *elenchos* in a far less unified way, insisting that the only thing common to all elenctic arguments is that they are refutative.[7] But even this much unity is difficult to sustain in the light of all of our texts because, in at least some of them, the refutative function seems peripheral to Socrates' real goals, which often leave the strongest impression that he is actually arguing *for* something rather than simply seeking to refute an interlocutor. For example, most of the argument in the *Crito* seems to be more of a shared deliberation than a simple refutation of Crito. And in the *Protagoras*, Socrates explicitly exhorts Protagoras to help him to "persuade humankind" (352e) that "being overcome by pleasure" or moral weakness is not possible. Indeed, in most of Socrates' encounters with his interlocutors, including especially the most recalcitrant ones, such as Callicles in the *Gorgias* and Thrasymachus in Book I of the *Republic,* Socrates is not merely arguing *against* what his interlocutors have proposed; he is plainly also arguing *for* an opposing view.

In an earlier work, we tried to show that absolutely nothing in our texts actually licenses attributing to Socrates anything that *he himself* would say was a *method* or that he would understand as *methodical.* In fact, we have now come to the conclusion that the entire enterprise of searching for the necessary and sufficient conditions of Socratic *elenchos* has been misguided. As we put the matter in our latest contribution to this subject:

> Plato fails to give the supposedly "Socratic method" so much as a name [...] and applies the one scholars have given it [*elenchos*] to any sort of refutation at all. [...] The most reasonable conclusion, we claim, is a purely negative one: there simply is no such thing as "the Socratic *elenchos.*" (Brickhouse and Smith 2002b, p. 155)

6. THREE PLATONIC VERSIONS OF SOCRATIC PHILOSOPHIZING

We have argued thus far that the Platonic dialogues generally regarded as the most reliable sources on Socrates do not provide him with anything like a "method" for teaching. But if we broaden our survey of Plato's dialogues to include two others, we will find that Plato actually manages to depict three distinct versions of Socratic questioning, and in each version something significantly different is going on. In the first version, which we have discussed already, Socrates insists that he himself has no particular knowledge or wisdom worth sharing, and accordingly claims not to know the answers to the very questions he asks (*Charmides* 165b-c; *Republic* I.337e, 354c; *Hippias Minor* 372a-e, 376b-c). Even so, Socrates plainly has beliefs he is willing to share, and at times seems eager to argue for his own beliefs and to contrast what he regards as their merits with the faults he finds in others' views. Moreover, his focus in these dialogues is exclusively *ethical* and is often marked by a focus on *definitions*.

The second version can be found in the *Meno*, a relatively short dialogue that shares many of the features of the dialogues we have been calling "Socratic." There we find Socrates once again depicted as someone who only challenges his interlocutor's pretense of wisdom and who does not possess positive doctrines of his own. But in what is almost certainly one of the most memorable scenes in that dialogue—one that has almost certainly helped to form modern notions about "Socratic education"—Socrates actually undertakes to *demonstrate* what is plainly a positive doctrine: All learning, he proclaims, is recollection, and so "teaching" would simply be provoking memory (*Meno* 81e-82b). Socrates provides a demonstration with a slave boy of how he can use questions in order, first, to refute the boy's conceit that he knows something when he doesn't (*Meno* 82b-84e), and then to *lead him* to the correct conclusions (*Meno* 84e-85b), which is supposed to prove that the slave boy had the true opinions within him all along, and only needed to have Socrates, as teacher, tease them out with the correct line of questions.

The difference between the example of Socratic questioning in this section of the *Meno* and what we found in the other dialogues we have discussed is not just the novelty of the doctrine of recollection; for in addition to this, we suddenly find a Socrates who plainly has some understanding of geometry and who can use that understanding to guide the slave boy to what Socrates himself clearly knows to be the right answer. In none of the other dialogues does Socrates give us any reason to think he is an expert at *anything*. Moreover the topic itself is not only not within the general area of ethics, it is also one that (other) early Platonic dialogues give us no reason to suspect that Socrates held any interest in, whereas here in the *Meno*, Socrates expertly guides the slave boy with sophistication and obvious facility. In this famous passage in the *Meno*, then, we find a new use of Socrates' practice of questioning: to employ one's own knowledge in such a way as to lead another along a path that will ultimately allow the other to gain the knowledge already had by the one who leads him.

Our third version is found in the *Theaetetus*, a dialogue generally regarded as one of Plato's later works. There, we find what might appear to be a return to the nondogmatic questioner of the earliest dialogues. But this appearance is deceptive, for several new elements are introduced in the *Theaetetus* that do not square well with what we found in the first dialogues we discussed here. For the first time, for example, Socrates describes his philosophical questioning as a distinct *craft* (*technē*), which he compares to the craft of midwifery (*Theaetetus* 149a-151d). Whereas midwives help others to deliver bodily children, Socrates helps others deliver the offspring of their souls. Similarly, just as the first judgment of the viability of a physical child is made by the midwife (who may even decide to promote a miscarriage—149d), so Socrates will test others' cognitive offspring to see if they are "beautiful things" (150d), or "not worth bringing up, a wind-egg, a falsehood [which should be] exposed to die" (161a). Most importantly, just as female midwives are women who are past conceiving themselves and are barren, so, Socrates claims, he is "barren of wisdom"; however, "with those who associate with me it is different" (150c-d8).

Several differences are worth noting here. First, in obvious contrast to the Socrates who earlier denied having technical knowledge of any kind (explicitly contrasting himself with those who do have such knowledge, for example at *Apology* 22d), the Socrates of the *Theaetetus*, though proclaiming himself in every *other* way barren of wisdom, actually does possess a valuable craft. Although he does not elaborate what procedures constitute his craft, we can be sure that, just as midwives require knowledge and skill to do what they do, so Socrates must be skilled in all of the techniques his craft requires.

Second, unlike the earlier Socrates, whose mode of questioning is mostly *ad hominem* and refutative, in the *Theaetetus*, Socrates' role is to assist the interlocutor by helping his interlocutor to "give birth," if necessary, by inducing and hastening labor (149d). The reason the oppositional aspect of Socratic questioning disappears in the *Theaetetus* is that he now clearly grants to others the capacity to "give birth" to the very wisdom Socrates lacks himself. Gone now is the earlier Socrates who claimed Delphic authority for recognizing himself as the wisest of men for his awareness of his own ignorance.

Third, when Socrates characterizes his cognitive midwifery in the *Theaetetus*, he makes it plain that he actually contributes *nothing* of substance to the conversations (161b). As we saw in our discussion above, the Socrates of the earlier dialogues is prepared to express and even argue for his own views; the "midwife" of the *Theaetetus*, however, positively refuses to contribute his own views, but instead assiduously avoids stating them.

In both the *Meno* and *Theaetetus*, Socrates could well qualify as a kind of teacher—but he would be a different kind of teacher in each case. In the *Meno*, as we have now seen, Socrates uses questions to teach positive facts about a subject, on the basis of knowledge he possesses and can bring his interlocutor also to possess.

In the *Theaetetus*, Socrates again lacks all such knowledge—as he did in the earlier dialogues—but he recognizes that others may have it "within them" in some sense, and can exercise a highly developed skill by which he can bring that knowledge "into the light," whereas without the assistance Socrates' midwifery provides to those who are "in labor" with some great idea, those capable of such knowledge cannot fully realize it. The knowledge that Socrates "brings into the light," in both dialogues, is in some way already "inside" the interlocutor. Socrates' skilled questioning, in both cases, makes occurrent what would otherwise remain occult.

7. The "Socratic Method" of Teaching: Modern Applications

If what we have said thus far is correct, one might have any of three different models of questioning in mind when talking of "the Socratic method of teaching" and each one of these would have some basis in the Platonic portrait of Socrates. Readers troubled by the primarily negative tone of our exposition thus far will be relieved to find that we are inclined to make qualified endorsements of *each one* of these three different models, for contemporary uses. In order to be clear on each application, however, let us distinguish them as follows: for the distinct models given in the *Meno* and in the *Theaetetus*, let us refer to these as "the *Meno* model" and "the *Theaetetus* model," respectively. As for the kind of questioning we find Socrates using in (at least most of) Plato's earliest dialogues, we have argued that there is no specific method there at all, but we are inclined to think that what Socrates does in these dialogues would most aptly be called "the Socratic model" (or even "the genuine Socratic model"); but since all are in some sense "Socratic" (as all are given to Socrates by Plato), let us call what Socrates does in the earliest dialogues simply "the testing model," as this model is the one Socrates uses to test others for wisdom.

The *Meno* model is perhaps most widely employed (and advocated for use) in the context of legal education.[9] This model of education was first introduced into legal education by Christopher Columbus Langdell, the dean of the Harvard Law School from 1870 to 1895 (Mintz 2006, pp. 476–77). Langdell would have his students read cases, and then in class, he would call upon the students to summarize the cases and would question them in ways designed to bring out the legal theories that informed and were revealed in them (Redlich 1914, pp. 12–13). In the next several decades, Langdell's "Socratic method" became standard practice in legal education (Patterson 1951, p. 1). Although there have been several criticisms of this method (Patterson 1951, pp. 22–23; Guinier, Fine, and Balin 1997; Cicchino 2001; Mintz 2006, p. 477), a recent study reports that 97 percent of law professors continue to use the "Socratic method" of legal education—based, again, upon the

Meno model—in their first-year classes, though this percentage steadily declines in second- and third-year courses (Friedland 1996, p. 27).

Outside of the legal context, one can also easily imagine the *Meno* model used effectively in contexts relevantly like the first context in which it appeared: Socrates' questioning of Meno's slave on a problem in geometry. Generally, the "Socratic" teacher in all such cases will use knowledge the teacher already has and will ask leading questions of the student to be guided, and will adjust those questions to expose errors in the student's initial responses and to lead the student to make more fruitful responses subsequently. This way of guiding students allows them to induce basic principles as a result of their own (guided) reasoning, rather than more passively learning them by rote memory from textbooks or class lectures. The more active engagement in discovering how such reasoning systems work is plausibly supposed to lead to the student gaining better and more lasting mastery in the subject area. The *Meno* model would appear to be generally useful in areas involving abstract reasoning, where someone expert in that area can guide novices to the recognition and application of principles by which expertise in the area may be gained.

Though many scholars interested in "Socratic education" have clearly distinguished what we are calling the *Meno* model from the more open-ended forms of Socratic questioning, they have generally failed to distinguish the *Theaetetus* model from the testing model,[10] and have sometimes thereby created a certain degree of confusion about the two models, and thus how each might successfully be applied.

The primary problem we find in failing to distinguish the *Theaetetus* model from the testing model may be found in various authors' insistence on the idea that in *true* Socratic teaching (which they generally distinguish clearly from the *Meno* model), there will be "an understanding of community, of a learning context of genuine affection and concern . . . fairly called 'friendship' or a kind of 'civic love' among interlocutors" (Cicchino 2001, p. 534). Those extolling this model of teaching emphasize the "collaborative, engaging communal inquiry of Socratic teaching" (Mintz 2006, p. 486) and say some studies show not only that all students enjoy significant benefits in learning, but also that there are particular benefits to females generally, and to minority females specifically (Strong 1997, p. 133; Mintz 2006, p. 486). They also note that students themselves are strongly supportive of this form of teaching over the perceived alternatives.

But this form of "Socratic teaching," in which teachers and students are engaged in a fully cooperative and collaborative form of inquiry, best fits the *Theaetetus* model (see Mintz 2006, pp. 486–87). It does not conform well at all to the testing model of the early dialogues. In Plato's earliest dialogues, it is actually quite uncommon to see the kind of collaboration between questioner and interlocutor that contemporary advocates of "Socratic teaching" extol.[11] In fact, the atmosphere of Socratic conversations is far more confrontational than collaborative, focused as it so often is on exposing the interlocutor's pretense of wisdom. The process is generally not enjoyed by the interlocutors, and their reactions are often tense and hostile. Let us not forget, in our haste to advocate the uses of "the

Socratic method" in our classrooms, that it was precisely because of Socrates' questioning ways that he was brought to trial, found guilty, and put to death.

But all of this is not at all to say that there is no good evidence for the sort of collaboration that contemporary advocates have in mind—for the evidence is plainly there in the *Theaetetus* in the account of Socratic questioning as midwifery. The midwife comes to the one "in labor" precisely to assist that person. The midwife has no special personal stake in the process of his or her own, but works with the "patient" in such a way as to give the best assistance possible, and to ensure the most successful outcome of their cooperation. So, too, the "Socratic" teacher does not undertake to inject his or her own views into the minds of the students, but rather to work with them to help them to develop their own ideas and to achieve personal growth—a kind of growth that will be shared only incidentally (and perhaps only infrequently) by the teacher him- or herself, but in which the teacher will play a critical role as questioner and (gentle, constructive) critic.

In suggesting that the *Theaetetus* model is "collaborative," we must be careful not to overstate the role played by Socrates, the midwife, in the process of discovery. It is true that the Socrates of the *Theaetetus* is honestly engaged with his interlocutor and has no desire to "steer" the discussion to a preconception Socrates already has about how it should turn out. However, the Socrates who poses questions and the interlocutor who answers, even on this model, are not on an equal footing, and this is not because Socrates has the right answers that he is not willing to disclose. On the contrary, he claims that it has been ordained by the gods that he be barren and hence he "has no wisdom of his own to be brought forth" (150d). Thus, in understanding that there is collaboration involved in the *Theaetetus* model, we must be careful not to obscure the fact that the effective Socratic midwife exercises a special skill that is intended to bring forth what is in the other party to the discussion—something that he, himself, wholly lacks. We doubt that many modern "Socratic teachers" would be willing to concede this point with respect to their own knowledge. And as for the putative communitarian aspect of this model, it may be that two or more persons can assume the role of midwife, but at least if we take what we see in the *Theaetetus* as our guide, the parties to the discussion will not switch roles, nor may they even be able to.

Another caveat is in order. In trying to understand the motives of the appropriately "Socratic" teacher, understood on the *Theaetetus* model, it would be a mistake to think that the sort of "intellectual growth" that is to be fostered is the mere formulation of new ideas or the recognition of previously unseen consequences of a student's antecedently held views. None of our sources about Socrates ever suggest that he was interested in promoting novel thoughts, however complex or pleasant. We always see Socrates directed by one thing, the truth, and thus, the only sort of intellectual growth that matters for him is growth toward the truth. Thus, his concern for the well-being of his interlocutor, which we see most plainly in the *Theaetetus* model, is concern that the interlocutor obtain wisdom and to expose mere appearance masquerading as wisdom. Finally, the truth Socrates always exhorts his interlocutors to pursue is truth in an objective sense, a truth that demands assent from all rational inquirers. In this respect, even the proponent of the *Theaetetus* model, properly understood, must part company with those who think it makes sense to talk of something being true for one person but not for another. Socrates was no relativist.

Thus, we see even in the *Theaetetus* model that Socrates (and the Socratic teacher) always recognizes some potential for conflict—after all, his commitment to an objective conception of truth as the goal of inquiry requires the Socratic midwife to inform the parent of the intellectual offspring that "it is a phantom and not truth" and that, accordingly, it must be abandoned (151c). Despite this potential for conflict—a potential that can even destroy the very community required for this sort of "Socratic" interaction to take place at all—the goal of the *Theaetetus* model of Socratic questioning is nonetheless a *productive* one, intended to bring new knowledge or wisdom about the truth to light. It is predicated on cooperative effort, and thus is best and most effectively undertaken between people who are on friendly and mutually trusting terms. Neither of these features is much in evidence in the examples of the testing model we find in Plato's earliest dialogues.

One powerful recent advocate of what we are calling the *Theaetetus* model of "Socratic" teaching is Sophie Haroutunian-Gordon (1991).[12] The specific area in which Haroutunian-Gordan advocates the use of "Socratic" teaching is literary interpretation and evaluation. As in the case of Socratic midwifery, Haroutunian-Gordon emphasizes that students *already have within them* all that they will require to engage in productive discourse with each other and with a Socratic questioner—even as they also gain from the insights provided in discussion with other members of their learning communities.

> They come to connect their own experiences with a circumstance they might never actually experience. By exploring and interpreting that situation, their lives acquire new meaning; they uncover relations between things they had not seen before. (Haroutunian-Gordon 1991, p. 14)

So this version of "Socratic" teaching not only fully realizes and makes useful what students bring with them into the classroom in the first place, it also makes them *more fertile* by allowing them to leave the classroom with more than they brought to it—none of which, however, may have come from any injection into the discussion of the Socratic questioner's own ideas. As Socrates said in the *Theaetetus*, just as the same craft applies to planting and to sowing crops, so too the midwife, though barren him- or herself, will engage in "reliable matchmaking" (150a). This occurs, in the modern context, when the "Socratic" teacher-midwife builds the disparate individuals who first come into a class into a true learning community that pursues the truth as if with one mind.

This is not to say, however, that the testing model *requires* a lack of community, or a mood of mistrust or hostility between the interrogator and the interlocutor. This sort of "Socratic" exchange may still have a place in contemporary society, of course, in congressional hearings, in courts of law, in investigative journalism, and in public or private debates, as well as many other situations in which we contest others' claims or expertise. Gaining experience in such debates was, in the ancient Athenian context, and is still in contemporary democracies, important to political efficacy. But even where the Socrates of Plato's early dialogues seems intent on refuting his interlocutors, he also emphasizes that *he* at least regards his efforts as cooperative (see, for example, *Charmides* 166c–d).

Generally more cooperative contemporary examples of the critical and refutative aspects of Socratic inquiry may be found in the presenter-plus-commentator format of most major philosophical meetings, and indeed, in most forms of contemporary philosophical discourse. Indeed, this sort of model would appear to apply to most forms of intellectual debate in which those engaged do not regard themselves as already occupying positions of sufficient knowledge—debates, that is, between people who are aware of their own cognitive limitations in the subject and who wish to inquire with others in order to overcome or at least mitigate those limitations, which is (at least supposedly) the condition that most philosophers today find themselves in, just as Socrates regarded his own condition to be. So most contemporary philosophizing, in the broadest sense of the word, is not the expert-asking-leading-questions pattern of the *Meno* model, nor does it consist in the "barren midwife, there only to assist others in giving birth to ideas" that we find in the *Theaetetus* model. Philosophy now, as it was with Socrates, consists in recognizing our own ignorance, but wishing to eliminate or at least diminish that ignorance.[13] So we examine one another's arguments with intense critical scrutiny, and (at least when we are on our best behavior!) we also regard those who give critical attention to our arguments as our colleagues and collaborators, in the hopes that our errors will be brought to light so that we may learn from them.

Some scholars, as we noted early in this chapter, have supposed there to be no positive or constructive role at all for Socratic refutations, and have supposed instead that their sole aim is exposing false claims to or the pretense of wisdom (see, e.g., Benson 2000). But we have argued elsewhere (e.g., in Brickhouse and Smith 1994, pp. 16–23; see also May 1997) that persistent efforts of this sort can begin to allow the one who persists to develop his or her ideas in ways that avoid the pitfalls and errors past refutations have illuminated. This may be seen as a form of "backing into the future"; but as unfruitful as that awkward image may make it seem, this way of trying to learn from one's ignorant mistakes, so as to become less ignorant, does seem to be the only available way for us to escape from ignorance where there is no one else we can turn to, to teach us (by the *Meno* model or any other) what they do—and we do not—know. In most areas of philosophy, at any rate, the condition of ignorance seeking to improve itself through refutation of the errors it produces continues to be the only game in town.

We see no reason, moreover, why this same idea of Socratic investigation could not find its way into classrooms, and we suspect that it already does—at least in higher education settings, where professors do not shy away from injecting their own ideas into classroom discussions (contrary to the *Theaetetus* model), but in which competing and contrary views are also given serious exposure and consideration (contrary to the *Meno* model), and challenges to all ideas from students are encouraged and considered carefully. Once again, though, if the activity is to be carried on in anything like a truly Socratic spirit, it must be a genuine inquiry whose goal is real refutation of what is false and real understanding of the truth. In such settings, teachers may play both roles: as Socratic questioner of students, and as interlocutor to take critical questions from students. As in ancient Socratic conversations, potentially all parties to this kind of debate can learn something from the debate—especially if an idea that seemed attractive to one or more parties to the debate is refuted. In secondary and primary educational settings, for obvious reasons, the influence of the teacher as a presumed "expert" whose own ideas are not subject to critical scrutiny may weigh against the more open-ended kinds of discussions the testing model would engender, for each input of the teacher's own ideas is likely to produce an end to discussion rather than to provide a focus for criticism. For these educational settings, as recent advocates have made their cases, something more like what we have called the *Theaetetus* model would be more applicable and more effective.

NOTES

1. Socrates did not write philosophy, and so our entire knowledge of him and his philosophy derives from the testimony of those who admired him (and, in a few instances, from those who regarded him less favorably). There are many such texts, by several ancient authors, and their depictions of Socrates are so varied that our access to "the historical Socrates" is actually much discussed and disputed as "The Socrates Problem." We have defended our own view—that the early or so-called Socratic dialogues of Plato are the best source for "Socratic philosophy"—in Brickhouse and Smith 2003. But whether or not we are right about this, the controversy over "The Socrates Problem" has little effect on our topic here, as it is plainly the Socrates of Plato's early or "Socratic" dialogues that people have in mind when they discuss the "Socratic Method" or "Socratic Teaching." These dialogues are (in alphabetical order): *Apology, Charmides, Crito, Euthydemus, Euthyphro, Gorgias, Hippias Major, Hippias Minor, Ion, Laches, Lysis, Menexenus, Protagoras,* and Book I of the *Republic*. Most also include the *Meno*, as well, though the theory that learning is recollection, which appears in that work, is generally recognized as Plato's own view (one he develops in more detail in several of his later works). In style, the *Theaetetus* is similar to the earlier works, though the subject matter and the ideas developed in that dialogue do not accord with those of the early group. We will have more to say about the *Meno* and *Theaetetus* later, and how and why they present importantly different views of Socrates as a teacher from those of the other dialogues mentioned here.

2. All translations provided herein are our own (from Brickhouse and Smith 2002a), unless otherwise noted.

3. So, see, for example, Stone 1987; for our own rebuttal, see Brickhouse and Smith 1987 and 1994, pp. 155–75.

4. See, e.g. Irwin 1977, p. 40; Burnyeat 1977; Santas 1979, pp. 120, 311 n. 26.

5. Such as Benson undertakes in Benson 1995.

6. After decades of negative reactions to Vlastos's proposal, there has very recently appeared at least some modest support for it. Alejandro Santana (2007) has recently argued that *sometimes* Socrates should be seen as arguing *for* the conclusions of *elenctic* arguments, and proposed several indicators of how we may know that the argument is constructive. From the fact that Socrates is prepared to draw positive conclusions in his arguments (if it is a fact), however, it does not follow that Socrates actually takes himself to be *proving* anything, so much as drawing out the logical consequences of claims he and or his interlocutors have agreed to.

7. This sort of approach is taken in Carpenter and Polansky 2002.

8. This and all of the following translations from Plato's *Theaetetus* are from M. J. Levett, revised by M. F. Burnyeat, in Cooper 1997.

9. We owe the remainder of our discussion of legal education to Mintz 2006, including the citations of others' work.

10. See, for example, Mintz 2006, esp. pp. 486–87, though a very useful source in general.

11. Indeed, perhaps the only example of such a collaboration in one of the earliest Platonic dialogues can be found in the *Crito*, but even here Socrates' lifelong friend cannot be said to find his "collaboration" with Socrates anything but wrenching, given the outcome of the conversation, which ends all of Crito's hopes that he might still save his friend from execution.

12. Haroutunian-Gordon actually never cites the *Theaetetus*; instead she mainly cites *Republic* 518b-d, but develops a view we regard as best aligned with the *Theaetetus* model.

13. One recent advocate of this picture of contemporary philosophizing is McEvoy 1999.

REFERENCES

Ahbel-Rappe, Sara, and Rachana Kamtekar, eds. (2006). *A Companion to Socrates.* London: Blackwell.

Benson, Hugh H. (1987). "The Problem of the Elenchus Reconsidered." *Ancient Philosophy* 7: 67–85.

——(1995). "The Dissolution of the Problem of the Elenchus." *Oxford Studies in Ancient Philosophy* 13: 45–112.

——(2000). *Socratic Wisdom: The Model of Knowledge in Plato's Early Dialogues.* Oxford: Oxford University Press.

——(2002). "Problems with Socratic Method." In *Does Socrates Have a Method? Rethinking the Elenchus in Plato's Dialogues and Beyond*, ed. Gary Alan Scott (pp. 101–13). University Park, PA: Pennsylvania State University Press.

Bloom, Allan. (1968). *The* Republic *of Plato.* New York: Basic Books.

Brickhouse, Thomas C., and Nicholas D. Smith. (1984a). "The Paradox of Socratic Ignorance in Plato's *Apology*." *History of Philosophy Quarterly* 1: 125–32.

——(1984b). "Vlastos on the Elenchus." *Oxford Studies in Ancient Philosophy* 2: 185–96.

——(1987). "Socrates' Evil Associates and the Motivation for His Trial and Condemnation." In *Proceedings of the Boston Area Colloquium in Ancient Philosophy,* vol. III, ed. J. Cleary (pp. 45–71). Lanham, MD: University Press of America; reprinted in *Socrates: Critical Assessments*, vol. II, ed. W. Prior (pp. 92–110). London: Routledge.

—— (1989). *Socrates on Trial*. Oxford and Princeton: Oxford University Press and Princeton University Press.

—— (1994). *Plato's Socrates*. Oxford: Oxford University Press.

—— (2000). *The Philosophy of Socrates*. Boulder, CO: Westview.

—— (2002a). *The Trial and Execution of Socrates: Sources and Controversies*. Oxford: Oxford University Press.

—— (2002b). "The Socratic Elenchos?" In *Does Socrates Have a Method? Rethinking the Elenchus in Plato's Dialogues and Beyond*, ed. Gary Alan Scott (pp. 145–57). University Park, PA: Pennsylvania State University Press.

—— (2003). "Apology of Socratic Studies." *Polis* 20: 108–27.

Burnyeat, M. F. (1977). "Examples in Epistemology: Socrates, Theaetetus, and G. E. Moore." *Philosophy* 52: 381–98.

Carpenter, Michelle, and Ronald Polansky. (2002). "Varieties of Socratic Elenchi." In *Does Socrates Have a Method? Rethinking the Elenchus in Plato's Dialogues and Beyond*, ed. Gary Alan Scott (pp. 89–100). University Park, PA: Pennsylvania State University Press.

Cicchino, Peter M. (2001). "Love and the Socratic Method." *American University Law Review* 50: 533–50.

Cooper, John M. (1997). *Plato. Complete Works*. Indianapolis: Hackett Publishing.

Fine, Gail. (1992). "Inquiry in the *Meno*." In *The Cambridge Companion to Plato*, ed. Richard Kraut (pp. 200–26). Cambridge: Cambridge University Press.

Friedland, Steven. (1996). "How We Teach: A Survey of Teaching Techniques in American Law Schools." *Seattle University Law Review* 20: 1–44.

Geach, P. T. (1966). "Plato's *Euthyphro*: An Analysis and Commentary." *Monist* 50: 369–82.

Guinier, Lani, Michelle Fine, and Jane Balin. (1997). *Becoming Gentlemen: Women, Law School, and Institutional Change*. Boston: Beacon.

Gulley, Norman. (1968). *The Philosophy of Socrates*. London: Macmillan.

Haroutunian-Gordon, Sophie. (1991). *Turning the Soul: Teaching through Conversation in the High School*. Chicago: University of Chicago Press.

Irwin, Terrence H. (1977). *Plato's Moral Theory*. Oxford: Oxford University Press.

—— (1979). *Plato: Gorgias*. Oxford: Oxford University Press.

—— (1995). *Plato's Ethics*. Oxford: Oxford University Press.

Kahn, Charles. (1986). "Plato's Methodology in the *Laches*." *Revue Internationale de Philosophie* 40: 7–21.

Kraut, Richard. (1983). "Comments on Vlastos." *Oxford Studies in Ancient Philosophy* 1: 59–70.

—— ed. (1992). *The Cambridge Companion to Plato*. Cambridge: Cambridge University Press.

Lesher, James. (1987). "Socrates' Disavowal of Knowledge." *Journal of the History of Philosophy* 25: 275–88.

May, Hope E. (1997). "Socratic Ignorance and the Therapeutic Aim of the Elenchos." In *Wisdom, Ignorance and Virtue: New Essays in Socratic Studies*, ed. Mark McPherran (pp. 37–50). Edmonton: Academic Printing and Publishing.

McEvoy, Martin. (1999). *The Profession of Ignorance, with Constant Reference to Socrates*. Lanham, MD: University Press of America.

McPherran, Mark I., ed. (1997). *Wisdom, Ignorance and Virtue: New Essays in Socratic Studies*. Edmonton: Academic Printing and Publishing.

Mintz, Avi. (2006). "From Grade School to Law School: Socrates' Legacy in Education." In *A Companion to Socrates*, ed. Sara Ahbel-Rappe and Rachana Kamtekar (pp. 476–92). London: Blackwell.

Nehamas, Alexander. (1986). "Socratic Intellectualism." *Proceedings of the Boston Area Colloquium in Ancient Philosophy* 2: 275–316.

O'Meara, D. J., ed. (1985). *Platonic Investigations*. Washington, DC: Catholic University of America Press.

Patterson, Edwin W. (1951). "The Case Method in American Legal Education: Its Origins and Objectives." *Journal of Legal Education* 4: 11–14.

Penner, Terrence. (1992). "Socrates and the Early Dialogues." In *The Cambridge Companion to Plato*, ed. Richard Kraut (pp.121–69). Cambridge: Cambridge University Press.

Polansky, Ronald. (1985). "Professor Vlastos' Analysis of Socratic Elenchus." *Oxford Studies in Ancient Philosophy* 3: 247–60.

Redlich, Josef. (1914). *The Common Law and the Case Method in American University Law Schools: A Report to the Carnegie Foundation for the Advancement of Teaching*. Bulletin Number 8. New York: Carnegie Foundation.

Santana, Alejandro. (2007). "Constructivism and the Problem of the Socratic Elenchos." *Ancient Philosophy* 27: 251–67.

Santas, Gerasimos Xenophon. (1979). *Socrates: Philosophy in Plato's Early Dialogues*. Boston: Routledge & Kegan Paul.

Scott, Gary Alan, ed. (2002). *Does Socrates Have a Method? Rethinking the Elenchus in Plato's Dialogues and Beyond*. University Park, PA: Pennsylvania State University Press.

Shero, L. R. (1927). "Plato's *Apology* and Xenophon's *Apology.*" *Classical World* 20: 107–11.

Stone, I. F. (1987). *The Trial of Socrates*. New York: Little, Brown.

Strong, Michael. (1997). *The Habit of Thought: From Socratic Seminars to Socratic Practice*. Chapel Hill, NC: New View.

Taran, Leonardo. (1985). "Platonism and Socratic Ignorance." In *Platonic Investigations*, ed. D. J. O'Meara (pp. 85–110). Washington, DC: Catholic University of America Press.

Vlastos, Gregory. (1971). "The Paradox of Socrates." Introduction to *The Philosophy of Socrates: A Collection of Critical Essays*, ed. Gregory Vlastos. Garden City, NY: Anchor Books.

—— (1985). "Socrates' Disavowal of Knowledge." *Philosophical Quarterly* 35: 1–31.

—— (1991). *Socrates: Ironist and Moral Philosopher*. Ithaca, NY, and Cambridge: Cornell University Press and Cambridge University Press.

—— (1994). *Socratic Studies*. Edited by M. F. Burnyeat. Cambridge: Cambridge University Press.

CHAPTER 11

EDUCATING THE PRACTICAL IMAGINATION: A PROLEGOMENA

AMÉLIE RORTY

"LET'S be practical," we say; and sometimes with added gravity, "Let's be reasonable."

In ordinary life, the call to practical rationality occurs in contexts where there is a problem that needs resolution, a problem that appears to have action in the offing. It may, however, also enjoin an attitude: to forgo anger or exasperation or to work cooperatively within the constraints of non-ideal situations. While the appeal is often made to individuals, it is also directed to decision-making groups, to academic committees, to corporations and unions, to political organizations and governmental agencies. The injunctions to practicality and to reasonableness carry normative force, even for those who voluntarily commit themselves to ends they regard as immoral. Other things being equal, we typically hold ourselves obliged to being reasonable, being practical, whatever our aims may be.

The appeal to practical rationality is a plea of enormous political significance in a liberal democratic state whose citizens are presumed to participate in governance, whose informal self-ruling associations play an important role in civic life, and whose citizens hold themselves responsible for acting in accordance with their conceptions of a good life. The abilities and habits of practical reason are, in all their forms, central to a flourishing society engaged in deliberation, not only in the political sphere but also in shared civic discussion and individual reflection.

Such deliberation engages a wide and heterogeneous range of cognitive skills. It is obviously engaged in the critical evaluation of plans, proposals, and policies. More constructively, it moves to answering the productive question, "What are the alternatives?" Courses and handbooks on critical reasoning typically distinguish critical and constructive or generative functions of practical reasoning.[1] Critical reasoning detects contradictions, ambiguity, invalid inferences, overgeneralizations, misleadingly emotionally charged analogies, questionable premises and assumptions, and undefined or vague contextualization. It often places an inference, a piece of reasoning, in context to reveal presumably unwarranted conclusions or unwanted consequences. But the skills of practical reason significantly extend beyond identifying and correcting fallacies charted by logic, semantics, and rhetoric. Their constructive exercise involves the kind of speculation that penetrates the surface or manifest content of practical proposals: they specify and articulate vague assumptions; they project the wide-ranging consequences of plans and proposals; they construct thought experiments; they map the interdependence of supportive proposals. They attempt to foresee the unforeseen. Although critical reasoning and constructive thinking are analytically and sometimes pedagogically distinguishable, they are conjoined. The actual processes of critical reasoning embed and involve some exercises of constructive practical reasoning—and vice versa: they are two aspects of the same process of hypothetical and counter-factual thinking.

But in what does constructive practical reasoning actually consist? What, exactly, does it involve? I want to persuade you that imaginative thinking is an essential ingredient within practical reasoning.[2] It is not an independent "creative" or "productive" faculty, whose sources and operations are psychologically distinct from other cognitive activities like believing, desiring, or being affected. It is neither an ornament designed to enrich or embellish practical reasoning nor a rhetorical instrument to lure persuasion. The habitual exercise of its various abilities, skills, and strategies are among the constituents of robust successful practical reasoning. There is nothing magical or mysterious about the activities of imaginative thinking. Like other cognitive skills, imaginative thinking may engage a wide range of heterogeneous and independent native abilities. Like them, its exercise can be improved by education; like them, it can be enhanced by practice, strengthened by strategic techniques. Like them, its effective and successful exercise depends on becoming deeply engrained as a habitual mode of thought. And like other cognitive skills, imaginative thinking can be substantively enlarged and enriched by being collectively and dialectically exercised.

It's all very well to claim that imaginative thinking is an essential ingredient in the activities of practical reasoning. How, exactly, does it work? What, exactly, does it do? We've been using OldSpeak in talking about the role of imaginative thinking in practical reason. It is tempting to postulate and reify a special faculty, "the imagination," as the source of inventive thinking. But constructive thinking does not emerge from a special faculty, a power of the mind. It comprises a wide set of heterogeneous independent cognitive, emotional, and rhetorical activities that can become habitual and that do not need to be motivationally prompted. Replace "the imagination" with "actively applying imaginative strategies" in your computer program. Without imaginative thinking, practical reason is empty. Without practical reason, imaginative thinking is undirected, unconstrained.

Since there is evidence that at least some of the skills and strategies of imaginative thinking can be acquired, taught, and strengthened, educators bear some responsibility for promoting its productive exercise.[3] They offer courses in what used to be called "rhetoric" and now goes under the name "critical thinking." Educators in all fields and at all levels also implicitly convey the imaginative abilities and skills of their particular fields, as they affect research in academic disciplines (e.g., theoretical physics, neurophysiology, and cultural studies), as well as in civic practices (e.g., journalism, architecture, and town planning). The skills of imaginative thinking pervade communication in the most austerely scholarly and experimental investigations, as well as in the rhetoric of political persuasion in all areas of life.

I

Cohen and Isaacs, old friends who had not seen each other for a long time, ran into each other in the Port Authority Terminal in NYC. "How are you, Isaacs?" asked Cohen, "Where are you off to?" "Me, I'm going to Newark to close a real estate deal. And you?" "I'm still in costume jewelry, and off to Princeton to see my customers there." Isaacs replies: "Ah, do you remember the great times when we were kids, how we used to go on boat trips on the Hudson with Rosie and how we used to fight over her?" As they continued reminiscing, Cohen's thoughts were elsewhere. "Isaacs is no fool. He says he is going to Newark for real estate. Real estate in Newark is dead, completely dead; and what there is, Isaacs couldn't touch. He's got no brief case, and is dressed to kill. I smell cologne. And why on earth did he mention Rosie? It comes back to me: I remember hearing Rosie is now a rich widow, living in East Orange. The sly rogue is going there to get connected with Rosie." So he said, "Congratulations, you old faker! Rosie would make a good match." "How on earth did you know?" gasped Isaacs. Cohen shrugged his shoulders, "It stands to reason."

Although Cohen is not primarily engaged in practical reasoning, his inferences provide an example of the role of imaginative thinking within the kind of inference that is ingredient in practical rationality. To be sure, Cohen's detection can readily be reconstructed in a sequence of logical steps, but it is unlikely that his cognitive process occurred in that form. It was Cohen's finely tuned imaginative association of ideas rather than the formal rigor of his inference that ensured the success of his detection. It is Hume, rather than authors of current textbooks on informal logic, who provides the best understanding of Cohen's gifts in practical reason.[4]

To be sure, adherence to rational standards of consistency and validity are essential to cogent thought and successful action. Practical reason is typically characterized as involving charting, selecting, and evaluating courses of action as means toward a critically established end that can itself be subject to review by reference to a more encompassing aim. Some philosophers think that practical reason moves to moral judgment and action because it is, when resolutely exercised, self-corrective. Others think that while individual agents may be both irrational and immoral, the conception of practical reason presupposes a rational agent concerned with the integrity of her aims. While both believe that the dictates of morality and those of systematically all-things-considered practical reason conceptually coincide, they concede that the limited exercise of practical reason can nevertheless be non-moral and even immoral. Whatever the conceptual or epistemic connection between morality and practical reason may be, a shrewd Mafioso or tyrannical demagogue can, in practice, be highly adept at imaginative practical reasoning.

II

Here is a simplified model of a standard case of practical reason: a person—call her Natasha—faces a difficult choice. Having newly graduated from Columbia Teachers College, she must decide among a number of career options: volunteer to work with Teach for America, become an administrator in the State Department of Education, or teach in an elite private school in Istanbul. Reflecting on her general aims and desires, she calculates the probability that her various options would satisfy her preferences. On this basis she selects the best option available to her, all things considered. This schematic characterization of practical reason is misleading: it is radically incomplete. Our options are rarely simply presented to us *de re*: we put them to ourselves *de dicto*, seeing them in this or that light, under this or that description. We narrow or expand them, rejecting or exploring alternatives. We are active in framing and characterizing our concerns; we are engaged in generating our options, constructing and defining them.

As they are typically described, the standard models of practical reason—Aristotle's practical syllogism, Mill's Methods of Differentiation, or Kant's application of the Principle of Universalizability—cannot by themselves generate the details of specific choices or actions. Aristotle fleshed out his formal model of practical reasoning with an account of the psychology of the *phronimos*, who characteristically perceives and describes particular situations in the right way at the right time, with the right emotional and motivational balance. Mill recognized that the successful exercise of the logic of the moral sciences depends on the development of well-educated cognitive habits; Kant's moral will commands the formal structure of the motive of actions without specifying the tenor or modality of their performance. The strict application of the categorical imperative involves working through the ramified details of a set of counterfactual suppositions. All these relatively formal methods of practical reason must be supplemented and substantiated by an educated imagination capable of specifying the details of particular courses of action. To make a reasonable choice, a choice that would suit her temperament as well as her aims and desires, Natasha needs an imaginative understanding of what her options would actually entail in experience. What would it be like for an American to teach in an elite private school in Istanbul? How would it differ from the daily life of a volunteer teacher working in an inner-city school? In order to have a sense of how her options might connect to her preferences, Natasha needs to be able to imagine the phenomenology of their experiential tenor. Her options become thickly identified and described in such a way as to engage her motives by the exercise of imaginative thinking. It is active in structuring her priorities.

Here's how this works. In trying to decide among her career opportunities, Natasha reflects on the general aims and values that guide her preferences. She wants to work with disadvantaged students; she wants to reform what she sees as flaws in the New York public school system; she would like to travel and to experience life in other cultures; she needs to repay her student loans; she has conventional ambitions and wants to make a mark for herself in the profession. Let's suppose that she also understands the details of her situation and the opportunities presently available to someone with her training and talents. As a graduate of Columbia Teachers College, she is of course also in command of the relevant logical skills required to make sound inferences. With values, facts, and logic on hand, what else does Natasha need to come to a constructive practical decision? [Let's call the initial list of the options imaginatively generated their *thin* semantic descriptions.] Roughly speaking, thin descriptions of options are identified by a set of conventional semantic descriptions of action-types as they might be identified by any random set of native speakers.[5] As they stand, they do not reveal their motivational salience—their relevance to her general preferences. Options are *intentionally* identified and specified by the *thick* descriptions of the features that set their salience or significance.

The thin descriptions of a person's options do not specify the way that she envisages or imagines her options. They do not in themselves indicate what attracts her to them or how she foresees their satisfactions. In order to make a decision, Natasha needs to engage in further, more detailed imaginative practical reasoning. The thicker, more detailed descriptions of Natasha's options include the description of what is salient to the way she envisages them, as indicating their connection to her long-range preferences. Her choice depends on being able to fill in the details of her descriptions of her options, to visualize the ways they would each affect the problems, preoccupations, and satisfactions of the next few years of her life. The activities of imaginative thinking are engaged in fleshing out the thin description of her options. Natasha's inventive talents and skills—her activity in envisaging and describing their phenomenological details—will make a significant difference in the weight she accords to each of her various options. To be sure, empirical information is also necessary: the process of ranking priorities among options cannot proceed without empirical data. But no amount of factual information about Natasha's various options—for instance, that the drop-out rate among teachers working in inner-city schools is 70 percent in the first year, or that women students in Istanbul are on strike, demanding to be permitted to wear head scarves—can help her connect these options with her preferences. In any case, it takes active and free-ranging imaginative thinking to determine what empirical information might be relevant to her choice. Natasha's desires and emotions need something to work on. The standard account of preference calculations presupposes and integrates the activity of the imagination.

Let's suppose that Natasha now has imaginatively thickened her description of her options she has constructed. She's on her way to ranking their priorities, but she is not there yet. She reasonably hopes to find a practical solution that fruitfully combines as many of her aims as possible, a solution that maximizes the compatible satisfaction of her preferences. She can attempt to coordinate her apparently incompatible options in a variety of ways: she can compartmentalize them; she can compromise and compensate; she can reframe the context of her situation and its options; or she can embed her initial thinly described options in the thicker description of an enlarged alternative. Each of these strategies employs the advantages of the fluid boundaries and focus of choices and actions.

III

Here are some of the imaginative strategies available to Natasha:

- *The Compartmentalizing Strategy:* While taking a prestigious administrative position in the State Department of Education, Natasha could also volunteer as a part-time intern in Teach for America. Compartmentalizing her options and attention in this way preserves the thin description of her options, though it may jeopardize their conjoined success. Because she believes that seriously engaged teaching requires full attention, she may fear that her compromise solution will shortchange her students. Under such circumstances, compartmentalizing requires the further and often continuous exercise of imaginative improvisation in juggling her attention and her schedules.
- *The Strategy of Compromise and Compensation:* Actively regretting that she cannot or will not herself participate in Teach for America, Natasha could attempt to organize some of her colleagues to urge their congresswoman to sponsor a bill to increase funding for the organization. The thick imaginative description of her strategy preserves and unites two of her original options. If

Natasha's integrative strategies are to be effective, she needs the skills of rhetorically inventive persuasion: knowing how to appeal to considerations that move her audience, how to construct metaphors and analogies that might elicit cooperation.[6]

- *The Strategy of Reframing:* Instead of envisaging her options as the first step in the choice of a profession, Natasha could think of them as descriptions of possible adventures. She could be indifferent about which alternative she chooses, just as she might if she were deciding whether to take a trip to Peru or to Albania, believing that it doesn't matter where she goes because she'll be able to make something interesting and worthwhile of her experience whatever she does. From that point of view, she could make her choice by throwing dice or consulting Tarot cards. Imaginatively reframing her situation, Natasha has transformed the initial constraints of her practical situation.[7]

- *The Strategy of Embedding:* Suppose that in the course of constructing the thick salient description of her options, Natasha finds that she is equally drawn to becoming influential in making educational policy and to enjoying the quite different pleasures of intellectually and politically significant journalism. Using the imaginative strategies of embedding, Natasha could attempt to find—or create—a media-outreach position as spokesperson for the Department of Education, a position that would permit her to articulate and refine its policies. With a further exercise of ingenuity, she could propose a project comparing multicultural educational innovations in the United States and Turkey that would take her to Istanbul for a few months of intensive research. Imaginatively embedding and uniting several of her goals within the scope of a more substantively detailed alternative, she would have enlarged the scope of her practical reasoning. It doesn't matter which of her preferences is dominant in forming the salient thick description of her choice. She can be indifferent about which of her attitudes is embedded in the others, indifferent about whether her proposal to do research in Turkey nets her the position of spokesperson for the Department of Education, or vice versa. In any case, it was the exercise of imaginative thinking that had made her reasoning more successfully practical.

It's all very well to claim that the imagination is an essential participant in the activities of practical reasoning. It inventively generates new options; it constructs the thick descriptions that link them to an agent's motivational structure; and it crystallizes an action solution that maximizes the compatible satisfaction of a number of distinctive options. But how, exactly does it work? What, exactly does it do?

Our brief sketch of several strategies for specifying the thick description of preferences and options suggests a rough list of such activities. The list is, of course, neither exhaustive nor mutually exclusive.

- Generating or enlarging alternative options of action (e.g., Natasha's ingenious extension of her options by constructing ways to combine them)

- Generating or enlarging the conventional conceptions of the affordances of objects[8]
- Specifying the sensory and phenomenological details of options (e.g., Natasha's projecting the sounds and sights of a day of teaching in an inner-city school)[9]
- Revising descriptions and interpretations of perceptions (e.g., seeing a person as eager rather than aggressive, ingenious rather than cunning, collaborative rather than manipulative)[10]
- Developing and specifying the implications of analogies (e.g., working through the details of historical analogies: "Remember Munich" or "Remember Vietnam")
- Tracing the consequences of competing policies (e.g., tracking ramifications of the long-range consequences of redistricting voting eligibility)
- Varying some of the variables that define or compose situations or contexts (e.g., envisaging the way that rearranging the seats of an inner-city classroom might change the dynamics of student interactions)
- Specifying the details of hypothetical thought experiments (e.g., Derek Parfit's mind-body switches, Judith Thomson's Trolley Problem, or Garrett Hardin's problem of lifeboat ethics)[11]
- Role playing, modeling, pretending, simulating[12]
- Applying a general rule or maxim to hypothetical cases (e.g., working through the ramifications of applying the principle "All men are created equal . . . endowed . . . with certain unalienable rights" to Iraqi-American prisoners of war)
- Reframing, extending, or narrowing contexts (e.g., transforming a zero-sum situation into one that is not limited by a ceiling on resources)
- Revising criteria for relevance in decision making (e.g., introducing new conditions for college admissions)[13]
- Introducing distinctions to bypass the force of polarized options (e.g., nurture vs. nature, good vs. evil)[14]
- Constructing idealized models of explanation[15]
- Combining and recombining ideas to construct a novel idea
- Constructing leading metaphors[16]

Some philosophers add empathy—sharing or identifying with the emotional attitudes of others, feeling their sorrow, sharing their joys, etc.—to this list of imaginative strategies.[17] Certainly, understanding the point of view of those whose values and preferences differ from our own is essential to all practical reasoning, quite independent of whether it has any moral significance. We would all have died of thirst and loneliness long ago if we were unable to construe the beliefs, motives, and attitudes of others, including our future selves. Such interpretive projections—"seeing" the mind in the gestures and expressions of faces or envisaging changes in one's own preferences—engage the activities of imaginative thinking. But while the capacity for imaginative empathy may be one of the preconditions for robustly constructive morality, it is far from sufficient. Imaginative understanding is one thing; sharing or identifying is another; and doing so in a morally constructive way is yet another.[18] What if my neighbor is seething with envy, rage, and hatred? What good—let alone what moral good—is served by my sharing his attitudes? Even worse, the skills of empathic imagination can be exercised by the tyrant and the sadist: it enables them to know what would hurt most. In any case, the claim of empathic sharing is presumptuous; at best, the empathic imagination of Abolitionists did not involve the outrageous presumption of thinking that they could share the experiences or the feelings of a slave.[19]

To be sure, the empathic exercise of the imagination does involve being able to perceive things from another person's point of view. It does so in two ways: minimally, it involves being able to project the perspectival phenomenology of a person's experience from knowledge of his history and situation.[20] It might, for example, involve being able to project an analogy that evokes the experience of an exiled Russian poet trying to find English words for making an appropriate apology or giving a compliment. Morally, it involves understanding the sources and rationale for values and interests that differ from one's own. It involves being able explain one's own perspective in terms that others—with very different outlooks—can understand.[21] Far from *sharing* emotions, such empathic imagination involves skills of phenomenological and intellectual interpretation—precisely when attitudes are *not* shared. We may bring comfort to the grieving when we grieve with them, but we should not presume to think that we can imaginatively actually share or experience their grief. The moral exercise of the imagination in empathy can be constructive and reconstructive; it cannot be replicative.

IV

Like the strategies used in basketball and chess, all of these imaginative strategies—including those of empathy—can be acquired: they can be taught, they can be imitated, they can be practiced. Brilliant and resourceful kindergarten teachers convey the techniques and strategies of imaginative practical reason. Without marking them as "moral education," they engage children in activities common to all successful practical enterprises: role playing, asking questions to elicit suggestions for inventive uses of ordinary objects (how many things can you do with a brick?), considering the consequences of hypothetical situations (how would things be different if our playground had been on the lakeshore? how would things be different for you if you had ten sisters and brothers?). This sort of education does not stop with kindergarten. Undergraduate courses in medical ethics can raise questions that elicit the strategies of imaginative thinking about preparing interns to address the needs and fears of indigent undocumented immigrant patients; courses in business ethics can raise questions that might enable employers to think imaginatively about how to address the concerns of their employees; courses in international economics can raise questions about the possible ramifications of outsourcing. Even—perhaps especially—those engaged in training military personnel can try to develop the improvisatory skills needed for situations of great danger and uncertainty. Rather than offering appeals to the imagination conceived as a distinct generative and somewhat mysterious poetic faculty, we need to integrate these sorts of skills, strategies, and habits *within* our textbooks and courses on critical thinking, *within* philosophic treatises on moral education, *within* our ordinary educational practices.

V

Let's suppose that you've now been convinced that ambivalence can sometimes be appropriate and constructive, and that imaginative thinking is essential to its proper preservation. You might still have three objections:

1. You might object that we don't need a Gothic account of the merits of ambivalence and the strategies and techniques of imaginative thinking to acknowledge the wisdom of keeping appropriate—though incompatible— attitudes in the space of reasons and values. Common sense is enough to remind us that we may in the future need opinions and values that we've rejected in the past.
2. You might further be uncomfortable about according the imagination so much latitude and power, arguing that, as I've described it, imaginative thinking has been made to encompass all thinking, including what was, in OldSpeak, called rational inference. Why suppose, you may rightly add, that the imagination is always constructive and productive? Isn't it often wild and distracting—indeed, sometimes downright destructive?
3. Finally, you might complain that preserving ambivalence is simply an active form of the kind of tolerant fallibilism advocated by Mill and Dewey. Farsighted fallibilism argues for retaining dissenting views in the space of reasons; sound prudence argues inclusiveness in community deliberation.

We can accede to the first two objections. There are many reasons in favor of developing the skills of imaginative thinking besides their use in preserving appropriate ambivalence: it is central to the robust exercise of any kind of reasoning. What OldSpeak called "the imagination" is implicated in every act of thinking, including those activities that OldSpeak classified as "desire" and "emotion."[22] We can, of course, reconstructively analyze and distinguish many different functions, structures, and styles of thinking. But in truth, as it lives and breathes, there is only one generic kind of thinking, and it engages the manifold activities of imaginative thinking along with those we artificially distinguish as the exercise of rationality.

Moreover, practical reasoning need not always serve moral or worthy aims. Indeed, if imaginative thinking were always essentially uncritical, unconstrained, and unfettered, it would be—as it is often feared to be—dangerous.

I didn't hope to persuade you that the imagination can take over the functions of practical reason; nor that it ensures or even necessarily contributes to the effective morality of decisions and actions. I only wanted to persuade you that it was a necessary ingredient in the operation of practical reasoning. It is not—any more than is rational inference—a self-corrective activity. The considerations that limit or constrain and direct it are in the nature of the case integrated with other functions of practical reasoning, with critical rationality and with constraints of relevant reasonableness.

The counsel to preserve ambivalence differs from Mill's version of minimal fallibilism. Mill argues in favor of intellectual tolerance for opposing opinions: he urges policies that would engage us in attempting to understand and to respect the grounds of intellectual difference. In a political context, it advocates ensuring that the conditions for open dialogue are available in the public sphere. Even when it acknowledges that morality is compatible with a wide range of morally permissible values and attitudes, it presupposes that the core system of moral evaluations is coherently unified. Preserving constructive ambivalence goes beyond open-minded tolerance and support for diversity: it demands actively engaging and accommodating and endorsing the terms of distinctive multivalent values. It does so without shouldering Mill's additional conviction that imaginative and critical deliberation ultimately converges in a unified moral system.

The imaginative skills exercised in preserving appropriate ambivalence are precisely those that are also needed to resolve tensions within a community. The ingenuity exercised in compromising, compensating, embedding, and reframing an individual's ambivalence can be applied to the problems of addressing public dissent. It involves describing and constructing public policies in terms that succeed in preserving and coordinating apparently incompatible perspectives and attitudes. As citizens in a pluralistic liberal democracy, notionally committed to acknowledging and respecting a wide range of occasionally conflicting value pre-ferences, the abilities involved in addressing appropriate ambivalence are among the civic virtues. Like other civic virtues, they encompass perceptual, imaginative, rhetorical, and conceptual skills. And like other civic virtues—courage, modera-tion, resourcefulness, fortitude—they can be misused.

It should by now be obvious—or at least clear—that all practical reasoning—and for that matter, all inquiry and justification—engages the varied cognitive activities conventionally encompassed and reified as "imaginative." Every step of critical thinking, of practical deliberation, of demonstration and persuasive justification involves working through hypothetical counterfactual inferences. When it is radically constructive, it can realign and revise conventional classifica-tions and fundamental categories. The strategies of imaginative thinking are not just stylistic ornaments in otherwise rigorous linear Bauhaus thinking. They are essential to the very process of any kind of reasoning, whether practical or theoretical, exploratory or demonstrative. Developing the capacities engaged in preserving the terms of ambivalence is central to integrating the rigor of rationality with the generative power of imaginative thinking. Rationality without the imagination is empty and sterile; the imagination without rationality is chaotic.[23]

NOTES

This paper is a section of *On the Other Hand: The Ethics of Ambivalence*—a work in progress—in which I argue that ambivalence is sometimes appropriate and justified. I offer examples of character traits about which we would do well to be ambivalent (e.g., integrity and courage); I also argue that we benefit from some commonly censured activities like self-deception and creating conflict. The active exercise of strategies of imaginative thinking enables us to preserve appropriate and constructive ambivalence. These skills can be analyzed and developed in much the same way that we acquire the habits of critical thinking and collaborative cooperation.

1. See Hugo Bedau and Sylvan Barnett, *Critical Thinking: A Brief Guide* (Boston: Freeman and Worth, 2004); Martin Gardner, *Fads and Fallacies in the Name of Science* (New York: Dover, 1957); S. Morris Engel, *With Good Reason* (New York: St. Martin's, 1994).

2. See Iris Murdoch, "The Idea of Perfection," in *The Sovereignty of the Good* (New York: Routledge, 1970); Sabina Lovibond, *Reason and Imagination in Ethics* (Minneapolis: University of Minnesota Press, 1983); Jonathan Adler, "Distortion and Excluded Middles" (unpublished lecture); Paul Harris, *The World of the Imagination* (Oxford: Blackwell, 2000); Gregory Currie and Ian Ravenscroft, *Recreative Minds: Imagination in Philosophy and Psychology* (New York: Oxford University Press, 2003); Michael Tye, *The Imagery Debate* (Cambridge, MA: MIT Press, 1991); Maurice Merleau Ponty, *Phenomenology of Perception* (London: Routledge, 2002). For an exhaustive account of the history and varieties of imaginative thinking, see Eva Brann, *The World of the Imagination* (Lanham, MD: Rowman and Littlefield, 1991); Sharon Bailin, *Achieving Extraordinary Ends* (Boston: Kluwer, 1988).

3. See Nigel Blake, Paul Smeyers, Richard Smith, and Paul Standish, eds., *Blackwell Guide to the Philosophy of Education* (Malden, MA: Blackwell, 2003), especially articles by Sharon Bailin, Harvey Siegel, and Maxine Greene; Maxine Greene, *Releasing the Imagination* (San Francisco: Jossey-Bass, 1995); Howard Gardner, *Multiple Intelligences* (New York: Basic Books, 2006), and *Frames of Mind* (New York: Basic Books, 1993); Sharon Bailin, ed., *Teaching and Learning Outside the Box: Inspiring the Imagination across the Curriculum* (New York: Teachers College Press, 2007).

4. See Don Garrett, *Cognition and Commitment in Hume's Philosophy* (New York: Oxford University Press, 1997), chap. 1.

5. See Clifford Geertz, "Thick Description: Towards an Interpretive Theory of Culture," in *The Interpretation of Culture* (New York: Basic Books, 1973), pp. 3–32.

6. See Avishai Margalit, *Rotten Compromise and Honorable Peace*. Tanner Lectures (Cambridge, MA: Harvard University Press, 2005).

7. See Erving Goffmman, *Frame Analysis* (Cambridge, MA: Harvard University Press, 1979); J. A. Fodor, *The Modularity of Mind* (Cambridge, MA: MIT Press, 1983); Z. W. Pylyshyn, ed., *The Robot's Dilemma: The Frame Problem in Artificial Intelligence* (Norwood, NJ: Ablex, 1987); D. Sperber and D. Wilson, *Relevance* (Cambridge: Blackwell, 1995); Avishai

Margalit, "Ideals and Second Bests," in *Philosophy for Education*, ed. Seymour Fox (Jerusalem: van Leer Foundation, 1983).

8. See J. J. Gibson, *The Senses Considered as Perceptual Systems* (Boston: Houghton Mifflin, 1966).

9. Merleau Ponty, *Phenomenology of Perception*; see the essays in Ned Block, *Imagery* (Cambridge, MA: MIT Press, 1984); E. Casey, *Imagining: A Phenomenological Study* (Bloomington: Indiana University Press, 1976); J.-P. Sartre, *The Psychology of the Imagination* (New York: Washington Square Press, 1966).

10. Murdoch, "The Idea of Perfection."

11. See Derek Parfit, *Reasons and Persons* (New York: Oxford University Press, 1984); Judith Thomson, "A Defense of Abortion," *Philosophy and Public Affairs* 1, no. 1 (1971): 47–66; Garrett Hardin, "Lifeboat Ethics," *Psychology Today* (Sept. 1974): 1–6; Roy Sorenson, *Thought Experiments* (New York: Oxford University Press, 1992); Martin Bunzl, "The Logic of Thought Experiments," *Synthese* 106 (1996): 227–40.

12. See Colin McGinn, *Mindsight* (Cambridge, MA: Harvard University Press, 2004); Shaun Nichols and Stephen Stich, *Mindreading* (New York: Oxford University Press, 2004); Kendall Walton, *Mimesis as Make Believe* (Cambridge, MA: Harvard University Press, 1990); Alvin Goldman, *Simulating Minds* (New York: Oxford University Press, 2006), chap. 11.

13. See Margalit, "Ideals and Second Bests."

14. See Adler, "Distortion and Excluded Middles."

15. See Gerald Holton, *The Scientific Imagination: Case Studies* (Cambridge: Cambridge University Press, 1987); Ulric Neisser, "Perceiving, Anticipating, Imagining," *Minnesota Studies in the Philosophy of Science*, vol. 9, C. Wade Savage, ed., Minneapolis: University of Minnesota Press, pp. 89–105; Nancy Nersessian, *Creating Scientific Concepts* (Cambridge, MA: MIT Press, 2008); N. J. Nersessian, "Model-based Reasoning in Distributed Cognitive Systems," *Philosophy of Science* 73, no. 5 (2006): 699–709; N. J. Nersessian, "Interpreting Scientific and Engineering Practices: Integrating the Cognitive, Social, and Cultural Dimensions," in *Scientific and Technological Thinking*, eds. M. Gorman, R. Tweney, and D. Gooding (Hillsdale, NJ: Erlbaum, 2005), pp.17–56; Christopher Hill, "Modality, Modal Epistemology and the Metaphysics of Consciousness," in *The Architecture of the Imagination*, ed. Shaun Nichols (New York: Oxford University Press, 2006), pp. 205–36; Tamara Szabo Gendler and John Hawthorne, eds., *Conceivability and Possibility* (New York: Oxford University Press, 2002).

16. See G. Lakoff and M. Johnson, *Metaphors We Live By* (Chicago: University of Chicago Press, 1980); Mark Turner and Gilles Fauconnier, *The Way We Think: Conceptual Blending and the Mind's Hidden Complexities* (New York: Basic Books, 2002).

17. See Carol Gilligan, *In a Different Voice* (Cambridge, MA: Harvard University Press, 1993); Nel Noddings, *Caring* (Berkeley: University of California Press, 2003). For a refined discussion of the moral force of empathy, see Stephen Darwall, "Empathy, Sympathy, Care," *Philosophical Studies* 89 (1998): 261–82.

18. See Bernard Williams, "Imagination and the Self," pp. 26–45 in his book *Problems of the Self* (Cambridge: Cambridge University Press, 1973).

19. Elizabeth Spellman, *Fruits of Sorrow: Framing our Attention to Suffering* (Boston: Beacon Press, 1997).

20. See Williams, "Imagination and the Self"; Richard Wollheim, "Imagination and Identification," in *On Art and the Mind* (Cambridge, MA: Harvard University Press, 1974), pp. 54ff; Tamara Szabo Gendler, "On the Relation between Pretense and Belief," in *Imagination, Philosophy and the Arts*, eds. Matthew Kieran and Dominic Lopes (London:

Routledge, 2003), pp. 125–41; Adam Morton, "Imagination and Misimagination," in *The Architecture of the Imagination*, ed. Shaun Nichols (New York: Oxford University Press, 2006), pp. 57–72.

21. See T. M. Scanlon, *What We Owe to Each Other* (Cambridge, MA: Harvard University Press, 1998).

22. An extended discussion of the role of imaginative thinking in preserving appropriate ambivalence is to appear in my in-progress work *On the Other Hand: The Ethics of Ambivalence*.

23. I am grateful to Jonathan Adler, Melissa Barry, Catherine Elgin, Steven Gerrard, Susan Russinoff, and Ronald de Sousa for stimulating and helpful discussions; Adler and Harvey Siegel for their helpful suggestions; and the donors of the William C. and Ida Friday Fellowship at the National Humanities Center for their generous support.

PART III

MORAL, VALUE, AND CHARACTER EDUCATION

CHAPTER 12

CARING, EMPATHY, AND MORAL EDUCATION

MICHAEL SLOTE

IN 1982, Carol Gilligan published *In a Different Voice: Psychological Theory and Women's Development*, a book that argued that women tend to approach moral issues in terms of caring for and emotional connection to others, whereas men more frequently think of moral questions in terms of justice, rights, and autonomy from others.[1] In 1984, Nel Noddings spelled out some of the features of a "feminine" ethics of caring in *Caring: A Feminine Approach to Ethics and Moral Education*.[2] Since then, the ethics of care (or caring) has become an increasingly visible way of thinking—both practically and theoretically—about morality; in fact, the ever-growing volume of books and articles on this subject—many critical, but many seeking for the best way positively to develop such an ethics—might well lead one to conclude that the ethics of care is the predominant form of feminist ethics at present. But care ethics also has deep historical roots. It is very much in keeping with the eighteenth-century moral sentimentalism of Hutcheson and Hume, with its central emphasis on benevolence and feeling, and moral sentimentalism itself was clearly influenced by Judeo-Christian ideas about kindness and love (*agape*).

Since Gilligan and Noddings were both educationists, it is hardly surprising that, almost from its inception, the ethics of care has been seen as relevant to the philosophy of education and, in particular, to moral education. But I believe that relevance has not been fully appreciated, and I would like here to draw out some of the implications an ethics of care has for moral education, in terms that are at least somewhat unfamiliar.

The relevance of caring for moral education is significantly mediated by considerations having to do with the nature, development, and moral implications of empathy, and so I want to spell out some connections between caring and empathy that bear crucially on issues of education. First, we have to say just a bit more about the nature of care ethics as it has developed in recent years in the work of many authors. Next, I will show the relevance of empathy to care ethics and to moral education based on such ethics. Finally, I want to discuss recent work by Nel Noddings in order to highlight some ways in which the relevance of caring to moral education may be relatively *independent* of questions of empathy.

1. THE ETHICS OF CARE

As I said above, there has been an enormous amount of work on care ethics since Gilligan's and Noddings's (first) books appeared. I can't possibly refer to *all* the highpoints of that literature in this brief compass, but let me at least mention some of them. Care ethics has largely developed in response to the idea of the difference between the way men and women approach morality. This idea has, of course, a history. Freud notoriously claimed that women lack the sense of justice that men have, and Lawrence Kohlberg's studies of moral development led him to conclude that women are by and large at a lower stage of moral development than men. But Gilligan pointed out that those studies were conducted entirely with male subjects, and she proposed that the differences Kohlberg detected between women and men should be seen as no more than that: differences, rather than a sign of male superiority. The title of her book shows you how important that conclusion was for her, and its importance for those developing an ethics of care subsequently is demonstrated by the emphasis they have placed on features of such an ethics that differ from and indeed are opposed to various elements of supposedly male ethical thinking.

Thus, males are supposed to prefer to use rationally justifiable abstract/universal rules or principles in dealing with specific moral problems; but according to an ethics of caring, the right way to deal with other people is to focus our attention directly on them. The ethics of care says we should be emotionally engaged with other people as individuals; we should be trying to help them and thinking about what would be good for them, rather than about moral principles or rules and what *they* say we should do. Also, according to such ethics, the basis of our desire to help others is not (some justification that derives from) the rational or reasoning side of our nature, but rather stems from our emotional capacities for engagement with and concern for other people—and from the high value we place on such engagement and concern as an ideal in our lives.[3] (Think of how even religious skeptics can be moved, e.g., by the idea that God is love.)

The stress care ethics places on (direct) connection with others also leads it to focus less on our rights *against* interference by others and more on what we owe to others, independently of voluntary choice. We have no decisive choice over what our parents do for us, but we can owe them gratitude nonetheless; and we may have no choice as to whether we may come upon a child drowning right in front of us, yet we are morally obligated to help such a child (at least if we can do so without enormous risk to ourselves). By contrast, and according to many care ethicists, traditional liberalism approaches morality via the assumption that our moral connections with others are contingent and voluntary (hence the popularity of social-contract theories). It stresses our fundamental autonomy or separateness from others, and that is perhaps why liberals frequently defend the right of people to engage in hate speech against blacks, Jews, and other groups by reference to the moral importance of autonomy/liberty—whereas an ethics of care that puts the primary stress on how well we are *connected* with others would tend to be morally opposed to such speech.[4]

Now in saying all this I have been going along with an assumption made by many care ethicists that has frequently been questioned. In her book *In a Different Voice*, Gilligan reports studies that purport to show that women and men, on the whole or on average, think differently about morality in the ways she indicated. But her methodology and results have subsequently been questioned, and new studies—some concluding that masculine-feminine differences exist, others just the opposite—have also been reported. It is impossible for us to engage with this literature in any serious way.[5] But it is worth noting that in work that appeared after *In a Different Voice*, Gilligan modified some of her original claims and pointed out, for example, that a great number of women seem to approach morality with the "voice" of justice rather than of caring.[6]

However, many of those who favor an ethics of caring do so independently of whether men and women are as different as Gilligan originally suggested. They point out that the ethics of care and the opposed putatively masculine standard "ethics of justice" are interesting in themselves as alternative ways of thinking about or dividing up the universe of morality. So one needn't assume male-female differences in order to find the ethics of care interesting and promising as a new way to think about morality. (This is something Gilligan herself says.)[7]

But those who find care ethics interesting and significant are somewhat divided about the implications or status of such an ethics. Some have said that the ethics of caring indicates a side of our moral thinking that has been neglected within Western ethics, but have concluded that such thinking can be harmonized or integrated with traditional justice/rights/autonomy thinking in or into a larger morality that takes in all of plausible or valid human moral thinking.[8] For such thinkers, the ethics of care offers an important corrective to earlier ways of thinking about morality—and may even constitute a more important or basic part of our morality than the part covered by justice/rights/autonomy—but is not and cannot aim to be a systematic total view of, or approach to, human morality.

Others, however, have disagreed, and Gilligan herself has suggested that a morality that stresses connection rather than separateness—which is what the ethics of caring is—should perhaps replace and supersede traditional "male" approaches to morality and thus represent in itself a more satisfying total ethical picture than anything previously available.[9] I myself favor this view of things, and part of my reason is that I think the ethics of care and the ethics of justice are incompatible in the judgments they deliver about particular cases or issues. As I indicated above, they appear to imply different judgments about whether the law ought to permit hate speech—arguably differing, for example, about whether neo-Nazis should have been allowed years ago to march in Skokie, Illinois, where many Jewish survivors of the Holocaust were living. If the ethics of care is inconsistent with that of justice, it can't be integrated or harmonized with the latter. Rather, the two are competitors or alternatives, and so it would seem that if the ethics of care is plausible, it has to be plausible as an account of morality as a whole—of questions about individual actions and also of questions about political and legal justice.

But how could this be possible? The ethics of care was originally promulgated as opposed to an ethics of justice, autonomy, and rights; and doesn't this mean that care ethics can have nothing to do with, has to dismiss or remain skeptical about, these three notions? If it does, then care ethics is in deep trouble, because almost all of us deeply feel that there are important questions of justice and the like that we as human beings and as philosophers need to address and find answers to. That is why, for example, so many defenders of care ethics prefer to think of it as complementing, rather than replacing, an ethics focused on justice. However, one may also think that an ethics of care might prefer to approach questions of justice and the like *on its own terms*. In other words, traditional moral theories have, for example, approached justice in certain ways, but an ethics of caring might have or develop its own conception or theory of justice, and in fact care ethicists or those closely allied with them have proposed views along these lines. Sara Ruddick has famously proposed that we think of social justice in terms of "maternal" thinking, and both Nel Noddings and (earlier) I myself have suggested that we can model justice on (various forms of) caring about people we don't intimately know.[10] Again, we have no space here to discuss these projects further, but the fact that they are possible and actually exist does strengthen the tradition of care ethics as a way of understanding morality generally. Having said all this, I would like now to begin focusing on empathy and its relevance both to care ethics and to care-ethical approaches to moral education.

2. Caring and Empathy

Noddings in *Caring* said that the caring individual is really focused on another person. Not only is such an individual's ordinary self-concern or self-interest "displaced" into a concern for the welfare of another person, but the kind of caring we value also involves our being "engrossed" in the reality of the other. That means, roughly, that someone who cares deeply or genuinely about another person is open and receptive to the reality—the thoughts, fears, desires, and so on—of the other human being, so that when he acts on behalf of (the good of) the person he cares about, he doesn't simply impose his own ideas about what is good in general or what would be good for that person. Noddings takes pains to distinguish engrossment from empathy, which she says involves a much less receptive and much more active attitude than engrossment. She sees the empathic individual as putting him- or herself into the shoes, into the position, of another person; and such presumably voluntary putting oneself into another constitutes a distinctively male way of doing things (think about it!) that stands in marked contrast with the more passive or at least receptive and feminine attitude she describes as engrossment. But here Noddings's usage is somewhat out of touch with the (then) recent psychological literature on empathy. What she calls empathy is actually just one kind of empathy studied by developmental psychologists, which they tend to call *projective* empathy. But, as the psychologist Martin Hoffman points out in *Empathy and Moral Development: Implications for Caring and Justice*, there are other forms of empathy. And one of them, which he calls mediated associative empathy, involves precisely the receptive and, if you will, more feminine character that Noddings says is constitutive of engrossment.[11]

We don't in fact really need the term *engrossment* in developing care ethics; we can talk of (the right sorts of) empathy, instead. But, more important still, the ethics of caring needs to pay more attention to the psychological literature on empathy than it has previously done. In what follows, I hope at least in part to explain why, but let me begin with some preliminary remarks about what the word *empathy* means. The term *empathy* didn't exist till early in the twentieth century, but it is used a great deal nowadays, and it may be helpful at this point to indicate briefly how empathy differs from sympathy. In colloquial terms we can perhaps most easily do this by considering the difference between (Bill Clinton's) feeling someone's pain, on the one hand, and feeling *for* someone who is in pain, on the other. Any adult speaker of English will recognize that *empathy* refers to the former phenomenon and *sympathy* to the latter. Thus, empathy involves having the feelings of another (involuntarily) aroused in ourselves, as when we see another person in pain. (Hume described this phenomenon without having a proper term to refer to it.) By contrast, *sympathy* involves feeling sorry or bad for someone who is in pain and wishing them well, and this can happen even if we don't feel their pain—just as one may feel bad for someone who is being humiliated while in no way feeling humiliated oneself.[12]

Much of the recent psychological literature on empathy is concerned with whether genuine altruism is possible. Many psychologists believe that it is, and the studies that have been done to show—or that putatively show—that altruism is possible typically attempt to do so by showing that (developing) empathy is a crucial factor in determining whether someone will act altruistically toward some-one in distress or in need. Hoffman, whose book offers an overview of recent studies of empathy, argues that individual empathy develops through several stages and that its connection with altruistic concern for others is more ambiguous or inchoate in the earlier stages of that development. A baby can feel distress and start crying at the distress and crying of another baby within hearing distance, and this operates via a kind of mimicry. But as the child gains conceptual/linguistic skills, a richer history of personal experiences, and a fuller sense of the reality of others, a more "mediated" form of empathy can be aroused in response to situations or experiences that are not immediately present and are merely heard about, remembered, or read about. It also becomes possible for the child deliberately to adopt the point of view of other people and see and feel things from their perspective. Although we sometimes speak of both these forms of later-developing empathy (and especially of the latter, *projective* type of empathy) as involving identification with the other, Hoffman and others insist that the identification isn't a total merging with or melting into the other: genuine and mature empathy doesn't deprive the empathic individual of her sense of being a different person from the person she empathizes with.

Empathy does, however, involve feelings or thoughts that are in some sense more "appropriate" to the situation of the person(s) empathized with than to (the situation of) the person empathizing. And as an individual's cognitive sophistication and general experience increase, he becomes capable of more and more impressive or sophisticated "feats" of empathy. For example, adolescents gradually become aware of the existence of groups or classes of people and the common goals or interests that may unite them, and this makes empathy with the plight, say, of the homeless or the challenged or various oppressed races, nations, religions, or ethnicities possible and real for them in a way that would not have been possible earlier on.

The recent literature on moral development offers a good deal of support, I believe, to the idea that caring for or about others works *via* empathy. Therefore, if, as care ethics says, it is morally incumbent on us to act caringly toward others, the development of empathy will be a crucial feature of the/a moral life. Till now, care ethics hasn't offered any distinctive systematic account of moral development and moral education, but if empathy is necessary to caring, then the ethics of care needs to borrow from the psychological literature on empathy if it wants to explain how caring attitudes and dispositions can be acquired and taught. I want to say a good deal more about these issues in what follows, but first I would like us to consider another kind of implication of what the literature on empathy and moral development tells us.

3. Ethics and Empathy

Hoffman and many others have pointed out that people tend to feel more empathy for near and dear than for strangers and also (though this is related) tend to feel more empathy for those whose pain or distress they are witnessing than for those whose pain or distress they merely hear about. Thus, although Hoffman says that, starting in adolescence, we have a tendency to feel some substantial empathy for disadvantaged groups or classes whose members we don't personally know; he also indicates that this empathy will typically be much less strong than what we feel toward those we do personally or intimately know. But this difference corresponds to a moral distinction ethicists of care are inclined to make and defend. In her early work, Noddings thought our relations with distant groups couldn't really be said to involve caring, but she now thinks otherwise, and certainly many ethicists, myself included, want to say that although we have a moral obligation to care about (and do something to help) unfortunate distant groups of people, we have a *stronger* obligation to care for or about (and do something to help) our own near and dear. So here the strength of the obligations entailed by care ethics corresponds to the strength of normal empathic reactions.

Similarly, an ethics of care is likely to claim that we have a stronger obligation to help someone whose distress we are witnessing than to help a person whom we don't know and whose distress we merely know *about*. Once again the difference in strength of obligation here seems to correspond to a difference in normal empathic responses, and one might well start to wonder whether distinctions regarding developed human empathy and caring based in such empathy can be used to demarcate more generally the kinds (or strengths) of obligation an ethics of care is plausibly committed to.

What originally led me in this direction was an article by Catholic thinker (and U.S. appellate judge) John Noonan on the bearing of empathy on the morality of abortion.[13] Noonan takes us beyond the usual questions concerning the rights of the fetus by asking us to consider how the idea of empathy with the fetus bears on the morality of abortion and, in particular, on the rights of the fetus. He says that the notion of

> [v]icarious experience appears strained to the outer limit when one is asked to consider the experience of the fetus. No one remembers being born, no one knows what it is like to die. Empathy may, however, supply for memory, as it does in other instances when we refer to the experiences of infants who cannot speak or to the experience of death by those who cannot speak again. The experience of the fetus is no more beyond our knowledge than the experience of the baby and the experience of dying. (p. 303)

Noonan argues, in effect, that we can empathize/sympathize with the fetus and that when we do so, we find the fetus to be "within the family of man." We accept, that is, its right to life.

However, what immediately struck me, when I started thinking about this article, was what a two-edged sword the idea of empathy can be within the abortion context. Yes, if the experience of the fetus is no more beyond our knowledge than the experience of the newborn baby, and if we empathize equally with them both, then we may well feel, with Noonan, that they ought to be treated the same (and that abortions are morally wrong). But *are* their experiences equally accessible to us? Do we or can we really or readily empathize as much with a fetus as with a (born) baby? It seems to me that there is reason to think not, and in that case the highly original notion of invoking empathy within the abortion debate may actually support some of the views of those who advocate a woman's "right to choose."

Noonan argues that defenders of the fetus need to make the fetus visible (in a way that people "out of sight" in prisons or mental hospitals, as well as blacks and other minorities, need to be made visible). However, even if we can make and have made the fetus literally visible through photographs, films, and even television in a way not possible in earlier eras, it is not clear that this bears univocally on the question of empathy. Very early fetuses and embryos look more like fish or salamanders or (at least) nonhuman lower animals than like human beings, and they lack experience, a brain, and even limbs. All this makes embryos and early-stage fetuses seem alien to us and helps explain why we tend to empathize more with the later stages than with the earlier.

It is also easier for us to empathize with (born) babies than with fetuses, even if the fetuses have been made (quasi-)visible and (quasi-)audible through films, television cameras, and the like. For such contact with the fetus is less immediate or direct than what we have even with a newborn baby. The baby is there, right in front of us, and we can hold her or look her in the eye, and such factors make empathy much easier than what we can experience, even with help from television, and so on, with regard to a fetus, embryo, or zygote. (The fact that babies *cry* also makes a difference to their empathizability.) So it is easier to empathize with a baby than with a fetus, and with a late-stage fetus than with an early-stage fetus or embryo, and these differences correspond fairly well to what most of us think about the moral issues involved here. Whether we think abortion is morally permissible or impermissible, most of us think it is morally worse to kill a newborn than to abort a fetus, and we think it is worse or morally less desirable to abort a late-stage fetus than to abort an early-stage one or an embryo or zygote. So in the area of abortion, it makes sense to suppose that what goes more against the grain of normal empathy and of caring based in such empathy is morally less acceptable. And something analogous is plausible regarding our various obligations to help others: as I indicated earlier, it seems worse—and goes more against the empathic grain—to deny help to someone whose distress we are actually witnessing than to do so in regard to someone whose distress we merely know about; and it also seems worse—and less in keeping with ordinary empathy or empathic caring—to deny needed help to our near and dear than to do so vis-à-vis people we don't personally know. An ethics of caring can and should take in all these distinctions (and make some relevant positive judgments as well, of course), so in the light of the recent psychology literature on empathy and its relation to altruism/caring, I believe that care ethics needs to invoke empathy as a criterion of moral judgments and moral distinctions more than its practitioners have previously realized.

Of course, there are a lot of other moral issues I haven't had time and won't have time to mention. But the reader might at this point be wondering, in particular, whether the notion of empathy is as useful to making commonsense deontological distinctions as it is to distinguishing how much we owe by way of beneficence or help to different people or groups of people. I have attempted to show elsewhere that considerations of empathy allow us to distinguish between killing (or harming) and letting die (or letting someone be harmed), so distinctions of empathy turn out (in what may be surprising ways) to be relevant to (the validity of) deontology; and there is every reason for an ethics of care that takes empathy seriously to accept and include deontological restrictions on killing, harming, breaking promises, and so on.[14] What we need to discuss now, however, is how an ethics of care contoured by distinctions of empathy should conceive moral education at home, at school, and elsewhere.

4. Moral Education Based on Empathy

Hoffman has very interesting and original views about how parents can best morally educate their children—views that rely heavily on children's capacity for empathy—and I believe that what Hoffman says has profound implications for moral education in schools. (Hoffman himself is not unaware of this.) Hoffman holds that the development of fully moral motivation and behavior requires the intervention of parents and others making use of what he calls "inductive discipline" or, simply, "induction." Induction contrasts with the "power-asserting" attempt to discipline or train a child through sheer threats (carried out if the child doesn't comply) and with attempts to inculcate moral thought, motivation, and behavior (merely) by citing, or admonishing with, explicit moral rules or precepts. Inductive training depends, rather, on the child's capacity for empathy with others and involves someone's noticing when a child hurts others and then intervening—in a nonviolent but firm manner—to make the child vividly aware of the harm that he or she has done, most notably by making the child imagine how it would feel to experience similar harm. This leads the child (with a normal capacity for empathy) to feel bad about what he has done. Hoffman believes that if such training is consistently applied over time, the child will come to associate bad feelings (guilt) with situations in which the harm he can do is not yet done, an association that is functionally autonomous of parents' or others' continued actual intervention and constitutes or supports altruistic "caring" motivation. He calls such habitual associations "scripts" and holds that they underlie and power (the use of) moral principles or rules that objectify (my term) such associations in claims like "hurting people is wrong."

Because caring arguably rests on empathy and induction centrally involves the human capacity for empathy, an ethics of care (especially one that makes its moral distinctions in terms of empathy) can use Hoffman's idea of induction as the cornerstone of its account of and recommendations for moral education. Power assertion and sheer moral admonition on the part of parents don't seem to make a child more caring, because they don't engage the capacity for empathy that is crucial to caring. But then if inductive discipline at home *can* make a child more sensitive to and more caring about the welfare of those around her, such lessons can certainly be continued at school: there is no reason a teacher cannot use induction in dealing with a child who has hurt another child, and there is reason to believe that such treatment is more helpful in leading the child to become a better (read: more caring) school citizen than making the child stay after school, taking away privileges, and other punishments are likely to be.[15]

In addition, inductive techniques don't have to be restricted to making a child more empathically concerned about those immediately around him (in school). I mentioned earlier that Hoffman regards our capacity for empathy, and empathic concern, for distant disadvantaged (groups of) people as coming into play during adolescence, and Hoffman in fact says a good deal about how inductive techniques can be and often are extended so as to bring about or enhance an older child's concern for (groups of) people in other countries or other parts of her own country.

For example, both parents and schools can expose children/adolescents to literature, films, or television programs that make the troubles and tragedies of distant or otherwise unknown groups of people vivid to them; and they can encourage their sensitivity to such people by asking children to imagine—and getting them into the habit of imagining—how they or some family member(s) would feel if such things were happening to them. Furthermore, families, schools, and countries could provide for more international student exchanges than now exist, with visiting students living with local families and attending local schools, thus bringing home to both visitors and those visited the reality and real humanity of those who might otherwise be just names or descriptions. Finally, parents and schools could inculcate in children the habit of thinking about and being concerned about the effects of their own actions and inactions—and those of their family, neighbors, and government—on the lives of people in other countries.

The part schools would play in the above-mentioned inductive processes could certainly be formalized in curricular/classroom terms, and it should be clear that and how doing so would favor the aims of moral education as seen from the point of view of an ethics of (empathic) caring. But it is perhaps worth pausing at this point to see how what I have just been proposing compares with what the two most prominent contemporary approaches to moral education—Kohlberg's cognitive developmentalism and character education—have to say.

Lawrence Kohlberg's Kantian/rationalist model of moral education stresses the development of moral reasoning and sees the capacity to reason abstractly with universal rules or principles as the highest attainment of mature morality.[16] But this whole idea was, of course, questioned by Gilligan when she criticized Kohlberg for basing his model of moral development on studies done exclusively with male subjects and then drawing the unwarranted conclusion that women tend to be morally inferior to—rather than merely different from—men. The ethics of care also specifically questions whether morality can be grounded in reason, in the human capacity for (practical) rationality, and this worry comes especially to the fore in reference to issues of moral behavior. Not merely defenders of caring but also many others involved in issues of moral education have questioned whether any amount of sophisticated or universal moral reasoning can actually motivate someone to *do* what she has concluded is morally obligatory or good. By contrast, the caring approach to moral development and moral education that I am suggesting makes the possible attainment of the disposition to act morally—that is, from caring concern for others—seem less problematic, because the psychological connection between empathy and active, motivated concern for people makes a certain intuitive sense to us.[17]

Character education, however, stresses habituation in a way that suggests a plausible sense of the need to tie moral knowledge to moral actions; and as with what we said about moral education based on the child's capacity for empathy, the adherents of the character education approach stress the importance or usefulness of literature to the moral-educative process. Character education believes it is important for a child to develop various (mostly moral) virtues, and it holds that reading/hearing stories in which heroes or saints demonstrate those virtues helps the child to develop those virtues for himself. Explicit recommendations of one or another virtue (and admonitions against one or another vice) are also supposed to be part of this process, and character education favors rewarding students who exhibit a given virtue in their actions and, indeed, holding prize competitions among students to see who best displays some virtue or virtues.

One criticism that has often been made—and that an ethics of empathic caring might also make—of competitions and prizes is that they appeal to students' self-interested or selfish motives; any supposed display of virtue is then not likely to be generalized to situations where no rewards are being offered for virtuous action, the very situations where virtue is most needed (and can be most clearly exemplified). Character education's reliance on verbal praise for virtues and verbal admonitions against vice is also motivationally suspect. It is not clear how such verbal and seemingly intellectual "interventions" can engage with the motivational capacities and dispositions of a child—except, most obviously, by way of a connection with the child's possible fear of and/or desire to please those who are verbally intervening. But then we have a case, basically, of power assertion, and, once again, it is not clear how such a technique of moral education can do more than make a child do what she thinks a grown-up wants when she thinks she is likely to be caught and punished (or at least not rewarded) if she doesn't do it. But this is not inherently moral, genuinely altruistic motivation, and we once again see illustrated how an inductive empathic caring approach makes (the development of) moral motivation understandable and attainable in a way other approaches seem unable to do.

In addition, character education seems to advocate (what Kohlberg has called) a grab bag of virtues, rather than a single and plausible overarching conception of moral education and morality. Since different proponents of character education propose different groups or lists of the virtues students need to be taught, the whole approach has been criticized for its inability to justify a single univocal curriculum for moral education, and it has been suggested that any given list is likely to reflect its proposer's parochial interests or values rather than something all students ought to learn. Now, Kohlberg's view doesn't have this problem because standards of moral reasoning have seemed, or once seemed, neutral as between different ethnic, religious, or cultural traditions. (That was one reason cognitive developmentalism originally displaced character education as an approach to moral education.) But an ethics of care doesn't have this problem either, because it proposes a single and highly unified standard both of morality and of (specifi-cally) moral education: the development of our capacity for empathic concern for other people.

However, it might be wondered at this point whether an ethics of caring serves the aims of moral education in a gender-neutral enough way. If caring and (presumably) empathy come easier to women than to men, won't explicit or systematic moral education for empathic caring come more easily to women than to men, and won't that mean that women may well end up doing an even greater share or proportion of the moral caring in society than they have in the past? But, then, since the oppression or unjust treatment of women in the past has depended in part on women's willingness and tendency to be more caring (of men) than men are (of women), won't moral education for empathic caring tend to make things morally worse or less just in society?

Well, not necessarily if we are aware of this very issue. Nowadays, women work outside the home much more than they used to, and men are taking a good deal more responsibility for child-rearing than they used to. But part of moral education (and here I anticipate some views of Noddings to be discussed further, just below) should include a special effort, in schools, at home, and elsewhere, to encourage the caring motivations and activities of boys. (This may make a difference to how much men are eventually willing to participate in child-rearing, and that, in turn, could make a *further* difference to how caring, and how moral, men come to be.)

There may be limits to how far caring motivations can be equalized between the genders because there is some evidence that testosterone makes men more aggressive than women and affects their capacity for empathy with others. But that doesn't mean that a moral standard of empathic caring doesn't apply equally to men and women or that both genders/sexes shouldn't be taught/encouraged as effectively as possible to meet that standard. Though the effects of testosterone may possibly give men some kind of overall moral excuse for falling short and allow us to infer that women are on average morally more capable than—even superior to—men, those very implications make most sense only against the background assumption that a single ethics of empathic care is valid for human beings generally.[18]

Finally, the patriarchal attitudes and actions that encourage women, but not men, to think they should be caring, and even selfless, are themselves criticizable by reference to a properly conceived ethics of care. As Gilligan points out in *In a Different Voice*, it is the way women and young girls aren't listened to, aren't heard, under patriarchy that makes them doubt their own desires, thoughts, and aspirations. But this means that patriarchal attitudes or societies show a lack of empathic concern for what women really think and want, and given what I have been saying above, this entails that those attitudes and societies can be morally criticized for what they do to women. Far from encouraging female selflessness, an ethics of empathic care offers us the means to criticize and work against the unjust, one-sided arrangements that prevail in patriarchal circumstances; and in that case, we have been given no reason to question and many reasons in support of an empathy-based care-ethical approach to moral education.

5. NODDINGS ON MORAL EDUCATION

Nel Noddings, who was, after all, the first to articulate an ethics of care, views moral education somewhat differently from what we have been suggesting above. Yet her views don't so much challenge as allow us to helpfully supplement and fill out the picture of moral education that has been offered here. For one thing, Noddings nowadays agrees that something like what Martin Hoffman calls induction is of value to moral education, and, like Hoffman and myself, she thinks literature is, too.[19] But although Noddings stresses the value of the moral virtue of caring for others, she also places great importance on the moral value of caring relations or relationships. If such relationships are good, then moral education should seek to encourage or enhance them, and, interestingly enough, that process involves virtues *other than* (empathic) caring. It is easier for someone to sustain their caring motivation and actions toward someone who is, for example, congenial, lovable, cooperative, fun to be with, and grateful for what he receives. So the moral desire to build and enhance caring relationships has to regard the just-mentioned traits as useful and even as virtues, and this takes us away from a narrow focus on the moral virtue of caring itself.

As Noddings herself indicates, to treat traits like lovability and being fun to be with as virtues is to assume that not all virtues have to be moral ones in some narrow sense of the term. But Noddings in any event demonstrates the moral relevance of such traits to the moral good of caring relationships. There is nothing here that an empathic caring view of the moral need challenge or repudiate. Caring about others is a moral virtue, but relationships in which one person primarily cares about another—for example, the mother-child relationship—can be morally desirable as well; and Noddings's discussion therefore broadens the purview of what we said earlier about the moral-educational implications of a caring approach to morality. Noddings and I, in fact, disagree about whether the value of caring relationships is ethically prior to that of the individual virtue of caring for others—she says it is, I say it isn't. But, as I am indicating, this difference needn't call into question what either Noddings or I want to say about moral education.

Now Noddings also stresses the need for schools to teach boys in particular how to care for others. She recommends that boys learn to care for, take care of, other children within the school context, but more radically, she also recommends that caring for others occupy the central place in school curricula. She thinks educating people to be caring and also lovable requires them to acquire important forms of competence, and she thinks that forms of competence that lack any connection with caring—as per the requirement that everyone do two years of algebra—should not be insisted upon in schools. Moreover, a large part of her emphasis on the teaching of caring in schools comes from her view (something that she says derives in part from the influence of John Dewey) that moral education requires the process of education itself to be moral. Schools that teach caring meet that requirement, presumably, because they make education as a whole an instrument of moral change for the better in society as a whole. But here Noddings's views about the connection between caring and useful competence, and about the lesser need for a coercive curriculum that requires forms of competence that are specifically unrelated to caring, go beyond my own competence to criticize or approve. Her views are fascinating and may be very important, but they don't themselves follow from the account I have offered of the ethics of empathic caring, and I am not in a position to say more than that.

What I can say and have said, however, is that if we conceive morality as empathic caring and make use of Martin Hoffman's ideas about inductive discipline, we enable care ethics to offer its own distinctive systematic view of and approach to moral education. And the value and validity of an ethics of care seems to me then, and by way of conclusion, to depend both on how well it stacks up against other approaches to morality or moral theory and on how plausible its implications for moral education are in comparison with those of character education and Kohlbergian cognitive developmentalism.

NOTES

1. Carol Gilligan, *In a Different Voice: Psychological Theory and Women's Development* (Cambridge, MA: Harvard University Press, 1982).
2. Nel Noddings, *Caring: A Feminine Approach to Ethics and Moral Education* (Berkeley: University of California Press, 1984).
3. Noddings, ibid., stresses these themes.
4. On liberal arguments for (permitting) hate speech, see Susan Brison, "The Autonomy Defense of Free Speech," *Ethics* 108 (1998): 312–39.
5. Gilligan cites subsequent studies that favor her "different voices" hypothesis, in "Reply," *Signs* 11 (1986): 324–33. Among the many later studies that call her view at least partially in question are: Mary Brabeck, "Moral Judgment: Theory and Research on

Differences between Males and Females," *Developmental Review* 3 (1983): 274–91; and Lawrence Walker, "Sex Differences in the Development of Moral Reasoning," *Child Development* 55 (1986): 511–21. (However, Gilligan cites articles that question Walker's conclusions in "Reply.")

6. See her "Moral Orientation and Moral Development," in E. Kittay and D. Meyers, eds., *Women and Moral Theory* (Totowa, NJ: Rowman and Littlefield, 1987), pp. 19–33.

7. Incidentally, I don't propose to discuss here the question of whether any differences there are between men's and women's moral thinking are due (more) to nature or (more) to nurture. But we shall below be discussing how boys and men might become more caring.

8. Three notable examples of this view are Virginia Held, "The Ethics of Care," in *The Oxford Handbook of Ethical Theory*, ed. David Copp (New York: Oxford University Press, 2006), pp. 548*ff*.; Marilyn Friedman, *What Are Friends For? Feminist Perspectives on Personal Relationships and Moral Theory* (Ithaca: Cornell University Press, 1993), chapter 5; and Annette Baier, "The Need for More than Justice," in Virginia Held, ed., *Justice and Care: Essential Readings in Feminist Ethics* (Boulder, CO: Westview, 1995), esp. p. 57. All three hold that the two modes of thought are not only consistent with one another but also capable of being *integrated* or *harmonized* within moral thought as a whole. However, this cannot be the case if the two are in conflict in the way I am suggesting in the text above.

9. See Gilligan's "Letter to Reader, 1993," in later printings of *In a Different Voice*, pp. xxvi–xxvii. My own work has consistently defended the notion that an ethics of care can cover all of (individual and political) morality. See, for example, my *Morals from Motives* (New York: Oxford University Press, 2001); but the project was pursued in earlier papers as well.

10. Sara Ruddick, *Maternal Thinking: Towards a Politics of Peace* (Boston: Beacon Press, 1989); Nel Noddings, *Starting at Home: Caring and Social Policy* (Berkeley: University of California Press, 2002); and my "The Justice of Caring," *Social Philosophy and Policy* 15 (1998), later incorporated into my *Morals from Motives*.

11. Martin Hoffman's *Empathy and Moral Development: Implications for Caring and Justice* was published by Cambridge University Press in 2000. Noddings has recently noted Hoffman's work and the similarity between engrossment and one kind of empathy he speaks about. See her *Educating Moral People: A Caring Alternative to Character Education* (New York: Teachers College Press, 2002), p. 151.

12. As Nel Noddings has recently pointed out to me, what I have just claimed about the distinction, in colloquial usage, between *empathy* and *sympathy* to some extent runs counter to what many dictionaries say about the historical derivation and usage of these two terms; see her *Starting at Home*, pp. 13*ff*. However, my own usage here will stick with what I said above (and believe to be true) about colloquial, ordinary English.

13. John Noonan, "Responding to Persons: Methods of Moral Argument in Debate over Abortion," *Theology Digest* 21 (1973): 291–307.

14. See my "Moral Sentimentalism and Moral Psychology," in D. Copp., ed., *Oxford Handbook*, pp. 229*ff*. However, the reader could (also) wonder at this point whether a reliance on empathy might lead to some *invidious* moral distinctions if, say, blacks are more empathic to blacks and whites to whites. I discuss this topic in my book *The Ethics of Care and Empathy* (New York: Routledge, 2007), but let me briefly say something here. Empathic solidarity shared by an *oppressed* group seems far from invidious, and the psychological and moral distinction between the solidarity of an oppressed group and that of a group of oppressors can itself be made by reference to the developmental tendencies of human empathy. In any event, and apart from past history, it is not implausible to suppose that a

certain degree of preference for one's own group is both empathically understandable and morally acceptable.

15. Hoffman thinks power assertion and admonition inevitably play a role in parental discipline, but holds that a preponderant use of inductive discipline is more likely to bring about individuals with moral, altruistic, caring motivation. For discussion of some of the evidence that favors this view, see Mark Davis, *Empathy: A Social Psychological Approach* (Madison, WI: Brown and Benchmark, 1994).

16. See, for example, Kohlberg, *Essays on Moral Development,* Vol. 1: *The Philosophy of Moral Development*; Vol. 2: *The Psychology of Moral Development* (New York: Harper and Row, 1981, 1984).

17. But the connection can be and has been questioned. It is, after all, a bit mysterious that when we feel another's pain, we frequently are moved to help the other rather than to run away and try to forget about their pain (which it is easier to do if you aren't immediately witnessing someone's distress).

18. For a popularized account of the effects of testosterone that surveys much of the recent scientific literature on this subject, see Louann Brizendine, *The Female Brain* (New York: Morgan Road Books, 2006).

19. See, for example, Noddings, *Educating Moral People*. But as far as I can tell, most care ethicists don't recognize the importance of induction to moral education conceived in care-ethical terms.

CHAPTER 13

KANTIAN MORAL MATURITY AND THE CULTIVATION OF CHARACTER

MARCIA W. BARON

> As a child I was taught what was right, but I was not taught to correct my temper. I was given good principles, but left to follow them in pride and conceit.... I was spoilt by my parents, who though good themselves, ... allowed, encouraged, almost taught me to be selfish and overbearing, to care for none beyond my own family circle, to think meanly of all the rest of the world, to *wish* at least to think meanly of their sense and worth compared with my own.
>
> —Fitzwilliam Darcy, in Jane Austen, *Pride and Prejudice*

LEARNING to be good, as Mr. Darcy reminds us, is much more than just learning correct principles. Being good involves having the right (or some set of right)[1] attitudes, feelings, and ways of viewing oneself and others.

It is sometimes supposed that this view—a view that I think is both right and important—is at odds with Kantian ethics.[2] My aim in this chapter is twofold: (1) to expand on what I will label "Darcy's truth"—meaning that to be good, it is not enough to follow good principles and (though Darcy didn't say this) to follow them from duty, for one also has to have the right attitudes and feelings—and (2) to explain why Darcy's truth is compatible with Kantian ethics.

I

Some fine-tuning of Darcy's truth is in order. First, I need to distinguish it from two positions with which it might be conflated. It might be confused with the position that to learn correct principles, one must (first) have the right (or some set of right) attitudes, feelings, desires, and affective responses. That is not what I intend by "Darcy's truth." I mean by it that being good actually involves having such feelings. They are not important merely as a prerequisite for becoming good. Indeed, whether they are a prerequisite to becoming good is not my concern here. It may be that some feelings need to develop before the child can reflectively affirm the principles and that others develop through acceptance of the principles and through acting on them; it may be that this differs considerably from one person to the next. I leave such matters to those with expertise on moral development. What I am claiming (and take Darcy to claim) is only that proper affect[3] is part of what it is to be good. Or put differently, proper affect is part of moral maturity.

Relatedly, I want to distinguish Darcy's truth from the view that our attitudes, longings, wishes, affective responses, desires, and so on are morally significant, but only insofar as they bear on how we act. I'll refer to this as the "restrictive" view. Someone who takes pleasure in the suffering of others (perhaps reads with intense delight about tortures inflicted and about the screams of the victims), but whose actions are in no way affected by that clandestine pleasure, is no worse, on the restrictive view, than someone who is pained by others' suffering but who does not take action to ameliorate their condition or prevent further suffering. Of course, the proponent of the restrictive view continues, our affective responses, our wishes, attitudes, and the like do usually affect how we act, and so they are morally significant—but only because of their effect on our actions. The proponent of the restrictive view thus agrees that holding correct principles does not suffice for moral goodness, but only because we will be more prone to violate them if our sentiments are morally deficient.

Darcy's truth (as I am interpreting it) is not so restricted. Our affective responses are morally significant even apart from their bearing on our actions.[4] That someone takes pleasure in the suffering of others is disturbing in and of itself; that someone finds the thought of raping or torturing exhilarating, even if we are somehow certain that he would in fact never rape or torture, would surely lower our estimation of him.[5] Or to take a less flat-footed example, we flinch, watching either the film *Capote* or *Infamous*, upon hearing Truman Capote bemoan the appeals of the killers' death sentences because he is anxious to finish and publish *In Cold Blood*, and cannot do so until either their sentences are commuted or they are executed.[6] Insofar as it appears that he prefers an execution to a commuted sentence because it provides a better ending to his book, this compounds our unease.[7] I very much doubt that our unease can be explained as a sense that someone who feels x, or fails to feel y, is therefore more likely to commit actions of type A.[8]

A second clarification: part of the insight in Darcy's truth is that we have a responsibility to cultivate in ourselves good desires, wishes, and affective responses, and to take care not to nourish the objectionable ones. We may not be able to extinguish them, and it may be unwise to try to do so; but we should not fuel them, either. Resenting those who have wronged us is not only permissible but may even be morally preferable to not resenting them;[9] but focusing one's attention on hating the wrongdoer, making a point of reciting to oneself all the terrible things the person has ever done, seeking out like-minded acquaintances to swap stories of how terrible the scoundrel is and thereby reinforcing one's conviction of his wickedness, creating an image of him and burning it in effigy, or otherwise stoking one's anger, is generally morally objectionable.[10] I emphasize this to bring out that the insight I see in Darcy's truth is not merely—or primarily—that having (by and large) good attitudes and affective responses in and of itself makes one, *ceteris paribus*, a better person than someone with (predominantly) objectionable attitudes and affective responses, but, rather, that we are responsible for cultivating our characters. We have a responsibility not to nurse grudges, not to endorse in ourselves (among other things) a smug sense of superiority, a racist outlook, a reckless love of danger, a cynicism that has the effect of giving one an excuse for never trying to improve things, or a readiness to believe whatever makes us feel good. It is true that there is a danger of overstatement here: we should not exaggerate the extent to which we can control our emotions and attitudes, or indeed the extent to which we ideally would control and shape them.[11] Nonetheless, there is shaping to be done, and the temptation to dismiss all such shaping as futile (or unnecessary or undesirable) needs to be resisted.

Arguably more important than the responsibility to cultivate one's own character, and more prominent in Darcy's remarks, is the responsibility to be mindful as teachers, parents, aunts, uncles, grandparents, neighbors—in short, as adults who interact with children—of what sentiments and attitudes we are (perhaps inadvertently) nurturing. The cultivation of morally desirable affective responses and attitudes is a vital part of good child-rearing and, more generally, of the moral education of children. Jane Austen's *Mansfield Park* gives us a vivid negative example, a sketch of a form of "moral education" that fosters smugness and (as Darcy put it in *Pride and Prejudice*) a wish to think meanly of the sense and worth of others. When Mrs. Norris's nieces remark to her on the "stupidity" of their cousin, Fanny—who, because of her parents' poverty, has come to live with them—Mrs. Norris agrees that she is stupid but observes,

> "I do not know whether it is not as well that it should be so, for though you know (owing to me) your papa and mamma are so good as to bring her up with you, it is not at all necessary that she should be as accomplished as you are;—on the contrary, it is much more desirable that there should be a difference."
>
> (Austen 1814/1992, p. 17)

A recent front-page article in my local newspaper also provides a good example of what not to do. The photo shows a 6-year-old standing on the hood of a car, wielding a baseball bat, his father holding the back of his shirt to prevent him from falling into the windshield that he is about to smash. The caption explains that they won "the silent auction for the coveted privilege of whacking the windshield during a church 'carbash.'" The "carbash" was a fundraiser to "help send kids to this year's Christ in Youth conference in Tennessee."[12] Although those who organized or attended the fundraiser may not agree, presumably we do not want to foster in children a delight in smashing up cars (or more generally, a delight in destruction). The problem is not (merely) that those who find such a thing intensely pleasurable are more likely to be, or grow up to be, destructive. It is plausible to suppose that they are, but even if they are not, finding such activities pleasurable is itself morally problematic. Similarly, even if Mrs. Norris had not led her nieces to treat Fanny badly, she would still have acted wrongly in endorsing their ill-founded view of their cousin as stupid, and in encouraging them to expect those of less moneyed circumstances to be stupid (and thus to interpret their words and actions accordingly) and to regard it as fitting that they be stupid.

A final point of clarification and fine-tuning: there is a risk that Darcy's truth will be interpreted as more extreme than, it seems to me, it should be (the aim here being not to ascertain precisely what Mr. Darcy meant, but rather to mine and hone the insight in his remarks). Whatever Darcy himself thought, Darcy's truth is best understood as *not* entailing that there is one correct set of attitudes, feelings, and affective responses that constitutes (one part of) moral goodness (or, if one prefers, simply goodness) in a (mature) person. There is a wide array of good attitudes and affective responses; but there are some that we should take care not to encourage in ourselves or in children, and others that it is a proper aim of moral education to cultivate. But it is no part of Darcy's truth to suppose that people's sentiments should be as carefully cultivated as possible (be it by themselves or by the adults who raise them).[13]

II

Among Kant scholars, that Darcy's truth is compatible with Kantian ethics would not be very newsworthy. I write for those who are not Kant scholars and whose understanding of Kant's ethics has been influenced by such remarks as the following, from a review in the *New Republic* of Manfred Kuehn's *Kant: a Biography.* Simon Blackburn writes:

> Kant's moral psychology is one in which duty is forever at war with blind and slavish inclination, which itself is always a species of self-love. Emotions and desires are the enemy. You score moral points only when duty wins over them, and just because it is duty. In most of Kant's moral writings, in fact, the less you care about other things and other people, the better.

Blackburn continues:

> Bliss, for Kant, is equated with complete independence from any inclinations or
> needs, including feelings of compassion and sympathy with others. But since as
> human beings we are unlucky enough not to have this freedom, we must be on the
> alert to slap our feelings down. We gain moral credit only when we do so. . . .
> Kant's ideal . . . is that you should try to be apathetic about your friends, and about
> everything else.   (Blackburn 2001, p. 35)

If Blackburn's characterization of Kant's ethics were accurate—even roughly so—
Darcy's truth would be incompatible with Kant's ethics. The old Darcy—Darcy as
he describes himself as having been prior to his morally transforming come-
uppance from Elizabeth Bennett—would have had nothing for which to reproach
himself (unless his temper got in the way of doing his duty). As long as he did what
was right, and acted on principle, what difference would it make—if Kant's ethics
were as Blackburn depicts it—that he followed those good principles "in pride and
conceit"? So what if he thought "meanly of all the rest of the world" and of "their
sense and worth compared with his own"?

Despite a renaissance in Kant scholarship that over the past twenty-five years
or so has corrected many misconceptions, inaccurate characterizations and misleading innuendos (though generally not as extreme as Blackburn's) abound. One
finds these in many discussions, but a particular common location is any discussion that contrasts virtue ethics to Kantian ethics to explain the appeal of the
former.[14] Thus, after noting some objections to Kant's ethics and "philosophical
liberalism," Nel Noddings and Michael Slote write in their contribution to the
Blackwell Guide to the Philosophy of Education that virtue ethicists "have urged a
return to . . . a moral domain that recognizes both a moral obligation to develop
one's character and personal potential and also a much messier, richer, and more
variable field of obligation to others" (2003, p. 343). The implication seems to be
that Kant's ethics does not occupy such a domain.[15] But Kant not only recognizes
but also emphasizes a moral obligation to develop one's character and personal
potential. This is evident especially in his *Metaphysics of Morals*. We also find in
that work a complex scheme of duties, to others and to oneself, one that it seems
implausible to criticize for lack of richness and especially implausible to fault for
insufficient "messiness."[16]

This is not the place to catalogue misrepresentations of Kant's ethics and set
the story straight.[17] Space is limited, so I will concentrate on showing that Kant's
ethics is quite hospitable to Darcy's truth.

III

The evidence that Darcy's truth, though certainly more naturally associated with
Aristotle's ethics, has a home in Kant's as well can be found in several of Kant's

works and several different aspects of Kant's practical philosophy. I'll focus on the following: the obligatory ends and certain duties they entail, articulated primarily in The Doctrine of Virtue (Part II of *The Metaphysics of Morals*), and Kant's remarks on education and related matters in *Lectures on Pedagogy* and *Anthropology*.

Kant holds that the happiness of others and one's own perfection are obligatory ends, ends that it is a duty for everyone to have (MS 385–86).[18] These ends entail various general principles of duty, which in turn entail—though with a fair amount of latitude—some moderately specific duties. We have a duty to promote others' happiness, but whose, how, and how much effort we are to put forth is (purposely) not stipulated; likewise, we have a duty to develop our talents, but which ones and how (and with what degree of zeal) we are to go about developing them are not stipulated. We also have a duty to improve ourselves in ways more distinctively moral—for example, to strengthen our sense of duty so that in the event of a conflict between duty and inclination, we will opt for duty over inclination. This duty has less latitude than the other duties just mentioned.

Although the obligatory ends entail distinct duties, the ends and their corresponding duties are not as distinct as might first appear. Each end shapes the other. The duty to perfect oneself acquires some additional content from the duty to make others' happiness one's end. Were we permitted to regard our characters as fixed points, beyond our power to change, the duty to make others' happiness one's end would be severely limited.[19] Likewise, the duty to make others' happiness one's end is more robust, thanks to the duty to perfect oneself. The duty to perfect oneself precludes smug self-satisfaction, complacency, or cynicism regarding the possibility of changing oneself. Because of this, I cannot escape or limit my duty to promote others' happiness by pleading that I lack sensitivity, do not know what to say to people when they are depressed or upset, or that I am hot-tempered. There is, to be sure, latitude in the duty to promote others' happiness, but it does not go so far as to allow us to seek to help others only in ways that we find easy (or convenient). (See Baron 1995, chap. 3; Baron and Fahmy 2009; Gregor 1963; and Herman 2007, chap. 9)

Even from this brief sketch it is evident that the obligatory ends entail more than simply duties to undertake certain types of actions and to refrain from certain others (and to do so for the right reason). They call upon us (albeit somewhat indirectly) to shape our characters affectively and attitudinally. If I have a tendency to hold grudges or to lose my temper easily, I'll need to strive to change that. Doing so requires more than mere behavioral changes. I must come to view what I perceive as slights as not the big deal that I now think they are; I have to train myself not to dwell on the "infuriating" remarks so-and-so made, or if I already have dwelt on them, to ratchet down the emotional reaction and (before long) to "drop it"; and I have to steer myself away from looking for slights in the first place.

Here is another way to see that adopting an obligatory end (focusing in particular on the obligatory end of others' happiness) calls for shaping one's character affectively and attitudinally. Part of what it is to have an end is that one finds certain features of the world salient. This is true of ends in general, but the process of coming to find certain features salient may work differently with ends that are suggested by our inclinations than with obligatory ends. When the end is suggested by inclination, we are already inclined to perceive the world in the relevant way; but when the end is obligatory, this might not be the case.[20] We may, therefore, need to bring it about that certain things become salient for us. This entails attuning ourselves more to the needs of others, to when we can help and how—whether to offer help, or simply to create an environment in which the people in question will feel comfortable requesting assistance; or alternatively, to help by facilitating independence, or (possibly but not necessarily different) by working with others to create a social and economic climate where many of the most serious hindrances to the pursuit of permissible ends one sets for oneself are greatly reduced.

The attitudinal dimension may be more obvious than the affective dimension of the character-shaping entailed by the obligatory ends, but for beings like us—rational beings who are not purely or merely rational, but human, and thus have an affective nature—it is virtually unimaginable that we would be properly attuned and responsive to the moral features of the world if we were affectively a mess.[21] Cultivation of one's character (by parents and others who help rear one and later by the agent herself) thus has to involve cultivation of affect.

It would be misleading to assert that this is the only reason, according to Kant, that we have a duty (albeit an indirect duty) to cultivate our compassionate feelings. There is room for debate over exactly why, on Kant's view, we have this duty, though I think one reason is that this is part of attuning ourselves to others' needs and to ways we might help.[22] Whatever the precise reason, Kant clearly holds that we have a duty to cultivate such feelings:

> But while it is not in itself a duty to share the sufferings (as well as the joys) of others, it is a duty to sympathize actively in their fate; and to this end it is therefore an indirect duty to cultivate the compassionate natural (aesthetic) feelings in us, and to make use of them as so many means to sympathy based on moral principles and the feeling appropriate to them.—It is therefore a duty not to avoid the places where the poor who lack the most basic necessities are to be found but rather to seek them out, and not to shun sickrooms or debtors' prisons and so forth in order to avoid sharing painful feelings one may not be able to resist.   (MS 457)

In addition, Kant holds that "human beings have a duty of friendship" (MS 469) and that friendship involves "each participating and sharing sympathetically in the other's well-being" (MS 469). He also speaks of a duty to cultivate a conciliatory spirit, duties of gratitude, duties not to be envious and not to take malicious joy in others' misfortunes, and a duty to be forgiving, all of which require that we shape our characters accordingly (see MS 458–60). Kant also asserts that it is a duty of virtue to "cultivate a disposition of reciprocity—agreeableness, tolerance, mutual love and respect" (MS 473). Also relevant is his discussion of "vices that violate duties of respect for other human beings"; these include arrogance (MS 465) and wanton faultfinding and mockery (MS 467). Part of self-cultivation, Kant implies, is to weaken whatever propensity we have to these vices.

In sum, Kant's duties of love, both in their basic conception and in the details he supplies, provide excellent evidence that Darcy's truth has a home in Kant's ethics. The virtues of social intercourse and our duties of respect for others further corroborate my claim. Our feelings and attitudes are morally significant, on Kant's view. Moreover, although some passages in his discussion of duties of love may be compatible with what I called the restrictive view, according to which the moral significance of feeling is limited to its effect on our actions, it is clear from other passages—for example, MS 469, on friendship—that the restrictive view is not Kant's view.

IV

So far the evidence I've put forward to show that Darcy's truth has a home in Kant's ethics stems from the obligatory ends. I focused primarily on duties entailed by the obligatory end of others' happiness, but because of the bearing the obligatory ends have on each other and the duties they each entail, my discussion has, at the same time, brought out some ways in which duties to oneself provide evidence that Darcy's truth is in no way in tension with Kant's ethics.

But there is more to be said about duties to oneself and how they show that Darcy's truth is not at odds with Kant's ethics. Their relevance is not limited to their bearing on our ability to promote others' happiness; the idea is not simply that in order to improve my skills at promoting others' happiness, or to remove barriers to doing so, I should cultivate my character so that I do not, for example, take pleasure in humiliating others. Cultivating my character—making myself more of a *Mensch*—is also inherently valuable. Some sense of its centrality to Kant's ethics can be gleaned from the following statement from Kant's *Metaphysics of Morals*: "A human being has a duty to raise himself from the crude state of his nature, from his animality (*quoad actum*) more and more toward humanity, by which he alone is capable of setting himself ends" (MS 387).[23]

This idea that we make ourselves human—that humanity has to be cultivated—is prominent in Kant's other works, as well, and is not confined to his explication of duties of self-perfection. It forms the core of his views on education. Just as one has a duty to raise herself from her crude state toward humanity, so likewise we are to educate children in a way that cultivates their humanity. Indeed, Kant writes, "The human being can only become human through education" (P 443).

What does Kant mean when he speaks of becoming human through education? In what sense of "humanity" is humanity to be cultivated? Those whose picture of Kant's ethics has been shaped by such caricatures as Blackburn's might expect that becoming human, for Kant, simply means developing a strong and clear sense of duty, and an ability and willingness to say no to any desire that conflicts with duty.[24] To those who think this, the fact that Kant emphasizes cultivating humanity would not seem to lend any support to my claim that Darcy's thesis is fully compatible with Kant's ethics.

So let's have a look at what we are supposed to be doing in cultivating our humanity, both individually and collectively. An assortment of quotations—a sampling, intended to be representative but not comprehensive—will provide an appreciation of at least part of what is involved in the cultivating of humanity in children (by adults, and gradually, by the children themselves), and in ourselves.

A. [T]he human being must learn not to let his inclinations become passions. (P 487)

B. The child must maintain friendships with others and not remain by itself all the time. Some teachers, it is true, are opposed to these friendships in schools; but this is very wrong. Children should prepare themselves for the sweetest enjoyment of life. . . . Children must be openhearted too, and as bright as the sun in their expressions. The cheerful heart alone is capable of rejoicing in the good. (P 484–85)

C. [A]bove all things one must beware never to bear grudges against children. (P 484)

D. For the thinker, the following maxims . . . can be made unalterable commands.

   1. to think *for ourselves*
   2. to think ourselves into the place *of every other man* (with whom we are communicating)
   3. always to think *consistently with ourselves.* (A 228)

I have quoted (A) because it might be thought to be damaging to my case. It might be thought to show that cultivating humanity is not at all about cultivating our affective nature, and indeed involves treating all feelings, inclinations, and emotions like weeds (though perhaps weeds in an organic garden)—to be eliminated as much as possible (though presumably without poisoning ourselves). If it did show that, Kant's emphasis on cultivating humanity would not lend support to my position that Darcy's truth has a home in Kant's ethics. But in fact what Kant is talking about in (A) and similar passages is not eliminating feeling, but moderating it.[25] The idea is to keep our inclinations under control, so that in the event of a conflict between duty and inclination, duty wins.[26]

That Kant does not hold that we should aim to eliminate inclinations is clear from his statement of his differences with the Stoics on this very matter. The Stoics, he says, "mistook their enemy, who is not to be sought in natural inclinations." Indeed, "natural inclinations are *good* . . . and to want to extirpate them would not only be futile but harmful and blameworthy as well; we must rather only curb them, so that they will not wear each other out but will instead be harmonized into a whole called happiness" (R 6: 58).[27]

Kant's unqualifiedly negative remarks about passions may have led some to think that he condemns affect in general. But his condemnation is limited to passions.[28] Passions are inclinations that have gotten out of control. They resist taming by reason and are serious hazards to one's moral health and one's happiness. Because they take over, blinding one to one's other ends (or to competing considerations), they thwart one's attainment of one's other goals. Kant's remarks in *Anthropology* about passionate ambition nicely illustrate this.

> A man's *ambition* can always be a bent of his inclination that reason approves of. But the ambitious man also wants others to love him, needs to have pleasant social relationships with them, to maintain his financial position and so on. If he is *passionately* ambitious, however, he is blind to these ends, though his inclinations still summon him to them, and overlooks the risk he is running that others will come to hate him or avoid him in society, or that his expenditures will reduce him to poverty. This is folly (making a part of his end the whole), which directly contradicts the formal principle of reason itself.   (A 266)

In sum, one aspect of the cultivation of humanity in oneself is taming one's inclinations, bringing them into harmony, and preventing them from becoming ungovernable. This and related features of self-government are crucial components of moral maturity, on Kant's view, and constitute goals that shape, or should shape, moral education.

Passages (B) and (C) hark back to the MS passages I discussed above, in III: part of cultivating humanity in oneself and in children is the cultivation of certain affective dispositions and attitudes, and the thwarting or subduing of others. Friendships are to be encouraged because friendship is "the sweetest enjoyment of life." Education should help children to be "openhearted"; being able to enjoy friendship—indeed, to enjoy life—requires that one not close oneself off to others; similarly, one cannot, except in a very limited way, promote others' happiness if one closes oneself off to others. Passage (C) calls to mind Kant's discussion in MS of our duties to cultivate proper attitudes toward others in general, so that we are not contemptuous, arrogant, envious, and so on; what (C) adds is that character-shaping needs to take into account proper attitudes to particular (types of) others, in addition to proper attitudes toward others in general. Presumably bearing grudges is in general to be discouraged, but grudges against a child are particularly unwarranted (probably because resentment of adults who have wronged us is more warranted than resentment of children, given that "infancy" is, when not a full-blown excuse, a mitigating factor). Moreover, grudges against children tend to be especially damaging, given children's dependence on adults and their lack, typically, of any option of escaping the adults who raise them, together with the enormous impact that those adults generally have on them.

I include (D) to call attention to another dimension of character cultivation, one that requires a way of thinking that is sharply at odds with the self-centeredness and arrogance that Darcy says his parents allowed and even encouraged in him. It is the second injunction—"to think ourselves into the place *of every other man* (with whom we are communicating)"—that particularly bears emphasis in this paper, though all three involve important character-shaping and should be taken very seriously by educators.[29] (Lest one think that the maxims in (D) are intended only for intellectuals, the following, from *Lectures on Pedagogy*, is pertinent: "to have trained one's children is not enough, rather, what really matters is that they learn to think" (P 450).[30])

We can see from Passages A–D that cultivating humanity is quite different from simply developing and maintaining a strong sense of duty (and a keen sense of what really is morally required). It entails training, shaping, and, yes, taming one's inclinations, but not trying to eradicate them; and it calls for shaping one's attitudes and patterns of thought in the ways suggested by (D). We are to think for ourselves, but this in no way entails ignoring others' opinions. Kant drives this point home in a section of *Anthropology* entitled "On Egoism," where he differentiates three types of egoism:

> The *logical egoist* considers it unnecessary to test his judgment by the understanding of others too, as if he had no need at all for this touchstone.   (A 128)

> The *aesthetic egoist* is a man content with his own *taste*, even if others find his verses, paintings, music etc. bad, and censure or even laugh at them. By isolating himself with his own judgment, applauding himself, and seeking the touchstone of artistic beauty only within him, he prevents himself from progressing to something better.   (A129–30)

> [T]he *moral egoist* is a man who limits all ends to himself, sees no use in anything except what is useful to him.   (A 130)

Kant concludes his discussion by articulating the "opposite" of egoism: "The opposite of egoism can be only pluralism, that is, the attitude of not being occupied with oneself as the whole world, but regarding and conducting oneself as a citizen of the world" (A 130).

Although he does not explicitly state that we have a duty to regard and conduct ourselves as citizens of the world, clearly the idea here is that this is part of moral maturity. His discussion of egoism, together with D, nicely encapsulates what cultivating humanity is all about. It also shows that not only is Darcy's truth compatible with Kant's ethics but, moreover, Darcy's specific vices (prior to his moral epiphany) are vices that Kant *can* recognize, compatibly with the rest of his theory, and indeed *did* recognize as vices.

V

A reader who grants that I've made my case—that Kant's ethics does not deny Darcy's truth, and indeed that Darcy's truth finds a home in Kant's ethics—might ask, "Why, then, have so many people gotten it wrong?"[31] This is a good question, though it is worth bearing in mind that the phenomenon is a familiar one, by no means limited to interpretations of Kant. A full answer would therefore note various reasons why it is easy for classics in philosophy to be misinterpreted, as well as reasons that apply especially to the case at hand. My answer will have to be brief and sketchy, and will focus primarily on the case at hand.

Part of the answer is that, as noted above, Kant's remarks on passions are easily misread as indicating that affect in general is to be suppressed—indeed, eradicated—as much as possible. Another is that in the *Groundwork* and the *Critique of Practical Reason*, Kant is concerned to emphasize that affect is not a suitable foundation for ethics, and thus his remarks on affect are primarily negative. Furthermore, at least one infamous remark, if read in isolation, seems indeed to say that we would be better off if we had no inclinations at all (see G 428, and the similar, though less hyperbolic KP 235). This is further complicated by the fact that in Section I of the *Groundwork*, Kant's account of acting from duty is (at least if read in isolation) easily misread as asserting that it is in general best to act whenever possible from duty alone.[32] Moreover, since that section of Kant's *Groundwork* is one that people often feel they understand better than the rest of the work, and since they often are less familiar with his other works (in particular, the Doctrine of Virtue), there seems to be an overconfidence among Kant's casual readers.[33] Another factor is the tendency, in discussing major philosophers, to group them together in ways that oversimplify and distort their views; the classification of Kant as a deontologist is a case in point (see Baron, forthcoming, and Wood, forthcoming).

Relatedly, virtue ethicists have frequently explained the attractiveness of their approach by using "deontology" as a foil; Kant is then quickly summarized in a way designed to highlight what virtue ethics has to offer. Those aspects of Kant's ethics that accord with the picture of him as a deontologist are highlighted; those that do not are typically ignored. (There is, of course, also a long history, perpetuated in many classes in nineteenth-century philosophy, of treating Kant as a foil to nineteenth-century continental philosophy. The contortions that this calls for partially overlap those involved in presenting Kant's ethics as a foil to contemporary virtue ethics.) When a philosopher is needed as a foil, resistance to listening to evidence that the interpretation that supports the "foil" is wrong can be quite strong.

But there may be another reason for resistance to reconsidering such interpretations of Kant as that presupposed in Blackburn's remarks. Allen Wood explains:

> In the course of presenting my reading of Kantian ethics, I have noticed one
> source of opposition to it that is especially worthy of mention. Many accept my
> view that Kant is a more appealing moral philosopher on my reading than on the
> traditional one. They may even reluctantly admit that it is better supported by the
> texts than they thought it could be. But they still resist, because they feel their
> philosophical world deprived of a significant inhabitant—namely, the stiff,
> inhuman, moralistic Prussian ogre everyone knows by the name "Immanuel
> Kant." They may not like him, but he plays an important role in their moral
> world—if not as the villain in a cautionary tale, then at least as the personification
> of a one-sided truth that becomes dangerous if we go that far. Without him,
> they feel disoriented. If this Kant did not exist, it would be necessary to invent
> him. They therefore think it might be better to keep the traditional interpretation

of his writings even if it is wrong—and even if the position it represents is unappealing—not despite, but even precisely because of that fact.[34]

If there is a strong psycho-philosophical (or simply psychological) need for the Prussian ogre version of Kant, nothing I have said in this paper will dislodge it. But I hope that those who have no such need have been persuaded that Kantian moral maturity involves having the right (or some set of right) attitudes, feelings, and ways of viewing oneself and others. I hope it is clear that it is the new Mr. Darcy—Mr. Darcy as he became after Elizabeth Bennett rejected his (first) proposal of marriage—not the old Mr. Darcy, who is the real Kantian.[35]

NOTES

1. I add this because I do not think that there is precisely one set of right attitudes; many sets are quite fine. See n. 11, below and the paragraph to which note 11 is appended.

2. See, among many sources, Williams 1976, pp. 225–26: "[I]f one is going to suggest that those things that a man does as the expression of certain emotions, can contribute to our view of him as a moral agent; if, further, one is going to say (as I have perhaps not yet said explicitly, but am very happy to) that one's conception of an admirable human being implies that he should be disposed to certain kinds of emotional response, and not to others; one has to try to answer the very powerful claim of Kant that this is impossible."

3. Throughout my paper I use *affect* to cover desire, emotion, inclination, longings, wishes, affective response (glee, sadness, intense sorrow, etc.), and the like. There is a danger that in the sections discussing Kant's work, it will be assumed that I mean by *affect* what Kant means by *Affekt*, so I want to clarify that that is not the case. I am using *affect* far more broadly. (See n. 28, below, for Kant's usage.)

4. I do not claim in this paper that we are morally responsible for our affective responses, though I claim that we have a responsibility to cultivate in ourselves morally appropriate desires, wishes, and affective responses, and to take care not to nourish the objectionable ones. (One might hold that we have the responsibility to cultivate them yet believe that our efforts are likely to be only partially successful, and that we therefore should not be held responsible for the actual affective responses we have unless, perhaps, we failed to make the appropriate effort.) For an excellent paper defending the view that we are morally responsible not only for cultivating our affective responses but also for the responses themselves, see Smith 2005.

5. It could be that we think less of him because we think that his conduct will be affected in some other, perhaps more subtle way, by taking pleasure in the thought of torturing someone; perhaps though he doesn't carry out his fantasies, he is a cruel taskmaster as a parent or teacher or coach. But again, I do not think that we think less of him only because of this. Indeed, it may be that we find certain of his actions objectionable especially because they reflect sadistic pleasures, rather than believing the sadistic pleasures to be objectionable only because we think they are likely to lead to heinous actions.

6. We flinch even though we do understand: we understand a writer being so overwrought by the project of writing his book, particularly a book on disturbing subjects,

and particularly a book that has taken years to research and write, that he wants desperately to finish it. I take this flinching to be telling, though of course it is possible that it does not track anything morally significant. But I take very seriously the view developed by (among others) Bernard Williams that flinching of this sort—flinching that is not explicable as a prejudice, or as reflecting a theoretical (or religious) commitment—usually is telling, and typically is a source of moral insight. See Williams 1976, chaps. 11 and 13; and Williams 1981, chap. 2.

7. I do not mean to assert here that Capote did prefer that they be executed; whether or not he did is not clear to me.

8. For a more extended discussion of both the restrictive and the stronger views, see Baron 2002b, especially pp. 244–48.

9. For discussion of the value of resentment, see Murphy and Hampton 1988, chaps. 1–2; and Walker 2004.

10. It is the stoking of the anger, the nurturing of the resentment, that is primarily objectionable, not the actions themselves. Indeed, we can imagine circumstances in which reciting to oneself all the terrible things the person has ever done might be a good idea— perhaps one is trying to get over what one realizes is an irrational and destructive emotional attachment to the other person.

11. Given my appeal to Jane Austen's work to develop my point, I want to note that I do not, in endorsing Darcy's truth, mean to endorse the degree of cultivation of feeling that she appears to endorse. Here I have in mind one particular character of Austen's, Fanny Price, of *Mansfield Park*. There is a moral fastidiousness, a judgmental self-consciousness about her every thought and feeling, that is certainly not something I regard as part of moral excellence, or as a mark of moral maturity. But see Grenberg 2007 for a more positive assessment of Fanny Price.

12. The headline for the piece is "Pathways," with the explanation that "Pathways is a weekly photographic column that captures those little moments that add up to a lifetime of memories." *Bloomington Herald-Times*, June 25, 2007, p. 1.

13. See n. 11, above.

14. I have elsewhere argued that the contrast between virtue ethics and Kantian ethics is overdrawn, both because of the misunderstandings of Kantian ethics and because of false dichotomies. See, in connection with moral education, Baron 1985. See also Baron 1997, and for an in-depth examination of virtue ethics, and an argument that the term is misleading and should be dropped, Nussbaum 1999.

15. See also Noddings 2002, where she contrasts the tendency, starting with Kant, "to restrict the moral domain to considerations of our duties and obligations to others" to the approach taken by ancient Greeks, and today by "character educators and care theorists" who "are concerned with the broader question, How shall we live?" As I and many others have argued, Kant is among those who understand ethics to be concerned with that question. I suspect it is because many of Kant's readers are familiar only with his foundational work, *Groundwork for a Metaphysics of Morals*, not with the work for which it laid the groundwork, *The Metaphysics of Morals*, that they are unaware that he is concerned with the question of how we should live. But I am at a loss to explain why anyone would think that Kant restricts the moral domain to considerations of our duties to others.

16. For discussion of this complex scheme of duties, see Baron 1995, chap. 2; Denis 2001; Hill 1992, chap. 8; and Gregor 1963.

17. For some of the many books and articles that correct such errors as Blackburn's, see Allison 1990; Baron 1995, 2002a, and 2006; Denis 2000; Guyer 1993; Herman 1993 and 2007;

Hill 1992, 2002, and 2007; Korsgaard 1996a and 1996b; O'Neill 1989; Sherman 1997; and Wood 1999, 2002, and 2008.

18. In citing Kant's works, I use the abbreviations and translations given below. All page references are to *Kants gesammelte Schriften, herausgegeben von der Deutschen Akademie der Wissenschaften* (Berlin: Walter de Gruyter and predecessors, 1902).

A   *Anthropology from a Pragmatic Point of View*, trans. Mary J. Gregor (The Hague: Nijhoff, 1974).

P   *Lectures on Pedagogy*, trans. Robert Louden. In Immanuel Kant, *Anthropology, History, and Education*, eds. R. Louden and G. Zöller (Cambridge: Cambridge University Press, 2007).

G   *Groundwork of the Metaphysics of Morals*. In Immanuel Kant, *Practical Philosophy*, trans. and ed. Mary J. Gregor (Cambridge: Cambridge University Press, 1996).

KP   *Critique of Practical Reason*. In Immanuel Kant, *Practical Philosophy*, trans. and ed. Mary J. Gregor (Cambridge: Cambridge University Press, 1996).

KU   *Critique of the Power of Judgment*. In Immanuel Kant, *Critique of the Power of Judgment* (Cambridge: Cambridge University Press, 2000).

MS   *Metaphysics of Morals*. In Immanuel Kant, *Practical Philosophy*, trans. and ed. Mary J. Gregor (Cambridge: Cambridge University Press, 1996).

R   *Religion within the Boundaries of Mere Reason*, trans. and eds. Allen Wood and George di Giovanni (Cambridge: Cambridge University Press, 1998).

WA   *An Answer to the Question: What is Enlightenment?* In Immanuel Kant, *Practical Philosophy*, trans. and ed. Mary J. Gregor (Cambridge: Cambridge University Press, 1996).

19. Indeed, the duty to make others' happiness one's end calls for some moral transformation (see Seymour 2007). For more on the obligatory ends, see also Baron 1995, 1997, and 2006; Baron and Fahmy, 2009; Gregor 1963; Herman 1993 and 2007; and Hill 1992 and 2002.

20. I draw in the preceding three sentences from Korsgaard 1996a, p.180; the entire paragraph overlaps with Baron 2006.

21. Of some relevance here is Kant's claim that there "are certain moral endowments such that anyone lacking them could have no duty to acquire them" for they "lie at the basis of morality, as subjective conditions of receptiveness to the concept of duty." The moral endowments are "moral feeling, conscience, love of one's neighbor, and respect for oneself" (MS 399).

22. For further discussion, see Baron 1995; Cagle 2005; Denis 2000; Guyer 1993; Seymour 2007; and Sherman 1997.

23. The sentence continues: "he has a duty to diminish his ignorance by instruction and to correct his errors." Lest we get the wrong idea about this duty to raise oneself more and more toward humanity, Kant clarifies: "And it is not merely that technically practical reason *counsels* him to do this as a means to his further purposes (of art); morally practical reason *commands* it absolutely and makes this end his duty, so that he may be worthy of the humanity that dwells within him" (MS 387).

24. They may also think that cultivation of character, if it means anything for Kant, would mean that even desires that do not conflict with duty are to be, as Blackburn put it, "slapped down"; however section III, above, makes it plain that that is not the case. Some passages in the first section of the *Groundwork* are sometimes read as supporting the "slap them down" view; for discussion of them, see Allison 1990; Baron 2002a; Herman 1993; Korsgaard 1996a and 1996b; and Wood 1999, among many, many works that discuss this matter. See also n. 17, above.

25. One might well differ with Kant on what amount of control is in order, and how "moderate" is optimal (and some differ with Kant over whether duty always ideally should win; see Williams 1982; Wolf, 1982 and 1986), but (except at the limit) that is a different disagreement from one over whether proper affect is a necessary part of being good. Disagreements about what type and intensity of affect are to be cultivated need to be differentiated from disagreements about whether cultivation of affect is part of a good moral education, and whether properly cultivated affect is part of what it is to be a good person.

26. I am using *duty* here and throughout my chapter as Kant uses *Pflicht*, to mean, in essence, what is morally required. This is different from the colloquial sense in which it makes sense to ask, "It is my duty, but is it what I really should do, morally?" See Wood 2008, chap. 9; and Baron 1995, chap. 1.

27. For other remarks registering some disagreement with the Stoics (here, a disagreement pertinent to passage B, above) see MS 484–85.

28. He has harsh remarks for emotions (or "affects," as Gregor translates *Affekten*) as well, though not quite as harsh as for passions. "An affect works like water breaking through a dam: a passion, like a stream that burrows ever deeper in its bed. An affect works on our health like an apoplectic fit; a passion, like consumption or emaciation. An affect should be regarded as a drunken fit—we sleep it off, though we have a headache afterwards; but passion, as a sickness that comes from swallowing poison" (A 252).

29. The maxims in (D) merit far more discussion than I give them in this paper. See KU 294–95, and Allen Wood's excellent discussion in Wood 2008, pp. 20–24.

30. This is from a section that begins, "The human being can either be merely trained, conditioned, mechanically taught, or actually enlightened." See also WA.

31. Thanks to Harvey Siegel for asking this question.

32. In addition, it is easy to read section I of the *Groundwork* as if Kant is offering a self-standing account of the moral worth of actions—or perhaps of the moral worth of both actions and persons—when his discussion of moral worth should be read as part of an attempt to develop the idea of a categorical imperative from that of the good will; Baron 1995, chap. 5.

33. This overconfidence encompasses a presumption that the works in Kant's practical philosophy that they know are of course the major works. Any works that do not corroborate the view that they take to be Kant's view must be peripheral—after all, if they were major works, they figure, surely they themselves would already be familiar with them. (Thus a response—from a philosopher of education, and certainly no expert on Kant's ethics—to a talk I gave several years ago on Kant's ethics: he informed me that my work on Kant was simply "nibbling around the edges.")

34. Wood 2008, p. xiv.

35. I am very grateful to Justin Brown, Sandra Shapshay, Harvey Siegel, and Allen Wood for their helpful comments on an earlier draft of this chapter, and to Dartmouth College for its hospitality during the summer of 2007, when I began this chapter.

REFERENCES

Allison, Henry E. (1990). *Kant's Theory of Freedom*. Cambridge: Cambridge University Press.

Austen, Jane (1814/1992). *Mansfield Park*. Hertfordshire, UK: Wordsworth Editions Limited.

—— (1813/2006). *Pride and Prejudice*, ed. Pat Rogers. Cambridge: Cambridge University Press.

Baron, Marcia W. (1985). "The Ethics of Duty/Ethics of Virtue Debate and Its Relevance to Educational Theory." *Educational Theory* 35: 135–49.

—— (1995). *Kantian Ethics Almost without Apology*. Ithaca: Cornell University Press.

—— (1997). "Kantian Ethics." In *Three Methods of Ethics: A Debate*, eds. M. Baron, P. Pettit, and M. Slote (pp. 3–91). Malden, MA: Blackwell.

—— (2002a). "Acting from Duty." In *Groundwork for the Metaphysics of Morals*, ed. and trans. Allen W. Wood (pp. 92–110). New Haven: Yale University Press.

—— (2002b). "Character, Immorality, and Punishment." In *Rationality, Rules and Ideals: Critical Essays on Bernard Gert's Moral Theory*, eds. Walter Sinnott-Armstrong and Robert Audi (pp. 243–58). Lanham, MD: Rowman & Littlefield.

—— (2006). "Moral Paragons and the Metaphysics of Morals." In *A Companion to Kant*, ed. Graham Bird (pp. 335–49). Malden, MA: Blackwell.

—— (forthcoming). "Virtue Ethics: An Opinionated Overview and Commentary." In *Perfecting Virtue: New Essays on Kantian Ethics and Virtue Ethics*, eds. Lawrence Jost and Julian Wuerth. Cambridge: Cambridge University Press.

Baron, Marcia W., and Melissa Seymour Fahmy. (2009). "Beneficence and Other Duties of Love in *The Metaphysics of Morals*." In *Blackwell Guide to Kant's Ethics*, ed. Thomas E. Hill, Jr. (pp. 211–28). Malden, MA: Blackwell.

Blackburn, Simon (2001). "Königsberg Confidential." *The New Republic*, April 23, 2001, pp. 34–37.

Cagle, Randy (2005). "Becoming a Virtuous Agent: Kant and the Cultivation of Feelings and Emotions." *Kant-Studien* 96: 452–67.

Denis, Lara (2000). "Kant's Cold Sage and the Sublimity of Apathy." *Kantian Review* 4: 48–73.

—— (2001). *Moral Self-Regard: Duties to Oneself in Kant's Moral Theory*. New York: Routledge.

Gregor, Mary J. (1963). *Laws of Freedom: A Study of Kant's Method of Applying the Categorical Imperative in the "Metaphysik der Sitten."* Oxford: Basil Blackwell.

Grenberg, Jeanine (2007). "Courageous Humility in Jane Austen's *Mansfield Park*." *Social Theory and Practice* 33: 645–66.

Guyer, Paul (1993). *Kant and the Experience of Freedom: Essays on Aesthetics and Morality*. Cambridge: Cambridge University Press.

Herman, Barbara (1993). *The Practice of Moral Judgment*. Cambridge, MA: Harvard University Press.

—— (2007). *Moral Literacy*. Cambridge, MA: Harvard University Press.

Hill, Thomas E., Jr. (1992). *Dignity and Practical Reason in Kant's Moral Theory*. Ithaca: Cornell University Press.

—— (2002). *Human Welfare and Moral Worth: Kantian Perspectives*. Oxford: Clarendon Press.

—— (2007). "Kantian Virtue and 'Virtue Ethics'." In *Kant's Virtue Ethics*, ed. Monika Betzler (pp. 29–59). Berlin: de Gruyter.

Korsgaard, Christine M. (1996a). *Creating the Kingdom of Ends*. Cambridge: Cambridge University Press.

—— (1996b). "From Duty and for the Sake of the Noble: Kant and Aristotle on Morally Good Action." In *Aristotle, Kant, and the Stoics: Rethinking Happiness and Duty*, eds. Stephen Engstrom and Jennifer Whiting (pp. 203–36). Cambridge: Cambridge University Press.

Murphy, Jeffrie G., and Jean Hampton. (1988). *Forgiveness and Mercy*. Cambridge: Cambridge University Press.

Noddings, Nel. (2002). *Educating Moral People*. New York: Teachers College Press.

—— and Michael Slote. (2003). "Changing Notions of the Moral and of Moral Education." In *The Blackwell Guide to the Philosophy of Education*, ed. Nigel Blake et al. (pp. 341–55). Malden, MA.: Blackwell Publishers Ltd.

Nussbaum, Martha. (1999) "Virtue Ethics: A Misleading Category?" *Journal of Ethics* 3: 163–201.

O'Neill, Onora. (1989). *Constructions of Reason: Explorations of Kant's Practical Philosophy*. Cambridge: Cambridge University Press.

Seymour, Melissa M. (2007). *Duties of Love and Kant's Doctrine of Obligatory Ends*. Ph.D. Dissertation, Indiana University.

Sherman, Nancy. (1997). *Making a Necessity of Virtue: Aristotle and Kant on Virtue*. Cambridge: Cambridge University Press.

Smith, Angela M. (2005). "Responsibility for Attitudes: Activity and Passivity in Mental Life." *Ethics* 115: 236–71.

Walker, Margaret. (2004). "Resentment and Assurance." In *Setting the Moral Compass: Essays by Women Philosophers*, ed. Cheshire Calhoun (pp. 145–60). New York: Oxford University Press.

Williams, Bernard. (1976). *Problems of the Self: Philosophical Papers 1956–1972*. Cambridge: Cambridge University Press.

—— (1982). *Moral Luck: Philosophical Papers 1973–1980*. New York: Cambridge University Press.

Wolf, Susan. (1982). "Moral Saints." *Journal of Philosophy* 79: 419–39.

—— (1986). "Above and Below the Line of Duty." *Philosophical Topics* 14: 131–48.

Wood, Allen W. (1999). *Kant's Ethical Thought*. Cambridge: Cambridge University Press.

—— (2002). "What is Kantian Ethics?" In *Groundwork for the Metaphysics of Morals*, ed. and trans. Allen W. Wood. (pp. 92–110). New Haven: Yale University Press.

—— (2008). *Kantian Ethics*. Cambridge: Cambridge University Press.

—— (forthcoming). "Kant and Agent-Oriented Ethics." In *Perfecting Virtue: New Essays on Kantian Ethics and Virtue Ethics*, eds. Lawrence Jost and Julian Wuerth. Cambridge: Cambridge University Press.

CHAPTER 14

THE PERSISTENCE OF MORAL SKEPTICISM AND THE LIMITS OF MORAL EDUCATION

ELIJAH MILLGRAM

"I see what morality requires me to do, but I don't know why I should do it." The tone of such remarks is not one of innocent invitation to inquiry, but rather resistance to or a rejection of moral commitment; call the attitude they express *moral skepticism*. It is not just as old as philosophy, but probably as old as ethics or morality itself,[1] and so, over the past two thousand plus years, moral philosophers have sought the arguments showing the skepticism to be a mistake. Plato's dialogues, especially the *Gorgias* and Book I of the *Republic*, are a useful reminder of its antiquity, and early members of a long list of theoretical constructions, each meant to give a convincing and substantive answer to the rhetorical "But *why* should I do it?"

Systematic philosophizing is almost inevitably led to the topic of education, and the strongest philosophers in the tradition have been systematic philosophers. And so it has been that, time and again, ethical theorists have turned to instruction to put in place the moral commitment that they took the antiskeptical arguments to warrant. Plato was preoccupied with the question of whether virtue could be taught, and over two thousand years later, John Stuart Mill—attentive enough to the importance of moral cultivation to argue for political liberty and gender equality on the grounds that they improve one's character—devoted much of the third chapter of his *Utilitarianism* to explaining why educational institutions that produce natural altruists are, in the long run, inevitable.[2]

The antiskeptical argumentation and the pedagogical follow-on were not independent projects. If moral education could never be more than brainwashing, moral skepticism would be correct. And whether or not moral expertise is a coherent or morally acceptable notion, brainwashing is now acknowledged to be a last resort; we would much rather avoid a scheme of educational allocation in which only experts-to-be receive more than mere brainwashing. Thus, the ideal has come to be instruction, supplied to every fully participating member of a society, that brings its pupils to a compelling appreciation of the force of the reasons—the *real* reasons—for morality. Over time, the catalog of heavy-handed experiments in improving the citizens' level of moral commitment, on one or another construction of what that ought to be, has become depressingly lengthy.

I want here to think about the persistence of moral skepticism in the face of all those theories, and all those attempts at teaching moral commitment. I will deploy materials from a recent account of moral standing to assemble an explanation for skepticism's tenacity. The account, I am going to suggest, has the consequence that, no matter how good it is, theory will not do away with moral skeptics. And it has the further consequence that, in the long run, even the last-resort fallback will not work: theoretically unambitious training will not do the job, either, and will not do so no matter how effective brainwashing techniques become. (That blanket claim will eventually be supplemented by a disturbing qualification.) Neither theory nor education will in the end do what so many philosophers have assumed they could, that is, anchor ethical commitment against skeptical second thoughts.

The explanation of moral standing that I will be using is due to Robert Nozick, and although the position I will draw out of it was not his, and is perhaps not one he would have endorsed, it would be a suitable tip of the hat to his life and work to describe it as Nozickian.[3] I will begin by summarizing and amending Nozick's treatment of moral standing.

I

Many people think that it is morally forbidden to kill other human beings (anyway, to kill them in order to eat them), but that it is fine to kill animals (and to kill them in order to eat them). Many people also think that this injunction or prohibition is directed toward, or applies to, human beings, but not to animals: while we do try to prevent animals from eating people, we do not take the animals to be violating a moral code when they do so.[4] A shorthand for these opinions is that human beings, but not animals, have *moral standing*; moral theories describe demands and evaluative judgments that cover, apply to, or stick to people, but not animals.

Of course, at different times and places people have held different views about who or what has moral standing; it is only recently that the line between those who have it and those who don't has been drawn to include all human beings, and at present there are controversies over whether to include some or all of the animals. I don't right now want to be inviting you to have a particular view on the subject but, rather, just to be introducing the notion.

Now, what accounts for moral standing? There is a long history of attempts to explain it *metaphysically*, by which I mean to account for it as an intrinsic feature of its possessors (which can then ground the demands of one's moral theory). For example, the Benthamite utilitarian view is that human beings have moral standing in virtue of their ability to feel pleasure and pain; the traditional Kantian view is that they have moral standing in virtue of being rational agents; a widespread religious view is that they have moral standing in virtue of having souls, or being created in the image of God. Nozick departs from this tradition by giving a *political* account of moral standing. The rules of a morality are the rules of a particular sort of game (where that term is meant in its game-theoretic sense, and so not as implying frivolity or fun); to have moral standing is to be a player in such a game.[5] On this conception of moral standing, it is not an intrinsic or metaphysical property of human beings. You might have moral standing in one morality game but not in another; you might have standing in no morality game at all. For instance, in the Nazis' morality game, Jews had no standing; in the ancient Greeks', perhaps barbarians had none.[6]

These games are sometimes framed by and effectively coextensive with institutional structures such as states or religious hierarchies, and in those cases moral standing may amount to an institutional status, such as citizenship or church membership. But this is not the general or even the normal case, because morality games often serve to manage and coordinate activity when such structures are lacking or unsuitable. Think of the norms of hospitality in nomadic cultures, or the role the Geneva Convention was once meant to play in European warfare. These functions may explain our own tendency to distinguish moral from political status.

One prominent and especially important feature of these games is that they can be expanded, in either of two ways.[7] If a winning coalition—Nozick calls it a "power subgroup"—of the players of a game so decides, they can admit new players (the abolition of slavery, after America's Civil War, might be a good example); alternatively, they can merge with other ongoing games. These decisions are not necessarily, or even usually, simple yes-or-no questions. Building a coalition that favors expansion, and which is able to carry the day, may involve complex negotiations, often resulting in provisos making (metaphorical or even literal) second-class citizens of the new entrants. Nozick points out under this heading that first-generation immigrants often accept living and working conditions below the legal minimum for other citizens; it is only under these conditions that the prior players of the game are willing to admit them. And when two different games, with two different sets of rules, are merged, compromise rules for the new game must be settled on to cover players formerly covered by the old sets of rules.

Morality games started long ago, and started small. Over time, expansion and mergers have created such large-scale coverage and integration that we tend to think that there is just one morality game in which everyone is a player. That tendency (along with the philosophical tendency to look for metaphysical foundations for aspects of our life that we regard as important) explains the prevalence of the notion that moral standing is an intrinsic property. But even now it is overstated to say that there is just one all-inclusive morality game. We only find it plausible to say so because we are likely to overlook those who are outside the very big game in which we are players. *Everyone* has moral standing—but to count as *someone*, you have to be a player in the game. Today, animals aren't players, and so we don't usually think of them as counterexamples to the claim that everyone has moral standing. Analogously, even though women and slaves couldn't participate politically, the ancient Athenians thought of themselves as a democracy, rather than an odd sort of oligarchy, because they didn't count women or slaves as possible political actors; large populations of disenfranchised children don't count against describing a regime as democratic nowadays, because we don't regard children as possible political actors.[8]

Moral standing is, in Nozick's account, a political and social achievement, and not one which we should take for granted. He reminds us that politicians sometimes try to build coalitions which will expel players from a morality game or will fracture one game into two, often along ethnic lines. But, he allows, the historical trend seems to be toward larger games, with more players, and that is, he agrees, overall a good thing.

Nozick has not been the only philosopher to take moral standing to be a political or conventional matter. The idea seems to be at work in Hume when he restricts the demands of justice to those who can make others "feel the effects of their resentment."[9] Some of the more recent Kantians describe themselves as "constructivists," and while they for the most part write as though the question of who is to engage in "construction" was already settled by the metaphysical fact of personhood, I read Rawls's last work as broaching the question of who counts, and doing so in a political rather than metaphysical spirit.[10] But Nozick's treatment is distinctive in explaining the scope of moral standing via a dynamic, multistage process.

II

Morality games are characterized in part by the fact that they impose norms on the players, and by the further fact that, while they typically penalize violations of their norms, their players are not responsive merely to the threat that penalties will be imposed; rather, they internalize the norms of the morality game.[11] The problem of moral skepticism is a live issue because such norms are not internalized to the point where they become one's deliberative norms, plain and simple (i.e., they are not internalized to the exclusion of other terms in which people can think about what to do). After all, if one's thought and deliberation were conducted entirely in terms of the norms of one's morality game, the question of why to be moral (asked in the characteristic tone of the moral skeptic) would never arise. Nozick gestures at both the social and evolutionary benefits of internalizing such norms; we observe that people do internalize norms, and we should not be surprised at that. The interesting question is, then, why norms do not get internalized *all the way.*[12]

Consider the process of expanding or merging morality games. Because players cannot be brought to consent if their interests and positions are not accommodated, building a winning coalition to support expansion or merger involves renegotiating the rules of the game[13] (as, for instance, when the negotiations create a new category of second-class participant as a condition of expansion). Renegotiation of this kind presupposes two further characteristics of the players.

First, they must have a certain distance from the norms they currently follow; after all, if they were fully and wholeheartedly committed to them, they would be unable seriously to consider abandoning them for other rules. (And if we think of the rules as covering, inter alia, who has moral standing, there is an important class of cases in which this is true by definition.) By way of illustration, suppose that in a particular morality game "modesty" and "knowing one's place" are terms used to describe conformity to norms governing the behavior of a group of second-class players, and suppose the players of the game are fully committed to those norms. Then proposals to change the norms in ways that upgrade the status of the second-class players will run aground on the emotionally entrenched objection that they foster immodesty and that the second-class players should know their place.

Second, the players must have available a set of interests, which can be to some extent understood as independent of the rules of their current morality game, in terms of which to conduct the negotiations. In referring to these as their *interests,* I do not mean to beg any questions as to just how egoistic or more narrowly self-interested they are. They might well be, as they were often in the past, religious or clan interests; the skeptical question, 'Why be moral?' does not always have to be asked from the point of view of personal prudence. Notice that there is a tricky question as to how to delineate the relevant notion of independence. The problem is that what plausibly count as interests of this sort may be constitutively intertwined with the rules of one's morality game. For example, property depends on rules to the effect that other people can't just walk away with it; social standing depends on rules that require various sorts of comportment. But I won't try to specify more tightly what I mean by independence just now.

Players who have the distance from the rules of their current morality game required for renegotiating those rules, together with interests in terms of which they can assess competing adjustments to the rules of their morality game, will be in a position to ask themselves: these are the demands of such-and-such a morality game, but why should I accept them? So they are players for whom moral skepticism can and may well arise. Why have we so persistently, over the course of past centuries, found such players?

Allow as a premise that size matters: larger morality games, when they do not absorb or merge with smaller ones, have often, over the course of history, simply crushed them.[14] Nozick entertains this possibility in an uncharacteristically delicate way, when he points out that norms that have made possible "a large coordinated society . . . contributed also to the society's ability to mobilize resources and physical force in its competitive relations with other societies" (2001, p. 291). The events themselves, however, are not delicate: because the players outside one's morality game have no moral standing, crushing smaller morality games has often meant exterminating their players. Because larger morality games have more players than smaller ones, and because, as they are absorbed or flattened, smaller morality games become fewer and farther between, when you, an observer, look around, the chances are that you will be in a larger rather than a smaller morality game.

Morality games grow by adding new players and by merging with other games.[15] These processes require the distance and interests that enable moral skepticism. (A bit of nuance: it is not that the ability to renegotiate one's morality game is identical to moral skepticism but, rather, that the preconditions of the former enable and so amount to a disposition to the latter.) So the preconditions of moral skepticism are produced and maintained by at least two kinds of selection effect: the likelihood that morality games that foster the preconditions of moral skepticism will displace those which don't, and anthropic selection, the likelihood that you will, as an observer, find yourself in a morality game that fosters those preconditions.[16]

If people naturally adopted the position that the rules of a morality game were to be accepted only to the extent that they served one's independently defined interest, moral skepticism would not have become a topic of philosophical discussion. Moral skepticism is experienced as a *problem* because the players of morality games do to some extent or other internalize the norms of their game. Those who do not internalize them at all we call sociopaths, and they are relatively rare. But, on the other hand, the players of morality games that emerge from the process we have just described also have, as part of the cultural tradition of the morality game they are in, the ability to stand back from the rules of their game and assess it against their interests. In a suitably reflective culture, the ensuing tension gives rise to philosophical theory meant to resolve it and, in even minimally self-aware cultures, to attempts to develop and reinforce internalizations of the norms of the game.

III

Here is an argument to the effect that deploying moral theory in order to eliminate moral skepticism is, over the long run, futile. Suppose you were to produce and disseminate a moral theory (supported by arguments that were as good as you like) that resolved the tension: your theory demonstrates that you ought to accept and abide by the rules of the morality game.

For a philosophical theory to extirpate the problem of moral skepticism from the lives of most people, it must spread widely and persuade those who become aware of it to adopt it. So suppose the argument spreads, convincing almost all players of the morality game in which it appears. If it is an argument for the rules of the morality game, then when the time comes to renegotiate those rules, players of the game will be handicapped by the extra allegiance the rules now enjoy: they will lack the distance from them that is the prerequisite for expanding the game. And so, in the long run, a morality game (a culture) in which people are susceptible to such theorizing and arguments will not be prepared to face down a competing game whose members are not susceptible. Lacking the ability to negotiate a merger, and lacking moral standing (from the point of view of the more powerful players of the other game), they will, sooner or later, be wiped out.[17] When we look around, after a suitably lengthy stretch of time, we will find morality games in which no such theory has shown itself to be effective.

This is not to say that arguments against moral skepticism will have *no* effects; indeed, they may temporarily ameliorate skepticism. But they will not nail down full allegiance to morality once and for all; after a while, such extreme effects will wash out. Moral theory is not the long-term solution to doubts and questions about the legitimacy of morality. Since producing once-and-for-all commitment to morality has been the (sometimes explicit, sometimes implicit) aim of moral theory of a certain stripe, moral theory of that stripe has been deeply misguided.

IV

Our argument against the long-term effectiveness of moral theory does not turn on how intellectually respectable the theory is. That means that even dropping our theoretical ambitions will not help. Let the content be so flimsy as to make of its inculcation no more than brainwashing: no matter the material of a moral curriculum, and no matter the methods of instruction, if it is effective in the short term in eliminating the ability to adopt the stance of the moral skeptic, the processes of selection to which we have pointed will work to neutralize its effects over the long term. We should expect to see moral education that is only weakly effective, and when we look around, that *is* what we see.

Still, the conclusion for which we have been arguing requires a bit of contouring. After all, why can't a morality game outgrow its competitors without relying on the sorts of mergers and expansions that require negotiation and compromise? To be sure, this is not an easy task: think of how even as militarily determined a regime as Rome's found it necessary repeatedly to renegotiate the terms of citizenship in order to co-opt new members.

For a morality game to increase the number of its players rapidly enough, relying only on nonnegotiated recruitment of outsiders and population growth, policies that strongly prioritize those tasks must be entrenched in the norms of the game. We are not unfamiliar with social institutions that emphasize proselytizing, or forced conversions, or large family size, and it is usual to hear those policies explained by their participants' moral certainty (often unflatteringly described as fanaticism). The surprise put on the table by the present argument is that the direction of explanation runs the other way: it is the content of the policies that makes moral certainty sustainable in the long term, for only policies dictating the aggressive expansion of a compromise-resistant morality game can keep it growing quickly enough to forestall its demise when it encounters other morality games that grow by mergers and acquisitions. In general, then, resistance to moral skepticism is not viable over the long term, but there is a disconcerting exception: when what the players of a game most value is increasing the number of players of their game, without renegotiating its rules.

V

You might think that even if, after two thousand plus years of trying, we do not have an argument that convincingly refutes moral skepticism, there is a consolation prize. It is easy to conclude from the history that no such argument is satisfactory from the purely logical point of view, and that that in turn is because moral skepticism is the *truth*. But we have seen that even if there were a sound and valid argument against moral skepticism, in the long run it would not be convincing anyway.[18] So we can tell ourselves that the philosophical constructions produced in the history of what was in fact a misguided endeavor may have been better, by formal lights, than we are tempted to suppose them to be.[19]

You might also think that if, even after all those efforts, what we see are only weakly effective programs of moral education, there is a second consolation prize. We tend to think of our educational institutions as dismal failures when it comes to this particular job.[20] It tends to be assumed that when moral education *is* done right, it is by accident, the effect of a charismatic or otherwise gifted teacher. It is easy to conclude that the track record is an empirical impossibility proof: that moral education is something that isn't done right because it *can't* be done right, at any rate systematically; which in turn means that the science of ethical education is somehow an incoherent enterprise; which further means that the corresponding part of philosophy of education is somehow a mirage rather than a genuine subject matter. But we have seen that even if fully effective programs of moral education have been implemented, we shouldn't expect to see them around anymore; they, or rather the places where they were implemented and worked, have been ploughed under and forgotten. Pedagogical incompetence may look like miserable failure when it is viewed locally and close up, but the society whose educational institutions are incompetent at firmly inculcating its moral principles lives to fight another day. We are the inheritors of traditions that yield only modest pedagogical success, because full success is weeded out over time. The consolation prize, accordingly, is that philosophers of education may have managed more truth in their theories of moral education than we have been prone to imagine.

There is a better, because more practical, way of facing up to the fact that much of our theorizing has been misdirected, namely, rethinking the job of moral pedagogy. Education, in the sense at hand, is not necessarily to be understood as the product of specialized institutions such as schools; nevertheless, one quick way to identify a widely prevalent conception of the task it has been set is to take a look at the contemporary ethics curriculum. Its textbooks reflect a set of presumptions as to what a successful ethical education is. Its bread and butter is teaching what the right thing to do is: in our present way of putting it, what the rules of the governing morality game require.[21] More ambitiously, it attempts to put students in a position to handle complex or tricky cases, by figuring out the morally correct decision for themselves—appealing, however, to the rules of the governing morality game. In especially ambitious cases, it attempts to equip students to argue about what the correct moral view (already really) is, and if the account of moral standing we are considering is on target, this means that the students are confused about what they are doing; I will return to this point momentarily. Finally, it has a homiletic dimension, meant to reinforce commitment to the rules of the morality game.

Perhaps there is a place for some suitably muted version of all of these enterprises, even if the point of moral education cannot reasonably be to commit people, wholeheartedly and irrevocably, to doing the right thing. And some philosophers seem to have backed away from the idea that full-fledged moral commitments are to be produced by teaching the young to appreciate the arguments. For example, when Rawls tells his readers that a "constitutional democracy must have political and social institutions that effectively lead its citizens to acquire the appropriate sense of justice as they grow up and take part in society,"[22] the task he turns out to be imposing is, by the lights of the tradition, unassuming: that of amplifying and shaping already available moral sentiments in a way that will produce *enough* commitment, spread out over society as a whole, to keep its institutions stable in normal, that is, relatively undemanding, circumstances. That is a long way from setting out to eliminate moral skepticism entirely.

However, if anything like the Nozickian account is correct, moral or ethical tuition needs to take on a further agenda, that of preparing players of the present morality game for changes in the rules, and especially for changes in how moral standing is delineated. If the power subgroup that negotiates such changes is not going to be a tiny and undemocratic elite, we must equip everyone to participate in renegotiating the terms of the game.[23] That means, among other things, training people to look out for their interests when the (not so much theorists or scholars, but) brokers and mergers-and-acquisitions specialists of ethics propose the deals necessary to keep our morality game growing fast enough to stay abreast of a never-ending arms race.

This sort of participation is contingent upon demystifying the terms in which such renegotiations have traditionally been broached. Attempts to redraw the scope of moral standing are almost always conducted in what we could call a proleptic register. In something like the way that parents tell children that good boys and girls brush their teeth (i.e., they announce a proposal as a fact, hoping thereby to make it so), attempts to include new individuals under the moral heading of personhood have normally been accompanied by the insistence that, as a matter of metaphysical fact, those individuals were really persons *already*. Likewise, and more depressingly, attempts to eject players from a morality game are generally accompanied by appeals to the alleged metaphysical fact that those being excluded are not really human beings. Equipping the players of our morality game to be clear-eyed negotiators means—and I acknowledge that this will seem like a lot to swallow—teaching them that the question is not, "Who is (already, metaphysically) a person?" but, "Who shall our morality game collectively designate and acknowledge as a person?"

If this does seem like a lot to swallow, that is because, from the perspective that treats moral standing as a metaphysical matter, it looks like a lapse into cynicism. (If you construe personhood metaphysically, it will sound to you as though we are being asked to agree that, while the candidates for admission are not really people, it pays to *pretend* that they are.) If mergers and expansions of our morality game are practically unavoidable, however, the commitment to a metaphysical conception of personhood is likely to express itself in a much more dangerous form of cynicism, which we can call *country club syndrome*. By that I mean an emotional posture adopted by older members of a club who have not reconciled themselves to the newly broadened membership; having had to accept the new level of inclusiveness, and regarding the previous exclusions as justified by the real inferiority of the formerly excluded, they respond by emotionally disinvesting in the club. This is not a stance any of us should want to see adopted toward the ever-widening morality game, and so perhaps the Nozickian account of moral standing adds three related items—both delicate and ambitious—to the agenda of philosophy of education: figuring out how to manage the shift from metaphysical to political conceptions of personhood, how to enable transparent public debate over revisions to the scope of moral standing, and how to do so without undermining the goodwill of its players for the morality game.

NOTES

I would like to thank Chrisoula Andreou, Alyssa Bernstein, Sarah Buss, Christoph Fehige, Erika George, Tom Herrnstein, Gregg Horowitz, Harvey Siegel, Cindy Stark, Leif Wenar, and an audience at the Intermountain Philosophy Conference at Brigham Young University for comments on earlier drafts of this Chapter, as well as Jon Bendor, Pepe Chang, and Ron Mallon for helpful conversation. This essay grew out of conversations at a Liberty Fund conference on Robert Nozick; I'm grateful to the Fund, to the participants for the lively discussion, and to the Australian National University's RSSS, for its hospitality.

1. The disjunction is meant to cover philosophers, such as Anscombe 1997, or Williams 1985, p.6, who contrast ethics with morality, and think of morality as a recent innovation. From here on out, I'll use the terms interchangeably.

2. Mill 1967–1989, vol. 10, pp. 227–33; vol. 18, pp. 260–75; vol. 21, pp. 259–340, esp. at pp. 288*ff.* Ryle 1966, p. 118, speculates that Plato took up the topic because it was standardly assigned for dialectical exercises and perhaps competitions; if true, that witnesses to a prevalent worry in the broader culture of the time about whether education could successfully inculcate ethical commitment.

3. Nozick 2001, chap. 5. Nozick describes his project as a "genealogy" of ethics, and thus joins Williams 2002 in conflating genealogies with state-of-nature arguments. However, as Nietzsche introduced the notion, a genealogy of an institution undercuts a functional account of it, by showing how functional interpretations supersede one another while leaving the workings of the institution more or less intact (1887/1976, Essay 2, secs. 12–14). State-of-nature arguments, by showing that an institution would be introduced to serve such-and-such a function, precisely do provide functional accounts of institutions. Nozick himself burst on the public scene with a state-of-nature argument addressing a perennial problem of political philosophy, that of the legitimacy of the sovereign state (1974); that argument took its moral theory for granted, and it is intriguing to see Nozick's attempt to deepen his treatment by the addition of a state-of-nature reconstruction of moral standing.

4. It is an interesting question whether these two lines are always drawn in the same place; what matters for now is that, with a handful of exceptions, the questions of who must obey the moral law and who is protected by it are not just given the same answer, but rarely distinguished from each other. I will shortly suggest that it's a merit of Nozick's account that it can explain their traveling together often enough to end up being called by the same name.

5. For a recent and related view, see Schapiro 2001.

6. For a terse description of the latter case, see Williams 2006, pp. 72f.

7. That the scope of moral standing does seem to expand has come in for notice—e.g., by Green 1969, pp. 217*ff*—who remarks on "the extension of the area of common good."

8. Nozick sometimes loses track of this point himself. When he's discussing norms that cover interaction with those outside the group (as opposed to giving a description of such interactions), he tells us they "*forbid* . . . interacting with [them] in a way that forces [them] to be worse off than if you or your group had not interacted with [them] at all" (2001, p. 264). But because those outside the group are outside the "domain of ethics" (they have no moral standing, in just the way that sticks and stones and plants have no moral standing), it is hard to see how that could be a general and effective requirement on such interactions: to be outside *such* a group is, generally, to go unrecognized, and so to fly under the radar of such a prohibition. That's compatible with its being a rule of some particular game that a specified class of nonplayers have to be treated in such-and-such a way, just as a morality game might have a rule that artworks, or Bibles, or Korans have to be treated in such-and-such a way. But normally, it is only *after* something has moral standing that one takes it to introduce moral limitations on one's options.

9. Although he does state that "we should be bound by the laws of humanity to give gentle usage to . . . creatures [who cannot]" (1777/1978, p. 190).

10. Rawls 1999; the contrast adapts the title of another of his well-known papers. Very quickly, to have moral standing, in Rawls's terminology, is to have basic human rights. Basic human rights are those whose violation (as a matter of empirical fact) is a marker of (and causally implicated in) a state's disposition to start nondefensive wars; because that disposition makes such a state a threat to a polity of "peoples," basic human rights are those that in a stable international order will warrant military or other intervention. The account thus uses the politics of the large-scale structures of a possible global political system to determine the moral standing of individuals.

For discussion of how the problem of moral standing looks to constructivists, see Williams 2005, chap. 2, esp. pp. 20f.

11. Or, more carefully, internalize *to one degree or another* the norms of the morality game (2001; p. 247, n. 17). Nozick adapts the notion from Hart 1997; he speculates that the disposition to internalize norms is the effect of a hardwired Chomskian module (p. 270), and that the belief that norms are binding may be due to a selection effect driven by the handicap principle (p. 273).

12. Nozick gestures at a number of explanations that are alternatives to the one I will focus on here: that a natural selection approach cannot specify the function of ethics tightly enough to support an argument, starting from the fact that human beings have undergone natural selection driven by that function, against feeling the pull of rational egoism (2001, pp. 269, 293); that evolution's "shaping is imperfect . . . given the occasionally large benefits of noncooperation or of betrayal of cooperative schemes" (p. 269); and that evolution might have as an equilibrium a mix of individuals, some with higher and some with lower levels of internalization (p. 263 and n. 63).

13. Because the outcome of tough negotiations should not be expected to take into account the interests of those who are not themselves negotiators, those protected by the rules of an updated morality game will normally be those to whom the rules apply (that is, the very players of the updated morality game). This is the promised explanation (see n. 4, above) of why "moral standing" is generally usable in both of these senses.

14. This claim is a good first approximation, and certainly requires qualification. However, notice that when we find, for instance, a handful of Spaniards toppling the Aztec and Inca empires, that is treated as a puzzle which deserves a special and dramatic explanation (Diamond 1999)—evidence that what the premise predicts is regarded as the normal case. Or again, as I write this, the theaters are showing a film about the Battle of Thermopylae; that battle is regarded as remarkable enough, well over two thousand years later, to be the subject of a movie. That it is remarkable is in part owing to its surprising outcome, given the numerical disparity of the forces and populations. The surprisingness of the outcome is further, if anecdotal, evidence as to what is regarded as the normal case.

We moderns have become accustomed to the phenomenon of smaller guerilla forces defeating much larger armies. So notice that this is a side effect of the process we are discussing. A guerilla underground may have a decent chance of prevailing because the most ruthless means—for instance, exterminating the population that serves as its support base—are not regarded as live options. Those options are not entertained because members of these populations have moral standing, that is, they are understood to be players in our shared morality game.

15. These are not always crisply distinguished options, but the contrast is real enough, and to get a sense of what it can amount to, compare the adjustments Belgian society is making to accommodate its large Moslem immigrant population with those it has made, and is making, to accommodate membership in the European Community.

16. For some discussion of anthropic selection effects, see Roush 2003.

17. Notice that a nihilistic philosophical theory, of the sort that makes allegiance to the norms of the morality game out to be just a mistake, should be expected to do no better. If it becomes effective in the lives of real people, then the selection effects—which, as Nozick points out, may be group selection effects (2001, pp. 253, 271, 282, n. 63)—operating in favor of internalized norms will also operate to eliminate the players whom the argument convinces, and the morality games in which the nihilistic theory becomes dominant.

We might wonder why the dispositions that give rise to moral skepticism couldn't be limited to the power players of a game. One reason is that when the power players negotiate a revision in the rules, they must be able to bring the remaining players on board once the deal is consummated. Another is that, because the negotiators can be expected to look out for their own interests first and foremost, a possible upshot of unbending naivete on the part of the others is being written out of the game entirely. (Recall the explanation for the coordination of the two aspects of moral standing, from n. 4 and n. 13.)

Might a preemptive and uncompromising universalism short circuit the argument we have just sketched? After all, if we adopt a moral theory that includes all possible political players up front (the meek, the disempowered, the poor, the proletarians), we will never need to expand the game to include anyone else. There are two reasons to doubt that this flanking move is viable. First, although this is hard to see in retrospect, the track record suggests that the players of such games are not good at exhaustively identifying possible participants. Maybe someday we will have good strategic reasons to expand our game to include classes of automatic devices; no one, not even the science fiction writers, is suggesting granting devices moral standing now, and one reason is that we cannot see clearly enough into our technological future to discern what devices could come to be political actors. (For this reason, we should also not be too quick to proclaim that the history of morality has reached a new stage, one to which the argument is irrelevant because there are no further opportunities for expansion.) Second, the morality game requires cooperation on the part of its players; the benefits it distributes entail costs paid. So designating all possible players as players, in the absence of arrangements that make real contributors of them, is no more than an empty promotion in title, and unlikely to be accepted by prior and contributing players.

18. Our argument is compatible with all the moral realism a metaethicist with such leanings could want, and even with all the moral realist epistemology he could want. The argument *does* assume that correctness of a moral theory, as Cornell moral realists understand it, confers little or no selective advantage.

To a traditional moral theorist, the argument I am developing may seem to be beside the point: whether or not morality is in the end fully endorsed by everyone, what matters is that it is *right*, and that the arguments for morality are valid and sound. The reason our agreement that they may have been counts only as a consolation prize is that the side effects of being in the right reopen the question of how much *just* being right matters.

19. There is perhaps another bonus that the Nozickian account promises to metaethicists. One way to look at the debate over internalism and externalism in twentieth-century moral philosophy is as an attempt to make sense of the outcome we have been sketching. It was widely assumed that understanding the possibility of moral skepticism would consist in articulating the respective logical types of the interest-based and norm-oriented reasons. (E.g., as when Williams 2001, made the former, "internal," reasons bottom out in the agent's motivations, and the latter, "external," reasons entirely without intelligible content; for a critical reconstruction of the argument, see Millgram 1996; for the earlier history of this debate, see Robertson 2001.) But if our story is plausible, it is quite possible that neither sort of reason is to be identified by distinctive logical features. The explanation of the tension

between the two functional classes of reasons does not require that they be of logically distinct types.

20. Here is a representative expression of this frame of mind, from someone who thought long and hard about education generally: "We believe, so far as the mass of children are concerned, that if we keep at them long enough we can teach reading and writing and figuring. We are practically, even if unconsciously, sceptical as to the possibility of anything like the same assurance in morals" (Dewey 1983, p. 291). The same author registers popular complaints about the efficacy of moral education by the schools, thus indirectly documenting the prevalence of the notion that this is something schools ought to provide, at pp. 268f.

21. When one turns to popular reference works or professional guidelines, one not infrequently finds simple checklists, as, for instance, the "Four Principles" approach in bioethics (Chadwick 2007).

22. Rawls 1999, p. 15.

23. This conclusion is closely related to recent argument that liberal states should develop skills that support autonomy in their citizens, but is not quite the same thing, because current conceptions of autonomy amount to specification of a role called for by the rules of a current morality game. For an overview of the recent back-and-forth, see the Symposium on Citizenship, Democracy, and Education, in *Ethics* 105(3), for April 1995; for some followup, see Brighouse 1998.

REFERENCES

Anscombe, G. E. M. (1997). "Modern Moral Philosophy". In *Virtue Ethics*, eds. R. Crisp, and M. Slote, pp. 26–44. Oxford: Oxford University Press.

Brighouse, H. (1998). "Civic Education and Liberal Legitimacy". *Ethics* 108(4); 719–45.

Chadwick, R. F (2007). "Bioethics". In *Encyclopedia Britannica*, Encyclopedia Britannica Online, http://www.britannica.com/eb/article-251773.

Dewey, J. (1983). "Moral Principles in Education". In *Essays on Pragmatism and Truth 1907–1909*, ed. J. A. Boydston, pp. 265–91. Carbondale: Southern Illinois University Press.

Diamond, J. (1999). *Guns, Germs, and Steel*. New York: W. W. Norton.

Green, T. H. (1969). *Prolegomena to Ethics*. Eds. A. C. Bradley and Ramon Lemos. New York: Thomas Crowell.

Hart, H. L. A. (1997). *The Concept of Law,* 2nd ed. Oxford: Oxford University Press.

Hume, D. (1777/1978). *Enquiries Concerning Human Understanding and Concerning the Principles of Morals*. 3rd ed., L. A. Selby-Bigge and P. H. Nidditch. Oxford: Clarendon Press.

Mill, J. S. (1967–1989). *Collected Works of John Stuart Mill*. Toronto/London: University of Toronto Press, Routledge and Kegan Paul.

Millgram, E. (1996). "Williams' Argument Against External Reasons". *Nous* 30(2): 197–220.

Nietzsche, F. (1887/1967). *On the Genealogy of Morals and Ecce Homo*, trans. and ed. Walter Kaufmann. New York: Vintage.

Nozick, R. (1974). *Anarchy, State, and Utopia*. New York: Basic Books.

——(2001). *Invariances*. Cambridge, MA: Harvard University Press.

Rawls, J. (1999). *The Law of Peoples: With 'The Idea of Public Reason Revisited.'* Cambridge, MA: Harvard University Press.

Robertson, J. (2001). "Internalism, Practical Reason, and Motivation". In *Varieties of Practical Reasoning.* ed. E. Millgram, pp. 127–151. Cambridge, MA: MIT Press.

Roush, S. (2003). "Copernicus, Kant, and the Anthropic Cosmological Principles". *Studies in History and Philosophy of Modern Physics* 34:5–35.

Ryle, G. (1966). *Plato's Progress.* Cambridge: Cambridge University Press.

Schapiro, T. (2001). "Three Conceptions of Action in Moral Theory". *Nous* 35(1): 93–117.

Williams, B. (1985). *Ethics and the Limits of Philosophy.* Cambridge, MA: Harvard University Press.

—— (2001). "Internal and External Reasons" (with postscript). In *Varieties of Practical Reasoning,* ed. E. Millgram, pp. 77–97. Cambridge, MA: MIT Press.

—— (2002). *Truth and Truthfulness.* Princeton, NJ: Princeton University Press.

—— (2005). *In the Beginning Was the Deed,* ed. Geoffrey Hawthorn. Princeton, NJ: Princeton University Press.

—— (2006). "Pagan Justice and Christian Love". In *The Sense of the Past,* ed. M. Burnyeat, pp. 71–82, Princeton, NJ: Princeton University Press.

CHAPTER 15

VALUES EDUCATION

GRAHAM ODDIE

MORAL education has received a great deal of attention in the philosophy of education. But morality is just one aspect of the evaluative, which embraces not just the
deontic concepts—right, wrong, permissible, obligatory, supererogatory, and so
on—but also the full range of concepts with evaluative content. This includes the
so-called thin evaluative concepts (e.g., *good, bad, better, worst*); the thick evaluative
concepts (e.g., *courageous, compassionate, callous, elegant, cruel, charming, clumsy,
humble, tendentious, witty, craven, generous, salacious, sexy, sarcastic, vindictive*); and
the concepts that lie somewhere between the extremes of thick and thin (e.g., *just,
virtuous, sublime, vicious, beautiful*). Value, broadly construed to embrace the entire
range of evaluative concepts, presents an educationist with some problems. Should
values be part of the curriculum at all? If so, which values is it legitimate for
educators to teach and how should they be taught?

1. THE CONTESTEDNESS OF VALUE
ENDORSEMENTS

Philosophers disagree wildly about the metaphysics of value, its epistemological
status, and the standing of various putative values. Given the heavily contested
nature of value, as well as of the identity and weight of particular putative values,
what business do we have teaching values? Perhaps we don't know enough about
values to teach them (perhaps we don't know anything at all[1]).

It might be objected to this argument against the teaching of values, from
value's contestedness, that value theory is no different from, say, physics, biology,

or even mathematics. There is much about these disciplines that is contested, but no one argues that that's a good reason to purge them from the curriculum. This comparison, however, is not totally convincing. True, philosophers of physics disagree over the correct interpretation of quantum mechanics, but there is little disagreement over its applications, its significance, or the necessity for students to master it. Similarly, even if there is disagreement over the foundations of mathematics or biology, few deny that we should give children a solid grounding in arithmetic or evolution.

The contestedness of value has been used to argue for a "fact/value" distinction that, when applied to educational contexts, leads to the injunction that teachers should stick to the "facts," eschewing the promulgation of "value judgments." Given the contestedness of values, an educator should pare her value endorsements down to their purely natural (nonevaluative) contents, indicating at most that, as a matter of personal preference, she takes a certain evaluative stance.

2. The Value Endorsements Informing the Educational Enterprise

Attempts to purge education of value endorsements are, of course, doomed. Value endorsements are not just pervasive, they are inevitable. The educational enterprise is about the transmission of knowledge and the skills necessary to acquire, extend, and improve knowledge. But what is knowledge—along with truth, understanding, depth, empirical adequacy, simplicity, coherence, completeness, and so on—if not a cognitive good or value?[2] And what is an improvement in knowledge if not an increase in cognitive value? Sometimes cognitive values are clearly instrumental— acquiring knowledge might help you become a physicist, a doctor, or an artist, say. But instrumental value is parasitic upon the intrinsic value of something else— here, knowledge of the world, relieving suffering, or creating things of beauty.

The enterprise of creating and transmitting knowledge is freighted with cognitive value, but episodes within the enterprise also express particular value endorsements. A curriculum, for example, is an endorsement of the value of attending to the items on the menu. It says, "*These* are worth studying." The practice of a discipline is laden with norms and values. To practice the discipline you have to learn how to do it *well*: to learn norms and values governing, inter alia, citing and acknowledging others who deserve it; honestly recording and relaying results; not forging, distorting, or suppressing data; humbly acknowledging known shortcomings; courageously, but not recklessly, taking cognitive risks; eschewing exaggeration of the virtues of a favored theory; having the integrity to pursue unwelcome consequences of discoveries. In mastering a discipline, one is inducted into a rich network of value endorsements.

The thesis of the separability of fact and value, and the associated bracketing of value endorsements, is not just tendentious (it precludes the possibility of facts *about* value) but also is so clearly unimplementable that it is perhaps puzzling that it has ever been taken entirely seriously. The educational enterprise is laden with value endorsements distinctive of the enterprise of knowledge and the transmission of those very endorsements to the next generation. Without the transmission of those values, our educational institutions would disappear. So, even if the value endorsements at the core of education are contested, the enterprise itself requires their endorsement and transmission.

3. THE PLACE FOR NONCOGNITIVE VALUE ENDORSEMENTS IN EDUCATION

To what extent does the transmission of cognitive values commit us to the teaching of other values? It would be fallacious to infer that, in any educational setting, all and any values are on the table—that it is always permissible, or always obligatory, for a teacher to impart his value endorsements when those are irrelevant to the central aims of the discipline at hand. For certain value issues, a teacher may have no business promulgating his endorsements. For example, the values that inform physics don't render it desirable for a physicist to impart his views on abortion during a lab. Physicists typically have no expertise on that issue.

But it would be equally fallacious to infer that cognitive values are tightly sealed off from noncognitive values. Certain cognitive values, however integral to the enterprise of knowledge, are identical to values with wider application. Some I have already adverted to: honesty, courage, humility, integrity, and the like. These have different applications in different contexts, but it would be odd if values bearing the same names within and without the academy were distinct. So, in transmitting cognitive values, one is ipso facto involved in transmitting values that have wider application.[3] This doesn't imply that an honest researcher will be an honest spouse—she might lie about an affair. And an unscrupulous teacher might steal an idea from one of his students without being tempted to embezzle. People are inconsistent about the values on which they act, but these are the same values honored in the one context and dishonored in the other.

I have argued that there are cognitive values informing the educational enterprise that need to be endorsed and transmitted, and that these are identical to cognate values that have broader application. However, this doesn't exhaust the values that require attention in educational settings. There are disciplines—ethics, for example—in which the subject matter itself involves substantive value issues. In a course on the morality of abortion, for example, it would be impossible to avoid talking about the value of certain beings and the disvalue of ending their existence. Here, explicit attention must be paid to noncognitive values. There are other disciplines—the arts, for example—in which the point of education is to teach students to discern aesthetically valuable features, to develop evaluative frameworks to facilitate future investigations, and to produce valuable works. Within such disciplines it would be incredibly silly to avoid explicit evaluation.

4. The Role of Inculcating Beliefs in Education

Grant that there are noncognitive values, as well as cognitive values, at the core of certain disciplines. Still, given that there are radically conflicting views about these—the value of a human embryo, or the value of Duchamp's *Fountain*—shouldn't teachers steer clear of explicitly transmitting value endorsements? Here, at least, isn't it the teacher's responsibility to distance himself from his value endorsements and teach the subject in some "value-neutral" way?

In contentious areas, teachers should obviously be honest and thorough in their treatment of the full range of conflicting arguments. Someone who thinks abortion is impermissible should give both Thomson's and Tooley's famous arguments for permissibility a full hearing. Someone who thinks abortion permissible should do the same for Marquis's.[4] However, even if some fact about value were *known*, there are still good reasons for teachers not to indoctrinate, precisely *because* inducing value knowledge is the aim of the course.

Value knowledge, like all knowledge, is not just a matter of having true beliefs. Knowledge is believing what is true for good reasons. To impart knowledge, one must cultivate the ability to embrace truths for good reasons. Students are overly impressed by the fact that their teachers have certain beliefs, and they are motivated to embrace such beliefs for that reason alone. So, it's easy for a teacher to impart favored beliefs, regardless of where the truth lies. A teacher will do a better job of imparting reasonable belief—and the critical skills that her students will need to pursue and possess knowledge—if she does not reveal overbearingly her beliefs. That's a common teaching strategy whatever the subject matter, not just value.[5]

The appropriate educational strategy may appear to be derived from a separation of the evaluative from the non-evaluative, but its motivation is quite different. It is *because* the aim of values education is value knowledge (which involves *reasonable* value beliefs) rather than mere value belief, that instructors should eschew indoctrination.

5. The Natural/Value Distinction Examined

In ethics and the arts, noncognitive values constitute the subject matter. But that isn't the norm. In many subject areas, values aren't the explicit subject matter. Despite this, in most disciplines it isn't clear where the subject itself ends and questions of value begin. Even granted a rigorous nonvalue/value distinction, for logical reasons there are, inevitably, claims that straddle the divide. It would be undesirable, perhaps impossible, to excise such claims from the educational environment.

Consider a concrete example. An evolutionary biologist is teaching a class on the evolutionary explanation of altruism. He argues that altruistic behavior is explicable as "selfishness" at the level of genes. His claim, although naturalistic, has implications for the value of altruistic acts. Suppose animals are genetically disposed to make greater sacrifices for those more closely genetically related to them than for those only distantly related, because such sacrifices help spread their genes. Suppose that the value of an altruistic sacrifice is partly a function of overcoming excessive self-regard. It would follow that the value of some altruistic acts—those on behalf of close relatives—would be diminished. And that is a consequence properly classified as evaluative. Of course, this inference appeals to a proposition connecting value with the natural, but such propositions are pervasive and ineliminable.

Here is an argument for the unsustainability of a clean natural/value divide among propositions. A clean divide goes hand in glove with the Humean thesis that a purely evaluative claim cannot be validly inferred from purely natural claims, and vice versa. Let N be a purely natural claim and V a purely evaluative claim. Consider the conditional claim C: if N then V. Suppose C is a purely natural claim. Then from two purely natural claims (N and C) one could infer a purely evaluative claim V. Suppose instead that C is purely evaluative. The conjunction of two purely evaluative (natural) claims is itself purely evaluative (natural). Likewise, the negation of a purely evaluative (natural) proposition is itself purely evaluative (natural).[6] Consequently, not-N, like N, is purely natural, and so one could derive a purely evaluative claim (C) from a purely natural claim (not-N). Alternatively, not-V, like V, is purely evaluative. So, one could derive a purely natural claim (not-N) from two purely evaluative claims (C and not-V).

Propositions like C are natural-value *hybrids*: they cannot be coherently assigned a place on either side of a sharp natural/value dichotomy. Hybrids are not just propositions that have both natural and evaluative content (like the thick evaluative attributes). Rather, their characteristic feature is that their content is not the conjunction of their purely natural and purely evaluative contents.

Hybrids are rife among the propositions in which we traffic. Jack believes Cheney unerringly condones what's good (i.e., Cheney condones X if and only if X is good), and Jill, that Cheney unerringly condones what's not good. Neither Jack nor Jill knows that Cheney has condoned the waterboarding of suspected terrorists. As it happens, both are undecided on the question of the value of waterboarding suspected terrorists. They don't disagree on any purely natural fact (neither knows what Cheney condoned); nor do they disagree on any purely evaluative fact (neither knows whether condoning waterboarding is good). They disagree on this: *Cheney condones waterboarding suspected terrorists if and only if condoning such is good.* Suppose both come to learn the purely natural fact that Cheney condones waterboarding. They will deduce from their beliefs conflicting, purely evaluative conclusions: Jack that condoning waterboarding is good; Jill that condoning waterboarding is not good. So, given that folk endorse rival hybrid propositions, settling a purely natural fact will impact the value endorsements of the participants differentially because natural facts and value endorsements are entangled via a rich set of hybrids.

I don't deny that there are purely natural or purely evaluative claims, nor that certain claims can be disentangled into their pure components. I am arguing that there are hybrids—propositions that are not equivalent to the conjunction of their natural and evaluative components. The fact that we all endorse hybrid claims means that learning something purely natural will often exert rational pressure on evaluative judgments (and vice versa). An education in the purely natural sciences may thus necessitate a reevaluation of values; and an education in values may necessitate a rethinking of purely natural beliefs.

6. Intrinsically Motivating Facts and the Queerness of Knowledge of Value

I have argued that natural and evaluative endorsements cannot be neatly disentangled in an educational setting for purely logical reasons. Still, it's problematic to embrace teaching a subject unless we have a body of *knowledge*. For there to be value knowledge there must be knowable truths about value. A common objection to these is that they would be very *queer*—unlike anything else that we are familiar with in the universe.

The queerness of knowable value facts can be elicited by considering their impact on motivation. Purely natural facts are motivationally inert. For example, becoming acquainted with the fact that this glass contains potable water (or a lethal dose of poison) does not *by itself* necessarily motivate me to drink (or refrain from drinking). Only in combination with an antecedent desire on my part (to quench my thirst, or to commit suicide) does this purely natural fact provide me with a motivation. A purely evaluative fact would, however, be different. Suppose it's a fact that the best thing for me to do now would be to drink potable water, and that I know that fact. Then it would be very odd for me to say, "I know that drinking potable water would be the best thing for me to do now, but I am totally unmoved to do so." One explanation of this oddness is that knowledge of a value fact entails a corresponding desire: value facts necessarily motivate those who become acoquainted with them.

Why would this intrinsic power to motivate be queer rather than simply *interesting*? The reason is that beliefs and desires seem logically independent—having a certain set of beliefs does not entail the having of any particular desires. Beliefs about value would violate this apparent independence. Believing that something is *good* would entail having a corresponding *desire*. Additionally, simply by virtue of imparting to your student a value belief you would thereby instill in him the corresponding motivation to act. How can mere belief *necessitate* a desire? Believing something good is one thing; desiring it is something else.

One response to the queerness objection is to reject the idea that knowing an evaluative fact *necessarily* motivates. Let's suppose, with Hume, that beliefs without desires are powerless to motivate. A person may well have a contingent independent desire to do what he believes to be good, and once he becomes acquainted with a good he may, contingently, be motivated to pursue it. But no mere belief, in isolation from such an antecedent desire, can motivate. That sits more easily with the frequent gap between what values we espouse and how we actually behave.

This Humean view would escape the mysteries of intrinsic motivation, but would present the educationist with a different problem. What is the *point* of attempting to induce true value beliefs if there is *no* necessary connection between value beliefs and motivations? If inducing true evaluative beliefs is the goal of values education, and evaluative beliefs have no such connection with desires, then one might successfully teach a psychopath correct values, but his education would make him no more likely to choose the good. His acquisition of the correct value *beliefs*, coupled with his total indifference to the good, might just equip him to make his psychopathic adventures more effectively evil.

There are two traditions in moral education that can be construed as different responses to the problem of intrinsic motivation. There is the formal, rationalist tradition according to which the ultimate questions of what to do are a matter of reason, or rational coherence in the body of evaluative judgments. But there is a corresponding empiricist tradition, according to which there is a source of empirical data about value, something which also supplies the appropriate motivation to act.

7. The Rationalist Response to the Problem of Intrinsic Motivation

Kant famously espoused the principle of universalizability: that a moral judgment is legitimate only if one can consistently will a corresponding universal maxim.[7] A judgment fails the test if willing the corresponding maxim involves willing conditions that make it impossible to apply the maxim. Cheating to gain an unfair advantage is wrong, on this account, because one cannot rationally will that everyone cheat to gain an unfair advantage. To be able to gain an unfair advantage by cheating, others have to play by the rules. So, cheating involves a violation of reason. If this idea can be generalized, and value grounded in reason, then perhaps we don't need to posit queer value facts (that *cheating is bad*, say) that mysteriously impact our desires upon acquaintance. Value would reduce to nonmysterious facts about rationality.

This rationalist approach, broadly construed, informs a range of educational value theories—for example, those of Hare and Kohlberg, as well as of the "values clarification" theorists.[8] They share the idea that values education is not a matter of teaching substantive value judgments but, rather, of teaching constraints of rationality, like those of logic, critical thinking, and universalizability. They differ in the extent to which they think rational constraints yield substantive evaluative content. Kant apparently held that universalizability settles our moral obligations. Others, like Hare, held that universalizability settles some issues (some moral judgments are just inconsistent with universalizability) while leaving open a range of coherent moral stances, any of which is just as consistent with reason as another. What's attractive about the rationalist tradition is that it limits the explicit teaching of value content to the purely cognitive values demanded by reason alone—those already embedded in the educational enterprise—without invoking additional problematic value facts.

There are two problems with rationalism. First, despite the initial appearance, it too presupposes evaluative facts. If cognitive values necessarily motivate—for example, learning that a maxim is inconsistent necessarily induces an aversion to acting on it—then the queerness objection kicks in. And if cognitive values don't necessarily motivate, then there will be the familiar disconnect between acquaintance with value and motivation.

Second, rational constraints, including even universalizability, leave open a vast range of substantive positions on value. A Kantian's inviolable moral principle—it is always wrong intentionally to kill an innocent person, say—may satisfy universalizability. But so, too, does the act-utilitarian's injunction to always and everywhere maximize value. If killing innocent people is bad, then it is better to kill one innocent person to prevent a larger number being killed than it is to refrain from killing the one and allowing the others to be killed. The nihilist says it doesn't matter how many people you kill, and this, too, satisfies universalizability. The radical divergence in the recommendation of sundry universalizable theories suggests that rational constraints are too weak to supply substantive evaluative content. Reason leaves open a vast space of mutually incompatible evaluative schemes.

8. THE EMPIRICIST RESPONSE TO THE PROBLEM OF INTRINSIC MOTIVATION

To help weed out some of these consistent but mutually incompatible evaluative schemes, value empiricists posit an additional source of data about value. They argue that detecting value is not a matter of the head, but rather a matter of the heart—of feeling, emotion, affect, or desire. It involves responding appropriately to the value of things in some way that is not purely cognitive. Many value theorists whose theories are otherwise quite different (Aristotle, Hume, Brentano, and Meinong, and their contemporary heirs) have embraced variants of this idea.[9]

Different value empiricists espouse different metaphysical accounts of value, from strongly idealist accounts (according to which values depend on our actual value responses) to robustly realist accounts (according to which values are independent of our actual responses). What they share is the denial that grasping value is a purely cognitive matter. Responses to value involve something like experience or perception. That is to say, things seem to us more or less valuable, these value-seemings are analogous to perceptual seemings rather than to beliefs, and value-seemings involve a motivational component, something desire-like.

What, then, are these experiences of value, these value-seemings? According to the Austrian value theorists (Meinong and his descendents), evaluative experiences are emotions. So, for example, anger is the emotional presentation of, or appropriate emotional response to, injustice; shame is the appropriate emotional response to what is shameful; sadness to the sad, and so on. Emotions are complex states that are necessarily connected with value judgments, but also with desires and nonevaluative beliefs. A much sparser theory of value experiences identifies them simply with desires.[10] That is to say, to desire P is just for P to seem good to me. To desire P is not to *judge* that P is good, or to *believe* that P is good. Something might well seem good to me (I desire it) even though I do not believe that it is good. Indeed, I might well know that it is not good (just as a rose I know to be white may appear to be pink to me). Value-seemings, whatever their nature, would provide the necessary empirical grounding for beliefs about value, while also providing the link between acquaintance with value and the corresponding motivations.

Imagine if you were taught the axiomatic structure of Newtonian mechanics without ever doing an actual experiment, or even being informed what results any such experiment would yield in the actual world. You might well come to know all there is to know about Newtonian mechanics, as a body of theory, without having any idea whether the actual world is Newtonian. But, then, why should you prefer Newton's theory to, say, Aristotle's, as an account of the truth? According to the value empiricist, values taught entirely as matters of reason alone would be similarly empty. By contrast, if value judgments have to be justified ultimately by appeal to some shared value data, and the value data consist of value experiences, then the job of a value educator would be, at least in part, to connect the correct evaluative judgments in the appropriate way with actual experiences of value.

9. The Theory-Ladenness of Value Data and Critical Empiricism

If pure rationalism seems empty of content, then pure empiricism seems correspondingly blind. Notoriously, people experience very different responses to putative values. Indeed, the highly variable nature of our value responses is the root of the contestedness of value, and it is often the major premise in an argument to the effect that either there is no such thing as value or, if there is, it cannot be reliably detected. If values education goes radically empiricist, and experiences of value (affect, emotion, desire, etc.) are the empirical arbiters of value, then an uncriticizable subjectivism, or at best relativism, looms, and the teaching of values would amount to little more than the teacher, like a television reporter, eliciting from her students how they feel.

This criticism presupposes a rather naive version of empiricism, according to which experience is a matter of passively receiving theory-neutral data that are then generalized into something like a value theory. A more promising model is provided by some variant of critical rationalism. Perceptual experiences are rarely a matter of passively receiving "theory-neutral" data, as a prelude to theorizing but, rather, are themselves informed and guided by theory. Even if there is a core to perceptual experience that is relatively immune to influence from background theory, the information that one gains from experience is partly a function of such theory. An experience in total isolation from other experiences to which it is connected by a theory rarely conveys significant information. If someone who knows no physics is asked to report what he sees in the cloud chamber, say, then what he reports will likely be very thin indeed and hardly a basis for grasping the nature of matter. So, enabling folk to have the right kinds of experiences—informative and contentful—which can then be appropriately interpreted and taken up into a web of belief, is in part a matter of teaching them a relevant background theory that makes sense of those experiences. This might be more accurately called a *critical empiricist* approach.

Given value experiences, and a critical empiricist approach to knowledge of value, values education would be, in part, a matter of cultivating appropriate experiential responses to various values; in part, a matter of refining and honing such responses; and in part, a matter of providing a framework that supports those responses and that can be challenged and revised in the light of further value experiences. Further, if experiences of value are a matter of emotion, feeling, or desire, values education would need to take seriously the training of folk in having, interpreting, and refining appropriate emotions, feelings, and desires. This would not in any way diminish the crucial role of logic, critical thinking, and rational constraints like universalizability. But it would open up the educational domain to cultivation and refinement of affective and conative states.

10. The Agent-Neutrality of Value and the Relativity of Value Experiences

The hypothesis of the theory-ladenness of experience is, unfortunately, insufficient to defuse the problem of the *radical* relativity in value experiences. Compare value experiences with ordinary perception. It is rare for a rose to appear to one person to be red and to another blue. But it is not at all rare for one and the same state of affairs to seem very good to one person and seem very bad to another. If these radical differences in value experiences are to be attributed simply to differences in the value beliefs that people hold, then value experiences are too corrupted to be of any use. Experiences too heavily laden with theory cease to be a reliable source of data for challenging and revising beliefs.

This problem can be sharpened by a combination of an idea endorsed by many empiricist value theorists (namely, that value is not what is desired in fact, but what it would be fitting or appropriate to desire), with a popular idea endorsed by most rationalist value theorists (namely, the agent-neutrality of real value). The *fitting-response thesis* says that something is valuable just to the extent that it is appropriate or fitting to experience it as having that value. The *agent-neutrality of value thesis* says that the actual value of a state or property is not relative to persons or point of view. So if something—a severe pain, say—has a certain disvalue, then it has that disvalue regardless of whose pain it is. It is bad, as it were, irrespective of its locus. These theses combined imply *the agent-neutrality of the fitting response to value.* If a state possesses a certain value, then it possesses that regardless of its locus. And a certain response to that value is fitting regardless of the relation of a valuer to the locus of the value. Consequently, the fitting response must be exactly the same response for any valuer. So ideally, two individuals, no matter what their relation to something of value, should respond to that value in exactly the same manner. The responses of the person whose responses are fitting are thus isomorphic to value, irrespective of the situation of that person or her relation to the value in question. Call this consequence of fitting-response and agent-neutrality, the *isomorphic-response thesis.*

Now, quite independent of the issue of theory-ladenness, the isomorphic-response thesis seems very implausible. Suppose that the appropriate response to valuable states of affairs is desire, and the more valuable a state of affairs, the more one should desire it. Then, the isomorphic-response thesis entails that any two individuals should desire all and only the same states to exactly the same degree. But clearly the states of affairs that people desire differ radically. Consequently, either we are all severely defective experiencers of value or one of the two theses that jointly entail the isomorphic-response thesis is false.

11. The Effects of Perspective, Shape, and Orientation on Perception

The fitting-response thesis looks implausible if value experiences are analogous to perceptual experiences. There is an objective state of the world that is perceiver-neutral, but perceivers have very different experiences of the world depending on how they are situated within it. First, there are perspectival effects: the farther away an object is, the smaller it will appear relative to objects close by, and that is entirely appropriate; objects *should* look smaller the farther away they are. Is there an analogue of distance in value space, and an analogue to perspective? If so, something might, appropriately, seem to be of different value depending on how far it is located from different valuers. Second, there are variable perceptual effects owing to the shape of objects and their orientation to the perceiver. An asymmetric object, like a coin, looks round from one direction but flat from another; but again, it *should* look those different ways. Is there anything in the domain of value analogous to shape and orientation?

Grant that pain is bad and that qualitatively identical pains are (*ceteris paribus*) equally bad. I am averse to the pain I am currently experiencing—it seems very bad to me. However, an exactly similar pain I experienced twenty years ago does not elicit such a strong aversion from me now. Nor does the similar pain I believe I will face in twenty years' time. I can have very different aversive responses to various pains, all of which are equally bad, and those different responses do seem fitting. The temporally distant pains are just further away, in value space, from me now. Time can, thus, be thought of as one dimension in value space that affects how values should be experienced.

Some people are close to me, and the pain of those close to me matters more to me than pain experienced by distant beings. If my wife is in severe pain, that appears much worse to me than if some stranger is in severe pain; and that response, too, seems appropriate. I know, of course, that my loved ones are no more valuable than those strangers, and I am not saying I shouldn't care at all about the stranger's pain. Clearly, the stranger's pain is bad—just as bad as my wife's pain—and I am somewhat averse to it as well. But suppose I can afford only one dose of morphine, and I can give it to my wife or have it FedExed to the stranger. Would it be inappropriate of me to unhesitatingly give it to my wife? Hardly. Someone who tossed a coin to decide where the morphine should be directed would be considered lacking normal human feelings. Persons are located at various distances from me, and since persons are loci of valuable states, those states inherit their positions in value space, and their distances from me, from their locus. And it seems appropriate to respond more vividly to states that are close than to those that are more distant.

Finally, we can think of possibility—perhaps measured by probability—as a dimension of value. Imagine this current and awful pain multiplied in length enormously. If hell exists and God condemns unbelievers to hell, then I am going to experience something like this for a very, very long time. That prospect is much worse than my current fleeting pain. And yet I am strangely unmoved by this prospect. Why? Because it seems very improbable to me. First, it seems improbable, given the unnecessary suffering in the world, that God exists. And if, despite appearances, a Perfect Being really exists, it seems improbable She would run a postmortem torture chamber for unbelievers. So, extremely bad states that are remote in probability space elicit less vivid responses than less bad states that have a higher probability of actualization. And that, too, seems fitting.

Of course, one might argue that these things should not appear this way to me, that the same pain merits the same response wherever it is located. But that's just implausible. As a human being, with various attachments, deep connections with particular others, and a limited capacity to care, it would be impossible for me to respond in a totally agent-neutral way to all pain whatever its locus: the pain of total strangers; pains past, present, and future; and pains actual as well as remotely possible. It would also be bizarre if one were required to randomly allocate one's limited stock of care regardless of the distance of the bearers of such pains. So, if a value that is closer should *appear* closer, and desires and aversions are appearances of value, then it is entirely fitting that desires and aversions be more sensitive to closely located values than to distantly located values.[11]

Distance is not the only factor affecting value perception. A valuer's orientation to something of value (or disvalue) may also affect perception. Take a variant of Nozick's famous case of past and future pain. You have to undergo an operation for which it would be dangerous to use analgesics. The surgeon tells you that on the eighth day of the month you will go into the hospital and on the morning of the ninth, you will be administered a combination of drugs that will paralyze you during the operation, scheduled for later that day, and subsequently cause you to forget the experiences you will have during the operation, including all the dreadful pain. You wake up in hospital, and you don't know what day it is. If it is the tenth, the operation was yesterday and the operation was twelve hours ago. If it is morning of the ninth, then you have yet to undergo the operation in twelve hours' time. So, depending on which of these is true, you are twelve hours away from the pain. Both are equally likely, given your information. You are equidistant from these two painful possibilities in both temporal space and probability space. You are, however, much more averse to the 50 percent probability of the future as yet-unexperienced pain than to the 50 percent probability that the pain is now past. This asymmetric response seems appropriate. We are differently oriented toward past and future disvalues, and that can make a difference how bad those disvalues seem.

What about the shape of value, and the effect of shape together with orientation on perception? Should the value of one and the same situation be experienced by folk differently if they are differently oriented with respect to it? Suppose that a retributive theory of justice is correct, and that in certain cases wrongdoers ought to be punished for their wrongdoing; that such punishment is some sort of suffering; and that the punishment restores justice to the victim. The suffering inflicted on the wrongdoer is, then, from the agent-neutral viewpoint, a good thing. Consider three people differently, related to the wrongdoer's receiving his just deserts: the wrongdoer himself, the wrongdoer's victim, and some bystander. It is fitting for the victim to welcome the fact that the wrongdoer is getting his just deserts. A neutral bystander will typically not feel as strongly about the punishment as the victim does, but provided she recognizes that the deserts are just, she should be in favor. What about the wrongdoer? His punishment is a good thing, but he has to be averse to the punishment if it is to be any sort of punishment at all. The difference in the victim's and the bystander's degree of desire for the just deserts can be explained by their differing distances from the locus of the value. But the differing responses of the victim and the wrongdoer cannot be explained by distance alone. Desire and aversion pull in opposite directions. Unless the wrongdoer is averse to his punishment, it is no punishment at all. Unless the victim desires the wrongdoer's punishment, it will not serve its full role in restoring justice.

Value is one thing, the appropriate response to it on the part of a situated valuer is another. The same value may thus elicit different responses depending on how closely the value is located to a value perceiver, the shape of the value, and the orientation of the valuer toward it. The thesis that the appropriate responses to value are experiences, which, like perceptual experiences, are heavily perspectival, defuses what would otherwise be a powerful objection to the agent-neutrality of value. If the appropriate response to an agent-neutral value were the same for all, then value would impose a wholly impractical, even inhuman, obligation on a person to effectively ignore his singular position in the network of relationships. Fortunately for us, experiences of agent-neutral values can legitimately differ from one valuer to another.

Interestingly, these features of value experience help explain the attraction of Nel Noddings's ethics of caring, perhaps the most prominent contemporary educational ethic in the empiricist tradition. For Noddings, the prime value seems to be caring relationships and fostering such relationships through fostering caring itself. But one is not simply supposed to promote caring willy-nilly, in an agent-neutral way. Rather, one is supposed to be attentive to the caring that goes on fairly close to oneself. Consequently, it would be bad to neglect one's nearest and dearest even if by doing so one could foster more caring relationships far away. But it is not just distance in the network of care that is important. I am located at the center of a particular network of caring relationships, and my moral task is to tend not just to the amount and quality of caring in my network but also to my peculiar location in the network. So, it would be wrong for me to neglect my caring for those close to me even if by doing so I could promote more or better caring among those very folk. I should not cease to care for my nearest and dearest even if by doing so I could promote higher quality caring among my nearest and dearest.[12]

12. Teaching Values on the Critical Empiricist Approach

Agent-relative responses to agent-neutral values are, thus, entirely appropriate on a critical empiricist conception of value. If this is right, it is not the job of an educationist to try to impose a uniform experiential response to all matters of value. Rather, it is to try to provide the necessary critical and logical tools for making sense of agent-neutral values in the light of our highly variable agent-relative responses, and to elicit and refine the fitting response to value in the light of a valuer's relation to it.

But this, of course, raises a difficult question for any would-be value educator. How is it possible to teach appropriate responses to value and coordinate such responses with correct value judgments? Partly, this is a philosophical question involving the nature of value and the fitting responses to it, and partly, it is an empirical question involving the psychology of value experience and the most effective ways to develop or refine fitting responses.

Let us begin with a fairly uncontroversial case. It is not difficult for a normal human being to appreciate the value of her own pleasures or the disvalue of her own pains. A normal child will almost always experience her own pain as a bad thing. There is no mystery here, given empiricism, for the child's aversion to pain is part and parcel of the experience of the pain's badness. Indeed, it is through aversion to states like pain, or desire for pleasure, that a child typically gets a grip on the concepts of goodness and badness in the first place, since the good (respectively, bad) just is that to which desire (respectively, aversion) is the normal and fitting response.

Correct judgments on the goodness of one's own pleasures and the badness of one's own pains thus follow rather naturally on the heels of one's direct experiences of those pleasures and pains. What about judgments concerning more remotely located goods and evils? Provided one has some capacity to empathize, one also has the capacity to experience, to some extent, the disvalue of another's pain or the value of another's pleasure, albeit somewhat less vividly than in the case of one's own. Clearly, normal people do have an innate ability, perhaps honed through evolutionary development, to empathize with others in these crucial ways.[13] Recent research suggests that this capacity may be realized by the possession of mirror neurons and that these structures have played a crucial role in the evolution of social behavior.[14] With empathy in place, there is the capacity to experience values located beyond oneself.

What may not always come so naturally, and what might conceivably require some tutoring, is that the exactly similar pains and pleasures of others must have exactly the same value and disvalue as one's own. Even for a good empathizer, given the perspectival nature of value experience, another's exactly similar pain will seem less bad than one's own. And the more distant the pain is, the less bad it will seem. One has to learn, at the level of judgment, to correct for this perspectival feature of value experience. That will mostly be a matter of learning to apply principles of reason—specifically, that if two situations are qualitatively identical at the natural level, they must be qualitatively identical at the level of value. Presumably, knowledge of the agent-neutrality of the goodness and badness of pain and pleasure will feed back into one's capacity for empathic response, enhancing and refining such responses. A defect in empathy may, thus, be corrected by becoming cognizant of the actual structure of value.

A person may, of course, have a very weak capacity for empathy, or even lack it altogether. This seems to be a feature of severe autism. Interestingly, an autistic person is often capable of using his experience of what is good or bad for him, together with something like universalizability, to gain a purchase on goods and evils located in other beings. His purchase on these more remote goods and evils lacks direct experiential validation, but he can still reason, from experiences of his own goods and evils, to judgments of other goods and evils. An autistic person may not thereby acquire the ability to empathize—just as a blind person may not be taught how to see—but he may still learn a considerable amount about value.[15] The value judgments he endorses will admittedly rest on a severely reduced empirical base, and that may never be enlarged by the theory, but the theory might still be quite accurate.

A more radical defect is exhibited by the psychopath, who seems to have no capacity to reason from his experience of his own goods and evils to goods and evils located elsewhere.[16] It is not clear how one might go about teaching value judgments or value responses to a psychopath. It might be like trying to teach empirical science to someone who has vivid experiences of what is going on immediately around him, but lacks any capacity to reason beyond that or to regard his own experience as a situated response to an external reality. Clearly there are limits to what can be taught and to whom.

13. Conclusion

Value endorsements and their transmission are unavoidable in educational settings, as they are everywhere. The question, then, is not whether to teach values but which values to teach, in what contexts, and how to teach them effectively. Clearly, the constraints of reason are crucial to the cultivation of a coherent set of value endorsements. But reason alone is insufficient. To access values we need some value data, experiences of value. And, to mesh motivation appropriately with value endorsements, value experiences have to be desiderative. This critical empiricist model of value knowledge suggests a model of values education that is richer and more interesting than either its rationalist or its naive empiricist rivals—one in which the cultivation and refinement of emotion, feeling, and desire and the honing of critical skills both play indispensable roles.

Of course, any teaching of values could go awry. That we are serious about teaching values, and that we attempt to do so with due respect for both reason and experience, does not guarantee that we will succeed. We ourselves may have got value wrong. Or, we might possess and try to pass on the right values, but our students reject them. Here, as elsewhere in the educational enterprise, there is always a risk that things might turn out badly despite our noblest intentions and sincerest efforts.

NOTES

1. Mackie 1977.
2. Putnam 2002.
3. Murdoch 1970.
4. All three are reprinted in Boonin and Oddie 2004.
5. Scheffler 1973 and Siegel 1997.
6. If not, then other troubling consequences flow.
7. Kant 2002.
8. Kohlberg 1981; Hare 1998; Simon, Howe, and Kirschenbaum 1972.
9. Oddie 2005, chap. 3.
10. Oddie 2005.
11. Oddie 2005, chaps. 3 and 8.
12. Bergman 2004.
13. Eisenberg 2006.
14. Singer 2006.
15. Kennett 2002.
16. Ibid.

REFERENCES

Bergman, R. (2004). "Caring for the Ethical Ideal: Nel Noddings on Moral Education." *Journal of Moral Education* 33: 149–62.

Boonin, D., and G. Oddie, eds. (2004).*What's Wrong? Applied Ethicists and their Critics.* New York: Oxford University Press.

Eisenberg, N. (2006). "Empathy-related Responding and Prosocial Behavior." In *Empathy and Fairness*, Novartis Foundation (pp. 71–79). Chicester: Wiley.

Hare, R. M. (1998). "Language and Moral Education." In: Hare, R. M., *Essays on Religion and Education* (pp. 154–72). Oxford: Clarendon.

Kant, I. (2002). *Groundwork for the Metaphysics of Morals*, edited and translated by Allen W. Wood. New Haven: Yale University Press.

Kennett, J. (2002). "Autism, Empathy and Moral Agency." *Philosophical Quarterly* 52: 340–57.

Kohlberg, L. (1981). *Essays on Moral Development*, vol 1. New York: Harper and Row, 1981.

Mackie, J. (1977). *Ethics: Inventing Right and Wrong.* New York: Penguin.

Murdoch, I. (1970). *The Sovereignty of Good.* London: Routledge.

Noddings, N. (1984). *Caring: a Feminine Approach to Ethics and Moral Education.* Berkeley: University of California Press.

Oddie, G. (2005). *Value, Reality and Desire.* Oxford: Oxford University Press.

Putnam, H. (2002). *The Collapse of the Fact/Value Dichotomy and Other Essays.* Cambridge, MA: Harvard University Press.

Scheffler, I. (1973). *Reason and Teaching.* London: Routledge

Siegel, H., ed. (1997). *Reason and Education: Essays in Honor of Israel Scheffler.* Dordrecht: Kluwer.

Simon, S. B., L. W. Howe, and H. Kirschenbaum. (1972). *Values Clarification: A Handbook of Practical Strategies for Teachers and Students.* New York: Hart Publishing.

Singer, T. (2006). "The Neuronal Basis of Empathy and Fairness." In *Empathy and Fairness,* Novartis Foundation (pp. 20–29). Chicester: Wiley.

PART IV

KNOWLEDGE, CURRICULUM, AND EDUCATIONAL RESEARCH

CHAPTER 16

CURRICULUM AND THE VALUE OF KNOWLEDGE

DAVID CARR

1. PHILOSOPHY AND CURRICULUM

ARGUABLY, the key issue of curriculum theory—that of how we might justify what we teach—is primarily a philosophical question. Insofar as the question of what we should teach and why we should teach it is about the worth of what is taught for human life or well-being, it undoubtedly belongs to that part of value inquiry broadly known as ethics or moral theory. However, to the extent that the content of the school curriculum is normally taken to be some or other body of knowledge or skills, and knowledge or skills are usually justified in terms of their objective truth and/or usefulness, the matter of justification would seem to be implicated in issues of the epistemic value of particular forms of knowledge. As we shall shortly see, some educational philosophers have thought that the obvious starting point for curriculum reflection is with questions about the epistemic status of this or that form of knowledge or skill. But, since forms of knowledge and skill are clearly of some social, political, and/or economic importance in human affairs—and since some theorists seem to have thought that there can be little more to the objectivity of knowledge and skills than their social and economic usefulness—the key issues of curriculum theory also have implications for political philosophy and theory.

2. PLATO, EDUCATION, AND CURRICULUM

It would also appear that the first place in which all of these curriculum questions are addressed in any systematic philosophical way is in such Platonic dialogues as *Gorgias, Republic,* and *Protagoras* (Hamilton and Cairns 1961). Indeed, the key philosophical question raised by Plato's teacher and mentor Socrates is effectively the educational question of how best for human beings to live their lives—more specifically, of how the young might be educated for positive living. It is well known that in the course of addressing this issue, Socrates took to task the educational philosophy of the ancient Greek sophists—in a way that remains highly relevant to contemporary concerns. For although the sophists held (broadly) that the good life consisted of the pursuit of *arete*—virtue or excellence—they appear largely to have construed such excellence in the nonmoral terms of worldly success. The truly excellent or enviable human agent would be he (rather, of course, than she) who had achieved great wealth, honor, and influence in the eyes of his peers. In consequence, only those arts or skills that conduced to the achievement of such success could be held to have much if any educational value. Specifically, for such sophists as Gorgias, the chief among such success promoting skills was *rhetoric* or the art of fine speaking by which others might be persuaded to support personal ambitions, particularly in the democratic assemblies of ancient Athens.

In short, rhetoric—as in popular modern psychology manuals—could help the practitioner to win friends and influence people. In the dialogues, Gorgias and others are fairly explicit that this is all that really matters about rhetoric: from this viewpoint, the sincerity or truth of fine words are of little account so long as personal advantage is effectively secured. It is this self-seeking view of "education" that Socrates challenges, arguing that lives of fulfilled ambition on the heels of finely worded deceit could not be regarded as virtuous or excellent lives—at least in terms of his own more moral conception of virtue. For Socrates, far from being excellent and admirable, the lives of materially prosperous or sensually sated but vicious tyrants are benighted and contemptible: no reasonable person recognizing the moral wretchedness or poverty of such lives could so want to live. For Socrates, the chief virtue or excellence is wisdom, the main goal of which is self-knowledge in the light of truth; hence, insofar as rhetoric is largely indifferent to the pursuit of truth, it can serve no genuine educational end. In this light, Plato's Socrates sets a new, morally revisionary educational agenda: since genuine virtue is nothing less than the wisdom of self-knowledge, the educational worth of any branch of study or learning resides not in its practical utility but in its contribution to the promotion of wisdom.

Socrates, of course, bequeathed to Plato the problem of showing how genuine knowledge of the good life, which for Socrates was the very essence of virtue, might be possible—not least in the face of the arguments (of, for example, Protagoras) that any and all so-called knowledge is relative to particular (individual or social) perspectives. Plato's heroic attempt to address this issue—via development of a form of dialectic that might disclose the very forms of goodness, virtue, and justice—is a fairly familiar story over which we cannot presently pause. Still, it is worth here observing that, although Plato's theory of forms is nowadays widely discredited, it ought not to be dismissed as merely a bogus attempt to secure the objective credentials of moral (and/or other) knowledge. On the contrary, Plato's theory of forms follows directly from a philosophically substantial doubt about the possibility of offering a purely empirical (or abstractionist) account of concept formation that has seldom been recognized, let alone addressed, by latter-day educational philosophers and social theorists (though this problem has, of course, been well recognized in the analytical literature of philosophical psychology; see, for example, Geach 1957).

At all events, we cannot take present leave of Plato without noting the wider social and political implications of his theory of knowledge for subsequent (medieval, modern, and contemporary) educational thinking and curriculum theorizing. First, Plato was not an educational egalitarian. Insofar as he took wisdom-conducive knowledge to be dependent on rational or intellectual abilities of an advanced order—to which he did not think that all had equal access—he proposed a highly selective education in which individuals neither should nor would be educated beyond their natural limits. But second, in view of the uneven distribution of abilities required for wisdom—and of the varying levels of educational achievement to which he thought this must inevitably lead—Plato held that individuals would also have to be differently positioned with regard to civic and political responsibilities. In short, since he thought that the wisdom required for responsible statesmanship could be cultivated only by those of requisite intellectual ability—and since it could make sense only for the wise few to rule the ignorant majority—he famously rejected democracy as a rationally optimum form of political order and association.

Plato, therefore, held that some kinds of study—those addressed to the largely theoretical discernment of allegedly objective knowledge—are superior to other (practical, technical, aesthetic) learning, and that individual ability to master such forms of knowledge in the course of advanced formal schooling rightly places some in positions of greater political authority and responsibility than others, if not in terms of greater social worth as such. Consequently, for Plato, higher education is and should be a positional good, even if public service is a concomitant of that good. It would also be hard to exaggerate the subsequent influence on educational and curriculum thinking of this idea—even on those who by no means share Plato's antidemocratic sentiments. In the particular context of British education (arguably shaped throughout much of its development by Platonic assumptions), it is somewhat ironic that the most significant of modern (postwar) official attempts to turn British schooling in a more egalitarian direction—the socialist-inspired 1944 Education Act—ushered in a selective system of schooling (constructed on the basis of an innatist conception of ability) in which those positively selected would be entitled to a superior form of academic education leading to greatly enhanced life opportunities. In consequence, the lives of generations of young people were shaped—many would say blighted—by the experience of rigid selection and consequent consignment at the age of 11 to either academic "grammar schools" or vocational, technical, or practical "secondary schools."

3. Educational Traditionalism and the Objectivity of Knowledge

Plato's conception of knowledge as an encounter with objective truth(s) also seems to be inherent (in tandem, perhaps, with rather crude didactic notions of knowledge transmission) in the rather loose position commonly referred to by educational theorists as "traditionalism." Broadly, on the so-called traditionalist perspective, genuine knowledge (as for Plato) affords insight into an order of reality that is not of our own making and that is therefore apt for discovery and appreciation (rather than invention or construction) via the grasp of objective (mind-independent) criteria of rational coherence and truth. Such understanding is precisely a means to the cultivation of personally formative intellectual, moral, and civil values, virtues, and sensibilities whose worth transcends mere utility. This is more or less the view of education defended by the great modern champions of the liberal education tradition—who are all in this (epistemological) sense traditionalists—although the liberal tradition inclines to a much broader (empiricist) view of what counts as knowledge from Plato. In this vein, defining education largely as the "transmission of culture," and culture as the "best that has been thought and said in the world," the nineteenth-century poet and cultural critic Matthew Arnold (arguably the founding father of modern liberal traditionalism) gave a key curriculum role (as, of course, Plato would not have done) to literature and the arts in the development of wisdom and broadly educated sensibility (see Gribble 1967).

At all events, a more or less Arnoldian conception of education as the introduction of the young to various forms of rationally grounded or objective understanding of ourselves, our (moral and other) association with others, and the world in which we find ourselves has informed the bulk of latter-day traditionalist thinking of a broadly liberal educational temper. It is prominent, for example, in the educational writings of such important and influential mid-twentieth century (British or British-based) cultural "elitists" (insofar as they often argued in a markedly Platonic manner for "alternative" vocational or nonacademic education for the masses) as T. S. Eliot, D. H. Lawrence, and G. H. Bantock, and in the works of such more recent American defenders of "great books" as Mortimer Adler, Robert Hutchins, William Bennett, Allan Bloom, and Harold Bloom. Of particular present interest, however, are the more egalitarian forms of such liberal educational and curriculum theorizing that emerged as part and parcel of the so-called analytical revolution in educational philosophy following the Second World War.

While the new liberal philosophy of education that developed in 1960s Britain owed more to the ordinary language "revolution" of such Oxbridge philosophers as Wittgenstein, Austin, and Ryle, its postwar American counterpart was broadly continuous with an equally distinctive pragmatist tradition of philosophical and educational thought going back (mainly) to John Dewey. However, the leaders of both movements—principally Richard Stanley Peters in Britain and Israel Scheffler in the United States—shared a broadly common view of education as primarily concerned with the promotion of critical rational autonomy. Irrespective of any deeper epistemological differences, they seem to have agreed that knowledge—conceived as rational inquiry into the meaning and truth of judgments—was the key condition of individual self-determination. This general idea led theorists in various places to try to develop philosophical curriculum frameworks grounded (variously) in "forms of knowledge" (Hirst 1974) or "realms of meaning" (Phenix 1964). A particularly influential account of this kind (perhaps more in Britain and in such parts of the British Commonwealth as Canada and Australia than in the United States)—the so-called forms of knowledge thesis of R. S. Peters's disciple and sometime collaborator Paul Hirst (itself owing much to the "ways of understanding" of Peters's London Institute predecessor Louis Arnauld Reid)—may here be taken as a sufficiently representative example (see Hirst 1974).

Following Peters's (1966) fairly sharp separation of education from (vocational and other) forms of training, Hirst argued that the curriculum of common elementary schooling should be primarily concerned with initiation of pupils into a specified range of time-honored forms of rational inquiry that were alleged to be logically distinguishable by virtue of their different and distinctive syntactical structures and truth conditions. He identified (mainly) seven "forms of knowledge" on which, so he argued, an "objectively" rational school curriculum might be constructed—namely, mathematical and logical knowledge, scientific inquiry, understanding of the social and/or human worlds, moral understanding, religious knowledge, aesthetic appreciation, and philosophical understanding. While Hirst appeared to regard epistemology as the proper starting point of curriculum theory, the precise epistemic status of the forms of knowledge was less clear, and Hirst seemed to draw on a variety of (not obviously compatible) realist, verificationist, and constructivist conceptions of meaning and truth; whether, for example, the so-called moral form of knowledge drew on moral realism, prescriptivism, or even emotivism was hard to determine. Later, under the influence of various "postanalytical" trends in social and political philosophy, Hirst repudiated the essentially academic slant of the forms of knowledge thesis. However, his original account had wide influence on curriculum policy and design in the 1960s and 1970s (see, for example, Scottish Education Department 1977), and may in some ways be considered the high-water mark of liberal traditionalist curriculum theorizing.

Although Hirst himself explicitly held that forms of knowledge are not the same as subjects—insofar as the same form of knowledge (such as the empirical) may be instantiated in different subjects (such as physics, chemistry, and biology), and different forms of knowledge (such as the mathematical, logical, ethical) may fall within the scope of the same subject (such as physics)—his forms of knowledge were nevertheless often taken to license subject-centered conceptions of curriculum. Indeed, insofar as forms of knowledge seemed to rest on problematic empiricist distinctions between the analytic and the synthetic, fact and value, theory and practice, and so on, it is not hard to see why the connection with subjects was so often made. If, on a forms-of-knowledge view, the deductive inference of mathematics differs from the inductive reasoning of physics, or if moral education involves the mastery of concepts that are quite logically disconnected from those employed in geography, it may seem less potentially confusing to study these disciplines in the logically pure isolation of separate subjects. To be sure, the very idea that knowledge can be logically divided in this way is questionable and has been trenchantly criticized by (among others) the British philosopher and educator Baroness Warnock (1977), who asked, *inter alia*, what might count as empirical scientific as opposed to, say, humanistic inquiry (an especially difficult question in relation to such studies as psychology). As we shall shortly see, such reflections may also suggest other ways of organizing the school curriculum than in terms of subjects.

4. Some Questions about Knowledge-Centered Curricula

In any case, curriculum theorizing grounded in the idea that education is primarily a matter of the learner's rational grasp of an essentially objective order of truth or reality is otherwise far from unproblematic. First, it seems to imply serious devaluation and/or denigration of the more utilitarian practical or vocational forms of school learning that most pupils are likely to require for useful and responsible lives. It cannot be doubted, moreover, that traditionalist conceptions of curriculum have often enshrined an elitist disdain for the practical—with socially divisive and economically damaging devaluing of those whose abilities, strengths, and inclinations lie in other than academic directions. But traditional knowledge-centered curriculum may also have promoted more normatively problematic moral and social values. For example, in the light of feminist and other critical theory, it is now evident that traditional academic curricula have fostered, whether by accident or design, a range of prejudices of race, class, gender, sexuality—often in the name of "objective" truth—in school subjects as diverse as history, science, literature, art, and religious education. Moreover, this is to take into account only the so-called formal curriculum of schooling, since the powerful influence on pupils' values of informal (explicit but not time-tabled) and hidden (more covert school ethos related) curricula should also be noted. In turn, however, this raises deeper epistemic questions about whether it is even meaningful to speak in terms of "objective" truth in such fields of inquiry as history and literature—or even science and mathematics—at all.

In this connection, one can hardly omit to mention two past thinkers whose roles in formulating these and other objections to traditional knowledge-centered curriculum theorizing are historically pivotal. The first of these is the eighteenth-century Swiss philosopher Jean-Jacques Rousseau, who is widely regarded as the founding father of progressive education and who had an inestimable influence on the romantic tradition and on several later strands of educational progressivism (as well as on the great enlightenment rationalist Immanuel Kant). Rousseau is far from skeptical about the possibility of objective human knowledge (he had little directly to say on epistemological questions as such), but he is deeply distrustful of the moral character and quality of conventional schooling—which he held to be largely a matter of indoctrination into the false values (of *amour propre*) upon which he took the unjust social divisions of civil society to be founded. Thus, in his key educational work *Emile* (1974), Rousseau argues for a "negative" (non-indoctrinatory) education largely focused on the mastery (through progressive "discovery" methods) of practical and useful "problem solving skills." While not directly influenced by Rousseau, these two ideas are certainly prominent in the "psychoanalytic" progressivism of two of the greatest twentieth-century educational experimentalists—the American Homer Lane and his chief disciple, the Scot A. S. Neill. Neill, in particular, was overtly contemptuous of academic learning and he made avoidance of any external compulsion or ideological (political or, especially, religious) influence the guiding principle of his school Summerhill (Neill 1968).

5. Dewey's Pragmatist Progressivism

However, the work of the pragmatist philosopher John Dewey (1915, 1916, 1938, 1958) has probably been more influential on latter-day nontraditional curriculum theorizing. Although significantly "progressive," Dewey is neither a libertarian (like Neill) nor an epistemic sceptic as such. Dewey's key objection to traditionalism is not so much to the human aspiration to knowledge (which he wholeheartedly shares) but to past (realist, empiricist, or positivist) conceptions of knowledge as some sort of mapping of human judgment onto the deliverances of human sense or (worse still) onto a supposed order of mind-independent reality. On the one hand, Dewey's conception of knowledge is a form of (social) constructivism that—true to its idealist (Hegelian) sources—stresses the local provenance and provisionality of all human knowledge claims. On the other, Dewey's no less evident commitment to the human value and utility of scientific explanation and understanding is expressed in what his distinguished pragmatist successor W. V. O. Quine (1953) has called a "naturalized epistemology." For Dewey, scientific theories and hypotheses are no mere tribal lore but important naturally emergent resources and tools for human survival that we neglect at our evolutionary peril. For Dewey, the trouble with the "passive spectator" knowledge of traditional (empiricist or correspondence) epistemology is precisely that it mistakes important and hard-won survival-conducive skills and capacities—the various forms of rationally developed human inquiry—for inert records of past experience.

All this, Dewey holds, has large implications for the school curriculum. First, if knowledge is not a matter of passive reception but of active engagement, so should learning also be. So, in Dewey's view, the teaching and learning of science, say, ought to be focused on the acquisition of skills of scientific method—of experiment and hypothesis-testing—more than on the memorization (for examination or other purposes) of scientific laws or "facts." Second, although Dewey does not think that knowledge is a matter of the mere reporting of experience, he does believe that it involves the development of skills apt for the solution of experientially encountered problems. In this light, the extant experience of the child is, for Dewey, the natural starting point for further learning. But third, in line with his rejection of passive spectator epistemology, Dewey is a "holist" about meaning, knowledge, and the curriculum. As he appears to believe (again, in the words of his pragmatist heir, Quine) that "our statements about the external world face the tribunal of sense experience not individually but only as a corporate body" (Quine 1953), he rejects the curriculum of discrete academic subjects associated with traditional schooling. Instead, he advocates a less "fragmented" approach to curriculum organization that aims for more holistically "integrated" or cross-disciplinary interplay between different modes of human (scientific, historical, geographical, moral, aesthetic, and so on) inquiry in the interests of more meaningful problem solving.

Dewey's famous "project" method (suggested by Dewey, though more fully developed by his disciple W. H. Kilpatrick) is constructed precisely around these three key notions of activity, experience, and holistic meaning. Indeed, the project method is—with a little support from Rousseauian discovery pedagogy and modern theories of cognition—the backbone of so-called process models of learning and curriculum. On a project or thematic view, the proper approach to school curriculum design and planning is not from the prepackaged subject but from the pupil's experience of real-life issues and problems. The Deweyan teacher is encouraged to start from the identification of a theme or topic that is within the existing experience or interest of pupils (such as, perhaps, the farm or the circus). It then falls to the teacher to stimulate further pupil curiosity by means of interesting questions about some aspect of the topic (concerning, perhaps, milk production or lion taming), the solution of which will require the learner to engage in active research or inquiry. These should also be questions that cannot be adequately addressed via recourse to the narrowly defined academic content of any given traditional subject; for example, understanding fully the enterprise of milk production may require a relatively "integrated" grasp of aspects of geography, biology, chemistry, economics, as well as some appreciation of the moral, social, political, and even aesthetic questions that such a complex human practice may raise. Ironically, despite Dewey's limited influence (with some notable exceptions) on British educational philosophy, a watered-down version of his topic approach to curriculum did have considerable impact on official UK policymaking in the progressive 1960s (Primary Memorandum 1965; Plowden Report 1967) that left a legacy of topic-based work in British primary schools.

All of these educational ideas are underpinned by Dewey's deep antipathy to any and all metaphysical or epistemological dualisms of knowledge and reality, mind and body, and theory and practice. For example, Dewey's views are evidently at odds with the distinction between educationally valuable knowledge for its own sake and noneducational, merely useful, vocational skills that seem to have gone hand in glove with traditional "forms of knowledge" curriculum theorizing. For Dewey, there can be no meaningful distinction between the educationally valuable and the practically or vocationally useful; for if a form of knowledge or understanding fails on the second count, it could hardly pass muster on the first. But another significant dualism to which Dewey is no less opposed is that between schooling and society—insofar as he regards social and political goals as integral to education. Indeed, notwithstanding the broadly idealist and anti-empiricist temper of Dewey's pragmatist epistemology, his views have nevertheless clear roots in the broadly liberal-democratic tradition of much post-Lockean Anglo-American political theory. Thus, in common with an empiricist such as J. S. Mill (and at odds with Plato), Dewey holds that education and democracy are not just compatible but also mutually supportive. In short, for Dewey, it is not just that without those habits of open critical inquiry that it is the prime task of education to promote, there could be no true democracy, but that in the absence of a wider social and political climate of democratic association, there could be no genuine education.

Any estimate of Dewey's educational influence needs serious qualification. On the one hand, many if not most educational academics would probably question the extent of its "real" influence on schools as agents of state policy. In this light, it may be said that state policy (in America as elsewhere) has pursued narrower agendas of social control in which aims of schooling are defined more in terms of economic productivity and measured by reference to the sort of pre-specified behavioral objectives and/or attainment targets (for the promotion of closed knowledge and skills) that owe more to the behaviorist learning theories of Watson, Thorndike, and Skinner (and to the educational and vocational applications of these of Ford and Taylor) than to Deweyan or other educational philosophy. In a fairly recent Dewey Society address (Eisner 2002), the influential American educator Elliot Eisner observed that in the twentieth-century battle for influence on American schooling, "Thorndike won and Dewey lost." On the other hand, it would be hard to overestimate the extent of Dewey's influence on the progressive liberal-democratic mainstream of academic American (and wider) educational philosophy and theory. From this viewpoint, there seem to be three key ideas— already touched on—that largely define a contemporary American orthodoxy of Deweyan curricular thought.

6. DEWEY'S INFLUENCE ON THE AMERICAN PROGRESSIVE MAINSTREAM

The first of these is the idea—departing from traditionalist emphases on knowledge and subjects—that curricular thinking should focus more on process than on content. A Deweyan conception of knowledge as useful problem-solving activity more than passive reception shifts the key educational question from the "what" to the "how" of effective learning. So, although Dewey did not himself formulate an explicit developmental theory, he does seem to have pointed educational philosophers and theorists in a psychological direction—in short, toward inquiry into the capacities and dispositions required for this or that successful learning. In this connection, there has been much synergy between post-Deweyan educational philosophy and the empirical theorizing of latter-day cognitive psychologists (something that is rather less conspicuous in British educational theory). Second, again departing from traditional views of schooling, Dewey clearly regards the curriculum as more than just the explicit or formally prescribed school syllabus. Dewey was one of the first to draw attention to those "collateral" forms of value or knowledge acquisition—that have been the main topic of the pioneering work of Phillip Jackson (1968) and others on school ethos and the "hidden curriculum." But third, as already noticed, Dewey also emphasizes the wider task of education and schooling to prepare pupils for their future roles as moral, economically productive, and democratic citizens. While these concerns are by no means foreign to traditional educational theories, Dewey's active conception of knowledge suggests a more radical conception of the good citizen as not just a product but also a critic of the received social order. So, before moving on to consider some educational and curricular trends that fall outside (or are even opposed to) this Deweyan progressive consensus, we may now look briefly at the work of a number of key American educationalists—with references, where appropriate, to related non-American developments—on whom the influence of Dewey is more or less evident.

One such important figure is Lawrence Kohlberg. Although primarily a cognitive psychologist, Kohlberg drew on a wide range of (not obviously consistent) philosophical influences including Plato, Kant, Habermas, Rawls, and also fairly clearly Dewey (see Kohlberg 1984). As is well known, Kohlberg elaborated a basically Piagetian account of moral development that regarded moral growth as a matter of (quasi-Kantian) progress from heteronomous to autonomous moral deliberation. However, Kohlberg also regarded the promotion of such development as not only the concern of some parts of the formal curriculum (history or social studies) but also as a whole school and/or curriculum matter. In this respect, the influence of Dewey (and perhaps also of Rawls and Habermas) is especially apparent in his later efforts to develop schools as "communities of justice" primarily concerned with creating the climate and conditions of rational interpersonal association that Kohlberg came to see as conducive to principled moral reasoning—now, however, conceived as the very essence and form of critical Deweyan democratic sensibility. Like Dewey, Kohlberg is interested less in the content of what children learn than in their acquiring a general disposition to learn in a critical, principled, and cooperative way.

However, despite lasting influence, Kohlberg's ideas have also attracted their fair share of criticism from both psychologists and philosophers. Some feminists, for example, were inclined to question any and all conceptualization of moral growth as a predominantly cognitive or intellectual matter, attributing this "prejudice" in part to Freud's account of moral conscience as post-Oedipal internalization of the incest taboo (which seemed to imply that since girls did not undergo any Oedipal crisis, they could never be mature moral agents). In opposition to this, they saw the female course of development—characterized by unbroken attachment to the mother and others—as the essence of positive moral growth. This was essentially the criticism leveled at cognitive stage theory by Kohlberg's student Carol Gilligan, who argued (Gilligan 1982) that his research (focusing, as it happened, mainly on boys) had biased the issue in favor of a male ethic of detached principle over a female ethic of affective and emotional attachment. This pointed Gilligan and others—notably for present purposes the educational philosopher Nel Noddings (see, for example, 1984, 2002)—in the direction of a so-called ethics of care. For Noddings, however, caring is not primarily an individual virtue to be cultivated by this or that pedagogical method, but an entire philosophy of education—if not a comprehensive social theory: healthy educational and social institutions are those that are characterized primarily by a climate or ethos of care. Noddings is also unsympathetic to traditional academic curricula as too coercive and focused on the development of disengaged rationality. But though, like Dewey, she is in favor of curricular scope for the development of individual interests and abilities, she also rejects any top-down social or vocational streaming of pupils. To this extent, Noddings's views are reminiscent of the British critic of liberal forms of knowledge education Baroness Warnock, also a pioneer of special education reform, who once argued that the main aim of the school should be to promote (at least) "one genuine enthusiasm" on the part of children (Warnock 1973).

Hailing from an arts and arts education background, Elliot Eisner's (see 1969, 1994, 1998) major influences include Herbert Read, Nelson Goodman, and Suzanne Langer, but he also draws heavily on the progressive aesthetic theories of Dewey in *Art and Experience* and elsewhere. Eisner's starting point is a critique of the almost exclusive focus on empirical reasoning and scientific method of enlightenment philosophy, and on the "associationist" learning theories and technicist or industrial conceptions of education and schooling constructed on these. Eisner developed his widely known notion of "expressive objectives" (Eisner 1969) largely by way of criticism of Benjamin Bloom's more famous taxonomy of "behavioural objectives." In pursuing a more explicit artistic metaphor for education that focuses on the importance of judgment and sensibility more than on mechanical calculation, emphasizes the intrinsic purposes of education, acknowledges the difficulty of separating educational ends from means, and recognizes the general creativity and unpredictability of genuine educational outcomes, Eisner's work seems to have affinities with the British critic of behavioral objectives and the pioneer of the "process curriculum," Lawrence Stenhouse (1969), who also defended the value of the arts in his 1970s Humanities Curriculum Project.

The psychologist Howard Gardner was also influenced by Nelson Goodman, from whom Gardner inherited leadership of the Harvard Project Zero. Gardner's (see 1985, 1993) international reputation is based on his opposition to a widely influential concept of intelligence (going back to such founding fathers of educational psychology as Binet and Burt, if not indeed to Plato) as a general intellectual capacity. It is to this that Gardner opposes his so-called multiple intelligences, which include the linguistic, the logical-mathematical, the spatial, the musical, the bodily-kinaesthetic, the interpersonal, and the intrapersonal (the last two of which have had much influence on Goleman's 1996 notion of "emotional intelligence"). Insofar as Gardner's account reflects the commonsense view that people have different talents that call for equal appreciation, it is consistent with the egalitarian and inclusive ideology of mainstream American progressivism. Thus, like Noddings (and Warnock 1977 in the UK), Gardner is unsympathetic to any procrustean submission of young people to uniform state-imposed models of curriculum and instruction of the kind to be found in much Western schooling. That said, Gardner's multiple intelligences seem to be themselves rather protean entities that may entail some category confusion between rather different ideas of ability, activity, and discipline. In the last resort, moreover, it seems that the curriculum implications of Gardner's multiple intelligences are not much clearer than those of any notion of general intelligence, for it remains unclear—especially if we take the view of the British curriculum philosopher John White (1973) that "ability should be a goal not a given"—whether we should encourage a child gifted in this or that respect to study more or less of what she is good at.

7. Some Radical and Conservative Curriculum Alternatives

Having identified, with rather broad brushstrokes, a number of key moments in what we have called the (Deweyan or pragmatist) progressive mainstream of modern American educational theorizing, it remains crucial to notice that there have been trends beyond this mainstream less directly influenced, if at all, by Deweyan or pragmatist sources. We shall, therefore, conclude this brief survey by examining two such broad trends—what we might call, respectively, the radical left and the conservative right of the liberal-progressive mainstream.

The more radical trend is primarily focused on the political and ideological dimensions and determinants of education and curriculum policy, and on the way these have been shaped—and been rendered variously unjust—by a variety of hegemonic interests of class, race, gender, and other kinds. While concerns with social justice, as we have seen, are by no means absent from curriculum theorizing in the progressive mainstream, a rather more radical perspective is brought to bear on these issues by writers who derive ultimate inspiration from Hegel and Marx, mediated by such Frankfurt critical theorists as Habermas, Adorno, and Marcuse. One key influence on the radicalism of such latter-day American educational theorists as Michael Apple, Henry Giroux, and Peter McLaren has undoubtedly been the emancipatory philosophy of the Brazilian radical educator Paolo Freire (1972)—sometimes linked to such so-called de-schoolers as Ivan Illich (1973). Generally, curriculum theorists of this ilk subscribe to the broadly post-Marxian view that so-called worthwhile knowledge has invariably expressed and promoted dominant ideology, and that institutionalized education or schooling has often served as the principal device for hegemonic control and exploitation of subaltern social groups or classes. From this view-point, the key purpose of curriculum theorizing is the radical reform of educational institutions and practices for the empowerment of the traditionally marginalized and disenfranchised.

For those of this persuasion, the latter-day triumph of neoliberal economy over its postwar communist adversary renders the post-Marxist critique more rather than less compelling—and this is clearly a key concern of the influential curriculum theorist Michael Apple. Although Apple is obviously on the side of genuine liberal democracy, he is no less opposed to what he takes to be a prevailing neoliberal ("right wing") conservatism of capitalist production and consumption. In his key works, such as *Ideology and Curriculum* (1979) and *Education and Power* (1982; see also 2000), Apple has been a leading contemporary critic of the coarse instrumentalism toward which much public education has tended under the influence of neoliberal economics—in particular, the substitution of economic and vocational for educational goals—and he has more lately been concerned to warn educators of the dangers of educational technology as all too often subservient to such goals. That said, Apple's radical critique of neoliberal manipulation is still firmly located in the rationalism of mainstream critical theory, and he has remained resolutely opposed to the kind of poststructuralist or postmodern turn taken by such more recent radical (and formerly critical theoretical) advocates of emancipation as Henry Giroux (1981, 1992). Indeed, in attempting to give political and educational recognition to the fullest possible diversity of human experience, Giroux's "border pedagogy" draws heavily on poststructuralist ideas of knowledge as "script" or narrative and on postmodern repudiation of grand narratives—to the extent of skepticism about the very objectivity of rationality as such. In this respect, there are clear points of contact with latter-day radical feminist critiques of "logicism" (rationality conceived as a tool of male control) and with the neo-Marxist relativism of the British educational sociologists of knowledge who opposed the "rationalism" of mainstream liberal education in the 1970s (see, for example, Young 1971). The basic trouble with such arguments, however, is that they are in some danger of cutting off the dialectical branch upon which they are sitting (and it is correspondingly unclear upon precisely what "grounds" such critiques might be mounted).

While such radicals seem located to the left of what we have called the progressive mainstream, another influential group of North American curriculum theorists could be regarded as standing to the right of it. The main concern of E. D. Hirsch, Allan Bloom, Diane Ravitch, Mortimer Adler, William Bennett, and others is that the progressive mainstream—reinforced by the generally leveling effects of popular culture—has greatly undermined traditional educational concern with the promotion of worthwhile content. While such educational conservatism does not always go hand in hand with political conservatism (which Hirsch, for example, explicitly disavows), it is generally hostile to progressive focus on the process rather than the substance of learning and on much progressive and radical debunking of received high culture as undemocratically elitist or indoctrinatory. For conservatives, progressive focus on the instrumental aspects of learning, with concomitant emphasis on the psychological mechanisms of knowledge acquisition, has fostered false ideas about the nature and value of learning: precisely, that how one learns matters more than what one learns, and that the value of what one learns is largely determined by considerations of personal interest, convenience, or utility. In turn, according to conservatives, this has led to generations of pupils and students who are not just functionally illiterate and innumerate but also culturally disinherited to the point of dangerous ignorance of the very democratic traditions and institutions in whose name they are being educationally shortchanged. Conservatives, therefore, urge a return to the didactic emphasis of traditional educational practice—and, in particular, to the initiation of young people into the great traditions of human reflection and achievement.

Two rather different works of educational conservatism—Allan Bloom's *The Closing of the American Mind* and E. D. Hirsch's *Cultural Literacy: What Every American Needs to Know*—appeared in 1987. Bloom's book, aimed at what he took to be the deplorable and hopeless state of American higher education, seems to be the rather more politically conservative of the two. It mounts a bitter tirade against what he takes to be the wholesale "dumbing-down" of American academia under a range of prevalent cultural and intellectual influences—not least, post-Nietzschean philosophy, feminism, and popular culture. While many of Bloom's arguments have evident force—not least his general defense of the educational need for objective standards of literary and other judgment and the point that those who are ignorant of the great moral and spiritual narratives and themes of general cultural inheritance are effectively debarred from appreciating any genuine past or present human wisdom—his tone is stridently elitist and colored by a rather Platonic disdain for the democratization of taste and sensibility that seems at times almost contemptuous of democracy itself. On the other hand, Hirsch's *Cultural Literacy* and its successor *The Schools We Need: And Why We don't Have Them* (1999), seem less concerned about the corruption of the academic elite and more about the effects of progressive educational trends on the general run of elementary schooled pupils—not least those already starting from positions of some social, cultural, and economic disadvantage. For Hirsch, it is such children, rather than those who are already the beneficiaries of culturally enriched lives, who stand to lose most by exposure to progressive educational speculations on child-centered learning, project methods, problem-solving skills, holistic understanding, and multiple intelligence. Again, there are evident links between the new American educational conservatives and other past educationally conservative movements: their general emphasis on the importance of the literary canon looks clearly back to Arnold's concept of education as initiation into "the best that has been thought and said in the world" and to the great-books tradition of Eliot and Leavis—and may even connect with the concerns of postwar British theorists of liberal education.

8. The Key Issues: Balance, Commonality, and Diversity

A number of key curriculum themes and concerns run through all the various curriculum theories and proposals considered to date. To begin with, there is clearly much in common between the American conservative curriculum perspectives lately aired, the forms of knowledge proposals of postwar British educational philosophers, earlier theorists of liberal education such as Arnold and Newman, and such ancient thinkers as Plato. The main point here seems to be that education—and therefore an educational curriculum—is more than just a matter of the learning of useful skills. As we have seen, many have been inclined to distinguish educational from other sorts of learning in terms of the personally developmental or "intellectual" benefits of intrinsically motivated appreciation of great cultural (scientific and/or artistic) achievement. Still, while there is much to this view, not least as a safeguard against more instrumental and philistine inclinations to regard the study of poetry (for example) as a useless curriculum frill, it is clearly prone to overstatement—and it has, as already noted, led to some academically elitist denigration of more practical or instrumentally useful curriculum pursuits.

Moreover, although this issue has in past curriculum and policy literature been liable to some unhelpful opposition or confrontation between advocates of learning for its own sake and learning as a means to other ends, it is probably the broad consensus that it is about both: it is likely that most educational policy-makers, professionals, and parents would welcome a place in the school curriculum for poetry *and* word-processing skills. A major challenge that this presents for contemporary educational philosophers, however, is that of conceiving a broader view of education in terms of which these different—intrinsic and extrinsic—features of development might be reconciled in some principled way. One common way in which contemporary educational philosophers have tried to address this problem is via a basically Deweyan or pragmatist erosion of the distinction between knowledge for its own sake and useful knowledge. Thus, for example, Richard Pring (a rare British Deweyan) has sought to bridge the alleged gap between education and training via a more liberal conception of vocational educational and a more pragmatic view of liberal learning (see Pring 1995). Others, however, more impressed by the liberal educational distinction than by Deweyan construc-tivist epistemology, have tried to address the issue via a distinction between education and schooling: on this view, although it may still be useful to regard education as the development of knowledge for its own sake, this is not the sole purpose of the public school curriculum that is concerned with promoting a wide variety of other more utilitarian ends (see Carr 1996).

But any such expansive view of the scope of the school curriculum—which allows for the inclusion of home economics as well as Shakespeare—evidently raises, if they were not conspicuous already, even more vexing issues regarding the connection of education and/or schooling to broader social, political, and eco-nomic goals. If it is proper to point young people in particular vocational directions, is it not also socially desirable that schools should assist them to be particular kinds of people? Indeed, the idea that schooling is implicated in moral and social education and training—in the personal formation of young people—is probably the generally prevailing educational view. But what can this mean in the normatively diverse conditions of contemporary plural societies in which there may seem to be precious little agreement about the nature of desirable moral formation and/or cultural identity? As we have seen, it is the major concern of radical educationalists that any and all curricula designed for common school-ing are likely to reflect the values of dominant ideologies (or those of neoliberal consumerism)—with the effect of marginalizing or belittling less dominant or subaltern cultural identities. But the alternatives to common curricula may seem no more promising. One possibility, that of broadening or "democratizing" the common school curriculum in so-called multicultural directions, is hard put to steer any principled course between the alternatives of condescending trivializa-tion of aspects of diverse cultures and no less unsatisfactory nonjudgmental recognition of all as equally valuable. However, the other main possibility (see, for example, MacIntyre 1987) of a plural pattern of educational provision in which the diverse (faith and other) values of different cultural constituencies might be recognized and celebrated in their own schools may seem no more appealing.

Indeed, the most commonly recognized danger of any such tendency toward culturally plural educational provision is that of creating further social divisions in a world in which there is already bloody confrontation between those of different cultures and creeds. From this viewpoint, it is probably safe to say that the main present-day political and professional trend—at least in developed liberal democracies—is toward some form of common schooling as a means to the promotion not only of a common body of economically useful knowledge and skill but of a common set of civic values and virtues whereby individuals of diverse cultural backgrounds and inheritances might see themselves as jointly contributing to the common good. Thus, while this concern is at least as old as Dewey, recent educational philosophers and theorists have been much exercised—often drawing on Dewey as well as on the insights of more recent political liberals such as Rawls—with the question of what citizenship might mean, or be made to mean, in circumstances of cultural diversity. In more practical terms, this has led to interestingly diverse views about how such common values and virtues might be promoted or fostered through the school curriculum. Whereas for some (see, for example, Crick 1999), the level of political literacy needed for effective contemporary democratic participation requires extending the curriculum to include additional political knowledge and skills, for others (see Pring 1999), a properly taught humanities-focused curriculum—of the kind already envisaged by such great apostles of the liberal tradition as Arnold—has already full potential for the development of the requisite moral and political sensibilities.

In conclusion, it is worth noting that, although these currently fashionable issues of liberal versus vocational, multicultural, and citizenship education have never been far from the concerns of curriculum theorists, they have somewhat displaced earlier postwar deliberations on the epistemic dimensions of curriculum content of the kind that primarily exercised the likes of Hirst. I suspect that this partly reflects a general trend on the part of educational philosophers (despite honorable exceptions)—probably under the influence of pragmatism, poststructuralism, and postmodernism (see Carr 1998)—toward regarding curriculum issues as of greater political than epistemological concern. On this view, since theories of knowledge are socially conditioned or constructed, there can be no objective epistemic grounds upon which to judge the worth of curriculum content and, therefore, nothing but competing political arguments for this rather than that content. Apart from the fact that such thinking is overstated, if not just mistaken, its consequences for neglect of the epistemological dimensions of the curriculum are certainly regrettable—not least insofar as philosophical explorations and analyses of the epistemic character of this or that body of school knowledge or skill may be regarded as of enormous value for helping field professionals to teach well what they teach. It might therefore be hoped that when the philosophical wheel comes full circle—as philosophical wheels inevitably do—such time-honored questions about the objective truth, meaning, and value of knowledge claims may reclaim their rightful place at the heart of philosophical reflection concerning the curriculum.

REFERENCES

Apple, M. (1979). *Ideology and Curriculum.* Boston: Routledge and Kegan Paul.

—— (1982). *Education and Power.* New York: Routledge.

—— (2000). *Official Knowledge: Democratic Education in a Conservative Age.* New York: Routledge.

Bloom, A. (1987). *The Closing of the American Mind.* New York: Simon and Schuster.

Carr, D. (1996). "The Dichotomy of Liberal versus Vocational Education: Some Basic Conceptual Geography." In *Philosophy of Education 1995,* ed. A. Nieman (pp. 53–63). Urbana, IL: Philosophy of Education Society.

—— ed. (1998). *Education, Knowledge and Truth: Beyond the Post-Modern Impasse.* London: Routledge.

Crick, B. (1999). "The Presuppositions of Citizenship Education." *Journal of Philosophy of Education* 33(3): 337–52.

Dewey, J. (1915). *The School and Society.* Chicago: University of Chicago Press.

—— (1916). *Democracy and Education.* New York: Macmillan.

—— (1938). *Experience and Education.* New York: Collier Books.

—— (1958). *Experience and Nature.* La Salle IL: Open Court.

Eisner, E. W. (1969). "Instructional and Expressive Educational Objectives: Their Formulation and Use in the Curriculum." In *Instructional Objectives,* eds. W. J. Popham et al. (pp. 1–31). Chicago: Rand McNally.

—— (1994). *Cognition and Curriculum Re-considered.* New York: Teachers College Press.

—— (1998). *The Kind of Schools We Need.* Portsmouth, NH: Heinemann.

—— (2002). "What Can Education Learn from the Arts about the Practice of Education?" *Encyclopedia of Informal Education.* Updated December 28, 2007, www.infed.org/biblio/eisner_arts_and_the_practice_or_education.htm.

Freire, P. (1972). *Pedagogy of the Oppressed.* Harmondsworth: Penguin.

Gardner, H. (1985). *Frames of Mind: The Theory of Multiple Intelligences.* New York: Basic Books.

—— (1993). *The Theory of Multiple Intelligences: The Theory in Practice.* New York: Basic Books.

Geach, P. T. (1957). *Mental Acts.* London: Routledge and Kegan Paul.

Gilligan, C. (1982). *In a Different Voice: Psychological Theory and Women's Development.* Cambridge MA: Harvard University Press.

Giroux, H. (1981). *Ideology, Culture and the Process of Schooling.* London: Falmer.

—— (1992). *Border Crossings: Cultural Workers and the Politics of Education.* London: Routledge.

Goleman, D. (1996). *Emotional Intelligence: Why It Can Matter More Than IQ.* London: Bloomsbury.

Gribble, J., ed. (1967). *Matthew Arnold.* Educational Thinkers Series. London: Collier Macmillan.

Hamilton, E., and H. Cairns, eds. (1961). *Plato: The Collected Dialogues.* Princeton, NJ: Princeton University Press.

Hirsch, E. D. (1987). *Cultural Literacy: What Every American Needs to Know.* Boston: Houghton Mifflin.

—— (1999). *The Schools We Need: And Why We Don't Have Them.* New York: Random House.

Hirst, P. H. (1974). "Liberal Education and the Nature of Knowledge." In *Knowledge and the Curriculum*, by P. H. Hirst (pp. 30–53). London: Routledge and Kegan Paul.

Illich, I. (1973). *Deschooling Society*. Harmondsworth: Penguin.

Jackson, P. W. (1968). *Life in Classrooms*. New York: Holt, Rinehart and Winston.

Kohlberg, L. (1984). *Essays on Moral Development: Volume I*. New York: Harper and Row.

MacIntyre, A. C. (1987). "The Idea of an Educated Public." In *Education and Values: The Richard Peters Lectures*, ed. G. Haydon (pp. 15–36). London: Institute of Education, University of London.

Neill, A. S. (1968). *Summerhill*. Harmondsworth: Penguin.

Noddings, N. (1984). *Caring: A Feminist Approach to Ethics*. Berkeley: University of California Press.

——— (2002). *Starting at Home: Caring and Social Policy*. Berkeley: University of California Press.

Peters, R. S. (1966). *Ethics and Education*. London: George Allen and Unwin.

Phenix, P. (1964). *Realms of Meaning*. London: McGraw-Hill.

Plowden Report. (1967). *Children and their Primary Schools*. London: HMSO.

Primary Memorandum. (1965). *Primary Education in Scotland*. Edinburgh: Scottish Education Department, HMSO.

Pring, R. (1995). *Closing the Gap: Liberal Education and Vocational Education*. London: Hodder and Stoughton.

——— (1999). "Political Education: Relevance of the Humanities." *Oxford Review of Education* 25: 71–87.

Quine, W. V. O. (1953). *From a Logical Point of View*. New York: Harper and Row.

Reid, L. A. (1986). *Ways of Understanding*. London: Heinemann Education for the University of London Institute of Education.

Rousseau, J-J. (1974). *Emile*. London: Dent.

Scottish Education Department (1977). *The Structure of the Curriculum in the Third and Fourth Years of the Secondary School* (The Munn Report). Edinburgh: HMSO.

Stenhouse, L. (1969). "The Humanities Curriculum Project." *Journal of Curriculum Studies* 1(1): 26–33.

Warnock, M. (1973). "Towards a Definition of Quality in Education." In *The Philosophy of Education*, ed. R. S. Peters (pp. 112–22). Oxford: Oxford University Press.

——— (1977). *Schools of Thought*. London: Faber and Faber.

White, J. P. (1973). "The Curriculum Mongers." In *The Curriculum: Context, Design and Development*, ed. R. Hooper (pp. 273–80). Edinburgh: Oliver and Boyd.

Young, M. F. D. (1971). *Knowledge and Control*. London: Collier-MacMillan.

CHAPTER 17

....

EDUCATION, DEMOCRACY, AND CAPITALISM

....

PHILIP KITCHER

Democracy cannot flourish where the chief influences in selecting subject matter of instruction are utilitarian ends narrowly conceived for the masses, and, for the higher education of the few, the traditions of a specialized cultivated class.

—John Dewey, *Democracy and Education*

I

....

DEWEY bequeathed to us a conception of philosophy quite different from the one most prominent in contemporary Anglophone philosophy.[1] Philosophy begins with study of the good life, aims to understand how opportunities for living well can be promoted by social institutions, and considers how young people, people with their lives before them, can best be prepared, as individuals and as citizens. Instead of taking metaphysics, epistemology, and the study of mind and language as core philosophical disciplines, Dewey's rival vision would see Plato, Rousseau, and Mill as large figures in a great tradition that focuses on questions of human and social development. In adopting that vision, we should add Dewey to the list, and embrace his explicit judgment that philosophy can be defined as the general theory of education.[2]

I want to explore some basic questions that arise in developing an approach to education within our liberal democratic tradition. I'll start with Mill, whose varied thoughts on human and social development offer a number of approaches to the aims of education that are apparently in tension with one another. Then, I'll try to show how Dewey develops some Millian themes in ways that are intended to reconcile the tensions. The result is an ambitious ideal for education that faces the obvious challenge that it's economically unfeasible. Dewey saw the challenge, and offered sketches of a response to it. I hope to make clear how deep and difficult the problem is.

II

First, we need a framework for discussion. An obvious way to characterize education would be to suggest that it provides young people with knowledge. That suggestion, however, is dangerous unless we adopt a broad conception of knowledge, one that embraces both certain kinds of practical abilities and the cognitive skills involved in extending knowledge once formal education is done. Whether or not a particular set of moral precepts ought to be inculcated in schools and universities, it's surely correct to judge that any system of education that routinely produced people incapable of reflective ethical decisions or of participating in reasoned exchanges with their fellow citizens would be, in virtue of that failure, inadequate. Similarly, too, an educational system that left its former students incapable of continuing to learn more, as human knowledge increases, would be recognizably unsatisfactory.[3]

We can, thus, divide the kinds of knowledge we expect good education to generate into three main types: knowledge of particular propositions that have been explicitly taught, habits and dispositions to judge and to act in private and in social contexts, and skills to acquire further knowledge of the first two types. Despite the great emphasis often placed on the first type of knowledge, one might view it as less important than the second, and take the third to be really fundamental.

The project of education explicitly recognizes the importance for each of us of the knowledge we acquire from others, and even the most superficial reflections on it reveal the overwhelming importance of public knowledge. What passes for the contemporary theory of knowledge is often focused on arcane puzzles about how individuals can be justified, but the dominant source of most of what anyone knows is our system of public knowledge. Nor is public knowledge adequately understood by assimilating our encounters with it to mundane cases of testimony. The student's interaction with the teacher is significantly different from your fleeting encounter with a stranger on the street from whom you request directions. The teacher's role is that of a conduit between the system of public knowledge and young people who, as yet, are uninitiated into the riches of that system.[4] Questions about authority with respect to the information transmitted in the classroom are not primarily questions about the credentials of teachers (such issues arise, but they are relatively straightforward), but about the status of the system of public knowledge itself. To understand the ways in which the educational project can be conceived, and how there can arise attractive conceptions of that project that are in tension with one another, it is useful to begin with the conception of a system of public knowledge.

Here's an obvious analogy. A society's system of public knowledge is like a gigantic library in which new documents are constantly deposited and from which the citizens can withdraw as much as they want, whenever they want it. Education both acquaints young members of the society with those parts of the library's contents on which the previous generation places particular emphasis and equips neophytes with the ability to seek out and understand the information they need. The contents of the library are built up in a society-wide collective project. Inquiries are directed toward those issues that seem, at the time when they are conducted, most pertinent to the needs of the citizens. The results of those inquiries are registered on the books if they meet standards of certification designed to balance the competing claims of providing as much information as possible and ensuring accuracy: notice that the society will, tacitly or explicitly, have to arrive at a trade-off here. The organization of the information provided is intended to dovetail with the ways in which young people are equipped with the skills for using the public resource. Ideally, the inquiries conducted should anticipate the questions to which citizens will need answers, the results of those inquiries should be maximally informative with minimal risk of misinformation, and the educational system should enable the citizens to discover, with no significant extra work, the answers they need.[5]

There are important philosophical questions about the character of current systems for public knowledge—questions that have been neglected in contemporary epistemology. Prominent among them are issues about how the agenda for inquiry should reflect the concerns of citizens, and about how to decide on standards of certification when citizens are committed to radically different ideas about good evidence.[6] Here, however, I'm concerned with the question of how the conception of education as setting up a connection between future citizens and a public system of knowledge gives rise to alternative visions of the aims of education.

III

Although John Stuart Mill doesn't offer as extensive an account of the ends of education as we find in other writers, his wide-ranging essays on aspects of social theory provide important suggestions about how education should be under-stood.[7] An obvious Millian perspective would start from "On Liberty," where Mill offers the picture of people ideally choosing for themselves their own plan of life, deciding what matters to them, what they are to pursue and how they are to pursue it. For Mill, the decision to shape your life in one way rather than another ought to be neither coerced nor blind. Provided that decisions made within the legally protected private sphere do not harm those outside it, the decisions should be free of external interference. The negative imperative—"No interference with the private choices of mature citizens!"—is accompanied by a positive directive. Young people who would not initially be able to make responsible decisions about what matters in their own lives are to be brought to the point at which they can seriously contemplate what projects and pursuits make most sense for them. A central task of their education is to enable them to decide on "their own good" and "their own way," basing their decision on a reflective understanding of themselves and of the genuine options that arise for them. Mill's emphasis on "experiments of living" derives from his thought that the reports of such experiments are essential con-tributions to human public knowledge. Over time, the menu of choices for new human beings increases, and it's important that education should give the young a clear idea of the range of possibilities. By itself, however, that's hardly enough, and equally crucial is the inculcation of abilities for reflective decision making—just those ethical habits of mind to which I've already briefly alluded.

An obvious worry about this first ideal is that it overemphasizes the individual in isolation from others. Elsewhere, however, Mill proposes that a principal task of education lies in preparing people for the role of citizen in a democracy, conceiving of this in terms of an ability to make informed and reasoned decisions about matters of public policy.[8] In societies with extensive division of labor, as well as stratification by socioeconomic class, there's likely to be a form of myopia in public decision making: citizens cannot understand the needs and concerns of their fellows, and cannot even fathom their own interests.[9] A crucial argument for the superiority of laissez-faire capitalism loses its cogency because a fundamental premise becomes dubious: we may no longer trust that individual citizens are the best judges of the impact of proposed courses of action on their own lives. At a minimum, then, the task of education is to correct for this myopia by enabling people to gain accurate information about the large issues that confront them. To this end they need an ability to recognize the likely consequences of proposed policies, not only for themselves but also for others. Further, they need to develop a capacity for identifying the predicaments of their fellow citizens and for respond-ing sympathetically to those predicaments. Once again, the development of such skills appears to presuppose a lengthy period of broad education, during which people are taught to analyze the effects of complicated interventions in a variety of areas, during which they also become acquainted with the very different ways in which their fellow citizens live.

Mill's analyses, however, aren't simply directed toward the status quo. He plainly believes that public knowledge is a great achievement of our predecessors—one on which we can build. At some moments in human history—for example, in the wake of the fall of Roman civilization in Western Europe—simply securing and retaining what had already been accomplished seemed a crucial project for scholars and for the society that supported them; but for us, one task of education is to identify and then train people who can continue expanding our knowledge, people whose contributions will become available to all our descendants. An obvious way to pursue this goal, manifested in the British educational policies under which I grew up, is to test and winnow, starting at whatever age educational psychologists see as the first point at which reliable markers can be spotted.[10]

Finally, there's a progressivist notion, clearly articulated by Mill, that envisages stages in human culture. The famous declaration of "On Liberty" that liberty is to be conceived in terms of "the permanent interests of man as a progressive being" rests on Mill's view that considerations of the good are dependent on the stage to which a society has developed—thus, there are circumstances in which the appropriate approach to the good is Bentham's hedonic utilitarianism (perhaps the circumstances of the early Industrial Revolution provide a case in point). As people attain higher levels of culture, the measures previously applied come to appear crude and inadequate. In the educational context, the aim of fostering flourishing human lives in the here-and-now sits beside the aim of creating a culture in which later beings will be able to attain to a style of flourishing that is beyond our current imaginings. So there's yet another perspective on education, one that takes its principal task to be that of producing people who can continue the progression of human culture.

Four perspectives are surely enough. Education might promote individual flourishing, or it might aim at the production of citizens who will participate well in current democratic institutions, or it might endeavor to expand public knowledge, or, finally, it might foster the advance of human culture. These are all attractive ideals, but it's not obvious that they can be reconciled: how do you promote individualism, citizenship, the advancement of knowledge, and the progressive development of human culture all at once?

IV

One way of reading *Democracy and Education* is to see Dewey as understanding what is attractive about the Millian ideals and recasting them so that they can be harmonized. Dewey explicitly claims to be able to reconcile goals that we might think of as incompatible: "if we analyzed more carefully the respective meanings of culture and utility, we might find it easier to construct a course of study which should be useful and liberal at the same time."[11] His reconciliation project can be interpreted as encompassing the four Millian perspectives I've distinguished.

For, in the first instance, Dewey contends that the Millian account of individual flourishing is doubly wrong: it starts by confining a single individual within a private, protected sphere, and it supposes some critical moment at which this individual freely chooses a life plan. Meaningful life, on Dewey's account, is committed, from the beginning, to joint activity, so that the isolated individual within the private sphere is a harmful fiction—one that should give way to overlapping, protected spheres in which clusters of individuals can cooperate. He insists, repeatedly, that social activity must be a constituent of any significant individual choice: "Any individual has missed his calling, farmer, physician, teacher, student, who does not find that the accomplishment of results of value to others is an accompaniment of a process of experience inherently worth while. Why then should it be thought that one must take his choice between sacrificing himself to doing useful things for others, or sacrificing them to pursuit of his own exclusive ends.... ?"[12] Moreover, we should see our lives not as proceeding according to some fixed plan on which we decide at some crucial time—the "defining moment"—but as following a trajectory that is constantly adapted to circumstances, and, most important, to the lives of others: "education is a constant reorganizing or restructuring of experience."[13] Both points are subsumed under the idea that our lives go better through our awareness of connections among aspects of our experiences, or as Dewey so often puts it, through the expansion and deepening of "meanings." Increased awareness enables forms of appreciation that matter intrinsically to us and also promote interventions that help us realize antecedent goals (as well as sometimes prompting us to change our aims).[14]

This reframing of Millian ideals is to be understood in terms of a conception of democracy richer than that espoused by Mill. Dewey rightly sees the process of voting as a superficial manifestation of democracy, and he envisages a broader process of social discussion through which people are brought to something like consensus.[15] Tocqueville's celebration of the New England town meeting lurks in the background.[16] Central to Dewey's thought is the conception of supplementing the methods for resolving factual disputes developed from the early seventeenth century on with an equally powerful method for addressing conflicts over values. From our twenty-first-century perspective, the thought that we possess a socially shared means of settling factual disputes already seems optimistic, not because contemporary theoretical critiques have exposed the inefficacy of the rules and standards that are employed in the sciences (broadly construed), in social and historical studies, in critical disciplines, in the law, and in everyday life, but because the recognized difficulty of squaring those rules and standards with prominent religious conceptions fosters an epistemological fragmentation of the public.[17] Dewey extends the claim that secular standards govern the societal acceptance of facts to the ambitious thought that conflicts in values can be decided through the detailed elaboration of the consequences of various options by people who are maximally sympathetic to the predicaments of all.[18]

Democracy, in Dewey's conception, involves the joint working through of the problems that arise at a given stage of society and culture, by people committed to the improvement of that society and that culture. The knowledge they ideally acquire in their education prepares them for understanding the connections within experience, whether centered on natural or social phenomena; gives them methods for pursuing further inquiry and addressing value conflicts; and simultaneously develops them as individuals and as citizens, since any meaningful trajectory for a life will be one that involves joint action, and, indeed, joint efforts to improve the culture. For Dewey, I suggest, individual flourishing is bound up with democratic participation, with contributing to and learning from public knowledge, and with playing a role in that progress of human life emphasized by Mill.[19] If there are particular places at which Millian tensions resurface, then those are to be seen as particular value conflicts, to be tackled in their context by means of the methods assembled by public knowledge and transmitted in the system of education.

A central task for a post-Deweyan theory of education is to articulate more clearly, and in more detail, the attempt at reconciliation I've just sketched. But I want now to turn to a different difficulty that arises for an approach to education along these lines, and perhaps for any descendant of Mill's liberal ideals. This problem, of which Dewey was well aware,[20] derives from the fact that, as the aims of education become more ambitious (as they surely do on Dewey's account), there are serious questions about their socioeconomic feasibility. I'm going to approach it by distilling a line of argument from the first great theorist of capitalism.

V

Adam Smith begins *The Wealth of Nations* by developing further a conception of human society that's already present in his predecessors, and even in Plato.[21] The production of goods by a society will be enhanced by assigning different roles to different people. (Plato's account seems to make the optimistic assumption that this can achieve maximal efficiency in a distribution that accords with the native talents of each.) Smith's guiding thought is that further efficiencies in production arise from decomposing the tasks to be performed ever more finely, so that each worker who participates in the process exercises an extremely specialized skill. With hindsight, it's easy to attribute to Smith the idea that economic growth, measured by the production of value, is driven by a double motor, in which technological innovations divide and streamline the tasks of production processes, and in which individual workers are trained to become especially attuned to discharging their assigned tasks in optimal time.

Over 800 pages later, however, Smith turns his attention to education, and he is almost driven to an unnerving reversal of his initial perspective. In accordance with the emphasis on training workers for their practical tasks, he opposes what he takes to be a wasteful form of education, one that has survived into his time as a relic of outmoded ideas. Although he recognizes that young men in the ancient world were drawn to a course of education whose guiding ideal is that of the individual's flourishing, his judgment is that the eighteenth-century programs that advertise themselves as aiming at this ideal are (at best) frivolous and useless luxuries for a tiny elite. They would no longer be sustained if the original conditions of ancient education were still in force and teachers had to live on the fees of their pupils: "A private teacher could never find his account in teaching, either an exploded and antiquated system of a science acknowledged to be useful, or a science universally believed to be a mere useless and pedantic heap of sophistry and nonsense."[22]

Smith proposes simultaneously to construct a system of public education that will be supported by the contributions of students (or, more exactly, by their parents) and to reform the curriculum so that it is geared to the needs of the commercial world: the "essential parts of education," delivering the abilities to "read, write, and account," are to be preserved and the useless "smattering of Latin" is to give way to "the elementary parts of geometry and mechanics."[23] Allegedly, study of these latter subjects will be valuable in the improvement of the common trades that most students will eventually practice.[24]

The trouble is that the intensification of the division of labor seems to tell against the idea of the system of education Smith envisages. If the guiding criterion for training the young is to equip them for the work they will carry out as adults, it's far from obvious that they'll need "the elementary parts of geometry and mechanics" or very much skill in reading and writing. It might be efficient to select a few especially talented young people whose applications of mathematical sciences to common trades or production processes would improve efficiency, but the vast majority of the young would seem to be able to manage with an extremely basic education.[25] Smith recognizes the plight of the ordinary worker as the division of labor becomes ever more minute:

> The understandings of the greater part of men are necessarily formed by their ordinary employments. The man whose whole life is spent in performing a few simple operations, of which the effects too are, perhaps, always the same, or very nearly the same, has no occasion to exert his understanding, or to exercise his invention in finding out difficulties which never occur. He naturally loses, therefore, the habit of such exertion, and generally becomes as stupid and ignorant as it is possible for a human creature to become.[26]

Now one might think that the "torpor" that Smith attributes to the ordinary worker results from the neglect of aspects of his education that would develop him as a human being. Precisely because the focus on efficiency in production has neglected the ideals advanced by Mill and consolidated by Dewey, the life of the worker is truly empty. Smith might be right to think that the memory of tags from Virgil would be of little value as the laborer stretches the umpteenth wire to form the umpteenth pin, but it's not obvious that reflection on the elementary parts of geometry and mechanics will serve better. Hence, the Smithian focus on education appears to acquiesce in the thought that mental death is simply the lot of most people under capitalism.[27]

It's tempting to suppose that the predicament Smith envisages is tied to a very specific form of early industrial capitalism, and that the problem goes away under the conditions of contemporary employment. That, however, would be to mistake the general form of the concern. On the one hand, we have an educational ideal of the type proposed by Mill and Dewey, one that emphasizes noneconomic facets of individual and social development. On the other, is the social strategy of assigning workers to roles in the cause of advancing net productivity. Assignments of this latter kind may embody far more flexibility than that recognized in Smith's analysis of a competent and efficient workforce—they may attend to the fact that workers may need to be able to change jobs and may require social skills for interacting with others. Yet even when that is recognized, it's still reasonable to worry that an efficient education for producing the needed workforce would pay no attention to major aspects of the Mill-Dewey ideal. It's not enough to build in some type of flexibility and socialization; it has to be the specific kinds of flexibility and social commitment that Mill and Dewey value. Hence, it's no adequate response to the Smithian worry to point out that most contemporary workers aren't in analogous situations to the toilers in the pin factory: although the workplace environment has changed, it's far from obvious that the alterations resolve the threat to human development.[28]

In fact, these passages in the *Wealth of Nations* are especially interesting for us because they contain the germ of a serious skeptical argument about a program like Dewey's. Stepping back from Smith's formulations, and from the details of the context in which he wrote, we find that there are several important ideas.

A. Economic well-being requires a continued intensification of the division of labor.
B. That intensification of the division of labor requires workers who are trained to highly specialized tasks.
C. A system of education that invests in programs guided by other ideals—in particular Dewey's ambitious package (or even its Millian elements)—will be less efficient at training workers for the highly specialized tasks they will be required to perform.
D. Efficient systems of education will produce workers, most of whose lives will be impoverished.

Smith offers us very specific versions of A–D, versions that are articulated with respect to his eighteenth-century preindustrial context. I shall shortly try to show that there are also versions that seem quite plausible in our twenty-first-century postindustrial context. But before doing so, it's worth making the underlying threat explicit. For it appears that A–C support a conclusion to the effect that societies that invest in systems of education that aim at Dewey's preferred goals will lose out in economic competition to societies that adopt more efficient systems of education. If that is so, Deweyan education can only be a temporary luxury, something a society can enjoy for a few generations before it loses the economic basis on which its inefficient system can be supported. The next task is to investigate whether this threat is genuine.

VI

Here's a very concrete version of the worry I derive from Smith. Suppose education is conceived in Dewey's way, so that a substantial part of educating children is devoted to preparing for joint social activity and to laying the basis for a broad appreciation of the varieties of human culture and cultures. Contrast this with a rival system that embodies Smith's emphasis on what is useful in the workplace. In this rival system, students with particular aptitudes for the disciplines that underlie contemporary economic life are identified as early as possible, and rigorously trained so that they arrive at the frontiers of the pertinent fields as soon as possible. Smithian students become workers who are either (1) more adept at discharging the tasks required by the most productive existing technologies; or (2) better able to improve those technologies; or (3) able to function equally well, for a longer time or at lower costs, as those trained by the system that lavishes time on Deweyan education (because of earlier induction into the workforce). Whichever of these advantages accrues to the Smithian rival, the society that implements it will do better in terms of its productivity, and its greater success in economic competition will eventually undermine the feasibility of Deweyan education.

Smith himself could not have advanced the argument in the form I've given, because it's crucial to his analysis that capital is best invested locally. In the most quoted passage of *The Wealth of Nations*, he argues that entrepreneurs will suffer disadvantages if they try to profit from ventures carried out in foreign countries, so that, under the assumption that opportunities for local investment are always at hand, they will always prefer "the domestic to the foreign trade."[29] In our world, the speed of global communication and the ability to direct and supervise a distant workforce make Smith's claim of disadvantage highly dubious. Hence, the stage is set for a comparison between systems of education implemented in spatially distant societies and for a competition based on the idea that capital can flow freely to any region that supplies the best-trained workers at the cheapest price.

You might think that there's an easy rebuttal to the argument. A long tradition of defenses of liberal education—anticipated, as we shall see, by Dewey's own remarks—emphasizes the thought that people who are trained as narrow specialists turn out to be less able at supplying the needs of productive economies. Those defenses are based on two main grounds: first, the thought that rapid shifts in technology make workers trained in narrow ways redundant; and second, the view that great breakthroughs in productive technology require habits of mind that are best developed by less utilitarian systems of education. Defenders will cite statistical studies showing the ways in which efforts to focus education too narrowly fail in one of these ways. Yet I think any serious discussion of educational ideas ought to wonder how far one can extrapolate from studies of this sort. For the serious issue is whether, for any Deweyan system of education, there is a Smithian alternative whose expected economic efficiency is higher, and that issue can't be settled by comparing particular educational systems that countries happen to have tried (comparisons that don't take into account: economic asymmetries among countries, or whether the systems in question are seriously Deweyan, or whether the economic context is akin to the current circumstances of global capitalism).

In effect, the classical defenses of liberal education focus on C, and deny that Deweyan education diminishes efficiency. On the face of it, these defenses are committed to a very strong claim, to wit that attention to goals that initially appear to be hard to achieve and strikingly different from those recommended by Smith—goals like the fostering of human individuality and the development of capacities for sympathy with fellow citizens whose situations differ widely—can be undertaken without loss of economic efficiency. The obvious worry is that doing more in domains without evident impact on economic success will have to be compensated for by doing less well in those aspects of education that are dedicated to fashioning a productive workforce.

Dewey saw clearly that a simple additive version of this idea won't do. In his incisive little book on moral education, he debunks the superficial thought that fostering an ability to make ethical decisions requires explicit teaching of ethical statements.[30] He notes, correctly I believe, that the ethical component of a system of education might lie in the way that the individual subjects are taught. To focus the point sharply, and perhaps in a more ambitious way than Dewey intended, we might envisage two systems of education that taught exactly the same explicit propositions and exactly the same nonethical cognitive skills, but differed in respect to their success at cultivating habits of ethical reflection and decision: in the extreme, one might realize the ideal of inculcating such habits as perfectly as we have reason to hope for, and the other might fail to do so at all.

It's now possible to formulate more exactly the lines along which a defense of Deweyan education should go. The ambitious form of the defense is to suppose that Deweyan education can succeed just as well as any Smithian rival, because it can achieve exactly the same Smithian goals, and do so in ways that realize the Deweyan ideals. A less ambitious version would deny exact equivalence, urging that although certain bodies of expertise may be less fully developed under a Deweyan regime, there will be compensating gains because of the inculcation of cognitive skills that turn out to be economically important—skills that are by-products of the efforts to realize Deweyan goals. So, in striving to educate people to find extended meanings in experience, we generate a class of workers among whom will be the great innovators of productive technology.

As I've already said, I don't think that existing comparisons of rival ways of educating people settle the general issue here, and a more refined consideration of the circumstances in which the Smithian argument arises for us may help to show why. Smith effectively concentrates on a particular type of worker, one assigned in the division of labor to a routine that can be learned by anyone. Although it's sometimes common to characterize such workers as "unskilled," the crucial point is that their skills are accessible to the vast majority of the population. Among such workers there's a continuum of cases, defined by the length of time and effort required to acquire the pertinent skills, but for simplicity, I'll introduce a dichotomous classification: some skills can be inculcated quickly and others take a long time and a great deal of training. Besides workers of this sort, there are others whose performance depends on their having talents that aren't widely shared. Simplifying again, I'll suppose that there's a class of workers who are able to perform complex tasks in economic production because they have abilities shared only by a few and because they have undergone a lengthy and demanding training. Within this class, I'll distinguish a subset whose role in the economy is to initiate new forms of technology.

Let me emphasize again that splitting the workforce into discrete classes is a grotesque oversimplification, one I introduce solely for the purposes of sharpening the argument with which we're concerned. We have four categories of work based on skills that are (1) obtainable by many and easily acquired; (2) obtainable by many and acquired only with considerable effort; (3) obtainable only by a few, with effort, and oriented to existing technology; and (4) obtainable only by a few, with effort, and directed at innovation. Call the four types of people "ordinary workers," "specialized workers," "elite workers," and "innovators," respectively.

Smith's original proposals about education consider only ordinary workers, and depend on his recognition that ordinary workers don't need extensive education. His pessimistic judgment of their likely fate expresses the thought that, even were they to be given extensive education, its effects would be blunted by the conditions of their work. Given the familiar criticism that education is needed to equip people for situations in which they have to acquire new skills, Smith might respond that there will always be a need for ordinary workers and that, under changing conditions, there will be no bar to their acquiring whatever new ordinary skills the new technologies demand.

The idea that education promotes a valuable flexibility is more pertinent to the situation of the next two classes, the specialized workers and the elite workers. Dewey's own version of the appeal to necessary flexibility tacitly presupposes that contemporary industry depends on the performance of these two groups: "an attempt to train for too specific a mode of efficiency defeats its own purpose. When the occupation changes its methods, such individuals are left behind with even less ability to readjust themselves than if they had a less definite training."[31] A simple model will bring out Dewey's point. Imagine two systems of education. The first, system A, wastes no time on any features that aren't found in the prevailing technology. The second, system B, provides a broader training in the background field in which the specialists' fields are embedded. (So, for a concrete example, one offers an in-depth immersion in a particular programming language, and the other provides extensive education in mathematics, logic, and computer science.) Assuming that new technology can be expected to be introduced when a specialist or elite worker is in mid-career, it isn't implausible to suppose that system B will prove superior to system A.

Unfortunately, however, this appeal to flexibility doesn't favor Deweyan education over Smithian rivals. What's crucial is to identify the background fields out of which new technologies are likely to come. So, system B provides specialized workers with background skills not directly pertinent to their first jobs, but relevant both to the initial specialties and to specialties that are likely to be needed when the original jobs are superseded. For the elite workers, the emphasis on background is even more important, since the identification of talent and the selection of those who are to acquire the elite skills will go better if the criteria for selection are framed in terms of the background field; otherwise there's a serious chance that people will be selected who can't be retrained under the new technologies, with consequent shortfall in the workforce. The trouble, however, is that the emphasis on broadening the training doesn't entail any consideration of the features on which Dewey (and Mill) place so much emphasis. Simply knowing a broader area of some science, or acquiring a broader set of practical or cognitive skills, need not, on the face of it, involve any serious development of abilities in ethical decision making, any contemplation of the possibilities for human lives, any expansion of sympathies with fellow citizens, any appreciation of the wider forms of human culture, or any contribution to the progress of democracy. Even when considerations of flexibility are introduced, Dewey's attractive goals look like expensive luxuries.

An obvious response would be to suggest that the account I've given only deflects the challenge that Smithian education is inflexible because it assumes a certain predictability in technological development. The difference between systems A and B lay in the fact that B focused on the "background field" out of which future technological developments were expected to come. To institute a Smithian version of system B would, thus, presuppose that we could mark out the pertinent field in advance, and because of the unpredictability of technology, this is impossible. We'd do better, so the argument goes, to cast our net very broadly and to frame a system of education along Deweyan lines. The point can be underscored by considering the fourth class of workers. If a society is to have a serious chance of training innovators, then, it's suggested, its educational system must acquaint them with the full extent of human thought and culture, so that they may be stimulated from any direction.

Unfortunately, it doesn't seem to me that any of this works. As Dewey saw so clearly, any system of education has to be selective[32]—it would be sheer folly to think that one could acquaint students with the full variety of human thought and culture. The issue between Deweyan education and Smith's utilitarian goals concerns the likely consequences for technological innovation of guiding the selection either by attention to the ideals of Dewey's rich notion of democracy or by offering a more specialized education in the sciences that form the contemporary background to technology. There's no evidence that the former is a particularly good approach, and under a situation of uncertainty, the most reasonable option would seem to be to institute a mixed system of education, one in which the vast majority of the population were educated under Smithian systems of education, aimed at producing ordinary workers, specialized workers, and elite workers, in the latter cases with appropriate emphasis on breadth of background field. A small number of especially talented young people might be offered a more extensive education in the hopes of encouraging their creativity; almost all of them would be directed toward the fields that underlie prevalent technologies, without any special concern for classroom time in areas that might improve them as democratic citizens, but a tiny minority would be educated in the Deweyan way, as a small experiment into whether this approach might generate the results presupposed by classic defenses of liberal education. Ironically, any stratified approach of this sort would be completely at odds with Dewey's fundamental emphasis on integrating education and democracy, and would further contribute to that fragmentation of the public of which he complained.[33] In effect, it would restore a fundamental division of the ancient world, a conception of the search for the good life as an occupation of the privileged few.

VII

So far, I've suggested that any Deweyan system of education (and probably any Millian system) has a more economically efficient Smithian rival. I want next, rather briefly, to attend to the last stages of the argument, and to the thought that there's a dynamic in global capitalism that will tend to eliminate Deweyan education.

Let me begin with a scenario that has probably already occurred to you as an illustration of some of my points. It's no secret that in some areas of the world, particularly in India, China, and other parts of East Asia, educational systems produce young people whose mathematical skills and knowledge of the physical and biological sciences greatly outrun those of their counterparts in North America and Western Europe. With the emergence of a very large potential workforce that can supply plenty of specialized workers and elite workers, probably at rates of pay cheaper, or no more expensive than, those demanded in the West, we can expect the migration of capital to South Asia and East Asia. Americans and Western Europeans may continue to figure in those parts of the economic sector that can't easily be exported, or as ordinary workers, or as innovators (to the extent that their systems of education supply innovators at higher rates). The ready replication of innovation will prevent any serious lag time between the emergence of new profitable technologies in any part of the world and their deployment in any other, so that the locations of greatest production will be those that supply the largest, cheapest, and most qualified army of specialist and elite workers. In these circumstances, the economic basis of Deweyan systems of education will be undercut: nations will have to go Smithian to compete.

I don't claim that this scenario is inevitable, but it seems to me plausible, if you believe the preceding steps of the Smithian analysis. If you suspend the happy belief that Deweyan education is economically as efficient (or more efficient) than more utilitarian schemes, then it's not a large step to conclude that the present conditions of global capitalism introduce a competition among systems of education in which Dewey's favorite will lose. In effect, there's a dynamic in capitalism that brings together two different ideas in Marx: the diagnosis of the plight of the worker in the 1844 *Manuscripts* and the abstract form of the intensified immiseration of the worker in *Capital*. The growth of capitalism inevitably undermines our best attempts to foster valuable forms of human life, attempts that conceive education as Dewey did.

VIII

But Dewey foresaw all this—or so I think. The central theme of *Democracy and Education* is that full commitment to democracy requires a very ambitious program of education, one that is no longer willing to "treat the schools as an agency for transferring the older division of labor and leisure, culture and service, mind and body, directed and directive class, into a society nominally democratic."[34] At two points, he clearly and explicitly sees "present economic conditions" as needing transformation if his educational program is to be realized.[35] So he would not see the Smithian challenge as requiring us to turn away from Deweyan education— that would be to give up on the project of democracy—but, rather, as a call to change economic conditions so that democracy and Deweyan education both become possible.

I end as I began, with an affirmation of the Deweyan conception of philosophy— and also with a brief defense. Dewey claimed that the central questions of philosophy were questions about how to live, both as individuals and in society. He saw these questions as arising at a wide variety of times and places, and as being focused by pertinent features of the social and cultural context. Philosophers respond to these more localized and precise forms of the general question, and their attempts to provide answers generate further issues—so arise the fields of metaphysics and epistemology, as ancillary domains that have to be explored to make progress on the fundamental issues. As that exploration proceeds, however, it's all too easy for technical issues to gain a life of their own, and for them to be pursued without any sense of the ultimate purpose. Philosophy ossifies, becoming removed from the needs of the ambient culture. Dewey invites his contemporaries—and us—to scrutinize the accepted agenda and accepted programs of philosophy, in the interests of addressing the most important questions as they arise within our own place and time.[36]

To accept that invitation is to place the general theory of education at the center of philosophy: to ask what is needed in our context for people to lead valuable lives, both individually and collectively. Posing those central philosophical questions again, we find, I suggest, the sorts of philosophical projects that have surfaced in this essay. The crucial questions for philosophers today have very little to do with consciousness and qualia, with the analysis of epistemic justification, with internalism or externalism about reasons, or with any of a multitude of other subjects that fill the pages of professional journals that attract a tiny, but oddly devoted, readership. Rather, our most important tasks are to articulate further the Deweyan connection between democracy and education, to probe more accurately the economic preconditions of democratic education, to expose as precisely as possible the sources of conflict between capitalism, as we now have it, and Dewey's ambitious project, and, on that basis, to conceive of ways of modifying the economic constraints. To identify, or re-identify, the project of philosophy in this way is only to take a tiny step toward carrying out this task, but I believe that it is a step worth taking.

NOTES

An earlier version of this essay was presented to the Philosophy and Education Colloquium at Teachers College, Columbia University. I am grateful to members of the audience for their comments and suggestions, and would like in particular to thank David Hansen, Megan Laverty, and Robbie McClintock. I am indebted to Terri Wilson for a number of valuable conversations about Dewey, and to Robbie McClintock for helpful written comments. The sage advice of Harvey Siegel has also enabled me to improve the final version.

1. The epigraph is from John Dewey's *Democracy and Education*, p. 192. I shall refer to this work as DE.

2. DE 328. I shall indicate briefly at the very end of this essay why I endorse Dewey's vision of philosophy. More extensive defenses are suggested in several essays that are currently forthcoming: "Mill, Education, and the Good Life," "Carnap and the Caterpillar," and most centrally, "The Road Not Taken."

3. Dewey emphasizes the importance of "learning to learn" (DE 45, 51). He also thinks of the moral aspects of education in terms of the acquisition of methods of ethical deliberation. See *Moral Principles in Education* (MPE), p. 3.

4. This formulation should not be read as supposing a one-way flow from the society's acquired wisdom to the passive initiate. I follow Dewey in thinking of education as a vehicle for reproducing, and modifying, the ideas of the background culture. See, for example, DE 75; I'll develop this theme more extensively below.

5. For two centuries or more, the systems of public knowledge of affluent societies have been so vast that selection, both in inquiry and in transmission, is inevitable. Dewey's discussions clearly appreciate the importance of this; see DE 187, 191, 286–87. In the context of inquiry, the necessity of selection, together with even a relatively modest democratic ideal leads to a demand for what I've called "Well-ordered science"; see my *Science, Truth, and Democracy*, chap. 10. For a more extensive discussion of this demand in connection with the idea of public knowledge, see my "Knowledge and Democracy," pp. 1205–24.

6. I discuss some of these questions in *Science, Truth, and Democracy*, "Science, Religion, and Democracy," and "Knowledge and Democracy."

7. Mill's most direct treatment of educational issues occurs in the Inaugural Address he delivered on his appointment as Rector of St. Andrews University (reprinted in volume 21 of Mill's *Collected Works*). That address articulates all the perspectives I'll attribute to Mill. I discuss it in more detail in "Mill, Education, and the Good Life." John Skorupski has independently come to a similar reading of Mill; see his *Why Read Mill Today?* (especially chaps. 1 and 2).

8. This perspective is most evident in Mill's *Considerations on Representative Government.* However, it's notable that the work also stresses the educative role of democracy itself, a theme that is readily interpreted in terms of the richer conception of democracy favored by Dewey.

9. See Mill, "Considerations on Representative Government," pp. 252–56, 296–301.

10. Of course, part of the British policy depended on studies, allegedly carried out by Sir Cyril Burt, that were said to reveal the stability of measurements of intelligence taken at age 10. Those studies turned out to be fraudulent. For a penetrating critique, see the work of Leon Kamin, beautifully summarized in R. C. Lewontin, Steven Rose, and Leon Kamin, *Not in our Genes.* I've given my own assessment of the ethical status of Burt's research in the introductory chapter of my *Vaulting Ambition.*

11. DE 258.

12. DE 122. See also DE 37, 93, 120–21. A more general recasting of Mill's themes about individual liberty and protected spheres is provided in the first chapter of his *The Public and its Problems* (hereafter, PP).

13. DE 76. The entire passage DE 76–79 wraps together Dewey's breakdown of the boundaries between the school and life and that between the school and society. He supposes both that education isn't preparation for some period in which its rewards will be reaped and that education is constitutive of the ways in which we live until our cognitive social lives end. Similar themes are sounded at many other places in his writings; see DE 20–21, 311; MPE 25; *The School and Society* (hereafter, SS), pp. 9, 10.

14. DE 75, 85, 120–21; SS 16.

15. See DE 87, 122, 359; also PP 147.

16. As in the case of Mill, Tocqueville's analysis of democracy in America is important for Dewey.

17. I develop this point in my "Science, Religion, and Democracy."

18. I offer this reconstruction of Dewey's approach to value conflict in my "The Hall of Mirrors."

19. I discuss Mill's commitment to the progress of forms of human life in "Mill's Consequentialism."

20. See, for example, DE 85, 86, 119, 122, 251–52.

21. See the discussion of the formation of city-states in Book II of Plato's *Republic.*

22. Adam Smith, *Wealth of Nations*, p. 838.

23. Ibid., pp. 842, 843.

24. There are, I think, some difficulties in reconciling Smith's thought that schools be supported by the contributions of parents with his conception of the curriculum. The assumption that people will perceive it to be in the interest of their children to study just these things—and not, rather, to acquire either something more minimal or the useless badges that mark out the socially superior—is open to debate. But my interest here lies in a different aspect of Smith's tangled views on education.

25. For Dewey's opposition to this educational approach, see MPE 24–25, DE 289, 318.

26. Smith, *Wealth of Nations*, p. 840. Smith's diagnosis here comes very close to that offered by Marx in "Alienated Labor." The three "economic and philosophical manuscripts"

that precede Marx's celebrated discussion are, in essence, Marx's own précis of Smith, and the opening sentence—"We have begun from the premises of political economy"—is completely justified. As I'll suggest in the text, Smith's own response to the diagnosis is quite inadequate, and it's tempting to envisage his having recognized that and rewritten the entire *Wealth of Nations*!

27. Dewey explicitly notes the problem of the alienation of the worker; see DE 205, 260, 314, 317.

28. I shall elaborate this point below. I introduce it here to forestall the misunderstanding that Smith's argument is linked to a very specific form of economic life.

29. Smith, *Wealth of Nations*, pp. 484–85. This discussion introduces the famous image of the "invisible hand," in arguing for the conclusion that production processes suited to the locale are always preferable. I'm not going to undertake a full critique of Smith's reasoning here.

30. MPE 1–4; see also DE 354–57.

31. DE 119.

32. DE 187.

33. There are many places in which Dewey attacks the idea of educationally generated class divisions; see DE 122, 136, 251–52, 260, 289, 318. These are transpositions into the educational context of the central theme of PP.

34. DE 318; see also DE 87, 192.

35. DE 98, 136.

36. I take this to be the call of *Reconstruction in Philosophy*, although the same themes pervade many of Dewey's other works (see, for example, *The Quest for Certainty*).

REFERENCES

Dewey, John. *Democracy and Education*. New York: Free Press, 1944.
—— *Reconstruction in Philosophy*. Boston: Beacon Press, 1948.
—— *The Quest for Certainty*. Volume 4 of *John Dewey: The Later Works*, series editor Jo Ann Boydston. Edwardsville, IL: Southern Illinois University Press, 1984.
—— *The Public and Its Problems*. Athens, OH: Swallow Press, 1985.
—— *Moral Principles in Education*. Carbondale: Southern Illinois University Press, 1975.
—— *The School and Society*. Carbondale: Southern Illinois University Press, 1980.
Kitcher, Philip. *Vaulting Ambition: Sociobiology and the Quest for Human Nature*. Cambridge, MA: MIT Press, 1985.
—— *Science, Truth, and Democracy*. New York: Oxford University Press, 2001.
—— "The Hall of Mirrors." *Proceedings and Addresses of the American Philosophical Association* 79, no. 2 (November 2005): 67–84.
—— "Knowledge and Democracy." *Social Research* 73 (December 2006): 1205–24.
—— "Science, Religion, and Democracy." *Episteme* 5 (2008): 5–18.
—— (forthcoming). "Mill, Education, and the Good Life." In *John Stuart Mill on the Art of Living*, ed. Ben Eggleston. New York: Oxford University Press.
—— (in press). "Mill's Consequentialism." In *Routledge Companion to Nineteenth Century Thought*, ed. Dean Moyer.

—— (in press) "Carnap and the Caterpillar." *Philosophical Topics* (special issue on Pragmatism).

—— "The Road Not Taken." In a volume of essays on pragmatism, eds. Martin Hartmann and Marcus Willaschek (unpublished manuscript).

Lewontin, Richard, Steven Rose, and Leon Kamin. *Not In Our Genes.* New York: Pantheon, 1984.

Mill, John Stuart. *Collected Works.* 33 Volumes. Toronto: University of Toronto Press, 1969–95.

—— "Considerations on Representative Government." In *On Liberty and Other Essays*, ed. John Gray (pp. 205–470). New York: Oxford University Press (World's Classics), 2002.

—— "On Liberty." In *On Liberty and Other Essays.*, ed. John Gray (pp. 5–130). New York: Oxford University Press (World's Classics), 2002.

Skorupski, John. *Why Read Mill Today?* London: Routledge, 2006.

Smith, Adam. *The Wealth of Nations.* New York: Modern Library, 2000.

Tocqueville, Alexis de. *Democracy in America.* London: Penguin, 2005.

CHAPTER 18

ART AND EDUCATION

CATHERINE Z. ELGIN

WHEN budget cuts loom, school committees target arts programs. They consider education for the arts a frill—something nice to have in times of plenty, but not mandatory if money is tight. Nor is financial exigency the only threat. In the current climate, where curricula are designed around state-mandated tests, schools see time devoted to arts education as time taken away from more important matters—namely, those that the states test. Evidently, with sharp limits on time and money, education for the arts is a luxury that schools can ill afford.

The idea that arts education is a frill is not new. Booker T. Washington argued that only after the African-American community had achieved prosperity should the arts be integrated into educational programs.[1] Nevertheless, the idea that the arts are peripheral to human well-being ignores the ubiquity of the arts. Unlike science, art is evidently a cultural universal. The earliest known paintings and drawings are over 14,000 years old. The earliest know musical instruments are 7,000 to 9,000 years old. Nor is prosperity a precondition for art. Frederick Douglass recalls,

> [The slaves] would make the dense old woods, for miles around, reverberate with their wild songs, revealing at once the highest joy and the deepest sadness. They would compose and sing as they went along, consulting neither time nor tune. The thought that came up came out, if not in the word, in the sound, and as frequently in the one as in the other.[2]

But rather than supporting the desirability of arts education, the ubiquity of art might serve as an argument against it. If people make art anyway, why should we devote scarce resources to teaching it? The slaves Douglass describes had no formal musical training. They made incredibly moving music without it. Why don't we just let art happen?

If this is a good argument against teaching art, it is an equally good argument against teaching language. Children learn their native language just by growing up around people who speak it. But no one would think that we, therefore, should let nature take its course and drop the study of English from the curriculum. We appreciate how education improves, strengthens, enhances, and extends the capacity to speak English that native speakers of the language bring to school. If school committees do not think the same about arts education, it is, I believe, partly due to misconceptions about education and partly due to misconceptions about art. Once these misconceptions have been corrected, the contribution of art to education and the value of education for the arts will be manifest.

Skepticism about the feasibility of art education is grounded in a suspicion that art is unteachable. Stereotypes to this effect abound. Talent is a gift—something that a few select people just have. Art results from inspiration, and there is no hope of teaching anyone how to be inspired. Art appreciation, on the other hand, is purely subjective, a matter of how art makes a person feel. There is no accounting for matters of taste. If these stereotypes are correct, education cannot do much for either the artist or her audience. Better we should spend our money teaching children the source of the Nile.

The misconception about education lies in the assumption that education consists mainly in information transfer. A student is an empty vessel into which the teacher pours justified true beliefs. The student thereby acquires a new store of knowledge. Since much art is nonpropositional, it does not consist of truths. Since most art contains no arguments, it does not convey justification. And even if art moves us in profound ways, it rarely engenders new beliefs. Works of art have little, if any, credible information to convey. "Construed as sources of knowledge," Mothersill writes, "the arts make a poor showing; as a means of acquiring new truths about the world or the soul, they are in competition with science and with philosophy."[3] In the competition, they do not fare well. But education does not consist entirely of information transfer. Students learn not just that $2 + 2 = 4$, but also how to add. They learn not just that *bei* in German takes the dative, but also how to use and recognize German dative constructions. They learn not just that people resent being patronized, but also how to take the perspective of a patronized person and understand how things feel from his point of view. So even if we concede that the arts are in general poor sources of reliable information, we should not too quickly exile them from the educational realm. They may be repositories of and vehicles for learning of other valuable kinds.

What of the charge that art is impervious to education? We should look at this from two perspectives: that of the artist and that of the audience. If inspiration is essential to art, and no one can teach others to be inspired, then a crucial aspect of artistry cannot be taught. No doubt, inspiration sometimes figures in the creation of art. But the assumption that art is entirely a product of inspiration is unfounded. Orchestral music provides an obvious counterexample. The members of an orchestra need to know how to tune their instruments, how to read music, how to play their instruments, and how to play together under the direction of a conductor. They need to recognize patterns, motifs, phrasings. They need to be sensitive to dynamics, rhythm, and pitch, as well as to what other players are doing. A composer needs to know a good deal about the capacities and limitations of the various instruments; about acoustic and tonal properties and their interactions; about melodic, harmonic, and rhythmic patterns and possibilities. Such matters can be learned, and some of them can be taught. Of course, there is no guarantee that a composer or performer of classical music who knows these things will be a good artist. But a composer or performer of classical music who is ignorant of or oblivious to such things is apt to be a bad artist.

Similarly in the visual arts. Students in the fine arts learn the powers and limitations of different media; the interactions of discrete factors; the effects of color, light, shade, shape, and form, as well as the effects of their various combinations and juxtapositions. Artists in all fields benefit from knowing about the history of their art—about what has been done, how it has been done, what succeeded, and what failed. Even if artistic talent is a gift, education can foster and develop a variety of artistic skills and abilities that figure in the exercise of that gift.

This might be an argument for the educational value of conservatories and art institutes, but most students are not going to be artists. Is there any reason to think that art should be part of the general curriculum? To answer that, we should consider the perspective of the audience. Although most of us will never be professional artists and relatively few of us will even be serious amateur artists, we are all members of audiences. For audiences for the arts do not consist exclusively of a cultural elite. They include everyone who turns on the television, goes to the movies, plugs in an iPod.

The conviction that audiences cannot be educated is grounded in the idea that art is, in Langer's terms, presentational rather than discursive.[4] In responding to art, she maintains, we respond to the sense-perceptible qualities an object presents—to its colors, shapes, and tones. Our responses may be purely sensory or they may be emotional, but they are not cognitive. If this is right, there is nothing to learn. And since taste is entirely subjective—a matter of how one feels about an experience—there is no need to learn either.

This viewpoint is wrong in several regards. First, both sensory and emotional responses can be educated. At a wine tasting, for example, one learns to detect nuances of flavor that one could not initially taste. Solfège trains the ear, enabling one to hear aspects of tones that were previously inaudible. And as we attend to our own and to other people's emotional responses, we learn to make distinctions that we could not originally make. We learn, for example, to distinguish between love and infatuation, where we once felt only an undifferentiated attraction. So even if art works were purely presentational, there would be something to learn. To be sure, simply telling a student that she should distinguish subtly different shades of blue that she cannot now tell apart is an unpromising pedagogical strategy. But students can, through a series of carefully crafted exercises, be brought to discern such subtle differences in color.

Nevertheless, one might ask, if responses to the arts are purely subjective, why should we bother? If there is no basis for saying that a crude reaction is worse than a refined one, the student was no worse off vis-à-vis her experience of the painting when she saw the blue as a single uniform color than when she saw it as a variegated field of subtly different shades.

Here it pays to turn to Kant.[5] He points out that our responses to art take the form of judgments. In talking about art, we do not simply express our personal feelings, as a person might when he says, "I don't like butterscotch." We make claims on others. If a person says, "This work is derivative," or "That work is splendid," he intimates that others should think so, too. We give reasons for our interpretations and evaluations of works of art. We take these reasons to hold generally, but recognize that they can be contested. In our discussions about art, we assume that there is such a thing as being wrong. Indeed, we take it that people can be wrong in a variety of ways. Although there are many acceptable interpretations of *Hamlet*, it is wrong to interpret it as a story about a boy and his dog. Nor do we deem every sensory or emotional response to a work of art acceptable. A person who finds Madama Butterfly's plight mildly amusing simply does not understand the opera. A person who is oblivious to the juxtapositions of tonality and atonality in *The Firebird* suite does not understand the piece. Our discussions about art reveal that we do not take aesthetic responses to be purely subjective. The question, evidently, is how can they be anything else?

The answer lies in rejecting the idea that lurks behind Langer's contention that the arts are not discursive. She is surely right in saying that. But we should not assume that if they are not discursive, the arts do not symbolize at all.[6]

Goodman argues that works of art are symbols with determinate syntactic and semantic structures. Syntax determines the identity of a symbol; semantics determines what, if anything, it refers to. If we construe works of art as symbols rather than merely as attractive (or unattractive) artifacts, many of the problems relating to art and education dissolve. For interpreting symbols is a cognitive matter, one that, in principle, education can influence. Moreover, the sorts of symbols used in the arts are also used in disciplines that fall squarely within the province of education.

In the arts and elsewhere, we construct and use symbols with different syntactic and semantic properties. Maps, pictures, charts, diagrams, and musical scores are familiar nonlinguistic symbols. At the syntactical level, a crucial difference is between symbols that belong to systems that consist of discrete, sharply differentiated characters and symbols that belong to systems that lack such differentiation. Every linguistically significant symbol in a written language consists of some combination of letters, spaces, and punctuation marks. The primitive elements are finite—indeed, extraordinarily limited—in number. Musical scores likewise consist of combinations of relatively few discrete and determinate primitive elements. Representational symbols, such as pictures and maps, on the other hand, are syntactically dense. The smallest difference in certain respects makes a difference to the identity of a representational symbol.[7] If a line on a map or a drawing were the least bit shorter, it would be a different symbol. But if the letter k were printed in a different font or size—as a k or a *k*, for example—it would still be a *k*.

At the semantic level, Goodman recognizes two basic modes of reference: denotation and exemplification. Denotation is the semantic relation in which a name stands to its object, a predicate stands to the members of its extension, a picture stands to its subject. Description and representation, thus, depend on denotation. Fictional symbols, such as unicorn pictures or the names of fictional characters, are denoting symbols that lack denotata. Their intelligibility, Goodman believes, derives from symbols that denote them. Because "Ahab-description" denotes the members of a specific collection of names and descriptions (predominantly, but not exclusively, those occurring in *Moby Dick*), those names and descriptions fix Ahab's fictive identity. We learn who Captain Ahab is by reading the novel, just as we learn who Captain Cook was by reading a biography. But whereas Captain Cook was who he was regardless of what the biographies say about him, the Ahab-descriptions in the novel constitute the character. They make Ahab the character that he is.

Some symbols, including works of abstract art, most instrumental music, and many dances, do not even purport to denote. They refer by other means. Prominent among these is exemplification, the relation between a sample or example and the features it is a sample or example of. To exemplify a feature, Goodman maintains, a symbol must both instantiate and refer to it. Under its standard interpretation, a fabric swatch exemplifies its pattern, color, texture, and weave. The swatch makes these features manifest and affords epistemic access to them. The swatch also has a vast number of unexemplified properties, such as a particular mass, age, and distance from Sheboygan, Wisconsin. It makes no reference to these.

Because commercial samples belong to regimented exemplificational systems, established practice and accepted precedent dictate which features the swatch standardly exemplifies. But even outside the arts, not all exemplars are so regimented. A teacher might hold a student paper up to the class as an example of particularly good or bad work. When he does so, the paper functions as an exemplar of the things he wants his students to notice. Depending on his current pedagogical objectives, it might exemplify its content, its form, its argumentative strategy, or even the neatness of the author's handwriting. Exemplars are selective. They point up, highlight, display, and convey some of their features by marginalizing, overshadowing, or downplaying others.

Exemplification plays a major role in the arts. Works of art exemplify some of their own properties, highlighting them and bringing them to the fore. A Mondrian painting, for example, exemplifies squareness. It not only consists of squares, it also points up this aspect of itself. *The Firebird* exemplifies tensions between tonality and atonality. It focuses attention on and heightens our sensitivity to such tensions. Representational works can also exemplify. Titian's portraits of Pope Paul III denote the Pope and exemplify decadence. Tolstoy's description of the Battle of

Borodino both describes the battle and exemplifies an attitude toward war. The songs Douglass describes both denote aspects of the slaves' lives and exemplify the intermingling of joy and bitterness. In the arts, a single symbol may simultaneously perform a variety of referential functions. And unlike commercial samples, exemplars in the arts typically do not belong to regimented systems. They function more like the student paper in that interpretation, which is far from automatic, is required to determine what they exemplify.

Denotation and exemplification need not be literal. Metaphorical symbols genuinely refer to their metaphorical subjects. "Bulldog" genuinely, albeit metaphorically, refers to Churchill, and "Churchill was a bulldog" is true under its metaphorical interpretation. Many people believe that metaphors are purely decorative. They are just "artsy" ways of saying things that could be expressed literally. But, as is well known, metaphors typically resist paraphrase. Although "Churchill was stubborn" is in the right neighborhood, it is less precise than "Churchill was a bulldog." Metaphors evidently are not just fancy paraphrases for accessible literal truths. They pick out extensions that are otherwise semantically unmarked.[8] Standard English contains no literal predicate for the class of people in the metaphorical extension of "bulldog." So metaphors extend our semantic and cognitive range. They enable us to say things that we strictly have no way to say literally. They function similarly in representational realms. A caricature of Churchill as a bulldog, in metaphorically depicting him as a bulldog, characterizes Churchill in a way that no literal portrait of Churchill would quite do.

Metaphor is not restricted to denotation. In referring to a feature it metaphorically possesses, a symbol metaphorically exemplifies that property. Thus, Churchill metaphorically exemplifies bulldoggedness when serving as an example of that trait. Expression, Goodman maintains, is a form of metaphorical exemplification. A work of art, functioning as such, expresses the properties it metaphorically exemplifies. Being inanimate, the *Pietà* cannot literally exemplify sorrow. But it can and does exemplify the property metaphorically. It thereby expresses sorrow.

Exemplification thus accommodates the properties Langer labeled presentational. Works may literally exemplify sensory properties and metaphorically exemplify emotional properties. Since exemplification is a device for exhibiting or displaying properties, we can say that the works present the properties in question. But, according to Goodman, literal exemplification by works of art is not restricted to sensory properties, nor is expression restricted to emotional ones. A painting, although literally immobile, may express movement. A fanfare, although literally invisible, can express brightness and color.

I have discussed Goodman's theory in some detail, because the construal of works of art as symbols helps explain what art education is, why education facilitates the creation and appreciation of art, and how understanding art interfaces with understanding of other kinds. A critical insight is that the symbolic devices used in the arts are also used in other disciplines. To deny that these devices function cognitively, then, would be to deprive ourselves of resources used in plainly cognitive domains, such as the natural and social sciences. But once we admit that they function cognitively in such domains, it is hard to deny that they do so in the arts.

If a work of art is a symbol, then to create a work of art is to devise a symbol. To create a work of art that conveys a particular insight is to devise a suitably effective symbol. Moreover, to understand a work of art is to interpret a symbol correctly. That requires mastering its syntax and semantics. The parallel to language is illuminating here. Students need to know how to read works in the nonverbal arts as well as in the verbal arts. So art education is analogous to literacy education. Learning how to read and write effectively requires mastering the syntax and semantics of a natural language. A student needs to learn the alphabet, the vocabulary, and the grammar. She must develop facility with using and recognizing not just literal descriptive locutions but also locutions that function in a variety of other ways. She must learn how to recognize and interpret metaphors, allusions, and other tropes. She must acquire the ability to construct and use them effectively. She has to learn how to tell whether something left unsaid is implicated by what is said. And she has to master the use of implicatures to convey more than she actually says. She even needs to acquire the ability to determine what to make of what is left unsaid in a particular passage. She must be able to tell what a particular passage exemplifies or expresses. And she must learn how to compose passages that exemplify and express what she wants them to.

All of this is familiar in the study of literature, but it is also critical in other areas. Political discourse, for example, is rife with metaphor, allusion, implicature, and expression. That a term for an ethnic group expresses contempt may be far more important to understanding a politician's remarks than knowing the exact boundaries of the group the derogatory term denotes. His failure to mention ongoing negotiations with adversaries may implicate that he is ready to go to war. To understand the political climate of an age, then, requires a complex array of linguistic abilities. Reading and understanding the primary source documents in history thus requires facility with symbols of different kinds.

The skills needed to understand literature are to a significant extent continuous with those needed to understand other uses of language. So it is perhaps not surprising that the study of literature is far more deeply integrated into standard school curricula than the study of any other art. But the syntactic difference between linguistic symbols and representational symbols might seem to suggest that mastering representational symbols is hopelessly difficult. If every difference between two marks constitutes a difference between characters—if, for example, every difference in the length or shape of a line makes it a different symbol—we will never be in a position to tell exactly what symbol confronts us. How can we hope to interpret a symbol if we cannot even be sure what the symbol is?

Luckily, such pessimism is unfounded. Students regularly master syntactically dense representational systems. Even if we ignore, for the moment, their facility with interpreting pictures, it is plain that they learn to read and make maps, charts, and diagrams. Maps represent such things as the course of a river, the height of a mountain, the location of a city, the boundaries of a state. In certain respects, every difference between marks makes a difference to the identity of a symbol on a map. So if, for example, the line representing the Nile had been shorter or thinner, it would have been a different symbol. The difference might, but need not, have been semantically significant. On a map purporting to show the precise source of the Nile, if the line representing the river had been shorter, it would have indicated that the river began farther north. If the thickness of a line representing a river is supposed to correlate with the river's volume, then representing it with a thinner line would have indicated that it was a smaller river. If, on the other hand, the source is only roughly indicated on the map, and there is no significance to the thickness of the lines indicating rivers, then these syntactic differences have no semantic consequences.

This is a familiar aspect of maps, and is one that students readily learn. Significant features of the terrain tend to be marked on maps. Features that are relevantly alike are represented in the same way. On a road map, for example, cities of the same size are apt to be represented with dots of the same size or the same color. On a political map, regions with the same voting patterns are apt to be represented in the same color. So cities that are represented in the same way on one map might be given distinct representations on another. In learning to make and read maps, students need to learn how to construct and interpret the nonverbal symbols. This involves more than recognizing that a blue line represents a river and a dot represents a city. It also involves, for example, recognizing what the map does not represent. Should they infer from the fact that the map records no city between Rochester and Syracuse that there is no city between the two? That there is no major city between the two? That there is no city with a significant Polish population between the two? It depends. Students need to know what sort of information the map is designed to convey in order to answer such questions. The crucial point here is that map reading and map making are readily learnable skills. That every difference in particular respects *can* make a difference is compatible with the fact that it is possible to learn how to recognize in particular cases which features actually *do* make a difference.

Syntactic density, then, is in principle no barrier to symbolic mastery. Students readily learn to read maps, diagrams, and charts. But, one might argue, all such symbols are highly regimented. Maps contain keys that tell the reader what is represented, how it is represented, and at what scale. Charts and diagrams are standardized as well. The problem with paintings, sculptures, and the like is that they do not provide such keys.

But art is not alone in this regard. To understand a political poster, it is as important to recognize that the illustration is derogatory as that the words are. To understand a politician's campaign speeches, one needs to recognize that some of his gestures express contempt and others express admiration. Properly interpreting his verbal, pictorial, and gestural tropes is critical to understanding what he is doing. The skills and abilities that students need to master symbols in other disciplines such as history and civics are thus the same, or continuous with those that they need to master artistic symbols.

Nevertheless, art arguably has more degrees of freedom than other disciplines. In history, geography, or physics, context sharply circumscribes, providing cues as to what aspects of a symbol are significant and what they are likely to symbolize. But a painting or a quartet (particularly a contemporary painting or quartet) could in principle symbolize just about anything via just about any of its features. This is a difference in degree, not in kind. At best, it would indicate that learning to interpret aesthetic symbols is more difficult than learning to interpret symbols used in other disciplines. But even this may be conceding too much. For even though art as such allows for symbolization along any dimension and to any degree of precision, it is not the case that every work of art symbolizes along every dimension and with every degree of precision. In learning to interpret works of art, as in learning to interpret other symbols, the student starts out with relatively simple symbols and works his way up to more difficult ones. In picture books for very young children, for example, the colors tend to be bright, the palette limited, the figures sharply defined, the mood clear. The picture of the woods near the witch's house may express scariness. But a three-year-old is not generally expected to decide whether they express eeriness, spookiness, or ominousness. If she recognizes that the picture depicts the woods and expresses scariness, she interprets it correctly. Even though scariness can be further divided into subcases, such as ominousness, eeriness, and spookiness, the symbol itself need not reflect these further distinctions. Just as we can say that something is scary without further refinements, a picture can *express* scariness without expressing any more refined sort of scariness. In that case, the child who takes the picture to exemplify scariness gets it right.

As he matures, the student encounters pictures that symbolize along additional dimensions and that belong to symbol systems that are capable of drawing finer distinctions. Eventually, he may be called upon to decide whether a work, such as Dürer's *Knight, Death and the Devil* expresses mere scariness or a more refined emotion such as eeriness, ominousness, or spookiness. Although the question is difficult, and any answer is controversial, the question is not obviously any more difficult or the answer any more controversial than, for example, deciding whether Lear's mad scene expresses genuine insanity, or rage, or fury. One way students advance is by learning to construct increasingly sensitive interpretations of works of art. As they learn, the standards of correctness rise.

Evidently, art education is possible. The sorts of symbols used in the arts are also used in disciplines that are uncontroversially part of the curriculum—history, English, geography, and so on. The skills needed to create and interpret works of art are also needed to create and interpret symbols in the other disciplines that use them. Creativity, talent, and genius are desirable in all disciplines, but no more necessary in art than in history, science, or geography. The fear that there is something about art that locates it outside the boundaries of education is unfounded.

This raises a further question. Not everything that can be taught should be taught. What reasons are there for saying that art should be part of the general curriculum?

One answer appeals to the intrinsic value of art. Making and appreciating art is an end in itself that need not be justified by any further goods it produces. Evidence for the intrinsic value of art comes from the ubiquity of art. Every culture produces and values art. Unlike commerce and technology, art as such seems to serve no further end. So it is at least plausible to think that art is valuable for its own sake. If this is so, then education that improves the ability to make and appreciate art is valuable because it enables students to achieve an intrinsically valuable end.

I consider this argument sound—in fact, decisive—but it faces a challenge. It is exceedingly difficult to provide a strong argument that something is intrinsically valuable. The challenger can always ask, "But, why should we value *that*?" Since an end in itself need serve no further end, there is nothing to be said about what intrinsic values are good for. When challenged to show that they really are good, there seems to be no way to mount a defense. So let us consider the idea that art education is good as a means.

A familiar justification appeals to the so-called Mozart Effect. Exposure to classical music is held to enhance general intelligence, as in a slogan, "Music makes you smarter." So parents are encouraged to expose their young children (even in utero) to classical music and to have them take music lessons from an early age, on the grounds that eventually this will pay off in higher SAT scores. But the research shows no such correlation.[9] There is a correlation between listening to classical music and a short-term improvement in specific spatial skills. This is an interesting neurological finding, but the improvement lasts only about fifteen minutes and the skills (in paper-folding tasks) are of no particular value for anything other than the insights about neurology they afford. The conviction that exposure to classical music enhances mathematical and engineering skills or general reasoning skills appears unfounded. The idea that it is but a short step from Suzuki violin to higher IQs is not supported by the evidence.

Instead of thinking of arts education as a cause of cognitive advances that have virtually nothing to do with art, as advocates of the Mozart Effect do, we do better to notice that skills and abilities acquired and developed through arts education are skills and abilities that figure in the mastery of other disciplines. A student who recognizes the irony in Molière's *Misanthrope* is apt to recognize irony in Plato's *Apology* or in Mencken's news reports on the Scopes trial. And, of course, the converse also holds. A student who recognizes Mencken's or Plato's irony is apt to be able to recognize irony in Molière.

Even if this is so, a problem remains: If we want students to understand irony in political commentators, why don't we just have them study political commentators? What is the point of a detour through the arts?

Although the same symbolic functions are performed by works of art and by symbols of other kinds, the locus of the constraints seems to be different. Maps, charts, and diagrams are standardized. There are external constraints, dictated by the functions these symbols are designed to perform, that determine how the symbols are to be interpreted—what aspects symbolize and to what degree of specificity. Because works of art set their own constraints, they can serve as laboratories of the mind.[10] A work of art can isolate particular features and present them in a purer or clearer form, or from a more telling angle than we are apt to encounter in daily life.

Because there is less regimentation, determining whether a particular aspect of a work of art is functioning symbolically, and what if anything it symbolizes, requires interpreting the work as a whole and figuring out what constraints it sets for itself. Because the symbols tend to be dense and replete, the answer to such questions may be indeterminate. Frequently, a work admits of multiple correct interpretations. Whether, for example, a given juxtaposition is significant depends on how it contributes to an interpretation of the work as a whole. Relative to one interpretation, it is significant; relative to another, it is not. So to make sense of a work, an interpreter needs to tease out possible interpretations and determine what is to be said for and against each of them. It requires a delicate balance of cognitive firmness and flexibility.

The capacity to strike such a balance is cognitively valuable across disciplines. It is particularly useful at the cutting edge of inquiry, where things are not nearly so regimented as our stereotypes pretend. How to represent the data, how to distinguish between signal and noise, and what to make of the data may be unclear and how to decide may be controversial. The skills and dispositions one acquires in interpreting works of art may provide a useful platform for interpreting cutting-edge results in the sciences.

Epistemologists often focus on cases where the evidence is, or might be, too sparse to warrant a conclusion. But frequently we face problems of plenty. We have a vast amount of data, but no obvious way to make sense of it. We do not know how to distinguish signal from noise, or relevant from irrelevant likenesses. Fiction can help. A work of fiction can contrive a situation that brings particular patterns or features or possibilities to the fore and makes readers aware of them. A painting with a fictive subject can do the same thing. A fictional symbol may exemplify a pattern that is present in the data, but that is easily missed because it is overlaid by other, salient factors. Once we have learned to discern the pattern, we can recognize it in ordinary life. *Oedipus Rex*, for example, exemplifies Aristotle's point that we should call no man happy until he is dead. Having seen the play, we can readily recognize other, more pedestrian cases of the precariousness of good fortune.

Nor is it only works of fiction that play this role. A work of art, representational or not, can exemplify features or patterns that obtain, but are not discerned in daily life. Once we learn to recognize them, they may be readily found. Douglass's discussion of the slave songs brings this out: "They told a tale of woe which was then beyond my feeble comprehension; they were tones loud, long, and deep; they breathed the prayer and complaint of souls boiling over with the bitterest anguish. Every tone was a testimony against slavery, and a prayer to God for deliverance from chains."[11]

By expressing the bitter anguish that slavery produced, the songs made manifest what should have been, but was not, obvious anyway. It is worth noting that Douglass does not emphasize the words of these songs. The loud, long, and deep tones convey the slaves' anguish. He says, "I have often thought that the mere hearing of those songs would do more to impress some minds with the horrible character of slavery than the reading of whole volumes of philosophy."[12] If he is even nearly right, the power of the arts extends vastly beyond the aesthetic realm. In that case, the capacity to create and interpret symbols such as the slave songs is crucial for reasons that have nothing to do with art.

This example might seem to make things too easy. Since we are firmly convinced that slavery is evil, a device that can move people to share our opinion seems to advance understanding. But songs, however moving, convey no evidence and provide no argument. At most, it seems, the songs get people to change their minds about slavery. They convey no warrant. The danger is that equally moving works could move people to endorse untenable conclusions.

If the songs or other works of art were supposed to make the entire case for a conclusion, the worry would be apt. At best, works of art highlight features, point up patterns, show or suggest unsuspected aspects of things that enable us to frame hypotheses. Except in rare, self-referential cases, a song or a story or a painting by itself does not demonstrate or provide evidence that things are as it intimates that they are. Still, framing hypotheses that are worth investigating is itself cognitively valuable. For we are unlikely to test hypotheses we have never framed. So even if art did no more than enable people to frame such hypotheses, it would be cognitively valuable. But sometimes it does more. By exemplifying particular features or patterns, works of art prompt us to formulate hypotheses for which we have ample evidence but might without the works never have framed.[13] In such cases they enable us to bring familiar facts together so that we can see what follows from them.

To insist that works of art are symbols that figure in the advancement of understanding might seem to underrate the subjective and emotional aspects of art. It might seem to make looking at the *Mona Lisa* like peering at a problematic x-ray. Is a line or shadow significant? What, if anything, does it represent? What, if anything, does it portend? Do others see the same things when looking at it as I do? If not, what should we make of that? But, one wants to insist, looking at the *Mona Lisa* is *not* like looking at a problematic x-ray. In the case of the x-ray, each radiologist should be as objective as possible. Each should attempt to draw conclusions for which he can give reasons that would be acceptable to other experts in the field. Consensus in interpretation is strongly desired. But in looking at the *Mona Lisa*, the viewer should not leave her subjectivity behind. Consensus is not necessary. The felt quality of her experience is important.

Can a theory that construes works of art as symbols do justice to this difference? I think it can. I earlier denied that art is purely subjective, for it is possible to misinterpret works of art. But this is not to say that subjectivity has no place in the interpretation of art. Encounters with the arts are reflective. We attend to the work, and to our reactions to the work. And we take it that our subjective reactions may be indicative of aspects of the work. If the *Mona Lisa* strikes us as mysterious, we consider why we are reacting that way. Our responses are Janus faced: they reveal something about the work and something about ourselves. And each of these reflects back on the other. The more we understand our responses, the more resources we have for understanding the works that evoke them; and the more we understand the works, the more sensitive and focused our responses can be. So subjective reactions are not the end of an aesthetic encounter, but they are a means to advance understanding of and through the encounter. Our feelings, like our sensations, are resources for interpretation. They indicate what and how a work symbolizes. Like other indicators, they can be misleading. So the sensibilities need to be educated. We need to learn when and how feelings are apt to mislead, and how to recognize when we are being misled. And we need to learn how to deduce what is actually the case from the misleading appearances. We do the same thing in perceptual cases. We have learned that the apparent shape of a tilted coin is not its real shape; and we have learned how to figure out its real shape from the apparent shape. The crucial point is that educating the sensibilities is not a matter of moving away from subjective responses; it is refining them so that, while they remain subjective, they become increasingly valuable cognitive resources. A connoisseur, like a good judge of character, is someone whose subjective responses are finely tuned to relevant features of their targets.

We have seen that a symbol-theoretic conception of art readily explains how art education is possible and why it is valuable. Dewey's conception of a means-ends continuum is useful here.[14] Rather than conceiving of the arts as mere means to some utterly independent end, as the advocates of the Mozart Effect do, we should see that they are at once both ends and means. Understanding works of art is worthwhile for its own sake. But it also provides a platform for further understanding, both of art and of other matters. We develop resources, perspectives, and motivations that enable us to ask questions and find answers that, without them, we could not have done. The end, then, becomes a means to formulating and pursuing further ends, both in the arts and elsewhere. Education for the arts facilitates this process.

NOTES

1. Booker T. Washington, "Industrial Education for the Negro," in *The Negro Problem: A Series of Articles by Representative Negroes of Today* (New York: AMS Press, 1970), p. 17; first published 1903.

2. Frederick Douglass, "Narrative of the life of Frederick Douglass," in *Douglass Autobiographies* (New York: Library of America, 1994), p. 8.

3. Mary Mothersill, *Beauty Restored* (Oxford: Clarendon, 1984), p. 8.

4. Suzanne Langer, *Philosophy in a New Key* (Cambridge, MA: Harvard University Press, 1976), pp. 79–102.

5. Immanuel Kant, *Critique of Judgment* (Indianapolis: Hackett, 1987), pp. 209–20.

6. Nelson Goodman, *Languages of Art* (Indianapolis: Hackett, 1976).

7. Density in this sense has nothing to do with obscurity. It has to do with the relation of symbols to one another. The real numbers are dense in this sense, in that between any two there is a third.

8. Sam Glucksburg and Boas Keyser, "Understanding Metaphorical Comparisons: Beyond Similarity," *Psychological Review* 97 (1990): 3–18.

9. F. H. Raucher, G. L. Shaw, and K. N. Ky, "Music and Spacial Task Performance," *Nature* 365 (1993): 611.

10. Catherine Z. Elgin, "The Laboratory of the Mind," in *A Sense of the World: Essays on Fiction, Narrative, and Knowledge*, eds. Wolfgang Huemer, John Gibson, Lucca Pocci (London: Routledge, 2007), pp. 43–54.

11. Douglass, "Narrative," p. 24.

12. Ibid.

13. David K. Lewis, "Truth in Fiction, Postscript," in *Philosophical Papers* (Oxford: Oxford University Press, 1983), vol. 1, p. 279.

14. John Dewey, *Democracy and Education* (New York: The Free Press, 1916), pp. 100–24.

CHAPTER 19

SCIENCE EDUCATION, RELIGIOUS TOLERATION, AND LIBERAL NEUTRALITY TOWARD THE GOOD

ROBERT AUDI

EDUCATION in science is enormously important, but even in parts of the world in which it is an element in required public schooling, it is often insufficiently integrated with education in the humanities. Philosophy of science has an obvious bearing on understanding scientific inquiry, but science education should also be properly integrated with some central points in metaphysics, ethics, and political philosophy. This view will be developed here mainly in relation to a branch of scientific inquiry that in recent years has been widely debated. I refer to evolutionary biology; and although this essay bears on science education in general, the United States will be the main case in point.

Evolutionary biology is a standard topic in science education in much of the world, but at least in the United States it remains controversial, especially among religious citizens. Many people have insisted that creationism be taught side by side with evolutionary theory, and the name "creation science" has been used to suggest that this demand does not imply that science instructors should endorse any religious position. The name "intelligent design" (ID) is also intended to imply that science teachers introducing that perspective—and perhaps even proponents of it—need not be committed to a religious position. It seems likely that the courts in the United States will continue to consider the merits of various positions on this issue.[1] A major focus of their considerations has been what constitutes neutrality toward religion. My aim here is to clarify the issue, to provide a conception of religious neutrality that does not undermine the kind of moral education that every society needs, and to propose a framework for scientific education that may reduce the tensions now causing difficulties both for education in science and for civic harmony.

1. Science and Scientific Method

There is no need here to define *science*, but I will assume that paradigms are the natural sciences, especially physics, chemistry, and biology. The term *science* also applies, however, to psychology and the other "human sciences," different though they are from the natural sciences. What all of these disciplines have in common that is particularly relevant to our topic is a use of *scientific method* and a tendency to foster what has been called *a scientific habit of mind*. Both notions are important for the overall issue of how evolutionary biology should be taught.

Scientific method is the subject of a huge literature. This chapter will discuss only three important elements that bear on the status of creationism and related views as candidates for scientific positions.

Testability

First, it is widely held that a scientific hypothesis (indeed, any statement belonging to the realm of science) must be observationally testable, in the sense that in principle some observations could confirm or disconfirm it. Such testability in principle is more than the mere logical possibility of testing but less than its technological feasibility. The notion cannot be precisely defined, but we may say that scientists tend to demand of a proposed hypothesis that those competent in the field to which it belongs can at least see what kinds of empirically possible observations—whether of natural events or events produced experimentally—would tend to confirm or to disconfirm it.

Testability has been identified with falsifiability.[2] There is certainly such a thing as falsification of a hypothesis to the satisfaction of competent judges; but falsifiability should not be considered equivalent to testability. Logically speaking, apart from special exceptions that are unlikely to be important for understanding scientific method, existential claims (those asserting the existence of something) can be verified and disconfirmed, but not falsified.[3] Suppose it is claimed that a human being will someday grow to a height of twenty feet. This is, in principle, verifiable but cannot be strictly falsified (it implies no contradiction nor even a contravention of laws of nature). There might be experiments that disconfirm it and well-confirmed theoretical grounds to consider it improbable, but such results would at most render it highly improbable. Similarly, logically speaking, universal propositions (of a scientific kind)—say, that all metals conduct electricity—can be (at least with high probability) falsified (by counterexample) but not verified, in the strong sense entailing that they are decisively established.[4]

Two further points should be added for even minimal clarification of the idea of testability in principle. The first bears on why "in principle" or some such phrase is essential. Consider the statement that a cup of sugar was unwittingly spilled in the Atlantic exactly 100 miles east of the Statue of Liberty. Given that by hypothesis no one could remember this, and given that sugar dissolves in water, only indirect evidences could be invoked, and without further information it is not clear what these evidences would be. (This hypothesis is not meant to be of scientific interest, but similar points hold for statements that are.)

Consider also what counts as observability. Take a psychological hypothesis to the effect that if I have a certain sequence of thoughts, I will next have a certain mental image. The entire test could be conduced mentally. Contrary to the usual assumption that observability must be through the five senses, here we have *experienceability* but not, strictly speaking, observability. Must we say that the experiment is not scientific? I doubt that; but whether we conclude this or not, there is something important for scientific inquiry that the example does not challenge—namely, that the confirmatory relevance of experience is crucial for scientific status.

Publicity

I have assumed both that mental phenomena hold scientific interest and that our mental lives are in a certain way private. To see how the latter assumption can be squared with the idea that science is "public," we might generalize our psychological hypothesis to the claim that *anyone* who has the relevant sequence of thoughts will have a certain image, where the thoughts are abstract but the image is of, say, a representation of Jesus. This generalization meets a kind of *publicity test*: any competent person could run the experiment and could give publicly observable testimony as to its outcome. Publicity is, in fact, the second element in a very common conception of scientific method—perhaps the standard conception of it if there is one. In part, this requirement is needed both to rule out epistemically prejudicial idiosyncrasy and to do justice to the cooperative character of scientific endeavor. If I discover a connection between silent utterance of certain sequences of words and the formation of certain mental images, this should be a result that is publicly testable even if each person seeking direct confirmation must ascertain the connection internally.

To be sure, if *reports* of the results could not be produced in the public domain where they are equally accessible to competent observers, we would not regard the experiment as meeting the publicity condition. It may be true that we cannot directly verify someone's report of an inner experience, such as imaging a person; but even to check on someone's perceptions of what is experienced in the public domain (such as the color of a precipitate), we have to rely on other perceptions, and here we count on sensory experiences to reveal properties of external objects. Those experiences are no less interior than images. Publicity implies a kind of intersubjectivity, but it does not require either perceptual infallibility or reliance only on nonmental phenomena.

Empiricality

A third element important in understanding scientific method is its restriction to empirical matters. The idea underlying the restriction is, in part, to set aside inquires in logic or pure mathematics (fields, to be sure, whose claims some believe to be broadly empirical). These fields may be viewed as nonempirical without being considered *un*scientific, nor are they. But, however competent in these fields some scientists may be, propositions of logic and mathematical are not usually considered the kinds that science investigates.[5] The contrast here is between the empirical and the *a priori*. There was a time when many would have said, following Kant, that *a priori* propositions are equivalent to necessary ones (those that, like the proposition that nothing is round and square, *must* be true) and hence science must be concerned with what is both empirical and contingent (not necessary). It seems clear, however, that a proposition could be necessary—for example, that water is H_2O—but not be *a priori*.[6] A necessary truth, then, might be discoverable empirically, even if the fact that it *is* necessary is not itself an empirical matter.

Suppose that necessary propositions are not beyond scientific confirmability. An important consequence follows—namely, that certain necessary theological propositions, which some take to include the proposition that God exists— might be scientifically confirmable. That God's existence is empirically confirmable has also long been held by proponents of the argument from design (roughly, the argument from the order found in nature to the existence of God as needed to explain it or at least as what best explains it). To be sure, theists need not take the existence of God to be necessary. In that case, an empiricality requirement alone would not even begin to rule out the scientific confirmability of theism.

Fallibilism, Experimental Rigorism, and Replicability

In addition to the three elements so far stressed—testability, publicity, and empiricality—fallibilism as a procedural attitude has been thought essential to scientific method. I call it procedural because the point is about scientific practice and the epistemic claims made in assessing it; the actual psychological disposition of scientists engaging in the practice is of secondary importance. In my view, however, procedural fallibilism is a better candidate to be a requirement of a proper *use* of scientific method than partly definitory of scientific method itself. A dogmatic person could use scientific method to confirm hypotheses and could even acquire knowledge through using it. But given the fallibility of both the procedures used and those who use them, the person would have an inappropriate attitude. If fallibilism as a procedural attitude is above all (roughly) an openness to the possibility of one's being mistaken even in what seems obvious or established, it is indeed necessary for a scientific attitude. But, clearly, fallibilism is appropriate in theology and other fields as well.

If we now note that in principle the occurrence of religious experiences can be predicted from theological assertions, we can begin to see that the kinds of demarcation criteria we have been considering do not strictly show that no theological hypothesis is observationally, or even experimentally, testable. To be sure, most theologians and many lay religious people have not staked their faith on predictions. But consider an example of a religiously significant prediction: that ardent believers who pray intensely and wholeheartedly will more often than not feel better immediately afterwards. This can actually be confirmed or disconfirmed. Suppose it is true. Its truth does not, of course, entail the existence of God, and many would say that the explanation of the pattern lies in secular psychology. Suppose for the sake of argument that this is true. It should be balanced by the point that it is common for clearly scientific hypotheses to be explainable in more than one way; so, just as different scientists may retain conflicting theories to explain data they agree on, theists may claim that the confirmation of this hypothesis remains *some* evidence for divine action in the world.

This brings us to a further presumptive requirement for scientific testability. Call it the *hostile-observer standard.* Its basis is the rigoristic idea that a scientifically respectable hypothesis should be testable by competent persons even if they are hostile to it or to the theory of which it is part. The point is not that hostility conduces to observational competence; rather, the idea is that a sympathetic observer is biased and bias affects perception, memory, interpretation, or other elements important for scientific confirmation. To be sure, a believer in God might happen to be hostile to the idea that prayer makes one feel better and hence could, by the hostile-observer standard, test the proposed prayer hypothesis. But someone hostile to theism itself could not do so in the direct way in question, since it is restricted to believers. One could get indirect evidence through testimony from believers, but the standard is supposed to be applicable to scientifically testable hypotheses. If hostility can interfere in this way with direct testing, it is not a basic requirement for scientific status.

The general point here is that it is a contingent matter whether there *is* anyone hostile to—or even neutral toward—a position under scrutiny; and its testability does not depend on this. More important, there are ways to eliminate the effects of bias—

which, of course, can interfere with the reliability of hostile as well as sympathetic observers (or experiencers) or even neutral ones who have some other potentially distorting characteristic. One way is repeated testing. Indeed, *replicability* under varying conditions and given different observers is one among other criteria for a genuinely scientific test. As with testability itself, however, this criterion is limited: the conditions needed for testing might not be realizable. This could be a special problem in biology, since species of living things change and can die out. Replicability is limited by mortality. We could discover the last living specimen.

The Demarcation Problem and Theological Testability

Suppose we set aside these difficulties of analysis and conceive scientific method as described in relation to the three criteria that, in some form, can withstand scrutiny: observational testability, publicity, and empiricality. We might then characterize a scientific claim (whether a hypothesis or a full-scale theory) as one that can, in principle, be confirmed or disconfirmed using this method. The problem here—commonly called the *demarcation problem*—is to distinguish scientific claims, in the broad sense of claims appropriately assessable by using scientific method, from others, such as those of logic, on one side, and theology, on another side. A great deal has been written on this problem.[7] All I can do here is further indicate the difficulty of ruling out certain kinds of claims, including some by creationists or intelligent-design theorists, as nonscientific. In the light of that, we can better assess how those views should be treated in public education.

It is commonly (though by no means universally) thought that theological claims are intrinsically untestable empirically.[8] But consider the claim that God will darken the sky at noon. This cannot be decisively established by observation, since the occurrence would only confirm it but would leave open what *caused* the phenomenon. Yet it is empirically confirmable and, more obviously, empirically disconfirmable (since the sun may shine as usual). Still (returning to our main subject), what of human origins? It could be claimed that we can confirm "God created the earth in 4004 BC" if this implies that we will find both faults in, say, carbon dating and develop a new dating system that pinpoints this time of origin. I do not see how this scenario can be shown inconceivable.[9]

Let us leave creationism aside for the time being. The intelligent-design view is more modest. In principle, *some* version of it might yield predictions about how our brains are constructed or how human beings would adjust to certain changes—predictions that could be confirmed or disconfirmed in months or a few years.[10] We do not, so far as I know, find such predictions emerging from ID theorists. Some critics would hold that the positions are not even clear enough for predictions of these sorts to be said to follow from them (or even made probable by them), in which case their observationally bearing out is not confirmatory. Even if this is so, there remains the idea that only what *best* (or well) explains observable phenomena is thereby confirmed. This idea raises more questions than can be pursued here. One is what counts as a good explanation; another is whether predictive power is a condition for qualifying as one. Still another is whether being best is enough: Why should the best of a number of *poor* explanations be supported at all by what it explains? (I assume for the sake of argument the legitimacy of a loose usage that may be controversial: that we can properly speak *at all* of explanations that are not wholly *factive*—i.e., contain only true explaining and explained propositions.)

Methodological vs. Metaphysical Questions

It should be evident that the elements of scientific method so far emphasized are methodological, not ontological. Neither the testability nor the publicity nor the empirical character of scientific hypotheses entails any substantive ontological conclusion, say that *only* natural events can be causes or that there *cannot* be an infinite chain of causes extending into the past. But it is commonly and plausibly held that a commitment to scientific method presupposes a commitment to *methodological naturalism*: roughly, the view that causes and explanations of natural phenomena should be sought in the natural world, paradigmatically in terms of what meets the other three criteria (testability, publicity, and empiricality) *and* does not presuppose supernatural agency, such as that of God taken as transcending nature and as creator of the universe.

Methodological naturalism neither affirms nor denies theism. In this, it is like liberal democracy itself, which is the kind of society that provides the context of our discussion. Methodological naturalism ethically constrains the conduct of scientific inquiry but implies no substantive conclusions of either science or, especially, metaphysics.

My formulation of methodological naturalism allows that scientific inquiry might posit causal elements, such as the Big Bang, which may be argued to require a supernatural cause. The point is that, methodologically and epistemically, one would need no evidence of any supernatural proposition in order to conduct scientific inquiry and confirm scientific hypotheses. One might, then, qualify as using scientific method to understand the world even if one takes the Big Bang to have a supernatural cause, provided one does not treat such a factor as essential in the content or confirmation of one's scientific work.[11] A methodological naturalist might even hold that *every* natural event, whether mental or physical, has a natural cause and even a sufficient naturalistic—indeed, perhaps physicalistic—explanation, *as well as* a theistic explanation, provided that the latter, supernaturalist claim is no part of one's scientific endeavor.[12]

Given this conception of methodological naturalism, the best response to the demarcation problem for purposes of this essay is to draw four tentative conclusions:

1. There very well may be no way to show that theological hypotheses are intrinsically untestable by observation or experience.[13]

2. It does not follow (and is not true) that, if they *are* observationally testable, they thereby represent good scientific hypotheses (or scientific hypotheses of any sort).

3. There is no good reason to think that every significant scientific hypothesis or theory in a given domain should be introduced into science teaching in that domain, especially at the pre-college level.

4. The common and not unreasonable commitment to methodological naturalism in the moderate form described above implies that any creationist or ID view that presupposes or self-evidently entails a supernaturalistic proposition is not a proper object of scientific appraisal. (This is not to say that scientific evidence cannot be in some way *relevant* to such a view.)

In the light of what we have so far seen, we might conclude that although there apparently are plausible methodological criteria of demarcation that many creationist or ID views do not satisfy, those criteria will not warrant a wholesale rejection of all possible hypotheses from those domains as nonscientific. Why, then, should some of them not be included in even public school (pre-college) courses seriously treating evolution?

2. The Scientific Habit of Mind

The point that a theological hypothesis is not intrinsically insusceptible of observational confirmation should be balanced by two others. One is that such hypotheses are not normally put forward in a way that makes it clear *how* they might be observationally confirmed. A second is that scientists working as such are commonly committed, even if tacitly, to methodological naturalism and hence view their work as concerned with understanding and predicting natural phenomena in terms of laws of nature and phenomena in the natural world. This is perhaps implicit in the standard use of the term "natural science" as contrasted with "the humanities," "theology," and "pure mathematics." We might go further and ask, "Is the scientific habit of mind naturalistic as opposed to supernaturalistic?" The question is important for science education because an affirmative answer would imply that the teaching of science is by its very nature not entirely neutral toward the truth of religious views.

By "the scientific habit of mind" I refer not just to an intellectual orientation but also to a practical commitment to using scientific method in the pursuit of empirical questions. Defining this idea would take much space, but the idea is sufficiently clear for my use of it here. I would add, however, that I take the scientific habit of mind to imply a tendency, even in nonempirical matters (such as questions of pure mathematics and, more controversially, ethics), to use what might be called *theoretical method* in important matters: a systematic attempt to seek evidentially relevant data, to try to explain them by appeal to theoretical notions, and to be willing to revise theory in the light of data and—sometimes—to reinterpret data in the light of theory. It is in part because the scientific habit of mind does imply this tendency to seek, in *any* domain of inquiry, an integration between theories (or generalizations) and data that developing it is educationally so valuable.

It may seem that even scientific *method* sets science at odds with religious commitment. For commitment to scientific method is easily taken to entail not only using experimentation as a central way of achieving knowledge but also maintaining that science alone can yield general knowledge, or at least any general knowledge outside logic and mathematics. This view is, if not a version, then a legacy, of positivism. Positivism is often said to be dead; but if it is, its ghost lingers. Surely the sound point in this vicinity is that scientific method is *applicable in principle* to any kind of empirical question about the world, probably *relevant* to all of these questions, and *needed* for some of them. This point is in no tension with classical theism, on which the universe is a creation of an omniscient, omnipotent, omnibenevolent God.

Indeed, for many religious traditions, including at least Christianity and Judaism, the scientific study of nature is readily viewed as an attempt to understand the world God created. Within these traditions one can view scientific inquiry as a use of reason conceived as a natural endowment from God. Even the most rigorous scientific inquiry can be seen as aimed at understanding nature viewed with a certain kind of reverence. Far from being necessarily in conflict with the scientific habit of mind, such a religious commitment can reinforce it.

What about the theory of evolution? The theory is clearly inconsistent with the account of creation given in Genesis interpreted *literally*. But literal interpretation of scripture is not required for a reasonable theology and is widely (and increasingly) rejected by educated Biblical interpreters. This is not to suggest that there can be no tension between scientific results and some scripturally based beliefs on the part of a religiously committed person. The point is that it is theologically implausible to view scripture as competing with scientific inquiry with respect to answering the same questions. One possibility, for instance, is to take the account in Genesis to be affirming (among other things, to be sure) the creative action and the sovereignty of God. These generic attributions are compatible with the theory of evolution.

But, one might reply, isn't the evolutionary account of our genesis physicalistic, and doesn't the physicalism in question entail a conception of human beings that is at odds with the dualistic view that some think is implicit in the Bible, or at least in the Christian tradition? I do not see that the evolutionary account is inconsistent with dualism, particularly the modest, *property dualism* on which mental properties are distinct from physical ones, even if—as on *substance monism*—there is only one kind of substance. For all that, I suspect that the closer biological science comes to explaining the origin and development of human beings, the more it will seem to some people that a physicalistic view of the human person is being confirmed. I find this association understandable, and its strength is part of what underlies some religious people's hostility to evolutionary biology. Nonetheless, the evolutionary account of human origins is genetic and biological, not metaphysical. Above all, providing physicalistic conditions (such as biochemical ones) for the genesis of biologically identified human beings leaves open whether or not they are wholly physical in *constitution*.[14]

Evolutionary science also leaves open two other important views. The first is that *normative* properties, such as being intrinsically good, being virtuous, and being obligatory, are not physical or even "natural." The second is that survival of bodily death does not have to be either rejected or understood in terms of, say, a resurrection body with physical properties appropriate to sustain personhood.[15]

If evolutionary science is neutral with respect to physicalism about our ultimate psychological constitution, presumably the scientific enterprise as a whole is, too. For plainly psychology and the other social sciences can be scientifically pursued without the assumption of physicalism about the human person; and the physical sciences certainly are pursued without this assumption.

3. Philosophical Naturalism

Many who have a scientific habit of mind are committed to something more: philosophical naturalism. Often the qualifier *philosophical* is omitted, but it will soon be clear that naturalism in a commonly accepted form, and in a version in which it is widely considered a worldview incompatible with theism, is a philosophical position.

There is no consensus about just what constitutes philosophical naturalism. In metaphysics, naturalism is both a reaction against supernaturalism (especially theism) and, in some versions, a rejection of mind-body dualism. In ethics, naturalism forswears irreducible concepts of value and obligation, or in more cautions versions, of irreducible moral and axiological *properties*. And in epistemology, naturalism is above all the attempt to account for knowledge and justification using notions amenable to scientific treatment, particularly commonsense observational concepts and concepts of physics and psychology. Epistemological naturalists tend to be more friendly than metaphysical naturalists toward countenancing a property dualism on which mental properties are distinct from physical ones. But neither kind of naturalism is committed to such property dualism. Indeed, nearly all naturalists consider some kind of materialism or, perhaps more broadly, physicalism, to comport with their ideals better than does property dualism.

Is there a unifying conception of naturalism in all these realms? One could be a naturalist in denying the existence of transcendent beings, but a nonnaturalist in the philosophy of mind, ethics, or epistemology. Indeed, holding a form of naturalism in any one of these domains may well leave one free to reject it in all the others. Perhaps philosophical naturalism in the main overall sense—a sense that might unify naturalism in these several domains—is roughly the view that nature is all there is, and the only basic truths are truths of nature. But how should *nature* be defined? Whatever nature is, it is not plausibly taken to encompass an omniscient, omnipotent, omnibenevolent God. But perhaps it can include (non-physical) mental phenomena, at least mental properties even if not minds conceived as nonembodied substances.

If not all philosophical naturalists are committed to physicalism about the mental, they typically do consider a physicalistic metaphysics to be an ideal we should try to achieve.[16] I will also take it that philosophical naturalism is not committed to empiricism, even if most of its proponents tend to be empiricists. Modern philosophical naturalists generally are committed, however, to what we might call the *epistemological sovereignty of science*: roughly the view that (1) scientific method, broadly understood to include the use of logic and mathematics, is the paradigm of a rational way to seek general knowledge; and (2) the sciences are the only authoritative source of general empirical knowledge, where empirical knowledge is understood to include any knowledge (or, loosely, justified true belief) concerning "the world," particularly the "external world" but on some views even the inner domain of consciousness. The associated metaphysical view would have as a major element a commitment to countenancing entities as real only if knowledge of them is possible in principle on the epistemological standard just formulated. Wilfrid Sellars may have had in mind both epistemological and metaphysical sovereignty when he said, "science is the measure of all things, of what is that it is and of what is not that it is not."[17] For many naturalists, this is an apt slogan.

It is ideas like this that easily create the impression that the teaching of science and, especially, of scientific method as a model of intellectual inquiry, imply a "religion of secular humanism" or at least some kind of secular religion. For, in monotheistic religions, it is God who is "the measure of all things." Even secular humanists, however, need not hold the strong version of philosophical naturalism suggested by Sellars (if any version at all). For they may certainly take normative questions, such as questions of what constitutes justice, to be nonscientific. Secularity in a theory does not imply its empiricality.

It should also be plain that one need not be a philosophical naturalist to be committed to scientific inquiry in answering questions that are within the purview of science. This commitment allows granting that there could be another route—say, through theology—to some of the same truths; but people with a scientific habit of mind will tend to want scientific evidence for important claims that are amenable to scientific appraisal even if they think there can be nonscientific access to their truth. It should be noted, however, that scientific inquiry has limitations even apart from the normative domain. I do not think that such inquiry extends to the question of why there is any universe at all. It is concerned with understanding patterns *in* the universe and, especially, with articulating laws and associated models that enable us to explain and predict events.

4. THE RELIGIOUS AND THE SECULAR

So far, I have argued that neither a commitment to scientific method nor the scientific habit of mind itself entails a commitment either to endorsing philosophical naturalism or to considering every theological statement intrinsically untestable by observations. This is certainly not to claim that, as usually pursued, creation science or even ID is indeed scientific, but I will use other grounds in arguing for conclusions about their position in the teaching of science. One concern is whether a commitment to them entails any religious commitments.

Defining *religion* is no easier than defining *science*. But again we do not need a definition, as opposed to important criteria. Here are nine criterial features, each relevant, though not strictly necessary, to a social institution's constituting a religion or (as applied to individuals) to an individual's having a religion: (1) appropriately internalized belief in one or more supernatural beings (gods); (2) observance of a distinction between sacred and profane objects; (3) ritual acts focused on those objects; (4) a moral code believed to be sanctioned by the god(s); (5) religious feelings (awe, mystery, etc.) that tend to be aroused by the sacred objects and during rituals; (6) prayer and other communicative forms concerning the god(s); (7) a world view according the individual a significant place in the universe; (8) a more or less comprehensive organization of life based on the worldview; and (9) a social organization bound together by (1)–(8).[18]

The richest paradigms of religion, such as Christianity, Judaism, Islam, and some of the theistic Asian religions, exhibit all of these features. In virtue of that, they are especially good cases to consider in relation to separation of church and state. Religions that take God to be omniscient, omnipotent, and omnibenevolent and so, in their different ways, claim a special authority in the lives of their adherents, are especially important for understanding church-state issues. It is these three divine attributes that I shall mainly have in mind in speaking of God here, and a proposition self-evidently entailing the existence of God so conceived is a paradigm of a (broadly) religious proposition. Less clear cases are propositions affirming (or self-evidently entailing) that a religion in the sense characterized is true, right, "the way" for humanity, or the like. The notion of a religious proposition is at least as vague as that of religion itself, but given such clarity as these notions have and in the light of what has been said here, the points made in this essay about the relation between the religious and the political and about education in science should be sustainable.

Should we countenance as a religion what has been called the "religion of secular humanism?" Clearly, it lacks many of the nine elements just listed. This is not to say that a religion must be theistic, but I will restrict my attention to theistic religions. Doing so will not prevent our seeing—in relation to some of the criteria just noted—why secular humanism is objectionable to many religious people. Much depends, to be sure, on what kind of view goes by that name. A crucial question is whether *secular* denotes the "nonreligious," in a sense implying a certain kind of independence of religion, or the "anti-religious," in the sense of "incompatible with religion," where *religion* is understood to embody theism.[19]

Philosophical naturalism is secular in the strong sense, not just the neutrality sense. Moreover, many who consider themselves humanistic and *non*-theistic are also philosophical naturalists. Since a strong association exists between naturalism and the scientific habit of mind, it is to be expected that unsophisticated science teachers and certainly unsophisticated conservatively religious parents of school-children will suspect many science teachers of being philosophical naturalists—or at any rate, atheists—and of injecting secularism in the strong sense into their teaching of certain subjects.[20] I have stressed that the scientific habit of mind does not require philosophical naturalism. This is not a point too subtle to be incorporated into science education. But how should it be incorporated into the teaching of science—and indeed, of certain other subjects—in the public schools of a free democracy?

5. SOME DIMENSIONS OF NEUTRALITY IN FREE DEMOCRACIES

Since my concern is with free democracies, I presuppose a significant degree of separation of church (meaning religious institutions) and state as part of a constitutional framework (even if there is no written constitution or only one that does not explicitly endorse this separation). Since preservation of religious liberty is a main concern of free democracies, the state should not interfere with churches. Here, I suggest three principles: first, a *liberty principle*, which says that (within limits) the state should permit the free exercise of religion; second, an *equality principle*, which says that the state should give no preference to one religion (or denomination) over another; and third, a *neutrality principle*, which says that the state should be neutral with respect to religion.[21] The liberty principle is crucial for the religious toleration essential in a free democracy, and the other two support that ideal in ways that will be suggested shortly.

All three principles are multidimensional and must be interpreted with great care, but it is the neutrality principle that especially needs comment now. Its most important function is to prevent governmental *favoritism* of the religious over the nonreligious (or vice-versa). Favoritism can occur even if, as the equality principle requires, no one religion is preferred over any other. Indeed, even if there is no discrimination (at least of a certain highly invidious kind) against the nonreligious, a measure of favoritism of the religious is possible. Suppose there is no established church. Those who have some religion could still receive preference in governmental appointments provided other things are equal. Thus, if a religious person is as well qualified for such an appointment as a nonreligious person, the former would be appointed. Then competition may be free and—some would argue—in a certain sense not unfair, since a nonreligious person would never fail to be appointed if *better* qualified than a religious competitor who was appointed. Still, the former would not have an *equal chance* of appointment, and this seems unfair relative to the nonreligious qualifications for the appointment that we are assuming. The point holds, if with less force, even if the favoritism other things equal ceases when a limited proportion of the appointments are filled by religious people (say the proportion they represent in the population).[22] (Similar issues arise for certain affirmative action policies, but I do not have space to pursue that issue separately.)

As to the liberty and equality principles, these (but apparently not the neutrality principle) are reflected in the First Amendment to the U.S. Constitution. The former is essentially stated therein; the latter is arguably the main underlying standard supporting the Establishment Clause.[23] I shall assume that the Founders were wise to prohibit an established church; and although this prohibition does not by itself entail endorsing state neutrality toward religion, it does indirectly support such a principle. (So does the liberty principle, in my view.)

Neutrality in Education Touching on Religion

Two points should be stressed immediately to prevent an overbroad interpretation of the neutrality principle. First, despite the close association between religion and ethics, and despite many people's thinking that ethical principles depend for their "validity" on religion (or at least on the existence of God), teaching ethics need not violate the neutrality principle. I have in mind teaching the kind of common-sense ethical principles that are expressed in the major ethical theories and, indeed, in the ethical (and nontheological) Ten Commandments, including the prohibitions of killing, stealing, and lying.[24] Second, neutrality toward the truth of religious doctrines does not imply that the state must view religion as unimportant. Not to teach *about religion* would be a drastic mistake, but one can teach about its content, development, and influence in, say, a history or literature class without endorsing or denying religious propositions. To be sure, doctrinal neutrality is compatible with attitudinal hostility. That stance toward religion is offensive to many citizens and inappropriate to teaching about religion in a free democracy.

Would the kind of moral education that goes with the points made here violate a sound liberal neutrality toward the good? In my view, moral education can observe at most a limited neutrality toward conceptions of the good: roughly, of human flourishing. The heading "conceptions of the good" includes the standards for what elements make life worth living and should underlie people's basic choices. Should a liberal democracy promote, for instance, such favorite candidates for major roles in the good life as friendship, knowledge, artistic expression, athletic activities, the beauty of the environment, and spirituality in general, even if not in religion? Rawls, among others, has argued that the liberal state should be neutral with respect to what he called "comprehensive" views of the good.[25] Although I do not believe he made at all precise what sort of conception this is, I will assume that a view of the good encompassing even the items just cited would count as comprehensive. Let us explore this position.

There is a wide range of views regarding the extent to which a liberal democracy may be committed to a large-scale conception of the good for human beings. One view is that no such conception is appropriate and that a religiously based conception of the good is simply a special case of one. A less restrictive view is that some presuppositions about the good may be commitments of a liberal democracy, but religious conceptions are not among them. It is true that there are theories, and general conceptions, of the good for human beings that are not an appropriate basis for the underlying structure of law in a liberal democracy. But the almost unrestricted exclusion of conceptions of the good favored by some neutralists is excessive.

Suppose for the sake of argument that we conceive morality as an institution directed essentially toward preventing or reducing evils.[26] This negative conception of morality is highly plausible as a partial guide in constitutional matters. We would still need an account of harms or of some still wider range of evils that can justify limitations on the freedom of citizens. For liberal democracy is clearly committed to supporting the maximal liberty citizens can exercise *without* producing certain harms (or a substantial likelihood of them).[27] Thus, even if a liberal state could be neutral toward the good, it could not be neutral toward the bad. It could not, then, be *value-neutral*.

There is, however, no sharp distinction, and perhaps no distinction in practice as opposed to principle, between a government's restricting liberty as a way to prevent harm and its doing so as a way of promoting some good. Consider our main subject, education. Compulsory education is essential to prevent the harms attendant upon ignorance. But education is surely one kind of good, and it is in practice impossible to provide it in a way that makes it effective in preventing harm yet is not inherently good. Even apart from that, can we reasonably design a required curriculum appropriate to a liberal democracy without making quite comprehensive presuppositions as to what counts as good human functioning, what skills are needed for good citizenship, and what is worth knowing for its own sake? Surely not. In determining the content and manner of compulsory education, there may be a huge range of values, including positive ones, toward which it is virtually impossible (and not necessary) for the state to be neutral. On this point there apparently is, and certainly can be, wide agreement among both many liberals who are methodological naturalists and endorse teaching evolutionary biology but not ID and, on the other side, those who think that ID, or even creationism, should also be taught.

Suppose, by contrast, that we do not assume that there are some kinds of things that are intrinsically good. Suppose further that we tie the goods suitable as a basis for structuring a liberal democracy to human nature—at least in the sense that we assume there are some things every rational person wants. Given how much our desires can be influenced by fashion, circumstance, and demagoguery, and given the growing specter of a technology that can alter our very genes, one wants moral and political theories that, in an overall way, at least, can provide standards for judging human desires independently of what they happen to be in a particular cultural and sociopolitical setting.[28] We must not leave social justice at the mercy of the contingencies of desire. Even if we can trust nature, we cannot in general trust its manipulators.

In resisting this line of thought, one might reply that although any plausible theory of the basis of liberal democracy affirms at least two values as essential constituents in such a society—namely, liberty and basic political equality—the state should be neutral on every other value and particularly toward overall conceptions of the good. This reply is at best of limited force. For just as we need some account of the good to decide what burdens to impose on the curricular freedom of students, we will need some account of the bad to determine limitations on the freedom of citizens in general. We need some kind of account or theory of the bad, especially of the kinds of harms or evils that warrant certain *restrictions* on liberty, as well as a theory of competence to vote in order to determine eligibility. Recall compulsory education, which surely is a requirement for assuring competence to vote, especially at the legislative level. The educational requirements for competent judges are higher still. One may certainly seek to design a political structure in which the state is as nearly neutral as possible about the good; but even if one affirms only the values of liberty and basic political equality as governing standards, there are drastic limits to how far this can go.

A limited liberal neutrality toward the good may, however, imply the soundness of the religious neutrality principle proposed above. This in turn implies that public schools should not teach creationism, which explicitly says that God created human beings, as a true position, since that would endorse a religious view. The equality principle would preclude doing this only on the contingent assumption that some religion denies God's creating the world, since otherwise one could teach it without favoring any one religion over any other. The neutrality principle does not, however, preclude noncommittally mentioning creationism; but doing this is neither necessary for good science teaching nor likely to be welcome to students and parents who wish the view to be presented as true.

If neutrality precludes teaching creationism, it also precludes *denying* such religious propositions as that God created the world. Doing this might also be proscribed by the liberty principle on the ground that it tends to reduce religious liberty, but certain kinds of denial need not have this tendency. In any case, to see the scope of a reasonable neutrality, we need a good understanding of what constitutes denial. The basic case of denial of a proposition—*direct denial*—is either asserting that it is false or affirming its negation. We should also recognize a notion of *indirect denial*; this might be equivalent to an assertion that is not a direct denial but does self-evidently and obviously entail one. Suppose a teacher said that if God created humanity, people would be less prone to evil than they are. Any normal adolescent could see this to imply that God did not create humanity. It would not be a religiously neutral assertion.

The issue becomes more complex, however, when the nonneutral implication is not obvious or self-evident, but is ascertainable by reflection on the part of a normal adult with the level of education reasonably sought for students in, say, the tenth grade or above. Imagine that a teacher considers a version of ID theory and composes a list of "evidences of divine action" in the genesis of humanity. The teacher indicates that the list includes all the significant kinds of evidence and then presents data in such a way as to yield a series of arguments, one concerning each kind of evidence, and each concluding that the relevant evidence is missing. At the end of this process—for instance, after half a dozen arguments are mounted—the teacher might say that we cannot rationally believe a view for which there is no relevant evidence. This might be fairly called an *implicit denial* of the religious proposition in question (in this case, the proposition that there has been divine action in the genesis of humanity). It might also be plausibly considered a failure of neutrality toward religion.

It will be no surprise that there are borderline cases. Suppose the teacher had concluded instead that there is no evidence of divine action in the genesis of humanity and that the probability of such action is very low. This is not neutral toward religion but is not a clear case of denying the religious view in question. If the teacher had simply said there is no evidence, we would not have denial, but would still have what would, in most contexts, be a breach of neutrality. Breach of neutrality, then, does not entail denial of a religious view. This makes neutrality more difficult to achieve. Two points must be added immediately.

First, just as breach of neutrality does not entail denial of a religious view, denying such a view—for one broad and common notion of a religious view—does not entail breach of neutrality toward religion. There are many statements in the Bible that are denied—if taken as literal descriptions of fact—by religious people whose mode of Biblical interpretation makes frequent appeal to symbolism, metaphor, and the ways of narrative. Some people may think that serious cosmic or ethical pronouncements by certain religious authorities are religious statements. It would be a mistake to define neutrality so broadly that denial of any of these statements entails breaching it. The same holds even for many theological statements; profoundly religious people, even within, say, Christianity, can disagree on theological matters. It turns out, then, that state neutrality toward religion in the sense in which it is a sound political ideal does not entail neutrality regarding every possible religion or every statement deemed religious. Given that almost any statement can be deemed religious by someone and that religious institutions can be built around indefinitely many sets of statements and practices, requiring such sweeping neutrality would be an unreasonable demand on both government in general and education in particular.

Second, neutrality is bi-directional, applying to affirmation as well as to denial of that to which it applies. Although the examples just given concern anti-religious breaches of neutrality, they may all be adapted to make similar points about pro-religious breaches. In neither case is it possible to characterize neutrality precisely. Practical wisdom is needed both in identifying it and in abiding by its demands.

The notion of neutrality is, however, clear enough to enable us to see that a commitment to scientific method does not entail violating neutrality. It does not even entail denying that God created the universe and humanity within it; hence, it does not oppose that minimal kind of creationism. If creationism is understood, as it usually is, in a way that renders it insusceptible of confirmation by scientific method as understood to incorporate methodological naturalism, then the neutrality principle does preclude teaching creationism as *science*. This is not to say that *nothing* a creationist holds may be considered a scientific hypothesis, but the hypothesis that God created human beings is surely not such a hypothesis.

6. TOWARD A RESOLUTION

In the light of what has been said about neutrality, how should science teachers in public schools be educated to observe a reasonable kind? Should they seek to distinguish (in their own words) the two kinds of naturalism we have discussed and explain the demarcation problem and why a sociopolitical rationale rather than a narrow conception of science must be brought to bear in designing pre-college education in science? Some science teachers could competently do this without saying or conveying anything objectionable to reasonable religious citizens. Would it, however, be needed for good science teaching? As formulated, these points might be an important element in teaching science and, indeed, some other subjects; but the points do not address intellectual and related learning concerns that students may have. What more might science teachers say?

I believe that those capable of teaching science competently at the level of evolutionary theory are also capable of saying something about the question of demarcation. They need not use that term or even try to distinguish science from other kinds of inquiry in any systematic way. They could, however, explain the empirical character of scientific inquiry and the roles of testability and publicity. They could also distinguish methodological naturalism from the metaphysical view that natural phenomena exhaust reality, and they could then note that a commitment, in doing science, to scientific method as including methodological naturalism is neutral with respect to theism and is not antitheistic. Doing this does not entail any substantive teaching about religion. Teaching about religion, however, as distinct from teaching theology or religion itself, is desirable in, for instance, the history curriculum, and the former kind of teaching too can be quite challenging.[29]

Beyond this, science teachers—especially below the college level—might note that evolutionary science does not require a physicalistic conception of the human person. Evolutionary science is compatible with dualism about mental and physical properties, and even with Cartesian dualism, on which human beings are a kind of unity of mental and bodily substances. That view, in turn, need not be combined with theism, though it easily leads to speculation about whether Cartesian minds are souls and have religious significance. Perhaps, then, these points in the philosophy of mind are, in most high schools, best left in readiness and not presented if they need not come up. But my sense is that part of the resistance by conservative theists to the teaching of evolutionary biology is the belief, or at least the sense, that it implies—or that endorsing it conveys the impression—that human beings are simply biological, hence in some sense physical, systems. This view is not incompatible with the possibility of resurrection, but it does imply the falsity of traditional dualistic conceptions of how resurrection may occur.

Third, high school science teachers can point to nonempirical disciplines and note that they are legitimate domains of inquiry with standards of genuine knowledge. I recommend that at least three in particular be noted: logic, pure mathematics, and ethics.[30] This can be done without mentioning theology, but there is no reason why that cannot be mentioned with an indication that it is not a subject for discussion in a science class. To be sure, most science teachers cannot be easily prepared to explain the possibility of theological knowledge or to consider whether any of it might be *a priori*. But that may apply almost as much to ethics, and in any case the main point to be conveyed is that knowledge need not be empirical or, even if it is empirical in the way some think ethical knowledge is, it need not depend on scientific inquiry.[31]

I have so far not considered ID, understood as the view that intelligent design best explains the empirical data concerning the history and biology of the human species. There is an ambiguity here that should be immediately exposed: the claim may be that (1) our history and biology exhibit a biological pattern that is of a *kind* that an intelligent designer might rationally choose; or that (2) it is of a kind that *has* been designed by an agent. Claim (2) does not entail that this agent is God, but proponents of ID surely have God in mind. Claim (1) may be more naturally interpreted philosophically than scientifically, but it is true that the needed description of our history and biology requires scientific inquiry. Claim (2) is not scientific if the agent referred to is taken to be supernatural. However, (2) can be argued to be, metaphysically, the best explanation of (1). A science teacher could point this argument out both without endorsement and with an indication that it is not an appropriate subject for discussion in a science class. Granted, pointing it out at all would be difficult to do without evincing a positive or negative attitude. For that reason among others (including facts about the students in attendance), some teachers should resist mentioning it.

A science teacher may also preface certain examination questions with such phrases as "According to the theory of evolution." This need not be presented as expressing suspended judgment, but it allows students for whom the theory (or the version introduced in the course) is religiously unacceptable to succeed on their exams without feeling that they are asserting religiously offensive falsehoods.

This cautionary suggestion does not imply that evolution is to be taught as "theory, not fact." That is a dangerous false contrast: a theory may be true, hence factual. The sound point here is that, where proof is understood rigorously, as in logic and mathematics, theories are confirmed or disconfirmed to some degree short of *proof*. In science teaching, as indeed in the humanities and social sciences, distinguishing proof from confirmation and from establishing high probability is a good thing to try to get across to students.

There is no reason that suitably trained science teachers cannot distinguish creationism from ID and explain how scientific method is apparently applicable to, at most, one of them. But for some teachers, such essentially philosophical discussion may be uncomfortable or impossible. Where, as is sometimes the case, it is inevitable, if only because students insist on bringing up methodological or ontological issues raised by evolutionary biology (and, if less often, by other branches of science), a useful corrective to one kind of misunderstanding is to point out to students that not all legitimate questions or disciplines are scientific. As I have suggested, logic is not; pure mathematics is not; and ethics is not. Scientific activity *depends* on the former two; and it should be *constrained* by the latter. Once students see that science is not the only source of knowledge and is not needed to legitimize every kind of question, they need not view the idea that theology is nonscientific as disparaging. In following the suggestions presented here, science teachers do not even need to say that there is no other conception of science.

The implication of all this is that education for teaching science should be enhanced. Philosophy is a desirable requirement here, especially philosophy of science or epistemology or, preferably, both. This proposal would impose some costs on teacher education. But in my view, it should be welcome, especially as things now seem in at least the United States, where pre-college education in science and, more broadly, in critical thinking, is generally (and I think plausibly) regarded as usually inadequate.[32]

7. Conclusion

I have suggested that there is apparently no plausible way to demarcate science from all of the nonscientific disciplines except by positing, in addition to testability and other traditional criteria, a commitment by scientists to a moderate methodological naturalism. Even this approach does not yield a sharp distinction. The more important point here, however, is that methodological naturalism is neutral with respect to theism and thus with respect to what is perhaps the core element in the kinds of religions that raise the most pressing problems for the teaching of science and, indeed, for the separation of church and state.

Even given the proposed methodological distinction between scientific and other kinds of inquiry, we cannot say that no *claims* important for creationism or, especially, intelligent design are scientifically appraisable. But the overall positions motivating most such claims would be readily seen by students as belonging to a theistic worldview; and, more important, their connection to such a view would typically appear sufficiently tight to create the impression that teaching these claims as true or plausible is an endorsement of theism. The theistic worldview and, similarly, propositions perceptibly presupposing it or self-evidently entailing it are not appropriate for discussion in public school science classes—at least as part of the science curriculum. This applies less at the college level than below it, and it does not generally hold for religiously affiliated schools. The constraint does not imply the overly restrictive view that science teachers in public schools should have no legal right to address these questions in a balanced way that does not imply violating religious neutrality. This kind of violation may occur positively, through teaching a religion or a religious doctrine, or negatively, through denying propositions that are theological or constitute religious doctrines. Such denial is not entailed, however, by denying the kind of scientifically appraisable proposition that, though testable within the constraints of methodological naturalism—as are claims of evolutionary science—is affirmed in some religious scripture or taken to be a religious truth by some people. Nonetheless, science teachers should not go out of their way to select for criticism empirical historical claims (or other empirical claims) important for religious people. It is one thing to have to deny the Genesis account of human origins; it is another to seek out scriptural or other religious claims for criticism when this is not required by teaching the scientific subject in question. Moreover, as desirable as critical discussion of religious positions may be, science classes in public schools are in general an inappropriate place for them.

The practical conclusions I have come to for pre-college science teaching, given my theory of the appropriate separation of church and state, call for a sensitivity by science teachers to what constitutes science, to the existence of nonscientific disciplines that are genuine fields of inquiry, and to the need to confine discussion to scientific issues in an atmosphere in which it is understood that doing so is neutral with respect to religion rather than hostile to it. The appropriate neutrality toward religion is entirely compatible with a sense of its historical importance and of its position in contemporary culture. It is also compatible with profound religious faith, on one side, or, on the other, deep dislike of religion. Good teaching calls on us to transcend commitments to either of these positions in teaching the young and impressionable. The right kind of transcendence does not entail hypocrisy; it can be an affirmation of values of mutual respect that are shareable by us all.

NOTES

....

Earlier versions of this paper or substantial parts of it were presented at the College of William and Mary's conference on the Future of Democracy in 2006, and, in 2007, at the annual meeting of the Society for Indian Philosophy of Religion, and at the Ian Ramsey Centre at the University of Oxford. For helpful responses I am grateful for comments from audiences on those occasions and, for detailed reactions, to Richard Cameron, Richard Liebendorfer, Harvey Siegel, Richard Swinburne, Roger Trigg, and, especially, Nicholas Wolterstorff, who provided a substantial commentary at the William and Mary Conference.

1. For recent discussion of the Supreme Court's decisions on the kind of neutrality in question, as well as for analysis of what constitutes such neutrality, see Kent Greenawalt, *Does God Belong in Public Schools?* (Princeton: Princeton University Press, 2005). For further discussion on neutrality and particularly on nonestablishment and on the related ethics appropriate to a liberal democracy, see Michael J. Perry, *Under God: Religious Faith and Liberal Democracy* (Cambridge: Cambridge University Press, 2003).

2. Karl Popper is the most widely known proponent of the falsifiability criterion. See esp. *The Logic of Scientific Discovery* (New York: Basic Books: 1959), originally published in German in 1934.

3. This has reference mainly to existential claims likely to be of scientific interest, such as that there is an as yet undiscovered planet. If we think of artificially simple cases, such as that there is a purple patch in my visual field, then my considering this introspectively and *not* finding one would in some good sense falsify the claim. But the solar system is not so easily scanned, and a planet could in principle escape discovery in a way a colored patch in consciousness apparently cannot.

4. This is not quite the same as the point that general ("scientific") propositions cannot be *proved*, in a sense implying a valid argument for them from premises that are at least beyond reasonable doubt. It is consistent with holding that they may be validly deduced from more comprehensive principles. For one thing, the relevant ones may not be beyond reasonable doubt; for another, this is not normally considered a kind of verification.

5. To be sure, the well-known work of W. V. Quine challenges the distinction made here and would instead simply provide distinctions among degrees of generality. Some such distinctions might serve my purposes here, but I have defended a stronger distinction in, e. g., chap. 4 of my *Epistemology* (London: Routledge, 2003).

6. The work of Saul Kripke and others has apparently shown this. See esp. his "Naming and Necessity," in *Semantics of Natural Language*, 2nd ed. (Synthese Library, Volume 40), ed. Donald Davidson and Gilbert Harman, pp. 253–355 (Dordrecht: D. Reidel, 1977). Cf. Aristotle's view that *scientia*, which includes knowledge of natural patterns, has the necessary as its object.

7. For discussion of the demarcation problem as bearing on (and generally supportive of) this essay, see Mike U. Smith, Harvey Siegel, and Joseph D. McInerney, "Foundational Issues in Evolution Education," *Science & Education* 4 (1995): 23–46; see esp. pp. 28–30. Some philosophers believe (as they may) that the demarcation problem is probably insoluble: "The prospects for this [drawing a line between science and non-science] are dim. Twentieth-century philosophy of science is littered with the smoldering remains of attempts to do just that." See Alexander George, "What's Wrong with Intelligent Design, and with Its Critics," *Christian Science Monitor*, December 22, 2005, p. 9. In his view, then, "either we should find alternatives to the courts to protect our curricula from bad science

[as opposed to nonscience] or we should start arguing in court that the separation of church and state would be violated by intelligent design's injection into the science curriculum on account of its predominantly religious motivation" (ibid.). Though slightly less pessimistic than George about the possibility of determining a reasonable demarcation, I agree (as will be evident in the text) that doing so is not the best way to proceed; but it will also be evident that I would put little weight on motivation.

8. In the postpositivist era, unfalsifiability was a common charge against theistic claims. See, e.g., Anthony Flew's challenge replied to in detail by John Hick in "Theology and Verification," *Theology Today* 17 (1960): 12–31.

9. It has been argued that theism—indeed, Christian theism—is testable eschatologically, i.e., by experiences one could have after bodily death in what would be reasonably considered a resurrection world. For the original statement of the case, see Hick, "Theology and Verification."

10. There are many versions of ID, and considering any of them in detail is beyond my scope here. But note the latitudinarianism of this general formula: "Intelligent Design is the hypothesis that in order to explain life it is necessary to suppose the action of an unevolved intelligence." See William A. Dembski and Michael Ruse, eds., *Debating Design: From Darwin to DNA* (Cambridge: Cambridge University Press, 2004), p. 3. This volume contains informative papers on both sides of the debate. For a more recent case that ID theory is committed to supernaturalism, see Elliott Sober, "Intelligent Design Theory and the Supernatural: The 'God or Extraterrestrials Reply,'" *Faith and Philosophy* 24, 1 (2007): 72–82. Further criticism of creationist and ID positions is provided by Philip Kitcher, *Abusing Science: The Case Against Creationism* (Cambridge, MA: MIT Press, 1982).

11. This requirement needs discussion. A scientist could, for instance, argue in a theological paper that the scientific findings imply divine action or even that proper confirmation of them presupposes that God guarantees the reliability of our sense-perception. But these points, even if true, are not part of the scientific account and would not prevent an atheist from understanding and confirming the scientific theory developed within methodological naturalist constraints.

12. The suggestion that there might be theistic as well as naturalistic explanations of the same events is not uncontroversial. Jaegwon Kim, e.g., has proposed the idea (which many scientifically minded thinkers find plausible) of the "causal closure" of the physical domain (entailing that every physical event has a causally sufficient condition), and he has argued that overdetermination (the presence of two independent causally sufficient conditions) cannot be posited between the mental [which would include divine fiats] and the physical. See, e.g., his *Mind in a Physical World* (Cambridge, MA: MIT, 1999). It should be added that even naturalistic explainability of all events in physical terms need not be understood so as to imply *determinism*; the explanatory laws in question need not be considered deterministic rather than statistical.

13. Cf. Daniel C. Dennett: "The postulation of invisible, undetectable effects that (unlike atoms and germs) are *systematically* immune to confirmation or disconfirmation is so common that such effects are sometimes taken as definitive. No religion lacks them, and anything that lacks them is not really a religion, however much it is like a religion in other regards." See his *Breaking the Spell: Religion as a Natural Phenomenon* (New York: Viking, 2006), p. 164. We have already seen reason to doubt these strong claims, and on the plausible eight-point characterization of religion given below, nothing in the concept of a religion implies them.

14. Some confirmation of the points here is found in a recent *New York Times* special section on evolution. The writer Cornelia Dean says, apparently without dissent,

"The idea that human minds are the product of evolution is 'unassailable fact,' the journal Nature said . . . A headline on the editorial drove the point home: 'With all deference to the sensibilities of religious people, the idea that man was created in the image of God can surely be put aside,'" June 26, 2007, p. F5. This passage exhibits poor reasoning: whether human persons are created in the image of God (in some metaphorical sense, presumably) is independent of how they are created biologically; God, understood as omnipotent, could produce such a result through evolution or in some other way.

15. Hick, "Theology and Verification," argues for the possibility of a resurrection body that sustains both personhood and individuality. I have critically assessed his case in my "Eschatological Verification and Personal Identity," *International Journal for Philosophy of Religion* 7, 4 (1976): 393–408.

16. Cf. Alan Donagan: "Naturalism can take as many forms as there are conceptions of nature . . . it has come to be accepted that, if there is nothing but nature, then there is nothing but matter in space-time. Naturalism has become materialism." See his "Can Anybody in a Post-Christian Culture Really Believe in the Nicene Creed?" in *Reflections on Philosophy and Religion*, ed. Anthony N. Perovitch, Jr. (Oxford: Oxford University Press, 1999), p. 24.

17. Wilfrid Sellars, "Empiricism and the Philosophy of Mind," in his *Science, Perception and Reality* (London: Routledge and Kegan Paul, 1963), p. 173 (originally published in *Minnesota Studies in the Philosophy of Science* 1 [1956]). In this paragraph and the previous ones on naturalism, I draw on my "Philosophical Naturalism at the Turn of the Century," *Journal of Philosophical Research* 25 (2000): 27–45.

18. These features are stressed by William P. Alston, in *Philosophy of Language* (Englewood Cliffs, NJ: Prentice-Hall, 1964), p. 88 (I have abbreviated and slightly revised his list). This characterization does not entail that a religion must be theistic, but theistic religions are my main concern (even in nontheistic religions, the relevant moral code tends to be given a somewhat similar privileged status in relation to appropriate items on this list, such as the worldview, the sacred and profane, and certain rituals, such as marriage). It is noteworthy that in *United States* v *Seeger*, 380 US 163 (1965), the Supreme Court ruled that religious belief need not be theistic; but for reasons that will become increasingly apparent below, theistic religions raise the most important church-state issues, at least for societies like those in the Western world. For discussion of the significance of *Seeger* in relation to church-state aspects of the foundations of liberalism, see Abner S. Greene, "Uncommon Ground," a review essay on John Rawls's *Political Liberalism* and on Ronald Dworkin's *Life's Dominion*, in *George Washington Law Review* 62, 4 (1994): 646–73.

19. An intermediate case would be secularism that does not deny the truth of theism but does deny that it provides knowledge of or justification for believing moral truths (or truth of other kinds). There are too many varieties to be sorted out here, but the two in the text are the most common.

20. For an indication of why "secular humanism" is objectionable to many theists, see Greenawalt, "Does God Belong," esp. pp. 81–84. Extensive related discussion of how liberal democracy should regard religious citizens and theocratic communities is provided by Lucas Swaine, in *The Liberal Conscience: Politics and Principle in a World of Religious Pluralism* (New York: Columbia University Press, 2006).

21. These three principles are explicated and defended in my *Religious Commitment and Secular Reason* (Cambridge: Cambridge University Press, 2000), esp. chap. 2, which discusses all three principles in the context of the theory of the basis of free democracy.

22. This point is supported in my *Religious Commitment*, esp. chap. 2.

23. We cannot plausibly hold that preference for one denomination entails establishment of it; but it tends in that direction and would be objectionable on similar grounds, such as encouraging discrimination against religions or denominations not favored by the government.

24. The commonsense ethical framework I refer to is set out and defended in my *The Good in the Right: A Theory of Intuition and Intrinsic Value* (Princeton: Princeton University Press, 2004), in which I also argue for basic moral principles having an *a priori* status of a kind appropriate to their being elements in the divine mind, rather than established by divine will.

25. See, e.g., Rawls, *Political Liberalism*, lectures IV and V.

26. For a plausible defense of this negative conception of morality, see Bernard Gert, *Morality* (New York: Oxford University Press, 1998); and for some critical discussion of the view (including a case that his theory is not as negative as he makes it sound), see my "Rationality and Reasons in the Moral Philosophy of Bernard Gert," in *Rationality, Rules, and Ideals: Critical Essays on Bernard Gert's Moral Theory*, eds. Walter Sinnott-Armstrong and Robert Audi (Lanham, MD: Rowman and Littlefield, 2002), pp. 73–88.

27. John Stuart Mill's famous harm principle in *On Liberty* is a prominent example of the kind of view in question.

28. I am, of course, implicitly rejecting an instrumentalist conception of rational action and of practical reason in general. Detailed arguments to this effect are given in my "Prospects for a Naturalization of Practical Reason: Humean Instrumentalism and the Normative Authority of Desire," *International Journal of Philosophical Studies* 10, 3 (2002): 235–63.

29. In many parts of Greenawalt, "Does God Belong," there are points and examples that indicate the difficulty of even teaching about religion in a neutral way.

30. The idea that these disciplines are nonempirical is not uncontroversial. It should not be rejected, however, on the ground that our justification for, say, a logical claim can be defeated by empirical considerations, such as conflicting testimony by respected peers to the effect that we are mistaken. Indefeasibility is not implied by nonempiricality. There is, however, wide agreement among moral philosophers that one cannot take ethical principles to be empirical simply on the basis of discovering an empirical account of the origin of our capacity or even inclination to hold them. Consider the claim that "as evolutionary biologists and neuroscientists peer ever deeper into the brain . . . they are discovering physical bases for the feelings from which moral sense emerges . . . For many scientists, the evidence that moral reasoning is a result of physical traits that evolve along with everything else is just more evidence against the existence of a soul" (see Dean, note 14 above, p. F8). Suppose these genetic claims are true. Nothing follows about what distinguishes valid from invalid moral reasoning or about what moral principles are true. Nor does anything follow concerning whether there is a soul conceived as non-physical.

31. Another case is the aesthetic. At least certain statements about literary works are either not empirical at all or are empirical in a way that does not make knowledge of them depend on scientific inquiry.

32. This conclusion is supported by Harvey Siegel's "The Rationality of Science, Critical Thinking, and Science Education," *Synthese* 80 (1989): 9–41. This paper bears directly on science education regarding matters in which, as for this essay, the relation between science and religion or science and values is in question.

....

CHAPTER 20

CONSTRUCTIVISMS, SCIENTIFIC METHODS, AND REFLECTIVE JUDGMENT IN SCIENCE EDUCATION

....

RICHARD E. GRANDY

THIS chapter consists of three parts. The first distinguishes among several kinds of views labeled "constructivist" and argues for the relevance to science education of cognitive and epistemic constructivism, and the irrelevance of ontological constructivism.[1] The second discusses historical conceptions of scientific method and argues that it is important to develop a much more complex account.[2] There are strong parallels between the two parts, the first drawing mainly on philosophy and cognitive psychology, the second on various forms of science studies. Both argue that proper understandings of what is involved in knowledge of science and in what "the scientific method" is mutually inform one another and portray a much more complex cognitive and social landscape than is usually recognized. Both argue for including more activities such as reading, writing, discussion, and debate of scientific issues in science education. In the final part, I first outline what I see as a close

connection between the expanded scientific method and research on the development of reflective judgment. I then raise and discuss serious concerns about whether
implementing the suggestions for science education are feasible, given apparent
constraints on cognitive development seen in the literature on reflective judgment.

1. Constructivisms: Cognitive, Metaphysical, and Epistemic

Since constructivisms are a dominant topic these decades in education (Cobb
1994b; Davis, Maher, and Noddings 1990; Driver, Asoko, Leach, and Scott 1994;
Fosnot 1993; Giannetto 1992; Glasson and Lalik 1992; Matthews and Davson-Galle
1992; Matthews 1998; O'Loughlin 1992, 1993; von Glasersfeld 1992), and since they
are also very controversial, it will be helpful to delineate some of the many
approaches that go under the title "constructivism." I believe this is a useful project
since it seems to me that there is not sufficient clarity about the variations on
constructivism, let alone their relations and implications. I also believe that an
understanding of the various elements and kinds of constructivism will be helpful
in evaluating what is required of teachers in implementing any curriculum that
incorporates some of the insights and important elements of constructivism.

. There is a wide range of terms, and I am sure I will offend some authors by
using the following distinctions rather than theirs. Here, I distinguish cognitive
constructivism, metaphysical constructivism, and epistemic constructivism.

Cognitive constructivism is the view that individual cognitive agents understand the world and make their way around in it by using mental representations
that they have constructed. What they could, in principle, construct at a given time
depends on the conceptual, linguistic, and other notational resources—for example, mathematics and graphing—at their disposal and on their current representations of the world that they have constructed through their personal history. What
they actually construct depends also on their motivations and on the resources of
time and energy available to devote to this particular task, as well as the social
settings in which they find themselves.

By *metaphysical* constructivism I mean the (collection of) view(s) that the
furniture of the world is constructed by us. This view can be subdivided into the
individualistic, which postulates individual constructions of individual worlds, and
the social, which postulates social constructions of shared worlds. This view
typically contrasts with metaphysical realism, the view that (much of) the furniture
of the world exists independently of minds and thoughts. There are some obvious
issues for the social sciences that I will not explore here, since social institutions are
clearly human creations; the implications for geography or psychology or human
biology are unclear and will also not be explored here.

Metaphysical realism itself comes in a range of positions on the optimism/ pessimism scale with regard to the knowability of the structure. Optimistic metaphysical realism holds that not only does the universe have an intrinsic structure, that God used a blueprint if you like, but that the structure is knowable, in principle, by humans—we could understand the blueprint. Less optimistic, though still guardedly hopeful, versions would be that we can develop representations that are approximately correct descriptions of some aspects of the universe. How either of these positions is justified philosophically is a matter we will not linger over here, for my main point is that these issues are irrelevant for science education once we understand fully the implications of cognitive constructivism.

A metaphysical realist who accepts cognitive constructivism must recognize that whatever knowledge is attained or even attainable about the ultimate structure of the universe must be represented in the constructions of the cognizer. While accepting cognitive constructivism has very important consequences for the teacher, which I will elaborate on shortly, once you have embraced cognitive constructivism, it makes very little difference what attitude you have toward the metaphysical realist issues. However independent of us the structure of the universe may be, what we can achieve by way of producing more knowledgeable students depends on the representations they can construct. This seems to me of great importance because, if constructivism is presented as a package that includes both cognitive constructivism and metaphysical antirealism, then teachers who have longstanding philosophical inclinations toward realism will find the package unpalatable. Cognitive constructivism is a relatively empirical theory that has strong evidential support from psychology, artificial intelligence, and education; metaphysical realism is a venerable philosophical doctrine supported by philosophical arguments, and it is subject to equally venerable philosophical objections.

Accepting cognitive constructivism has very significant consequences for understanding the tasks, and the demands of the tasks, required of the science teacher (Bloom 1992). All science teachers have, and must necessarily always have had, a philosophy of science—a set of beliefs about the nature of scientific inquiry, of scientific progress, of scientific reasoning, of scientific data, theories, and so on. Often this has been at least somewhat unconscious and implicit, often acquired unreflectively along with the content knowledge in science classes. And often, in the past at least, this philosophy of science incorporated beliefs in the continuous linear progress of science, in the empiricist inductive scientific method, in the immutability of scientific facts, in scientific realism, perhaps even metaphysical realism, and so on. It has often included the philosophy of science education that is described as direct teaching (Duschl 1990) or, as I think of it, the modified Dragnet theory of teaching. Unlike the old *Dragnet* television show, we don't just give them the facts, but on that model we do just give them the facts, definitions, and theories, and nothing but the facts, definitions, and theories.

Whatever the remainder of one's philosophy of science, accepting cognitive constructivism means recognizing that each student constructs a representation based on his experience, including but by no means limited to his teacher's verbal input. The teacher must assess the extent to which the student's representation is isomorphic to the teacher's, but of course cognitive constructivism applies reflexively and teachers have no direct infallible access to students' representations but instead construct their own representations of students' representations. Since a typical student motivation, for better or worse, is to please the teacher, it may also be valuable for the teacher to construct a representation of the student's representation of the teacher's representation.

There are important developmental questions about both students and teachers that I will turn to in the final part, but first I want to make some more general philosophical points about the process. Teachers are necessarily pursuing this process under time constraints and must repeatedly balance the potential value of further exploring the student's representation in all of its detailed uniqueness against categorizing the student's representation as sufficiently similar to others seen in the past to allow a particular course of further instruction to be developed without further investigation.

Of course, that is only part of the task, for the teacher may well need to understand also why the student has constructed that particular representation. The divergence from the desired kind of representation may result from lack of the tools to construct an alternative, lack of accepted evidence that the current representation is insufficient, or lack of motivation to construct an alternative (Ames 1990). The next step to bringing about desired change will likely depend on which of these factors is prevalent, and this implies that the teacher must have an understanding of motivational psychology, of the evidence the student accepts, of what the student counts as evidence, and of what conceptual tools the student can make use of. If this is correct, the conceptual change movement (cf. Chinn and Samarapungavan 2008; Krajick 2008) was in the right direction, but the process of instigating conceptual change in the student is more complicated than was probably initially recognized.

2. Objectivity and Change

Some science educators are unwilling to pronounce any student representation a "misconception." The reasons for this reluctance are important to analyze and understand. There is a very important positive aspect to this taboo, which stems from the insight that students produce the best representations that they are capable of producing at the time, given their information and conceptual and motivational constraints. The student is not to be *faulted*. But if we are unwilling to evaluate representations, unwilling to judge some representations and understandings as more accurate, more general, more consistent than others, then there is no reason to teach "science." Why spend our time on such a frustrating activity if we do not think that the student is, in principle, capable of a representation that is in some important sense an improvement? If the representations of the teachers or of the scientific community are not in some judgmental way better than those of neophyte students, then there is nothing to teach and time would be better spent on teaching spelling.

Having said that, and emphasizing the difference between judging the representation and judging the student, we should note that the fact that the teacher sees room for improvement does not mean that the best way to proceed is by directly criticizing the student's representation. One important aspect of the cognitive constructivist view is that the student's repertoire typically includes more than one way of representing a situation. Just as we can draw various maps representing various aspects of the world—highways, rainfall, elevation, population—the cognitive agent represents any situation in sundry ways. We recognize now that it is not just a matter of enabling the student to construct a Newtonian representation of a situation, but that there is the further project of ensuring that the Newtonian representation, rather than the intuitive physics representation, is applied. There is nothing wrong with having multiple theories or representations; the best known examples are the use of Newtonian physics for large slow objects, and relativity or quantum mechanics for the very fast or very small. This use of multiple representations is probably ubiquitous in the sciences— Cartwright (1983) cites a number of such cases, including six competing mathematical treatments of quantum damping (p. 78*ff*) as part of her argument for the ontological priority of causes over laws. But there is an important and somewhat elusive element of expertise in knowing what representation to deploy. And, most important, there is abundant evidence that students continue to deploy intuitive versions of Aristotelian physics after training at the college level in Newtonian mechanics (Bruer 1993, pp. 130*ff*).

It will be helpful to distinguish, using Megill's terms, absolute from disciplinary objectivity. Absolute objectivity was the goal of some of the mathematical explorations of inductive logic during the heyday of logical positivism, and it has long been a philosophical Holy Grail. Like metaphysical realism, it is irrelevant, in my view, to the process of science pedagogy, since absolute objectivity is at best an ideal and in the classroom we are but beginning the process of developing a sense of objectivity. Absolute objectivity requires criteria of validity that are invariant over time or culture or discipline. In contrast, it seems to me that a very worthwhile, and by no means easy, goal is to develop and nurture disciplinary objectivity.

> Disciplinary objectivity emphasizes not universal criteria of validity but particular, yet still authoritative, disciplinary criteria. It emphasizes not the eventual convergence of all inquirers of good will but the proximate convergence of accredited inquirers within a given field.   (Megill 1991, p. 305)

Megill qualifies his adjective *disciplinary* with a footnote saying that many of the criteria tend to be even more specific than disciplinary—that is, originating from subdisciplines. This is important for the culture of the classroom, since the discipline that we can hope students will construct is not professional biology or geology, but an age-appropriate variant of that, which is also limited by the constraints on time, equipment, and other resources. The goal is to create in the classroom a subculture that is in some appropriate ways related to the discipline under study.

3. EPISTEMIC CONSTRUCTIVISM: INDIVIDUAL OR SOCIAL?

In my presentation of constructivisms and their relations in the first section, I ignored *epistemic* constructivism—the view that knowledge is constructed by us rather than directly imbibed from the environment. This seems to me a reasonable consequence of cognitive constructivism, though a thorough defense would require a detailed discussion of the various possible analyses of knowledge. Rather than engage in that enterprise, I would like to flag an important aspect of the use of the term "construction" that has, I think, been insufficiently remarked on. The use of the term "constructivism" is arguably a metaphor extending to the abstract a notion that makes good physical sense: we construct dams, buildings, airplanes.

What I want to note is that, in the case of physical construction, there are always important constraints on the construction process if we are constructing for some useful purpose and not simply to expend time and energy. Some methods of construction are more efficient than others, some are faster, some are slower and more expensive but produce a more enduring product. Many shoddy methods of construction produce nothing of value. Surprising little discussion has been expended on the issue of the methods and materials of construction that go into constructing representations of scientific objects, data, and theories.

Accepting that knowledge is constructed, a natural metaphysical question that arises at this point is whether one sees the scientific group or the individual as the basic unit of analysis and explanation of knowledge. Two fairly representative but divergent positions are the following, which are, or were, held by two distinguished philosophers of science who were once colleagues at the University of Minnesota:

> What I propose . . . is a much more thorough going contextualism than the one which urges us to remember that scientific inquiry occurs in a social context, or even that scientists are social actors whose interests drive their scientific work. What I urge is a contextualism which understands the cognitive processes of scientific inquiry not as opposed to the social, but as themselves social. This means that normativity, if it is possible at all, must be imposed on social processes and interactions, that is, that the rules or norms of justification that distinguish knowledge (or justified hypothesis-acceptance) from opinion must operate at the level of social as opposed to individual cognitive processes.   (Longino 1992, p. 21)

In contrast:

> The conclusion is simple. The most promising approach to a general theory of science is one that takes individual scientists as the basic units of analysis. It

follows that we must look to the cognitive sciences for our most basic models, for it is these sciences that currently produce the best causal models of the cognitive activities of individual human agents.   (Giere 1989, p. 8)[3]

The view I am advocating accepts neither model, but sees the continuing dynamic interaction between group and individuals as critical (cf. Cobb 1994a, 1994b; Driver et al. 1994 for related arguments). "Although learning science involves social interactions . . . we have argued that individuals have to make personal sense of newly introduced ways of viewing the world" (Driver et al. 1994, p. 11). Objective knowledge is the result of an interactive process between individuals and community. It is essential to see that, although a group is in an obvious sense constituted at a given time by a set of individuals, as a group changes over time members are attracted to the group or become part of it because of the properties of the group as a whole. The group, and the perception of the group, shapes the cognitive behavior of those who join it. Moreover, epistemic evaluation seems appropriate for both individual and group processes, although the units and the measure of evaluation differ.

4. Individual, Society, and History

For either individual or social construction of science more is needed than theories, data, and instruments. What are missing are the epistemic connections that relate theories to supporting data, conflicting theories, anomalous data, and equivocal data. The concept of a data domain as developed by Ackermann (1985), and of the importance of anomalous data (Chinn and Brewer 1993) within that domain, needs to be emphasized. While the individual has some freedom to argue against the grain of the scientific community, to a large extent what can be taken as data and what is disqualified, what is strong evidence and what is weak evidence, is always judged against the background provided by the community's experience with the theories, data domain, and instruments in question. The data domain may be very refined, as in the case of professional-level well-established sciences, or much more in flux, as it will be in the classroom scientific community; but the demarcation between what counts and what does not, however fluctuating it may be over time, is critical to the ongoing enterprise. And initiation into the process of constructing data, evaluating data, citing data, and contesting data are all part of the individual's skills in the social setting.

The role of history of science in science teaching has received much attention (e. g., Aikenhead 1992; Gil-Perez and Carrasosa-Alis 1992; Niedderer 1992; and Matthews 1998 and further references there), and I cannot resist adding a few sentences on how the conception above relates to the use of history. The history of the development of a particular scientific theory or conception—e.g., the Copernican system, plate tectonics, or Darwinian evolution—is one or more routes by which reasonable inquirers arrived at a conclusion. The starting point for late-twentieth-century students is not the same as for the historical inquirers. The most obvious example is that most students 'know' that the earth goes around the sun when they come to science class, even though they are frequently unable to develop the appropriate conclusions from that knowledge. The reasons are complex, but they include in most cases the fact that they bring to bear a version of intuitive physics. This latter has many resemblances to the sophisticated neo-Aristotelian physics of the sixteenth century, but it would be a mistake to treat them as identical. And the motivations of sixteenth- and seventeenth-century intellectuals were different in many very important respects from those of our current students.

On my view, knowing the history of a scientific development provides the teacher with a set of arguments and experiments and an epistemic route from one cognitive locus to another. This is often an important part of the tool kit that can be used to assist learners in constructing their own representations more satisfactorily. But as I have outlined above, the history of science by itself is far from sufficient for the teacher confronted with a very complex set of tasks. I see the extent of the utility of history of science as being subject to possible empirical study. A second point is that independent of issues of bringing students' constructions to a different state by calling on the same arguments and experiments that were historically used, reflection on the history of science can itself provide important fodder for the epistemic learning mill. The concepts of data, anomalous data, questionable data, and so on can be illustrated in the history of science as well as in classroom productions. This is another step in forging the cultural links between the classroom inquiry and the larger scientific process.

5. Conclusions about Constructivism

I have argued that we can distinguish the claims of cognitive constructivism from those of metaphysical constructivism. Cognitive constructivism has strong empirical support and indicates some important directions for changing science instruction. It implies that teachers need to be cognizant of representational, motivational, and epistemic dimensions that can restrict or promote student learning. Metaphysical issues are irrelevant to the pedagogical enterprise except when explicit philosophical issues arise. The resulting set of tasks for a science teacher is considerably larger and more complex than that associated with the older more traditional conception, but the resources of cognitive sciences and the history of science can provide important parts of the teacher's intellectual tool kit. (An older but lengthier discussion of these topics is in Grandy 1998.)

A critical part of this conception of science education as informed by cognitive constructivism is that students must develop the skills to participate in the epistemic interchanges that take place in scientific communities. They must be provided opportunities and materials to develop those skills and the classroom community must have the appropriate features of an objective epistemic community. Thus far I have been focusing on development; in the next section I turn to some more general analyses of the scientific method.

6. Scientific Method

In matters of science education, the guiding conception for the scope and sequence of curriculum materials is that of the "scientific method." Grounded in narrow interpretations of positivistic views about scientific inquiry, the accepted scientific method is based on a view that doing science is primarily a matter of doing experiments.

Twentieth-century philosophy of science can be partitioned into three major developments: an experiment-driven enterprise, a theory-driven enterprise, and a model-driven enterprise. The *experiment-driven* enterprise gave birth to the movements called logical positivism or logical empiricism, shaped the development of analytic philosophy, and gave rise to the hypothetico-deductive conception of science. The image of scientific inquiry was that experiment led to new knowledge that accrued to established knowledge. How knowledge was discovered and refined was not on the philosophical agenda, only the final justification of knowledge was deemed important. This early-twentieth-century perspective is referred to as the "received view" of philosophy of science.

At an NSF sponsored conference on teaching scientific inquiry (hereafter TSI), at Rutgers in 2005,[4] an interdisciplinary group discussed at length what "scientific inquiry" includes, and it ended with the following list:

posing questions
refining questions
evaluating questions
designing experiments
refining experiments
interpreting experiments
making observations
collecting data
representing data
analyzing data
relating data to hypotheses/models/theories
formulating hypotheses
learning theories
learning models

refining theories
refining models
comparing alternative theories/models with data
providing explanations
giving arguments for/against models and theories
comparing alternative models
making predictions
recording data
organizing data
discussing data
discussing theories/models
explaining theories/models
writing about data
writing about theories/models
reading about data
reading about theories/models

If we contrast this list with the traditional Scientific Method, we have:

1. Make observations
2. Formulate a hypothesis
3. Deduce consequences from the hypothesis
4. Make observations to test the consequences
5. Accept or reject the hypothesis based on the observations

We can see that, although all of these involve cognitive tasks, only the last involves an epistemic task. By contrast, many of the activities on our first list include social or epistemic elements. In fact, many of the items on the list involve all three.

For example, writing about a theory is obviously a cognitive task, but it also requires social judgment since the writer is writing for an audience (Norris and Philips 2008). Writing for an audience requires that the writer have a nuanced and detailed conception of the belief and motivational structures of the reader. If the writer does not engage the motivational structure of the reader, the reader will read superficially, if at all. If the writer does not engage the reader's belief structure in a relevant way, the reader's beliefs will not change and the reader may not even pay attention to the arguments. The task is also epistemic because the presumptive point of the writing is to adduce evidence that will encourage belief in or doubt about the theory, so it is essential to the writing task that one makes epistemic judgments about the relations between evidence and theory.

Similarly, although one can formulate ideas in solitude, if one is part of a scientific or classroom community in which there is an ongoing discussion of a question against a background of shared theoretical assumptions, then what counts as a relevant conjecture, inference, or hypothesis is constrained by social and epistemic considerations.

At the professional level of science education, there is a tension between ensuring that everyone who is given the formal credentials of the discipline shares the fundamental values and concepts so that the coherence of the discipline is preserved, and ensuring that innovative thinkers who may question even fundamental values and concepts are not excluded so that the possibility of creative innovation is preserved. In other words, both the group, as a group, and the individuals who constitute it must have appropriate characteristics in order for there to be a significant cognitive activity worth calling "scientific knowledge."

One analysis of the role of the group is that of Longino (1994), who lists four conditions for a community to meet in order for a consensus to qualify as knowledge:

1. There must be publicly recognized forums for the criticism of evidence, of methods, and assumptions and reasoning.
2. There must be uptake of criticism. The community must not merely tolerate dissent; its beliefs and theories must change over time in response to the critical discourse taking place within it.
3. There must be publicly recognized standards by reference to which theories, hypotheses, and observational practices are evaluated and by appeal to which criticism is made relevant to the goals of the inquiring community. . . .
4. Finally, communities must be characterized by equality of intellectual authority. What consensus exists must be the result not of the exercise of political or economic power, or of the exclusion of dissenting perspectives, but a result of critical dialogue in which all relevant perspectives are represented. This criterion is meant to impose duties of inclusion; it does not require that each individual, no matter what her or his past record or state of training, should be granted equal authority. . . .   (Longino 1994, pp. 144–45)

These requirements were written with the professional community, not the classroom, in mind, but I think they are a reasonable set of guidelines for the classroom scientific community on a smaller scale. There are a number of crucial and vague terms, but while these can be fleshed out in somewhat more detail, the exact details will have to be developed and negotiated in each individual case. Although one can formulate ideas in solitude, if you are part of a scientific community in which there is an ongoing discussion of a question against a background of shared theoretical assumptions, then what counts as a relevant conjecture, inference, or hypothesis is constrained by social and epistemic considerations.

7. Expanding the Scientific Method

One way that Richard Duschl and I (Duschl and Grandy 2008) have framed the debate about the nature of scientific inquiry is in terms of seven tenets of logical positivism. It is important not to simply reject logical positivism, without under-standing it and building on the valuable elements. Otherwise we risk losing some of both the insights provided and the perspectives on some of the oversimplifications that are involved. Similarly, I do not reject the idea of scientific method, but want to radically supplement it. I also organize the seven tenets in table 20.1 to contrast the "received view" of the nature of science with the "revised view."

The organization of the table's rows and columns is meant to highlight the reactions, objections, and insights the seven tenets occasion. Consideration of both the insights and limitations of logical positivism and early "Kuhnian" responses to logical positivism have expanded our perspectives about the nature of science, the growth of scientific knowledge, and the goals/limitations of science. For each of the seven tenets I contrast the "traditional" and the "revised" views for the nature of science. Reading down the traditional "Received Views" column paints a picture of the commitments held by the logical positivists. Reading down the "Revised Views" column reveals commitments from those adhering to naturalized philosophical views that stress more descriptive and historically based approaches to understand-ing the scientific processes. The "Revised Views" items stress the dialectical process-es/practices of science and do so with respect to conceptual as well as methodological changes in scientific inquiry. The main points from the seven tenets table provide a basis for an expanded scientific method; they include:

- The bulk of scientific effort is not theory discovery or theory acceptance but theory improvement and refinement.
- Research groups or disciplinary communities are the units of practice for scientific discourse.
- Scientific inquiry involves a complex set of discourse processes.
- The discourse practices of science are organized within a disciplinary matrix of shared exemplars for decisions regarding the (a) values, (b) instruments, (c) methods, (d) models, and (e) evidence to adopt.
- Scientific inquiry has epistemic and social dimensions, as well as conceptual.
- Changes in scientific knowledge are not just in conceptual understandings alone; important advancements in science are also often the result of technological and methodological changes for conducting observations and measurements.
- What comes to count as an observation in science evolves with the introduction of new tools, technologies, and theories.
- Theories can be understood as clusters of models where the models stand between empirical/conceptual evidence and theoretical explanations.
- Theory and model choices serve as guiding conceptions for deciding "what counts" and are an important dynamic in scientific inquiry.
- Rubrics for a rational degree of confirmation are hopeless; dialogue over merits of alternative models and theories is essential for refining, accepting, or rejecting them and are not reducible to an algorithm.

Table 20.1 Nature of science: seven tenets

Traditional tenets from logical positivism	Received views	Reasons for revised tenets	Revised views
1. There is an important dichotomy between contexts of discovery and contexts of justification.	Logical positivism's focus was on the final products or outcomes of science. Of the two end points, justification of knowledge claims was the only relevant issue. How ideas, hypotheses, and intuitions are initially considered or discovered was not relevant.	Theory change advocates value understanding the growth of knowledge. Perhaps the most important element Kuhn and others added is the recognition that most of the theory change is not final theory acceptance, but improvement and refinement.	The bulk of scientific inquiry is neither the context of discovery nor the context of justification. The dominant context is theory development and conceptual modification. The dialogical processes of theory development and of dealing with anomalous data occupy a great deal of scientists' time and energy.
2. The individual scientist is the basic unit of analysis for understanding science.	Logical positivists believed scientific rationality can be entirely understood in terms of choices by individual scientists.	Kuhn's inclusion of the scientific community as part of the scientific process introduced the idea of research groups or communities of practice as being the unit of scientific discourse. This shift from individual to group produced negative reactions from many philosophers. Including a social dimension was seen as threatening the objectivity and rationality of scientific development. Teams of scientists engage in investigations.	Scientific rationality can be understood in terms of dialogic processes taking place as knowledge claims and beliefs are posited and justified. Scientific discourse is organized within a disciplinary matrix of shared exemplars; e.g., values, instruments, methods, models, evidence.

3. There is an epistemologically significant distinction between observational and theoretical (O/T) languages based on grammar.	Logical Positivism focused on the application of logic and on the philosophy of language to analyze scientific claims. Analysis void of contextual and contingent information produces a grammar that fixes criteria for observations.	The O/T distinction debate showed that our ordinary perceptual language is theory laden: what we see is influenced by what we believe. New theories leading to new tools and technologies greatly influenced the nature of observation in science and the representation of information and data.	What counts as observational shifts historically as science acquires new tools, technologies, and theories. Science from the 1700s to the present has made a transition from a sense perception dominated study of nature to a tool, technology, and theory-driven study of nature.
4. Some form of inductive logic would be found that would provide a formal criterion for theory evaluation.	There exists an algorithm for theory evaluation. Given a formal logical representation of the theory and data, the algorithm would provide the rational degree of confirmation the data confer on the theory.	Seeking an algorithm for a rational degree of confirmation is hopeless. Scientists working with the same data can rationally come to differing conclusions about which theory is best supported by given evidence. There is ongoing debate about how much variation is rational and how much is influenced by other factors.	Dialogue over the merits of competing data, models, and theories is essential to the process of refining models and theories as well as accepting or rejecting them.
5. Scientific theories can most usefully be thought of as sets of sentences in a formal language.	Logical positivists advocated the position that theories are linguistic in character and could be described with deductive-nomological procedures.	Model-based views about the nature of science embrace, where hypothetical-deductive science does not, the dialogic complexities inherent in accounts of science. Scientific representations and explanations take many different forms: mathematical models, physical models, diagrams, computation models, etc.	Modern developments in science, mathematics, cognitive sciences, and computer sciences have extended the forms of representation in science well beyond strictly linguistic and logical formats. One widespread view is that theories should be thought of as families of models, and the models stand between empirical/conceptual evidence and theoretical explanations.

(continued)

371

Table 20.1 (continued)

Traditional tenets from logical positivism	Received views	Reasons for revised tenets	Revised views
6. Different scientific frameworks within the same domain are commensurable.	Logical positivists sought to establish criteria that supported the claim that there are normative dimensions to scientific inquiry. The growth of scientific knowledge is a cumulative process.	Science communities are organized within disciplinary matrices. Shared exemplars help to define science communities. Scientific frameworks on different sides of a revolutionary change are incommensurable. Hypothesis testing takes place within more complex frameworks requiring more nuanced strategies for representing and reasoning with evidence.	Different scientific frameworks within the same domain share some common ground. But they can disagree significantly on methodology, models and/or relevant data. The issue is the extent to which knowledge, beliefs, reasoning, representations, methods, and goals from one research domain map to another research domain. The social and epistemic contexts are complex indeed.
7. Scientific development is cumulatively progressive.	Logical positivists held that the growth of scientific knowledge is cumulative and continually progressive. Scientists work with common theory choices.	Theory choice is an important dynamic of doing science and it influences how investigations are designed and conducted. On what grounds (e.g., rational vs. irrational) scientists make such choices is a matter for further research and debate.	The Kuhnian view that "revolutions" involve the abandonment of established guiding conceptions and methods challenges the belief that scientific development is always cumulatively progressive. New guiding conceptions inform what counts as an observation or a theory. Such changes reinforce beliefs that all scientific claims are revisable in principle. Thus, we embrace the notions of the "tentativeness" of knowledge claims and the "responsiveness" of scientific practices.

The expanded scientific method, then, would be inclusive, not exclusive, of the three sequential twentieth-century images of the nature of science: Hypothetico-deductive experiment driven science; Conceptual Change theory driven science; Model-based driven science. The expanded scientific method recognizes the role of experiment and hypothesis testing in scientific inquiry, but emphasizes that the results of experiments are used to advance models and build theories. Thus, the expanded scientific method makes a further recognition that the practices of scientific inquiry involve important dialogic and dialectical practices that function across conceptual, epistemic, and social dimensions.

8. Demarcating Science?

Any characterization of scientific method—enhanced, expanded, or otherwise—raises the question of whether science as a way of knowing is distinct from other ways of knowing that also involve conceptual, epistemic, and social discourses. Philosophers of science refer to this issue as the demarcation between science and other forms of inquiry, and making a clear demarcation was a primary goal of the logical positivist movement. Note that there are two related but somewhat distinct demarcation questions. First, some individuals see a distinction between legitimate science and activities that purport to be scientific but are not—for example, astrology, creation science, and the like. Second, there are some who see a distinction between scientific inquiry and other forms of legitimate but nonscientific activities, such as historical research or electrical engineering. Some TSI conference participants felt strongly that it not only is possible to make a sharp general demarcation but also that it is an important part of teaching science to teach that demarcation. Other participants were skeptical that such a demarcation is possible.

Several participants at the conference suggested that scientific inquiry involves mechanistic explanations. This is clearly too narrow, as magnetism and gravitation are not mechanical. Another suggestion was that scientific explanations are causal. This suggestion has two problems; one is that it seems to rule out statistical explanations that are not necessarily causal. The second is that three centuries of debate over the nature of causation in philosophy have produced no consensus on what constitutes causation.

Another suggestion was that scientific explanations/hypotheses must be testable. While this seems right in spirit, decades of attempts by philosophers to make this concept precise have also consistently failed.

Another group of participants argued that the distinction between scientific and nonscientific hypotheses is real, but is not a matter for which we can formulate explicit rules. For them, the only individuals able to appropriately make the distinction between testable and nontestable hypotheses are those who are deeply embedded in the practices of the specific science and have sophisticated knowledge. Today there are domains of science that do not begin inquiry with stating hypotheses but, rather, are guided by patterns of discovery from huge data sets (e.g., human genome project).

I am not suggesting that it is impossible to distinguish scientific inquiry from pseudoscience. But I believe that to the extent that the distinction can be made, it has to be made locally, from the perspective of the particular field at a specific time. A naturalized approach to understanding science means that researchers observe what scientists do, not just what scientists say about what they do. The naturalized approach to the history of science strongly suggests that the nature of scientific activities has changed over time, and I expect change to continue. Knowledge of the relevant scientific principles and criteria for what counts as an observation are important elements in distinguishing scientific claims and developing demarcation capacities—for example, distinguishing science from pseudoscience. However, I am skeptical that a general demarcation criterion can be abstracted from the concrete historically situated judgments.

Moreover, history suggests that at times new hypotheses or theories may provoke disagreement about testability even among the most expert scientists. Mach and others rejected atomism as unscientific around the turn of the century (Brush 1968). The majority of earth scientists rejected continental drift as unscientific during the 1920s and later (van Waterschoot van der Gracht 1928; LeGrand 1988). On the present scene, many physicists regard string theory as the most important breakthrough since quantum mechanics. Others disagree—one recent book title states that string theory is "not even wrong" because it makes no testable predictions (Woit 2006; Smolin 2006). The expanded conception of scientific method derives from reflection on progress in various areas of science studies. But if we are to draw implications for education, we need to consider the abilities and limitations of learners at various stages.

9. EXPANDED SCIENTIFIC METHOD AND COGNITIVE DEVELOPMENT: PARALLELS

There is a strong correlation between the elements of the expanded scientific method discussed above and the stages of development of reflective judgment as delineated by King and Kitchener (1994). The first three stages, which they label "pre-reflective," are:

1. Concrete single category belief system. Knowledge is a copy of reality.
2. There is a concrete reality which is knowable, though at least some parts are only known (knowable) by experts.

3. A belief that in some areas even authorities may not currently have the truth, but a belief that knowledge will be manifest in concrete data at some future time.   (King and Kitchener 1994, pp. 47–57)

There then follow two stages that they label "quasi-reflective":

4. One cannot know with certainty.
5. Knowledge claims are never absolutely certain or unqualifiedly true, people may "know" relativized to their perspective, interpretation, etc.   (1994, pp. 58–66).

The label "reflective thinking" is applied to two final stages:

6. Knowing is a process which requires action on the part of the knower. Many issues are not resolvable but some beliefs or justifications are better than others, at least in some domains.
7. "While reality is never a 'given,' interpretations of evidence and opinion can be synthesized into epistemically justifiable conjectures . . . . Knowledge is constructed using social skills of critical inquiry or by synthesizing evidence and opinion into cohesive and coherent explanations for beliefs about problems. It is possible, therefore, through critical inquiry or synthesis, to determine that some judgments . . . have greater truth value than others or to suggest that a given judgment is a reasonable solution for a problem." (1994, p. 70, cf. 66–74)

10. Expanded Scientific Method and Cognitive Development: Problems

Traditional scientific method appears to be primarily at level 3, while the expanded method I have been discussing involves level 7. There are clear parallels between our expanded method and King and Kitchener's reflective judgment, but theirs is a developmental scale that conflicts with most philosophers' conception of the development of reflective judgment and the use of the expanded method. Most philosophers think of the educational issue as a problem of moving the learner away from the absolutist copy theory of knowledge to the much more nuanced and complex reflective judgment theory of knowledge without overshooting and having the learner adopt relativism. Thus, the philosophical picture of the three positions is:

Absolutism → Reflective judgment → Relativism

whereas King and Kitchener's scale indicates that cognitive development requires a path *through* relativism:

Absolutism → Relativism → Reflective judgment

This raises the possibility that, for some individual learners, the path through relativism to reflective judgment may not be completed, and it is unclear whether, at least for purposes of science education, it is better for them to be stage 5 relativists or stage 3 believers in authority. And since the King and Kitchener scale is the product of numerous studies on various populations, it is important to look at their results to assess the likelihood of relativist outcomes, as well as to evaluate how much of the expanded scientific method can be taught at various educational levels. There is no point in redesigning curricula to incorporate elements of the expanded method if learners are incapable of mastering the concepts and abilities at that stage.

The King and Kitchener data across several studies (see their Table 6.5, pp. 154–55) suggest that high school juniors on average are slightly below level 3, and that most university students move on average into the high 3 or low 4 level range. Hofer and Pintrich (1997, p. 101) summarize some of the pooled data as showing that "mean scores of both first-year college students and college sophomores were 3.6, with a mean for juniors of 3.7 and seniors at 4.0, not quite half a stage higher than first year students" (1997, p. 101). The only groups that scored on average above level 5 were adults several years beyond college graduation, and the only groups that scored above level 6 in general were doctoral students. There is some reason to think that education rather than unguided development is relevant, in that evaluations of *adult* college students also show a mean of 3.6 the first year and 4.0 as seniors.

11. EXPANDED SCIENTIFIC METHOD AND COGNITIVE DEVELOPMENT: SOLUTIONS?

Above, I raised the concern about how much of the expanded scientific methods should be incorporated for various developmental levels. But there is also another important issue. One immediate implication is that we have to rethink whether prospective K-12 teachers can adequately master the required reflective judgment while they are undergraduates; it appears that most cannot. This indirect evidence is confirmed by research by Windschitl (2008). But before we become too pessimistic, it is important to note that while King and Kitchener describe these as "stages," they do not find them as rigid as the traditional Piagetian stages. They recognize that at any given time a learner may function at one level on one task and at a higher level on a different task, leading them to attribute to a learner a "reflective range" that includes both an upper bound and a prototypical level. These findings seem to be corroborated in a smaller but more longitudinal study (Magolda 2002).

And at least in its applications to science education, we must be aware that we probably are not working with optimal curricula and materials. Most science education is based on the traditional conception of scientific method, and it appears that it is possible that curricula that incorporate richer elements of the enhanced scientific method can be more successful. For example, Samaparungavan (1992, p. 24) found that "even 7 year olds could use metaconceptual criteria such as the range, empirical consistency, and logical consistency of theories when the theories did not violate their beliefs." Also, evaluations of individual stages of reflective development are open to debate (Elby and Hammer 2001).

12. CONCLUSION

In the first section, I argued that constructivist perspectives on cognition and knowledge are important for pedagogy, but that metaphysical constructivism is irrelevant. This insight emphasizes that it is of great value for learners to be actively involved in the learning process and that science education must pay close attention to where the learner begins the process. In the second section, I argued that work in various fields of science studies leads to a much broader conception of scientific method, less exclusively focused on experimentation and more inclusive of various skills such as reading about, writing, and discussing scientific ideas; evaluating data; comparing alternative models; and so on. In the third section, I noted the strong parallel between both the constructivist view of scientific beliefs and the expanded scientific method and the stages of development of reflective judgment as delineated by King and Kitchener. The slow trajectory to reflective judgment, typically not completed until the learners are in their mid-20s, if at all, raises serious research questions about how much of the expanded method can be effectively included in a curriculum. It also raises the serious concern about whether teachers can master the nuances of reflective judgment that are prerequisite to teaching it.

NOTES

1. Some of the funding for the research in this section was provided by a grant from the National Science Foundation (MDR-9055574) to the University of Pittsburgh and the Educational Testing Service. The opinions expressed do not necessarily reflect the positions or policies of NSF, and no official endorsement should be inferred.

2. Many of the ideas in this section were developed in collaboration with Richard Duschl, and also with the participants in an interdisciplinary conference in February 2005

on the nature of scientific inquiry supported by NSF grant ESI #0343196. The opinions expressed do not necessarily reflect the positions or policies of NSF, and no official endorsement should be inferred. See Duschl and Grandy 2008 for more information on the conference.

3. Giere subsequently changed his views significantly; see Giere 1999.

4. The proceedings of the conference appeared as Duschl and Grandy 2008.

REFERENCES

Ackermann, R. J. (1985). *Data, Instruments, and Theory: A Dialectical Approach to Understanding Science.* Princeton: Princeton University Press.

Aikenhead, Glen. (1992). "How to Teach the Epistemology and Sociology of Science in a Historical Context." In *Second International HPS&ST Proceedings*, vol. 1, ed. Skip Hills (pp. 23–34). Kingston, Canada: University of Kingston Press.

Ames, C. A. (1990). "Motivation: What Teachers Need to Know." *Teachers College Record* 91: 409–21

Bloom, Jeffrey. (1992). "Contextual Flexibility: Learning and Change from Cognitive, Sociocultural, and Physical Context Perspectives." In *Second International HPS&ST Proceedings*, vol. 1, ed. Skip Hills (pp. 125–34). Kingston, Canada: University of Kingston Press.

Bruer, John T. (1993). *Schools for Thought: A Science of Learning in the Classroom.* Cambridge, MA: MIT Press.

Brush, Steven. (1968). "Mach and Atomism." *Synthese* 18: 192–215.

Cartwright, Nancy. (1983). *How the Laws of Physics Lie.* Oxford: Clarendon Press.

Chinn, C., and W. Brewer. (1993). "The Role of Anomalous Data in Knowledge Acquisition: A Theoretical Framework and Implications for Science Instruction." *Review of Educational Research* 63: 1–50.

—— and A. Samarapungavan. (2008). "Learning to Use Scientific Models: Multiple Dimensions of Conceptual Change." In *Teaching Scientific Inquiry: Recommendations for Research and Implementation,* ed. Richard A. Duschl and Richard E. Grandy (pp. 191–225). Rotterdam: Sense Publishing.

Cobb, Paul. (1994a). "Constructivism in Mathematics and Science Education." *Educational Researcher* 23: 4.

—— (1994b). "Where Is the Mind? Constructivist and Sociocultural Perspectives on Mathematical Development." *Educational Researcher* 23: 13–23.

Davis, Robert B., Carolyn Maher, and Nel Noddings, eds. (1990). *Constructivist Views on the Teaching and Learning of Mathematics.* Reston, VA: National Council of Teachers of Mathematics.

Davson-Galle, Peter. (1992). "Primary Philosophy of Science." *Second International HPS&ST Proceedings*, vol. 1, ed. Skip Hills (pp. 239–44). Kingston, Canada: University of Kingston Press.

Driver, Rosalind, Hilary Asoko, John Leach, and Philip Scott. (1994). "Constructing Scientific Knowledge in the Classroom." *Educational Researcher* 23: 5–12.

Duschl, Richard A. (1990). *Restructuring Science Education: The Importance of Theories and Their Development.* New York: Columbia University Press.

—— and Richard E. Grandy, eds. (2008). *Teaching Scientific Inquiry: Recommendations for Research and Implementation*. Rotterdam: Sense Publishing.

Elby, Andrew, and David Hammer. (2001). "On the Substance of a Sophisticated Epistemology." *Science Education* 85(5): 554–67.

Fosnot, Catherine. (1993). "Rethinking Science Education: A Defense of Piagetian Constructivism." *Journal of Research in Science Teaching* 30(9): 1189–201.

Giannetto, E. (1992). "The Relations between Epistemology, History of Science and Science Teaching from the Point of View of the Research on Mental Representations." In *Second International HPS&ST Proceedings*, ed. Skip Hills (pp. 359–74). Kingston, Canada: University of Kingston Press.

Giere, R. (1989). "The Units of Analysis in Science Studies." In *The Cognitive Turn*, eds. S. Fuller et al. (pp. 3–11). Dordrecht: Kluwer.

—— (1999). *Science without Laws*. Chicago: University of Chicago Press.

Gil-Perez, Daniel, and Jaime Carrasosa-Alis. (1992). "Approaching Pupil's Learning to Scientific Construction of Knowledge: Some Implications of the History and Philosophy of Science in Science Teaching." In *Second International HPS&ST Proceedings*, vol. 1, ed. Skip Hills (pp. 403–18). Kingston, Canada: University of Kingston Press.

Glasson, George, and Rosary Lalik. (1992). "Social Constructivism in Science Learning: Toward a Mind-World Synthesis." In *Second International HPS&ST Proceedings*, vol. 1, ed. Skip Hills (p. 427–34). Kingston, Canada: University of Kingston Press.

Grandy, Richard E. (1998). "Constructivisms and Objectivity: Disentangling Metaphysics from Pedagogy." In *Constructivism in Science Education*, ed. Michael Matthews (pp. 113–22). Dordrecht: Kluwer.

Hofer, Barbara K., and Paul R. Pintrich. (1997). "The Development of Epistemological Theories: Beliefs about Knowledge and Knowing and Their Relation to Learning." *Review of Educational Research* 67(1): 88–140.

King, Patricia M., and Karen S. Kitchener. (1994). *Developing Reflective Judgment: Understanding and Promoting Intellectual Growth and Critical Thinking in Adults and Adolescents*. San Francisco: Jossey-Bass.

Krajick, J. (2008). "Commentary on Chinn and Samarapungavan's Paper." In *Teaching Scientific Inquiry: Recommendations for Research and Implementation*, ed. Richard A. Duschl and Richard E. Grandy (pp. 226–32). Rotterdam: Sense Publishing.

Le Grand, H. E. (1988). *Drifting Continents and Shifting Theories*. New York: Cambridge University Press.

Leinhardt, G., and M. Steele. (2005). "Seeing the Complexity of Standing on the Side." *Cognition and Instruction* 23: 87–163.

Longino, H. (1992). "Essential Tensions—Phase Two: Feminist, Philosophical and Social Studies of Science." In *The Social Dimensions of Science*, ed. E. McMullin (pp. 198–216). Notre Dame, IN: University of Notre Dame Press.

—— (1994). "The Fate of Knowledge in Social Theories of Science." In *Socializing Epistemology: The Social Dimensions of Knowledge*, ed. Frederick F. Schmitt (pp. 135–57). Lanham, MD: Rowman & Littlefield.

Magolda, Marcia. (2002). "Epistemological Reflection: The Evolution of Epistemological Assumptions from Age 18 to 30." In *Personal Epistemology: The Psychology of Beliefs about Knowledge and Knowing*, ed. Barbara Hofer and Paul Pintrich (pp. 89–102). Mahwah, NJ: Earlbaum.

Matthews, Michael, ed. (1998). *Constructivism in Science Education*. Dordrecht: Kluwer.

Matthews, Michael, and Peter Davson-Galle. (1992). "Constructivism and Science Education: Some Cautions and Comments." In *Second International HPS&ST Proceedings*, vol. 2, ed. Skip Hills (pp. 135–44). Kingston, Canada: University of Kingston Press.

McMullin, E., ed. (1992). *The Social Dimensions of Science*. Notre Dame, IN: University of Notre Dame Press.

Megill, Allan. (1991). "Four Senses of Objectivity." *Annals of Scholarship* 8: 301–20.

Morris, Edgar. (1992). "Characteristics of the Mind from a Social Constructivist Perspective." In *Second International HPS&ST Proceedings*, vol. 2, ed. Skip Hills (pp. 195–200). Kingston, Canada: University of Kingston Press.

Niedderer, Hans. (1992). "Science Philosophy, Science History and the Teaching of Physics." In *Second International HPS&ST Proceedings*, vol. 2, ed. Skip Hills (pp. 201–14). Kingston, Canada: University of Kingston Press.

Norris, Stephen, and Linda Philips. (2008). "Reading as Inquiry." In *Teaching Scientific Inquiry: Recommendations for Research and Implementation*, ed. Richard A. Duschl and Richard E. Grandy (pp. 233–62). Rotterdam: Sense Publishing.

O'Loughlin, Michael. (1992). "Rethinking Science Education: Beyond Piagetian Constructivism Toward a Sociocultural Model of Teaching and Learning." *Journal of Research in Science Teaching* 29(8): 791–820.

—— (1993). "Some Further Questions for Piagetian Constructivists: A Reply to Fosnot." *Journal of Research in Science Teaching* 30(9): 1203–207.

Samarapungavan, Ala. (1992) "Children's Judgments in Theory Choice Tasks: Scientific Rationality in Childhood." *Cognition* 45: 1–32.

Smolin, Lee. (2006). *The Trouble with Physics: The Rise of String Theory, the Fall of a Science, and What Comes Next*. Boston: Houghton Mifflin.

van Waterschoot van der Gracht, W. A. J., ed. (1928). *Theories of Continental Drift: A Symposium*. Tulsa: American Association of Petroleum Engineers.

Von Glasersfeld, Ernest. (1992) "A Constructivist Approach to Experiential Foundations of Mathematical Concepts." In *Second International HPS&ST Proceedings*, vol. 2, ed. Skip Hills (pp. 551–71). Kingston, Canada: University of Kingston Press.

Windschitl, M. (2008). "Our Challenge in Disrupting Popular Folk Theories for 'Doing Science'". In *Teaching Scientific Inquiry: Recommendations for Research and Implementation*, ed. Richard A. Duschl and Richard E. Grandy (p. 292–303). Rotterdam: Sense Publishing.

Woit, Peter. (2006). *Not Even Wrong: The Failure of String Theory and the Continuing Challenge to Unify the Laws of Physics*. London: Jonathan Cape.

....

CHAPTER 21

EMPIRICAL EDUCATIONAL RESEARCH: CHARTING PHILOSOPHICAL DISAGREEMENTS IN AN UNDISCIPLINED FIELD

....

D. C. PHILLIPS

The twentieth century has seen considerable progress in education. It has also witnessed the birth of research in education, and has watched the delicate infant grow into a fair-sized, rather noisy and undisciplined child. But so far the child has contributed very little to the progress, which has come about rather by other means . . . research in education has achieved very little up to the present, and it is fairly true to say it is taken seriously mainly by those who are engaged in it.

—C. D. Hardie, "Research and Progress in Education"

THESE words, written in 1965 by C. D. Hardie, the acerbic pioneer of analytic philosophy of education, give a depiction of the field of educational research the general thrust of which—apart from some details—would be endorsed by many commentators forty years on. The field is now noisier and more undisciplined than Hardie would have thought possible; and it is no longer accurate to characterize it as "fair-sized"—the American Educational Research Association (AERA) has about twenty-five thousand members, most of whom take their work quite seriously. Even the U.S. Department of Education views the field seriously—so much so that it has taken the bold step of giving official imprimatur to a small set of research designs and, in effect, has imposed an embargo on many others, which is a level of political involvement with the nitty-gritty of research that has rarely, if ever, been encountered in a democratic society. (This matter will be revisited in due course.) The issue of whether the field has achieved anything substantive is a matter of ongoing controversy, but there are some commentators who have passed a harsher judgment even than Hardie and who have accused the empirical research enterprise as having put forward only truisms and trivialities (Barrow 1984; Egan 1983, 2002; Smeyers 2007; for a counter, see Phillips 2005); some researchers, however, have been confident that the scientific basis for such things as "the art of teaching" has been revealed (see Gage 1978, 1994).

Clearly, if spawning controversies and attracting the attention of a major branch of the U.S. government are any indication, something of interest is taking place; and the following discussion shall survey the field seriously enough to do some philosophical probing. The aim is twofold. First, I hope to provide a more nuanced overview than is often given of the research terrain and its intellectual and methodological disputes. For, probably much more than for other branches of applied research, empirical educational research is a hotly contested, sometimes reviled, ideologically saturated field that possesses enormous and yet largely untapped potential for contributing to the improvement of society;[1] without having an adequate grasp of the nature of the field, philosophers run the risk of discussing an irrelevant artifact. Second, I aim to identify and clarify some of the more prominent philosophical issues that cut across this contested terrain. The discussion will proceed in point form, starting with issues relating to the complexity of the field and to its politicization; these points are followed by assessments of the criticisms of empirical research offered by members of the philosophy of education community—an amorphous group whose members, it is important to note, self-identify as philosophers, although this sometimes is not their primary or even secondary area of expertise and professional activity. The chapter culminates in a discussion of several philosophically rich issues that are of relevance across many of the research traditions in the field. For reasons that will quickly become obvious, examples of exemplary pieces of empirical research shall not be discussed in detail—which is a good segue to the opening section.

1. The Problem of Selecting Exemplary Research

It might be expected that an essay on the topic of empirical educational research would open with an analysis of several examples of exemplary or groundbreaking work; but to take this tack would be to court philosophical disaster unless some important background has been covered. There are several interrelated reasons for this, apart from the sheer difficulty of giving brief yet clear accounts of the intricacies of good work. The first of these reasons is that the enormous number of topics on which research has been done raises the thorny issue of the criteria that would be used to select some cases to serve as exemplars. (Perhaps methodological rigor? But judged by whom—fellow travelers or methodological rivals? Social relevance? But judged by the rich and powerful, or by the needy and oppressed? Philosophical acumen? But judged by which philosophers? "General quality?" But judged by theorists or by practitioners?) Second, and most important, topics and research methodology are often tightly interrelated, in that many research questions are amenable for investigation only by a limited set of methods; and as already indicated, the choice of methodologies has become politicized. This has the consequence that selection of examples of exemplary research reveals not only one's methodological sympathies but one's political or ideological sympathies as well; and any proffered exemplars are bound to draw fire from those researchers who favor other methodologies and who have other ideological, political, or value preferences.

All this can be put in loosely Kuhnian terms: in such an enormous field as educational research, it is not surprising that there are many alternative research "paradigms," and adherents of any one of these are likely to reject "exemplars" chosen from the others—after all, paradigmatic work must come from one's own paradigm.[2]

2. The Scope of Educational Research

Despite what has just been said, the enormity of the task facing a philosopher commenting on issues in educational research is easily downplayed, for the myth is surprisingly persistent that the field is solely oriented toward doing research to improve the performance of practitioners, who by and large are thought of as classroom teachers. But, as argued above, philosophers need to grasp the true scope of the field, with its diversity of topics and methodological approaches—in its scope, the field of educational research parallels the entire panoply of the social sciences. A good place to start developing an adequate picture is the program of the

2006 Annual Meeting of AERA (San Francisco, April 7–11, 2006). Not including maps and other appendices, this document has 479 pages, and (by quick calculation) it lists more than 9,000 presentations. In opening this telephone-directory look-alike at random (pp. 170–73), the following were among the topics or research foci revealed (as I did not attend these parallel sessions, I can provide no further clarification):

- A poststructuralist analysis of teaching practices in mathematics
- An inquiry into whether standards-based mathematics tests measure students' conceptual understanding
- The problems faced in leading standards-based reform in rural high schools
- An investigation of gender-identity contestation and transformation in a community of practice
- A case-study investigation of use of technology to enhance pluralistic thinking in a feminist classroom
- A study of the effectiveness or otherwise of same-gender groupings in eighth-grade science classrooms
- Cultural diversity and approach responsiveness in problem-based language learning
- Narrative construction of self through tools and signs
- A longitudinal study of factors influencing high school students' pursuit of college math/science majors
- Using popular film to investigate whiteness with teachers
- The effects of course-taking and extra-curricular activities—a structural equation modeling approach
- U.S. federal statistical data and the advancement of educational research
- Small schools within an urban high school
- Direct and indirect effects of SES and instructional practices on student achievement

In addition to the great diversity of topics, methodologies, and political/ideological positions that leap out here, it is also worth pointing out that researchers working in different niches have different aspirations for their research—a matter that is only imperfectly illustrated by the topics listed. Some researchers wish to discover nostrums for specific educational problems, or wish to determine whether a solution (that is, a specific program or intervention) proposed by a policymaker or educational reformer actually "works" in a particular setting or is a fad. Others are dedicated to understanding in depth a particular setting or the affordances and constraints facing an individual in a specific setting, and again the issues of generalizability and theory-building are set aside. Yet another grouping of researchers is interested in determining (via a variety of outcome measures) the overall impact on a district or state system of varying an input factor such as teacher starting salary or class size—work that might have widespread policy implications and also might be the foundation of an economic theory. And certainly there are some who are interested in discovering the general social or psychological mechanisms by which treatments or inputs produce results.

This divergence in research aims has caused much confusion for over a century; the literature is replete with contradictory charges that cover the spectrum from the complaint that educational research is too ivory tower and theoretical, to the opposite complaint that it is too focused on issues of practice and is not theoretical enough. The philosophical issue of whether educational phenomena at these various levels are amenable to theoretical description on a par with, for example, that which has proved to be possible with physical phenomena or economic ones, has received some philosophical attention, but not much; and although some interesting thoughts have been put forward by researchers themselves, these have received virtually no philosophical attention.

3. THE HEATED NATURE OF DEBATES WITHIN THE FIELD OF RESEARCH

There is one other revealing feature of the field of educational research that does not emerge clearly from the list of topics given above—namely, the heat with which the debates about theoretical constructs and especially methodology have been conducted. Undoubtedly there are fields within the natural sciences that harbor vigorous internal disputes, and that also draw the contumely of "outside" spectators who have stakes in some of the work in that field, or in its supposed implications— evolutionary biology being the current prime example. But it is arguable that when the debates of the past decade or two are taken into account, the field of educational research actually takes the prize, both for the range of issues and criticisms that are forthcoming from "inside" and "out" and for the intensity—occasionally verging on impropriety—with which criticisms and defenses are mounted.

There is no great mystery about this level of intensity, and it reveals what is not an incidental but an essential aspect of the field. In the eyes of many, educational research serves as handmaiden to the educational policy-forming communities, which in turn are among the chief sites in modern democratic societies where the great emotionally charged issues of economic and political equity, including the empowerment of women and minorities, are fought out. (There is some indication of this in the earlier listing of topics from the AERA program.) The nature and content of the formal education of children also is contested territory, where the rights of parents to shape what and how their offspring are taught can come into conflict both with the rights of those children to a liberal education and with the interest of the liberal civic state in producing an enlightened citizenry via compulsory education of the young. In such a complex and charged climate, even the smallest (or micro) educational decisions can become highly politicized; and the products of empirical research inevitably come to be viewed as resources that can be used selectively to marshal public opinion either pro or con.

The remarks above serve to explain why many individuals become intensely skeptical about the products of all research, and why research and its "findings" are seen as belonging to the social world of political struggle, not to the epistemic world of producing sound warrants for belief. And these remarks also throw light on another prominent feature of the world of educational research: when a field of research is highly politicized, the analyses of the practice of science given by the radical sociologists of knowledge, and by such thinkers as Foucault and Gramsci, who stress sociopolitical rather than epistemic factors, possess more appeal than otherwise might be the case. This leads directly to the next point.

4. The Politicization of Research Methodology

Political and ideological differences, or perceived differences, are often argued explicitly, but sometimes the conflict is carried out via "proxies." In the case of the deep divisions about educational policies and practices, for the past couple of decades the battle has been pursued on both fronts—explicitly, but also via proxies in the area of research methodology, the proxies being pro and con regarding the adoption of rigorous science as the model that educational research should aspire to emulate.

Thus, the use of the modifiers "empirical" or "rigorously scientific" have been vigorously contested; as one critic put it, to speak of empirical or scientific educational research is to be guilty of adopting "your father's paradigm," which presumably is not complimentary (Lather 2004). In the eyes of critics like this, these labels carry important and contestable sociopolitical connotations and are not merely methodological in nature—they convey a false picture of research as being objective or value-free; they give a false sense that policies supported by the research are the only ones possible and that these policies are assailable only by the deluded; and finally, use of these labels leads to the denigration of modes of inquiry that are rooted in the humanities or in feminist theory, or that can be gleaned from the work of such late natives of the Continent as Foucault, Derrida, Baudrillard, and Gadamer, among others. (Some examples of work in one or other of these genres can be found in the listing given earlier from the AERA program.) In 1997, the then editor of the *British Educational Research Journal* and a co-author wrote in support of a broadly postmodern methodological alternative to the dominant empiricist/scientific mode; the following passage nicely illustrates the close bond between methodology and sociopolitical commitments:

> [This new approach] could be located within an emerging body of educational, feminist, postcolonial and anthropological research which recognizes, and tries to

work within, the necessary *failure* of methodology's hope for certainty, and its dream of finding an innocent language in which to represent, without exploiting or distorting, the voices and ways of knowing of its subaltern "subjects." Such work . . . tries to practice what could be called a methodology, and a politics, of disappointment . . . disappointment—of certainty, clarity, illumination, generality—is both a choice and an inevitability; something to be both resigned and committed to.   (Stronach and Maclure 1997, pp. 4–5)

The arguments offered by the critics to justify such things as the claim that objectivity needs to be rejected even as an ideal, or that it is an imposition to require that research findings or interpretations of findings need to be adequately warranted, are too often "quick and dirty" or "deep and murky," or else they are nonexistent and their place taken by name-calling—it is not uncommon for those who push for objectivity as an ideal or insist upon competent warrants (a Deweyan notion) to be called "positivists," the implication being that this is a "knock-down" argument.[3]

It is safe to say that, on all sides of the debates over methodologies and their implications, there is mutual incomprehension mingled with distrust. As indicated above, the critics of traditional empirical work see it as bankrupt, as an arm of conservative social policy, and they reject its supposed virtues of objectivity and scientific rigor as missing the point. Instead, educational research should move, as Lather mysteriously asserts, "toward a Nietzschean sort of 'unnatural science' that leads to greater health by fostering ways of knowing that escape normativity" (Lather 2004, p. 27). On the other hand, mainstream empirical educational researchers—who view themselves as a species of applied social scientists—do not see the point of the more radical criticisms of their work mentioned above, and not surprisingly many simply pay no heed. This group of researchers is not unified, however, for as will be seen in the following section, a philosophically dubious wedge has been driven into them recently by no lesser agent than the U.S. government.

5. Imposition of the "Gold Standard" in the Name of Scientific Rigor

Adding fuel to the fire—indeed, turning it from a fire into a conflagration—and conferring a degree of face-validity on the political analyses of research given by the critics, a subset of empirical educational researchers have been in the eye of the storm because of their single-minded advocacy of scientific rigor, which they characterize extremely narrowly. Crucially, they have identified rigor—and sometimes scientific worthiness—with the use of *one* particular research method, which has lost them the support of empirical researchers who use other methods, and who might otherwise have been allies against the radical attacks on empirical research outlined above. This so-called "gold standard" methodology is the randomized controlled experiment or field trial (RFT), which of course is an instantiation of at least one of J. S. Mill's "methods of logic." Chief among its virtues—the one that endears it to the U.S. government—is the (supposed) fact that it can authoritatively establish that a program or intervention or treatment did, or did not, cause an observed effect; this, it is claimed, is precisely the kind of information needed for the rational shaping of educational policy. Researchers who are advocates of the "gold standard" often go on to deliver a very backhanded compliment to their empiricist colleagues; for they suggest that other empirical research methods are useful, at best, only in "building up" to RFTs or in "augmenting" them (Mosteller and Boruch 2002, p. 4)—the idea being, roughly, that such things as qualitative case studies might generate interesting causal hypotheses, but that these remain merely hypothetical until supported by rigorous RFTs. To add insult to injury, two of the leading advocates for the use of RFTs have been quite denigratory when referring to the contributions that could be made to this research enterprise by philosophers, social theorists, and the like: "Even throat-clearing essays at times contribute to understanding" (Mosteller and Boruch 2002, p. 4).

Insults aside, it is important to note the serious narrowing of the purpose of inquiry that is embodied here: the aim of rigorous educational research simply is to establish whether or not treatments or programs are causally efficacious, and other aims common in science such as unraveling causal mechanisms or developing and testing theories, or even the initial development of treatments that are likely to work, are ignored (see Phillips 2006a).

It is also worth pointing out that, although many of the vocal advocates for use of the "gold standard" are researchers based in the United States, the same approach has strong support in the UK and Europe, where "evidence-based policy" and "what works" are catchphrases, and where it is held that the "evidence" and the "working" are determined most reliably by strong experimental studies paralleling those that are performed in the medical sciences to establish which particular treatments are effective. A few philosophers of education are starting to pay attention to the assumptions here, though not particularly effectively.[4]

As hinted above, there has been an astounding twist of fate in the United States, one that gives further support to the charge that methodology and politics are closely intertwined in fields like education. Around the turn of the millennium, the arguments and pronouncements of this pro-"gold standard" group of researchers found favor among those in power in the conservative political circles in Washington, who viewed the field of educational research as lacking rigor, and as too influenced by ideology (views for which, admittedly, there is some evidence from an evaluation of research in the UK; see Tooley and Darby 1998). Unfortunately, this ideological sensitivity on the part of the politically powerful does not extend to recognition of how their *own* ideology influences policy and (mis) shapes research. Thus, since the early years of the Bush (junior) administration, federal educational research funding in the United States has been available only for the conduct of RFTs, which means that empirical work using *any other methodology* goes unfunded. This is a draconian policy indeed, especially when promulgated in the name of scientific rigor. The U.S. National Academies of Science, through its executive arm, the National Research Council (NRC), tried to liberalize this funding policy by issuing a report that made room, in the name of science, for such things as ethnographic research, but to no avail (NRC, 2002; for documentation of the relevant pieces of legislation and debates over both the federal funding policy and the motives behind the NRC report itself, see Phillips 2006b.) It also is of some interest that the NRC report was interpreted by some of the radical critics of research as being, in fact, part of the conservative political weaponry deployed to suppress dissident voices, rather than an abortive effort to liberalize the notion of "science" that was being abused by supporters of the "gold standard."[5]

In the years since the promulgation of the "gold standard" funding policy, the nature of rigor in various types of quantitative and qualitative research has been much discussed, as has the nature of science, and the mischaracterization of the history and methods of science that follow upon adoption of the RFT as the "gold standard" of scientific work. It has been pointed out that Galileo, Newton, Darwin, Crick and Watson, and Hawking would not be regarded as doing rigorous, fundable scientific work under the U.S. Department of Education definition (Phillips 2006a). A few members of the broad philosophy of education community have been actively involved in the debates provoked by imposition of the "gold standard," but in general the domain of research has not been a major focus of interest—for reasons that now shall be examined.

6. Philosophers of Education on Empirical Research

It is natural to assume that the relationship of philosophers of education to educational research parallels the relationship between philosophers of science and the research fields that they philosophize about. But this is a mistaken assumption. The point is, about five decades ago, philosophical discussion of research in the natural sciences underwent a change. As Peter Machamer characterized it, "Philosophers of science could no longer get along without knowing science and/or its history in considerable depth. They, hereafter, would have to work within science as actually practiced, and be able to discourse with practicing scientists about what was going on" (Machamer 2002, p. 9). Harold Kincaid expressed a similar view concerning philosophical work about the social sciences, but he suggested that there had been a slight time lag and that the transformation has been more recent (Kincaid 2002, p. 290).

This new approach, however, has produced only the faintest of ripples on the waters of philosophy of education, where the detailed examination of empirical educational research is given short shrift—if any shrift at all (Phillips 2005). Examination of cases of research beyond a superficial level are rare, although not nonexistent (see, for example, Barrow 1984; Egan 1983; Phillips and Nicolayev 1978; Phillips 1983; Smeyers 2006);[6] when research is mentioned, *a priori* pronouncements (especially condemnations of the field as either trite or bankrupt) are common, and consideration of how researchers would likely respond to these charges is lacking.

By and large, then, the focus is on conversing with other philosophers of education—after all, why bother to talk with empirical researchers when their work is futile? In 2006, the *Journal of Philosophy of Education* (*JPE*) published an unprecedented two-issue symposium on "Philosophy, Methodology, and Educational Research"; the first paragraph of the editors' introduction (Bridges and Smith 2006, p. 131) stresses the importance of fostering engagement among philosophers, researchers, and policy-framers. However, about halfway down the first page the tone changes. Rather than initiating a dialogue in which philosophers and researchers *both* might learn something, the language implies that *only the researchers* stand to learn anything; for what is stressed is the view that philosophy is a "central and essential part of research" in education and the social sciences (p. 131)—whereupon the discussion turns to a litany of defects in research that the essays in the *JPE* will expose. There is no mention of the issues arising in the work of researchers that philosophers might find stimulating to ponder.

Of course, there is nothing at all wrong with discussing what other philosophers have said about educational research, and indeed there might be much to learn; but at some point there needs to be grounding in reality. Examples of the research itself need to be examined (but selection bias needs to be avoided), and if defects are detected, mere assertion is not sufficient. Careful analysis is required to establish that these indeed are defects; the views of researchers about the aims and methods of work in their field need to be considered in more than "sound-bite" depth; and if a posit of methodology is rejected on philosophical grounds, some consideration needs to be given to what alternatives remain. In the absence of such grounding, the efforts of philosophers will have an ethereal quality and will have little impact on the thinking of researchers or those who use the products of research. Analysis of the *JPE* symposium, I believe, supports this general concern.[7] Indeed, one of the essays in this symposium actually develops in fine style the same points being made here; Martyn Hammersley argues that, although philosophy can contribute much to the field of educational research, currently researchers do not pay it sufficient attention; furthermore, "there are important limits to philosophy's contribution"; and finally, "it could be argued that philosophers do not make sufficient use of the theoretical ideas and empirical evidence generated by social scientists" (Hammersley 2006, p. 283).

7. PHILOSOPHICAL CRITICISMS OF THE EMPIRICAL RESEARCH ENTERPRISE

Many in the philosophy of education community would respond to the charge made above that—unlike their colleagues in philosophy of science—they do not have sufficient acquaintance with the nitty-gritty of the substance of research, by arguing that substance is precisely what is missing in the field itself. Thus, there is little point in adopting the new approach to research exemplified in the natural and social sciences—namely, being well-versed in the substantive and technical issues of the field and taking these seriously—if, in fact, the field is bereft of merit. And indeed they are right; little is to be achieved by continuing the present discussion unless this charge itself can be shown to be chimerical.

First, a small methodological matter needs to be resolved and a minor historical point made. Methodologically, it must be insisted that a case either way on this important issue cannot be made by deliberately selecting examples that "prove the point." The argument is not about the existence of some individual cases of trite or chimerical research, but rather is about the *preponderance* of research—whether there is reason to believe that most (or a reasonable proportion of) research can never, in principle, be anything but a waste of time and other resources. The bar is high.

The historical point will serve as segue to the main discussion. Harold Kincaid, in his survey of the field of philosophy of social science, made the point that in the past—up until the "revolution" in orientation of the field with respect to its treatment of real cases of research—the literature in philosophy of social science "concerned largely what the social sciences can or cannot do, what they must be like or never could be. Those views were typically defended on broad conceptual grounds.... However, these arguments claimed more for purely philosophical considerations than they can deliver" (Kincaid 2002, p. 290). The parallel with philosophy of education's treatment of educational research is striking. Philosophers of education, on those rare occasions when they have deigned to look at empirical educational research, have been concerned "largely with what educational research can or cannot do, what it must be like or never could be." And the philosophical arguments that have been advanced "claimed more for philosophy of education than they can deliver."

The main arguments against, or criticisms of, the research enterprise are as follows.

Triviality

The charge of triviality is usually brought against a few particular instances of research, and then on that limited basis the charge is generalized to cover the whole genre—clearly an illicit move. Furthermore, the charge itself is vague, but it seems to boil down to one or other of the following: the findings were true by definition (and therefore did not need empirical investigation); or they were so well known as to be truisms, and hence were not worth the effort to investigate. Despite being extremely weak, these objections warrant careful discussion, as they have carried undue weight not only among philosophers of education but also in the lay community.

It is true by definition that all bachelors are unmarried; and it also is true that when a class has been tested, not all students in that class can be at or above average (except in Lake Wobegon), provided that all those who were tested did not obtain the same score. It would make no sense at all to empirically test these assertions, and to my knowledge no educational researcher has been deranged enough to do so. It also is difficult to conceive of live examples in education where such empirical folly could be practiced. Nevertheless, the charge of "true by definition," although unfounded and based on a faulty analysis, is not uncommon. Thus, one commentator recently claimed that it was true by definition that meaningful material is easier to remember than nonmeaningful (Egan 2002, chap. 5)—an assertion not borne out by any dictionary I possess; and another (Barrow 1984, p. 182) has stated that "praise to some extent lessens anxiety by definition," which again is absent from my dictionaries, and about which I found the following thought-experiment decisive: I imagined that I had just been praised by Vice President Cheney. What we have here are cases of mistaken identity—findings that are so obvious, so evidently truisms, that those who are incautious take them for definitional truths.

Unfortunately, there are several catches with respect to truisms. First, judgments of "obviousness" are heavily context or situation dependent. It may be obvious to a dietician that my eating habits are dangerous, but—lacking the background knowledge—it is not obvious to me that my heavy consumption of chocolate is not beneficial. It might not have been obvious to parents of, say, two hundred years ago, that meaningful material was easier to learn than nonmeaningful. Philosophers of education who are skeptics about the usefulness of empirical educational research do not see the force of this simple point about contextualization; and they suffer from a lack of historical perspective on the development of the sciences that would have sensitized them to the fact that history is littered with the bodies of theories that at one time seemed incontrovertibly true. If these had been immunized against skeptical probing, on the grounds that they were so obvious that further inquiry would be a waste of time, intellectual progress would have been stalled—and we would still accept the obvious truths that the earth is at the center of the solar system and that bloodletting is the cure for a large range of ailments (possibly including anemia).

Paul Smeyers falls into this trap; he outlines a qualitative research study of teachers in their first professional year, and after summarizing the researchers' set of findings, he writes:

> let me be blunt about this, is it really more than truisms, more than "common sense." . . . Their general conclusions are very similar to the relationship between

> speeding and accidents, drinking and driving, being depressive and suicidal, and so forth and so on . . . one may wonder whether [sic] in what sense this kind of research is helpful at all.   (Smeyers 2007)

In addition to the point above, that what is obvious to Paul might not be obvious to Peter or to Denis (who have different background knowledge), it also needs to be pointed out that this is a selective list that establishes nothing about the triviality of research *in general*. In the interest of balance, Smeyers might well have discussed research on massed versus distributed practice of mathematics skills, on phonics versus whole-language approaches to beginning reading instruction, or on the impact of instruction in integrated versus single-sex classrooms on the mathematics achievement of girls (and are boys affected the same way?). Are the likely findings here quite so obvious? And even in those cases (if any) where the answers are obvious, there is the issue of the nature of the social or psychological or cultural mechanisms that are operating to produce these nonsurprising results. Or do these regularities occur without any mechanisms being operative?—which is an important question about the metaphysics of the social world.

But there is another point that could be brought to Smeyers's attention, and this brings us to the second catch concerning truisms—namely, that humans are quite fickle when it comes to judging whether a factual claim or a purported finding is "obvious" or "trivial." Empirical work has shown that assertions of purported facts, and of their direct contradictories, are both likely to be judged by the nonexpert as so obvious as to make further inquiry a waste of time and resources (Gage and Berliner 1988, pp. 13–15). So an interesting counterfactual surfaces here: if the researchers cited by Smeyers had produced an opposite set of findings, would he also have judged these to be mere "common sense"?

Perhaps the moral for the wise philosopher is that whether or not a result is obvious is irrelevant to its epistemic status, and is irrelevant to any practical or theoretical role it might be called upon to play.

Value Discourse Settles Everything

It is a commonplace of philosophy of education that the very concept of "education" has values built into it; as Paul Hirst and Richard Peters stressed many decades ago, to educate a person is to change him or her for the better, a connotation that the term "training" does not possess—a person may be trained and end up worse, as when he or she is trained by the military or the KGB (Hirst and Peters 1970). Teachers, policymakers, administrators, and researchers all work in value-laden contexts, although some individuals are more aware of this than others. Philosophers of education have been particularly aware of the role value considerations play in shaping policies, practices, and aims, but occasionally they have gone too far. Thus, David Carr, who states in a recent book that "the forms of human association characteristic of educational engagement are not really apt for scientific or empirical study at all" (Carr 2003, pp. 54–55), has also asserted in a fit of philosophical daring-do that examination of values and social norms will provide answers to many (perhaps all?) questions one could desire to raise about such a basic process as human learning, and certainly such inquiry trumps the need for most (or all?) empirical research on the topic:

> it is mistaken to construe human conceptual learning, or knowledge-acquisition, as a quasi-naturalistic process... apt for investigation via some kind of empirical science: on the contrary, any meaningful (human) educational learning (rather than animal training) is a matter of *normative* initiation into socially constructed and/or constituted rules, principles and values that no statistically conceived processes could even begin to explain. (p. 132)

It is hard to judge this passage as anything but one long non sequitur, with a fathomless swipe at a nonspecified "statistically conceived process" in the tail.[8] All humans are initiated into socially developed normative frameworks, but the facts that they were *socially* developed and that they are *normative*, seem to have no bearing on the issue of whether these processes can be studied "naturalistically." A process of initiation (for example, a nurse's introduction to care of the infirm, and the need for sensitivity and awareness of the potential for many situations to cause embarrassment) is a process in the world, and it can be observed, discussed, even measured (how many times with patient X did this nurse act curtly—using some convention for identifying curtness?), and certainly as a process it has the potential to be improved—and improved not merely on *a priori* or philosophical grounds. Furthermore, empirical study of a normative process might be necessary for ethical reasons—for there might be a number of alternative ways the initiation could proceed, and one of these might be more effective, have less negative unintended side effects, and be less of a drain on scarce societal resources than the other alternatives, so that it would be immoral not to adopt it, *if only we knew which one it was.*

A simple educational example illustrates the point: Moral and value deliberations might determine that children ought to be taught to read, but the pressing empirical question remains: *how* should this teaching proceed? For currently there are two rival methods of attaining this same morally desirable end—whole language and phonics—and there are pros and cons with respect to each. Indeed, it would be *immoral* to adopt one of these methods if it was less effective, or had more harmful side effects, than the other, and these things are not determinable by moral or other *a priori* inquiry but by empirical work.

Other Arguments

The literature contains a number of other objections to empirical educational research that are worth noting. One, by Kieran Egan, in essence depends on an idiosyncratic notion of self-referentiality coupled with a strong notion of educational determinism, both of which can be questioned; but the thing that emerges with greatest clarity is again the strong antipathy that exists among some philosophers of education to empirical (and in this case, psychological) research. The argument runs as follows: Human behavior may be shaped by our nature, which is in part biological but is in large part cultural; but culture is shaped by educators whose task is to pass it on to the rising generation. Thus, "regularities discovered by psychologists are products of the kinds of forces that it is the educator's job to shape"; thus, "all empirical research based on any psychological theory has no implications for education" (Egan 1983, pp. 135, 139). Apart from the fact that the first premise can be challenged (biological, including neural, mechanisms are probably more influential than Egan was then, or is now, willing to concede), the argument requires not only that cultural mechanisms are completely dominant in the shaping of human behavior but also that in turn they are fully shaped/transmitted by educators. But even if these improbable assumptions are granted, still the conclusions do not follow; a researcher studying a social practice that is fully culturally determined might, nevertheless, throw light on this practice and learn something about it that is of use to someone in some context—and after all, major branches of anthropology owe their existence to the view that cultural practices can be studied in a rigorous way. It seems likely that Egan's background assumption here is that we learn about cultural practices by participating in them, and there is nothing else to research; and his metaphysics allows no room for mechanisms (especially psychological ones) that are involved in the production of human behavior—that are the link between the cultural context and the behavior of individuals.

8. The Sociocultural Context

Egan is just one of many in education and the social sciences who recognize the importance of the sociocultural context in which the developing individual is located and in which the mature individual lives and acts, and who have come under the influence of Vygotsky's work on the role of cultural tools in shaping the mature mind. But within the large group that has been influenced by these ideas, there seems to be no unanimity about the consequences that are claimed to follow concerning the conduct of empirical social science and educational research. A nuanced position was developed by Brian Fay in his *Contemporary Philosophy of Social Science* (1996); crucially, he does not believe that cultural embeddedness undermines the possibility of doing worthwhile social science inquiry, but rather it means that methods of inquiry must be adopted that are not based on the natural science model: "social scientists have historically sought to claim the mantle of science and have modeled their studies on the natural sciences," but this has "run out of steam" (Fay 1996, p. 1). It needs to be said that his case hinges on what, precisely, he understands the "natural science model" to be, for on some accounts of this model it readily can cover inquiry into cultural influences (see, for example, Phillips and Burbules 2000, chap. 4). Fay's reformulated social inquiry would be hermeneutical, interactionist, process-oriented, aware of human agency and cultural embeddedness, and anti-dualistic (Fay 1996, chap. 11).

Kenneth Howe is in close agreement; he also stresses the importance of human agency, attacks the excesses of what he calls "neoclassical experimentalism," and concludes by advocating a position that presumably Fay would be able to endorse—"mixed-methods interpretivism" (Howe 2004, pp. 43, 54). Lincoln and Cannella take a different tack: "contemporary methodological conservatism" (their version of Howe's "neoclassical experimentalism") is "much criticized and largely discredited," one of the reasons being that research which meets the gold standard—namely, a RFT or related "quantitative" study—cannot deal with the complexities of educational contexts,

> especially considering the farrago of subtle social difference produced by gender, race, ethnicity, linguistic status, or class. Indeed, multiple kinds of knowledge, produced by multiple epistemologies and methodologies, are not only worth having but also demanded if policy, legislation, and practice are to be sensitive to social needs.   (Lincoln and Cannella 2004, p. 7)

Although the call for "multiple epistemologies" seems liberally eclectic, it is not quite clear what to make of it, given their quite negative evaluation of the worth of the experimental/quantitative tradition.[9] (In a footnote that criticizes my own work as being positivistic, they also make clear that they support—as I do not— "emergent epistemologies which seek to frame research via clearly nonobjective lenses"; see Lincoln and Cannella 2004, fn. 2).

It is possible to hold the view canvassed by Fay, Howe, and many others that to understand individual actors, hermeneutic or interpretive methods must be used, without being forced to demote into insignificance the role that can be played in social and educational inquiry by naturalistic, quantitative/experimental types of inquiry. First, it is difficult to deny that the individual human actor usually acts for reasons, and these in turn are meaningful within a given context or culture—as the anthropologist Clifford Geertz put it, we all are caught up in webs of meaning that we ourselves have helped to create—and it takes acts of interpretation to reveal and make these reasons understandable. As mentioned earlier, some commentators (including Geertz himself; see Geertz 1973) regard this as being so different from the approach taken by researchers in the quantitative/experimental framework that it constitutes a separate nonnaturalistic paradigm. But second, be this as it may, the fact that at the micro-level in society—the level of individual human actions—interpretive methods play an important role does not mean that at the macro-level there are no regularities that can be found by the use of traditional naturalistic methods. (Physics, of course, can provide examples of macro-regularities that emerge from a background of micro-randomness; and Nobel laureate economist Thomas Schelling has an engaging example of a regularity in the behavior of human groups that emerges from a background of random individual micro-behavior—namely, the filling of auditoria. See Schelling 1978, chap. 1.) Critics of empirical educational research have a pronounced tendency to ignore the importance of these macro-regularities, the knowledge of which is vital for policy development and implementation across the many fields of educational endeavor. But if no general regularities existed, we would be bogged down in a welter of particulars and even effectively teaching a classroom of twenty-five fifth-graders would become a virtual impossibility.

9. ANOTHER MAJOR DEBATE AMONG RESEARCHERS: QUALITATIVE VERSUS QUANTITATIVE METHODOLOGIES

If the past two decades of research-oriented journals, handbooks (ever-popular in education), and research association conference programs are given even cursory perusal, what emerges quite clearly is the deep interest in the respective merits of the qualitative versus quantitative research traditions.[10] There was a time when the former was characterized as *ideographic* and the latter as *nomothetic;* but the debate has moved on and now has a strong methodological flavor. The focus today is largely on their respective canons of rigor and criteria of validity, the threats to validity that research studies in each tradition face, the issue of the generalizability and replicability of the findings of work in each tradition, and above all the epistemological underpinnings and scientific status of each. All of these issues have philosophical elements that quickly come to the fore, and it is interesting to see how many researchers themselves (rather than philosophers of education) have been engaged in the debates.

Quantitative researchers are accused of having an approach to these issues that reveals they are positivists or possibly postpositivists, and also that they are realists, who believe the educational researcher (perhaps like the astronomer) is separate from, and does not affect, the situation being studied and measured.[11] Furthermore, it is suggested that things that are not readily measurable—such as salient features of the sociocultural context in which educational phenomena occur—are, of necessity, ignored by quantitative workers (who often treat context as a "nuisance variable," of which more below.) On the other hand, qualitative researchers face the charge of being subjectivist, and often of being unscientific—or worse, of perhaps being postmodernists. For while being sensitive to the role played by sociocultural context in shaping human behavior—the charge runs—they lack clear criteria for judging the truth of the claims that they make, and in some cases even deny that "truth" is relevant to their work. Measurement-phobia is common in these circles. (Actually, the situation is even more complex, for some qualitative inquirers have been influenced by positivistic assumptions—see Denzin and Lincoln 1998, chap. 1—while many postpositivists have little in common with the positivists and are favorably disposed toward some types of qualitative inquiry; see Phillips 2000; Phillips and Burbules 2000).

The following extract from the introductory chapter to an influential work on qualitative research written by two nonphilosophers is informative; they argue that many qualitative researchers, but not all,

> reject positivist and postpositivist criteria when evaluating their own work. They see these as irrelevant to their work, and contend that these criteria reproduce only a certain kind of science, a science that silences too many voices. These researchers seek alternative methods for evaluating their work, including verisimilitude, emotionality, personal responsibility, an ethic of caring, political praxis, multivoiced texts, and dialogues with subjects. In response, positivists and postpositivists argue that what they do is good science, free of individual bias and subjectivity.... [They] abstract from this world and seldom study it directly. They seek a nomothetic or etic science based on probabilities derived from the study of large numbers of randomly selected cases.
>
> (Denzin and Lincoln 1998, p. 10)

Clearly, there is much philosophical underlaboring of a raw kind to be done here; but it is to be hoped that it is also clear that pinning down the precise epistemological and ontological differences between qualitative and quantitative inquiry (if there are any such differences) would be to perform an important service for the research community at large.

This clash between qualitative and quantitative inquiry has often been cast in Kuhnian terms. Questions such as the following arise: "Are qualitative and quantitative approaches different paradigms?" "Can a researcher validly use both kinds of methods in the one study or is the attempt to use a so-called 'mixed or multimethod design' a Quixotic attempt to breach the gulf of incommensurability?" Thomas Schwandt commented, in his *Qualitative Inquiry: A Dictionary of Terms*, that after Kuhn's work became popular,

> it was particularly fashionable to talk about the qualitative versus quantitative "paradigm debate" in the social sciences.... The term offered a convenient conceptual shorthand for pointing to apparently significant differences in methodologies. It was not always entirely clear, however, what the term actually meant in this context.   (Schwandt 1997, p. 108)

One of the few philosophers of education who has been an active participant in these "paradigm debates" (or as they were also known, "paradigm wars") is Kenneth Howe, and on a number of occasions he has defended the position that—by the turn of the millennium—became widely accepted and allowed a semblance of peace to descend; this was the "compatibilist" view that there is no epistemic bar to using both qualitative and quantitative methods in the one piece of research (for example, see Howe 2003, esp. chap. 3). Howe argued that compatibilism granted something to what he calls "the interpretivist paradigm," and also granted something to "the positivist paradigm," and thereby "avoids running aground on either the positivist or interpretivist methodological islands" (p. 38). As a "friendly amendment" I would suggest that Howe drop the use of "paradigm," for two reasons: first, these orientations toward research—by whatever names they are called—are certainly not Kuhnian-like paradigms and certainly are not incommensurable; and second, while using different methods to collect different types of data, these two approaches are not even incompatible, at either a commonsense or an epistemic level—for both approaches hold, speaking loosely, that researchers must provide warrants for the assertions that are made, that competently gathered empirical evidence of various types will be an important part of any such warrants, that these warrants must be able to withstand searching public scrutiny, and that no warrant confers absolute certainty on an assertion. At any rate, the peace of the new millennium meant, to many, that their hero John Dewey was vindicated for, of course, his epistemology gives support to the compatibilist position; and positive talk about "multi-methods" research designs proliferated.

However, it also should be noted that the peace is not universal, for there have been hold-outs to the consensus. Hanan Alexander, writing in the *JPE* symposium, remarked that the truce between the warring sides was based on a weak epistemology:

> For the dual epistemology thesis never adequately addressed the question of how it is possible to embrace the findings of research grounded in a qualitative orientation given the empiricist demand for randomization and generalisability, or conversely, how quantitative results can be meaningful given the hermeneutic critique of positivism and post-positivism.   (Alexander 2006, p. 208)

Clearly, there are problems with the position developed here. First, the outbreak of peace did not necessitate that the combatants accept some type of "dual epistemology"; Howe and other commentators have been quite clear about this (Howe 2003, chap. 3; Phillips and Burbules 2000). Second, empiricism has been mischaracterized badly—there is no general demand that randomization and generalizabilty be achieved in *every empirical study*; rather, these arise in very specific contexts, most notably in the design and execution of RFTs where it is important to avoid selection of a biased sample, but where the design possibilities also open the opportunity to increase external validity. Third, it is far from agreed that the "hermeneutic critique" proscribes the use of *all* quantitative data—when, how, and by whom did the total ban on measurement and the use of numbers get enacted? And the fact that numerical data need to be interpreted is, of course, symptomatic of a difficulty that faces *all* educational researchers and not solely those who perform experiments—namely, that any data at all, whether from observations, interviews, or tests or other measurements, requires interpretation, and interpretation that can be solidly warranted. It is not clear that all qualitative researchers have responded to the "hermeneutic challenge" in more stellar fashion than have their quantitative brethren.

10. Controversies about Causation in Educational Processes

It is appropriate to end this chapter with a brief discussion of an issue (or set of issues) that lurks behind many of the controversies about educational research. This is the issue of causation—the role it plays in social and educational life, the forms that causal mechanisms take, how causal processes can be discovered, and how causal claims can be warranted. Although some researchers have made major, sophisticated contributions—notably Cook and Campbell (1979) and Cook (1993)—there remains much for philosophers to do here, and since what follows is barely more than a mere listing of some key issues, the discussion shall proceed by way of "bullets."

- Students, parents, teachers, administrators, and policymakers all act for reasons (at least, most of the time), and included in their reasons for acting are their beliefs, values, and their situational analyses. It is now generally accepted (post-Davidson) that reasons in this broad sense are causes, and it seems evident that we can bring about a change in a person's behavior (a causal process) by giving him or her new reasons, new beliefs, and so on. If we did not hold such a view, there would seem to be little point in taking the trouble to educate the rising generation (or to write philosophical essays). While there is reluctance on the part of some philosophers of education, and some educational theorists with postmodernist predilections (sometimes these are the same people), to concede that reasons are causes (see, for example, Smeyers 2006, p. 103, who states that the "paradigm of causality" only applies to human actions by "changing the meaning of 'causality'" so that the concept incorporates reasons), the issue for many of those who study individuals or small groups—essentially qualitative researchers, especially those of interpretivist persuasion—is the methodological one of how the causal explanations that they produce can be warranted. Observation and qualitative inquiry in general is limited in its ability to identify the reasons for a person's actions, although it is not completely ineffective (and it should be noted that Joseph Maxwell, an informed qualitative researcher, has strongly challenged on philosophical grounds the "dismissal of qualitative research as a rigorous means of investigating causality," Maxwell 2004, p. 3). An alternative, narrative research, has undergone a period of popularity, but the issue of how to determine the veracity of a person's account that describes why he or she acted in a certain way has not been settled, and some researchers simply accept at face value any story that is told to them (Phillips 2000, chap. 4). Even the well-established field of ethnography faces methodological difficulties (Hammersley 1992 provides a refreshing discussion of these).

- Advocates for the use of the RFT as the "gold standard," who also generally endorse the restricting of research funds to support only this type of research, justify their position by two arguments: first, only a randomized controlled experiment can establish that a treatment or intervention caused an effect—a position they trace back to the classic monograph by Campbell and Stanley (1963), but which originates in Mill's methods of logic; and second, that causal evidence generated by RFTs has been a successful basis of policy in the medical and public health areas, and education deserves no less. Both of these arguments have provoked heated discussion: it has been pointed out that the history of science reveals a number of ways in which causal claims have been defended; it has also been noted that the causal inferences relied upon in everyday life have not in general been warranted by RFTs (one recent tongue-in-cheek paper in the *British Medical Journal* points to the shocking fact that the causal efficacy of parachutes has not to this day been supported by a RFT; see Smith and Pell 2003). The point also has been noted that law courts count observer testimony as relevant to the determination of whether or not a person perpetrated (that is, caused) a crime; and finally, the so-called medical model of decision making has been severely attacked, and this has led to further attention being paid to the complex relationship between evidence and policy (see Moss 2007).
- Supporters of the "gold standard," and those who use it as a basis for funding policy, overlook the enormous scientific and policy values of not only establishing that a treatment T caused the observed effect E, but also of discovering the biological, psychological, or social causal mechanism that is at work.[12] For without knowledge of the underlying mechanism, a policy that mandates use of T could well meet with failure (the policy will in general be successful only if the conditions allowing the functioning of the underlying mechanism are also present); furthermore, the stability of the relation between T and E cannot even be guaranteed absent knowledge of the mechanism that links them (as Weber 2007, nicely shows).
- There is an interesting difference in the way that the sociocultural context in which all humans live has been conceptualized. Most qualitative researchers, as well as many philosophers, regard this context as part of the causal nexus that influences individuals; as Brian Fay put it, "Agents become agents only by being enculturated and socialized into a particular culture and society... which continue to provide the means in and through which agents can act" (Fay 1996, p. 69). In contrast, many quantitative researchers adopt the definition of "cause" advocated by Paul Holland in what is regarded as a classic article, "Statistics and Causal Inference" (Holland 1986). This article gives an analysis of the experimental model in great technical depth, and in a section titled "What Can Be a Cause?" Holland writes as follows: "Put as bluntly and as

contentiously as possible, in this article I take the position that causes are only those things that could, in principle, be treatments in experiments" (Holland 1986, p. 954). Many readers of this paper have become convinced that sociocultural background factors, which are hard to conceive of as "experimental treatments," are not causes, and they are treated often as something like nuisance factors. At the very least a misunderstanding with qualitative researchers arises. While agreeing that sociocultural factors are indeed causes, I also have some sympathy with Holland, and I offer the suggestion that his words have not been read carefully enough—he is elucidating the logic of the experimental model, and *within this framework* he is insisting (offering a stipulative definition? or is it reportive?) that a cause is always a treatment—the whole point of the experimental design is to maximize the authority with which it can be said that this particular treatment caused/produced this effect. Trouble arises only if Holland is interpreted as legislating the general use of "cause."

There is more that deserves to be said about causation and education; for example, the discussion has not touched on the fact that educational policies can be conceived of as causal recipes. But it is hoped that enough has been covered to indicate the potential of the topic to generate issues of great philosophical interest.

11. CONCLUSION

This chapter has covered rather convoluted terrain, and its purpose may have become obscured, so in concluding I shall be as blunt as possible. It has not been my intention to produce a blanket defense of the work of empirical educational researchers against philosophical criticism, for indeed there is much to criticize and if there are errors or confusions or conceptual blunders, these need to be exposed. But my main purpose has been to suggest several other things: Educational research raises many of the issues familiar to philosophers of social science, but raises them in a socially relevant but highly charged and complex context, and philosophers might find this both refreshing and challenging once they become familiar with the topography of the field; empirical researchers have done some important work on difficult issues that raises substantive, but more especially methodological, issues that could profitably engage the attention of philosophers; and crucially, *both* the research and philosophical communities stand to gain from this informed attention, for it is my belief that members of the former will think about their work with greater clarity and members of the latter group will be led down interesting philosophical paths.

NOTES

Some of the ground covered in this essay has been traversed in other recent publications; see Phillips 2005, 2006a, 2006b. However, the present discussion reworks or completely restates much of this material, profiting from feedback and from further time for reflection; and there is much that is new.

1. But even this is contested by some who see the field as chimerical, and others point out that the link between research findings and policies is quite complex.

2. For an entertaining but ultimately frustrating example of the diversity of approaches to educational research, see the introductory text by Paul 2004; adherents of different approaches each comment upon the same set of examples of "research/inquiry."

3. For example, see Lincoln and Cannella 2004, fn. 2, where for sinning in this way I am labeled a positivist and my arguments not even referred to—this, despite my having written at length about the demise of positivism and my admiration of Popper!

4. Thus, a philosophical research group that has been meeting annually in Belgium recently produced a volume aimed at critiquing the "what works" doctrine (Smeyers and Depaepe 2006), but in the judgment of the present author the book is far too diffuse to be an effective response to a key volume written in support of the doctrine (Mosteller and Boruch 2002). Indeed, this latter volume is not mentioned at all by Smeyers and Depaepe. In 2007, Gert Biesta published an essay on "Why 'What Works' Won't Work" that purports to be a knock-down critique of that approach, but during the course of the essay it becomes clear that it is incorrectly titled, for Biesta's conclusion is a modest one that few would oppose—"an *exclusive* emphasis on 'what works' will simply not work" (Biesta 2007, p. 22, emphasis added). It is also worth noting that this essay appears in a philosophy of education journal where it is unlikely to come to the attention of those who most need to read it.

5. Four journals—only one of them in philosophy of education, and two of the others being research oriented—have devoted special numbers to the discussion of the NRC report. The majority of responses were quite negative. See *Educational Researcher* (2002), *Qualitative Inquiry* (2004), *Educational Theory* (2005), and *Teachers College Record* (2005). I should note that I was a member of the NRC writing panel.

6. These discussions are not of equal quality, but they do take one or more cases of research seriously. It is not an exhaustive list.

7. Including introductory essays, there are twenty-one pieces in this two-issue symposium. Three or four of these are on issues directly related to the conduct of research; the others rarely (if ever) cite, let alone discuss, actual examples of mainstream empirical research. A few are not about research at all. The vast majority of references in all the papers are to views of other philosophers. However, this is not to say the essays were uninteresting or uninformative, but they were more informative about the views of philosophers than about research.

8. Presumably, the swipe is intended for the RFT; but experiments are not accurately characterized as "statistically conceived," but rather are attempts to instantiate John Stuart Mill's methods of logic, especially the "method of difference." Many researchers who carry out RFTs use statistics, but their use is not mandatory. The remark is yet another indication of the great antipathy that exists within the philosophy of education community toward much empirical educational research.

9. For a helpful discussion of this troublesome notion, see Siegel 2006.

10. It is important to note that the labels used here are themselves a matter of deep contention, and mask important differences within each "camp." So the labels are used here

with hesitation and purely for convenience. Roughly, "qualitative" refers to a broad family of approaches, including ethnographies, studies using observational techniques, interview data, and questionnaires; "quantitative" covers true and quasi experiments, correlational studies, and the like.

11. Many educationists—philosophers as well as researchers—hold erroneous ideas about positivism. See Phillips 2004.

12. Social mechanisms and their importance are well discussed in Hedstrom and Swedberg 1998.

REFERENCES

AERA. (2006). *2006 Annual Meeting Program: Education Research in the Public Interest.* Washington, DC: American Educational Research Association.

Alexander, H. (2006). "A View from Somewhere: Explaining the Paradigms of Educational Research." *Journal of Philosophy of Education* 40: 205–21.

Barrow, R. (1984). *Giving Teaching Back to Teachers.* Sussex: Wheatsheaf.

Biesta, G. (2007). "Why 'What Works' Won't Work: Evidence-Based Practice and the Democratic Deficit in Educational Research." *Educational Theory* 57 (1): 1–22.

Bridges, D., and R. Smith, eds. (2006). "Special Issues: Philosophy, Methodology, and Educational Research. Parts 1 and 2." *Journal of Philosophy of Education* 40: 131–286; 417–574.

Campbell, D., and J. Stanley. (1963). *Experimental and Quasi-Expherimental Designs for Research.* Chicago: Rand McNally.

Carr, D. (2003). *Making Sense of Education.* London: Routledge-Falmer.

Cook, T. (1993). "A Quasi-Sampling Theory of the Generalization of Causal Relationships." *New Directions for Program Evaluation* 57: 39–82.

—— and D. Campbell. *Quasi-Experimentation: Design and Analysis Issues for Field Settings.* Chicago: Rand McNally.

Denzin, N., and Y. Lincoln, eds. (1998). *The Landscape of Qualitative Research.* Thousand Oaks, CA: Sage.

Egan, K. (1983). *Education and Psychology.* New York: Teachers College Press.

—— (2002). *Getting it WRONG from the Beginning.* New Haven, CT: Yale University Press.

Fay, B. (1996). *Contemporary Philosophy of Social Science.* Oxford: Blackwell.

Gage, N. L. (1978). *The Scientific Basis of the Art of Teaching.* New York: Teachers College Press.

—— (1994). "The Scientific Status of the Behavioral Sciences. The Case of Research on Teaching." *Teaching and Teacher Education* 10: 565–77.

—— and D. Berliner. (1988). *Educational Psychology,* 4th ed. Boston: Houghton Mifflin.

Geertz, C. (1973). *The Interpretation of Cultures.* New York: Basic Books.

Hammersley, M. (1992). *What's Wrong With Ethnography?* London: Routledge.

—— (2006). "Philosophy's Contribution to Social Science Research on Education." *Journal of Philosophy of Education* 40(2): 273–86.

Hardie, C. D. (1965/1973). "Research and Progress in Education." In *Philosophy of Educational Research,* ed. H. S. Broudy, R. H. Ennis and L. Krimerman (pp. 87–101). New York: Wiley.

Hedstrom, P., and R. Swedberg. (1998). *Social Mechanisms: An Analytical Approach to Social Theory.* Cambridge: Cambridge University Press.

Hirst, P., and R. Peters. (1970). *The Logic of Education.* London: Routledge and Kegan Paul.

Holland, P. (1986). "Statistics and Causal Inference." *Journal of the American Statistical Association* 81: 945–60.

Howe, K. (2003). *Closing Methodological Divides: Toward Democratic Educational Research.* Dordrecht: Kluwer.

—— (2004). "A Critique of Experimentalism." *Qualitative Inquiry* 10(1): 42–61.

Kincaid, H. (2002). "Social Science." In. *The Blackwell Guide to the Philosophy of Science,* ed. P. Machamer and M. Silberstein (pp. 290–311). Oxford: Blackwell.

Lather, P. (2004). "This IS Your Father's Paradigm: Government Intrusion and the Case of Qualitative Research in Education." *Qualitative Inquiry* 10(1): 15–34.

Lincoln, Y., and G. Canella. (2004). "Dangerous Discourses: Methodological Conservatism and Governmental Regimes of Truth." *Qualitative Inquiry* 10: 5–14.

Machamer, P. (2002). "A Brief Historical Introduction to the Philosophy of *Science.*" In *The Blackwell Guide to the Philosophy of Science,* ed. P. Machamer and M. Silberstein (pp. 1–17). Oxford: Blackwell.

Maxwell, J. (2004). "Causal Explanation, Qualitative Research, and Scientific Inquiry in Education." *Educational Researcher* 33: 3–11.

Moss, P., ed. (2007). *Evidence and Decision-Making.* 106th Yearbook, Part 1, of the National Society for the Study of Education. Malden: Blackwell.

Mosteller, F., and R. Boruch, eds. (2002) *Evidence Matters.* Washington, DC: Brookings Institution Press.

National Research Council (NRC). (2002). *Scientific Research in Education.* Washington, DC: National Academies Press.

Paul, J. (2004). *Introduction to the Philosophies of Research and Criticism in Education and the Social Sciences.* Upper Saddle River, NJ: Pearson/Merrill/Prentice-Hall.

Phillips, D. C. (1983). "On Describing a Student's Cognitive Structure." *Educational Psychologist* 18(2): 59–74.

—— (2000). *The Expanded Social Scientist's Bestiary.* Lanham, MD: Rowman and Littlefield.

—— (2004). "Two Decades After 'After the Wake: Postpositivistic Educational Thought.'" *Science and Education* 13: 67–84.

—— (2005). "The Contested Nature of Educational Research (and Why Philosophy of Education Offers Little Help)." *Journal of Philosophy of Education* 39(4): 577–97.

—— (2006a). "Muddying the Waters: The Many Purposes of Educational Inquiry." In *The SAGE Handbook for Research in Education,* ed. C. Conrad and R. Serlin (pp. 7–21). Thousand Oaks, CA: Sage.

—— (2006b). "A Guide for the Perplexed: Scientific Educational Research, Methodolatry, and the Gold versus Platinum Standards." *Educational Research Review* 1: 15–26.

—— and N. Burbules. (2000). *Postpositivism and Educational Research.* Boulder, CO: Rowman and Littlefield.

—— and J. Nicolayev. (1978). "Kohlbergian Moral Development: a Progressing or Degenerating Research Program?" *Educational Theory* 28: 286–301.

Schelling, T. (1978). *Micromotives and Macrobehavior.* New York: Norton.

Schwandt, T. (1997). *Qualitative Inquiry: A Dictionary of Terms.* Thousand Oaks, CA: Sage.

Siegel, H. (2006). "Epistemological Diversity and Education Research: Much Ado About Nothing Much?" *Educational Researcher* 35(2): 3–12.

Smeyers, P. (2006). "The Relevance of Irrelevant Research; The Irrelevance of Relevant Research." In *Educational Research: Why 'What Works' Doesn't Work,* ed. P. Smeyers and M. Depaepe (pp. 95–108). Dordrecht: Springer.

—— (2007). "On the Limits of Empirical Educational Research, Beyond the Fantasy: A Rejoinder to D. C. Phillips." In *Philosophy, Methodology and Educational Research*, ed. D. Bridges and R. Smith (pp. 333–50). Oxford: Blackwell.

—— and Depaepe, M. (2006). *Educational Research: Why 'What Works' Doesn't Work*. Dordrecht: Springer.

Smith, G., and J. Pell. (2003). "Parachute Use to Prevent Death and Major Trauma Related to Gravitational Challenge: Systematic Review of Randomized Controlled Trials." *British Medical Journal* 327: 1459–61.

Stronach, I., and M. MacLure. (1997). *Educational Research Undone: The Postmodern Embrace*. Buckingham: Open University Press.

Tooley, J., and D. Darby. (1998). *Educational Research: A Critique*. London: OFSTED.

Weber, E. (2007). "Social Mechanisms, Causal Inference, and the Policy Relevance of Social Science." *Philosophy of the Social Sciences* 37: 348–59.

PART V

SOCIAL AND POLITICAL ISSUES

CHAPTER 22

EDUCATING FOR INDIVIDUAL FREEDOM AND DEMOCRATIC CITIZENSHIP: IN UNITY AND DIVERSITY THERE IS STRENGTH

AMY GUTMANN

IN the epilogue to *Democratic Education*, I outline a democratic approach to multicultural education and illustrate some of its practical implications for schooling in the United States.1 The approach is broadly applicable because it is informed by a democratic ideal of civic equality: individuals should be treated and treat one another as equal citizens, regardless of their gender, race, ethnicity, or religion.

More or less civic equality distinguishes more from less democratic societies. Democratic education—publicly supported education that is defensible according to a democratic ideal—should educate children so that they are capable of assuming the rights and correlative responsibilities of equal citizenship, which include respecting other people's equal rights. In short, democratic education should both express and develop the capacity of all children to become equal citizens.

Multicultural education in democracies can help further civic equality in two importantly different ways: first, by expressing the democratic value of tolerating cultural differences that are consistent with civic equality; and second, by recognizing the role that cultural differences have played in shaping society and the world in which children live. Not all education that goes by the name "multicultural" serves the ideal of civic equality in one of these two ways, but democratic multicultural education can (and I argue should) do so. Toleration and recognition of cultural differences, I argue, are both desirable parts of multicultural education.

If toleration and recognition of cultural differences are both democratically desirable, then the stark contrast often drawn between a liberal politics of toleration and a nonliberal politics of recognition represents a false dichotomy. Liberal democracies can defend a set of multicultural educational practices that exhibit both toleration and recognition of cultural differences, depending on their content and social context.

To defend a politics of toleration and recognition, we must differentiate among cultural practices, since not all cultural practices deserve to be tolerated, let alone recognized as parts of a democratic culture. In a democracy, a defensible standard of differentiation by publicly supported schools emerges from asking whether the practices are consistent with educating children for equal citizenship. As a general rule, democratic education should tolerate or recognize the teaching of cultural differences that aid, or at least do not impede, the education of children as civic equals. Democratic education defends the many kinds of multicultural education that are consistent with the aim of expressing the civic equality of citizens and educating children for civic equality. In a democracy, citizens are empowered to disagree about what educational practices are defensible on democratic grounds, and consequently to deliberate over their disagreements. Deliberative disagreement among a diverse citizenry is an important part of the ongoing public education of multicultural democracies.

In this chapter, I examine how well civic equality, toleration, and recognition travel in multicultural democracies, and what their implications are for different forms of diversity. If multicultural democratic education is now a movement worldwide, and if it is defined by widely shared democratic aims, it also faces a tremendous variety of cultural, socioeconomic, and political conditions even within democracies. In many parts of the world, such as Western Europe, multicultural education programs have developed largely to accommodate relatively recent (post-World War II) immigrant populations. In countries such as Belgium, Canada, the Netherlands, and South Africa, the debate over multicultural education revolves as much around the demands of more settled ethnic, religious, and linguistic minority groups, each of whom claims authority over its "own" children's education. In the United States with regard to Native Americans, and in Canada with regard to the Inuit and other "First Peoples," as in many other countries, multicultural education is also concerned with the needs of indigenous populations that have been oppressed and marginalized by the larger country in which they exist. In still other situations in some of the same countries—the United States is a particularly conspicuous case because of its legacy of slavery—historically oppressed, nonnative minorities make special claims in the name of multiculturalism on an educational system.

These examples and myriad others indicate that minority populations that make claims on multicultural education are enormously varied. They are varied in more complex ways than is generally recognized. Some theorists have argued that indigenous groups have claims to a politics of recognition while immigrant groups do not. Immigrant groups, they argue, come to a country voluntarily and therefore can be expected to give up more of their native culture while indigenous groups were forced to integrate when they should have been permitted to perpetuate their culture. The problem with this argument is that it grossly simplifies, to the point of distorting, the condition of many immigrant as well as indigenous populations. Many immigrants were forced to escape their native countries and had little if any choice as to where to go. We cannot justifiably treat immigration either today or in the past as a purely voluntary phenomenon. Nor can we assume that the descendants of immigrants or indigenous populations face the same conditions as their ancestors. Some turn out to be better and others worse off than their ancestors with regard to the relevant democratic standard of civic equality.

Depending on their socioeconomic situation, members of immigrant and indigenous groups may be treated more or less as civic equals, and find themselves more or less free to remain in a country and cultivate the culture of their choice. If voluntary residence is the basis for a democracy's refusal to recognize a group's distinctive culture, then almost all groups have some legitimate claim to recognition, not only toleration. This is because citizenship is largely not a voluntary phenomenon. Voluntarism is not the primary dimension by which to judge claims of toleration and recognition. Civic equality is. If claims to toleration and recognition are assessed on grounds of civic equality, then among the most significant variations between groups will be their tolerance or intolerance of their dissenting members and other groups. A rule of thumb might be: a democracy should tolerate and recognize those cultures that are compatible with mutual toleration and respect within and across cultural groups.

Even limiting ourselves to democratic societies for the sake of focus, we notice how varied cultural groups are with regard to their willingness and ability to live together in a context of mutual toleration and respect. The principle of civic equality is general enough to be applicable as a starting point for multicultural education to all democratic societies. Yet educators, who have practical aims, also need to be able to move from the general to the specific. Just as educational policies unsupported by democratic principles remain arbitrary and unjustified to the people who are bound by them, general principles unlinked to educational policies and practices remain practically impotent and pragmatically untested. Any theory of democratic multicultural education, therefore, should be both principled and adaptable to variations among groups and contexts. It needs to probe the implications of diverse cultures and conditions for its own commitment to educating children for civic equality and for the freedom to choose their way of life.

1. Aiming for Civic Equality

The fundamental commitment of a democratic approach to publicly funded education (which I call democratic education, for short) is as follows: All children—regardless of their cultural background, ethnicity, race, gender, or religion—are entitled to an education adequate to equal citizenship. The issue that immediately arises within democratic education is that citizens often reasonably disagree about what constitutes an education adequate to equal citizenship.

Deliberative democracy can make a virtue out of the necessity of such disagreement. The virtue is that democracies that respect reasonable disagreement can creatively combine unity and diversity in democratic education. Effective education is locally delivered, although oversight mechanisms range from the local to the national and even international. Diverse communities can institute many variations on the common theme of educating children for equal citizenship. Creative tensions—multicultural variations on the theme of democratic education—all accept civic equality as an aim, but elaborate in innumerable ways not only on the means to more civic equality but also on the other valuable ends of education. Civic equality is a general aim of education that leaves room for democratic education to defend a great deal of diversity.

Not all disagreements in democratic societies, however, produce creative tensions in democratic education. Destructive tensions occur when dominant members of the government or opposition groups subordinate the very aim of educating children as civic equals to perpetuate their own power. In such instances, group power or culture is confused with the legitimate authority to educate. Children are then implicitly treated as the mere vehicles to transmit power or culture from one generation to the next. Educators then assume a position of absolute authority over the education of their "own" children. This practice impedes the civic equality of these children as well as their ability to develop the tools to choose their life. Whereas creative tensions propel changes in how democratic multicultural education is conceived and designed out of a shared aim of better educating children for both civic equality and the ability to choose one's life, destructive tensions challenge these very aims.

Although destructive tensions threaten democratic education, toleration permits the profession of certain destructive positions. The democratic hope is for more creative and fewer destructive challenges. Civic equality calls for an education that empowers adults as equal citizens, and that empowerment entails (among other things) the freedom to disagree about the demands of democratic education. All we can say here is that it is a reasonable democratic hope that disagreement within the bounds of equal toleration and recognition will be on balance creative.

The diverse kinds of multicultural groups further highlight creative and destructive challenges to educating children for civic equality in multicultural democracies. Toleration and recognition of diversity should be structured as unifying practices when they aim at educating all children for civic equality. Not all multicultural practices, however, share this aim. How can democrats differentiate between multicultural practices that do and do not educate children for (more or less) civic equality? To answer this question, I draw primarily on the United States for examples because it has experienced large and recurrent cycles of immigration, has substantial indigenous communities, has a large linguistic minority, and also contains major groups of historically oppressed citizens. All of these features make it useful in developing a principled yet context-sensitive approach to multicultural education. That said, I also draw on other national contexts, and welcome scholars who focus on other countries to add both critically and constructively to this project.

Whatever examples we draw upon, two separate questions need to be asked:

- How can democratic education strive for civic equality under conditions of diversity?
- Do some multicultural conditions successfully challenge the democratic framework itself, and suggest the need for a guiding principle other than civic equality in some contexts?

Before considering these questions, I should clarify the terms *multicultural education, toleration,* and *recognition.*

2. MULTICULTURAL EDUCATION: TOLERATION AND RECOGNITION

To consider what kinds of multicultural education are defensible, we need to use the term *multicultural* in a way that is not polemical or question-begging. Anything multicultural is sometimes said to rely on a belief in moral relativism. Tying multicultural education to moral relativism indefensibly narrows the use of the term and thereby prejudices multicultural education in many people's minds (both for and against). *Multicultural,* as I use it here, refers to a state of schooling, society, or the world that contains many cultures that affect one another by virtue of the interactions of people who identify with or rely upon these cultures. A culture consists of patterns of thinking, speaking, and acting that are associated with a human community larger than a few families.

Multicultural schools and societies are by no means new. As interdependence, communication, and commerce have expanded, most societies and the world have become increasingly multicultural. Individuals themselves are multicultural; they rely upon many cultures, not only one, in living their lives. Individuals are also more than the sum of their cultural identities; they are creative agents who use many cultural resources to live lives that are not simply the product of external cultural forces. Individual identities can therefore express diverse, interdynamic cultures and they can also express their own creative way of interpreting those cultures.

To force anyone to choose between being multicultural and being a free agent is therefore a false forced choice. We must not assume that any individual is completely constituted by a combination of cultural identities. People can creatively constitute their identities, but they cannot do so *de novo*. People are born within complex social contexts, and they become human agents by interacting with other people within culturally loaded contexts. Human creativity and choice operate against a background of interactive and dynamic cultural resources. Cultures offer contexts of choice,[2] but since human beings are creative multicultural agents, they can reinterpret the various contexts of choice in which they live.

A standard debate over how best to respond to diverse cultural resources and identities within a single democracy often poses a stark choice between two options. The first is privatizing differences in order to realize a public realm unified around principles—such as equal liberty and opportunity—that are often (misleadingly) called culturally neutral principles. The second option is publicly recognizing differences and thereby dividing the public realm into equally valuable but separatist cultural group identities. The two options offer very different understandings of the nature of citizenship and mutual respect among individuals who identify with various cultural groups. Either citizens should tolerate their cultural differences by privatizing them and acting in public as if cultural differences do not exist, or they should respect their cultural differences by publicly recognizing them and treating all as equally valuable but separate group identities.

The first response to multiculturalism is often identified as supporting liberal values, which are considered culturally neutral, and the second response as opposing them and substituting culturally specific values for culturally neutral ones. This opposition between toleration and recognition, as I argue in *Democratic Education*, is misleading. Also misleading is the contrast between culturally specific and culturally neutral values. No values are culturally neutral in the sense of being equally conducive or acceptable to all cultures. Yet some values can be defended from the vantage point of many—even if not all—cultures that are common in and across democracies. The latter phenomenon—which might be called cross-cultural principles—should not be confused with culturally neutral principles. Toleration and recognition, moreover, are not diametrically opposed. In their most democratically defensible forms, toleration and recognition of cultural diversity are compatible.

Toleration at its best implies that individuals be given the right to practice their cultural differences in private, but it does not require citizens or states to treat individuals as if their cultural differences were irrelevant to their public standing.[3] Recognition at its best implies respect for various cultural differences—for example, by integrating the cultural contributions of diverse groups into the history curriculum—but recognition does not entail treating all cultural practices or contributions to history as equally valuable.[4] Taken at their best, toleration and public recognition are compatible in both theory and practice.

Of course, some practices that are defended on grounds of toleration or recognition may be indefensible. Tolerating or recognizing the equal value of a cultural practice such as female genital mutilation when it is a form of torture practiced on young girls is not what toleration or recognition justifiably calls for. A democratic educational system has a responsibility to recognize racist and other discriminating ideologies for what they are, and not treat them as having positive public value in the school curriculum or elsewhere in public life just because some people value them. To be even minimally decent, a democracy cannot tolerate every practice that every cultural group, subgroup, or individual deems desirable on cultural grounds. Democracies need to ask whether cultural practices respect the civic equality of individuals. Civic equality should serve as the guiding principle for applying both toleration and recognition in multicultural contexts.

Democratic education should recognize important cultural contributions of different groups. Democracies also should tolerate diverse cultural practices that may offend some people's sensibilities but that do not violate anyone's rights to civic equality. Toleration and public recognition of cultural differences are, therefore, two different responses to two different sets of issues that arise partly out of cultural differences.

In its educational system, a democracy should not only tolerate cultural differences that are consistent with educating children for civic equality but should also recognize the cultural contributions of different groups. Why? Because such recognition helps express the civic equality of (and respect for) members of different cultural groups. A democracy that aims to educate children for civic equality, therefore, must not be opposed to publicly recognizing cultural differences, as any good multicultural curriculum reflects, yet it must be opposed to ceding rights to cultural groups to engage in practices that oppress individuals (whether insiders or outsiders to the group) in the name of recognizing cultural difference.

A defensible response of democratic education to multicultural diversity, therefore, incorporates both toleration and recognition. It rejects the dichotomy "privatize and tolerate or publicly recognize" when it comes to terms with the fundamental phenomenon of a world in which all societies and individual identities are increasingly multicultural. What sorts of steps should educational systems take both to recognize and to tolerate multicultural diversity? I will outline the approaches of recognition and toleration, both of which are important to any successful multicultural education initiative, but each of which has a special role and therefore independent ethical relevance.

3. PUBLIC RECOGNITION THROUGH CURRICULAR DESIGN

"Old" minority groups, including indigenous groups and historically oppressed groups like African Americans, have special claims on the shape of national educational curricula. For them, the principle of recognition has a historical dimension: it requires that the wrongs they suffered as well as the goods they contributed to society be acknowledged alongside those of the majority groups. The implications are enormous for democratic education, since most of the curriculum, as well as the culture of the school more generally, needs to be alert to the demands of multicultural recognition.

To teach U.S. history, for instance, largely without reference to the experiences, including the oppressions and the contributions of Native Americans, African Americans, Latino Americans, and Asian Americans, constitutes a compound failure. The failure is intellectual: that of not recognizing the historical role of many different cultures, the contributions along with the oppressions of individuals who identify with those cultures. But the failure is more than intellectual; it is also a moral failure judged by democratic principles. It morally damages democracy—and expresses a lack of respect for individuals by virtue of their group identity—to convey a false impression that their ancestors have not suffered wrongs or contributed goods in making society what it is today.

Why do historical wrongs inflicted on members of minority groups need to be recognized alongside their contributions? Again, the reasons are both intellectual and ethical. Learning the history of the oppression of slaves, for example, in the United States is crucial to understanding the past and analyzing contemporary social realities. Assessing the past and present also depends on coming to terms with oppression. Democratic ethics cannot do without a citizenry that is capable of being critical of its past partly (but not only) in order to construct a better future.

Something analogous can be said about the value of including women's voices in the curriculum for both intellectual and ethical reasons, which are closely connected. Like other oppressed groups, and partly owing to their oppression, women have some distinct experiences and sensibilities that call for recognition. When textbooks excluded women's voices and experiences, they conveyed the false impression that women have contributed little or nothing to the cultural resources that should be accessible to everyone in a democratic society. Conveying this impression is also an ethical wrong: it imposes an extra burden on members of oppressed groups, making it more difficult for them to be empowered to share as civic equals in shaping their society. Negative stereotyping of women and minority groups is exacerbated by their absence from, or negative stereotyping within, school curricula and educational practices more generally. Men as well as women develop falsely unequal impressions of their civic worth, public standing, and social entitlements.

Even apart from any probable effects, excluding the contributions of different cultures constitutes a moral failing in its own right. Exclusion represents a failure to respect those individuals as equal citizens who identify with less dominant cultures. The most basic premise of democratic education—respect for all individuals as civic equals—calls for a history that recognizes both the oppressions and the social contributions of individuals. To overlook the ways in which minorities have been oppressed by, or contributed to, society is to disrespect not only those cultures but, more fundamentally, also the individuals who identify with the cultures. Democracy owes equal respect to individuals as civic equals, not to groups, but disrespecting some groups conveys disrespect to the individuals who identify with those groups.

Equal respect can be manifest in various parts of a school curriculum. Literature can no longer be taught as a field that belongs exclusively, or even largely, to "dead white males." Toni Morrison takes her place beside the greatest male novelists, as the literary voice of an African-American woman, but not only as that. Morrison is also a great literary voice who can be appreciated across many cultures. Such cross-cultural appreciation is another contribution of multicultural recognition and a manifestation of equal respect for individuals, whether they are women or men, this color, ethnicity, religion, or that. Equal respect entails the inclusion of books such as *Beloved* in school curricula that represent the oppression of groups in literary as well as historical form.

Multicultural aims for the curriculum legitimately extend beyond history and literature. Some schools, for example, make it a point of teaching math in a multicultural way by representing different cultures in the word problems assigned to students. Traditional math can be well taught in ways that capture the cultural imaginations of students.[5] Nothing is lost and something valuable is gained in the process. Schools can sensitively introduce students to different cultures by recognizing how different groups celebrate the New Year, and by analyzing both the similarities and differences in holiday celebrations. Once again, the intellectual and the ethical can mutually reinforce one another, as they should, in democratic education without infringing on anyone's legitimate freedom.[6]

Democratic education supports a "politics of recognition" based on respect for individuals and their equal rights as citizens, not on deference to tradition, proportional representation of groups, or the survival rights of cultures.[7] The practice of history textbook publishing in the United States has often perverted this politics of recognition. Succumbing to strong market and political pressures, publishers sometimes produce history textbooks that include only positive references to traditional American heroes and only enough references to people of politically prominent ethnicities to achieve proportional representation. These practices are counterproductive to engaging students in learning about the history and politics of their society, an engagement that is essential to teaching the skills and virtues of democratic citizenship and respecting every individual as an equal citizen.

Practices like these are not the inevitable product of a democratic process. Democratic processes can be, and in some states actually are, more deliberative and more conducive to developing the deliberative skills of democratic citizenship. Several states, Tennessee and Virginia among them, along with various inner-city public schools and elite private schools, have demonstrated this. They were sufficiently impressed to adopt a textbook that can serve as a model for deliberative democratic education. *A History of US* by Joy Hakim presents American history as a series of narratives that are inclusive and accurate.[8] With an engaging and broadly accessible style, its content is relatively complex. Equally important, the narratives highlight the relevance to democratic citizenship of choices that individuals and organized groups make in politics.

When texts and teachers present narratives of ethical choices in politics, they set the stage for students to think about those choices as democratic citizens. A multicultural history should not imply—let alone claim—that vastly different beliefs and practices are equally valuable. Diverse beliefs and practices are subjects of understanding and evaluation. Appreciating the importance of a multicultural curriculum is only the prologue to teaching skills of understanding and evaluation. The value of any belief or practice cannot simply be assumed; it must be assessed.

Appreciation, understanding, and evaluation are three capacities of democratic citizenship that multicultural education can cultivate. Classrooms that include students from diverse cultural backgrounds can facilitate such cultivation, especially if teachers engage their students in deliberating about their commonalities and differences. Teachers who are attuned to the desirability of deliberation in multicultural classrooms, and find ways of making such deliberation productive of appreciation, understanding, and evaluation of commonalities and differences, are models of democratic educators. This is because open-minded learning in a multicultural setting—to which students bring diverse presuppositions and convictions—is a prelude to democratic deliberation in a multicultural society and world. Democratic deliberation, and the open-minded teaching that anticipates it, encourages all citizens to appreciate, understand, and assess differences that are matters of mutual concern.

4. TOLERATING DIVERSITY WITHOUT ENDORSING EVERY DIFFERENCE

Not all matters that are important to us as individuals are—or should be—of mutual concern for citizens in a democracy. Democratic education calls for public recognition when its absence would be discriminatory or disrespectful—as in the case of textbooks that exclude the contributions and experiences of oppressed minorities or women. Some cultural practices, such as whether or how individuals worship, should not be matters of mutual concern among citizens. For people to be free to live their own lives, some of their cultural practices must also be free from public regulation and even scrutiny. Multicultural education, therefore, should not suggest that every cultural difference needs to be a matter of mutual concern.

To the extent that there is a mutual concern about religious worship, for example, it is directed not at appreciating, understanding, and assessing competing cultural practices but at tolerating them. The mutual concern is that citizens tolerate religious differences that do not harm others, not that they endorse or otherwise assess or mutually justify those differences by a common ethical standard. To put the same point somewhat differently, toleration of diverse ways of worshiping is what is mutually justifiable in a deliberative democracy, not the diverse ways of worshiping themselves. A multicultural world includes a wide range of conceptions of the good life, none of which needs to be mutually justifiable to all citizens. Why? In a decent democracy, the state does not dictate or regulate belief. (If the manifestation of belief directly harms others—for example, by leading people to sacrifice others for the sake of salvation—then coercion may be justified but only when aimed at protecting the equal liberty of others.) For many people, religious belief constitutes some of their deepest ethical commitments. To coerce or regulate such commitments is to not respect the persons who hold them. In addition, the state has no expertise in deciding the "right" way to worship. It, therefore, should leave such decisions to individuals to decide according to their own deepest convictions. Freedom of worship, therefore, can be considered a basic right of democratic citizenship and honored as such in democratic education.

A democratic state takes toleration seriously to the extent that it does not impose ways of worshiping and the like on students in publicly subsidized schools. It, therefore, does not publicly recognize one way or the other of worshiping as proper or improper in its own right. It leaves citizens free to worship as they choose provided that they respect the equal liberty of others. Worship is then "privatized" only in the very specific sense that it is not a matter of state endorsement or recognition of its "rightness." Worship still can be a public matter in the broad sense of being an overtly social activity, which is publicly protected by law.

Hard questions arise in multicultural education with regard to religious freedom—for example, when individuals or groups want to manifest their religiosity in various ways within public schools. Should a democratic state tolerate manifestations of religion within public schools? Religious toleration is extremely important to the just treatment of all minorities who diverge from the dominant ways of worship. But religious toleration becomes especially salient in the way in which a democratic government treats recent immigrant populations with unfamiliar ways of manifesting their religiosity. These groups typically do not demand a separate school system or public recognition (in the sense of endorsement) of their particular religions. What they typically do demand is toleration based on an equitable rather than an unfairly skewed interpretation of the toleration principle. The demand for a fair application of democratic principles applies to decisions as basic as who will be educated and how. Recent French history offers a paradigmatic example of public conflict over what constitutes a fair interpretation of the principle of toleration.

The "affair of the scarf" began in France when three Muslim girls attended their public high school in Creil, France, wearing hijab or chador—head coverings that are demanded by some interpretations of orthodox Islam. French public schools are, by law and centuries-long tradition, secular. A 1937 law prohibits the wearing of religious symbols in government-run schools, but yarmulkes and crucifixes have been permitted on grounds that they are "inconspicuous" religious symbols.[9] Not surprisingly, given its greater unfamiliarity to mainstream French culture, the hijab was considered "conspicuous." The principal in Creil insisted that the three girls remove their hijab or be expelled from class. When they refused and were expelled from class, the controversy became national, and soon international, by its audience.

Some democrats defend expulsion because religious garb that symbolizes civic inequality—not least the inequality of women—must be excluded from public schools. A democracy is responsible for publicly educating children to become civic equals, and one way of doing so is to keep all differentiating dress that symbolizes civic inequality out of public schools. Other democrats respond by denying that the hijab must be interpreted in a way that blocks educating Muslim girls for civic equality, which after all is the aim of democratic education. These democrats oppose expelling children for wearing religious symbols when they are otherwise willing to be publicly educated as civic equals. They find the expulsion wrong in principle and counterproductive in practice to democratic ends.[10] In an equal but opposite response to those who defend the expulsion, these democrats agree that a democracy is responsible for publicly educating children to become civic equals despite their religious differences, but they argue that religious toleration within public schools is a principled means toward this important end.

A democratic rationale for tolerating religious differences, as this example suggests, is to help citizens understand that many disagreements in public life are compatible with sharing a society as civic equals. It is important to note that this rationale is not well captured by the notion of privatization. To tolerate the wearing of yarmulkes, crucifixes, and hijab in public schools would be neither to privatize these religious symbols nor to publicly endorse them. Rather, it would be to demonstrate that religious differences can be accommodated within public schools as long as they do not block the aim of educating children as civic equals. The controversy over the hijab can then be viewed as one of democratic disagreement: agreement on the end of civic equality but disagreement on the justifiable and practical means of achieving the end.

A question that called for democratic deliberation was the following: Would the willingness or the refusal of the French public school system to tolerate the hijab be more conducive to educating Muslim girls for civic equality? If educators and citizens alike publicly ask this question, then they can publicly deliberate over their disagreements, and their answers—even if divergent, as answers often are in a democracy that protects free speech—will be guided by a manifestly shared commitment to educating for civic equality. What policy within the range of options available to French society is more likely to aid in educating Muslim girls for civic equality? This question is very different from the racist response of those who argued for the immediate expulsion of all Muslim immigrants from France and the closing of the borders to people who do not share a French pedigree.

Multicultural education can demonstrate that symbols have different meanings to different people in different contexts. A hijab does not need to be viewed as a symbol of gender inequality, even if it is now widely viewed as such.[11] The meaning of symbols varies and changes over time and in cultural contexts. Recognizing various symbolic interpretations as reasonable is a prelude to considering how a system of public schooling can best aid in educating children of different religious and cultural backgrounds for greater civic equality.

Some critics disparagingly call toleration of this sort "funny-hat liberalism."[12] They argue that it is little more than a pretense for accommodating ways of life that dissent from liberal orthodoxy. The price paid by orthodox Muslim parents for agreeing to educate their girls on tolerant terms may be a dilution of an orthodox religious way of life. Even if this is the case, it does not damage the position of democratic education. Democratic education does not aim to preserve or even to be equally conducive to all ways of life. Were the hijab accommodated in French public schools in the spirit of democratic education, the schools would do so for the sake of educating all children as equal citizens with diverse religious views and practices, not for the sake of perpetuating orthodox Islam (or any other secular or religious way of life).

Toleration in the service of civic equality cannot claim to support cultural or religious ways of life on their own terms, since not all cultural or religious perspectives embrace toleration. Toleration is not culturally neutral, and saying so is not a critique of toleration. A culture itself does not have a right to equal support by a democratic government just because it is a culture. Democratic governments owe children equal rights to be educated for civic equality (and as civic equals). If some cultural perspectives would deny children this right, democratic education will find itself at odds with parts of these cultures. But democratic education need not, therefore, be at odds with all of any culture. It is the responsibility of publicly supported schools to educate all students as civic equals. By asking how best to educate the Muslim girls for civic equality, democrats challenge themselves to apply the principle of toleration in an equitable manner, which does not unnecessarily exclude some children because their religious symbols are more conspicuous or controversial in their meaning than others.

Conditions like those that gave rise to the "affair of the scarf" have led many critics of multicultural education to ask whether public school systems can successfully strive for civic equality under conditions of cultural diversity. The analysis above suggests that a lot depends on the nature of the diversity and the democratic response. The challenge of combining religious toleration with an education for civic equality is greater, for example, the less willing orthodox religious parents are to educate girls equally with boys to prepare them for public life and the professions.

The analysis above also suggests that the challenge of multiculturalism to democratic education depends far less on the extent to which the group is newly arrived or not in the society, or indigenous or immigrant, than on the extent to which its commitments and identity are compatible with civic equality. "Civic equality within what society?" is another question to ask of any government that restricts the cultural content of schooling to the dominant culture or cultures. I cannot pursue this question at length in this essay, but I can say, based on the analysis above, that toleration and recognition, taken together, leave room for great cultural variation in democratic education. Civic equality within any and all democracies is what democratic education supports. Any group that is willing and able to constitute itself as a democracy, and provide an education that aims at civic equality for students, has full ethical standing. Indigenous groups that constitute themselves democratically, therefore, can make strong claims for educating their own children in their own culture and consistently for civic equality. To the extent that dominant groups fail to educate children for civic equality, their claims over other groups are without ethical standing. Unity without the aim of civic equality is an authoritarian, not a democratic, value.

Democratic education, therefore, depends on a commitment to civic equality by diverse groups in diverse societies. A commitment to civic equality, in turn, depends in practice on interpreting toleration and recognition in fair ways so as to provide all children, whatever their ethnicity, religion, race, or gender, with the education that they deserve. Diversity per se does not make striving for civic equality difficult. A lack of commitment to civic equality and fair accommodation of diversity does.

5. Challenges to the Aim of Civic Equality

The largest normative question remains: Do some multicultural conditions successfully challenge the democratic framework itself, and suggest the need for a guiding principle other than civic equality? I have already suggested that the framework of democratic education is a kind of principled pragmatism (or what I have also called "pragmatic idealism"). It does not insist on realizing civic equality against all odds. Rather, it aims at civic equality and, therefore, judges to what extent (and how best) it can be realized in particular contexts, all of which are nonideal but some are far less ideal than others.

Some democratic contexts may be so far from ideal for democratic education, however, as to challenge the very aim of civic equality itself. Consider, for example, a democracy where the dominant nationality is far more liberal and democratic toward its own than toward other subordinate and historically oppressed nation-alities, who are themselves relatively illiberal and undemocratic. The United States vis-à-vis Native Americans and Israel relative to Palestinians are two complex and troubling examples for democratic education. The United States devolved educational (and other political) authority to the local level of Native American tribes, but it is far from clear that progress toward civic equality (internal to the tribes or between them and the larger society) has resulted. Nor is it clear what a better alternative might have been (or is today).

In Israel's case, many people who otherwise disagree agree that two culturally distinct nations—Israel and Palestine—are needed for minimum stability in the area. Moreover, the absence of ongoing violence is a necessary (but not sufficient) precondition for teaching children to tolerate rather than hate one another, and to recognize each nation's right to exist. Even with two nations, however, the challenge of educating children for civic equality will be formidable, since the nations will probably be radically unequal in liberty and opportunity, an issue that democratic education does not adequately address when it focuses only on education within the boundaries of a single nation. The education systems in these two possible neighboring states will also have to find ways to recognize and tolerate minority students from the other (formerly adversary) nationality. The Israeli-Palestinian example is important not only for what it can tell us about the preconditions of educating children for civic equality—some peaceful and minimally unified society is necessary. The example also alerts us to the larger challenge of educating children to respect members of other societies as human beings who are equally deserving of civic equality, but who are denied such standing because they were born or raised somewhere else.

Many groups in many societies, including many democracies, do not accept the principle of civic equality. Indeed, many find the principle threatening to their valued way of life. What is the justifiable response of democratic education to such groups? We need to distinguish between the demands of insular groups who peacefully ask (almost) only to be left alone and those of separatist groups who typically insist, often violently, on far more. The Amish are a paradigmatic case of the former kind of (almost always agrarian) group, who ask for no welfare benefits, do not vote, and want above all to live a communal way of life free from the political authority of the larger democracy. They expect to be protected against violence, and they pose no threat of violence to the larger society. In this sense, the "social contract" that they request is quite reciprocal.

Peaceful groups like the Amish pose a problem for democratic education only if and when (as is often the case) their educational system offers far less preparation for exercising one's freedom and opportunity—which was afforded some parents who insist on denying it to their children—than the education that would otherwise be offered by the larger society. Democratic principles are compromised if the group is permitted to educate their children as they see fit, with no constraints whatsoever, but the compromise has far fewer ramifications for the larger democracy than a capitulation to the demands of a violent separatist group. Nonetheless, democracies do compromise an important principle of educating all children within their borders to the status of equal citizens when they decide to exempt some insular groups from this democratically justifiable requirement. When democracies do make such exemptions, they should recognize that they are effectively placing the value of a particular communal way of life above the value of a democratic education.

The problem posed to democratic education by violent separatist groups is far greater to the extent that they threaten the unity of the society and are likely to teach their children intolerance and disrespect for their neighbors. Deferring to the demands of a group simply because it represents a different culture cannot be justified by democratic principles. Only pragmatic necessity can justify such deference on grounds that no better alternative is available. The goodness of alternatives must be measured by defensible democratic principles, not by the aims or claims of the violent separatist group. If possible, a legitimate democratic state facing an intolerant separatist movement should effectively defend its authority with the aim of guaranteeing greater civic equality to all than would be afforded by the separatist alternative. One important means of guaranteeing greater civic equality is offering all children a publicly subsidized education that promotes tolerance and mutual respect across many multicultural lines.

Some historically oppressed groups are viewed as challenging the aim of teaching all children as civic equals when they actually further it. They distrust the authority of the democratic government that has treated them oppressively in the past. Rarely is oppression overcome once and for all, and the legacy of a long history of oppression must be taken seriously by any decent democracy. When historically oppressed minorities press claims on public education, they often do so in the name of civic equality. Some historical inequalities, especially those that have been compounded by decades of slavery, de jure and then de facto discrimination, create conditions under which equal treatment cannot constitute treatment as an equal.

The claim that equal treatment is all that is needed may be a sincere interpretation of the ideal of an education for civic equality, but it is not an adequate interpretation. It is naïve to think that nothing more or different is needed to educate African-American children as civic equals than newly arrived Swedish-American immigrants.[13] Neither toleration nor recognition of cultural contributions is likely to suffice to educate children who continue to be negatively and falsely stereotyped by large segments of society simply by virtue of the color of their skin.

The situation of identity groups whose members continue to suffer from negative stereotyping and consequent discriminations calls not for an alternative to the aim of civic equality but, rather, for creative interpretations of what civic equality demands of educational practices and institutions, and what can be realized over time in particular contexts. The democratic defense of civic equality itself requires more ambitious efforts to attend to the needs of members of perennially disadvantaged groups.

CONCLUSION

Educating children for civic equality is an ambitious aim for any democracy, and not one that by its very nature can ever be realized once and for all. More rather than less civic equality is all that a democrat can realistically aim for over time. If more civic equality is better than less, then democrats have a guiding principle that can help us evaluate educational practices and institutions. Striving for civic equality in democracies under multicultural conditions is not an all-or-nothing end. It is a question of practical judgment as to what educational practices are more or less conducive to greater civic equality.

The practical implications of civic equality, moreover, vary across groups. The claims to civic equality advanced by different groups cannot be treated identically because the content of their demands and their relationship to democratic ideals are far from identical. Some groups—indigenous groups and other minorities with a domestic history that extends back in time, for example—have legitimate claims to be recognized for contributions to the country's history. Some of these same groups, but not others, also are entitled to educational aid to overcome the injustice of accumulated disadvantage. What such justifiable demands share is the aim of educating children for civic equality.

Although I have not had the time to catalog the full range of justifiable demands of cultural groups, it is worth noting that long-term linguistic minorities may lay claim to special resources to help preserve their language and culture if they themselves are too poor to afford to do so on equal footing with other citizens. This is because civic equality does not permit a state to deprive its less affluent citizens, against their will, of the institutional structures on which their cultural and linguistic practices have come to rest.

Some immigrant groups may require little more than toleration and well-trained teachers who know how to help children learn a new language and adjust to a strange and likely somewhat scary environment. Well-trained teachers are often no small feat to find, especially when the profession of teaching is underpaid relative to others of similar social value. Relatively affluent and well-educated immigrants pose less of a challenge than the more common situation of children from poor and uneducated immigrant families. The children of affluent immigrant parents may need little special aid in education. Yet they, too, have justifiable claims to recognize their cultural heritage in the teaching of world history and literature, for example. Democratic education undermines the ideal of civic equality if it conveys to students that only citizens of their society are deserving of equal respect and fair treatment. The more interrelated and interdependent democratic societies are in the world, the more important the full range of multicultural contributions becomes in democratic education. In all these examples, the aim is to educate all children as far as feasible to equal citizenship.

Civic equality and individual freedom, I have shown, are both defensible and desirable aims of publicly funded education. Part of the responsibility of a democratic society to ensure the adequate education of all citizens consists of providing political opportunities in which citizens who identify with diverse groups can deliberate democratically about their differences. Democratic education responds to these contextual challenges of multicultural groups within a society, and to diverse multicultural societies, by supporting democratic deliberation within societies, among other important matters, about how public schooling can best educate all children as civic equals.

Multicultural conditions, as we have seen, can challenge the very aim of educating children for civic equality. Democracies are variously multicultural, and the varieties of groups make a difference in the kind of education and the progress toward civic equality that can realistically be expected at any time. When groups deny the value of civic equality, democracies cannot simply deny their responsibility to further civic equality for children of these groups. The interests of children must be considered, which is yet another reason any settlement with insular or separatist groups should be assessed on democratic grounds that aim to treat all individuals as civic equals. Democratic education is committed not to tolerating but to opposing educational programs that perpetuate civic inequality or intolerance.

Unity and diversity in multicultural education, therefore, go together, not like love and marriage, since democracies are not happy or unhappy families; they are far more diverse than most families. Unity and diversity in education go together like citizens and democracies. Toleration and recognition of diversity—within principled limits—make democratic unity possible. Disagreements about the limits of diversity fuel creative and destructive tensions within the unity. The more the creative tensions overwhelm the destructive ones, the better off a democracy will be and the more constructive work democratic educators will have cut out for them.

NOTES

An earlier version of this article appeared in *Diversity and Citizenship Education: Global Perspectives*, ed. James Banks (San Francisco: Jossey-Bass/Wiley 2003), pp. 71–96. Reprinted with permission of John Wiley & Sons, Inc.

1. Amy Gutmann, *Democratic Education* (Princeton: Princeton University Press, 1999).

2. "Familiarity with a culture determines the boundaries of the imaginable. Sharing in a culture, being part of it, determines the limits of the feasible." Joseph Raz and Avishai Margalit, "National Self-Determination," in *Ethics in the Public Domain: Essays in the Morality of Law and Politics*, by Joseph Raz (New York: Oxford University Press, 1994), p. 119.

3. See Susan Mendus, *Toleration and the Limits of Liberalism* (London: Macmillan, 1989).

4. See Charles Taylor, "The Politics of Recognition," in *Multiculturalism: Examining the Politics of Recognition*, ed. Amy Gutmann (Princeton: Princeton University Press, 1994), pp. 25–74.

5. See some examples at http://mathforum.org/alejandre/mathfair/about.html.

6. A variety of ideas regarding multicultural curricula, including the treatment of holidays, can be found at http://www.kidlink.org/KIDPROJ/MCC/ and http://jeffconet. jeffco.k12.co.us/passport/index.html.

7. Compare the perspective of Charles Taylor, "The Politics of Recognition," in *Multiculturalism and "The Politics of Recognition"* (Princeton: Princeton University Press, 1992), pp. 25–37. Taylor claims that cultural communities are entitled to survival, protected by the state, as long as the cultures respect basic individual rights. (Taylor does not consider cases where so few people want the culture to survive that it would take a heroic effort on the part of the state, even against its own citizens' reasonable democratic will, to secure its survival.)

8. See a discussion of this book in comparison to other trends in teaching history in the essay by Alexander Stille, "The Betrayal of History," *The New York Review of Books*, June 11, 1998, pp. 15–20.

9. *New York Times*, November 12, 1989, p. 5, and December 3, 1989, p. 17.

10. For a variety of views, see Susan Moller Okin and respondents, in *Is Multiculturalism Bad for Women?* ed. Joshua Cohen, Matthew Howard, and Martha C. Nussbaum (Princeton: Princeton University Press, 1999).

11. For an Islamic perspective on headscarves, and on "the affair of the scarf," see Aziza Y. al-Hibri, "Is Western Patriarchal Feminism Good for Third World/Minority Women?" in *Is Multiculturalism Bad for Women?* ed. Joshua Cohen, Matthew Howard, and Martha C. Nussbaum (Princeton: Princeton University Press, 1999), pp. 41–46.

12. For a critique conveyed by this term and a discussion of the hijab case, see Anna Elisabetta Galeotti, "Citizenship and Equality: The Place for Toleration," *Political Theory* 21 (November 1993), pp. 585–605.

13. For data on contemporary discrimination and negative stereotyping of African Americans, see David O. Sears, Jim Sidanius, and Lawrence Bobo, eds., *Racialized Politics: The Debate about Racism in America* (Chicago: University of Chicago Press, 2000); and Donald R. Kinder and Lynn M. Sanders, *Divided by Color: Racial Politics and Democratic Ideals* (Chicago: University of Chicago Press, 1996).

CHAPTER 23

MAPPING MULTICULTURAL EDUCATION

MEIRA LEVINSON

MULTICULTURAL education is a conceptual mess. It stands in for people's political aspirations, but has no independent meaning or value—despite its advocates' pretences (and beliefs) to the contrary. This is not to say that the various meanings and values attached to multicultural education by its various proponents are themselves worthless; to the contrary, they are often both plausible and compelling. But these meanings and values neither derive from nor are clarified by the concept of "multicultural education" itself. Furthermore, "multicultural education" is saddled with so many different conceptions that it is inevitably self-contradictory both in theory and in practice; even in its most well-intentioned, assiduous, and effective implementation, it cannot simultaneously achieve all of the goals it is called upon to serve. Thus, I shall argue in this chapter, "multicultural education" has no independent identity or value beyond the various goals, practices, or content to which others attach it, and to know that an education is called "multicultural" is to know little if anything about its form, content, or aims.

This is, admittedly, a curmudgeonly way to begin an essay about multi-cultural education. Why write about something that I claim is intrinsically muddled and even self-contradictory? There are two important reasons to do so. First, "multicultural education" is used so frequently, and often with such potent political consequences, that it is important to come to grips with its multiple possible meanings, to recognize its various uses by different advocates and organizations, and to make sense of the ways these meanings and uses may reinforce, undermine, and/or simply bypass each other. If we have a conceptual map of what "multicultural education" is used to mean, then we will be far better equipped to comprehend and evaluate claims made about, against, and on behalf of multicultural education in philosophical, educational, and policy literature. Second, as I noted above, many of the aims and practices attached to "multicultural education" often are quite valuable and hence worth promoting—but in the confusion of so many meanings attached to multicultural education, their value may get lost in the mix. Too often, for example, one politically unpopular or conceptually incoherent version of multiculturalism is used as an excuse to reject other approaches to multicultural education out of hand, even though the latter are in fact totally separate from and even potentially in conflict with the former. Furthermore, at least as problematically, achievement of one version of multicultural education is frequently cited as an excuse not to pursue other, often more challenging and transformative, goals and practices—even though the latter may be more important and desirable. In sum, therefore, it is crucial that we "map" multicultural education as a set of concepts, practices, and goals, even if the map proves to include somewhat contradictory directions and in fact requires outside intervention to clarify one's direction in the first place.

Section I begins to construct this map by surveying the different uses and meanings of "multicultural education" as articulated by three groups: political and educational philosophers, educational theorists (or as I sometimes call them, educational multiculturalists), and educational practitioners. Section II examines some of the inconsistencies and potentially serious contradictions among the aims, calling into question the conceptual coherence of "multicultural education." Section III then highlights some potential tensions among the aims, practices, and content of multicultural education. I show that promotion of toleration and mutual respect, for example, may actually be better achieved by *not* teaching students about "others" than by teaching students about other cultures' very different ways of life. Relatedly, certain central multicultural goals may be more easily achieved in segregated rather than integrated settings—exactly the opposite of what almost any self-respecting advocate of multicultural education would favor.[1] I conclude with a brief reflection on multicultural education's potential practical importance despite its conceptual incoherence.

1. Mapping the Aims of Multicultural Education

One of the reasons that "multicultural education" has such a multiplicity of meanings is that it has been embraced and developed by a number of different groups of thinkers who tend not to read each other's work (or seemingly even know of each others' existence). In this section, I will try to map out the work of three such groups who are particularly relevant to readers of a handbook on philosophy of education: political and educational philosophers, multicultural educational theorists, and educational policymakers and practitioners. Let us start with the philosophers.

Multicultural education tends to be invoked in the political and educational philosophy literature for three purposes. First, multicultural education is used to respond to claims by minority groups within a community or nation for group rights or accommodations. Will Kymlicka notably defends this notion in *Multicultural Citizenship*, arguing, "[W]e should aim at ensuring that all national groups have the opportunity to maintain themselves as a distinct culture, if they so choose. This ensures that the good of cultural membership is equally protected for the members of all national groups" (Kymlicka 1995: 113; see also Young 1990; Tamir 2002). These minority group preservation programs may be voluntary, as when Hispanic families are given the choice about whether to enroll their children in bilingual or English immersion programs; or they may be involuntary, as when the National Curriculum in Wales requires instruction in Welsh language, literature, and culture; or when all non-Anglophone (and all immigrant, whether Anglophone or not) children in Quebec are required to attend Francophone schools. They are unusual in American public schools, although they do occasionally arise, as in this example from the New York state curriculum: "Communication in Native languages takes place primarily to share expression of ideas, thoughts, and feelings to preserve Native cultural ideology" (New York State 1996: Standard 1, Checkpoint A, Native American Languages). More frequently we see them in the form of accommodations of minority religious groups' requests to be exempted from certain curricula or classes, as when conservative Christian students are exempted from biology or gym class (see, e.g., *Moody* v. *Cronin*)—or most drastically, in the case of Amish students' exemption from any formal schooling after eighth grade on the grounds that continued school attendance would fundamentally threaten the continuation of the Amish way of life (*Wisconsin* v. *Yoder*). Interestingly, such educational exemptions are rarely referred to as multicultural education (a fact which we will return to below), but they are logical extensions of the explicitly multicultural goal of preserving minority group cultures.

Second, multicultural education is invoked by liberal political theorists and philosophers of education as a means of promoting children's development of autonomy. As Rob Reich argues, "Multicultural education fosters minimalist autonomy by (1) creating and enhancing the possibility of critical and independent reflection, and (2) making vivid to the student a diversity of cultural practices and values, which themselves may come to represent real and meaningful options that the student could choose and seek to adopt or pursue" (2002: 132). Thus, multicultural education helps students develop autonomy in two ways: it gives them a set of new options for how to lead their lives by expanding their "experiential horizons" (2002: 184) and it spurs them into reflecting critically on their current lives by placing their received "practices and values" in sharp relief against alternative or opposed ones. It is worth noting that these aims aren't propounded solely by philosophers, although they articulate them most clearly. Consider Montana's English curriculum: "Literature is a primary vehicle to widen and extend our experiences, to make us more aware of other individuals, issues, cultures and viewpoints and, thus, ourselves, our own cultures and our own attitudes. Literature moves us out of our personal spheres and extends our understanding as we change" (Montana Office of Public Instruction 1999). Furthermore, we should note that this approach to multicultural education may provide benefits beyond students' development of autonomy per se. By expanding the realm of human achievements to which they are exposed, multicultural education may strengthen students' understanding of the world and their access to meaningful ideas, practices, and ways of life, whether or not they become more autonomous as a result (Appiah 1996). Thus, exposure to a variety of valuable achievements and ways of life may be justified on autonomy grounds or simply as a good in itself.

Finally, multicultural education is invoked by philosophers as a means to promote the civic good. Multicultural education does this in four related ways.

1. It is thought that as students learn about other cultures, they will come to tolerate them, and hence also tolerate people who live within that culture (see, e.g., Gutmann 1996). This is probably the most familiar and universally embraced purpose of multicultural education—often to the neglect of all other purposes, much to some multiculturalists' regret. New South Wales' "Making Multicultural Australia" Web site explains, for example, that its purpose is to help teachers "promote cultural diversity and tolerance"; although many other purposes are also articulated along the way (such as providing "information on the contributions that different cultural groups have made to the development of Australian society"), they generally are tied back to the goals of promoting "tolerance" and "community harmony" (NSW Department of Education and Training and Office of the Board of Studies NSW 2007).

2. It is hoped that with tolerance will also come respect. Often, respect is thought to be promoted by teaching students about the achievements of other cultures, including their contributions to the nation. This explains California's mandate that first graders will "[u]nderstand the ways in which American Indians and immigrants have helped define Californian and American culture" (California Department of Education 2000: 1.5.2), and the English National Curriculum's "Respect for All" Web site's reminder, "Respect for diversity can be promoted in all subjects by drawing examples from different countries, cultures and communities and encouraging pupils to focus on the way human diversity enriches our lives" (Qualifications and Curriculum Authority 2007b). By helping students develop respect for other cultures or ways of life, and therefore for their fellow

citizens, multicultural education promotes the civic good by increasing civic harmony.

3. Liberal philosophers argue that in coming to respect different groups within the polity, individuals also become more open to considering different viewpoints within public deliberation and debate. Stephen Macedo articulates this idea as follows: "All children should be made aware of the ethnic, racial, and religious diversity that constitutes our society so that they can think as citizens and so that they will not live in a mental straitjacket at odds with freedom" (Macedo 2000: 240). New York State seems to be gesturing toward this aim in the following English Language-Arts standard: students are expected to "understand that within any group there are many different points of view depending on the particular interests and values of the individual, and recognize those differences in perspective in texts and presentations" (New York State 2003: Standard 3.1, Intermediate, 5–8). This increase in open-mindedness promotes civic cooperation.

4. Finally, political liberals emphasize that because multicultural education has taught them to be aware of people's differences, citizens become more aware of what constitutes a "public reason" (Rawls 1993)—meaning a reason that lots of people will recognize as legitimate, regardless of their religious or cultural differences, as opposed to a sectarian claim within public discourse. Because they are respectful of these differences, they become more willing to rely on public reasons and to insist that others do so as well. This awareness of and commitment to public reasons promotes civic reasonableness and civic equality. Thus, Macedo ultimately argues,

> A liberal civic education will insist that children learn that it is possible for fellow citizens who affirm the political supremacy of liberal values to disagree deeply about other matters: not only cultural tastes, but also deep religious convictions. A liberal pluralistic multiculturalism will insist on the good of political respect for many different religions and cultures, while acknowledging the political authority of a shared point of view. Multiculturalism properly understood is an important part of a liberal civic education.   (2000: 260)

Educational theorists tend to have a significantly different agenda from that of political theorists when they discuss multicultural education. Most notably, educational multiculturalists view the philosophers' approach to multicultural education as being overly, even exclusively, individually oriented and curriculum-based. Multicultural education, they argue, is not simply about tinkering with the content of the curriculum—adding topics here to encourage toleration of others, or developing a new course there so as to promote autonomous thinking and perspective taking. As Sonia Nieto comments, "Many people assume that multicultural education is little more than isolated lessons in sensitivity training or prejudice reduction, or separate units about cultural artifacts or ethnic holidays. . . . If conceptualized in this limited way, multicultural education will have little influence on student learning" (Nieto 2001: 383). James Banks agrees, deriding both what he calls the "contributions approach" and the "additive approach." "The contributions approach often results in the trivialization of ethnic culture, the study of their strange and exotic characteristics, and the reinforcement of stereotypes and misconceptions" (Banks 2001a: 231). The additive approach, too, "usually results in the viewing of ethnic content from the perspectives of mainstream historians, writers, artists, and scientists because it does not involve a restructuring of the curriculum. The events, concepts, issues, and problems selected for study are selected using mainstream-centric and Eurocentric criteria and perspectives" (2001a: 232).

Rather, these educational theorists argue, multicultural education should be transformative, restructuring and regrounding the curriculum, and more important, reorienting the school as a whole to instantiating and promoting social justice and real equality. Banks, who is the grandfather of the multicultural education movement in the United States, explains,

> To implement multicultural education in a school, we must reform its power relationships, the verbal interaction between teachers and students, the culture of the school, the curriculum, extracurricular activities, attitudes toward minority languages, the testing program, and grouping practices. The institutional norms, social structures, cause-belief statements, values, and goals of the school must be transformed and reconstructed. (Banks 2001b: 22)

Thus, although the goal of using multicultural education to teach antiracism, which all educational theorists embrace and which Sonia Nieto describes as being "at the very core of a multicultural perspective,"[2] may seem related to political theorists' notion of using multicultural education to teach mutual toleration and respect, Nieto argues against mere curricular inclusiveness: "Being antiracist and antidiscriminatory means paying attention to all areas in which some students are favored over others: the curriculum, choice of materials, sorting policies, and teachers' interactions and relationships with students and their families" (2000: 305–306).[3]

The result of this transformation not only of the curriculum but also of the formal and informal structures and orientation of the school is generally intended to be twofold. First, educational multicultural theorists hope to promote *societal* transformation and reconstruction, specifically with regard to eliminating racism, prejudice, and discrimination. Banks's highest form of multicultural education, for example, is the "Social Action Approach," for which he sets this goal: "A major goal of the social action approach is to help students acquire the knowledge, values, and skills they need to participate in social change so that victimized and excluded ethnic and racial groups can become full participants in U.S. society and so the nation will move closer to attaining its democratic ideals. . . . In this approach, teachers are agents of social change who promote democratic values and the empowerment of students" (Banks 2001a: 236). Likewise, noted multicultural theorists Carl A. Grant and Christine E. Sleeter distinguish five approaches to multicultural education, labeling the most desirable one, "Education That Is Multicultural and Social Reconstructionist" (Grant and Sleeter 1999). This approach, they explain, "deals more directly than the other approaches have with oppression and social structural inequality based on race, social class, gender, and disability. Its purpose is to prepare future citizens to reconstruct society so that it better serves the interests of all groups of people, especially those who are of color, poor, female, and/or with disabilities" (Grant and Sleeter 2001: 68–69).[4]

The other aim that educational theorists of multiculturalism highlight is that of promoting equal educational opportunity for all students. "Multicultural education is an idea, an educational reform movement, and a process whose major goal is to change the structure of educational institutions so that male and female students, exceptional students, and students who are members of diverse racial, ethnic, language, and cultural groups will have an equal chance to achieve academically in school" (Banks 2001c: 1; see also Gay 2001; Banks and Banks 2004). For this purpose, the point of changing the curriculum, pedagogy, and school structure in response to nonmainstream groups' beliefs, norms, and practices is not so that others can learn about these groups, but so that members of the groups themselves will be more likely to achieve, since they presumably will respond more favorably to schools that are "culturally congruent" (Gay 2000) or "culturally relevant" (Ladson-Billings 1994) rather than culturally alien. In this respect, multicultural education is aligned *with* the groups being taught, as opposed to being *about* them. "Pedagogical equality that reflects culturally sensitive instructional strategies is a precondition for and a means of achieving maximal academic outcomes for culturally diverse students" (Gay 1995: 28).

In certain respects, therefore, the educational multiculturalists and the philosophers are aligned. Both groups embrace one aim of multicultural education as strengthening historically marginalized and/or minority communities, although educational multiculturalists tend to be more concerned with cultural empowerment (e.g., Ladson-Billings 1994), while philosophers focus more on how multicultural education may promote cultural preservation.[5] Furthermore, many educational theorists embrace notions of civic solidarity and the value of gaining multiple perspectives:

> Multicultural movements have defined the main purpose of curriculum as social improvement . . . for equality and justice, and a belief that education should fuel democratic actions. Broadly speaking, multicultural movements challenge the United States to live up to its ideals of justice and equality, believing that this country has the potential to work much better for everyone. As tomorrow's citizens, children in schools should learn academic tools and disciplinary knowledge resources from vantage points of multiple communities. Further, young people should develop some sense of solidarity across differences that enables working toward closing the gap between the nation's ideals and its realities.   (Sleeter 2005: 15)

As this quotation demonstrates, however, these values are embedded within a thoroughgoing egalitarian commitment to social justice: students should learn to understand others' perspectives and to respect others not merely so as to treat each other as civic and political equals, which is the goal articulated by the political philosophers cited above, but also so as to be motivated to act on others' behalf—actively to pursue social and political equality. This latter aim is more politically partisan, insofar as it privileges the goal of civic equality over other equally democratic goals such as liberty. Hence, the apparent alignment among the various goals should not be mistaken to imply total consistency among them.

Finally, there are three aims for multicultural education that tend to be promoted mostly by educational practitioners (teachers, administrators, and curriculum developers) rather than theorists, as well as one aim that is articulated by all three groups (political and educational philosophers, educational theorists, and educational policymakers and practitioners) alike. This latter aim is that of righting the historical record—education that incorporates multicultural perspectives, it is generally agreed by now, is more accurate than education that presents only one perspective, especially but not only when the single perspective is that of the dominant group. Thus, Gary Nash, a historian who has written a number of popular textbooks for school children, comments, "multicultural approaches enhance, rather than diminish, the quality of historical analysis in the classroom" (Nash 1996: 183). Similarly, Rob Reich attests, "Multicultural education corrects the ethnocentric and chauvinist education so typical of years past, and as such is a truer representation of the history and current composition of the United States" (Reich 2002: 131; see also Susan Wolf's essay in Okin, Cohen, et al. 1999).

One of the aims primarily promoted by educational practitioners had its heyday in the 1980s and early 1990s and since then has slipped from view—namely, using multicultural education to increase the self-esteem of nonmainstream students.[6] A second aim, however, is alive and well—namely, increasing students' interest in what they are learning by emphasizing how it relates to their own lives. (This aim has been a recurring theme of educators over many generations; its most recent instantiation has carried over from the 1960s, when both students and teachers started demanding that the curriculum be "relevant.") This is obviously related to culturally relevant teaching, as mentioned above, but it tends to have a somewhat more limited focus. Culturally relevant teaching incorporates multiple aspects' of students' "cultures," including learning styles, language patterns, social roles and mores, and so on, in order to help students achieve in the classroom. Educators' concerns with emphasizing the relevance of curriculum to students' own lives tend to center more on content: teachers use students' knowledge of and interest in rap, for example, to introduce poetic devices such as assonance, internal rhyme, or meter. Multicultural education is seen in this respect as a tool for helping students see themselves and their interests in the curriculum, not as a cudgel to reshape all aspects of curriculum, pedagogy, and practice.

The final aim that multicultural education is sometimes asked to serve is that of enabling students to succeed economically in a multicultural world by teaching them to be comfortable in a diverse workforce and skillful at integrating into a global economy. Thus, New Jersey justified its world languages curriculum by asserting, "To support the growth of New Jersey's dynamic economy as we move into the twenty-first century, our state needs educated citizens whose multilingual abilities and multicultural sensitivities prepare them to work in a pluralistic society and a global economy. As countries became increasingly inter-dependent, it is essential that we actively promote proficiency in world languages to improve cross-cultural understanding" (State of New Jersey 1996: Introduction, World Languages; see also State of Delaware 1995: Geography Standard 3). The multicultural theorist Jim Cummins rather tendentiously makes a similar argument:

> Corporate America wants people . . . who can work cooperatively across cultural, linguistic, and racial boundaries to solve problems using this information. It might appear obvious then that our schools should be aiming to produce critical and creative thinkers who are knowledgeable about and sensitive to other cultural perspectives. Any student who emerges into our culturally diverse society speaking only one language and with a monocultural perspective on the world can legitimately be considered educationally ill prepared and perhaps even 'culturally deprived.'   (Cummins 2000: xiv; see also Feinberg 1998: 129–30)

In sum, multicultural education can serve a broad range of possible goals, and has been called on to do so by various constituencies. Because I will be returning to these various goals in subsequent sections of this essay, let me summarize them here:[7]

- Preserve minority group culture
- Foster children's development of autonomy through:
  - Expanding their "experiential horizons" by exposing them to new options
  - Posing alternative beliefs, values, ways of life, etc., that spur students to reflect critically on their own lives
- Increase students' exposure to humankind's highest accomplishments
- Promote the civic good by teaching:
  - Toleration
  - Mutual respect
  - Civic cooperation and open-mindedness
  - Commitment to use of "public reason"
- Promote social justice and equity by:
  - Implementing antiracist education
  - Teaching students to be attuned to and to fight against social, political, and economic inequality and injustice
  - Teaching students in a "culturally congruent" manner
- Right the historical record
- Foster sense of national unity by demonstrating contributions made by each group
- Increase self-esteem of nonmainstream students
- Increase students' interest in a subject or discipline by emphasizing how it relates to their own lives
- Enable students to succeed economically in an integrated, multicultural workplace and globalized economy

2. MULTICULTURAL TENSIONS

These aims may be generally admirable, and well justified each on its own terms as plausible interpretations of "multicultural education," but they are both theoretically and practically incompatible with one another in numerous ways. That's not necessarily an indictment of multicultural education, of course. It could be that some of these characterizations of multicultural education's purposes are misguided, partial, or subordinate to others; once we clear those out of the way, it could be that what's left—multicultural education's overriding goals—are consistent, coherent, and compatible. My purpose in this section and the next, however, is to demonstrate that this isn't true. First, there are numerous internal inconsistencies between various goals that have considerable claim to being central to any account of what "multicultural education" might mean; and second, there are incompatibilities among *goals*, *practices*, and *content* that are reasonably considered to be central to multicultural education.

Let's start by considering the first potential aim of multicultural education listed above: preserving minority groups' cultures. In contrast to many of the other goals, which are clearly promoted by an inclusive curriculum and/or pedagogy that teaches about or responds to a wide variety of groups, preserving a minority culture may require the implementation of an *exclusive* curriculum that teaches the beliefs of the minority group culture *instead of* the beliefs of other groups. Some religious groups, for example, request this kind of multicultural accommodation in order to prevent their children from encountering (from their perspective) impure, untrue, and/or blasphemous ideas, norms, and practices. These were the grounds given by fundamentalist Christian parents for requesting an alternative reading program for their children in the now-canonical case *Mozert* v. *Hawkins*. To this extent, multicultural education aimed at preserving minority cultures may work in opposition to other goals, such as increasing individual autonomy or promoting mutual respect (by exposing children to a wider variety of alternative views and beliefs). This is not true, however, in all cases; some minority cultures, by contrast, may require a more *inclusive* curriculum for their preservation, as in Wales, for example, where Welsh language, literature, and culture are taught *in addition* to English.

Another contrast worth reflecting upon when considering multicultural education's appropriateness for preserving minority groups, especially within the public school, is whether the curricular adjustments are mandatory or optional. Contrary to what one might think, this distinction does not map neatly onto exclusive vs. inclusive curricula. To take the Welsh National Curriculum again, all students living in and attending public schools in Wales are required to take Welsh as a means of attempting to revitalize the language and culture. Thus, this is an example of a mandatory, inclusive multicultural curriculum. In Quebec, on the other hand, all families who are not native Quebecois Anglophones are required to send their children to Francophone schools as a means of preserving and strengthening Francophone Quebecois culture. This constitutes, therefore, a mandatory, exclusive multicultural accommodation. It is possible, as well, to have voluntary, exclusive approaches, whereby families choose to pull their children out of science or reading classes, say, in order to expose them to a minority religious perspective exclusively and protect them from encountering different or contradictory perspectives, as the *Mozert* parents tried to do. (Whether this can be considered "voluntary" from the child's perspective, however, is questionable, and is an issue that I have addressed in detail in Levinson 1999.) Voluntary, inclusive curricula are also possible in the form of electives and after-school programs. Even if one is sympathetic, therefore, to minority groups' claims for public assistance in their cultural preservation, one would need to decide which of these kinds of curricular accommodations are desirable for a public school to provide.

Additional potential conflicts arise when one considers the relationship between minority group preservation, on the one hand, and social justice and equity, on the other. As Susan Moller Okin points out in *Is Multiculturalism Bad for Women?* many minority (as well as majority) groups are deeply inegalitarian in their treatment of and mores concerning men and women. When multicultural claims are pressed to explain or (worse) excuse behavior that violates egalitarian norms—Hmong men's kidnapping of young girls excused as culturally acceptable "bride snatching," for example (Okin 1999: 18–19)—social justice and equity are clearly violated. The same may be true for group-respecting forms of multicultural education. To assist groups in preserving their cultures, whether through exclusive or inclusive and voluntary or mandatory means, schools may end up reinforcing these same deep gender (and other) inequalities.

These concerns are not new ones. Philosophers have discussed many of these dilemmas in debating the meaning and justification of multiculturalism itself. But I would argue that they have not been taken as seriously as one might hope by educational theorists, especially the group of "multicultural educationalists" I discussed in section I. For it is not only explicitly group-oriented justifications of multicultural curricula that fall into these dilemmas about inclusion and exclusion and the preservation or reinforcement of culturally grounded inequalities. Even multicultural education that is specifically egalitarian and justice-oriented in intent—namely, "culturally congruent" education that is intended to foster especially minority student achievement by incorporating familiar cultural practices, norms, referents, and language into the curriculum, pedagogy, and culture of the school—may end up similarly raising dilemmas about inclusive and exclusive education as well as reinforcing culturally grounded inequities.

To take the equity-oriented concerns first, how does one truly teach both equitably and in a culturally congruent fashion when students come from a culture that values "assertive" or "macho" boys but decries "bossy" or "aggressive" girls? How does a school incorporate cultures that use *pimp* and *pimpin'* as positive nouns and verbs for boys or men, but (and?) *ho* and *bitch* as derogatory terms for women? What about a culture that values lighter skin over darker skin, or one that describes homosexual behavior as a desecration of God's holy vessel, or one that holds women who are raped responsible for bringing shame upon their family? The educational challenges here are numerous. Of course, the same challenges arise with regard to teaching members of majority cultures; sexism, racism, homophobia, and other inegalitarian expressions of prejudice and discrimination are by no means limited to or necessarily even more predominant in minority groups. But proponents of multicultural education as culturally congruent education frequently seem to ignore the fact that the same inegalitarianism that afflicts majority group cultures also may arise within minority group cultures, and that reinforcing minority students' cultural practices and presuppositions in order to help them achieve may simultaneously reinforce inegalitarian and even racist or sexist norms and behaviors.

I say "frequently" because multicultural educationalists admittedly have acknowledged this problem at times—although they then seem unwilling or unable to confront it head-on. Sleeter asks, for instance, "Should empowerment mean teaching these students to recognize and reject sexism, thereby accepting the teacher's definition of the world, or should it mean developing their power to examine the world and act upon it for themselves, which might not involve questioning sexism and could even strengthen it?" (Sleeter 1991: 19). Her answer to this dilemma, however, is to assert that all people's "perceptions"—students' and teachers' alike—"embody self-interest and personal experience . . . ; nobody's definition is universal or neutral" (1991: 19–20). Thus, even though she declares elsewhere in the essay that "*empowerment* and *multicultural education* are interwoven, and together suggest powerful and far-reaching school reform" in order to achieve "the emancipation of oppressed people" (1991: 2, 22), she is remarkably loathe to take a stand on what that might look like if it means overturning the views of "members of oppressed groups" (1991: 21). This is because the aim of enabling student achievement by teaching in a culturally congruent manner actually shares with the aim of preserving minority group cultures a profound discomfort with making judgments—especially critical judgments—about any culture, especially one that is marginalized or whose members are relatively disempowered. (See Taylor 1992 for an especially insightful critique of the sources and incoherence of this discomfort.)

Furthermore, I would argue that some of the most effective, empowering, and egalitarian culturally congruent teaching of minority students may be found in segregated rather than integrated schools. This takes us back to the exclusivity vs. inclusivity issue raised above. The more culturally diverse a classroom is, the harder it is to teach all students in that classroom in a culturally congruent manner. Culturally congruent education includes adjustments in questioning styles (see Delpit 1995), spoken and written language, choices of texts and other curricular materials, classroom culture, communication with parents and family members, means of establishing authority in the classroom, incorporation of students' interests, and more, in response to students' backgrounds, norms, and experiences. All of these play into the "transformation" of education "so that students from racial, cultural, language, and social-class groups will experience equal educational opportunities... [and] equal status in the culture and life of the school" (Banks 2005: viii). If students' incoming backgrounds, norms, and experiences are fairly homogeneous, then educators can relatively easily adjust their curriculum and practices to capitalize on their students' strengths and meet their students' needs. If the student body is extremely diverse, on the other hand, then this is much harder to achieve. Hence, from the perspective of taking multicultural education to mean culturally congruent teaching, culturally exclusive (segregated) educational settings may actually be more conducive to successful multicultural education than culturally inclusive and integrated settings are.

I think this explains, in fact, some of the ambivalence exhibited by African Americans and others about how much effort should be put into the cause of integrating schools. In a 1998 survey, African-American survey respondents joined white respondents in ranking racial diversity second from the bottom of their preferred characteristics for a good school (Public Agenda Foundation 1998), while black mayors in Seattle, Denver, St. Louis, and Cleveland have attempted to dismantle desegregation practices in their cities (Hochschild and Scovronick 2003: 48–49; see also Massey and Denton 1993). Gloria Ladson-Billings (1994), who champions many of the aims of multicultural education, acknowledges in her classic *The Dreamkeepers* the appeal of segregated schools, thanks primarily to their greater potential for culturally relevant education. In the same vein, as one African-American veteran teacher explained in an interview in the early 1990s, "we were able to do more with the black students in all-black schools.... I got disillusioned with integration because I could not get to my people and tell them all the things that they needed to know." He now enjoys working with the de facto segregated Upward Bound program "because once again, in addition to teaching mathematics, I have the opportunity to get to my people to talk to them and tell them all the important things that I used to preach to black children when I taught in segregated schools. It's as if I have come back home" (Foster 1997: 6, 7, 11). Vanessa Siddle Walker (1996) documents similar strengths of segregated education in her history *Their Highest Potential*, and I would argue that evidence from both historical and contemporary freedom schools and from historically black colleges and universities supports this contention, as well (Levinson forthcoming).

This is not to claim that segregated education is actively desirable all things considered, or even that multicultural education is better achieved under segregated conditions. To the contrary, I remain a firm supporter of integrated schools and I believe that most advocates of multicultural education would be astonished and appalled to be told that multicultural education was best achieved under segregated conditions. This is in part my point. Multicultural education's goals and practices are—at least with respect to preserving minority groups' cultures or teaching in a culturally congruent manner to achieve social justice, as I have shown, and I would suggest in many other cases, too—at a minimum inconsistent and more likely fundamentally at odds with one another.

3. CONTENT, GOALS, AND PRACTICES: A WOBBLY TRIUMVIRATE

One of the reasons that advocacy of segregated education seems so much at odds with what we assume multicultural education is about is that embracing diversity would seem to be at the heart of any plausible understanding of the concept. What could multicultural education be about if not learning to accept, understand, and ultimately embrace the rich human diversity that surrounds us? This clearly does lie at the heart of many of the goals listed above: antiracism, toleration, respect, expanded horizons, celebration of the contributions made by diverse peoples, and so on. In this section, I want to turn to one of these goals—that of fostering toleration—in part because it might be thought of as a minimal standard for multicultural education. Clearly, few advocates would be willing to stop at mere toleration as the final goal for multicultural education, but it is hard to imagine any—whether philosophers, multicultural theorists, or educators—who would reject the promotion of toleration as a step on the road to multicultural education. Hence, whereas one might argue that section II focused on overly expansive, exclusive, or demanding conceptions of multicultural education's goals, here we will focus on a minimal goal: multicultural education should help students become more tolerant of each other. Even under such a minimalist conception of multicultural education's purposes, however, I will argue that it potentially conflicts with diversity-inclusive content. In other words, encouraging toleration may not be best realized through teaching multicultural content—in which case, one has to ask whether multicultural education has any core meaning at all.

There are three forms of tolerance that students can learn

1. They may learn to tolerate others because "they don't know any better"—this is the basis for many people's toleration of "white trash," or of the "rednecks" down the road, or of "those Chinese people who eat chicken feet." This idea is also pithily if idiosyncratically expressed in Georgia's high school character education curriculum, which specifies that students must learn "Tolerance: the allowable deviation from a standard. Indulgence for beliefs or practices differing from or conflicting with one's own" (Georgia Department of Education 1997). Although most of us would reject these grounds for teaching toleration, its influence can be insidious (even outside of Georgia!), as the following veteran teacher notes: "I've seen white teachers let black kids misbehave and then when I ask them why they say, 'I thought that was part of his culture.' ... It's a lack of understanding that what's right and what's wrong is wrong for blacks as well as whites; an unwillingness to take risks and really get involved with black children" (Foster 1997: 61). It's clear that this is not a productive basis for teaching toleration, both because it can lead to incorrect generalizations about a group (such as that black

culture tolerates misbehavior) and because "they don't know any better" cannot set the grounds for respect, which is ultimately needed to promote the civic goods of harmony, cooperation, and equality.

2. A second and more productive ground for toleration is learning to tolerate others because "underneath it all we're all the same"; for example, we are all human beings possessing intrinsic worth and dignity. This is the purpose, I assume, of the following first-grade social-science standard in California: "Students... [r]ecognize the ways in which they are all part of the same community, sharing principles, goals, and traditions despite their varied ancestry" (California Department of Education 2000: 1.5.1). When multicultural education is used to teach this form of toleration, it usually takes a comparative turn: students may study kinship structures, religious beliefs and practices, foods, or coming-of-age ceremonies of various groups with an eye to learning to appreciate both the differences and the similarities. The strength of this approach is that once they learn to be tolerant based on a recognition of intrinsic common attributes, students will be inclined to be tolerant of all people, not just those they have specifically met and/or learned about. The weakness of this approach, however, is that it runs the risk of trivializing real differences in order to emphasize our commonality: toleration becomes a lesson on the order of, "They eat tortillas, whereas we eat blintzes, and that group eats mu shu." With the best of intentions, teachers may be inclined to teach, for example, "Allah is just like God, only with a different name"—without teaching the ways in which the Islamic, Christian, and Jewish notions of God truly do differ and even conflict. It is extremely easy to give into this temptation, even when one knows better. Soon after the attacks on September 11, 2001, for instance, my student Marvin was researching Islam in order to prepare for an in-class debate about whether we should go to war in Afghanistan. (I was teaching eighth-grade humanities at the time.) "Dr. Levinson, did you know that 'Islam' means 'peace?'" Marvin asked me excitedly. "Muslims are just like everybody else because we all want peace; that's the basis of their religion!" I readily agreed with him because I was hoping students would develop and/or maintain tolerant attitudes toward Muslims. My approach did nothing, however, to teach him about the real differences between Islam and Christianity (Marvin's religion), and hence he (and the rest of the class) remained ill-equipped to maintain tolerant attitudes when they learned, for example, about some of the harsher aspects of *sharia.*

3. This brings us to the third way that students may learn to be tolerant, which is by coming to understand the *reasons* for a group's differences. This provides a deeper and more stable basis for toleration (and ultimately potentially for respect), because it helps students learn to engage with real differences in belief and orientation. Unlike with (1) or (2), they learn to understand another person's (or group's) perspective. For example, a person—let's call her Molly—may be offended the first time she meets an Orthodox Jewish man who refuses to shake her hand, let alone give her a hug hello. But when she learns that he believes that he

should not touch a woman who is not his wife, then she becomes tolerant of his behavior because she realizes he's not intentionally being rude. Understanding his reasons doesn't necessarily lead her to respect his behavior—Molly can understand, and hence be tolerant of, his behavior but still think, "He should just get over this"—but it is more likely to ground a respectful relationship than (1) and even possibly than (2).

Multicultural education ideally aims at both (2) and (3)—and hence also aims to replace toleration on the grounds of (1) with toleration on the grounds of (2) and (3). As I mentioned above, we need (2)—toleration based on appreciation of our common human attributes—because there are only so many different groups, and only so many different behaviors/norms/ceremonies/etc. of each group, that schools have the time, opportunity, or knowledge to teach about. Hence, it's unreasonable to expect that students (or adults) will tolerate all groups on the grounds of understanding the reasons for their differences; there has to be a more fundamental assumption of toleration based on shared characteristics (common humanity, we all love our children, etc.) that sets the foundation for the hard task of then learning the reasons for differences.

We cannot rely only on (2), however, because, as I noted above, it runs the risk of trivializing real differences; teachers end up teaching or emphasizing superficial differences in order to get at fundamental similarities. This is dangerous since cultural groups do differ fundamentally from each other. Proselytizing door-to-door, taking multiple wives, endorsing sex discrimination, caring for one's child as a stay-at-home father, living according to *sharia*, eating dogs and rats, calling out responses at the theater or the movies, not believing that Jesus is the son of God, choosing to put one's mother in a nursing home, expecting to live with and be cared for by one's children when one is old, choosing to be a single professional mother—all of these may be experienced by children (and adults) as being fundamentally different from how they lead (and believe it's appropriate to lead) their lives. If a child never learns to be tolerant of fundamental differences as a result of understanding people's reasons for adopting and endorsing these behaviors, i.e., (3), then she will have a hard time being tolerant of others who really do seem fundamentally different. Of course, which of these are taken to be fundamental differences depends on one's perspective. A few years ago, one of my students asked out of the blue, "Do Chinese people really eat rats?" Since I had just read Peter Hessler's (2000) account of dining on various species of rat in China, I couldn't in good faith say no, but it was clear that if I said yes, I would confirm his suspicion that Chinese people were at least bizarre, and probably repellant. Luckily enough, another student, who reveled in her Jamaican background, commented that she loved eating goat curry, even though she knew others found it gross. This (plus the knowledge that the more we talked about food, the more off-track they could get my American history class) inspired other students to reveal what "weird" foods were eaten in their cultures, and to express pride in these differences; as a result, what began as apparently a fundamental difference between "us" and the "Chinese other" became normalized into a superficial difference.[8]

Not all cultural differences can or should be normalized, however, and not all can necessarily be handled even by (3), teaching others the reasons behind these differences. Returning to the example of the Orthodox Jew above, it is relatively easy for Molly to learn to tolerate his not shaking her hand because once she knows the reason, she can interpret it as one way his culture expresses fidelity, which is a value Molly shares. In this respect, Molly ultimately tolerates his behavior because she sees it arising out of a shared value—because in this respect at least, underneath it all they're the same: they both believe in the value of fidelity. If Molly discovers, however, that fidelity is expressed in this way (not touching other women) because women are viewed as temptresses, and hence as in some way unclean, then her newfound understanding of his behavior confronts her with a fundamental difference. She doesn't interpret the gendered world the same way at all, so what Molly at first might have seen as rude ("why won't he shake my hand?"), and then at second glance seen as a somewhat old-fashioned but charming way of demonstrating fidelity to his wife ("oh, he'll touch only her, how sweet"), now at third glance she sees as a slap in the face to herself and half the world's population ("he won't shake my hand because I'm inherently unclean?!"). The true test of Molly's toleration of difference is her remaining tolerant even now—now, note, that she's learned *more* about his beliefs, rather than less.

As this example reveals, learning about others does not necessarily guarantee that we will become more tolerant of their behavior or beliefs, let alone more respectful of them. The more we learn, the more different and the less deserving of toleration someone, or some group, may seem. In this respect, multicultural education understood as multicultural content is both a tool and a potential hindrance to promoting mutual toleration and respect. Does this mean that multicultural education is the wrong tool to use in achieving the aims of promoting toleration and respect? I don't think so. But its implementation is much more complex than is usually acknowledged.

We just saw how multicultural *content* may be a useful approach to achieving an important *goal* of multicultural education (in this case, promoting toleration), but that it is more complex than is usually assumed. I want now to turn to another example in which neither the *content* nor *practices* of multicultural education (such as culturally congruent teaching) seem to be evident—where they are in fact consciously rejected, to a certain extent—but which may achieve some of the central *goals* of multicultural education more consistently than most self-consciously multicultural schools. I am thinking here of the network of more than 50 KIPP charter schools that has expanded across the United States over the past five or so years. Students who attend a KIPP school participate in an extended school day that keeps them away from home, and often from their neighborhoods as well, from early in the morning until late in the afternoon. They follow similar rigorous academic curricula that leave relatively little room for individual teacher discretion in comparison to some other schools. Students attending KIPP schools are overwhelmingly black and/or Hispanic, and the vast majority are poor; to this extent, KIPP schools are often less diverse than other schools in the district. As soon as students enter a KIPP school, they are taught to "SLANT": Sit up straight, Listen, Ask and answer questions, Nod their head if they understand, and Track the speaker. KIPP elementary and middle schools usually attempt to prepare students for and place them in exclusive private/independent schools, as well as in select public schools (often ones that require an exam or place other barriers to entry). Almost all of these target schools have a student body that is predominantly white and middle class. Although reliable data are only just becoming available, it appears that KIPP students do much better on standardized measures of academic performance and go onto college at significantly higher rates than comparable students who attend non-KIPP schools in the same district (KIPP 2007; KIPP Academy Lynn Charter School 2003).

It is arguable that KIPP schools help students achieve more of the goals of multicultural education—including helping students develop autonomy (especially by expanding their universe of options), become more empowered citizens, and achieve economic competitiveness, as well as promoting equity and social justice by helping thousands of poor, minority students gain admission to and succeed in highly selective secondary schools and colleges—than do most other schools in the country. They do so, however, by explicitly teaching students what and how they need to know, do, and behave to succeed in the majoritarian culture of these selective schools—in other words, arguably, how to fit into the culture of the white, middle-class, educated elite. (Tough 2006; see Hochschild and Scovronick 2003, chap. 7, for a related argument.) Some multicultural education theorists thus reject approaches like KIPP's (Sleeter 1991). But this rejection strikes me as being reflexive rather than thoughtful. James and Cherry Banks define multicultural education as "a field of study designed to increase educational equity for all students that incorporates, for this purpose, content, concepts, principles, theories, and paradigms from history, the social and behavioral sciences, and particularly from ethnic studies and women's studies" (Banks and Banks 2004: xii). If schools such as KIPP "increase equity for all students" without incorporating content, principles, or paradigms based in ethnic and women's studies—and, let's pretend for the sake of argument, in fact increase equity far better than most schools that do incorporate ethnic and women's studies content and paradigms—then does the fault lie with schools like KIPP, or with the operative conception of multicultural education?

4. CONCLUSION

Multicultural education is a powerful idea. It has rallied many to take up the causes of improving the education of students who have suffered far too long in uncaring and ineffective schools, combating racism, giving appropriate recognition to the many groups and peoples who helped build and shape our national history and culture, and limiting majoritarian impulses to quash minority ways of life. As such, multicultural education deserves to be celebrated. But it is also an empty idea, at least taken solely on its own terms. It embraces so many laudable goals, practices, and types of content that they frequently contradict each other both in theory and in practice. Proponents of one vision of multicultural education chastise proponents of other visions for getting multicultural education wrong—but all conceptions of multicultural education, whether minimalist, maximalist, or in between, introduce complexities, complications, and potential contradictions of their own. Multicultural education is probably best thought of as an abbreviation or stand-in for other values that we hold regarding the aims, practices, and content of education. This approach sometimes can work, and may even be effective at rallying people who would normally be at odds with one another to work together in service of a shared (or apparently shared) goal. But its practical use as an umbrella term that fosters warm and fuzzy feelings of unity (at least among certain groups) shouldn't be confused with its theoretical coherence, of which there is little to none. When we see references to "multicultural education," therefore, we must always ask what is actually meant, and realize that the term may obscure as much as it enlightens.

NOTES

I have discussed my ideas about multicultural education with numerous people, many of whom have also generously commented on various drafts I've written about the topic. I am grateful to the following people for having helped me clarify my thoughts about multicultural education, although I hasten to add that none read (nor, hence, bear any responsibility for) this exact chapter: Rob Reich, Mica Pollock, Prudence Carter, Liz Canner, Larry Blum, Robert Fullinwider, Jennifer Hochschild, Michael Marder, Cynthia Levinson, Sanford Levinson, Marc Lipsitch, Michael Merry, Eamonn Callan, Walter Feinberg, Denis Philips, Howard Gardner, Chris Higgins, Sarah Tsang, Jack Dougherty, Jasmine Mahmoud, Lindy Hess, James Foreman, Pam Gordon, and participants in seminars, workshops, or other presentations I gave at Harvard, Cornell, Teachers College, Stanford-Illinois Philosophy of Education Summer Institute, University of Texas at Austin, and Radcliffe Institute for Advanced Study. I am also grateful for the financial and intellectual resources provided by Spencer Foundation/National Academy of Education and Radcliffe Institute for Advanced Study.

1. Although Kymlicka (1995: 59–60) does notably support voluntary segregated schools for Native Americans and native Hawaiians.

2. Although multiculturalism and antiracism are frequently mentioned in the same breath, Larry Blum (1999) points out that they have rather different value bases.

3. It should be noted that not all philosophers limit their multicultural critique to curricula alone. With reference to protecting minority groups' rights and cultures, Kymlicka explains, for example, we must "examine the structure of institutions (e.g., the language, calendar, and uniforms that they use) and the content of schooling and media, since all of these take the majority culture as the 'norm'" (Kymlicka 1999: 33).

4. It's worth noting that I've given no examples of this aim in U.S. state standards, as it would be politically suicidal for a state board or department of education to say that a goal of the curriculum is to "reconstruct society" or to empower teachers as "agents of social change." Even explicit discussion of racism as an ongoing, present challenge as opposed to something of merely historical interest is unusual in state curriculum frameworks in the United States, although other countries make the link much more readily (see, e.g., the U.K.'s Qualifications and Curriculum Authority 2007a).

5. It should be noted that political theorists interested in multiculturalism have also written a tremendous amount about the empowerment of minority or marginalized cultural groups, but this work tends not to be linked to writing on multicultural *education*.

6. Self-esteem has been decoupled from multicultural education both because the concept itself became an object of public derision thanks to its overuse and misuse in the 1990s (Owens and Stryker 2001) and because psychologists' research on self-esteem has demonstrated conclusively that self-esteem is an extremely complex construct that has little to do with, say, hearing positive things about their "group" or "I am special" mantras (Covington 2001).

7. These aims could obviously be broken up and recombined in a variety of ways.

8. I should note that these examples provide support for my contention at the end of section II that diverse, integrated schools may have tremendous value, including in promoting some goals of multicultural education. These discussions, and efforts to promote tolerance and mutual respect, are far easier in an integrated setting where children can become friends with each other and experience commonality (worries over tests, love of basketball, dislike of a teacher, treating others nicely) in a natural setting and then confront some of their differences. With a shared basis of experience, and an experience of common humanity already, it's an easier and safer basis on which to respect difference. (See Pettigrew and Tropp 2000 for a comprehensive meta-analysis of research supporting this conclusion.) In a segregated setting, on the other hand, there is a greater sense of "otherness" about the groups one is being taught about.

REFERENCES

Appiah, K. A. (1996). "Culture, Subculture, Multiculturalism: Educational Options." In *Public Education in a Multicultural Society*, ed. R. K. Fullinwider (pp. 65–89). Cambridge: Cambridge University Press.

Banks, J. A. (2001a). "Approaches to Multicultural Curriculum Reform." In *Multicultural Education: Issues and Perspectives*, 4th ed., ed. J. A. Banks and C. A. M. Banks (pp. 225–46). New York: Wiley.

—— (2001b). "Multicultural Education: Characteristics and Goals." In *Multicultural Education: Issues and Perspectives*, 4th ed., ed. J. A. Banks and C. A. M. Banks (pp. 3–30). New York: Wiley.

—— (2001c). Preface. *Multicultural Education: Issues and Perspectives*, 4th ed., ed. J. A. Banks and C. A. M. Banks (pp. 1–2). New York: Wiley.

—— (2005). Series Foreword. In *Un-Standardizing Churriculum: Multicultural Teaching in the Standard-Based Classroom*, by C. E. Sleeter (pp. vii–xi). New York: Teachers College Press.

Banks, J. A., and C. A. M. Banks. (2004). *Handbook of Research on Multicultural Education*, 2nd ed. San Francisco: Jossey-Bass.

Blum, L. (1999). "Value Underpinnings of Antiracist and Multicultural Education." In *Systems of Education: Theories, Policies and Implicit Values (Education, Culture, and Values)*, Vol. 1, ed. M. Leicester, C. Modgil, and S. Modgil (pp. 3–14). London: Falmer Press.

California Department of Education. (2000). "History-Social Science Content Standards for California Public Schools, Kindergarten Through Grade Twelve." Retrieved February 16, 2009, from http://www.cde.ca.gov/be/st/ss/documents/histsocscistnd.pdf.

Covington, M. V. (2001). "The Science and Politics of Self-Esteem: Schools Caught in the Middle." In *Extending Self-Esteem Theory and Research: Sociological and Psychological Currents*, ed. T. J. Owens, S. Stryker, and N. Goodman (pp. 351–74). Cambridge: Cambridge University Press.

Cummins, J. (2000). Foreword. In *Affirming Diversity*, by S. Nieto (pp. xiv–xvi). New York: Longman.

Delpit, L. (1995). *Other People's Children*. New York: The New Press.

Farkas, S., and J. Johnson. (1998). "Time to Move On: African American and White Parents Set an Agenda for Public Schools." Report for Public Agenda Foundation. Retrieved February 17, 2009, from http://www.publicagenda.org/files/pdf/time_to_move_on.pdf.

Feinberg, W. (1998). *Common Schools/ Uncommon Identities*. New Haven: Yale University Press.

Foster, M. (1997). *Black Teachers on Teaching*. New York: The New Press.

Gay, G. (1995). "Curriculum Theory and Multicultural Education." In *Handbook of Research on Multicultural Education*, ed. J. A. Banks and C. A. M. Banks (pp. 25–41). New York: Simon & Schuster Macmillan.

—— (2000). *Culturally Responsive Teaching: Theory, Research, and Practice*. New York: Teachers College Press.

—— (2001). "Educational Equality for Students of Color." In *Multicultural Education: Issues and Perspectives*, 4th ed., ed. J. A. Banks and C. A. M. Banks (pp. 197–224). New York: Wiley.

Georgia Department of Education. (1997). "Values and Character Education Implementation Guide." Retrieved February 17, 2009, from http://chiron.valdosta.edu/whuitt/col/affsys/valuesga.html.

Grant, C. A., and C. E. Sleeter. (1999). *Making Choices for Multicultural Education: Five Approaches to Race, Class, and Gender*, 3rd ed. New York: Wiley.

—— (2001). "Race, Class, Gender, and Disability in the Classroom." In *Multicultural Education: Issues and Perspectives*, 4th ed., ed. J. A. Banks and C. A. M. Banks (pp. 59–81). New York: Wiley.

Gutmann, A. (1996). "Challenges of Multiculturalism in Democratic Education." In *Public Education in a Multicultural Society*, ed. R. K. Fullinwider (pp. 156–79). Cambridge: Cambridge University Press.

Hessler, P. (2000). "A Rat in My Soup." *The New Yorker*, July 24, pp. 38–41.

Hochschild, J., and N. Scovronick. (2003). *The American Dream and the Public Schools*. New York: Oxford University Press.

KIPP. (2007). "KIPP: Knowledge is Power Program." Retrieved October 12, 2007, from www.kipp.org.

KIPP Academy Lynn Charter School. (2003). "KIPP Academy Lynn Charter School Final Application." November 14, 2003. Retrieved October 11, 2007, from http://www.doe.mass.edu/charter/approved/0429.pdf.

Kymlicka, W. (1995). *Multicultural Citizenship*. Oxford: Oxford University Press.

—— (1999). "Liberal Complacencies." In S. M. Okin, *Is Multiculturalism Bad for Women?* ed. J. Cohen, M. Howard, and M. C. Nussbaum (pp. 31–34). Princeton: Princeton University Press.

Ladson-Billings, G. (1994). *The Dreamkeepers: Successful Teachers of African American Children.* San Francisco: Jossey-Bass.

Levinson, M. (1999). *The Demands of Liberal Education.* Oxford: Oxford University Press.

—— (forthcoming). *The Civic Empowerment Gap* [title pending]. New York: Metropolitan/ Henry Holt.

Macedo, S. (2000). *Diversity and Distrust: Civic Education in a Multicultural Democracy.* Cambridge, MA: Harvard University Press.

Massey, D. S., and N. A. Denton. (1993). *American Apartheid: Segregation and the Making of the Underclass.* Cambridge, MA: Harvard University Press.

Montana Office of Public Instruction. (1999). Montana Standards for Literature. Retrieved October 15, 2007, from http://www.opi.mt.gov/pdf/standards/ContStds-Literature.pdf.

Moody v. Cronin. F. Supp., C.D. Ill. 484: 270 (1979).

Nash, G. (1996). "Multiculturalism and History: Historical Perspectives and Present Prospects." In *Public Education in a Multicultural Society: Policy, Theory, Critique,* ed. R. K. Fullinwider (pp. 183–202). Cambridge: Cambridge University Press.

New York State Education Department. (1996). "Learning Standards for Languages Other than English." Retrieved October 15, 2007, from http://www.emsc.nysed.gov/ciai/lote/ pub/lotelea.pdf.

—— (2003). "New York State Learning Standards: English Language Arts." Retrieved March 7, 2003, from http://www.emsc.nysed.gov/ciai/ela/elals.html.

Nieto, S. (2000). *Affirming Diversity: The Sociopolitical Context of Multicultural Education,* 3rd ed. New York: Longman.

—— (2001). "School Reform and Student Learning: A Multicultural Perspective." In *Multicultural Education: Issues and Perspectives,* 4th ed., ed. J. A. Banks and C. A. M. Banks (pp. 381–401). New York: Wiley.

NSW Department of Education and Training and Office of the Board of Studies NSW. (2007). "Making Multicultural Australia." Retrieved October 16, 2007, from http:// www.multiculturalaustralia.edu.au/purpose/index.php.

Okin, S. M. (1999). *Is Multiculturalism Bad for Women?* Princeton: Princeton University Press.

Owens, T. J., and S. Stryker. (2001). "The Future of Self-Esteem: An Introduction." In *Extending Self-Esteem Theory and Research: Sociological and Psychological Currents,* ed. T. J. Owens, S. Stryker, and N. Goodman (pp. 1–9). Cambridge: Cambridge University Press.

Pettigrew, T. F., and L. R. Tropp. (2000). "Does Intergroup Contact Reduce Prejudice? Recent Meta-Analytic Findings." In *Reducing Prejudice and Discrimination (Claremont Symposium on Applied Social Psychology),* ed. S. Oskamp. Mahwah, NJ: Erlbaum.

Qualifications and Curriculum Authority. (2007a). "Respect for All." Retrieved October 17, 2007, from http://www.qca.org.uk/qca_6753.aspx.

—— (2007b). "Respect for All Ethos." Retrieved October 22, 2007, from http://www.qca. org.uk/qca_6756.aspx.

Rawls, J. (1993). *Political Liberalism.* New York: Columbia University Press.

Reich, R. (2002). *Bridging Liberalism and Multiculturalism in American Education.* Chicago: University of Chicago Press.

Siddle Walker, V. (1996). *Their Highest Potential: An African American School Community in the Segregated South.* Chapel Hill: University of North Carolina Press.

Sleeter, C. E. (1991). *Empowerment through Multicultural Education*. Albany: State University of New York Press.

———— (2005). *Un-Standardizing Curriculum: Multicultural Teaching in the Standards-Based Classroom*. New York: Teachers College Press.

State of Delaware, Department of Education. (1995). "Content Standards." *Social Studies Framework*. Retrieved February 16, 2009 from, http://www.doe.k12.de.us/infosuites/ staff/ci/content_areas/socialstudies.shtml.

State of New Jersey. (1996). "New Jersey World Languages Curriculum Framework." *New Jersey Core Curriculum Content Standards*. Retrieved February 17, 2009, from http:// www.nj.gov/education/frameworks/worldlanguages/.

Tamir, Y. (2002). "Education and the Politics of Identity." In *A Companion to Philosophy of Education*, ed. R. Curren (pp. 501–508). Oxford: Blackwell.

Taylor, C. (1992). *Multiculturalism and "The Politics of Recognition."* Princeton: Princeton University Press.

Tough, P. (2006). "What It Takes to Make a Student." *New York Times Magazine*. Retrieved June 2, 2009 from http://www.nytimes.com/2006/11/26/magazine/26tough.html? pagewanted=print.

Wisconsin v. Yoder. U.S. Supreme Court. 406: 205 (1972).

Young, I. M. (1990). *Justice and the Politics of Difference*. Princeton: Princeton University Press.

CHAPTER 24

PREJUDICE

LAWRENCE BLUM

PREJUDICE and stereotypes are often grouped together as ways that we misrelate to our fellow humans, based on their group identities. Stereotypes often generate prejudices; if I regard group *X* as stupid, venal, or dishonest, I am likely to have an antipathy toward group *X* that constitutes prejudice. Prejudices generally involve stereotypes also; if I have antipathy toward group *Y,* I am likely to attribute certain negative characteristics to them in a stereotypical way. Similarly, both stereotypes and prejudice pose educational challenges. Both involve irrationality in beliefs about human groups, and both involve violating appropriate regard and respect for our fellow human beings. Avoiding these moral and epistemological pitfalls is an important task of education.

Yet prejudice and stereotypes are distinct phenomena and require distinct treatment. People can stereotype without necessarily being prejudiced. They may hold various stereotypic associations with various groups without either having any negative affect toward the group or assessing the group negatively. This is partly because stereotypes can be positive, attributing a generally favorable trait to the group—blacks being good athletes, Asians being good students, and so on. The stereotype is still objectionable, as all stereotypes are, but does not necessarily involve prejudice. But even negative stereotypes do not necessarily rise to the level of actual prejudice, which is a more robust negative attitude toward the group. So someone might think that Asians are devious and untrustworthy, yet not form an actual prejudice against Asians based on that attribution. In this entry, I will be focusing on prejudice, and will discuss stereotypes only incidentally.

The linguistic origin of *prejudice* lies in *prejudgment,* or making a judgment prior to having adequate evidentiary basis for it. But the contemporary notion of prejudice involves an affective component as well as a judgmental one. If I judge group *X* to have such and such characteristics, though I have little basis for doing so, yet if I have no feeling for or against group X, I would not be spoken of as prejudiced against group X. At the same time, a pure antipathy toward group X without any accompanying evaluations or judgments ("I'm not saying there is anything wrong with Mexicans—I just hate them") would not generally be spoken of as prejudice either, though this is not a very common phenomenon.

Prejudices can be favorable toward a group, not only antipathetic to them. However, of greater concern from a moral and educational perspective is the much more common phenomenon of prejudice as "prejudice against," and I will from this point on use *prejudice* only with this meaning.

Of the two components of prejudice, negative affect and (unwarranted) negative evaluation/judgment, neither has causal or definitional primacy. Judging or stereotyping group X as lazy, dishonest, and foolish can lead to antipathy toward its members; but an antipathy can be primary and can give rise to negative judgments that appear to rationalize the antipathy.

Almost anything can be a target of prejudice or stereotyping—individual persons, types of music, cities—but the study of prejudice has generally focused on human groups, or persons as members of such groups, no doubt because these are very common forms of prejudice and present moral challenges as harmful or disrespectful to persons. (If I am prejudiced against baseball, there seems no harm in this.) So human groups and human persons will be our subject. Yet the way that human persons are the target of prejudice allows for other related and derivative targets. Someone who dislikes blacks may also, derivatively, dislike what she regards as black characteristics, or characteristics she associates with blacks, in other persons or things (Piper 1990). For example, she may dislike hip-hop styles, when exhibited by whites or other nonblacks. That is, prejudice against blacks can involve prejudice against "blackness," which the subject can see in nonblacks. Prejudice does not require that the connection between black persons and the characteristic or object in question be in any way a valid one, only that the subject make that connection in her own mind; if someone dislikes a kind of music because she associates it with blacks, when in fact the music is Greek in origin, this dislike is still, for that person, part of prejudice against blacks.

Not all hostility toward human groups is prejudice, for some of it is justified. Prejudice must be unjustified; that is part of why it is morally wrong. Hostility toward Nazis is justified and, more generally, hostility to groups defined by a commitment to bad beliefs or actions is justified. Of course, it is not always easy, or possible, to determine what is bad in the sense required here. But most groups are not united around a bad project in this way; and ethnic, racial, religious, and national groups—those with which prejudice research has been primarily concerned—are not, so that antipathy toward them is always unjustified and is prejudice. And antipathy toward whole groups based on the bad behavior or characteristics of only some of its members is a paradigm of prejudice.

Since prejudice is, by definition, wrong or bad, people seldom avow prejudices as such, though they might avow an attitude they recognize others to view as prejudice. So there are two different ways prejudice can fail to be acknowledged.

One is that persons can hold antipathies toward a group, but regard those antipathies as warranted; they wrongly believe that the group in question possesses traits that warrant the group antipathy—Mexicans as lazy, Muslims as terrorists, Jews as greedy and cheap, and so on. So such persons acknowledge the antipathy but not that this constitutes prejudice.

A second very common way that prejudices can be unacknowledged is that a person might harbor antipathy toward a group and have negative evaluations of the group, yet be unaware of doing so. There is an important historical dimension to this form of nonconscious prejudice that can be illustrated in the case of racial prejudice. For centuries in the United States, holding antipathetic or disparaging views of black people was expected and normal among the white majority; this was true as well toward other nonwhite groups, and (in the early part of the twentieth century) toward many (white) immigrant groups also. Such negative assessments of whole ethnic groups were not thought to be wrong or misplaced. Over time, and largely because of the challenges to these prejudices spearheaded by blacks and, later, other racial and ethnic minorities, the idea that it was wrong to hold such views became normative, especially in public venues but in many personal ones as well. This development resulted in an incentive for people to be prejudice-free and to be thought to be prejudice-free.

This incentive did not result in the disappearance of racial and ethnic prejudices, although the striking diminishing of certain avowed prejudices (e.g., in opposition to racial integration) on opinion surveys from, say, the 1930s until today surely reflects some reduction in actual prejudice. But another effect of the incentive was the mere reduction in overt expressions of prejudice, both because many people learned to express their prejudices in a way that would not garner social disapproval and because many people masked their possession of those prejudices from themselves. As a result, it is much more difficult to discern when someone has racial prejudices than in earlier periods. And unconscious prejudice raises distinct moral issues. If someone does not know she is prejudiced do we not think of her as less responsible for her prejudice than if she is aware of that prejudice and accepts it? (Of course, she could be aware of it and be in the process of attempting to rid herself of it also.)

1. Delimiting "Prejudice"

Sometimes the term "prejudice" is used to encompass any and all negative affect toward human groups. This can be misleading, in two different ways. First, some negative feelings toward a group are so intense and extreme that the word *prejudice* seems too pallid to capture them. To say that Southern whites who lynched African Americans were "prejudiced" against them seems too weak for attitudes that would prompt such conduct, just as it would be to say that Hitler was "prejudiced" against

Jews. Although prejudices can themselves be of different strengths or intensities—someone can be more prejudiced against gays than Latinos, for example, and person A can be more prejudiced (against a given group) than person B—there seems to be some maximal threshold, not necessarily specifiable in any definitive way, beyond which the sentiment or attitude in question becomes something worse than prejudice. Similarly, some negative affect seems to be too weak or minimal to count as prejudice—for example, a mild discomfort in the presence of a member of the outgroup. It is not that such discomfort should be regarded as an acceptable feeling, only that the term "prejudice" implies something stronger.

A different potential confusion about the scope of *prejudice* relates to its standard definition, which I have accepted, as involving a negative affect and evaluation toward the group in question. Not every objectionable and unwarranted attitude toward human groups satisfies that definition. During Jim Crow segregation, many whites who employed blacks as servants felt genuine affection and care toward their employees; they did not have a "negative affect" such as antipathy, hostility, or dislike toward them. And yet they generally made the racist assumption that blacks' proper role in life was to serve white people, and that this was true of these valued servants as well. Obviously, this is an entirely morally objectionable view of blacks. So, objectionable attitudes toward a group do not always involve negative feelings toward the group. One can demean or patronize a group without such negative feeling. However, the ideology that blacks' proper place is to serve and be deferential to whites does tend to generate hostility and hatred toward those particular blacks who defy or fail adequately to conform, in whites' minds, to this expectation.

That objectionable racial attitudes do not necessarily involve antipathy or other negative affect illustrates a larger point about prejudice that applies beyond the domain of race. Objectionable sexist attitudes toward women can exemplify this point as well, as when women are seen as delicate flowers requiring male protection, objects of display for successful or powerful men, being ill-suited to "male domains" of work, and so on.

It would be morally arbitrary to confine a concern with objectionable and unwarranted individual attitudes toward groups to those involving negative affect toward the group. That subcategory is not necessarily more objectionable in any general sense than the disrespect involved in regarding group X as suited only to serve a "superior" group. And in fact, most psychologists studying prejudice often tacitly include the broader category of objectionable attitudes toward groups in their theories and research, even when their official definition of *prejudice* restricts it to negative affect. I will, therefore, take both the broader and the narrower category as my concern here, attempting to be clear about which is being discussed, while recognizing that the word *prejudice* as ordinarily used does not reliably track that broader view.

This lack of clarity about the appropriate scope of prejudice research arises in an acute and productive way in contemporary theories of racism or racial prejudice. As mentioned earlier, social psychologists and political psychologists recognize that expression of overt racial prejudice is no longer socially acceptable in most venues, but that actual prejudice has not declined to the same degree as its overt expression. New theories about the character of objectionable racial attitudes attempt to come to grips with the subtler or less blatant forms of these attitudes. For example, an important finding from opinion research is that some white people express opposition to the idea that the government should do anything to improve the situation of black people, but they do not express anything like the same hostility to black people themselves, either individually or as a group. There is a lively scholarly debate about whether the former view should be interpreted as a new form of racial prejudice, a perhaps unconscious displacement of a now-stigmatized prejudice into an acceptable political stance. (The names "modern racism" and "symbolic racism" have been used to label such a view.) Others draw a sharper distinction between traditional racial antipathy and political ideology.

Without weighing in on this complex dispute, there certainly seems a distinction worth making between an antipathy toward a group itself and its actual members, and an opposition toward the legitimate interests that that group presents in the political arena. The former may seem more objectionable than the latter; but this does not mean that the latter is acceptable. Suppose someone is opposed to the government's (at any level) doing anything to rectify the legacy of racial injustice from which blacks in the United States and elsewhere currently suffer. There may be different reasons that someone might hold such a view, ranging from straight prejudice against blacks to a pure libertarian ideology that thinks the government should be no more than a "minimal state." (Those reasons are explored in the literature just mentioned.) Nevertheless, the view itself is morally problematic, in that it involves blindness to or a failure to be moved by injustice. The exploration of prejudice should be concerned also with blindness to injustice (toward particular groups), and why some people have this blindness, as well as with other similar types of morally objectionable attitudes. It needs to be clear that it is not only racial animus that renders a resulting political stance or attitude morally problematic. That persons can hold principled political stands from which it follows that there should be no state action to address injustice does not shield such persons from moral criticism, although the criticism will have a different character than the charge of personal prejudice, depending, in part, on its source.

2. THE DIVERSITY OF PREJUDICES

Is prejudice a single phenomenon or many distinct phenomena? We have seen that prejudices encompass a range of distinct objectionable psychic phenomena—antipathy, disrespect, denial of humanity, opposition to justice. In her book *The Anatomy of Prejudices*, Elisabeth Young-Bruehl decries a tendency in psychology research about prejudice to think of prejudice as a unitary psychic phenomenon, as suggested by the title (and content) of Gordon Allport's classic (1954) work, *The Nature of Prejudice*. Young-Bruehl suggests a different sort of plurality than yet discussed, within the general category of "prejudice" and in contrast to Allport's view. Allport held that people who were prejudiced against a given group (when that group was a fairly widespread target of prejudice) tended to be prejudiced against all "out-groups." (An "out-group" is a group of which a given person is not a member.) Young-Bruehl argues, by contrast, that prejudices against different groups have differing psychological characteristics or structures, even when all of them share the same prejudice-defining psychic state, such as antipathy. So, she suggests, antipathy toward Jews and (in its recent forms in the U.S.) Asians and Asian Americans generally involves envy of their purported special capacity for success and (in the case of Jews) a view of them as pollutants who, in extreme forms of this antipathy, should be eliminated from the society in question. By contrast, she suggests, antipathy toward blacks involves projecting onto blacks sexual desires that the subject cannot acknowledge, then finding their resultant purported sexual nature fearful and threatening, and, in consequence, the group as uncivilized. Sexism she sees as exemplifying a third psychic configuration based on a fear of difference, and of that difference inside oneself (i.e., men fearing the feminine in themselves).

Young-Bruehl's specific psychoanalytically based analyses do not always seem convincing as full accounts of prejudice against the groups she discusses. Although she is correct to say that, in the United States at least, there is a tradition of sexualizing both black men and black women as part of anti-black prejudice, other dimensions of anti-black prejudice do not fit that prototype. The idea that blacks are meant to serve whites does not necessarily (though it can) have such a sexual component. And the stigmatizing of blacks evidenced in whites' refusal to live in neighborhoods with more than a "tipping point" of blacks has much more to do with associating blacks with crime, lowering of property values, and poor educational attainment and commitment than with sexuality. Neverthe-less, Young-Bruehl's larger point about the different psychological characteristics of prejudice against different groups is a salutary one and responds to the evident fact that some persons are prejudiced against only some groups but not others. They can have hostilities based on sexual orientation but not race, or vice versa, or gender but not nationality, and so on. In addition, they can have prejudices within those categories against some groups but not others (blacks but not Asians, etc.). This fact is not, however, inconsistent with a part of Allport's point—that some persons are prejudiced against all, or many, out-groups, within or across many categories.

Another related source of plurality within prejudice is in the group identities of subjects of prejudice against a particular group. For example, anti-gay prejudice among blacks might take a different form—that is, have a different psychic structure—than anti-gay prejudice among whites. For blacks, it might often be bound up with a threatened masculinity related to the historical difficulty during the era of slavery that black males had in finding work that could support their families. Anti-Jewish prejudice might have a different character among marginal white farmers who have never met a Jew but scapegoat Jews as the cause of their problems; among upper-class Protestants who view Jews with disdain as aggressive upstarts without good breeding; among blacks who know Jews as shop owners in their communities; and among Islamist Muslims. Just as the plurality among the targets of prejudice dovetails with the plurality of psychic structures of prejudice, so does a plurality in the group identities of the subjects of prejudice.

Particularly noteworthy in subject-plurality is reactive prejudice—that is, prejudice against members of groups that are victimizing one's own group. The category of reactive prejudice does not include antipathy toward the actual persons who are victimizing one or one's group; such antipathy is warranted and so does not count as prejudice. Perhaps such warranted hostility can be extended, if in lesser form, to members of the victimizer's group who support the victimizing, even if they do not take part in it. But (reactive) prejudice is involved when one is hostile to any or all members of the group in question simply because of their shared membership with the victimizers. Hostility of blacks toward all whites, or almost all whites (except those known not to be racist), or gays toward straights, are examples of reactive prejudice. Some argue that such prejudice is excusable and not really wrong. I think it would be preferable to see it as wrong but of lesser fault than nonreactive prejudice (that is, standard-issue prejudice, in any of the many forms mentioned above). It is always wrong to be hostile to another human being without warrant; it offends a norm of human respect. But it is more forgivable to do so if one's group is being targeted for victimization or discrimination by members of another group as members of that group, and with at least the passive support of many other members of said group, so that one cannot easily tell if the particular member in question falls into the set of passive supporters.

Reactive prejudice is not merely any prejudice on the part of a subordinate or nondominant group; rather, it is only when directed against the victimizing group. When directed against, say, another subordinate group, this is an entirely different dynamic, with different moral implications, as when blacks are prejudiced against Jews or gays, or gays against blacks or Mexicans. Subordinate status is not, purely in itself, a mitigating factor in the blameworthiness of prejudice.

As the phenomenon of reactive prejudice suggests, to the different forms of diversity so far mentioned—in the subject group, in the target group, and in the psychic character of prejudice—must be added a consequent fourth form: moral diversity. Not all manifestations of prejudice are equally morally wrong, blame-worthy, or otherwise problematic. Ceteris paribus, intense hostility to group X is worse than mild hostility; hatred is worse than dislike. Some groups are more vulnerable (within a given society) than others because of their small numbers, lack of economic or political power, frequency of being a target of prejudice, history of victimization, and the like. Ceteris paribus, prejudice against a more vulnerable group is morally worse than prejudice against a less vulnerable one. The more vulnerable group (or individual) is more likely to be harmed by the prejudice, both materially and psychologically, than is the nonvulnerable or less vulnerable group. For example, prejudice against Christians is, in the United States, less bad than prejudice against Muslims; prejudice against whites, than prejudice against Mexican Americans.

3. TOTALISTIC AND SELECTIVE FORMS OF PREJUDICE

We have defined the targets of prejudice as groups, or individuals in relation to their group identity or membership. This formulation needs some refinement. Some prejudices do encompass an entire group; every member of the group is regarded with equal hostility or disdain, or their justice-related interests are opposed. Let us call this a "totalistic" form of prejudice. However, when groups are in close interaction with one another, prejudices often take a more selective character, in which differentiations are made within the group. For example, in the United States, young black males are generally much more stigmatized and objects of more intense prejudice than, say, older black women. One can understand this as the subject viewing the subgroup as more representative of the larger group (young black males being viewed as "more black," or as representing what the subject sees as paradigmatically black, compared to other subgroups). A variation of this selective prejudice is when members of a group are accepted but only insofar as they do not do something to mark themselves as members of that group, even if the subject recognizes that they are members. So, blacks who do not call attention to their blackness by, for example, braiding their hair in dreadlocks, wearing African clothing, advocating for black interests, talking in African-American dialect, and the like, are accepted, while those who do engage in such behaviors are the target of prejudice. Here, the subject does not fail to recognize that the former group members actually are black. (However, "I don't see you as black" is one way of expressing this sort of prejudice, offered as if it were a compliment, but we do not think the utterer of this comment actually fails to recognize the person in question as black, according to standard racial classification practices.) But the subject is more prejudiced against those who call attention to their blackness.

Something similar applies to a selective form of anti-gay prejudice, and it represents an advance, though only a very partial one, from the totalistic homophobia that targets every gay person equally. In the selective form, certain gay people are accepted—those whom the subject does not regard as calling attention to or showing pride in their gayness, for example, by acting or talking in ways seen by the subject as gay, advocating for gay rights, and so on. Older forms of acceptance of only those Jews seen as "not too Jewish" exemplify this selective prejudice.

Clearly, selective prejudice does involve objectionable attitudes toward the whole group itself, even if it takes a nontotalistic form, in which certain subgroups are not the target of standard prejudicial attitudes of hostility, derision, disgust, and the like. For the subject is not able to accept members of the group who embrace that membership.

4. Theories of the Causes of Prejudice

If prejudice is to be understood as objectionable attitudes (evaluations plus affect) toward human groups, one wants to know what gives rise to such attitudes. This question is important also for educational purposes, as we want to know how to employ education to prevent or reduce prejudice; knowing what causes prejudice will help us to do that. Philosophy cannot supply this information; only social science can. But we can differentiate different categories of explanation—individual/psychological, social, and historical.

Psychological theories locate the causes of prejudice in features of individual personality. Perhaps the best-known of such theories was propounded in the 1950 study, *The Authoritarian Personality*, which claimed that persons who are rigid, conventional, strongly submissive to authority, and aggressive toward inferiors are likely to be prejudiced (toward all out-groups, it was claimed). Prejudice is thus seen as a kind of individual pathology.

Social explanations locate the sources of individual prejudice in social structures and circumstances. Individuals internalize views dominant in their societies, or in the subcultures in which they live, of salient social groups. (What causes a certain society to hold the views of particular groups that they do hold requires further explanation, such as the historical perspective attempts, in part, to supply.) Prejudice thus becomes part of normal socialization, like learning conventional greetings, expectations of personal distance, and accepted social values. On this account, someone's holding prejudices tells us little about that person's individual psychology.

The social approach encompasses two different emphases. One is how an individual's overall level or type of prejudice is linked to the norms of her society or subculture. A second is how an individual's prejudices might differ in different social circumstances. A 1952 study of white West Virginian miners found that when working in the mine, the workers accepted blacks as equals and accepted integration, but in community life "above ground," inequality and segregation were the norm. These two emphases within social explanations of prejudice pull in different directions but are not strictly incompatible. Some prejudices could be relatively stable and situationally independent, by virtue of their deriving from norms entrenched in their larger social contexts, while others could be situationally variable.

The third category of explanation is historical. Some, perhaps most, current prejudices have long histories. Jew hatred arose out of early Christianity, and was affected by the dispersal of Jews throughout Europe and Asia in the centuries around the birth of Christ, resulting in Jews being a religious minority in the lands in which they resided. These and other factors help to explain the forms and prevalence of Jew hatred (or what since the late nineteenth century is called "anti-Semitism") in the modern world. In the West, prejudice against blacks can only be understood in the historical context of the African slave trade and slavery in the New World, colonialism in Africa, segregation in the United States, and apartheid in South Africa. That history bears heavily on the current situation of blacks and the character of prejudices against blacks. For example, it explains why prejudices against blacks contain such a heavy component of the idea that blacks are inferior to whites, which is less present in other ethnic prejudices and prejudices of other categories such as sexual orientation and immigrant status. On the other hand, gender prejudice—prejudice against women—also has a long history and that history also contains a strong element of the idea that women are inherently inferior to men in important human traits.

The three categories of explanation—individual, social, historical—pull in different directions and have different implications for attempts to mitigate prejudice. If prejudice's causes are individual, attempts to address them through education and changes in child-rearing practices are appropriate. But if the causes are social in character, it will be necessary to change social arrangements and structures through policy and perhaps social movements. This difference is highlighted in one prominent theory of prejudice, called "social dominance" theory. On this view, societies in which some groups are more favorably positioned than others develop and adopt ideologies that rationalize that inequality—for example, by viewing some groups as inferior to others (either biologically or culturally). That ideology will then be pervasive within the society and will thus be adopted by individuals and groups, although to significantly different extents, in part dependent on whether the individual is a member of a dominant group or a subdominant one. Although social dominance theory does not explicitly draw this implication, it would seem to follow from it that if a society becomes more egalitarian in its social arrangements, and mitigates the inequities between social groups, its resultant ideology will change in a less hierarchy-rationalizing direction; such a more egalitarian society will, then, produce diminished prejudice within the society overall.

Of course, trying to make one's society more equal through social policy or social movement can be regarded as a worthy goal independent of its impact on prejudice. And, indeed, the focus on prejudice has itself been criticized for focusing exclusively on individuals and their prejudices, and thereby diverting attention from attempts to make societies themselves less unequal.

Although the individual, social, and historical approaches to prejudice causation can be at odds with one another, they are not really incompatible; indeed, one would expect an overarching theory of prejudice to contain all three. The historical is necessary to understand why the social factors—institutional devaluing of blacks, widespread stereotypes of Jews and Muslims, and the like—are present and how they operate. And the individual level can be combined with the social in two ways. One is to say that the same prejudice can have multiple causes. Some people are prejudiced against gays because they cannot acknowledge their own homosexual impulses, and suppressing those impulses results in antipathy toward gay people; but others simply absorb the less intense and emotionally volatile form of anti-gay prejudice pervasive in all but a small number of communities in the United States. A second way of combining them is to say that the individual and the social sources can coexist in a single person; to oversimplify a bit, perhaps everyone in a given community who is not gay shares a certain degree of anti-gay antipathy, but some individuals in that community are much more homophobic than others, and this difference is due to individual factors. In fact, social dominance theory itself is concerned both with general social prejudices generated by inequality-rationalizing ideologies and also with explaining individual differences in the degree and form of such prejudices.

5. Is Prejudice Ineradicable?

How can education contribute to reducing prejudice? Before addressing this question we must make sure that prejudice can be reduced, that it is not an inevitable and ineradicable part of human nature. Several distinct theories claim or strongly suggest that it is. One claims that the drawing of a boundary between in-group and out-group, with an attendant favoritism toward in-groups, is universal. A second says that natural selection favored small groups with strong in-group protective impulses, and that human beings inherit that tendency. A third focuses on a claim that our brains are hardwired to view social reality in terms of simplified group categories, which inevitably distort the complex reality of our world and render stereotyping, hence prejudice, inevitable. This last claim belongs to a discussion of stereotyping that cannot be undertaken here. The evolutionary claim in the second stance would also take us too far afield. But the view somewhat shared between the first and second claim, about the inevitability of in-group and out-group boundaries, warrants a brief discussion.

Attachment to particular groups does seem a virtually universal feature of human nature, and necessarily brings with it a differentiating between in-group and out-group members. Nevertheless, the character of sentiments toward out-groups seems extremely variable and wide-ranging, encompassing amiable competitiveness, benign indifference, prejudicial and inaccurate stereotyping, hostility, and hatred. The mere distinguishing between in-group and out-group does not by itself dictate what sort of attitudes and sentiments will be generated by that distinction, and certainly does not require prejudice against out-group members. Perhaps it is more likely, everything else being equal, that prejudice will develop toward out-groups than in-groups; but this tells us nothing about the possibilities of reducing or even eliminating prejudice, through education or other means. Moreover, making an in-group/out-group distinction is perfectly consistent with the existence of attitudes that are indifferent to or transcend that distinction, such as a sense of obligation to or solidarity with one's fellow citizen, fellow human being, fellow sufferer, and so on.

Furthermore, the boundary between in-group and out-group can be drawn in a large number of ways, and some are much more likely than others to generate prejudice. In a racially and ethnically mixed group of students in the same class, neighborhood, or club, in-groups can form along lines that transcend race and ethnicity, and can either supplant, or exist alongside, in-groups defined by ethnicity itself. The former types of in-group (in a racially mixed neighborhood, for example) are not likely to generate common forms of ethnic and racial prejudice, although they may generate other deleterious forms of rivalry and prejudice.

The distinction between in-group and out-group is sometimes conflated with the notion of ethnocentrism. And the latter is sometimes thought to be universal (and is sometimes, then, contrasted with racism, which exists only where a notion of race has developed, a notion that is not historically or culturally universal). But ethnocentrism is only one very particular form of in-group/out-group distinction, one that is based on a sense of ethnos, or ancestral-cultural identity, and involves the idea that one's ethnos is better than other ethne. But not everyone is part of such an ethnos, especially in a world of extensive ethnic mixing such as our own. And not everyone who is part of such an ethnos invests much in that distinction or identity. So ethnocentrism is not universal.

6. Educational Responses to Prejudice: The Contact Hypothesis

We can divide educational approaches to the reduction of prejudice into curricular and noncurricular forms. Let me begin with the latter.

Students' contact in school with members of out-groups clearly merits attention for its potential to reduce prejudice against those groups (and perhaps out-groups more generally). Indeed, many people think of prejudice as depending centrally on ignorance of the other, so that contact with those others will automatically reduce prejudice as well. Psychologists have long recognized the falsity of this assumption. The psychology of prejudice and its generally attendant stereotyping are much too complex for contact with others to result automatically in the reduction of prejudice against and stereotypes of the group in question. For one thing, prejudices and stereotypes are not mere conscious hypothetical generalizations about groups that are readily open to confirmatory or disconfirmatory evidence. They are psychic structures and cognitive schemas that exist at least partly at levels of consciousness not directly susceptible to straightforward cognitive engagement. Often there is an emotional investment in prejudices and stereotypes not directly susceptible to cognitive treatment through disconfirmation. Moreover, there is not a tight fit between the individual and group level; persons can be prejudiced against group *X* while nevertheless thinking well of and liking particular members of group *X*. And on the other side, persons can change their conscious view of group *X*, while nevertheless continuing to react to particular encountered members of group *X* in prejudicial ways.

For these and other reasons, social psychologists in the late 1940s and 1950s concerned with improving intergroup relations and countering prejudice developed the "contact hypothesis"—a theory about the conditions that must obtain for contact between members of two different groups between which (in either or both directions) there is some extant prejudice to result in a reduction of that prejudice. The issue addressed by the contact hypothesis became particularly salient after the *Brown* v. *Board of Education* decision (1954) and the attempts at school desegregation that followed in its wake. Although it did not originate with him, the contact hypothesis was elaborated by and is most closely associated with Gordon Allport's *Nature of Prejudice* (1954). It has remained an important research paradigm in social psychology, often linked with the tortuous fate of desegregation attempts over the years, in response to the changing legal standing of such attempts. (In 2007, the U.S. Supreme Court in the *Parents Involved* case shrank almost to nothing the ability of school districts to facilitate racial desegregation through the explicit use of race in assigning students to schools.)

The four conditions most generally accepted as facilitating the translation of contact into prejudice reduction are cooperation, equal status, individualized contact, and authoritative support. I will discuss the first three of these. First, cooperation. Students from different groups must engage in activities that require them to cooperate with one another for an aim shared by all. Further research has also found that unless the group is successful in attaining that shared aim, the desired prejudice reduction is much less likely to occur; indeed, failure often leads to members of one group blaming the other for the mixed group failure and so may even intensify prejudice, at least temporarily. A plausible explanation for the positive effect of cooperation is that it creates a superordinate identity, transcending the ethnic (or other in-group) identity. The superordinate identity is able to compete with the ethnic identity and give the students who adopt that identity a sense of "we-ness" defined by the cooperating group and its success that counters the prejudicial ethnic in-group/out-group dynamic.

A second condition is equal status among the group participants. If the co-operating group contains students from groups of differing social status (wealthy/nonwealthy, white/black, native speaker/immigrant, and the like), who also have differential abilities to achieve the group goal that align with the differences in social status, the cooperative activity is likely to simply reinforce the stereotype that the lower status group is less competent. To reduce prejudice, the members of the cooperating group must see one another as equals and equal contributors.

Two dimensions of social status must be equalized in order to achieve this result. One is equal social status on dimensions extrinsic to the task at hand. In a hierarchical society, by definition this condition will not be met by choosing random members of the differing groups; since some racial desegregation in schools brings largely middle-class whites and largely working-class or poor blacks and Latinos together, the equal status condition is challenging to meet. However, it can be partially realized by careful selection of the students in the cooperating group—for example, having white and black students, or native and immigrant students, of a similar class background put into the same cooperative groups, even if these are not representative of those groups in the school.

The second dimension is equal status within the cooperative in-class group itself. That is to say, students from each of the ethnic/racial groups must be perceived by members of the other group(s), as well as by themselves, to be equally competent at and contributory to achieving the group goal. One way this condition can be achieved is through the so-called jigsaw method, in which each student is given a distinct task that differs from all the others and is able to become an "expert" in this task, and all the tasks are essential to achieving the overall group aim (Stephan 1999, p. 63). The members of the group will then be dependent on each other and will perceive each other as competent and contributory no matter what their ethnic group. This condition can trump the need for extra-school equal status which, as we saw, can be difficult to achieve (Stephan 1999, p. 42).

The third condition for contact to have a positive impact on prejudice is that the students get to know one another across group lines, that the contact not be too fleeting or superficial, and that the group identity which is the subject of the prejudice not be made too salient. (This is called "personalization" or "individualization.") That form of contact allows students to break through their prejudice and stereotypes at least in relation to the particular other students, to gain information about these students that allows them to see the limitations of their previous images of the group, and thus to increase the likelihood of reducing the prejudice at least to some extent.

7. Educational Responses to Prejudice: Curricular Approaches

On the curricular side, there are two obvious candidates for academic material with some claim to reducing prejudice. One is information about particular groups that are the likely target of the prejudices of the students in the school. This might differ from school to school, depending on the demography of the area; some communities will have significant numbers of Mexicans, Hmong, Filipinos, and so on, and others not. But some groups should be taught about, independent of their numbers in the local population, just because of their national or international historical importance or their general vulnerability to prejudice—blacks, gays, Muslims, Mexicans, and women, for example.

The assumption here is that if students who are prejudiced or stereotyping of group X learn more and thus gain accurate information about group X, this will reduce their prejudice and stereotyping. This effect can take place in two ways. One is a correction of misinformation about the group—recognizing that blacks are not just or mainly drug dealers, criminals, or unemployed; that gays are not, disproportionately, child molesters; that women are as capable at men; and so on. The second is an encouragement of empathy for the group through seeing the world from its perspective, in light of its particular history, struggles, cultures, and so on. This is not a matter of information so much as of learning to take the point of the view of members of out-groups.

No doubt the study of groups will often have this desired effect. But we should not overstate its likelihood, as prejudice and stereotypes are only partly accessible to rational methods. Moreover, not everything one learns about a given group will be flattering to the group, and some further knowledge of a group may have the unfortunate effect of seeming to confirm the stereotypes the students bring to the class. If, for example, students learn that the unemployment rate among young black males is three times that of whites of the same age, for some this might play into a stereotype of black males as lazy and unreliable as workers, even though the inference from the former to the latter is not valid. Despite this point, the temptation to present material about a stigmatized group that is entirely favorable to it or to shun material that might "play into" a stereotype or prejudice should be resisted. As important as the goal of reducing prejudice is, methods for doing so that do not violate truth or accuracy must be employed.

A second domain of curricular learning is prejudice and stereotypes themselves; the processes by which people acquire them; their damage to their targets and their distorting effects on their possessors; the historical sources of various stereotypes and prejudices; and the universalistic values of respect, truth, and humanitarianism that they violate. This domain of learning should include the differences in types of prejudice discussed earlier—in psychic structures dependent on differences in the subjects and targets of prejudice, in social factors and histories, and so on. Presumably such knowledge will make students more reflective, better able to identity their own prejudices and stereotyping, and by recognizing the ways that these can survive disconfirming evidence and other rational processes, render the students more sophisticated about how to combat their own stereotypes and prejudices—for example, by becoming better at recognizing when they are falling back into these prejudices and stereotypes after attempting to reject them.

There are age-appropriate ways of presenting both these domains—information about groups, and about prejudice itself—from elementary school on, keeping in mind that prejudices are responsive to the course of cognitive, emotional, and moral development. In high school, the standard disciplines might seem to provide greater scope for the study of particular groups—in social studies, history, and literature classes—than for the study of prejudice and stereotypes, which seems to belong to psychology or philosophy, or subjects not generally taught in high school. At the same time, units on prejudice can be included in any number of subjects, and some curricular initiatives, such as that of the professional development organization Facing History and Ourselves, have found creative and effective ways of weaving prejudice reduction and the study of prejudice and stereotypes into high school and junior high school history, social studies, and literature curricula.

. One might include a third general domain of academic study in addition to groups and prejudice. If one accepts, even to some degree, the outlook of the "social dominance" theorists, students learning about social inequality, how it has arisen, what sustains it, and how one goes about reducing it through political action will help them to understand an important source of prejudice and how to counter it. Ultimately, making the society more just, and thus political action toward that goal, may have the most longstanding effect on reducing the sources of prejudice.

8. The Character of Prejudice Reduction as an Educational Goal

How should we conceive of the goal of educational initiatives regarding prejudice? To put it another way, what exactly is "prejudice reduction" as an educational goal? Let us consider two different prominent views of prejudice and their implications for this question. The first is the related theories of "stereotyping with compunction" of Patricia Devine and of "implicit prejudice" of Mahzarin Banaji. These views posit that certain associations between groups and positive or negative traits are widely shared in a given society. The trait, or the general negativity or positivity implied by it, is automatically triggered in most people's minds when the group in question (e.g., blacks, women, gays, immigrants) is "primed"—that is, when it is brought into a subject's explicit consciousness. However, most persons are unaware that they have these associations. (Banaji sees the associations as more definitively unconscious than does Devine.)

Studies have linked these associations, which Banaji (1994) calls "implicit prejudice," to discriminatory behavior. For example, one study showed that implicit prejudice against blacks correlated with prescribing (in a laboratory context) less adequate medical treatment for blacks compared to whites, when both were having a heart attack. (Since numerous data show that blacks actually receive inferior health care to whites, this laboratory study is likely to bear on the real world conduct of medical professionals.) So this implicit prejudice is consequential, even though it may exist at a level below that of explicit awareness.

Devine (1989) thinks that the group associations, which she refers to as a "stereotype," are relatively impervious to conscious intervention, and do not change much in the society at large over time. But she does think that people's conscious beliefs about the traits possessed by groups, and beliefs about how one should act toward members of the groups in question, are, or can be, relatively independent of the stereotype; and she believes that such beliefs control how we actually act toward the group in question. So if the doctors in the study just mentioned became aware of their previously unconscious negative associations with blacks, they can try to ensure that their beliefs about when patients warrant treatment are responsive not to their knowledge of the patient's racial identity but solely to his condition.

In line with much opinion research on whites' racial views (as we noted earlier), Devine argues that in the United States, whites' personal beliefs about blacks have become much more positive over time, in contrast to the relatively unchanging negative stereotype of blacks. An obvious educational implication of this view is that while attempting to rid students of the stereotypic associations themselves (acquired through socialization) is a fruitless endeavor, we should try to help students to adopt nonracist and egalitarian beliefs, and to recognize the challenge of maintaining such beliefs in light of their persistent stereotypic associations. Since beliefs are capable of trumping associations in determining our conduct, according to Devine, it is much more important to affect beliefs than associations.

Banaji (1994) refers to the associations themselves (between a group and negative characteristics) as "implicit prejudice." This use of the word *prejudice* seem misleading to me, and likely to distort the educational challenge involved in prejudice reduction. A prejudice is a more robust attitude than a mere association, consequential as that association may be for behavior; it requires some significant degree of cognitive investment, as implied in the "evaluative" aspect of prejudice, though perhaps less than that required for actual belief in the association. To say that someone is prejudiced against blacks implies that he genuinely views blacks in a negative light, not merely that he makes involuntary associations in his mind between blacks and negative traits (such as laziness or criminality). Banaji's qualification of these associations as "implicit" is, of course, meant to be a way of marking this distinction from more conscious and acknowledged prejudices; but the retention of *prejudice* just confuses the matter.

On the other hand, Devine's (1989) somewhat educationally optimistic focus only on conscious belief seems to understate the challenge of prejudice reduction. The adoption of egalitarian beliefs, or positive beliefs about a particular group, is only part of the challenge of affecting actual prejudices, as we have seen. Some students who consciously adopt nonprejudicial beliefs may still carry around prejudices and stereotypes (and not merely automatic associations with little cognitive investment).

Thus, the challenge of prejudice reduction through education is a fairly complex and daunting one. Explicit instruction as well as appropriately structured contact with out-groups can definitely help, though it is by no means guaranteed to succeed. A more minimal goal, but still a very significant one, is to enforce rules that promote civil and respectful conduct toward out-groups. For example, because homophobia is rampant among high school students, simply ensuring that a publicly identified gay student is treated respectfully and is not harassed and vilified would be an important accomplishment, even if it were not accomplished through a direct assault on anti-gay prejudices. However, it is also important to recognize the important falsehood that Allport (1954) noted in his book, in a context in which Southern whites were resisting legally mandated desegregation, in the statement that laws cannot affect personal attitudes, only conduct. Allport saw that laws do indeed affect attitudes over time. Once people begin to behave in a certain way, and become accustomed to doing so, eventually they tend to adopt attitudes that are consonant with that behavior. (Of course, this result is not inevitable or universal.)

REFERENCES

Adorno, T. W., Else Frenkel-Brunswick, Daniel Levinson, and R. Nevitt-Sanford. *The Authoritarian Personality.* New York: Norton, 1969 (1950).

Allport, Gordon. *The Nature of Prejudice.* Reading, MA: Addison-Wesley, 1954.

Banaji, Mahzarin, and A. G. Greenwald. "Implicit Stereotyping and Prejudice." In M. P. Zanna and J. M. Olson (eds.), *The Ontario symposium, Vol 7: The Psychology of Prejudice.* Hillsdale, NJ: Erlbaum, 1994.

Blum, Lawrence. *"I'm Not a Racist, But . . . ": The Moral Quandary of Race.* Ithaca, NY: Cornell University Press, 2002.

—— "Stereotypes and Stereotyping: A Moral Analysis." *Philosophical Papers* 33, no. 3 (November 2004): 251–90.

Devine, P. G. "Stereotypes and Prejudice: Their Automatic and Controlled Components." *Journal of Personality and Social Psychology* 56 (1989): 5–18.

Jones, Melinda. *Social Psychology of Prejudice.* Upper Saddle River, NJ: Prentice-Hall, 2002.

Pettigrew, Thomas F. "Prejudice." In Stephan Thernstrom (ed.), *Harvard Encyclopedia of American Ethnic Groups.* Cambridge, MA: Harvard University Press, 1980.

Piper, Adrian M. S. "Higher-Order Discrimination." In O. Flanagan and A. Rorty (eds.), *Identity, Character, and Morality: Essays in Moral Psychology* (pp. 285–310). Cambridge, MA: MIT Press, 1990.

Sears, David O., Jim Sidanius, and Lawrence Bobo (eds.). *Racialized Politics: The Debate About Racism in America.* Chicago: University of Chicago Press, 2000.

Stangor, Charles (ed.). *Stereotypes and Prejudice: Essential Readings.* Philadelphia: Psychology Press, 2000.

Stephan, Walter. *Reducing Prejudice and Stereotyping in Schools.* New York: Teachers College Press, 1999.

Young-Bruehl, Elisabeth. *The Anatomy of Prejudices.* Cambridge, MA: Harvard University Press, 1996.

CHAPTER 25

EDUCATIONAL AUTHORITY AND THE INTERESTS OF CHILDREN

ROB REICH

How should authority over the education of children be distributed in a liberal democracy? The standard answer to this question has been obvious: parents possess the authority to educate their children, either because parents possess rights to supervise the upbringing of their children or because parents are the best fiduciary agents to meet the needs and promote the interests of their children. And for most of modern history parents—in practice, fathers—have indeed possessed sole authority over the education of their children.

And if parents fail to provide education? Despite the absence of laws to remedy such a failure, J. S. Mill famously considered it almost "a self-evident axiom, that the State should require and compel the education, up to a certain standard, of every human being who is born its citizen" (Mill 1975, p. 97). But it was not until the mid-nineteenth century that states began to provide publicly funded schools and to pass compulsory education laws. Thus entered the authority of the state to compel parents to provide an education for their children.

Today, educational authority is typically divided between parents and the state. In this chapter I argue that educational authority should be shared among not two but three parties: parents, the state, and children themselves. I begin by considering how parental authority over children and educational authority over children are distinct. Parents do not have rights to direct the education of their children, even if, as is the case in U.S. law, they do have rights to direct the upbringing of their children. I then consider a trilogy of independent interests in education: parental interests, state interests, and children's interests. Children's interests ought not be subsumed under those of their parents or of the state. I show the implications of these independent interests for educational authority, and I conclude with a brief consideration of how children might in practice exercise authority over their education.

1. Separating Educational Authority from Parental Authority

Liberal democratic states grant wide latitude to parents to raise their children as they see fit, subject to limits in case of abuse or negligence. Some believe that parental liberties to raise children as they see fit extends, more or less axiomatically, to parental authority over education.[1] But educating a child through formal schooling is not coextensive with directing the upbringing of a child. Educating is not the same as parenting. To demonstrate this, consider, first, an appeal to legal arguments from U.S. Supreme Court cases and then an appeal to straightforward moral argument.

The landmark case *Pierce v. Society of Sisters* (1925) announced that "the child is not the mere creature of the state," that parents and guardians possess the liberty "to direct the upbringing and education of children under their control," and that, therefore, parents must have the right to opt out of public schooling.[2] This case is often cited in defense of parental rights over their children's education. Yet the Court in *Pierce* was unambiguous about the right of the state to regulate schools. This authority is vested in the state regardless of whether parents have been shown to be deficient. *Pierce* contains the uncomplicated declaration: "No question is raised concerning the power of the State reasonably to regulate all schools, to inspect, supervise, and examine them, their teachers and pupils; to require that all children of proper age attend some school, that teachers shall be of good moral character and patriotic disposition, that certain studies plainly essential to good citizenship must be taught, and that nothing be taught which is manifestly inimical to the public welfare" (268 U.S. 510).

Similarly, the more recent *Wisconsin v. Yoder* case (1972), which excused Amish parents from several years of compulsory schooling laws, found that "There is no doubt as to the power of a State, having a high responsibility for education of its citizens, to impose reasonable regulations for the control and duration of basic education" (406 U.S. 205).

Court decisions in the United States ascribe powers of regulation to the state with respect to education that do not parallel the power of the state with respect to parenting and child welfare. In the case of schooling, reasonable regulations are constitutional and do not demand any proof of educational misconduct. In the case of parenting, the state has to demonstrate abuse or neglect before it can intervene within the family on behalf of the child.

The more fundamental argument against equating parental authority and educational authority is a moral one. Publicly provided schools and the justification of compulsory attendance laws are founded on the interests of the state in promoting able citizenship and the state's responsibility to protect the interest children have in an education for autonomy. Whatever parents do in the course of raising their children certainly has profound effects on their children's future citizenship and autonomy, but the justification of parental supervision of the general upbringing of their children is not founded on claims of citizenship or autonomy but, rather, on something like the fiduciary duty of parents and the family's interest in intimacy (Brighouse and Swift 2006).

To put the point bluntly, the moral justification of what parents do for their children is different from the moral justification of what teachers do to educate children. The state can intervene in the lives of families when it can demonstrate that parents have abused or neglected their child. But the authority of the state to enforce regulations with respect to schooling is present even when parents are uncontestedly loving and caring. To see the difference in the brightest contrast, consider home-schooling, where parents are simultaneously teachers. In home schools, the role of parent and teacher is combined, but just because parents in their actions as parents have greater protection from state supervision and regulation does not mean that when parents serve as teachers their actions should be similarly free from supervision and regulation. The zone of liberty and privacy that protects parents' actions in the home as they raise their children is not equivalent when it comes to home-schooling parents' actions in the home as they educate their children. Moreover, the common welfare of society is at stake in schooling in a way that it is not at stake with respect to the penumbra of activities that we call parenting.

2. A Trilogy of Interests: Parents, State, and the Child

Once we distinguish parental authority over children from educational authority over children, it is easy to see that both parents and the state have legitimate interests in the education of children. In practice, educational authority is some balance between parental authority and state authority, with different historical and legal settings leading to different institutional arrangements to strike this balance. But I argue that this is an incomplete picture. In determining who should wield authority over education, it is not only parents and the state who have interests at stake. Children, who are subject to the education and thus the most directly affected by educational decision making, also have an interest. This interest may conflict with those of their parents or the state. To decide how educational authority ought to be apportioned among parents, the state, and perhaps children, we need first to consider the nature of the interests of parents, the state, and the child in education.

Parents' Interests in Education

Parents obviously have very strong interests in the education of their children.[3] In the abstract, these interests are twofold, grounded in the self-regarding interests of the parents themselves and in the other-regarding claim that since children are dependent for their well-being on others, parents are best situated to promote their welfare. Consider each in turn.

Children are not mere extensions of their parents; they are not their parents' property. But we can acknowledge this truth while also giving due weight to the self-regarding interests of parents, or what Eamonn Callan calls the "expressive significance" of child-rearing. Parenting is for many people a central source of meaning in their lives. As Callan puts it, "Success or failure in the task [of parenting], as measured by whatever standards we take to be relevant, is likely to affect profoundly our overall sense of how well or badly our lives have gone" (Callan 1997, p. 142). Raising a child is never merely a service rendered unto another person, but the collective sharing of a life. If we think in commonsensical terms that adults often have children in order to fulfill their goal to have a family, and to live life as part of a family, the sense in which child-rearing is something in the self-regarding interest of parents becomes clearer. It would be inconceivable for some people to lead what they would consider a good and flourishing life without having children with whom they have a close and abiding relationship, which is in part defined by the sharing not only of certain activities and rituals but also of values and interests.[4] Because schooling plays so important a role in cultivating the values and interests of children, the state cannot simply be indifferent to the interests of parents in how their children are educated.

Of course, the parental interest in exerting authority over the educational provision of their children is also grounded in the other-regarding interest of the children themselves. Children are dependent beings, not yet capable of meeting their own needs or acting in their own interests. Parents, it is generally believed, are best situated (better situated than the state and the children themselves) to act in the best interests of their children, or, in an alternative formulation, to promote their general welfare. In modern society, the welfare of a child depends in part on being educated. Therefore, as the guardian of their children's best interests or welfare, parents have an interest in the education that their children receive.

There is a problem with the "best interests" or "general welfare" standard, however. Despite the fact that the "best interest of the child" is the coin of the realm in legal decision making about children, it is not logically necessary that a child's *parents* are the agents who will best act on these interests. Others—grandparents, aunts and uncles, or state officials—might be better able to promote the welfare of the child. And, of course, when parents are clearly negligent or harmful to their children, whether intentionally or not, the state intervenes and awards guardianship to a relative or foster care family or, in the most dire situation, to the state itself. Who is to say, then, that parents are best suited to pursue the best interests of children?

One answer to this question is to consider the possible alternatives, all of which appear to be worse.[5] The more telling problem with the "best interest of the child" standard is that the best interest of a child does not admit of a singular answer in a society characterized by value pluralism, as all liberal democratic societies are. How does one define "best interest"? The answer depends on a particular view of the good life. Secular parents (or state authorities), for example, may define the best interest of a child in a very different manner than that from deeply religious parents. But we need not view this only as an issue of religious difference to see it as a problem. People may differ drastically on their interpretation of "best interest" in nonreligious terms. Given plural conceptions of the good life, there will be no readily identifiable consensus about the best interest of the child in all cases.

In light of this fact, one response is to suggest that parents are ideally situated not to realize the best interests of their children, for that is an inevitably contestable standard, but rather to meet the basic developmental needs of their children, the content of which appears to admit of a more objective answer. The basic developmental needs of the child include shelter, food, protection, and, not least, nurture, affection, and love. These the parents are surely in the best position to provide, at least when compared to the state and the children themselves. The difficulty for parents, however, is that when the needs of children are reduced to such an elementary and unobjectionable level, they do not yield any corresponding interest in control over educational provision. Whereas the "best interest" standard clearly implicates some parental interest in having a say in or perhaps even directing the educational environment of children, the lesser "basic developmental need" standard has no such implication. Shelter, food, protection, and love are responsibilities of a child's primary caregiver; not, or at least not to a large degree, of a child's teacher. An interesting dynamic emerges. The greater substance one packs into the notion of a child's needs and interests, the greater claim one has to influence the education of the child but the less likely that there will be objective agreement about what these needs and interests are. Conversely, the less substance one packs into the notion of a child's needs and interests, the more likely one will be able to secure objective agreement about them, but only at the cost of failing to justify an interest in educational provision.

Ian Shapiro forwards an interesting solution to this problem, arguing that the liberal democratic state should possess ultimate authority in meeting the basic interests of a child, which include security, nutrition, health, and education, while parents should possess ultimate authority in meeting the best interests of a child, which concern a full vision of the good life (Shapiro 1999, pp. 85ff). When parents thwart the realization of a child's basic interests, the state properly intervenes in parental decision making. If conflicts about the education of children arise, parents cannot wield a trump card based solely on their understanding of a child's interests.

State's Interests in Education

Like parents, the state has very strong interests in the education of children. In the abstract, these interests are twofold. First, the state has an interest in providing children a civic education. Second, the state has an interest in performing a backstop role to the parents in assuring that children receive a basic education sufficient to allow them to become adults capable of independent functioning. Both of these interests serve to justify a role for the state in exercising educational authority over its youngest citizens.

Historically, the civic interest of the state in providing and regulating education for children is familiar, and in American legal doctrine, well established. The *Pierce* and *Yoder* cases, cited earlier, acknowledge that the state possesses a fundamental interest in educating for citizenship. Similarly, in its landmark *Brown v. Board of Education* decision, the Court opined, "Today, education is perhaps the most important function of state and local governments."[6] What is the scope of the state's interest in civic education? Unsurprisingly, opinions differ. The scope of civic education is a matter of intense debate, and political theorists have interpreted the demands of civic education in very different ways. On the more demanding end of the spectrum, some argue that the state must teach children not only basic literacy but also knowledge of public policy issues; the conclusions of contemporary science; a foundation in world and national history; the structure and operation of federal, state, and local government; and a broad palette of critical thinking and empathy skills necessary to facilitate democratic deliberation amid a multiplicity of competing interests and among diverse races, religions, and worldviews (Arneson and Shapiro 1996, pp. 376ff). Others indicate that the state's civic interest in education lies more generally in assuring that children will have the opportunity and capacity to participate in public institutions and will come to possess a number of political virtues, such as tolerance, civility, and a sense of fairness (Rawls 1993; Macedo 2000). And on the less demanding side of the spectrum, some argue that civic requirements are more minimal, encompassing the teaching of tolerance, leaving, as Galston puts it, "maximum feasible accommodation" of diversity (Galston 2002, p. 20).

I explore this to acknowledge that there exists disagreement about how wide or narrow the scope of civic education should be. Yet even this acknowledgement underscores the simple point that, on any reading, the state does indeed have legitimate interests in educational authority based on providing children with the capacities to become able citizens, however citizenship and citizenship education are defined. While there is room for reasonable disagreement about the scope of civic education, no one seriously doubts that the state has an interest in some form of it. And, of course, seen historically this has been the central and abiding rationale for the public provision of schooling and the passage of compulsory attendance laws.

Beyond providing a civic education, the state also has an interest in education because it must perform a backstop role to parents in ensuring that children receive some basic minimum of schooling such that they can develop into adults capable of independent functioning. By "independent functioning" I do not mean to imply anything about individualism or detachment from parental or communal relationships. I mean it in the sense that, because parents will die and no longer be able to provide for and support them, all children (except in exceptional circumstances) need to grow into adults who possess a baseline set of social, emotional, and intellectual competencies that enable them to navigate and participate in the familiar social and economic institutions of society. I have in mind here things like the need to acquire reading skills and basic mathematical literacy so that, as an adult, they can do things as mundane as read street signs and as important as fill out a job application.

In modern society, educational attainment and academic achievement have become increasingly important to independent functioning. We would rightly consider a child unfairly deprived if he or she were denied the opportunity to be educated. While compulsory attendance laws arose in part to ensure that children received a civic education and to complement child labor restrictions, it is no exaggeration to claim that today educational attainment is essential simply to becoming an independent adult who is able to find a place in the workforce.[7] These educational outcomes, it should be emphasized, are different from the exercise of citizenship, having to do not with the capacity for participation in political arenas and mechanisms but with the capacity to lead a life amid the main social and economic institutions of society.

Now, while educational attainment may be necessary to acquiring the competencies essential for independent functioning as an adult, we cannot conclude from this fact that the state must control and regulate all educational provision. On the contrary, since parents almost always share this interest in educational attainment, and wish for their children to develop into independent adults in the sense indicated above, and since parents are better situated than the state to know their children's particular learning needs and capacities, the state properly exercises authority over the aspects of education necessary to becoming an independent adult in a backstop role. Pursuant to this task, the state provides and regulates publicly funded schools for those parents who wish to send their children to them. It also legislates that children shall attend schools until a specified age. But since the education necessary for developing into independent adulthood can be satisfied by a wide variety of curricula, pedagogies, and environments—any number of educational arrangements could lead to the desired outcome—parents should have on this matter wide discretion to choose or influence the form and content of the education that they believe best suits their children. There is, in short, a moral argument in favor of school choice that rests on the liberty interests of parents (Reich 2007).

The state thus possesses two distinct interests in the education of children: first, that children receive a civic education; and second, that children develop into adults capable of independent functioning. On this analysis, the parents and the state share the second interest but not necessarily the first. State interests most often clash with parents' interests where civic education is concerned.[8] Parents and the state may clash, for example, on their respective interpretation of what civic education requires, or in some cases, parents may reject aspects of civic education altogether. As the *Yoder* case, controversies over head scarves in public schools, clashes over the place of minority language education, and the rancor over the teaching of intelligent design all show, conflicts between parents and the state with respect to how children should be educated to become citizens are by no means uncommon; indeed, they appear endemic to liberal democracies.

Such conflicts lead to a set of very difficult questions. Should the state's interest in developing citizenship trump parents' interests in education when parents do not share the state's civic goals for their children? Can the state sometimes tolerate, if the stability of the state is not threatened, parents who will not provide an education that develops requisite citizenship capacities? Must children attend public schools in order for civic education to be most effective? At the very least, the clashing of parents' interests and the state's interests leads to questions about how such interests might best be balanced, how such usually overlapping but occasionally competing interests may yield a just distribution of educational authority. But to seek an answer is as yet premature; we have yet to consider the independent interests of children.

Child's Interests in Education

I consider this much to be uncontroversial: both parents and the state have clear interests in education that lead to legitimate claims to exert authority over educational provision. As I stated at the outset, social and legal institutions in liberal democracies typically consider these to be the only interests at stake. But as the subjects of the educational process, children have independent interests in education as well. They naturally have an interest in developing into adults capable of independent functioning, in the sense indicated above. They also have an interest in their prospective autonomy as adults.

Two prefatory comments. First, though the content of these interests may overlap with those of either the parents or the state, they are nevertheless independent interests. In certain circumstances, these independent interests may place children in conflict with their parents or with the state. Children's interests in education potentially conflict with their parents' interests when, for example, parents seek through the educational environment (and elsewhere) to satisfy an expressive interest in molding their children into certain persons without regard to the will of the children themselves. Think, for example, of the parent who wishes to shield his or her child from exposure to anything contrary to the convictions of the parents; certain cases of homeschooling in the United States reflect parental desires to educate their children in sole accordance with the will of the parents (Reich 2002, chap. 6). Children's interests in education may also conflict with the state's interests in cases—for example, like *Tinker* v. *Des Moines Independent Community School District*, where the right of students to express themselves politically in schools clashed with the power of the state to control the educational environment of the school.[9] Because of the possibility of conflict, it is important to identify children's interests as distinct and not subsume them under those of their parents or of the state.

Second, the fact that children are needy and dependent justifies a certain amount of parental and state paternalism with respect to educational provision, and also often necessitates that persons other than the child be able to represent his or her interests. Acknowledging the fact that children have independent interests in education does not mean that children are best suited to promote these interests; nor does it mean that they are able, especially at young ages, even to articulate them. But neither the problem of children's neediness and dependence nor the problem of who shall represent children's interests invalidate those interests. It merely points to the need for debate about when paternalism over children is no longer justified and when, developmentally, children might capably represent themselves, especially in cases where interests conflict.

Turning, then, to delineating the child's interests in education, the first interest should seem obvious: a child has an interest in education because education is necessary to developing into an adult capable of independent functioning. Again, I do not mean to imply anything potentially controversial about independent functioning. A child rightly expects to develop a set of competencies that make it possible for him or her to navigate and participate in the main social and economic institutions of society, including of course entering the labor force. The state and presumably the child's parents wish for this, too. Except in the most unusual circumstances—where, for example, a child is severely disabled or mentally handicapped and cannot be expected to become capable of independent functioning, or when parents abuse or neglect their children in obvious and uncontroversial ways—all three parties (parent, state, and child) would seem to share this interest.

It is a child's prospective interest in autonomy that may be controversial and may not be shared. Every child in a liberal democratic state, I claim, has an interest in becoming autonomous.[10] And because autonomy describes a character ideal that is an achievement rather than an inheritance, it requires an education of a certain sort for its cultivation. Some parents or cultural groups may resist such an education because they do not wish for their children to become autonomous.

But to resist the cultivation of autonomy in children would be to undermine the conditions of legitimate consent and stability in a liberal society. One justification for educating for autonomy is rooted in the terrain of every person's public or political life. For the exercise of state power to be legitimate and stable over time, citizens must autonomously consent, across generations, to the principles of justice upon which the state is founded. If persons, as citizens, are to be able freely and without coercion or indoctrination to make decisions about the political structures that will govern them, if they are to be able to contest and perhaps resist the exercise of state power, and if they are to be able sympathetically to engage other citizens in democratic deliberation, they will need to acquire the skills and habits of autonomy.

A separate justification for educating for autonomy is rooted in the terrain of every person's private or personal life. Becoming autonomous is necessary, albeit not sufficient, to lead a good and flourishing life in a liberal society.[11] This is so for two reasons. First, autonomy is necessary to establish the conditions of self-respect that enable a person to see his or her ends as valuable and worth pursuing. Without a capacity to subject our ends to critical reflection, and thereby to come to cleave to them autonomously or to revise or reject them autonomously, we may fail to acquire the confidence that these ends are deserving of our approbation. It is hard to see how we could live a flourishing life without having the self-respect that our own ends are worthy. Second, autonomy is necessary to avoid the inculcation of, as Callan (1997) argues, a servile disposition such that a child comes to subordinate his or her will to another person or persons. If we do not possess our own ends, in the sense that we have autonomously endorsed them, we risk becoming servile to those who would provide ends for us. But precisely because children are independent persons and the property neither of their parents nor of the state, they ought not to be socialized so as to be made servile to their caretakers or educational providers. Neither parents nor the state can justly attempt indelibly to imprint upon a child a set of values and beliefs, as if it were an inheritance one should never be able to question, as if the child must always defer and be unquestioningly obedient. In short, children must become autonomous as a condition of achieving self-respect and in order to escape the condition of servility. And both self-respect and the supersession of servility are conditions of leading a good and flourishing life. Becoming autonomous, therefore, while of course not guaranteeing the living of a good life, is in the eudaemonistic interest of children, as of all persons.

What can we conclude from this general survey of the interests of the parents, the state, and the child in education? In almost all cases, each party shares the goal of educating children to become adults capable of independent functioning. Indeed, many view the primary function of education to be the provision of capabilities, competencies, encouragement of talents, and fostering of academic achievement so as to allow children to develop into adults who will be able to function on their own in society—able, that is, to secure work, care for themselves, and seek and develop their own interests. In fact, a harmony among parents, the state, and child may in practice very often extend across all interests. The parents' self-regarding interests may coincide with the state's interest in developing the capacity for children to exercise the rights of citizenship; the child's interest in becoming autonomous may coincide with the parents' expressive interests and the state's interest in citizenship.

But this harmony of shared interests is not inevitable. As we have seen, the interest of the state in fostering citizenship may not be shared by the parents.

Likewise, a child's interest in becoming autonomous may not be shared by parents. At this point, one might object that, while the state and the child do have these conflicting interests, only parents possess actual rights with respect to their children's education. This is a matter of some controversy,[12] and the position tends to conflate, as I showed earlier, parental authority over their children with educational authority. I contend that, even on the assumption that parental interests in education rise to the level of rights, in addition to whatever other rights parents have over their children's education, the respective interests of the state and the child remain. The state may take steps to promote certain civic virtues in children, and children should develop the capacities of autonomy that entitle them, especially as adolescents, to a proto-right to self-governance. These two claims hold if parental rights are vindicated. They also hold, *a fortiori*, if there are no parental rights.

Put simply, no one set of parents', state's, or child's interests can trump the others and justify sole authority for any party over educational provision. Neither parents, nor the state, nor children themselves should unilaterally and without a countervailing balance direct and control the educational environment of children. Given the triad of interest-holders and the significance of their respective interests, a theory of educational authority claiming that only the interests of one party mattered could potentially establish a kind of parental despotism, state authoritarianism, or child despotism. Any defensible theory of educational authority will strike some balance among the three parties.

How should the balance of educational authority be struck? This seems to me a question that is impossible to answer theoretically. There is ample room for democratic decision making about the proper distribution of educational authority, and many institutional arrangements of schooling, along with a variety of governance structures, are likely to be able to meet the interests of all three parties and to be consistent with the requirements of justice. A precise institutional blueprint for education, and the distribution of authority over it, cannot be generated from philosophical principle.

What we can do from the level of theory is examine the limits of parental, state, and the child's authority. My own view is that parental interests in choosing schools for their children can indeed co-exist with the promotion of the state's interests in civic education and the child's interests in autonomy (Reich 2002, 2007). So long as schools embody an ethos that does not shut out diversity and that develops citizenship and autonomy, parents should be free to choose among schools on the basis of how they want their children to be educated. This would include a great diversity of schools, including public, private, religious, and home schools. To be sure, it rules out some undiscriminating forms of choice, such as schools whose view of democratic citizenship is threadbare and ignores the child's interest in autonomy. And it rules out schools that would refuse to expose children to and engage them with value diversity. Democratic citizenship and autonomy can be fostered only when children become aware of the existence of other ways of life, and moreover, when they engage intellectually with such value diversity. The liberal state should be wary of parents whose choices are made solely on the basis of shielding them from any and all competing views. To allow this would indeed establish a kind of parental despotism over children. But the elimination of school choice would establish a state despotism over parents.

But what of the child's authority over his or her education? As the liberal state seeks to protect the freedom and equality of all citizens, including children, it must see that it is possible for children to make decisions about the kind of lives they wish to lead. I conclude with a brief exploration of the most contentious aspect of my analysis: that children ought to possess some authority over their own education.

3. CHILDREN'S VOICES IN LEGAL CONTEXTS

It is easy enough to claim that children's interests are independent of those of their parents and of the state; the moral case seems clear. But how to translate or realize the moral claims of children in an institutional or legal framework? How should children themselves exercise authority over their own education? Do their independent interests in education yield a claim to controlling their own education? This is a difficult question, for while very young children clearly are incapable of exercising educational authority, it is nevertheless true that older children are capable of making informed and reasonable choices about their education, and about many other things as well.[13] If children were to decide unilaterally, a six-year-old might elect to attend a private school or home school (or no school at all) rather than a public school. But the preference of such a young child cannot be decisive, else children would not need guardians at all. But if a fifteen-year-old were to decide that he or she wanted to attend a public school rather than be homeschooled, or attend a public school rather than a private school, or be homeschooled rather than attend public or private school, should, and if so, how, ought this preference be evaluated?

A court case in Virginia raises the question of what the state should do when older children wish to attend public school and their parents wish to homeschool them.[14] Jennifer Sengpiehl had been homeschooled for many years when, in her teenage years, she began to ask her parents to permit her to attend the local public school. Her parents refused and continued to educate her at home, at which point Jennifer's behavior began to deteriorate. In an attempt to teach her a lesson about obedience, her parents called the police after she had vandalized her bedroom and brandished a knife at her father. The involvement of the police led to a juvenile court date, where unexpectedly the judge ruled that Jennifer should attend a public school. Because the court records of juveniles are sealed, it is impossible to know the details of the case in order to assess the rationale of the judge's ruling and in order to make an informed judgment in Jennifer's case about how continued homeschooling or public schooling would or would not meet the parents', the state's, and the child's interests in education. Traditional jurisprudence has viewed questions about educational authority over children as a contest or balancing act between the interests of parents and the state. Should the court have presumed to weigh Jennifer's own preferences about how her interests in education could best be met?

On the view I have defended here, if conflicts about education reach the court, judges must not presume an identity of interests between children and their parents. They should act with discretion in soliciting the voice of the child when there is reason to believe that a child may be autonomous and that the expression of a child's preferences in a legal context will not cause more harm than good. Because the ultimate resolution of any case will concern the child, as the subject of schooling, most directly, there are often reasonable grounds to inquire about children's preferences. This was the reasoning behind Justice Douglas's dissent in *Yoder*, where Douglas insisted that "if an Amish child desires to attend high school, and is mature enough to have that desire respected, the State may well be able to override the parents' religiously motivated objections" (*Wisconsin* v *Yoder*, 406 U.S. 205, at 242). And a wide range of U.S. cases offer ample legal precedent not only to solicit the opinions of children but also to accord them significant weight. In cases concerning custody disputes, for example, courts routinely ask children for their preferences. In disputes over the medical and mental health treatment of children, courts often evaluate the child's capacity to consent to or refuse the treatment in question. In cases when juvenile delinquents assert or waive their rights, courts must attempt to ascertain whether the child has asserted or waived his or her rights voluntarily and knowingly. And though it is controversial, many courts allow teenage girls who demonstrate maturity to seek and obtain an abortion without the consent or even notification of their parents. American jurisprudence demonstrates an inconsistent treatment of the position of children in legal proceedings, yet the presence of children's voices in courtrooms—independent of those of their parents—is far from unprecedented.

A key factor in deciding whether or not to solicit the views of a child in cases concerning conflicts over educational authority should be the expectation that a child has approached or achieved autonomy. Obviously, a child's age is crucial here. As a general rule, the older the child, the more likely that the child will have approached a threshold level of autonomy such that his or her preferences are deserving of respect, and therefore of significant weight. The younger the child, the less likely that his or her preferences issue from an autonomous source. Thus, courts might rightly presume to hear the voice of Jennifer Sengpiehl, a sixteen-year-old, but not to solicit the views of elementary-school-age children.

Even when judges have reason to expect that a child may be autonomous, they must still consider the possible harm to a child who is put into a potentially adversarial relationship with his or her parents and cultural group leaders, such as religious authorities. Should courts ask children to articulate views that, if opposed to those of their parents, will almost surely strain the relationship they have with some of the most important people in their lives? According to children an independent status, and assigning weight to a children's views, may potentially disrupt familial and communal bonds. Jennifer Sengpiehl was already at odds with her parents before her case reached the courtroom, but I doubt that the situation improved after the court ruled that, contrary to her parents' preferences, she should attend a public school. Since children have a clear interest in the ongoing love and support of those people with whom they have the closest ties, courts should be wary about the possible consequences of introducing open conflict between children and their family and community. When judges have good reason to believe that soliciting the views of a child will lead to real psychological trauma or physical harm, they should proceed with caution. And if they anticipate that the incorporation of a child's preferences will not play a significant role in the final outcome of the case, they should perhaps reconsider, or forgo, the solicitation of the child's opinion.

It must be said, however, that the charge that attributing legal standing to children and listening for their independent views will harm them by producing conflict within familial and communal relationships is itself a dangerous position. As feminist scholars have noted, such objections have been used to justify domination and hierarchy in cases concerning criminalizing rape within marriage and treating girls as the equals of boys within the family (Okin 1989). Moreover, in some instances, such as Jennifer Sengpiehl's case, there is likely already to be familial or communal strife, and what the child is often seeking is protection of her considered interests, not a muzzle, because it is believed that the continued expression of her beliefs will introduce still more conflict. Courts should be wary not to compromise the position of the most vulnerable and least powerful, the children, in an ostensible attempt to forestall potential harm to them. And they should be especially wary not to discount or ignore the position of children, and their interest in becoming autonomous, because the preferences of their parents are couched in claims about the importance of cultural maintenance or stability.

The upshot is that judges must make a judgment call about when to solicit the views of children within a courtroom, taking into account the likelihood of a child's autonomy and an assessment about the possible negative consequences to the child. The interests of children should never be subsumed under those of their parents, but there need not be an automatic expectation that if a case reaches the courtroom, children should be called upon to express their preferences. Of course, a judge's decision to solicit the expression of children's preferences says nothing about how much weight these preferences should be accorded. It may be that a judge solicits the view of an older teenager only to determine that the view was not expressed autonomously. Perhaps the child was under extreme pressure from his or her parents to articulate a particular position or preference, or perhaps the child aimed merely to please, or displease, his or her parents. When children do not appear to be autonomous, their views should not carry significant weight, and the state must defend its own interpretation of the child's interests in education. When children do appear to be autonomous, however, their preferences should become a factor in the decision calculus of the court. And when there is firm evidence that children have achieved autonomy, they acquire in my view a proto-right to self-governance. Their considered views about educational authority should weigh heavily in the mind of a judge who must consider how to balance the interests of the parent, state, and child in education.

NOTES

1. Some rest this authority in the claim that parents have a natural right to authority over education. Others view parental rights over education to stem from the liberties of adults and their interests in forming children as they see fit. See Gilles 1996, for instance. "I submit that the deference we extend to parental educational choices should approach (though not necessarily equal) the deference we give to the self-regarding choices of adult individuals" (p. 939). For similar views, see Milton Friedman 1962 and Charles Fried 1978, p. 152. Amy Gutmann offers a summary of this class of argument under the label of "the state of families" (Gutmann 1987, pp. 28*ff*).

2. *Pierce v. Society of Sisters*, 268 U.S. 535.

3. By using the term "parents" I do not mean to privilege biological parents over other kinds of parents. A more general, and for my purposes synonymous term, would be "guardians."

4. For a similar argument, see Brighouse and Swift 2006.

5. There are some plausible alternatives, of course, most famously the communal child-rearing described in Plato's *Republic* or, more recently, the communal parenting on kibbutzim. But such possibilities are highly unlikely ever to be implemented on a wide scale in modern society.

6. *Brown v. Board of Education*, 347 U.S. 483 at 493 (1954).

7. Evidence of the importance of educational attainment can be seen in the booming rates of high school attendance and graduation in only the past fifty years. As recently as 1950, only one-third of Americans twenty-five years and older had attained a high school degree. In 2000, the result was 85 percent. The source for these figures is the *A Half-Century of Learning: Historical Statistics on Educational Attainment in the United States, 1940–2000*," Table 5a, "Percent of the Total Population 25 Years and Over with a High School Diploma or Higher by Sex, for the United States, Regions, and States: 1940–2000." Accessible at: www.census.gov/population/socdemo/education/phct41/table5a.xls.

8. It is tempting to think that, when clashes occur between parents and the state with respect to ensuring the development of children into independent adulthood, it is because the state is acting in its backstop role, intervening in the face of negligent or abusive parents. But the reverse is far more likely. Parents often allege that the state is negligent or abusive in providing schools of such low quality that their children are effectively disabled from acquiring the necessary competencies to becoming an independently functioning adult in society. Parents routinely and justly decry public schools that fail to teach their children to read and write, that fail to keep their children physically safe, that evince a callous disregard for or ignorance of their children's distinctive needs and interests, and so on. It is not only the state that seeks to hold parents responsible for helping to develop their children into healthy adults; parents also seek to hold the state responsible for providing good schools in the service of the same goal.

9. *Tinker v. Des Moines Independent Community School District*, 393 U.S. 503 (1969).

10. I defend this claim at length in Reich 2002.

11. For an extended argument on this point, see Raz 1986.

12. For the pro-parental rights position, see Friedman 1962; Gilles 1996; Brighouse and Swift 2006; for the anti-parental rights position, see Dwyer 2001.

13. A large body of research indicates that the decision-making competence of late adolescents does not differ significantly, if at all, from that of adults. One psychologist notes that "in so far as denial of autonomy has been based on assumptions of incompetence (in decision-making, related to matters such as psychotherapy, abortion, medical treatment, and contraception), current psychological research does not support such an age-graded distinction" (G. Melton, as cited in Hill and Holmbeck (1986), p. 148). Similarly, in a literature review, Susan Silverberg and Dawn Gondoli (1996, p. 50) conclude that "the evidence available to date suggests that adolescents—at least once they reach age 16—have acquired a host of critical decision-making skills that are comparable to those of adults." More recent neurological research, however, on brain development in adolescence suggests that adolescence are more prone to risk-taking even as rational capacities are equivalent to those of adults; see Reyna and Farley 2006 and Steinberg 2007. These studies, older and newer, lend support to the claim that the preferences of adolescents, if expressed in a legal context, should not be assumed to be immature or unreasonable, though perhaps more prone to risk-taking.

14. See Walsh 1998; Glod 1998. See also Salamone 2000, p. 223.

REFERENCES

Arneson, R., and Ian Shapiro. (1996). "Democratic Autonomy and Religious Freedom." In *NOMOS XXXVIII: Political Order*, ed. Ian Shapiro and Russell Hardin (pp. 365–411). New York: New York University Press.

Brighouse, H. (2000). *Social Justice and School Choice*. Oxford: Oxford University Press.

—— and Adam Swift. (2006). "Parents' Rights and the Value of the Family." *Ethics* 117(1): 80–108.

Brown v. Board of Education, 347 U.S. 483 (1954).

Callan, E. (1997). *Creating Citizens: Political Education and Liberal Democracy*. Oxford: Clarendon Press.

Dwyer, J. (2001). *Religious Schools vs. Children's Rights*. Ithaca, NY: Cornell University Press.

Fried, C. (1978). *Right and Wrong*. Cambridge, MA: Harvard University Press.

Friedman, M. (1962). *Capitalism and Freedom*. Chicago: University of Chicago Press.

Galston, W. (2002). *Liberal Pluralism: The Implications of Value Pluralism for Political Theory and Practice*. Cambridge: Cambridge University Press.

Gilles, S. (1996). "On Educating Children: A Parentalist Manifesto." *University of Chicago Law Review* 937: 937–1034.

Glod, Maria. (1998). "An Education in the Courts; Couple Fights Order on Teen's Schooling." *Washington Post*, November 7, B1.

Gutmann, A. (1987). *Democratic Education*. Princeton: Princeton University Press.

Hill, John, and Grayson Holmbeck. (1986). "Attachment and Autonomy during Adolescence." *Annals of Child Development: A Research Annual*, Vol. 3, ed. Grover Whitehurst (pp. 145–89). Greenwich, CT: Jai Press.

Levinson, M. (1999). *The Demands of Liberal Education*. Oxford: Oxford University Press.

Macedo, S. (2000). *Diversity and Distrust: Civic Education in a Multicultural Democracy.* Cambridge, MA: Harvard University Press.

Mill, J. S. (1975). *On Liberty,* ed. David Spitz. New York: Norton.

Okin, Susan Moller. (1989). *Justice, Gender, and the Family.* New York: Basic Books.

Pierce v. Society of Sisters, 268 U.S. 510 (1925).

Rawls, J. (1993). *Political Liberalism.* New York: Columbia University Press.

Raz, J. (1986). *The Morality of Freedom.* Oxford: Clarendon Press.

Reich, R. (2002). *Bridging Liberalism and Multiculturalism in American Education.* Chicago: University of Chicago Press.

—— (2007). "How and Why to Support Common Schooling and Educational Choice at the Same Time." *Journal of Philosophy of Education* 41(4): 709–25.

Reyna, Valerie, and Frank Farley. (2006). "Risk and Rationality in Adolescent Decision Making: Implications for Theory, Practice, and Public Policy." *Psychological Science in the Public Interest* 7(1): 1–44.

Salamone, R. (2000). *Visions of Schooling.* New Haven: Yale University Press.

Shapiro, I. (1999). *Democratic Justice.* New Haven: Yale University Press.

Silverberg, Susan, and Dawn Gondoli. (1996). "Autonomy in Adolescence: A Contextualized Perspective." In *Psychosocial Development During Adolescence,* eds. Gerald Adams, Raymond Montemayor, and Thomas Gullotta (p. 50). Thousand Oaks, CA: Sage.

Steinberg, Lawrence. (2007). "Risk Taking in Adolescence: New Perspectives From Brain and Behavioral Science." *Current Directions in Psychological Science* 16(2): 55–59.

Tinker v. Des Moines Independent Community School District, 393 U.S. 503 (1969).

Walsh, Mark. (1998). "Court Sends Girl to Public School Against Parents' Wishes." *Education Week,* November 25.

Wisconsin v. Yoder, 406 U.S. 205 (1972).

PART VI

APPROACHES TO PHILOSOPHY OF EDUCATION AND PHILOSOPHY

CHAPTER 26

PRAGMATIST PHILOSOPHY OF EDUCATION

RANDALL CURREN

THERE are different ways of doing philosophy in general, and different ways of doing philosophy of education in particular. Many are broadly analytical, in the sense that they are predicated on the idea that philosophical problems can and should be addressed at least in part through methods of logical, linguistic, epistemic, and normative analysis, including diverse and more or less formal methods of articulating the structure of theories, institutions, practices, and other objects of inquiry. Within this loosely defined analytic style of philosophy, there are countless substantive disagreements and diverse methodological standpoints on the utility and propriety of drawing on empirical research, literature, the history of philosophy, and analytical apparatus from other disciplines. This methodological diversity has many sources, including most importantly the nature of the objects of inquiry and questions at issue. Philosophy of education, being a philosophy *of* something, where that something is a domain of human *practice*, is a subfield of philosophy in which many of the questions at issue have a practical edge, and many of the most useful answers that might be given would be no less *informed* than philosophically adept. Abraham Edel, a pragmatist and student of John Dewey (1859–1952), argued many years ago that analytic philosophers of education should integrate "the empirical, the normative, and the contextual (especially the socio-cultural) *within* the analytic method" (Edel 1973, p. 41).[1] This has largely come to pass, though it would be overly optimistic to suppose that philosophers of education have uniformly adopted the most promising approaches characteristic of other subfields of practical philosophy.

Pragmatist philosophy and analytic philosophy are not fully disjoint forms of philosophy. There are, and have long been, analytic pragmatists, beginning with Charles Sanders Peirce (1839–1914), the founder of pragmatism and preeminent logician of his day, and analytic neo-pragmatists, including Hilary Putnam (1995), Susan Haack (1993), and Robert Brandom (1994, 2000). Varying degrees of sympathy for pragmatist ideas have been evident in instrumentalist accounts of scientific theories, deflationary theories of truth, functionalist theories of mind, and fallibilism and contextualism regarding epistemic justification, all of which have been debated in analytic philosophy for decades—so much so that one might be forgiven for thinking that the viable remains of pragmatism were long ago absorbed into the mainstream, the postphilosophical pragmatism of Richard Rorty (1931–2007) notwithstanding.[2]

In the preface to their landmark *Readings in Philosophical Analysis*, Herbert Feigl and Wilfred Sellars acknowledged Peirce as having "more to say to us than many who are writing today" (Feigl and Sellars 1949, p. vi). In his introduction to the volume, Feigl wrote that:

> Empiricism, Skepticism, Naturalism, Positivism, and Pragmatism [disregarding some of William James's own tender-minded deviations] are typical thought movements of the worldly, tough-minded variety. Respect for the facts of experience, open-mindedness, an experimental trial-and-error attitude, and the capacity for working within the frame of an incomplete, unfinished world view distinguish them from the more impatient, imaginative, and often aprioristic thinkers in the tender-minded camp.   (Feigl 1949, p. 3)

Feigl wrote with regard for pragmatism as a source of the flowering of analytic philosophy, and went on to identify Peirce's *pragmatic maxim* as a useful formulation of the criterion of (factual) meaningfulness advocated by logical empiricists (known in the era of the Vienna Circle as logical positivists):

> If we cannot possibly conceive of what would have to be the case in order to confirm or disconfirm an assertion, we would not be able to distinguish between its truth and its falsity. In that case we would simply not know what we are talking about. C. S. Peirce's pragmatic maxim, formulated in his epoch-making essay, "How to Make Our Ideas Clear," has essentially the same import. . . . If and only if assertion and denial of a sentence imply a difference capable of observational (experiential, operational, or experimental) test, does the sentence have factual meaning.   (Feigl 1949, p. 9)

In the paper Feigl refers to, Peirce presents his pragmatic analysis of meaning as an alternative to the Cartesian standard of *clear and distinct ideas*, and aims to chasten metaphysics and apriorism in much the way that other empiricists have (see Kloesel 1986, p. 257ff). Years later, in "What Pragmatism Is," he refers to himself as a positivist and leaves no doubt as to why:

> [Pragmatic analysis] will serve to show that almost every proposition of ontological metaphysics is either meaningless gibberish . . . or else is downright absurd; so that all such rubbish being swept away, what will remain of philosophy

will be a series of problems capable of investigation by the observational methods of the true sciences.   (Peirce 1905, p. 171)

Bertrand Russell's announcement of a parallel assault on misguided metaphysics, in "On Denoting," would strike many as tame by comparison (Russell 1905).[3]

If pragmatist philosophy and analytic philosophy have shared considerable common ground, it is nevertheless true that the pragmatist and analytic movements have had different and distinctive histories. Most obviously, pragmatism was in the early decades of the twentieth century a widely discussed public philosophy, allied with the progressive and legal realism reform movements, and engaged with matters of urgent social and political concern.[4] Crucial to this was a rejection of *a priori* endorsements of universal principles or values, and a meliorist or reform-minded embrace of an evolutionary and experimentalist conception of social, political, and legal institutions.[5] The adequacy of institutions would be judged on the basis of their consequences in the existing social context. Through decades in which analytic philosophy was precluded from social commentary by its epistemological focus and meta-ethical noncognitivism—that is, the view that moral judgments are devoid of propositional content—pragmatism about values was understood to entail a kind of progressive cognitivism that preserved a role for philosophy in reasoned social criticism. Most important for our purposes here, pragmatism was closely associated with American philosophy of education through much of the twentieth century, owing very much to the dominating influence of John Dewey.

The main questions to be addressed here are: What distinguishes the philosophies of education advanced by pragmatists? What reliance do these philosophies place on distinctively pragmatist methods or doctrines? Does pragmatism have something distinctive to offer contemporary philosophy of education?

1. Pragmatism: Meaning, Truth, and Inquiry

Pragmatism was conceived at the "Metaphysical Club," where Peirce first presented his pragmatic maxim, in Cambridge, Massachusetts, in the 1870s. The group that convened philosophical discussions there included William James, the mathematician Chauncey Wright, Oliver Wendell Holmes and two other lawyers, the historian John Fisk, and the "scientific theist" Francis Abbott. The evolution studies of Charles Darwin and the empiricism of John Stuart Mill were influential in this group through Wright, who was himself known to Darwin for his work on evolutionary adaptation in plants (Wiener 1949, p. 31).

Peirce brought to this group the perspective of a chemist, physicist, mathematician, and logician, and formulated his maxim in a way that spanned matters of fact or experimental methods, relations of ideas or formal systems, and human practices broadly. He began from Alexander Bain's definition of *belief* as a disposition to act or "rule for action," which suggested to him the fundamental pragmatist doctrine that thought ("rational cognition") and action ("rational purpose") are in some sense inseparable.[6] Embedding this in a hard-nosed naturalism about human nature, which accepted the fact of biological, social, and institutional evolution, he and his pragmatist followers came to regard thought and ideas as instrumental and properly measured by instrumental success. This was understood in a way consistent with an embrace of experimental empiricism in science and human affairs, and an understanding of axioms through their deductive consequences in formal systems. Empirical hypotheses have observational consequences, legal rules and institutional policies have consequences for human well-being, and mathematical and logical propositions have inferential consequences. Peirce's pragmatic maxim treats these consequences as not only the *measure* but also the *meaning* (and *limits of meaning*) of the hypotheses or beliefs in question. If a belief is a behavioral disposition or habit, what could a belief's content consist of but the hypothesis that certain consequences would accompany the believer's actions in the various circumstances that could arise? An assertion without discernible consequences through which it could be tested would be empty words.

Axioms implicitly defined within their systems in this way lose any claim to *a priori* synthetic (descriptive) certainty, as those of Euclidean geometry did when geometries grounded in alternative axioms were invented. Governments and their laws lose any claim to self-evident authority. Science, which might have been thought to rest on unshakeable certainties, is seen to be the experimental and fallible enterprise that it is. This realism about the sciences did not diminish it in the eyes of the pragmatists, despite the conclusions Peirce drew in applying his account of belief and meaning to the nature of truth and reality. Let us note his formulation of the account in "How to Make our Ideas Clear," and trace its application to judgments of truth and reality:

> [T]he whole function of thought is to produce habits of action.... What the habit is depends on *when* and *how* it causes us to act. As for *when*, every stimulus to action is derived from perception; as for the *how*, every purpose of action is to produce some sensible result. Thus, we come down to what is tangible and practical, as the root of every real distinction of thought, no matter how subtle it may be; and there is no distinction of meaning so fine as to consist in anything but a possible difference of practice.   (Kloesel 1986, p. 265)

Consider, then, my belief that the loaf I've baked is smaller than a breadbox, and my related belief that a breadbox is a good place to store bread. What do these beliefs come to, according to Peirce? Most obviously, that I may try to place the loaf in a breadbox, if I have one at hand, expecting to see that the loaf will fit inside with the box closed, and expecting to find that if I return a day, or two, or three later, and feel and taste the bread, that I will find it not unpleasantly stale or nibbled by mice, but wholesome and intact. Less obviously, the belief that the loaf is smaller than a breadbox would entail expectations about what I would observe if I set about measuring the two—expectations about the possibility of finding a container into which the loaf would fit but the breadbox would not, and so on. The meaning of a belief is in this way cashed out as a function of possible actions and anticipated outcomes.

What happens when one subjects assertions about truth and reality to pragmatic analysis? If beliefs about truth have any meaning, it would be because they, too, are testable, and their meaning would be reducible in some sense to the methods and consequences by which they are tested. However, testing the belief, "It is true that p" would seem to be no different from testing p itself. Faced with this, one could regard assertions of truth as redundant or devise some other deflationary or metaphysically cautious account of the language of truth. Peirce holds, rather more contentiously, that "the ideas of truth and falsehood, in their full development, appertain exclusively to the scientific method of settling opinion" (Kloesel 1986, p. 272). He then holds that:

> [T]he processes of investigation, if only pushed far enough, will give one certain solution to every question to which they can be applied. . . . Different minds may set out with the most antagonistic views, but the progress of investigation carries them by a force outside themselves to one and the same conclusion. This great law is embodied in the conception of truth and reality. The opinion which is fated to be ultimately agreed to by all who investigate, is what we mean by the truth, and the object represented in this opinion is the real.   (p. 273)

It is in this way that truth and reality come to be defined by pragmatists in terms of agreement within a community of inquiry, but it need not have been so. The conclusion is a *semantic* analysis of the terms "true" and "real," and it is not entailed by Peirce's pragmatic maxim, or even the conjunction of the maxim and his "great law" concerning the eventual convergence of scientific opinion.[7]

It is the pragmatic method of analysis that Peirce and James both identify as the heart of pragmatism, so much so that Dewey remarked that in reading *Pragmatism* (James 1907), "one frequently gets the impression that he conceives the discussion of the other two points [the nature of ideas and truth; the nature of reality] to be illustrative material, more or less hypothetical, of the method" (Dewey 1908/1990, p. 377). The method, James says, is "The attitude of looking away from first things, principles, 'categories,' supposed necessities; and of looking towards last things, fruits, consequences, facts" (James 1907, pp. 54–55). It is a "method" much in harmony with earlier forms of empiricism, and distinguished from them primarily by the insistence that knowledge is a product not of passive perception, but of active interventions in the world that leave a mark on it.

In this brief introduction to pragmatism, we find five elements that became recurrent themes of the movement: (1) a rejection of apriorism and certainty, and a corresponding embrace of fallibilism, empirical and experimental methods, and the ideal of a community of scientific inquiry; (2) a naturalistic and evolutionary perspective on reality in general and human nature in particular; (3) an associated instrumentalism about thought, language, knowledge, values, and institutions; (4) an associated account of meaning, deployed as a tool of philosophical analysis, in the form of the pragmatic maxim; (5) accounts of truth and reality as products of inquiry.

To these we may now add, with qualification: (6) a commitment to secular democratic individualism or liberal democracy. Although James had pronounced democratic sympathies, the same could not be said of his European followers (Wiener 1973). Moreover, there is nothing in the five primary elements of pragmatism that would compel an embrace of democracy; nothing that would preclude a naturalistic, evolutionary, instrumentalist embrace of a quite *undemocratic* Social Darwinism, or Social Spencerism, as some would have it.[8] The social "Darwinist," Herbert Spencer, defined the pedagogical doctrines of progressive education more than anyone else (Cremin 1961, p. 91; Egan 2002), and it is far from evident that the adoption of pragmatist commitments would have given him any reason to revise his social and political views. An instrumentalist or consequentialist view of institutions becomes progressive in an egalitarian or social democratic way only if one adopts an egalitarian view of what kinds of consequences matter. Dewey did just that in adopting an egalitarian and eudaimonistic form of consequentialism, a liberal individualist vision of social experimentation as a vehicle of individual flourishing and social progress, and an associated developmental conception of democracy (Dewey 1916, 1939/1989; Gouinlock 1986; Held 1987, pp. 85–104; Campbell 1995). Dewey conceived of democracy as a form of social life in which "cooperative intelligence" can freely operate through social experimentation and progressive adjustments of goals and policies in light of collective deliberation grounded in the experience of every member of society. It is the form of social life that provides the best setting for continued individual "growth"—for the "liberation of powers," yielding "a progressive growth directed to social aims"—according to Dewey, and he proposed the same test of adequacy for other institutions, including schools (Dewey 1916).[9] In this vision, the empirical spirit of pragmatism is tethered to democracy through a conception of the processes of democratic social life modeled on the norms of a scientific community, and the idea that participation in those norms is conducive to personal growth. Though not quite inevitable, the union endured and commitment to democracy became a staple of American pragmatism.

2. James, Dewey, and the Philosophy of Education

It is in the work of William James that we first encounter a semblance of what might be thought of as a pragmatist philosophy of education. James was induced to deliver a series of lectures to the teachers of Cambridge, Massachusetts, in 1892, and these appeared together as his *Talks to Teachers on Psychology* in 1899. Elements of pragmatism had been evident in his writings on cognition as early as 1885, and one sees some evidence of pragmatist ideas in these lectures, though one also finds elements of the educational ideas of Locke and Spencer. Although the originating premise of the lectures is that they would draw pedagogical lessons from James's monumental *Principles of Psychology* (James 1890/1983), he remarks in the opening lecture that "there *is* no 'new psychology' worthy of the name. There is nothing but the old psychology which began in Locke's time, plus a little physiology of the brain and senses and theory of evolution, and a few refinements of introspective detail" (James 1901, p. 15).

Pragmatist ideas are most evident in the lectures on "The Child as a Behaving Organism," "Education and Behavior," and "Native Reactions and Acquired Reactions," where James asserts that the stream of consciousness that fills our waking hours has the primary function of producing action. "[M]an," he says, "is primarily a practical being, whose mind is given to him to aid in adapting him to this world's life" (James 1901, p. 24). He argues that this view of the mind has the virtue of being most consistent with the physiology of the brain and an evolutionary view of our place in the animal kingdom. It follows that education is "the organizing of *resources* in the human being, or powers of conduct which shall fit him to his social and physical world," or, more simply, "*the organization of acquired habits of conduct and tendencies to behavior*" (p. 27). By way of illustration, James describes the child's "training in good manners" (pp. 34–35) and cites the educational ideal of the German universities of his time: to turn men into "efficient instrument[s] of research" (p. 28).

The limitations of this instrumentalism about the mental life and its training are especially apparent in the lecture on the acquisition of ideas, which James describes as "inner objects of contemplation," gathered in experiences, and abstracted and grasped in relation to one another by the mind (pp. 88–89). Education is said to "fill the mind little by little, as experiences accrete, with a stock of such ideas" (p. 88), and an educated mind is said to be "the mind which has the largest stock of them, ready to meet the largest possible variety of the emergencies of life" (p. 89). Advice for teachers enters with the suggestion that children are disposed to assimilate different kinds of ideas at different ages: "sensible properties of material things" during the first seven or eight years of life, and only later in adolescence "the more abstract aspects of experience," such as the sciences and "moral relations" (pp. 89–90). James borrows from Herbert Spencer—and, broadly speaking, Jean-Jacques Rousseau—in encouraging the teacher to "feed" the growing mind what it "shows a natural craving" for at each age (p. 90)—namely, activities of making and doing to develop knowledge of the "material world" in the early years, and "verbal material" or "verbal reproduction" after the onset of adolescence "even in the natural sciences, so far as these are causal and rational, and not merely confined to description" (p. 91).

To his credit, James criticizes progressive educators who would too long immerse children in hand work, keeping them from the more abstract studies "the mind craves" (p. 92), but there is much in this little lecture and its companions to disappoint and lower expectations about the educational import of pragmatism. The conception of the natural sciences and how to teach them is not recognizably that of a pragmatist, who might be expected to display some enthusiasm for experimental methods and rather less enthusiasm for "verbal reproduction." The account of learning stages is an echo of Spencer's immensely influential principle of putting the concrete before the abstract, the empirical before the rational (see Egan 2002, esp. pp. 18–19). The narrowness of its vision of what is learned in the early years—"sensible properties of material things"—is remarkable, and barely comprehensible except as a reflection of Locke's account of *simple ideas* as the building blocks of all knowledge.10 If anything, James's view exhibits *less* of the pragmatist's characteristic focus on conduct than Rousseau's stage theory. In Rousseau's version the stages are not defined by the acquisition of concrete or empirical ideas versus abstract or rational ideas, but by a series of forms of motivation: the child is first moved by pleasure and pain, later by consideration of what is useful in achieving chosen ends, and finally by a consideration of what is right and wrong. All told, it would be an immense stretch to find a pragmatist philosophy of education in James's *Talks to Teachers*. The little work expected of pragmatism yields barely more than an abstract characterization of education as training calculated to produce desirable habits.

The image of a characteristically pragmatist philosophy of education—an image well entrenched through the later twentieth century—is predicated almost entirely on Dewey's philosophy of education.11

Dewey's philosophy of education is shaped by three fundamental commitments: a naturalistic and evolutionary conception of human nature and human affairs; a high regard for the methods and norms of experimental, scientific inquiry; and a conception of democracy as a form of social life consistent with individual growth, experimentation with new social forms, and collective control of society's evolution. Building on prior developments in pragmatism, Dewey regards mind as a function of a complex organism and ideas as tools that facilitate human activity and the management of experience (Dewey 1910/1978, 1925/1958). The various further products of mind, including languages, theories, institutions, cultures, and the personalities that presuppose all of these, are similarly tools or instruments grounded in the biological nature of human beings, equipping us to better manage what we experience, and to exercise further control of ourselves and the development of our societies. Our freedom owes much more to the cultural resources that enable us to evaluate, define, and direct our actions than to any natural gifts we might have. Philosophy, being a product of mind and cultural resource of the kind in question, is understood to be a tool for examining how we think, for furthering our development, and for responding to the public's problems and advancing the work of social reconstruction. Education, broadly construed, is the means through which such tools of inquiry and growth are disseminated, and it is for this reason the most fundamental vehicle of social reconstruction. In this scheme, philosophy becomes both an educative endeavor and one to which philosophy of education is central. It is also a scheme in which the methods of philosophy of education become at least in part *experimental*, as Dewey's did through the operation of his Laboratory School at the University of Chicago. The results of the experiments conducted there contributed to such publications as *My Pedagogic Creed* (1897/1972), *The School and Society* (1900), and *The Child and the Curriculum* (1902).

If the influence of Peirce's conception of philosophy is apparent here—his view that "what will remain of philosophy will be a series of problems capable of investigation by the methods of the true sciences"—his conceptions of thinking and inquiry are similarly apparent in Dewey's account of the nature of (effective) inquiry presented in *How We Think* (1910/1978). According to this account, effective thinking or inquiry can be analyzed as a five-part sequence. We (1) begin from an emotional response to an unsettling situation, (2) move on to an intellectual response, (3) generate a hypothesis that promises a resolution of the felt tension, (4) examine the hypothesis by reasoning and identification of consequences that flow from it, and finally (5) test the hypothesis empirically by arranging to observe whether the anticipated consequences actually occur. Dewey understood this experimentalist account of thinking to apply to the examination of *value* as well as more obviously testable matters. He held that one participates in a kind of character education in learning the norms of inquiry that regulate effective thinking and the behavior of scientific communities, and in submitting to those norms in the process of testing forms of conduct and coming to understand their consequences.

In light of this account of effective thinking and associated notion of character formation, Dewey holds that an educational institution is one in which individuals learn and use the skills of experimental inquiry, observing the norms of open communication characteristic of scientific communities. These norms include:

> willingness to hold belief in suspense, ability to doubt until evidence is obtained; willingness to go where evidence points instead of putting first a personally preferred conclusion; ability to hold ideas in solution and use them as hypotheses to be tested instead of as dogmas to be asserted; and (possibly the most distinctive of all) enjoyment of new fields for inquiry and of new problems.
>
> (Dewey 1939/1989, p. 112)

In schools, this implies engaging students in developing both the skills and the attitudes essential to scientific inquiry, which are necessarily exercised in the context of a *community of inquiry*. Science is not a solitary affair, but one essentially involving cooperation with other investigators, who ideally observe not only the norms noted above but also those pertaining to honest, respectful, and intelligent dialogue. Dewey holds that classrooms should themselves be communities of inquiry in which students will come to exhibit the requisite skills and virtues. He also holds that this is essential to individual growth, or open-ended, self-directed development—holding out "growth" in this sense as an ideal compatible with Darwinian evolution, unlike the Aristotelian ideal of flourishing, which involves the idea of fulfilling the potential entailed by a fixed species-essence. He further insists that this is vital to democracy: "Until what shall be taught and how it is taught is settled upon the basis of formation of the scientific attitude, the so-called educational work of schools is a dangerously hit-or-miss affair as far as democracy is concerned" (Dewey 1939/1989, p. 115).

What democracy requires above all is improving the quality of public discourse, and seeing that the free flow of information is not impeded by divisions of class, occupation, or sect, so that society itself operates according to the norms of scientific inquiry. Operating in this way, it becomes a mode of social organization conducive to the growth of its members, as well as effective in pursuing public projects and "flexible readjustment of its institutions" through cooperative inquiry and social experiments (Dewey 1916, p. 99). Put somewhat differently, democracy as Dewey conceives it would provide individuals with a basis for controlling their own development, and provide societies with the means to collectively control their own evolution. The requisite "freer interaction between social groups" (p. 86) was pursued by Jane Addams and other participants in the progressive *social settlement* movement, which allowed people of diverse fortunes to live in close proximity, learning from each other and pursuing common projects. Engaging diverse students in working together in schools was similarly a goal for schools. Dewey argued that the separation of vocational and academic education, the former producing "mere skill in production" and the latter "a knowledge that is an ornament and a cultural embellishment," must be eliminated in favor of "a course of study which should be useful and liberal at the same time" (pp. 256, 258).[12] He also argued strongly for co-education of males and females, and opposed the splitting off of religious communities into separate schools.

In applying these ideas, Dewey took the problems of education in the formative years of the American public school system as a point of departure. These included the loss of opportunities for informal education associated with industrialization, new mass media that made it easier to saturate the public with propaganda, and the rapid evolution of society that threatened to make current ideas and skills obsolete. The first problem was to be addressed, along with other pervasive shortcomings of traditional schools, by eliminating the separation of schooling and life. Dewey held that learning, which is functional and thus highly motivated in life, can be made much more so in schools with the right combination of "child-centered" observance of natural forms of learning and "teacher-centered" selection of curricula responsive to student needs and interests. This would require the elimination of drilling and other forms of information delivery that fail to engage students in active inquiry, and the elimination of narrow vocational training, in favor of forms of inquiry learning that combine practical and academic components. The third problem is also largely addressed through these means, since no one would be consigned to a narrow curriculum of manual skills that could easily become obsolete. Everyone would learn the skills of experimental inquiry and the critical and reflective skills and attitudes those entail, and they would be taught to grow and continually adapt. The second problem would also be addressed through the development of these skills, which Dewey took to be essential to robust public debate, and through eliminating the authoritarian management of classrooms, which invited passivity and conformity. Cooperative inquiry would henceforth be encouraged, instead of suppressed as a form of cheating, and cooperation with the school's purposes would be achieved largely through voluntary acceptance of the norms of activities gladly engaged in.

Writing in 1938, Dewey surveyed the trajectory of the progressive education movement and took some pains to distinguish his own educational vision from both progressive and "traditional" schooling. At its core, progressive education holds that schools should educate the "whole child" through methods that allow learning to occur in accordance with natural patterns of learning, which is to say in a natural sequence and manner, and motivated and guided by the child's natural desire to learn (Zilversmit 1993, p. 18). Dewey shared much of the progressive embrace of natural patterns of learning, but insisted that teachers still have a role to play in selecting curricula and establishing classroom norms of inquiry and cooperation (Dewey 1938). The shared commitments are evident in Dewey's desire to diminish the separation of learning from life, of academics from self-directed activity; in his embrace of learning through inquiry; in the room he leaves for child-directed learning; and in his endorsements of the basic progressive, Spencerian, and Rousseauian principle that the educator "has to find ways of doing consciously and deliberately what 'nature' accomplishes in the early years" (Dewey 1938, p. 74).

3. Pragmatist Philosophy of Education in Extremis

Dewey's educational ideas remain influential at several foci of advocacy, including the community of inquiry and cooperative learning models (Lipman 2003; Slavin 1995), Lawrence Kohlberg's just community model of moral education (Power, Higgins, and Kohlberg 1989), and various related models of classroom management and discipline. More generally, it is no exaggeration to say that progressive educational ideas can be counted on to reassert themselves as new and revolutionary every few years, as the insistence on the *naturalness* of basing literacy instruction on "whole language" has done for at least a century and a half now.

Setting aside the enduring influence of Dewey's philosophy of education, and the educational ideas of the progressive movement, there remains the question of whether there is a distinctively pragmatist approach to philosophy of education.

Let us note, first, that in the survey just concluded we found little evidence of the pragmatist method of analysis, embodied in the *pragmatic maxim*, playing any role in producing substantial results in philosophy of education. We saw it deployed in James's lectures to little effect, and we can reasonably ask whether an unflinching deployment of it would not suggest most obviously a form of *behaviorism*. Peirce offered a variety of formulations of his basic conception of meaning, but the one announced in "How to Make Our Ideas Clear" is exhibited in dispositional analyses of traits such as hardness. Applied to persons, this yields logical behaviorism, or the view that mental attributes are behavioral dispositions. E. L. Thorndike, a student of James's and colleague of Dewey's, endorsed the latter's instrumentalism and developed the theory of operant or instrumental conditioning, later reworked by B. F. Skinner. The prospects along this path are no longer inviting, and it is not surprising that philosophers of education sympathetic to pragmatism now repudiate them.[13] The application of Peirce's method of analysis to formal systems lends support to a different kind of mental functionalism, also embraced by logical empiricists and computational modelers, as well as pragmatists or pragmatic sympathizers such as Sellars and Brandom. Regarding the terms in a formal system as implicitly defined within the system (*a la* Peirce), one can model beliefs and other mental items as defined by functional roles in a "system" that explains what a person does. There is a more generous conception of empirical significance at work here, and it is certainly progress to abandon logical behaviorism in favor of cognitive models, but at this level of abstraction we are still very far from doing philosophy of education.

Suppose we regard pragmatism not as a method of analysis, as Peirce and James did, but as a philosophical orientation defined (as it was at the end of section I) by experimentalism, evolutionary naturalism, instrumentalism, and pragmatist theories of meaning, truth, and reality. Would this yield Dewey's philosophy of education, or might it just as readily lend itself to a behaviorist view of education? The answer, surely, is that it requires a great deal of selectivity and oversight to accept Dewey's philosophy of education as the essence of what pragmatism yields in the domain of philosophy of education. It is organized around some pragmatist themes, but it would be quite a leap to regard it as typical of what one could construct from pragmatist starting points. It does not depend fundamentally on any *distinctively* pragmatist doctrines, and it does depend on a good deal that is not essentially pragmatist—above all, the legacy of Rousseau, filtered through a tradition of pedagogical experiments and the writings of Spencer.

Reviewing the canonical elements of pragmatism, and allowing the addition of democracy, those that are evident in Dewey's educational thought are: (1) an embrace of experimental science; (2) a naturalistic view of human nature; (3) an embrace of democracy. What is noteworthy about these commitments is that they are now so widely shared that holding them does not mark one as a pragmatist. The early pragmatists were among the revolutionaries who adopted a broadly naturalistic, scientific, and (sometimes) liberal democratic outlook, but they were not the only ones, and we are now nearly all naturalists and democrats.

Most of us accept the fact of evolution, though we may doubt that the transient existence of species has the revolutionary implications for philosophical methodology that Dewey supposed. Most of us are advocates of secular liberal democracy, though we may not favor Dewey's particular conception of democracy as a form of society modeled on scientific communities. We all accept that cognition is embodied and situated—that bodies and societies provide contexts for thinking and learning.[14] Whatever we think about science, we are all or nearly all fallibilists. It is thus hard to see anything distinctively pragmatist in a commitment to Dewey's starting points. By contrast, the doctrines that do remain distinctively pragmatist—such as Dewey's insistence that inquiry does not reveal an independently existing world, but instead alters and makes it what it is in the interaction—play no significant role in his philosophy of education.

There continue to be advocates of pragmatism in philosophy of education, but it is debatable whether they have absorbed the basic pragmatist message about how to do philosophy any more than other philosophers of education have. It is not unusual for contemporary neo-pragmatists or pragmatist sympathizers in educational theory to echo Dewey's themes—the misbegotten quest for certainty, misguided authoritarianism in classroom management, learning through inquiry, art in the education of the whole person, and the wisdom of abjuring fixed ends in education—yet to do this without particular attention to the empirical methods, context, and consequences recommended by pragmatism. What distinguishes neo-pragmatism in philosophy of education today is not its practical edge but its recourse to pragmatist sources and an associated and problematic embrace of systematic philosophy as the key to doing deep or truly philosophical practical philosophy (see, e.g., Arcilla 1995; Burbules 1995; Neiman 1995; Standish 2003). Misbegotten attempts to glean educational lessons from metaphysics and epistemology are not the exclusive province of neo-pragmatism, but the underlying methodological tendency has surely been encouraged by an exaggerated estimation of the extent to which Dewey simply *applied* pragmatism to education.[15]

Several decades ago, analytic philosophers became impatient with the state of meta-ethics and the obstacle it posed to philosophical engagement with practical affairs. Some dove directly into analytical engagement with practical issues, some turned to work in normative ethical and political theory more or less engaged with applications, and others made new attempts within meta-ethics to find a rational basis for regarding morality as reason-giving. These developments gave rise to a variety of ways of pursuing engaged ethical, social, legal, political, and educational philosophy, more or less grounded in systematic analyses of such concepts as desert, well-being, and integrity, more or less grounded in normative theories of ethics and justice, and more or less systematically grounded in relevant empirical sources. The pragmatist focus on context and consequences in evaluating institutions, laws, and policies is not inconsistent with such approaches to practical philosophy, provided they are indeed serious about getting the facts right and do not ignore the current common wisdom in moral theory that consequences matter. If my characterization of the patterns of contemporary neo-pragmatism in

philosophy of education are correct, then it follows that to the extent contemporary analytic philosophers of education adhere to Edel's advice to integrate "the
empirical, the normative, and the contextual (especially the socio-cultural) *within
the analytic method*" (Edel 1973, p. 41), it is *within* analytic philosophy that the
basic pragmatist message about how to do philosophy of education lives on. This is
no longer Dewey's "time when America was still a symbol of the dawn of a better
day and was full of hope infused with courage," but it is within the vigorous and
informed debates of analytical liberalism, cast in terms fit for a wider public and
policy arena, that there is promise of something reaching "beyond the confines of
technical philosophy" (Dewey 1949, p. xiv).

What the pragmatist vision of a science of ethics would seem to condemn most
in the present landscape of philosophy of education is recourse to speculative
philosophy that impairs the effectiveness of arguments for educational reform by
burdening them with unnecessary and contested theoretical baggage, when what is
needed is evidence and analysis. It is hard to imagine that, in the circumstances we
face today, Dewey would have prized the transmission of his ideas, or attempts to
find some educational import in contemporary pragmatist theories, over direct
normative investigations of corporate influences in schools (Brighouse 2007),
racially integrated schooling (Blum 2007), or interventions to prevent forced
marriages of school age girls (McAvoy 2008).[16] If philosophy is a tool, then let it
be sharp and efficient in cutting to the chase.

NOTES

....

I owe thanks to John Bennett, Robert Holmes, and Harvey Siegel for helpful comments on a
penultimate draft of this chapter.

1. Edel (1908–2007) was a doctoral student in philosophy at Columbia University in
the 1930s, during the final years of John Dewey's teaching career there. His book *Ethical
Judgment: The Use of Science in Ethics* (1955) is characteristic of pragmatist ethical theory, in
its regard for morality as a human product in a contingent and changing world, and its view
that *a priori* absolutes must be set aside and everything tested by experience, using science
and its methods.

2. See Rorty 1979, 1991. Some accounts of the nature of pragmatism find a cleavage
between *reform* and *revolutionary* pragmatism, and see little plausibility in Rorty's attempts
to claim the authority of those in the former camp for his own revolutionary variety. See
Migotti 1988; Haack 1996; and Mounce 1997. The earliest pragmatists, Peirce and William
James (1842–1910), regarded pragmatism as an analytical methodology, not a substantive
philosophy, but their views differed in ways that gave rise to more or less revolutionary
doctrines within pragmatism, with the revolutionary elements descending from James and
his disciple, the English literary humanist Ferdinand (F. C. S.) Schiller (1864–1937).

3. For further discussion of the similarities and connections between pragmatism and
logical empiricism and positivism, see Wiener 1973. Morton White details the "scientific
outlook" shared by Dewey, Oliver Wendell Holmes (1841–1935), and other pragmatists, and

refers to the writings of positivists and operationalists as "half-critical, half-supporting" (White 1947, p. 5). For good general histories of pragmatism, see Wiener 1949 and Thayer 1968.

4. In addition to progressive education and progressive law, the movement embraced "social settlement" in distressed communities as a form of direct action to facilitate social improvement. See Addams 1902/2002, 1910/1990; Deegan 1988.

5. On the hostility of progressive reform theorists to abstract principles and "formalism," see White 1947. "Formalism," as White describes it, is in many respects the very foe attacked by pragmatists: an outlook that treats logic, deduction, and *a priori* principles as a substitute for experience, historical understanding, and an application of scientific methods. The reform-minded legal realists of the early twentieth century adopted characteristic pragmatist stances in: (1) criticizing legal principles of the nineteenth century, for their insensitivity to contemporary conditions and for being barriers to social progress; (2) holding that the meaning of legal rules or principles is determined, not by their intuitive moral content or derivation from higher principles, but by the practice and consequences of applying them. See Pound 1910, 1911; Llewellyn 1930. Industrialization and consequent changes in the nature of employment had, in fact, profoundly altered the kinds of cases coming before courts and the relationships between the litigants, with the result that principles designed for accidents between strangers frequently produced devastating outcomes for workers. A good example of this was the application of the principle of *contributory negligence* to disabling injuries arising from workplace hazards. Workers who had complained of hazards that were not their fault, not remedied, and from which they suffered were denied compensation on the grounds they were aware of the hazards and chose to stay on the job, thereby exposing themselves to the risks that eventuated in their injuries. For documentation of this and other examples, see White 1980. Holmes, though very much a pragmatist in his analysis of law (Holmes 1881), did not join the ranks of the reformers until his famous dissent in *Lochner* v. *New York*, a 1905 decision that, in the name of freedom of contract, struck down a law limiting the work week of bakers to 64 hours.

6. Peirce referred to Bain as the "Scottish ancestor of pragmatism" (Wiener 1949, p. 68). Focusing on pragmatism as a tradition of American cultural criticism, one might identify Ralph Waldo Emerson as another "grandfather" of the movement (West 1989).

7. Nor does anything follow about the nature of *truth* from the defeasibility of *evidence*, the proposition that evidence is never so conclusive as to produce certainty. All that follows from defeasibility is that we can't be absolutely certain of the truth of what we assert. It is often held (by nonphilosophers) that philosophers have shown that nothing is absolutely certain—that it is always possible that new evidence may force us to revise our beliefs—and it is just as often held that it follows from this that there is no "absolute truth." This is a *non sequitur*, and it lends nothing but obscurity to the issue to append the qualifier "absolute" to "truth."

8. Herbert Spencer used the expression "survival of the fittest" before and more persistently than Darwin did, and unlike Darwin he used it in opposing public schools and defending ruthless capitalist exploitation of the poor. His conception of adaptation was Lamarckian, moreover, so it is doubly unjust to call the repugnant view he popularized "Social Darwinism" (see Egan 2002, pp. 23*ff*).

9. The reference to individual powers being both liberated and directed to social aims signifies a fusion in Dewey's thought of the individualistic liberty of Mill with a more collectivist Hegelian notion of freedom as voluntary constraint by the norms of cooperative endeavors.

10. Spencer's principle seems to be a crude application of the Lockean premise that simple ideas must be gathered through experience before the mind can work upon them to produce "conceptions of a higher and more abstract order," as James so succinctly puts it (James 1901/1983, p. 89).

11. One may credit Dewey's collaborator, George Herbert Mead (1863–1931), and his various intellectual descendants, with secondary roles.

12. Morton White finds evidence of a direct influence of Thorstein Veblen's *Theory of the Leisure Class* (1899) in Dewey's appraisal of ornamental learning (White 1947, p. 98).

13. Jim Garrison and Alven Neiman may be right in saying that "Thorndike's victory internationally is one of the major reasons most educators completely ignore pragmatism," but they give no indication of recognizing the extent to which Thorndike's behaviorism embodies a pragmatist approach (Garrison and Neiman 2003, p. 26).

14. It is worth noting that pragmatists err in assuming that Descartes' mind-body dualism precludes a role for the body in the affairs of the mind. See Schmitter, Tarcov and, Donner 2003, pp. 78–79, and related references.

15. In the 1960s, when analytic philosophy of education was getting under way, Harper & Row launched The Philosophy of Education Series, consisting of texts "furnish[ing] authentic presentations of major contemporary philosophies as they relate to, or impinge upon, educational practice" (Bayles 1966, p. x). The series began with a volume on pragmatism by the series editor, and included others on idealism, existentialism, and realism. Philosophers of education look back in horror on the age of "isms," but the assumption that one can find educational "applications" in just about *any* work of philosophy has been harder to shake.

16. For commentary on a recent attempt to find educational import in Brandom's inferentialist pragmatism, see Curren 2008.

REFERENCES

Addams, Jane. (1902/2002). *Democracy and Social Ethics*. Urbana, IL: University of Illinois Press.
—— (1910/1990). *Twenty Years at Hull House*. Urbana, IL: University of Illinois Press.
Arcilla, René. (1995). *For the Love of Perfection: Richard Rorty and Liberal Education*. London: Routledge.
Bayles, Ernest. (1966). *Pragmatism in Education*. New York: Harper & Row.
Blum, Lawrence. (2007). "The Promise of Racial Integration in a Multicultural Age." In *Philosophy of Education: An Anthology*, ed. Randall Curren (pp. 266–82). Oxford: Blackwell.
Brandom, Robert. (1994). *Making it Explicit: Reasoning, Representing, and Discursive Commitment*. Cambridge, MA: Harvard University Press.
—— (2000). *Articulating Reasons: An Introduction to Inferentialism*. Cambridge, MA: Harvard University Press.
Brighouse, Harry. (2007). "Channel One, the Anti-Commercial Principle, and the Discontinuous Ethos." In *Philosophy of Education: An Anthology*, ed. Randall Curren (pp. 208–20). Oxford: Blackwell.

Burbules, Nicholas. (1995). "Authority and the Tragic Dimension of Teaching." In *The Educational Conversation: Closing the Gap*, ed. J. Garrison and A. G. Rud Jr. (pp. 29–40). Albany: State University of New York Press.

Campbell, James. (1995). *Understanding John Dewey.* Chicago: Open Court.

Cremin, Lawrence. (1961). *The Transformation of the School: Progressivism in American Education, 1876–1957.* New York: Knopf.

Curren, Randall, ed. (2007). *Philosophy of Education: An Anthology.* Oxford: Blackwell.

—— (2008). "Inferentialism Goes to School." In *Philosophy of Education 2007*, ed. B. Stengel (pp. 125–27). Urbana, IL: Philosophy of Education Society.

Deegan, Mary Jo. (1988). *Jane Addams and the Men of the Chicago School, 1892–1918.* New Brunswick, NJ: Transaction Books.

Dewey, John. (1897/1972). *My Pedagogic Creed.* In *Early Works of John Dewey, 1882–1898, vol. 5: 1895–1898*, ed. J. A. Boydston (pp. 84–95). Carbondale: Southern Illinois University Press.

—— (1900). *The School and Society.* Chicago: University of Chicago Press.

—— (1902). *The Child and the Curriculum.* Chicago: University of Chicago Press.

—— (1908/1998). "What Pragmatism Means by 'Practical.'" In *The Essential Dewey, Vol. 2: Ethics, Logic, Psychology*, ed. L. Hickman and L. Alexander (pp. 377–86). Bloomington: Indiana University Press.

—— (1910/1978). *How We Think.* In *The Middle Works, 1899–1924, Vol. 6: 1910–1911*, ed. J. A. Boydston (pp. 177–355). Carbondale: Southern Illinois University Press.

—— (1916). *Democracy and Education.* New York: Macmillan.

—— (1925/1958). *Experience and Nature.* New York: Dover.

—— (1929). *The Quest for Certainty.* New York: Minton, Balch.

—— (1938). *Experience and Education.* New York: Collier.

—— (1939/1989). *Freedom and Culture.* Buffalo, NY: Prometheus Books.

—— (1949). Foreword. In *Evolution and the Founders of Pragmatism*, by Philip P. Wiener (pp. xiii–xiv). Cambridge, MA: Harvard University Press.

Edel, Abraham. (1955). *Ethical Judgment: The Use of Science in Ethics.* Glencoe, IL: Free Press.

—— (1973). "Analytic Philosophy of Education at the Crossroads." In *Educational Judgments*, ed. James Doyle (pp. 232–57). London: Routledge.

Egan, Kieran. (2002). *Getting It Wrong from the Beginning: Our Progressivist Inheritance from Herbert Spencer, John Dewey, and Jean Piaget.* New Haven: Yale University Press.

Feigl, Herbert. (1949). "Logical Empiricism: Positivism, Not Negativism." In *Readings in Philosophical Analysis*, ed. Herbert Feigl and Wilfred Sellars (pp. 3–25). New York: Appleton-Century-Crofts.

—— and Wilfred Sellars, eds. (1949). *Readings in Philosophical Analysis.* New York: Appleton-Century-Crofts.

Garrison, Jim, and Alven Neiman. (2003). "Pragmatism and Education." In *The Blackwell Guide to Philosophy of Education*, ed. Nigel Blake, Paul Smeyers, Richard Smith, and Paul Standish (pp. 21–37). Oxford: Blackwell.

Gouinlock, James. (1986). *Excellence in Public Discourse: John Stuart Mill, John Dewey, and Social Intelligence.* New York: Teachers College Press.

Haack, Susan. (1993). *Evidence and Inquiry: Towards Reconstruction in Epistemology.* Oxford: Blackwell.

—— (1996). "Pragmatism." In *The Blackwell Companion to Philosophy*, ed. N. Bunnin and E. P. Tsui-James (pp. 643–61). Oxford: Blackwell.

Held, David. (1987). *Models of Democracy.* Stanford, CA: Stanford University Press.

Holmes, Oliver W. (1881). *The Common Law.* Boston: Little, Brown.

James, William. (1890/1983). *The Principles of Psychology.* Cambridge, MA: Harvard University Press.

—— (1901/1983). *Talks to Teachers on Psychology and to Students on Some of Life's Ideals.* Cambridge, MA: Harvard University Press. (Incorporates the 1899 work *Talks to Teachers on Psychology.*)

—— (1907). *Pragmatism,* ed. F. Burkhardt and F. Bowers. Cambridge, MA: Harvard University Press.

Kloesel, Christian J. W., ed. (1986). *Writings of Charles S. Peirce: A Chronological Edition, Vol. 3, 1872–1978.* Bloomington: Indiana University Press.

Lipman, Matthew. (2003). *Thinking in Education,* 2nd ed. Cambridge: Cambridge University Press.

Llewellyn, Karl. (1930). "A Realistic Jurisprudence—The Next Step." *Columbia Law Review* 30: 431–65.

McAvoy, Paula. (2008). "Should Arranged Marriages for Teenage Girls be Allowed? How Public Schools Should Respond to Illiberal Cultural Practices." *Theory and Research in Education* 6(1): 5–20.

Migotti, M. (1988). "Recent Work in Pragmatism: Revolution or Reform in the Theory of Knowledge?" *Philosophical Books* 29: 65–73.

Mounce, H. O. (1997). *The Two Pragmatisms: From Peirce to Rorty.* London: Routledge.

Neiman, Alven. (1995). "Pragmatism: The Aims of Education and the Meaning of Life." In *Critical Conversations in Philosophy of Education,* ed. W. Kohli (pp. 56–72). New York: Routledge.

Peirce, Charles. (1905). "What Pragmatism Is." *Monist* 15(2): 161–81.

Pound, Roscoe. (1910). "Law in Books and Law in Action." *American Law Review* 44: 12–36.

—— (1911). "The Scope and Purpose of Sociological Jurisprudence." *Harvard Law Review* 24: 591–619.

Power, F. Clark, Ann Higgins, and Lawrence Kohlberg. (1989). *Lawrence Kohlberg's Approach to Moral Education.* New York: Columbia University Press.

Putnam, Hilary. (1995). *Pragmatism.* Oxford: Blackwell.

Rorty, Richard. (1979). *Philosophy and the Mirror of Nature.* Princeton: Princeton University Press.

—— (1991). *Objectivity, Relativism, and Truth.* Cambridge: Cambridge University Press.

Russell, Bertrand. (1905). "On Denoting." *Mind* 14: 479–93.

Schmitter, Amy, Nathan Tarcov, and Wendy Donner. (2003). "Enlightenment Liberalism." In *A Companion to the Philosophy of Education,* ed. Randall Curren (pp. 73–93). Oxford: Blackwell.

Slavin, Robert. (1995). *Cooperative Learning: Theory, Research, and Practice,* 2nd ed. Boston: Allyn and Bacon.

Standish, Paul. (2003). "The Nature and Purposes of Education." In *A Companion to the Philosophy of Education,* ed. Randall Curren (pp. 221–31). Oxford: Blackwell.

Thayer, H. S. (1968). *Meaning and Action: A Critical History of Pragmatism.* New York: Bobbs-Merrill.

Veblen, Thorstein.(1899). *The Theory of the Leisure Class.* New York: Macmillan.

West, Cornel. (1989). *The American Evasion of Philosophy: A Genealogy of Pragmatism.* Madison: University of Wisconsin Press.

White, G. Edward. (1980). *Tort Law in America.* Oxford: Oxford University Press.

White, Morton. (1947). *Social Thought in America: The Revolt against Formalism.* Boston: Beacon Press.

Wiener, Philip P. (1949). *Evolution and the Founders of Pragmatism*. Cambridge, MA: Harvard University Press.

—— (1973). "Pragmatism." In *Dictionary of the History of Ideas: Studies of Selected Pivotal Ideas*, ed. P. Wiener (pp. 551–70). New York: Charles Scribner's Sons.

Zilversmit, Arthur. (1993). *Changing Schools: Progressive Education Theory and Practice, 1930–1960*. Chicago: University of Chicago Press.

CHAPTER 27

FEMINIST PHILOSOPHY AND EDUCATION

NEL NODDINGS

OVER the last thirty years, feminist philosophy has grown in quantity, if not in influence. Its growth has followed (roughly) the three generations of feminist thought described by Julia Kristeva (1982). In the first, emphasis is placed on women's oppression, and equality with men is the main goal. In the second, concentration is on women's agency, and questions are raised about uncritical assimilation into the male world. In the third, feminist philosophers critique previous generations of thought, and suggest new (or defend old) patterns of thought. These categories are better interpreted as centers of concentration than as "generations" because we find them scattered across the decades of activity in feminism. In what follows, I use this structure to organize the chapter. I use the last section to concentrate on feminist critiques in philosophy of education.

1. WOMEN'S OPPRESSION

Feminist scholars treat a great variety of topics, but the issue of women's oppression and long struggle for equality is of central importance. It may, indeed, be regarded as the defining feature of feminism. The history of feminist philosophy confirms this interest, but it also reveals conflicts that have arisen from feminist commitments. A pessimist might describe the pursuit of feminist philosophy as a no-win project. In fact, Margaret Urban Walker (2005) has recently made comments to that effect. A woman who chooses to do feminist philosophy may find herself rejected as a philosopher.

There have always been women philosophers. (See the four-volume history of women philosophers edited by Mary Ellen Waithe, 1987, 1989, 1991, 1995; see also a special issue on American women philosophers in *Hypatia*, Spring 2004.) But for the most part, they have been ignored in their own period, co-opted by male writers, and discarded entirely over time. Walker comments on the fate of Diotima, reputedly the teacher of Socrates: "she did not just disappear from the history of philosophy. She was reduced to a figment of that great man's imagination" (2005, p. 155). We will probably never know whether Diotima was a real person.

For today's women philosophers, a conflict arises in the choice to do feminist philosophy. Walker says of it, "It is a kind of philosophy, not a female or feminine activity," and it "is a method, not a topic" (2005, p. 157). But there is little agreement on this. Some women philosophers are analytic philosophers, and for them feminist philosophy is more a set of topics than a method. (See the special issue of *Hypatia* devoted to analytic feminism, Fall 2005.) Clearly, there are also feminist existentialists and pragmatists as well. Insofar as it is a method in itself—like, say, existentialism or pragmatism—it runs the same risk as other methods, that of relative isolation as a specialty, but the risk is enormously increased by the fact that most of its practitioners are women.

There are, however, excellent examples of feminist philosophy as method. One of the best known is "standpoint epistemology" (Harding 1996; Hartsock 1983; Hekman 1997). As method, standpoint epistemology holds that we get nearer to a true objectivity if we look at phenomena and situations through a variety of perspectives. We should give up the faulty, largely fictitious notion of a neutral or universal perspective. As one perspective in the category of standpoint epistemology, feminist epistemology looks at the world through the eyes of women. This does not in itself imply a loss of "objectivity" because it admits at the outset that, to achieve objectivity (if that is possible), we need the perspectives of all stake holders.

Still, there are problems. In educational philosophy, Barbara Thayer-Bacon (2000) has given a useful and persuasive account of standpoint theory and the difficulties it faces. In particular, it risks re-inscribing some of the features found so objectionable in traditional philosophy, such as privileging certain voices within the feminist community. How can anyone speak from the standpoint of all women? It is an open question whether these difficulties can be avoided. For present purposes, feminist standpoint epistemology offers an example of feminist philosophy as *method*. It is *not* a set of topics.

There is some risk, too, in rejecting the notion that feminist philosophy is a female activity. Thirty years ago, as feminist theory got a new start, feminist scholars often talked about solidarity with other women; they pledged themselves to interdisciplinary work within academe and to social efforts in the larger community. However, this is not the way to get ahead in universities, and women scholars had to blend their feminist work with approved specialties in other fields. They were challenged with the question: Are you a scholar or an activist? Answering that question changed the tone of feminist studies.

An important element of solidarity has remained among feminist philosophers within the academy. Black feminists have contributed to both liberal and radical feminist philosophy. (See, for example, Patricia Hill Collins 1990, 1995; also the essays by Kimberle Williams Crenshaw and bell hooks in Meyers 1997.) Their work has influenced the direction of discussions not only on race and equality but also on family, community, and schooling (Walker 1996).

The struggle with the question—scholar or activist?—helps to explain why so much feminist philosophy falls into the category of social or political philosophy. Much of this work has helped to keep the original feminist commitment alive. Alison Jaggar, for example, has described feminism as political philosophy. She notes that "feminist political philosophers . . . use both traditional and nontraditional categories in attempting to describe and evaluate women's experience" (1983, p. 7). Issues concerning childbirth, love, maternal work, childcare, and sexuality are brought into philosophical discourse. "By seeking to extend the traditional domain of political philosophy, contemporary feminism challenges both existing political theories and our conception of political philosophy itself" (Jaggar 1983, p. 7). This line of thinking remains strong today. Feminist philosophers may, for example, identify themselves as Marxist, liberal, radical, or socialist (Tuana and Tong 1995).

The effects of this work have been felt across disciplinary lines. Feminist theologians, nursing theorists, historians, psychologists, anthropologists, sociologists, and legal theorists have all contributed to the analysis of human life as embodied in women (Noddings 1990). However, the real social effects seem to emerge primarily from the social sciences. In a recent comprehensive work on women's well-being, there is no sign of influence from feminist philosophy (Bianchi, Casper, and King 2005), and a check of the indexes of books in political philosophy often reveals mention of "children's rights" or "families" but rarely anything on women, feminism, or bodies of any sort.

That said, there does appear to be a revival of interest in creatural existence within philosophy, and philosophers of education have contributed to this literature (O'Loughlin 2006). One feature of this revival is increased attention to emotions and everyday life in education (Boler 1999; Noddings 2003b). Questions have been raised about the traditional curriculum and why it is virtually devoid of topics that have been central to women's lives (Martin 1984, 1985, 1992; Noddings 1992/2005, 2006a).

Feminist philosophy has also exerted considerable influence through critiques of traditional philosophy. Susan Moller Okin (1979) has given us accounts of male philosophers who supported women's equality and of others who spoke powerfully against it. Her critique of Rousseau is especially important for educators. For years, it was not unusual for philosophers of education to extol Rousseau as the philosopher of freedom and his *Emile* as the book that describes an appropriate education for free citizens. However, one could hardly hold this view unreservedly after reading Book 5 of *Emile*. In that book, Rousseau advocates an education for Sophie that should keep her subservient to Emile. She is not to think for herself, and she is to be both sexually alluring and chaste—"both virgin and prostitute" (Okin 1979, p. 101).

Critiques of science have also been prominent in feminist philosophy. The most convincing acknowledge the enormous success of science while noting its domination by males and male thinking. Evelyn Fox Keller puts it well in describing two different discourses on science: "One an increasingly radical critique that fails to account for the effectiveness of science, and the other a justification that draws confidence from that effectiveness to maintain a traditional, and essentially unchanged, philosophy of science" (1985, p. 6).

From this perspective, several goals for feminist philosophy of science might be established: (1) to open scientific fields to women; (2) to show how science might be improved by expanding its methods; (3) to transform the scientific description of women and women's experience; and (4) to encourage interdisciplinary work within the sciences and between science and the humanities.

Jane Roland Martin (1985), concentrating specifically on education in her critiques, also gives us a devastating evaluation of Rousseau's recommendations for women's education. In addition to critiques of Rousseau, Plato, Wollstonecraft, Beecher, and Gilman, Martin is particularly interested in the connection between feminist theory and philosophy of education. If we are serious about education for *human* life, why in our curriculum planning do we persist in ignoring topics and activities central to female lives?

I, too, have discussed this question (Noddings 1992/2005, 2006a). For example, I have offered an analysis of evil from the perspective of women (Noddings 1989). It is clear, however, that this is *a* woman's view and not that of all women. Women have suffered for centuries under a succession of myths fabricated by men, myths blaming the origin of evil on women—on Pandora, Eve, witches, and lamias. Ridding religion of these pernicious myths is crucially important (Daly 1974), and philosophers and educators should give more attention to the sort of religious education that might accomplish this (Noddings 1993). Moreover, without the distraction and mystification of theological views of evil, we might look more clearly at the human condition and work toward the reduction of moral evil.

Feminist commitment to the alleviation of suffering and the elimination of oppression has led quite naturally to a concern for the welfare of other oppressed groups. Feminist philosophers are actively engaged in the identification and analysis of the oppression experienced by racial minorities, the disabled, and homosexuals. See, for example, special issues of *Hypatia* devoted to race: 22, no. 2 (Spring 2007); to maternal bodies 21, no. 1 (Winter 2006).

This is commendable, but it triggers another conflict for feminists. If we work for the elimination of such a wide range of oppression, will we thereby dilute efforts to improve the condition of women as a specific group? This was the dilemma faced by feminists during and after the Civil War. Having worked hard for the abolition of slavery, feminists were then betrayed when politicians decided to push for the voting rights of black men and postpone consideration of women's suffrage

(Ward and Burns 1999). Neither Elizabeth Cady Stanton nor Susan B. Anthony lived to see the justice they had worked for so many years to achieve.

Most feminists today defend decisions to work against all forms of oppression. They do this in full knowledge that even today women earn only 75 percent of what equally qualified men earn for roughly the same work, and we still do most of the housework and childcare. Women are still discriminated against in religious institutions that would collapse without their support. Of all groups, perhaps, women are the most complicit in our own oppression. The reason for this docility is probably that there are rewards as well as penalties in women's subservience, and many white women in the Western world—certainly most of those writing about oppression—are reasonably well-off economically. When others are suffering so much more obviously, it is hard to push one's own case, but this is a continuing dilemma for feminists.

Still another dilemma for feminists trying to overcome women's oppression is the question of how to fit into the world created by men. Much of feminist philosophy has its roots in liberal philosophy, and one of its main aims is to achieve equality for women. In education, there has been a steady and largely successful campaign to increase the participation of women at all levels of education but, again, the outcomes are not all rosy. Insisting on the inclusion of women in social studies texts, for example, has resulted in an "add women and stir" approach. The test for inclusion seems to be whether any woman, however obscure, has contributed anything to the activities dominated by men. This is very different from changing the curriculum to include tasks and interests traditionally associated with women. The male-structured curriculum remains, and women are fitted into paragraphs here and there.

This observation reminds us of a deeper, more lasting conflict. The problem was posed in the 1930s by Virginia Woolf. On the one hand, Woolf wanted to increase opportunities for women in the public world. She prescribed a "room of one's own" for women writers, and confessed to killing that obsequious creature, the Angel in the House. But she worried about the sort of world women would perpetuate if they joined the procession of educated men:

> Do we wish to join that procession, or don't we? On what terms shall we join
> the procession? Above all, where is it leading us, the procession of educated
> men? . . . What is this "civilization"? What are these ceremonies and why should we
> take part in them? What are these professions and why should we make money out
> of them? Where in short is it leading us, the procession of the sons of educated
> men?   (1938/1966, pp. 62–63)

Her questions still trouble us.

2. Women's Agency

Although women have suffered (and still suffer) oppression, they have also exercised agency, and historians have led the way in bringing attention to women's agency (Beard 1946/1962; Kerber 1997). In philosophy, women's agency often appears in views that develop a distinctive way of approaching social problems. Taking Woolf's questions seriously, these views seek a transformation of the society in which women will be equal partners and citizens (Offen 1988).

The ethic of care (Held 1995; Noddings 1984/2003) is an example of feminist philosophy that recognizes the dignity and moral importance of women's traditional work and uses it to articulate an alternative approach to moral life and thought. Relation, response to needs, familial care, and social responsibility were all elements of eighteenth-and nineteenth-century women's movements. Wollstonecraft (1792/1975) argued for the rights of women (particularly with respect to education), partly on the grounds that women would be better wives and mothers if they had better education. Similarly, Ellen Key (see Offen 1988) argued for state support for all mothers, and the great suffragists of Britain and the United States often emphasized women's sensitivity to human need as a reason to accord voting rights to women. Besides the standard suffragist arguments for extending the vote (equality, representation), advocates argued strongly that the moral orientation of women would bring a more humane and sensitive approach to public life. Most of us today reject the idea that women are morally superior to men, just as we reject the centuries-old claim that preceded it: that women are morally inferior because of some lack in reasoning power. But, that caveat aside, it is a fact that there is a measurable gap between men and women on social issues; women, in general, *do* vote more liberally on social issues than men. Still, neither the utopian improvement predicted by feminists nor the rational disaster predicted by misogynists has come to pass.

Formal articulation of an ethic of care began in the 1980s—in psychology (Gilligan 1982), philosophy (Noddings 1984/2003), nursing (Watson 1979), and sociology (Waerness 1984). Interestingly, none of these writers seemed aware of each other's work at the time of initial writing. An intellectual history of caring and care ethics cannot be undertaken here, but it is important to note that the work was interdisciplinary from the start. By the late 1980s, scholars writing on the ethic of care recognized and drew on one another's work.

My own work was strongly influenced by the relational philosophy of Martin Buber (1958/1970, 1965), and it was some time after the publication of *Caring* (1984/2003) that I became aware of feminist connections. In contrast, Sara Ruddick (1989) acknowledges the influence of many feminists, among them Jean Baker Miller (1976), Nancy Chodorow (1978), Adrienne Rich (1976), Dorothy Dinnerstein (1976), Iris Murdoch (1970), and Simone Weil (1977).

The publication of Gilligan's *In a Different Voice* (1982) triggered a wide range of debate. Questions were asked about the gender differences suggested by the study, and a lively debate arose over the perceived conflict between justice and caring. Both Ruddick and I explicitly stated that men are capable of caring and of maternal thinking, and Gilligan was careful to point out that, although the care-response was discovered in interviews with women, this did not imply that it is the exclusive property of women. Some of us now think that we were too quick to downplay gender differences and that much more should be done in this area.

Current thinking acknowledges the need for both justice and caring (Katz, Noddings, and Strike 1999; Tronto 1993), but interesting questions remain. Which is primary? Must they be applied in different domains? Are they reasonably applied in phases? I have argued that caring provides the foundation for a sense of justice (Noddings 2002b), and Okin's critique of Rawls implies a similar claim (Okin 1989). We can ask also whether decisions made using principles of justice leave important human concerns unfinished. For example, if the firing of a teacher is justified on principle, is there no further moral obligation to that teacher? I have argued that, in many such cases, caring picks up where justice leaves off.

A division of application by domain—public or private sphere—is not convincing. Feminist philosophers have shown both that caring is useful in the public domain and that justice is applicable in the private domain (Held 1993; Tronto 1993). The key point for application of caring-for is direct contact between the carer and the cared-for. This requirement limits both opportunity and obligation. If we are not in a position to receive the response of the cared-for, there can be no caring relation. However, we can *care-about* others when there is no direct contact, and this caring-about may be guided by principles of justice. But it must be guided also by the intention to establish or maintain conditions under which caring-for can take place.

For the past few years, a lively discussion has been conducted over the connection between care ethics and virtue ethics (Noddings 2000, 2006b; Sander-Staudt 2006; Slote 2000). The two are similar in several respects. Both put little emphasis on rules and principles as guides to moral action. Virtue ethics looks to the character of moral agents; care ethics depends on an ethical ideal of caring that is constructed over years of acting as one-caring. But a difference emerges even here. Care ethics puts emphasis on natural caring that requires no *moral* effort on the part of carers. In natural caring, we respond as carers because we are genuinely moved by the needs of the cared-for and want to respond to them. Effort—sometimes great effort—may be required in meeting the needs, but no moral effort is required as motivation.

When the motivation of natural caring fails, ethical caring must be summoned, and how effectively this can be done depends on the strength of the ideal of caring present in the carer. On this, care ethics and virtue ethics agree; only the terminology differs. However, another difference appears. An agent acting on ethical caring may act as though she would act in natural caring, but she has an additional task and that is to exercise whatever virtues are needed to restore conditions that will support natural caring. Virtually all of us prefer to be cared-for, or treated well, out of love or concern. We are made uneasy by generous acts done out of duty or righteousness. Ethical caring is admirable, even necessary, but it poses a risk to caring relations. The carer's attention is too concentrated on herself.

Both care ethics and virtue ethics recognize caring as a virtue, but care ethics anchors the virtue in the caring relation. Someone who regularly establishes caring relations may be said to exhibit the virtue of caring. He or she may rightly be said to be a caring person. In a caring relation, both carer and cared-for contribute. The cared-for must recognize the efforts of the carer as caring in order to complete the relation. No matter how great the carer's efforts, if the cared-for does not recognize those efforts, there is no caring relation. This does not mean that the would-be carer deserves no moral credit for her efforts. It means that something has gone wrong; it may be the fault of the carer, of the cared-for, or of the situation in which they find themselves. In teaching, the situation is often at fault. Teachers try to care, and students claim that they want care, but there are no caring relations (Noddings 2006b). I'll return to this problem in the last section, when we look at the contributions of philosophy of education to feminist philosophy.

Care ethics and virtue ethics also agree that it is impossible for any moral agent to care for everyone. An early criticism of my version of caring claimed that it was provincial, too tightly tied to the inner or family circle. This arose mainly through a misunderstanding. I said—and still insist—that we cannot care-for everyone; caring-for requires direct contact, some means of receiving a response of recognition from the cared-for. But this does not mean that we cannot care-about strangers and people at a distance, and I believe that we often have an obligation to care-about others. Slote (1998) approaches this difficult problem by prescribing "balanced caring"—caring-for (and caring-about) those close to us and also for distant others whose needs have come to our attention. Care ethics speaks of caring-for in direct encounters and caring-about in cases where no direct encounter is possible. But once again, care ethicists are guided by the perceived need to work toward conditions under which caring-for can flourish. It is not enough, for example, to pay for food that may or may not reach the hungry. We must somehow evaluate the effects of our efforts, and even getting food to the hungry is not enough; we have to ask what might be done to establish conditions under which fewer such emergencies will occur. Probably, virtue and care ethicists are largely in agreement on this.

Some critics argue that care theory needs to say more about the obligation to care (Engster 2005). This is true, but it must be done with caution. Slote (1998) handles this problem carefully in his discussion of balanced caring. Attempts to define the distribution of our caring duties more closely may actually warp the underlying conception of care. Caring as a moral orientation, described phenomenologically, contains an embedded concept of obligation—to respond to those who address us. It is—like every thoughtful conception of obligation—loaded with conflicts, and these should be discussed, but there can be no formula (within care theory) to eliminate them.

Recently, some writers have argued that caring should be redefined as a practice. As such, it can be said to have particular aims (Engster 2005). This strikes some of us as dangerous, because what is actually done by carers differs not only across cultures but, more basically, across situations and individuals (Okin 2003). In the attempt to redefine caring as a practice instead of a moral orientation, the deepest contributions of care theory may inadvertently be lost. Caring may be reduced to *caregiving* or *caretaking*.

This move—to describe caring as a practice—may indeed aggravate fears expressed earlier by feminist critics who worried that an emphasis on caring valorizes a genderized virtue and may thus lead to the continued exploitation of women. This objection to care ethics was raised early on at an APA symposium on Caring. Thoughtful comments along these lines were made by Claudia Card, Barbara Houston, and Sarah Hoagland (see the account in *Hypatia* 5, no.1 [Spring 1990]). It seemed to be answered by clarifying caring as a moral orientation, not simply a series of caregiving acts. But another answer is to teach boys as well as girls to engage in the practices associated with caring so that the orientation may develop in both. Feminist philosophers rightly want to avoid an Aristotelian position on virtue—one that separates male and female virtues, elevating the male over the female. This concern illustrates again a persistent difference between liberal feminism and the more radical feminism of care theory. With Virginia Woolf, we are ambivalent about joining the procession of educated men without changing the destination of the procession.

Part of the debate between virtue ethics and care ethics appears in discussions of Confucianism. Again, there are striking similarities. Both put great emphasis on relationships (Herr 2003; Star 2002). But the requirements of caring in Confucianism are governed more by formal relationships than by the encounter, address, and response of care ethics. Daniel Star notes "that Confucian ethics is better thought of as a virtue ethics than a care ethics" (2002, p. 98). He argues strongly for the distinctiveness of care ethics. In contrast, Chenyang Li (1994) supports some virtue ethicists in analyzing care ethics as a type of virtue ethics. Henry Rosemont (1997), too, declares that Confucian ethics is compatible with feminist ethics, primarily because of their common interest in social relationships. Probably most care theorists agree with Star that the difference in approaches to relationships makes the two ethics distinct.

One important similarity between Confucian and care ethics is their emphasis on the motivational importance of emotion or feeling. The work of Mencius underscores the basic role of *commiseration* in moral life. His famous example of the response of observers to the plight of a child about to fall into a well is meant to illustrate how "good" human beings react directly to perceived need. They do not consult principles, nor do they refer to formal relationships; they leap to save the child.

3. CRITIQUES AND APPLICATIONS IN PHILOSOPHY OF EDUCATION

Philosophy of education should be an ideal domain for the analysis and application of feminist philosophy. As Dewey pointed out years ago, there is a sense in which philosophy *is* philosophy of education, and he also suggested that our schools should be mini-societies that reflect our best conception of what our larger society should be. For an introduction to feminist philosophy of education, readers might consult the volume edited by Lynda Stone (1994). This collection of classic pieces includes work on self and identity, education and schooling, knowledge and curriculum, teaching and pedagogy, and diversity and multiculturalism.

Woolf's concern about joining the procession of educated men is especially pertinent in education itself. It seems clear that educators and policymakers have addressed the concern with an enthusiastic endorsement of women's inclusion in the affairs of men. Most of our colleges and universities are now co-educational, and in high school girls now outnumber boys in advanced mathematics classes. These seem to be positive steps, and liberal feminists see much to celebrate. Radical feminists and care theorists, however, express some reservations.

Liberal feminists are concerned, of course, by the continuing wage gap between women and men, and they deplore the paucity of women at the highest levels of business and government. They are also troubled by the sexism and violence suffered by women in the military. Their basic mission is to achieve equality in the man-made world.

Feminist philosophers of education have raised questions about the single-minded drive for equality. When the curriculum is constructed entirely around the knowledge arising from male experience, women are excluded even if they are allowed to participate (Martin 1982). The traditional activities and concerns of women do not appear in the curriculum. Where, for example, do we find parenting, making a home, love, marriage, and caregiving? Educators have long regarded such topics as nonintellectual—things to be learned with ease at home—but feminist philosophers of education have pointed out that these topics can be as intellectually challenging as any others and have the added merit of addressing the problems of real life (Noddings 1984/2003, 2003, 2006a). We are not even close to achieving a gender-inclusive curriculum.

How should gender be treated in educational theory and practice? (On this question, see the probing analyses in Diller, Houston, Morgan, and Ayim, 1996.) A gender-blind approach would, by default to the status quo, be an approach constructed by and for males—technically open to both males and females without discrimination. Thinking of this sort led to questions about why women lagged behind men in mathematics and science. The accepted answer was *discrimination*, and the remedy was to encourage—even push—young women to take more math and science courses in high school and college. Policymakers and educators, eager to escape the charge of discrimination, did not think to ask what young women are *interested* in, what *they* want to do. At the secondary-school level, the goal has been accomplished; more girls than boys are taking advanced math classes. However, girls still score significantly lower on the math SAT, and they now score somewhat lower on the verbal SAT as well.

A worry arises that girls are being pushed into subjects that may not hold great interest for them and discouraged from following occupational lines at which they might excel. This is not a simple matter. Thoughtful people welcome expanding opportunities for girls, but "opportunity" sometimes becomes "coercion." It is one thing to encourage girls who are interested and talented in mathematics; it is quite another to suggest that intelligent girls are "too good" for literature, early childhood education, or social work.

A fundamental problem, as Morwenna Griffiths (2006) has pointed out, is a hegemonic masculinity. That hegemony continues to dominate educational thought and practice, as it dominates all of public life. Consider, for example, the everyday matter of dress. It is entirely acceptable today for a woman to wear pants suits in professional settings. It is close to unthinkable for a man to appear at the office in skirt, blouse, pearls, and high heels. It is more acceptable for a woman to act like a man than for a man to act like a woman. The goal should not be to reverse this hegemony, nor should it be to forge a gender-neutral society. The philosophical problem is to analyze attributes of both traditions, identify what is humanly excellent in each, and suggest ways in which we can learn from one another. Some work along these lines has been discussed by Rhoads and Calderone (2007) with respect to gay, lesbian, bisexual, and transgendered students, but not with respect to women as a dominated group.

Seeking a healthy convergence, we might return to concerns about the career opportunities proffered to high school students. Policymakers worried that girls were "lagging behind" boys in mathematics, but they expressed no concern that boys rarely choose careers in the so-called caring professions. Nor is there great concern that salaries in those professions continue to lag behind those in the traditionally male professions. The issues here are complicated, but the initial impetus for feminist studies in academe—solidarity with our sisters—seems to have been lost or, at least, weakened. Now it is to the advantage of successful women to have poorly paid women clean their houses and care for their children.

A problem that can be identified in much of the preceding discussion is the conundrum of difference. Physical differences exist. But *gender,* in contrast to sex, is a social construct, and difference in the context of gender has always been defined as difference *from* the masculine norm. Difference, as Catherine MacKinnon (1987) has so forcefully argued, is a sign of and a product of dominance. However, there *are* gender differences that are products of centuries of cultural evolution, and some of these—extended maternal love, for example—are rooted in biology. Thus, it might be wiser to work toward the elimination of unfounded hierarchy in discussions of difference than to ignore difference entirely. When a difference is identified, it is beneficial to ask whether each element has its place or whether one is likely to contribute more to human well-being. MacKinnon is right that, historically, gender differences have been decided *a priori* in favor of males. Not nearly enough work is being done by philosophers of education on the conceptual problems associated with gender differences.

Feminist philosophy of education has had some influence through care ethics on moral education. It might be expected that because of the similarities between care ethics and virtue ethics, moral education from the care perspective would have much in common with character education (Noddings and Slote 2003). The potential is there (see Slote, this volume). What stands in the way is character education's longstanding practice of trying to teach the virtues directly. First, since the time of Socrates, doubts have been raised about the possibility of doing this. But, second, care theory probes beneath the surface of the named virtues to find what supports them. For example, I have asked the question: Are the virtues always virtuous? (Noddings 2002a). Slote (1992) is also interested in what lies behind the various virtues, but his purpose is primarily to develop a stronger foundation for virtue ethics. We agree (I think) that the underlying test for a virtuous act is its intention, coupled with its effect in bringing harm or good to other people.

One model of moral education based on care ethics involves modeling, dialogue, practice, and confirmation (Noddings 1984/2003, 2002a). The first element, modeling, is common in most schemes of moral education. Teachers must *show*, in their own conduct, the ways in which they want students to behave. *Dialogue* has several purposes. It is through dialogue that teachers come to know their students, and it is in dialogue that teachers raise questions, suggest possibilities, and guide students toward moral thinking. *Practice* gives students opportunities to employ the moral knowledge and skills discussed. Dialogue and practice working together may be considered acts of *induction* as Martin Hoffman (2000) has described it. The purpose is to develop a capacity for *empathy* (see Slote, this volume) or, as expressed by care theorists, for *engrossment* or receptive *attention*. Finally, the care model posits *confirmation*, a teacher's continuing efforts to help students realize their own best selves.

The first three elements have been widely accepted in moral education (Charney 1992; Stengel and Tom 2006; Watson 2003), but confirmation is rarely mentioned. I have described confirmation as "one of the loveliest ideas in moral life" (Noddings 2006a, p. 113). To recognize in another a better self struggling to realize itself is indeed a lovely act. But confirmation cannot be done by formula; it is not a strategy. To confirm another, we need to know that other reasonably well. It requires the establishment of caring relations. Philosophers of education are now giving considerable attention to the importance of relations in teaching (Bingham and Sidorkin 2004; Johnston 2006; Sidorkin 2002; Thayer-Bacon 2000).

Summing up what we have reviewed in feminist philosophy and philosophy of education—and with the understanding that reasonable people may differ on what they see in looking at the field—it seems that feminists are concentrating now on upgrading "first generation" ideas on liberal feminism and equality. Radical feminism and agency are still discussed, but much attention seems to be directed at equality in professional life, multicultural problems, and problems of sexual minorities. This is much needed work, but the trend is reminiscent of what happened to mid-nineteenth-century feminists: a morally driven delay in the development of feminist ideas that might transform the whole social/political domain.

REFERENCES

....

Beard, Mary R. (1946/1962). *Woman as a force in history.* New York: Collier Books.

Bianchi, Suzanne, Lynne M. Casper, and Rosalind Berkowitz King (Eds.). (2005). *Work, family, health, and well-being.* Mahwah, NJ: Erlbaum.

Bingham, Charles, and Alexander Sidorkin (Eds.). (2004). *No education without relation.* New York: Peter Lang.

Boler, Megan. (1999). *Feeling and reason in the arts.* New York: Routledge.

Buber, Martin. (1958/1970). *I and Thou*, trans. by Walter Kaufmann. New York: Charles Scribner's Sons.

——(1965). *Between man and man.* New York: Macmillan.

Charney, Ruth. (1992). *Teaching children to care.* Greenfield, MA: Northeast Foundation for Children.

Chodorow, Nancy. (1978). *The reproduction of mothering.* Berkeley: University of California Press.

Collins, Patricia Hill. (1990). *Black feminist thought.* Boston: Unwin Hyman.

——(1995). Black women and motherhood. In *Justice and care*, ed. Virginia Held (pp. 117–38). Boulder, CO: Westview Press.

Daly, Mary. (1974). *Beyond God the father.* Boston: Beacon Press.

Diller, Ann, Barbara Houston, Kathryn Pauly Morgan, and Maryann Ayim. (1996). *The gender question in education.* Boulder, CO: Westview Press.

Dinnerstein, Dorothy. (1976). *The mermaid and minotaur: Sexual arrangements and human malaise.* New York: Harper.

Engster, Daniel. (2005). Rethinking care theory: The practice of caring and the obligation to care. *Hypatia* 20(3): 50–74.

Gilligan, Carol J. (1982). *In a different voice.* Cambridge, MA: Harvard University Press.

Griffiths, Morwenna. (2006). The feminization of teaching and the practice of teaching. *Educational Theory* 56(4): 387–405.

Harding, Sandra. (1996). Rethinking standpoint epistemology: What is "strong objectivity"? In *Feminist epistemologies*, ed. Linda Alcoff and E. Potter (pp. 49–82). New York: Routledge.

Hartsock, Nancy. (1983). The feminist standpoint: Developing the grounds for a specifically feminist historical materialism. In *Discovering reality*, ed. S. Harding and M. B. Hintikka (pp. 283–310). Dordrecht: D. Reidel.

Hekman, Susan J. (1997). Truth and method: Feminist standpoint theory revisited. *Signs* 22(2): 341–65.

Held, Virginia. (1993). *Feminist morality.* Chicago: University of Chicago Press.

——(Ed.). (1995). *Justice and care.* Boulder, CO: Westview Press.

Herr, Ranjoo Seodu. (2003). Is Confucianism compatible with care ethics? *Philosophy East and West* 53(4): 471–89.

Hoffman, Martin. (2000). *Empathy and moral development: Implications for caring and justice.* New York: Cambridge University Press.

Hypatia. (1990, Spring). Symposium on caring. *Hypatia* 5(1): 101–26.

——(2004, Spring). Special issue: Women in the American philosophical tradition 1800–1930. *Hypatia* 19(2).

——(2005, Fall). Special issue: Analytic feminism. *Hypatia* 20(4).

——(2006, Winter). Special issue: Maternal bodies. *Hypatia* 21(1).

—— (2007, Spring). Special issue: The reproduction of whiteness: Race and the regulation of the gendered body. *Hypatia* 22(2).

Jaggar, Alison, M. (1983). *Feminist politics and human nature*. Totowa, NJ: Rowman & Allanheld.

Johnston, D. Kay (2006). *Education for a caring society*. New York: Teachers College Press.

Katz, Michael, Nel Noddings, and Kenneth Strike (Eds.). (1999). *Justice and caring: The search for common ground in education*. New York: Teachers College Press.

Keller, Evelyn Fox. (1985). *Reflections on gender and science*. New Haven: Yale University Press.

Kerber, Linda. (1997). *Toward an intellectual history of women*. Chapel Hill: University of North Carolina Press.

Kristeva, Julia. (1982). Women's time. In *Feminist theory: A critique of ideology*, ed. N. O. Keohane, M. Z. Rosaldo, and B. C. Gelpi (pp. 31–54). Chicago: University of Chicago Press.

Li, Chenyang. (1994). The Confucian concept of jen and the feminist ethics of care: A comparative study. *Hypatia* 9(1): 70–89.

MacKinnon, Catherine A. (1987). *Feminism unmodified*. Cambridge, MA: Harvard University Press.

Martin, Jane Roland. (1982). Excluding women from the educational realm. *Harvard Educational Review* 52(2): 133–48.

—— (1984). Bringing women into educational thought. *Educational Theory* 34(4): 341–54.

—— (1985). *Reclaiming a conversation*. New Haven: Yale University Press.

—— (1992). *The schoolhome: Rethinking schools for changing families*. Cambridge, MA: Harvard University Press.

Meyers, Diana Tietjens. (Ed.). (1997). *Feminist social thought: A reader*. New York: Routledge.

Miller, Jean Baker. (1976). *Toward a new psychology of women*. Boston: Beacon Press.

Murdoch, Iris. (1970). *The sovereignty of good*. London: Routledge & Kegan Paul.

Noddings, Nel. (1984/2003). *Caring: A feminine approach to ethics and moral education*, 2nd ed. Berkeley: University of California Press.

—— (1989). *Women and evil*. Berkeley: University of California Press.

—— (1990). Feminist critiques in the professions. In *Review of research in education 16*, ed. Courtney B. Cazden (pp. 393–424). Washington, DC: American Educational Research Association.

—— (1993). *Educating for intelligent belief or unbelief*. New York: Teachers College Press.

—— (2000). Two concepts of caring. In *Philosophy of Education 1999*, ed. Randall Curren (pp. 36–39). Urbana-Champaign: University of Illinois.

—— (2002a). *Educating moral people*. New York: Teachers College Press.

—— (2002b). *Starting at home: Caring and social policy*. Berkeley: University of California Press.

—— (2003). *Happiness and education*. Cambridge: Cambridge University Press.

—— (1992/2005). *The challenge to care in schools*, 2nd ed. New York: Teachers College Press.

—— (2006a). *Critical lessons: What our schools should teach*. New York: Cambridge University Press.

—— (2006b). Caring as relation and virtue in teaching. In *Working virtue: Virtue ethics and contemporary moral problems*, ed. Rebecca Walker and Philip J. Ivanhoe (pp. 41–60). Oxford: Oxford University Press.

Noddings, Nel, and Michael Slote. (2003). Changing notions of the moral and of moral education. In *The Blackwell guide to philosophy of education*, ed. Nigel Blake, Paul Smeyers, Richard Smith, and Paul Standish (pp. 341–55). Oxford: Blackwell.

Offen, Karen. (1988). Defining feminism: A comparative historical approach. *Signs* 14(1): 119–57.

Okin, Susan Moller. (1979). *Women in Western political thought*. Princeton: Princeton University Press.

—— (1989). Reason and feeling in thinking about justice. *Ethics* 99(2): 229–49.

—— (2003). Poverty, well-being, and gender: What counts, who's heard? *Philosophy and Public Affairs* 31(3): 280–316.

O'Loughlin, Marjorie. (2006). *Embodiment and education: Exploring creatural existence*. Dordrecht: Springer.

Rich, Adrienne. (1976). *Of woman born*. New York: W. W. Norton.

Rhoads, Robert A., and Shannon M. Calderone. (2007). Reconstituting the democratic subject: Sexuality, schooling, and citizenship. *Educational Theory* 57(1): 105–21.

Rosemont, Henry Jr. (1997). Classical Confucian and contemporary feminist perspectives on the self: Some parallels and their implications. In *Culture and self: Philosophical and religious perspectives East and West*, ed. Douglas Allen (pp. 63–82). Boulder: Westview Press.

Ruddick, Sara. (1989). *Maternal thinking: Toward a politics of peace*. Boston: Beacon Press.

Sander-Staudt, Maureen. (2006). The unhappy marriage of care ethics and virtue ethics. *Hypatia* 21(4): 21–39.

Sidorkin, Alexander M. (2002). *Learning relations*. New York: Peter Lang.

Slote, Michael. (1992). *From morality to virtue*. New York: Oxford University Press.

—— (1998). Caring in the balance. In *Norms and values*, ed. Joram G. Haber and Mark S. Halfon (pp. 27–36). Lanham, MD: Rowman & Littlefield.

—— (2000). Caring versus the philosophers. In *Philosophy of education 1999*, ed. Randall Curren (pp. 25–35). Urbana-Champaign: University of Illinois.

Star, Daniel. (2002). Do Confucians really care? A defense of the distinctiveness of care. *Hypatia* 17(1): 77–106.

Stengel, Barbara S., and Alan R. Tom. (2006). *Moral matters: Five ways to develop the moral life of schools*. New York: Teachers College Press.

Stone, Lynda. (1994). *The education feminist reader*. New York: Routledge.

Thayer-Bacon, Barbara. (2000). *Transforming critical thinking*. New York: Teachers College Press.

Tronto, Joan. (1993). *Moral boundaries: A political argument for an ethic of care*. New York: Routledge.

Tuana, Nancy, and Rosemarie Tong (Eds.). (1995). *Feminism and philosophy*. Boulder, CO: Westview Press.

Waerness, Kari. (1984). The rationality of caring. *Economic and Industrial Democracy* 5(2): 185–212.

Waithe, Mary Ellen. (Ed.). (1987–95). *A history of women philosophers*, 4 vols. Dordrecht: Kluwer Academic.

Walker, Emilie V. Siddle. (1996). Interpersonal caring in the "good" segregated schooling of African-American children. In *Caring in an unjust world*, ed. Deborah Eaker-Rich and Jane A. Van Galen (pp. 129–46). Albany: State University of New York Press.

Walker, Margaret Urban. (2005). Diotima's ghost: The uncertain place of feminist philosophy in professional philosophy. *Hypatia* 20(3): 153–64.

Ward, Geoffrey C., and Ken Burns. (1999). *Not for ourselves alone: The story of Elizabeth Cady Stanton and Susan B. Anthony*. New York: Alfred A. Knopf.

Watson, Jean. (1979). *Nursing: The philosophy and science of caring.* Boulder, CO: Colorado Associated University Press.

Watson, Marilyn. (2003). *Learning to trust.* San Francisco: Jossey-Bass.

Weil, Simone. (1977). *Simone Weil Reader,* ed. George A. Panichas. Mt. Kisco, NY: Moyer Bell Limited.

Wollstonecraft, Mary. (1792/1975). *A vindication of the rights of woman,* ed. Carol H. Poston. New York: W. W. Norton.

Woolf, Virginia. (1938/1966). *Collected essays,* vol. 2. London: Hogarth Press.

CHAPTER 28

POSTMODERNISM AND EDUCATION

NICHOLAS C. BURBULES

1. OVERVIEW

IT represents a challenge to produce an encyclopedic entry on postmodernism, or its impact on educational theory, because there is nothing approaching a consensus on what "postmodernism" is. First, it has come to be an umbrella term for a host of quite different theoretical positions. Richard Rorty's version of neo-pragmatism; Michel Foucault's or Jean-Francois Lyotard's versions of poststructuralism; Jacques Derrida's deconstructive philosophy; Hans Gadamer's hermeneutical phenomenology; Jurgen Habermas's critical theory; and the diverse feminisms of Nancy Fraser, Seyla Benhabib, Donna Haraway, and Luce Irigaray—plus many more examples— have all been referred to with the label "postmodern," even though most of these writers do not use the term to describe themselves. It would certainly be a stretch to find any set of theses that all of these thinkers share. Even a Wittgensteinian "family resemblance" definition that could encompass them all would have to be extremely general and vague. Hans Bertens's (1986) overview of the literature emphasized instead the plurality of postmodernisms. Added to this is the use of "postmodern" as a qualifier, sometimes attached to worldviews that do not seem "postmodern" at all: postmodern Marxism; postmodern Christianity; and even postmodern conservatism.

Second, it seems to be of the nature of postmodernism to resist any formal characterization of theses that could prescribe a coherent, assertive position. Postmodernism, if anything general might be said of it, represents a certain kind of critical attitude, most often defined in relation to what it is not. It has been described as a denial of meta-narratives; a reaction against Enlightenment values and rationality; an extreme form of antirealism or social constructivism; or a radical assertion of difference and nonnormativity. These are not just negative or critical views toward particular traditional philosophical claims; they question at a more fundamental level the very possibility of developing a coherent, comprehensive alternative theoretical position.

Third, it may be a misnomer even to characterize this thing "postmodernism" as an "ism" in the first place. The term, after all, originated not as a philosophical theory but as a description of movements within art and architecture (Harvey 1992; Jameson 1991). Many writers refer instead to postmodernity or the postmodern condition. In other words, what comes first is not an assertive theoretical stance, but a constellation of social and cultural changes that, it is claimed, have made the maintenance of certain traditional beliefs, values, and hopes problematic. Here, I believe we move closer to the crux of the matter. As I have written elsewhere, when Lyotard (1984, p. xxiv) provides his famous one-sentence definition of postmodernism, "Simplifying to the extreme, I define postmodernism as incredulity toward metanarratives," he does not mean (as he is frequently taken to mean) a rejection of meta-narratives or a conclusively worked out refutation of them. He means, quite literally, "incredulity"—an inability to believe them any longer, even if we once could (Burbules 1996). It means an ambivalent and ambiguous internal relation to modernity, not outgrowing or surpassing it. Postmodernists are creatures of a modernist society and culture who have lost faith, of a certain sort, in its ability to deliver on its promises. The causes of the postmodern condition are variously taken to include the Holocaust, globalization, and the myriad prospects of sudden and virtually worldwide catastrophe (whether through nuclear, biological, viral, or climate-related causes). Science and technology have not solved these problems, and have often exacerbated them. The most advanced democratic and liberal societies have proved to be among the worst in ignoring or perpetuating these problems. A reasoned consensus across cultures and religions that might adjudicate common human interests and values seems as far away (and sometimes further away) than ever. The postmodern condition, in this context, then, represents a kind of disenchantment with the spirit of the Enlightenment, not a rejection or refutation of it.

The quotation that best captures this ambivalence is Gayatri Spivak's comment on deconstruction: "If I understand deconstruction, deconstruction is not an exposure of error, certainly not other people's error. The critique of deconstruction, the most serious critique in deconstruction, is the critique of something that is extremely useful, something without which we cannot do anything" (Spivak 1993, p. 27). Similarly, Lyotard writes, "What then is postmodernism? . . . It is undoubtedly part of the modern. Everything that is received must be suspected" (Lyotard 1992, p. 12). In short, the very possibility of a "postmodern critique" is grounded in the conditions of modernity: Kant's critical philosophy, Hume's skepticism, Descartes' radical doubt, Marx's ideology-critique, Nietzsche's nihilism, Kierkegaard's existentialism, Dewey's pragmatism, Wittgenstein's reflections on doubt and certainty—even logical positivism and analytical philosophy, in a certain sense—all reflect a modernist skepticism toward traditions and received "foundations" of truth. What is different about these modernist philosophies is the aspiration to undertake such a critical exercise in order to arrive at a truer, clearer, more honest account of things. But that is just what postmodernism doubts.

This is a different kind of "critique"—an auto-critique, if you will, not of another's beliefs and traditions but of one's own. It is pulling the rug out from under one's own feet. It is most assuredly not a matter of demonstratively refuting another position and replacing it with a better one; because this very sort of endeavor, and the narrative of progress that implicitly underlies it, is part of what postmodernism wants to put into question. This attitude, sometimes described as a kind of pervasive irony, takes back with one hand what it seems to give with the other. One way to summarize this is that postmodernism is not, in a strict sense, "post" anything. It is a changed relationship of modernity with itself; as Zygmunt Bauman puts it, "living with ambivalence" (Bauman 1991). Or, as Lyotard puts it, "'Postmodern' simply indicates a mood, or better a state of mind" (1986–87, p. 209).

2. The Postmodern Condition

One important element of postmodernity is a growing awareness of the radical diversity and potential incommensurability of the different cultural forms of life that sustain groups and individuals—not in fact an increase in such differences but an increased sensitivity to these differences. In the current world, media, mobility, and new forms of communication and popular culture have brought diverse cultures into much closer proximity with one another. The nature of many global political and economic interdependencies has been to force the effort of engaging and reconciling conflicting beliefs and values—it is, generally speaking, no longer enough simply to co-exist. Now, it is a mistake to assume that incommensurability is the inevitable consequence of such encounters; but speaking practically, people do sometimes reach the limit of their ability or willingness to understand one another, or to pursue potential agreement with one another. In the face of such a realization, the modernist optimism that continued conversation can be successful in uniting or reconciling diverse perspectives and values has been thrown into doubt. For philosophers like Jacques Derrida and Emmanuel Levinas, the irreducibility of the Other to our understanding is the presumed starting point of such encounters.

A second element, related to the first, is a certain destabilization of the assumption of a coherent, consistent identity. Theories of performative and constructed identities emphasize much more the fluidity and context-dependence of even seemingly fixed biological categories like sex and race, let alone more obviously cultural identifications. Theories of hybridity emphasize the increasingly blended and boundary-blurring combinations that people find in themselves. Like the issue of difference, above, it is not only that such liminal selves are becoming more commonplace, but also that people are becoming increasingly aware that such liminality and hybridity may have always been the unrecognized norm, and not the exception. Reflections like these look at the supposedly unshakeable certainly of Descartes' "I think, therefore I am," and ask "Who is the 'I' speaking here?"

A third element is an understanding that dynamics of asymmetrical power distort and compromise even the best of human intentions; and that these dynamics are ubiquitous across the formal and informal structures of life in which humans are engaged. State, institutional, and corporate entities shape even the domain of seemingly personal or private choices. In the current world, technical systems of surveillance, manipulation, and control are increasingly widespread and subtle. We participate in these, consciously or unconsciously, nearly all the time. Not all of these manifestations of power are necessarily pernicious. But their ubiquity should sensitize us to the power dimensions of even apparently benign acts; to the limits of good intentions; to the deep culpability we all have within a world society that implicates us in a web of contingencies and interactions whose consequences are, in some degree, always harmful to someone; and to the dubious adventure of seeking a path toward any utopia that promises a better life for all.

A fourth element concerns language, and the particular way in which discourse—the patterns of language in use—colors and shapes our ways of living and being in the world. Postmodernism partakes of a radical nominalism. Our practices of communication, explanation, justification, truth-telling, and so on (and our apparently nonverbal practices as well) are always partly expressions of the particular language or languages we have. But because our languages are diverse, and noncongruent, there will always be a limit on any particular discursive system as a standpoint, in a place and time, within which one can try to describe all matters of truth, value, and so forth; such matters will always be to some extent the expressions of this language, and this place and time. This realization does not lead to relativism, necessarily; for there usually is a good deal of overlap or intertranslatability among different discursive systems. But this stance gives postmodernism a pervasive skepticism toward standard conceptions of realism, reason, justice, or objectivity.

These elements, along with others, underlie the postmodern incredulity toward some of the promises (or presumptions) of the Enlightenment. Each is a disturbed and disturbing suspicion—a loss of faith, I've called it—in universal claims and disinterested points of view. Dominant conceptions of Truth and Justice appear as the expressions of socially and institutionally privileged voices, not as grounding points. The kinds of arguments that philosophers have offered in support of such claims are, from the postmodern standpoint, insufficiently reflective about their own contingency and particularity.

3. Criticisms of Postmodernism

The emphasis here on a characterization of postmodernism as a kind of incredulity is meant to explain why some of the common criticisms of postmodernism may fail to hit the mark. David Carr (1998, p. 8) decries "the postmodern assault on knowledge and truth." My friend and editor here, Harvey Siegel, offers, in response to Wilfred Carr's characterization of postmodernism, several criticisms of that account:

> First . . . [the] postmodernist wants to reject the possibility of objective knowledge, but apparently regards it as an objective fact about the world that a subject's knowledge of that world is always "preinterpreted" and that such knowledge is therefore never objective. . . .
>
> Similarly, the postmodernist insistence that there is "no privileged position that enables philosophers to transcend the particularities of their own culture and traditions" seems itself to speak from such a position, since it seems to be making an assertion concerning all philosophers, cultures, and traditions. . . .
>
> Third, "foundationalist philosophy" is specified in such vague and general terms that it would be hard to locate a clear advocate of it in the contemporary literature. . . .
>
> Fourth, the postmodernist's argument against the possibility of objective knowledge is a strikingly weak one. . . . Does it really follow . . . that because my knowledge of trees, atoms, and people is always situated within my conceptual scheme, that there aren't trees, atoms, and people which exist independently of my scheme?   (Siegel 1998, p. 30)

I believe that Siegel is right in identifying a failing in accounts of postmodernism that, often in a rather celebratory way, proclaim the end of traditional philosophy, particularly the end of epistemology. There is, as he says, something self-undermining about assertive, conclusive claims about the impossibility of certain kinds of knowing and valuation—claims which themselves brook no exception.

But I have also suggested that many of the writers whose ideas are the deeper source of postmodern claims do not write this way: they are not "rejecting" or "assaulting" anything, and in the more thoughtful of these sources there is a tone that is very much the opposite of the triumphalist claim to have surpassed or defeated modernism, knowledge, or truth in any sense. In those cases, I would suggest, varieties of transcendental argument or claims that postmodern positions are self-contradictory lose some traction, because the most compelling postmodern writers are not making the kinds of definitive, sweeping assertions that would subject them to such criticisms. They are concerned, not with denial or refutation, but with the expression of a radical doubt. Spivak, whom I cited earlier, is perfectly aware that she needs to invoke the standards and rhetoric of argumentation in order to frame the skeptical questions she wants to pose toward them; and she admits the discomfort of trying to occupy both stances simultaneously. It is troubling, as Spivak makes clear, to doubt that which is necessary to one's life and mode of thinking. Wittgenstein (1969), in another context, makes clear the limits of the possibility of doubt—for there are epistemic conditions that make doubt itself possible (and these cannot be doubted, at least not all at once).

Another set of criticisms starts from the other side and attacks the characterization of a "postmodern condition" that supposedly throws into doubt the metanarratives of modernity. These counterclaims are usually more overtly political and historical than philosophical: "History has not stopped, we are not in a circular gravity. We do not accept that there is nothing left to do except survive along the remnants, nor do we accept that all struggles must be localized. Most crucially, we are not incredulous toward metanarratives" (Beyer and Liston 1992, p. 378).

Particularly for scholars of a Marxian theoretical bent, which emphasizes so strongly the difference between "ideology" and the material, economic conditions that provide an objective basis to social-class conflict, the postmodern suspicion, if not hostility, toward general theories threatens an enervating acquiescence to a social order they see wracked by fundamental injustices (see also Cole and Hill 1995). Politically, one must know whose side one is on and whom one is against. Hybridity and the fluidity of differences may make for provocative theoretical discussions, but they distract from the fundamental divides in power and privilege that shape modern society, which need to be diagnosed clearly and challenged directly.

Postmodernists, in response, deny that postmodernism is inherently apathetic or hostile to social or political action. What is at stake, rather, are conflicting notions of activism and justice; and strategic disagreements about the effective focal points of political intervention. Totalizing theory, even socialist theory, supported some of the worst forms of totalitarianism in the twentieth century. Belief that one is seeing clearly the "objective conditions" that others refuse, or are unable, to recognize has often led to political vanguardism and ends-justify-the-means strategies. Many of the leading figures of postmodern theory lived through the turbulence of 1968 in France and elsewhere, and were shaped by those events; this partly explains their "incredulity." Beyond this, a politics of difference is still a politics, just of a different kind: not given to binary characterizations of oppressors and oppressed; looking at power in its multiple and often conflicting dimensions; treating social distinctions and categories of identity as needing to be questioned and deconstructed, not reified. This is a politics that emphasizes cultural alongside economic factors, and which is suspicious of state interventions intended to create greater equality, freedom, and social justice. Admittedly, what constitutes a more just alternative to this state of affairs is often not so clear; and one of the areas in which we see this limitation to postmodernism is in the field of education.

4. POSTMODERNISM AND EDUCATION

Andy Green wrote, "There is clearly no such thing yet as a postmodern theory of education" (Green 1997, p. 8). Despite the apparent open-endedness of that "yet,"

Green was obviously skeptical about whether there ever could be such a thing: "Postmodernism has little of value to offer educational theory but it has many dangers" (Green 1997, p. 20).

Indeed, it is reasonable to wonder whether the term "a postmodern theory of education" is doubly contradictory: first, as already addressed here, because it is far from clear whether postmodernism can, or wants to, offer a "theory" of anything, as such. But at a deeper level, the endeavor of education seems to contain within it normative assumptions and values that rest uneasily within a postmodern sensibility. "Education" is, on any conceivable account, some activity or process intended to move the development and learning of people in a desired direction—a direction that, if many analytical philosophers of education are correct, intrinsically contains within it the idea of human betterment. Certainly a postmodern perspective can provide (and has provided) a critical angle on such efforts: What does "betterment" mean? Within whose cultural norms and interests? For which students? Who decides what knowledge, values, and dispositions of character are worth acquiring? How are the activities of teaching structured or distorted by elements of unequal power? What happens when educational practices get embedded in the bureaucratic, state-governed, and disciplinary structures we call "schools"? It appears that education is, in Foucault's terminology, intrinsically "normalizing," at least to a degree, and it seems impossible to imagine any system of education that would not be subject to that criticism. But then a deeper question arises: In what ways is a normalizing education necessarily bad? Isn't "normalizing," in part, just what we expect from education—in the sense of socializing learners into participation within a given social formation? Again, we are in an ambivalent space.

But when one turns to what might be a more prescriptive, alternative account, postmodernism seems to founder on its own auto-critique: On what basis could such prescriptive, alternative conceptions rest? What generalizability could they have? How could they possibly flourish within the institutional structures and constraints of schools as they currently exist? As Rousseau discovered in the *Emile*, even an attempt at completely natural and unfettered education for freedom inevitably brings in elements of social constraint.

Nevertheless, many thoughtful scholars have tried to provide just such a positive, "postmodern" account of education. Stanley Aronowitz, for example, wrote:

> Following from the dialectical relationship of knowledge and practice, postmodern educators believe the curriculum can best inspire learning only when school knowledge builds upon the tacit knowledge derived from the cultural resources that students already possess. . . .
>
> Perhaps more controversial is the fostering by postmodernists of the claims to intellectual validity of marginal discourses in the sciences and social sciences, especially those that refuse, on philosophical or ideological grounds, to observe accepted algorithms of inquiry. At issue is the question of diversity in ways of producing knowledge and, more broadly, the validity of the distinction between legitimate intellectual knowledge and other kinds of knowledge. . . .

One can imagine a postmodern high school. One of its more distinctive features is that what is studied is a matter of local decision making. Higher bodies—state and local school boards, principals and department chairs—may propose courses, texts, and pedagogies. And parents may express their concerns and try to influence what is taught and how. But the students and teachers have final authority. (Aronowitz 1991, pp. 15, 17, 20)

Whatever the merits of these proposals, however, one might ask what "postmodernism" adds if the main policy impacts are simply to reinforce fairly conventional understandings of progressive education, multiculturalism, and respecting teacher autonomy. Indeed, what is most striking about these recommendations, from a certain point of view, is how much they re-inscribe most of the actual practices and structures of schooling, simply mobilized in the service of a broadly left-democratic sensibility. This isn't to reject them, but one does wonder what makes them distinctively "postmodern."

Robin Usher and Richard Edwards approach the problem in a different way:

The very rationale of the educational process and the role of the educator is founded on the humanist idea of a certain kind of subject who has the potential to become self-motivated and self-directing, a rational subject capable of exercising individual agency. The task of education has therefore been understood as one of "bringing out," of helping to realize this potential. . . .

It is because postmodernism presents no foundational standpoint and no new theory that it teaches us to be skeptical of all systematic theorizations. . . . The implication is that it is precisely by adopting a postmodern argument that we can open ourselves through critical dialogue with others and with texts, to all varieties of educational tradition. (Usher and Edwards 1994, pp. 24–25, 29, 31)

This is more clearly postmodern in its spirit, because it emphasizes the indeterminacy of educational outcomes once one adopts a skeptical stance toward all meta-narratives. Nigel Blake, Paul Smeyers, Richard Smith, and Paul Standish add: "How could philosophers ever ask again, 'Who is the educated man?' as if there might be an answer for all times and cultures" (Blake et al. 1998, p. 5). What these latter authors are asking, in contrast with Aronowitz, is not only how to forge "postmodern" educational processes and curricula that question or contest prevailing meta-narratives but also what is much more challenging: What might it mean for education to proceed without any meta-narratives concerning itself?

The conditions of postmodernity discussed previously—an increased awareness of, and sensitivity to, radical and sometimes incommensurable difference; the instability of a fixed or consistent sense of identity; the pervasive analysis of power relations as constitutive of human interactions; and the indeterminacy and limits of language as a medium for adjudicating competing claims of truth and value—all go to the very heart of any possible account of education. How do we decide what "necessary" curricula or canons of learning might entail? How do we argue for an account of human betterment in the absence of any normative beliefs about what it means to be human? How do we navigate teacher-learner relations when power, privilege, and partisan interests always hover as considerations in the background?

How do we use language as a medium of communication and instruction while also problematizing the gaps and cultural particularities built into any language that we might have?

It may be well enough, in the context of higher education, for example, to argue that these very considerations might become part of a critically reflective pedagogy that, in true postmodern spirit, is also always partly deconstructing itself. But it is harder to see how this perspective sustains a general account of education—one that can address the learning of children, that allows for the mastery of basic literacy and thinking skills, that provides a basis of cultural understandings sufficient to posing the kinds of deeply problematizing questions called for by a postmodern sensibility. One needs to know a great deal about one's own culture and traditions, as well as those of others, in order for a theory of difference to have resonance, for example. In short, it is doubtful whether the capacity for a postmodern outlook on things can be developed, educationally, in a consistently postmodern matter. Once again, then, we find ourselves "living with ambivalence."

REFERENCES

Aronowitz, Stanley. (1991). *Postmodern Education.* Minneapolis: University of Minnesota Press.

Bauman, Zygmunt. (1991). "Postmodernity, or Living with Ambivalence." In *Modernity and Ambivalence.* (pp. 231–45). Ithaca, NY: Cornell University Press.

Bertens, Hans. (1986). "The Postmodern Weltanschauung and its Relation to Modernism: An Introductory Survey." Republished in *A Postmodern Reader,* ed. Joseph Natoli and Linda Hutcheon (pp. 25–70). (Albany, NY: State University of New York Press, 1993.

Beyer, Landon, and Daniel Liston. (1992). "Discourse or Moral Action: A Critique of Postmodernism." *Educational Theory* 42(4): 371–93.

Blake, Nigel, Paul Smeyers, Richard Smith, and Paul Standish. (1998). *Thinking Again: Education After Postmodernism.* Westport, CT: Bergin and Garvey.

Burbules, Nicholas C. (1996). "Postmodern Doubt and Philosophy of Education." In *Philosophy of Education 1995,* ed. Alven Neiman (pp. 39–48). Urbana, IL: Philosophy of Education Society.

Carr, David. (1998). "Introduction." In *Education, Knowledge and Truth: Beyond the Postmodern Impasse,* ed. David Carr (pp. 1–15). New York: Routledge.

Cole, Mike, and Dave Hill. (1995). "Games of Despair and Rhetorics of Resistance: Postmodernism, Education, and Reaction." *British Journal of Sociology of Education* 16 (2): 165–82.

Green, Andy. (1997). "Postmodernism and State Education." In *Education, Globalization, and the Nation State* (pp. 7–28). New York: St. Martin's.

Harvey, David. (1992). *The Condition of Postmodernity: An Enquiry Into the Origins of Cultural Change.* New York: Blackwell.

Jameson, Fredric. (1991). "The Cultural Logic of Late Capitalism." Republished in *A Postmodern Reader,* ed. Joseph Natoli and Linda Hutcheon (pp. 312–32). Albany, NY: State University of New York Press, 1993.

Lyotard, Jean-François. (1984). *The Postmodern Condition: A Report on Knowledge* Minneapolis: University of Minnesota Press, 1984.

—— (1986–87). "Rules and Paradoxes, and Svelte Appendix." *Cultural Critique* 5: 209–19.

—— (1992). *The Postmodern Explained.* Minneapolis: University of Minnesota Press.

Siegel, Harvey. (1998). "Knowledge, Truth, and Education." In *Education, Knowledge and Truth: Beyond the Postmodern Impasse,* ed. David Carr (pp. 19–36). New York: Routledge.

Spivak, Gayatri Chakravorty. (1993). "In a Word." Interview with Ellen Romney, quoted in Judith Butler, *Bodies that Matter: On the Discursive Limits of "Sex."* New York: Routledge.

Usher, Robin, and Richard Edwards. (1994). *Postmodernism and Education.* New York: Routledge.

Wittgenstein, Ludwig. (1969). *On Certainty.* New York: Harper.

INDEX